2010 NEW YORK YANKEES

MEDIA INFORMATION & RE...

Official Publication of the New York Yankees •

Yankee Stadium• One East 161st Street • Bronx, NY ...
Media Relations: (718) 579-4460 • Fax: (718) 293-8414
E-mail: media@yankees.com, credentials@yankees.com

Jason Zillo – Director, Media Relations and Publicity
Jason Latimer – Manager, Media Relations and Publicity
Michael Margolis – Manager, Media Relations and Publicity
Lauren Moran – Coordinator, Media Relations and Publicity
Kenny Leandry – Assistant, Media Relations and Publicity
Germania-Dolores Hernandez – Administrative Assistant

Produced by: Yankees Media Relations Department

Contributors: *Baseball Reference, Brigette Bielefeld, Alex Cotto, Steve Densa, Ken Derry, Kristina Dodge, Elias Sports Bureau, Ariele Goldman Hecht, Ian Johns, Pat Kelly, Paul A. Kopp, Mike Macchione, Nate Maciborski, Tony Morante, National Baseball Hall of Fame and Museum, James Petrozzello, Lou Rocco, Alfred Santasiero III, Bill Shannon, Craig Tapper, Alex Trochanowski, David Vincent.*

Photos throughout book courtesy of the New York Yankees, Getty Images, Photo File and the Library of Congress.

Printing: Creative Print Services, www.creativeprint.com
Layout & Design: Aaron Babcock, Barnstorm Creative Marketing, gobarnstorm.com

Table of Contents

George M. Steinbrenner III (1930-2010)

From 1973 until his passing on July 13 of this year, George M. Steinbrenner III created a legacy of winning unmatched by his peers. His foresight, drive and commitment permanently transformed not only the Yankees organization, but the game of Baseball.

It was more than 37 years ago, on January 3, 1973, that a group of businessmen formed and led by Mr. Steinbrenner purchased the New York Yankees from CBS for a net price of $8.7 million. It took just five years for his aggressive leadership to turn the organization back into World Champions. In his time as Principal Owner of the club, the Yankees won more pennants (11) and World Series (7) than any other team in baseball, while posting a Major League-best .566 winning percentage (3,364-2,583-3 record) over the stretch.

In addition to the team's on-field success under the direction of Mr. Steinbrenner, the New York Yankees consistently shattered franchise and league attendance records at home and on the road. In 2009, they drew 3,719,358 fans in their first season of play in the current Yankee Stadium, topping the American League in attendance for the seventh straight season (2003-09). The Yankees remain the only franchise in Baseball history to draw more than 4 million fans at home in four consecutive seasons (2005-08).

In recent years, Mr. Steinbrenner's foresight into both sports and business continued to build the value and prominence of the franchise, positioning it for the future. In 2002, *Sporting News* named him the No. 1 "Most Powerful Man in Sports." *Forbes* magazine has consistently listed the Yankees as the most valuable franchise in all of Baseball. Mr. Steinbrenner's vision led to the creation of YankeeNets, which owned the New Jersey Nets and New Jersey Devils and ultimately led to the launch of the YES Network, a trailblazing enterprise that has been the nation's most watched regional sports network for the past seven years. Most recently, Mr. Steinbrenner teamed with long-time friend and Dallas Cowboys owner Jerry Jones, creating Legends Hospitality, LLC, a new concession and merchandising company which currently operates at the Yankees' and Cowboys' new stadiums.

In 2006, his participation in the groundbreaking ceremony for the new Yankee Stadium underscored his role as the principal impetus in moving the much-anticipated facility towards its opening in 2009.

Mr. Steinbrenner's tenure of over 37 years exceeded that of any other New York Yankees owner by 13 years (Colonel Jacob Ruppert purchased the Yankees with Tillinghast L'Hommedieu Huston in January 1915, bought out Huston in 1922, and maintained sole ownership in the club until his death in January 1939—a total of 24 years). During Mr. Steinbrenner's time as the sole Principal Owner of the Yankees, the other 29 Major League clubs had over 100 owners or ownership groups.

Mr. Steinbrenner's success in the sports world began at an early age. He was a multi-sport athlete at Culver Military Academy (where he is in the Athletic Hall of Fame) and at Williams College. He began his successful coaching career as an assistant football coach at two Big Ten universities, Northwestern and Purdue. Then he assembled championship basketball teams in the National Industrial and American Basketball Leagues. In 2002, he was honored with the prestigious Gold

Medal Award from the National Football Foundation and College Hall of Fame for a lifetime of "outstanding commitment, dedication and dynamic leadership in his business, as well as his personal life."

Mr. Steinbrenner devoted as much time and effort to the U.S. Olympic Committee (USOC) as he did to his many other sporting endeavors. He was on the U.S. Olympic Foundation Board from 1986-2002 and served as Chairman over the last six years of his tenure. He also was Chairman of the 1989 Olympic Overview Commission, which was created to evaluate the structure and efforts of the U.S. Olympic program, and served as Vice President of the USOC from 1989 to 1992. As a result of his distinguished service, he was presented with the General Douglas MacArthur USOC Foremost Award and the F. Don Miller United States Olympic Award. In 2005, the U.S. Olympic Foundation created the George M. Steinbrenner Sports Leadership Award in his honor, which celebrates a member of the U.S. Olympic family who has made outstanding contributions to sport.

Mr. Steinbrenner was a member of the Baseball Hall of Fame's Board of Directors and served on the NCAA Foundation Board of Trustees beginning in 1990.

Most of Mr. Steinbrenner's philanthropic endeavors were performed without fanfare. However, he was repeatedly recognized by the communities in which he immersed himself. In 1993, he earned the Tampa Civitan Club's "Outstanding Citizen" Award, and in 1998, Tampa Law Enforcement named him "Citizen of the Year" for founding a scholarship fund for the children of slain law enforcement officers. In addition, Mr. Steinbrenner was honored as an "Outstanding New Yorker" by the New York Society of Association Executives in 1997 and credited in 2009 by the Museum of the City of New York as one of the "New York City 400," recognizing "people who have helped create the world's greatest city since its founding in 1609."

In February 2008, the Tampa City Council and the Board of the Hillsborough County Commissioner's Office both passed resolutions endorsing the renaming of Legends Field in Tampa after Mr. Steinbrenner to pay tribute to his numerous contributions to the area. On March 27, 2008, Mr. Steinbrenner—joined by his family—pulled down a curtain draped above the outfield scoreboard to unveil the new name for the Yankees' spring training home: George M. Steinbrenner Field.

In the fall of 2009, George M. Steinbrenner High School was opened in Lutz, Fla. The school was named after Mr. Steinbrenner by the Hillsborough County School Board in recognition of his philanthropic involvement in the community, particularly with the school system.

He is survived by his wife, Joan; sisters Susan Norpell and Judy Kamm, children, Hank, Hal, Jennifer and Jessica; and his grandchildren.

On September 20, prior to the team's game vs. Tampa Bay, the Yankees unveiled a monument in Mr. Steinbrenner's honor in Monument Park, reflecting the special connection, appreciation and responsibility that he felt toward Yankees fans.

GEORGE M. STEINBRENNER III
JULY 4, 1930 – JULY 13, 2010

New York Yankees Principal Owner
"The Boss"
1973 - 2010

Purchased the New York Yankees on January 3, 1973. A true visionary who changed the game of baseball forever, he was considered the most influential owner in all of sports. In his 37 years as Principal Owner, the Yankees posted a Major League-best .566 winning percentage, while winning 11 American League pennants and seven World Series titles, becoming the most recognizable sports brand in the world. A devoted sportsman, he was Vice President of the United States Olympic Committee, a member of the Baseball Hall of Fame's Board of Directors and a member of the NCAA Foundation Board of Trustees. A great philanthropist whose charitable efforts were mostly performed without fanfare, he followed a personal motto of the greatest form of charity is anonymity.

Dedicated by the New York Yankees
September 20, 2010

Bob Sheppard "The Voice of Yankee Stadium"

Bob Sheppard will forever be the "The Voice of Yankee Stadium." With his instantly recognizable elocution — in which each syllable was given meticulous attention — Sheppard provided a soundtrack of irreproachable dignity to Yankee Stadium for 57 years.

Sadly, he passed away on July 11, 2010, at his home in Baldwin, N.Y., with his wife, Mary, by his side. He was 99 years old.

Born in Ridgewood, Queens, Sheppard began his tenure as Yankees public address announcer on April 17, 1951—Opening Day of Joe DiMaggio's final season and the day of Mickey Mantle's Major League debut. Among the approximately 4,500 baseball games he worked over his tenure with the Yankees were an incredible 121 consecutive postseason contests (1951-2006), including 62 games in 22 World Series.

Sheppard's incredible career behind the microphone started when he volunteered his services for a charity football game in Freeport, Long Island, in the late 1940s. An executive from the Brooklyn Dodgers football team of the All-America Conference was at the game. He liked Sheppard's style ("clear, concise and correct") and hired him. The football Dodgers folded after just one season at Ebbets Field (1948), but one of their opponents—the New York football Yankees—heard Sheppard's booming voice and offered him their PA job at Yankee Stadium. Baseball's Yankees discovered him as a result and offered him their PA role for the 1950 season. Though he turned down their offer due to conflicts with his teaching schedule, he changed his mind the following year.

In addition to his baseball duties, Sheppard was the public address voice for the New York football Giants for 50 seasons—from their move to Yankee Stadium in 1956 until his retirement after the 2005 season. Sheppard also served the New York Titans of the American Football League at the Polo Grounds, the New York Stars of the World

Football League at Downing Stadium, the New York Cosmos soccer team, and St. John's University's basketball and football teams. Sheppard also handled PA duties for five Army-Navy football games in Philadelphia.

Some of the events he listed as the most memorable of his incredible career were: Don Larsen's perfect game in Game 5 of the 1956 World Series on October 8, 1956; Roger Maris' 61st home run on October 1, 1961; Reggie Jackson's three home runs in Game 6 of the World Series on October 18, 1977; and the Giants-Colts overtime NFL Championship Game on December 28, 1958.

Sheppard attended St. John's College, which eventually became St. John's University. Always a talented athlete, he received a full athletic scholarship to the school, playing quarterback on the football team all four years. He later enrolled at Columbia University, where he received his master's degree in speech and worked his way up from teacher-in-training to substitute teacher to permanent teacher to department chairman. In order to supplement his teaching salary, Sheppard played semiprofessional football on Sundays in Long Island with the Valley Stream Red Riders and the Hempstead Monitors, earning $25 a game.

In 1998, Sheppard was presented with the prestigious William J. Slocum "Long and Meritorious Service" Award by the New York chapter of the BBWAA as well as the "Pride of the Yankees" award by the ballclub. The Yankee Stadium media dining room was named "Sheppard's Place" prior to the 2009 season to commemorate his legacy.

On May 7, 2000, a plaque was dedicated to Sheppard in Monument Park of the original Yankee Stadium to commemorate his 50th anniversary season.

The native New Yorker was elected to the St. John's University Sports Hall of Fame, the Long Island Sports Hall of Fame and the New York Sports Hall of Fame. He was awarded honorary doctorates from St. John's University (Pedagogy) and Fordham University (Rhetoric), and in 2007, received St. John's' Medal of Honor, the highest award that the university can confer on a graduate.

Sheppard also made cameo appearances in numerous motion pictures and television shows, including *61**, *It's My Turn, It Could Happen to You, Anger Management, Seinfeld* and *Mad About You.*

Sheppard announced his final game at Yankee Stadium on September 5, 2007, a 3-2

SHEPPARD'S FIRST LINEUP CARD
April 17, 1951

Boston Red Sox	New York Yankees
Dom DiMaggio, CF	Jackie Jensen, LF
Billy Goodman, RF	Phil Rizzuto, SS
Ted Williams, LF	Mickey Mantle, RF
Vern Stephens, 3B	Joe DiMaggio, CF
Walt Dropo, 1B	Yogi Berra, C
Bobby Doerr, 2B	Johnny Mize, 1B
Lou Boudreau, SS	Billy Johnson, 3B
Buddy Rosar, C	Jerry Coleman, 2B
Billy Wright, P	Vic Raschi, P

Yankees victory over the Seattle Mariners.

On September 21, 2008, Sheppard provided a valedictory in the bottom of the seventh inning of the final game at the original Yankee Stadium. Unable to say goodbye in person as he continued to recover from an illness that had kept him away from the Stadium since the final weeks of the 2007 season, Sheppard gave his tribute through a taped segment played on the video board. He recited, "Farewell, old Yankee Stadium, farewell / What a wonderful story you can tell / DiMaggio, Mantle, Gehrig and Ruth / A baseball cathedral in truth."

Departed Yankees

Other members of the Yankees Family who passed away during the 2010 season.

Oscar Azocar

Ralph Houk

Stanley Kay

Dick Kraft

Jim Roland

Ralph Houk managed the Yankees to World Series appearances in each of his first three seasons at the helm of the Yankees, including back-to-back championships in 1961-62.

2010 Yankees HOPE Week

The New York Yankees were proud to share their second annual HOPE Week (Helping Others Persevere & Excel) in 2010, a unique week-long community program bringing to light five remarkable stories intended to inspire individuals into action in their own communities.

Each day from Monday, August 16, through Friday, August 20, the Yankees reached out to an individual, family or organization worthy of recognition and support. Though each day's celebration culminated at Yankee Stadium, outreach often took place away from the Stadium, allowing the Yankees to personally connect with individuals and highlight their success.

Initiated in 2009, HOPE Week is rooted in the fundamental belief that acts of goodwill provide hope and encouragement to more than just the recipient of the gesture.

A unique aspect of HOPE Week is that every player on the roster, Manager Joe Girardi and his coaching staff, General Manager Brian Cashman along with many front office employees, participated in the outreach during the week.

Equally significant during HOPE Week is gaining publicity for the highlighted causes and organizations. The greatest challenge facing many not-for-profits is generating interest, awareness and funding for their missions.

Additionally, the Yankees Foundation made a $10,000 donation to non-profit organizations associated with each day's participants.

The Yankees encourage all their fans to get involved…Give HOPE!

On **Monday, August 16**, the Yankees kicked off HOPE Week by surprising 13-year-old quadruple amputee Jorge Grajales of Ridgewood N.J., with a pool party and barbecue, which included generous donations from Stop & Shop and Party City. Mariano Rivera, Nick Swisher and Brett Gardner, along with Yankees coaches Kevin Long and Mike Harkey enjoyed an afternoon with Jorge, his foster parents John and Faye Dyksen, and his family and friends. Originally born in Panama, Jorge lost all of his limbs as an infant due to an infection. Since age 3, the Dyksen family has taken him into their home for three-quarters of the year through a program called Healing the Children. At that evening's game, Jorge and the Dyksens were

Nick Swisher and the Yankees kicked off HOPE Week with a swimming party for Jorge Grajales.

honored during pregame ceremonies and Jorge threw out the first pitch.

During an April 26 White House ceremony honoring the team's 2009 World Series championship, President Barack Obama officially announced the return of HOPE Week in 2010. In conjunction with HOPE Week, the White House's Corporation for National and Community Service awarded honorees "President's Volunteer Service Awards," bestowed by the President to salute volunteers who strengthen the nation's culture of service. At the conclusion of the week, the Yankees were honored with the President's Volunteer Service Award, given "in recognition and appreciation of commitment to strengthening the Nation and for making a difference through volunteer service."

On **Tuesday, August 17**, the Yankees reached out to Morris Plains, N.J., resident Jane Lang, who has been blind since birth. Manager Joe Girardi, players Joba Chamberlain, Chad Gaudin and David Robertson, along with former Yankee Tino Martinez surprised Lang at her house and joined her on her normal trek to

Joba Chamberlain [R] escorts Jane and Clipper through Herald Square and down to the D train.

Yankee Stadium, using public transportation. Once at the Stadium, Jane received a private tour of Monument Park, with former Yankee Paul O'Neill, where she felt some of the monuments and plaques for the first time. She then went on a private tour of the Yankees Museum and felt the 2009 World Championship Trophy as well as one of Babe Ruth's bats. Prior to the game, Jane and her Seeing Eye dog, Clipper, delivered the lineup card to home plate with Joe Girardi, who also escorted Jane around the base paths following the game.

On **Wednesday, August 18**, the Yankees reached out to Sierra Leone-native, civil war survivor and recent high school graduate Mohamed Kamara. CC Sabathia, General Manager Brian Cashman and Hall of Famer Reggie Jackson took Mohamed on a surprise tour of the New York Stock Exchange during the morning bell ringing. The Yankees then escorted Mohamed to City Hall, where the group was joined by Derek Jeter, Marcus Thames and Curtis Granderson before meeting with Mayor Michael Bloomberg. Following their trip to City Hall, the Yankees and Mohamed visited the United Nations where His Excellency Mr. Shekou M. Touray, Permanent Representative of Sierra Leone to the United Nations, spoke with Mohamed and the Yankees in a private meeting and accompanied the group on a tour of the General Assembly Hall.

[L-R] Brian Cashman, Reggie Jackson, Mohamed Kamara and CC Sabathia pause for a moment on the New York Stock Exchange floor during the morning bell ringing ceremony.

On **Thursday, August 19**, the Yankees reached out to children and supporters of "Beautiful People." The organization was founded by Peter Ladka of Warwick, N.Y., who – though he had two perfectly healthy children of his own – wanted to reach out to children and families with special needs to make them feel more a part of the community. Yankees players and coaches were paired with special-needs children from the Beautiful People organization in a baseball game on the field at Yankee Stadium following the club's game vs. Detroit. The Yankees, the children and their families also enjoyed an on-field barbecue catered by Hard Rock Cafe and dessert from Dylan's Candy Bar and Turkey Hill.

Jorge Posada and the Yankees buddied up with participants of Beautiful People for the group's game on the Yankee Stadium field.

On **Friday, August 20**, the Yankees reached out to the Arias sisters, Johanna and Melida, who have overcome hardships and homelessness and made their lives better through education and hard work. Two years ago, with their family struggling, Johanna chose to pass up college at Syracuse University in order to work so she could provide for her sister and mother. This fall, Melida began her freshman year at Baruch College in Manhattan and hopes to become the first member of her family to graduate college. Yankees players Alex Rodriguez, Robinson Cano, Ramiro Pena, Francisco Cervelli, Sergio Mitre, David Robertson and Bench Coach Tony Pena surprised Melida at her job at Wendy's in the Bronx, and then took both sisters on a surprise shopping spree at DKNY in Manhattan to outfit Melida for her freshman year of college and Johanna for future professional opportunities.

At that evening's game vs. Seattle, Brian Cashman presented paid internship offers to both girls – Melida with the Yankees and Johanna with Lincoln Hospital in the Bronx. Melida also received a laptop computer courtesy of TekServe and both sisters received gift bags with items donated by Dooney & Bourke, Helen Ficalora and Nike. The girls' mother, Maria, was presented with $1,000 in gift cards from White Rose.

Melida (L) and Johanna (R) pose with some of their new wardrobe at DKNY in Manhattan.

2010 Season Summary

RETURN TO THE POSTSEASON: With their win on 9/28 at Toronto, the Yankees clinched a spot in the 2010 postseason…are entering the postseason as the Wild Card for the fourth time (also 1995, '97 and '07)…are making their 15th postseason appearance in the last 16 seasons (1995-07, '09)…will be their 49th postseason appearance all time, most for any franchise.

HOME COOKIN': The Yankees were 52-29 (.642) at home in 2010, tying Detroit for the second-highest home winning percentage in the American League behind Minnesota (53-28, .654)…the Yankees completed their first two seasons at Yankee Stadium with a 109-53 (.673) record, marking the most wins and highest home winning percentage over the stretch…according to the Elias Sports Bureau, their 109 victories are the most by a Major League team in its first two seasons at a particular venue, surpassing the previous mark of 106 shared by the 1909-10 Philadelphia Athletics (Shibe Park) and the 1997-98 Atlanta Braves (Turner Field).

The Yankees became the second team among Baseball's current 30 franchises to advance to the postseason in each of their first two seasons in their current stadium, joining Atlanta (1997-98 at Turner Field)…in 2009, became the third team to win the World Series in their first season in their current stadium (also the 2006 St. Louis Cardinals and 1912 Boston Red Sox) – credit: Elias.

COMEBACK KIDS: The Yankees led the Majors with 48 come-from-behind wins this season, seven of which were by three or more runs…had six wins this season when trailing at the end of the eighth inning.

SUPPORT SHOWS: The Yankees had a total attendance of 3,765,803 at home during the 2010 season, marking the highest home attendance for any Major League team in 2010…the Yankees also led the Majors averaging 46,491 per game…surpassed their home attendance figures for the 2009 regular season (3,719,358 total / 45,918 per game)…marked the eighth consecutive season the Yankees led the AL in attendance…the organization also led the Majors in road attendance (2,830,138)…the Yankees' combined draw of 6,595,941 fans topped the American League for the 12th consecutive season.

DUELING LEFTIES: With LHPs CC Sabathia (21-7, .750) and Andy Pettitte (11-3, .786) the Yankees pitching staff featured multiple left-handers each with at least a .750 winning percentage and a minimum 20 starts for just the second time in franchise history…the 1953 combo

of Whitey Ford (18-6, .750) and Eddie Lopat (16-4, .800) also accomplished the feat in 1953.

TRIPLE YOUR PLEASURE: The Yankees collected 32 triples in 2010, matching their highest total since 2000 (also 2007)…Brett Gardner and Curtis Granderson each recorded seven triples, marking just the second time since 2000 the Yankees have had teammates each with at least 7 triples (also 2007: Melky Cabrera-8, Robinson Cano-7).

GOLD CALIBER: The Yankees led the Majors with a .988 fielding percentage, committing just 69 errors – the fewest for any Major League team in 2010…marked the Yankees' highest fielding percentage for any season and fewest errors for any non-abbreviated season (previous low was 83E in 2008).

The Yankees' primary infielders in 2010 (Teixeira, Cano, Jeter, Rodriguez) combined for a .994 fielding percentage (19E, 2,931TC)…according to the Elias Sports Bureau, all Yankees infielders were charged with 27 errors this season, the fewest of any ML team at those positions.

SS Derek Jeter led all Major League shortstops in fielding pct. in 2010 (.989) while 2B Robinson Cano led all AL second basemen with a .996 fielding pct…became the first teammates to finish a season as the fielding leaders at SS and 2B (in either league) since Omar Vizquel/Roberto Alomar for Cleveland in 2001…the last Yankees to accomplish the feat were Phil Rizzuto/Jerry Coleman in 1949 (Credit: Elias).

ARMED AND DANGEROUS: The Yankees collected 32 outfield assists in 2010, the sixth-most among AL teams…had 15 OF assists all of last year – fewest by any Major League team…OF Brett Gardner (12) tied for second in the Majors in OF assists behind Cleveland's Shin-Soo Choo (14)…along with RF Nick Swisher (10), the pair became the first Yankees teammates with at least 10 outfield assists in a season since 1975 (Bobby Bonds-12 and Roy White-11).

YANKEES HONOR ICONS: The Yankees are honoring former Principal Owner/Chairperson George M. Steinbrenner III and longtime Yankees PA announcer Bob Sheppard with commemorative patches…Mr. Steinbrenner's patch is affixed on the left breast of the Yankees' uniforms, over the players' heart…it is also being worn by all Yankees minor league affiliates…Sheppard's patch is being worn on the left sleeve…in addition, the team is wearing a black armband on their left sleeve to honor the passing of Ralph Houk.

MOST PITCHES SEEN IN 2010	
1. Boston	25,528
2. YANKEES	24,972
3. Arizona	24,742
4. Tampa Bay	24,618
5. Atlanta	24,259

BEST BULLPEN ERA AFTER THE ALL-STAR BREAK	
1. San Diego	2.70
2. San Francisco	2.78
3. **YANKEES**	**2.86**
4. Cleveland	2.95
5. Atlanta	2.99

FOR STARTERS: The Yankees had five pitchers each record double-digit wins this season (Burnett, Hughes, Pettitte, Sabathia and Vazquez)...joined Minnesota (six pitchers) and Tampa Bay (five) as the only teams to feature at least five such pitchers in 2010...last time the Yankees had five pitchers each with at least 10 wins was 1999 (Clemens, Cone, Hernandez, Irabu, Pettitte).

Entered the All-Star break with three pitchers with at least 11 wins – LHP CC Sabathia (12-3), LHP Andy Pettitte (11-2) and RHP Phil Hughes (11-2) – for the first time in franchise history, according to the Elias Sports Bureau...became just the third trio of teammates in AL history to accomplish the feat (also the 1970 and 1971 Orioles, with Mike Cuellar, Dave McNally and Jim Palmer in each season).

WINNERS AGAIN: The Yankees' clinched the franchise's 18th straight winning season in 2010 (since 1993)...according to the *Elias Sports Bureau*, only two previous teams ever had 18 or more consecutive seasons above .500: the Yankees from 1926-64 (39 seasons) and the Baltimore Orioles from 1968-85 (18 seasons).

TEAM DIVERSITY: Seven Yankees players scored at least 70R in 2010 (Cano, Gardner, Granderson, Jeter, Rodriguez, Swisher and Teixeira), tying the 1933, '36, '38, '77, '98 and '07 Yankees for the second-highest such total in franchise history...only the 1939 Yankees (eight) had more players with 70 or more runs...the Yankees had five players with at least 90 runs (Cano, Gardner, Jeter, Swisher and Teixeira), the most teammates to reach the plateau for any Major League team this season...had five Yankees play at least 150 games in 2010, marking their second straight season accomplishing the feat and the most for any team in Baseball this season...matched their most in a season since the start of the Expansion Era (since 1961).

· 2B Robinson Cano (103R), SS Derek Jeter (111R) and 1B Mark Teixeira (113R) became the fourth trio of infield teammates to each score at least 100R in consecutive seasons – also 1999-2000 Cleveland Indians (R. Alomar, J. Thome, O. Vizquel), 1936-38 Yankees (F. Crosetti, L. Gehrig, R. Rolfe) and 1929-30 Philadelphia A's (M. Bishop, M. Cochrane, J. Foxx).

CHART TOPPERS: The Yankees currently have Baseball's top active hits leader (SS Derek Jeter–2,926H) and top active home runs leader (3B Alex Rodriguez–613HR)...according to research from the Elias Sports Bureau, it is the first time both such leaders were teammates since the 1995 Cleveland Indians ended their season with Dave Winfield (3,110H) and Eddie Murray (479HR) on their roster...Seattle's Ken Griffey, Jr. led both categories prior to Jeter surpassing him this season in hits...in addition, Rodriguez leads all active players with 1,831RBI.

FIRST THINGS FIRST: The Yankees featured 11 players on their active roster this season that were selected in the first round or supplemental first round of the First-Year Player Draft – Berkman, Brackman Chamberlain, Hughes, Jeter, Moseley, Rodriguez, Sabathia, Swisher, Teixeira and Wood.

Alex Rodriguez hit his 600th career home run on 8/4 vs. Toronto.

RESUME CHANGERS: The Yankees defeated three pitchers who threw a no-hitter earlier in the 2010 season, defeating Philadelphia's Roy Halladay on 6/15 at Yankee Stadium, Oakland's Dallas Braden on 9/2 at Yankee Stadium and Tampa Bay's Matt Garza 9/20 at Yankee Stadium.

STADIUM SLUGFEST: On June 5, boxing returned to the Bronx as the Yankees and Top Rank boxing presented a world title fight between undefeated World Boxing Association super welterweight champion Yuri Foreman and three-time world champ Miguel Cotto at Yankee Stadium...Cotto defeated Foreman with a ninth-round TKO to win the WBA Super Welterweight title in front of 20,272...televised live by HBO, it was the first prizefight in the Yankees' home since Muhammad Ali won a unanimous decision over Ken Norton on 9/28/76 at the original Yankee Stadium.

BRONX BOOMBOX: Yankee Stadium hosted its first concert on September 13, when JAY-Z and Eminem played the first night of a two-show run...was the second stop of a home-and-home series featuring the rappers...the two sold-out shows marked the first concert at the Yankees' home since Pink Floyd played in June 1994.

GRIDIRON GREATS: Following this season, Yankee Stadium will play host to two premier college football events beginning with the revival of the Notre Dame-Army rivalry on November 20...the two historic programs met 22 times at the original Yankee Stadium – the previous home of the New York Yankees – with the Irish holding a 14-5-3 record in games played from 1925-29, 1931-46, and 1969...in addition, Yankee Stadium will be home to the New Era Pinstripe Bowl on December 30, 2010, which will be nationally televised by ESPN. The bowl game will pit the Big East team with the third-best conference record against the Big 12 team with the sixth-best conference mark after excluding the conferences' respective BCS teams from consideration.

Follow your team wherever you are.

Get highlights, scores, and stats on the nation's fastest mobile broadband network.

AT&T IS THE EXCLUSIVE TELECOMMUNICATIONS PARTNER OF THE NEW YORK YANKEES.

Rethink Possible™

1.866.MOBILITY - ATT.YANKEES.COM - VISIT A STORE

TEXT **YANKS** TO **4663** FOR EXCLUSIVE YANKEES CONTENT, HIGHLIGHTS, AND MORE DELIVERED TO YOUR WIRELESS PHONE!

Joe Girardi

28 Manager
Opening Day Age: 45

Full Name
Joseph Elliott Girardi

Birthdate
October 14, 1964

Birthplace
Peoria, Ill.

Resides
Purchase, N.Y.

College
Northwestern University

Career Highlights
BBWAA
N.L. Manager of the Year
▸ 2006

Sporting News
N.L. Manager of the Year
▸ 2006

N.L. All-Star Team
▸ 2000

At the Helm in 2010

▸ The 2010 season marked his third as Manager of the New York Yankees, guiding the club to a 95-67 record, their second consecutive postseason appearance and 15th playoff berth in the last 16 years…was the second-best record in the AL behind Tampa Bay (96-66) and the third best in the Majors, also trailing Philadelphia (97-65)…spent the final 69 days of the season (from 7/18 on) within 2.5 games (either ahead or behind) of Tampa Bay.

▸ Led the Yankees to a Major League-high 48 come-from-behind wins, their second straight season leading the category (51 in 2009)…collected six wins when trailing after the end of the eighth inning, one more than their total from last season.

▸ Did not lose more than four straight games during the 2010 season, one of just two teams to not record a losing streak of at least five games this season – also Minnesota…the Yankees were the last team in the Majors to suffer a three-game sweep, with their first and only instance coming 9/10-12 at Texas.

▸ Won 30 series, tying for the second-most in the AL with Tampa Bay, behind Minnesota (31).

▸ The Yankees were 52-29 (.642) at home, tying Detroit for the second-highest home winning percentage in the American League behind Minnesota (53-28, .654)… completed their first two seasons at Yankee Stadium with a 109-53 (.673) record, marking the most wins and highest home winning percentage over the stretch.

▸ Led the Majors with a .988 fielding percentage and committed only 69 errors, setting a franchise record for highest fielding percentage and fewest errors in any non-abbreviated season…since taking over in 2008, the Yankees lead the Majors with a .987 fielding percentage

▸ Earned his 200th win as Yankees Manager on 4/17 vs. Texas…recorded his 300th career managerial win on 5/31 vs. Cleveland.

▸ At 45 years old, was the third-youngest manager in the Majors at the conclusion of the season, behind Cleveland's Manny Acta (41) and Seattle's Daren Brown (43).

▸ Was ejected three times in 2010…has been ejected 14 times in his career, 11 times as a Manager (nine as Yankees manager), 10 times as a Yankee (also 8/6/99 as a player).

> ### Wise Beyond his Years
> In 2009 Joe Girardi became the youngest manager in Yankees history to win a World Series and the fourth-youngest in the Majors over the last 30 years (1980-2009) behind Minnesota's Tom Kelly (1987 and '91), the White Sox's Ozzie Guillen (2005) and the Mets' Davey Johnson (1986).

Managing/Coaching Career

▸ Was named the 32nd manager in club history on 10/30/07, becoming the 17th Yankees manager to have played for the club and fourth former Yankees catcher to skipper the team (also Bill Dickey, Ralph Houk and Yogi Berra).

▸ Led the Yankees to their 27th World Championship in 2009 in his second season as Manager, becoming the ninth Yankees manager to win a World Series… in his postseason managerial debut, joined Ralph Houk and Billy Martin as the only three Yankees to play for and manage a World Championship team… also joined Houk, Bob Lemon and Casey Stengel as the only four Yankees managers to win a World Series in their first postseason as a manager.

▸ Led the club to a 103-59 regular season record, marking the Majors' best record in 2009 and the Yankees' most wins since 2002 (103-58)… became the eighth Yankees manager to collect at least 100 wins in a full season, joining Miller Huggins, Joe McCarthy, Casey Stengel, Ralph Houk, Billy Martin, Dick Howser and Joe Torre… joined McCarthy, Houk, Martin and Howser as the only five Yankees skippers to accomplish the feat within their first two full seasons with the team… finished third in AL Manager of the Year voting with 34 total points, including four first-place votes.

▸ Is one of two current Major League managers who have both played for (1998 Yankees) and managed (2009 Yankees) teams that won at least 100 games in a season, joining Lou Piniella, as a player with the Yankees (1977-78, '80) and managers of the 2001 Mariners—credit: *Elias Sports Bureau.*

▸ ⊠At 45 years old, became the youngest manager in Yankees history to win a World Series and the fourth-youngest in the Majors over the last 30 years (1980-2009) behind Minnesota's Tom Kelly (1987 and '91), the White Sox's Ozzie Guillen (2005) and the Mets' Davey Johnson (1986).

▸ Led the Yankees to an 89-73 record in his debut season as the club's skipper in 2008…the Yankees ranked fifth in the Majors in fielding percentage (.986), committing their fewest errors in any non-abbreviated season (83).

▸ Was named the 2006 National League "Manager of the Year" by the Baseball Writers Association of America and the Sporting News, joining the Houston Astros' Hal Lanier (1986) and the San Francisco Giants' Dusty Baker (1993) as the only managers to win the honor in their managerial debuts…guided the Florida Marlins to a 78-84 record in his first season as a Major League manager.

▸ Became the first manager to improve his club's record above .500 after falling at least 20 games below the .500 mark during the same season (20 games under .500 on 5/21 (11-31), but then went 62-41 through 9/12 to improve to 73-72).

▸ Managed Anibal Sanchez's no-hit performance on 9/6/06 vs. Arizona…was the fourth no-hitter that Girardi has been a part of, having caught two (Dwight Gooden's on 5/14/96 and David Cone's perfect game on 7/18/99) and being a teammate in one (David Wells' perfect game on 5/17/98)… according to the *Elias Sports Bureau*, Girardi became the first person since Jeff Torborg to both catch and manage a no-hitter.

▸ Made his coaching debut in 2005, serving as bench coach and catching instructor on Joe Torre's New York Yankees staff…assisted in guiding the Yankees to a 95-67 (.586) record and the American League East title.

ACTIVE MANAGERS TO WIN WORLD SERIES IN THEIR FIRST POSTSEASON

JOE GIRARDI	NYY, 2009
Ozzie Guillen	CWS, 2005
Terry Francona	BOS, 2004
Mike Scioscia	ANA, 2002

DID YOU KNOW? Joe Girardi and Yogi Berra are the only Yankees catchers to be behind the plate for two regular season no-hitters. Girardi was the catcher for Dwight Gooden's no-hitter on 5/14/96 vs. Seattle and David Cone's perfect game on 7/18/99 vs. Montreal. Berra caught both of Allie Reynolds' no-hitters in 1951.

Playing Career

▸ Played parts of 15 seasons as a catcher in the Major Leagues with the Chicago Cubs (1989-92 and 2000-02), Colorado Rockies (1993-95), New York Yankees (1996-99) and St. Louis Cardinals (2003)…was a member of three World Series Championship teams in New York (1996, 1998-99) and played in a total of six postseasons with the Cubs (1989), Rockies (1995) and Yankees (1996-99).

▸ In 1,277 career Major League games, batted .267 (1,100-for-4,127) with 454 runs, 186 doubles, 36 HR and 422 RBI, finishing with a .991 career fielding percentage while throwing out 27.6% of potential base stealers…batted .184 (21-for-114) with 2 triples and 1 RBI in 39 career postseason games.

▸ Saw his first Major League action in 1989 as the Cubs' Opening Day catcher…was the first rookie catcher to start a season opener for the Cubs since Randy Hundley in 1966…was selected to Baseball Digest's All-Rookie Team…played in four games of the 1989 NL Championship Series against San Francisco, recording one hit.

▸ Was acquired by the Yankees on 11/3/95 from the Rockies in exchange for LHP Mike DeJean…hit a career-high .294 with 2 HR and 45 RBI for the World Series Champions.

▸ Was the catcher for Dwight Gooden's no-hitter on 5/14/96 vs. Seattle…in his final season as a player with the Yankees, caught David Cone's perfect game on 7/18/99 vs. Montreal.

▸ POSTSEASON: Appeared in 39 career postseason games as a player, most among all current American League managers…among Major League skippers, only Dusty Baker (40G) played in more postseason games as a player…had two triples during the 1996 postseason, including a run-scoring three-base hit off Greg Maddux in Game 6 of the World Series at Yankee Stadium.

JOE GIRARDI

Personal/Miscellaneous

▶ Graduated high school in 1982 from the Spalding Institute (Ill.), where he was an All-State selection in baseball.

▶ Graduated from Northwestern University in 1986 with a bachelor's degree in industrial engineering… was a three-time Academic All-American and two-time All-Big 10 selection at catcher… received the 2007 Distinguished Alumni Award from the Northwestern University Department of Industrial Engineering and Management Sciences.

GIRARDI'S CAREER MANAGERIAL RECORD

Year	Club	Position	W	L	Pct.
2006	Marlins	Fourth	78	84	.481
2008	YANKEES	Third	89	73	.549
2009	YANKEES	First	103	59	.636
2010	YANKEES	Second*	95	67	.593
Totals			**365**	**283**	**.563**
Totals w/NYY			**287**	**199**	**.591**

*Wild card winner

▶ Established his own charity, Catch 25, which is dedicated to providing support to families and individuals across the country who have been challenged with ALS, Alzheimer's, cancer and fertility issues…Catch 25 provides assistance through scholarships, financial aid and charitable donations and is devoted to serving children and adults that may not otherwise have the financial and emotional support they may need…hosts the annual "Remember When, Remember Now" benefit along with Michael Kay at the Grand Central Oyster Bar in New York City, helping raise funds for his charity and Alzheimer's research… his father, Jerry, suffers from the disease…see www.joegirardi.com for more information.

▶ Received the Community Leadership Award from the New York City Chapter of the Alzheimer's Association at its annual "Forget-Me-Not" gala on 6/1/09.

▶ Received the Sweetwater Clifton "City Spirit" Award from the New York Knicks on 11/22/09 for serving as a good Samaritan by stopping to aid a stranded motorist on his way home following the final game of the World Series… was the recipient of the Ben Epstein "Good Guy Award" in 1997, presented annually by the New York chapter of the BBWAA… was honored at the 2007 Lou Gehrig Sports Award Benefit Dinner.

▶ Joined New York City Mayor Michael Bloomberg and Roberto Clemente, Jr. in placing the first "pitch" on 7/29/08 at the 3rd Annual Gracie Mansion Tee Ball Game… hosted by the Mayor's Office, Little League Baseball and the Roberto Clemente Foundation, the game featured five teams, one from each New York City borough and promoted youth exercise as well as team-building sports.

▶ Joined the Alliance for Downtown New York on 6/15/10 to unveil a new granite sidewalk marker in the Canyon of Heroes commemorating the Yankees' ticker-tape parade honoring the team's 27th World Series championship

▶ Following his retirement as a player in 2004, Girardi joined the YES Network as an analyst and won an Emmy Award for hosting YES' "Kids on Deck" series…in 2007, he rejoined YES, working as an analyst on Yankees broadcasts…also worked with FOX during the regular season and postseason…Girardi gained broadcast experience as a member of ESPN Radio's team for the 2003 National League Division Series.

▶ He and his wife, Kim, have three children, Serena (10), Dante (9) and Lena (3).

Girardi's Major League Playing Career

Year Club	AVG	G	AB	R	H	2B	3B	HR	RBI	SH	SF	HP	BB	SO	SB	CS	E	OBP	SLG
Minor League Totals	.284	323	1128	152	320	42	13	21	136	7	6	7	88	181	28	10	34	.339	.393
Major League Totals	.267	1277	4127	454	1100	186	26	36	422	81	23	25	279	607	44	31	77	.315	.350
NYY Totals	.272	379	1283	147	349	72	9	8	153	32	8	9	80	172	20	12	19	.317	.361

Drafted by the Chicago Cubs in the fifth round of the 1986 First-Year Player Draft.

Girardi's Division Series Record

Year	Club/Opponent	AVG	G	AB	R	H	2B	3B	HR	RBI	BB	SO	SB
1995	COL vs. ATL	.125	4	16	0	2	0	0	0	0	0	2	0
1996	NYY vs. TEX	.222	4	9	1	2	0	0	0	0	4	1	0
1997	NYY vs. CLE	.133	5	15	2	2	0	0	0	0	1	3	0
1998	NYY vs. TEX	.429	2	7	0	3	0	0	0	0	0	1	0
1999	NYY vs. TEX	.000	2	6	0	0	0	0	0	0	0	1	0
Division Series Totals		**.170**	**17**	**53**	**3**	**9**	**0**	**0**	**0**	**0**	**5**	**8**	**0**

Girardi's League Championship Series Record

Year	Club/Opponent	AVG	G	AB	R	H	2B	3B	HR	RBI	BB	SO	SB
1989	CHC vs. SF	.100	4	10	1	1	0	0	0	0	1	2	0
1996	NYY vs. BAL	.250	4	12	1	3	0	1	0	0	1	3	0
1998	NYY vs. CLE	.250	3	8	2	2	0	0	0	0	1	0	0
1999	NYY vs. BOS	.250	3	8	0	2	0	0	0	0	0	2	0
LCS Totals		**.211**	**14**	**38**	**4**	**8**	**0**	**1**	**0**	**0**	**3**	**7**	**0**

Girardi's World Series Record

Year	Club/Opponent	AVG	G	AB	R	H	2B	3B	HR	RBI	BB	SO	SB
1996	NYY vs. ATL	.200	4	10	1	2	0	1	0	1	1	2	0
1998	NYY vs. SD	.000	2	6	0	0	0	0	0	0	0	2	0
1999	NYY vs. ATL	.286	2	7	1	2	0	0	0	0	0	1	0
World Series Totals		**.174**	**8**	**23**	**2**	**4**	**0**	**1**	**0**	**1**	**1**	**5**	**0**
POSTSEASON TOTALS		**.184**	**39**	**114**	**9**	**21**	**0**	**2**	**0**	**1**	**9**	**20**	**0**

Dave Eiland

58 Pitching Coach
Opening Day Age: 43

Full Name
David William Eiland

Birthdate
July 5, 1966

Birthplace
Dade City, Fla.

Resides
Wesley Chapel, Fla.

Coaching Career
▸ Completed his third season as Yankees pitching coach in 2010, marking his eighth season in the Yankees organization.
▸ Guided a staff that featured five pitchers with at least 10 wins apiece, one shy of the franchise record…the Yankees staff featured two pitchers (Sabathia and Hughes) with at least 18 wins in a season for the first time since 2002 (Mike Mussina: 18-10 and Davis Wells: 19-7), and two left-handers (Sabathia and Pettitte) with a winning percentage at .750 or above for just the second time, also Whitey Ford and Eddie Lopat in 1953 (min. 20 starts).
▸ His 2009 staff posted a 4.26 ERA in 2009, their lowest mark since 2003 (4.02)…3.94 ERA after the All-Star break…struck out 1,260 batters, the second-highest total in franchise history behind the 2001 total of 1,226K (credit: *Elias*)…their .251 opponents batting average was the second-lowest in the AL behind only Seattle (.247).
▸ Yankees starters (Burnett, Pettitte and Sabathia) worked to a 3.43 ERA in the 2009 postseason, holding the opposition to 3ER or less in 12 of their 15 playoff games…tossed at least 6.0IP with no more than 3ER allowed in each of their first seven starts of the 2009 playoffs, marking the best such stretch to start a postseason in franchise history.
▸ Spent 2007 as the pitching coach at Triple-A Scranton/Wilkes-Barre, where his staff ranked second in the International League with 1,101 strikeouts, tied for second with 13 shutouts and had the third-lowest ERA (3.64)…joined the Major League staff upon completion of Scranton's season.
▸ Previously served as the pitching coach for Double-A Trenton in 2005 and 2006…began his coaching career as the pitching coach for short-season Single-A Staten Island in 2003 and 2004.

Playing Career
▸ Appeared in 92 career Major League games (70 starts) over 10 seasons with the Yankees (1988-91, '95), San Diego Padres (1992-93) and Tampa Bay Devil Rays (1998-2000), going 12-27 with a 5.74 ERA (373.0IP, 238ER)…allowed a home run to his first-ever batter faced in the Majors on 8/3/88 at Milwaukee (Paul Molitor)…also homered in his first Major League at-bat on 4/10/92 off the Dodgers' Bob Ojeda.
▸ Underwent two Tommy John surgeries, forcing his retirement in 2002.
▸ Was originally selected by the Yankees in the seventh round of the 1987 First-Year Player Draft…earned Yankees "Minor League Pitcher of the Year" honors in 1990 as well as International League "Pitcher of the Year"…was selected to the Topps and *Baseball America* Triple-A All-Star teams.

Personal
▸ Married (Sandra) and has two daughters, Nicole and Natalie…played baseball and football at the University of Florida in 1985…transferred to the University of South Florida in 1986 to play baseball, earning All-Sun Belt Conference honors and preseason All-American honors…lettered three seasons in baseball, football and basketball at Zephyrhills (Fla.) High School and had his number retired in 2008…is active in charity work with the Pediatric Cancer Foundation.
▸ Served as Kevin Costner's body double in *For Love of the Game*.

Eiland's Career Major League Pitching Record

Year	Club	W-L	ERA	G	GS	CG	SHO	SV	IP	H	R	ER	BB	SO
1988	YANKEES	0-0	6.39	3	3	0	0	0	12.2	15	9	9	4	7
1989	YANKEES	1-3	5.77	6	6	0	0	0	34.1	44	25	22	13	11
1990	YANKEES	2-1	3.56	5	5	0	0	0	30.1	31	14	12	5	16
1991	YANKEES	2-5	5.33	18	13	0	0	0	72.2	87	51	43	23	18
1992	SAN DIEGO	0-2	5.67	7	7	0	0	0	27.0	33	21	17	5	10
1993	SAN DIEGO	0-3	5.21	10	9	0	0	0	48.1	58	33	28	17	14
1995	YANKEES	1-1	6.30	4	1	0	0	0	10.0	16	10	7	3	6
1998	TAMPA BAY	0-1	20.25	1	1	0	0	0	2.2	6	6	6	3	1
1999	TAMPA BAY	4-8	5.60	21	15	0	0	0	80.1	98	59	50	27	53
2000	TAMPA BAY	2-3	7.24	17	10	0	0	0	54.2	77	46	44	18	17
Minor League Totals		109-58	3.42	248	241	33	8	0	1421.2	1404	627	540	261	815
AL Totals		12-22	5.84	75	54	0	0	0	297.2	374	220	193	96	129
NL Totals		0-5	5.52	17	16	0	0	0	75.1	91	54	45	22	24
Major League Totals		12-27	5.74	92	70	0	0	0	373.0	465	274	238	118	153
NYY Totals		6-10	5.23	36	28	0	0	0	160.0	193	109	93	48	58

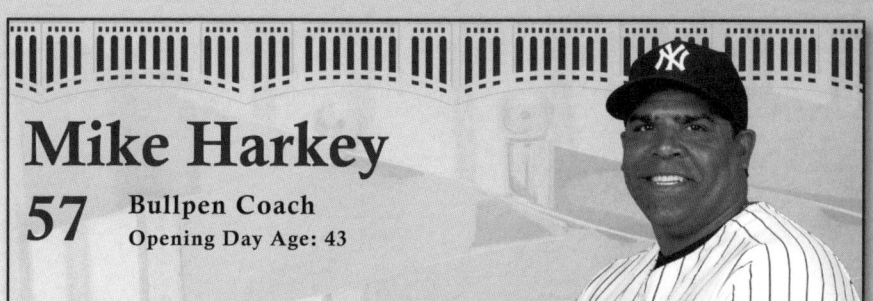

Mike Harkey

57 Bullpen Coach
Opening Day Age: 43

Full Name
Michael Anthony Harkey

Birthdate
October 25, 1966

Birthplace
San Diego, Calif.

Resides
Chino Hills, Calif.

Career Highlights
Sporting News
Rookie of the Year
▶ 1990

USA Today
Minor League Player of the Year
▶ 1988

Coaching Career
▶ Served his third season as Yankees bullpen coach in 2010…Yankees relievers combined for a 3.47 ERA, third-lowest in the AL, and held opponents to a .230 batting average, second-lowest in the AL…the Yankees were 81-2 when leading at the end of the eighth.
▶ Yankees relievers led the Majors in 2009 with 40 wins and tied for first with 51 saves, ranking second in opponent's batting average (.231) and fifth in strikeouts (483)…were 71-2 when leading after the end of the sixth inning.
▶ In 2008, the Yankees' bullpen collected a Major League-high 523K and recorded their lowest ERA (3.78) since 2002 (3.64).
▶ Is his second Major League coaching position, having served as bullpen coach for Joe Girardi with the Florida Marlins in 2006.
▶ Was the pitching coach for the Triple-A Iowa Cubs of the Pacific Coast League in 2007.
▶ Spent six seasons (2000-2005) as a pitching coach in the San Diego Padres organization, making stops at Single-A Rancho Cucamonga (2000), Single-A Fort Wayne (2001, '03), Single-A Lake Elsinore (2002, '04) and Double-A Mobile (2005).

Playing Career
▶ Appeared in 131 career Major League games (104 starts) over eight seasons with the Cubs (1988-93), Colorado Rockies (1994), Oakland Athletics (1995), California Angels (1995) and Los Angeles Dodgers (1997), going 36-36 with a 4.49 ERA (656.0IP, 327ER).
▶ Was named *Sporting News* 1990 "NL Rookie of the Year" after posting a 12-6 record with a 3.26 ERA in 27 starts for the Cubs…selected as *USA Today* "Minor League Player of the Year" in 1988…made his Major League debut at age 21 on 9/5/88 at Wrigley Field recording a no-decision in Game 2 of a doubleheader vs. the Phillies.
▶ Was a first-round pick by the Cubs in the 1987 First-Year Player Draft (fourth overall)…was originally selected by the San Diego Padres in the 18th round of the 1984 First-Year Player Draft, but chose to attend college.

Personal
▶ Married (Nikki) and has two sons, Tony and Cory, and a daughter, Miani…Tony is a junior infielder for Cal State Fullerton and Cory recently is in his junior season as a tight end with UCLA…played baseball at Cal State Fullerton, earning all-American honors as a junior…graduated from Ganesha High School in Pomona, Calif.

Harkey's Career Pitching Record

Year	Club	W-L	ERA	G	GS	CG	SHO	SV	IP	H	R	ER	BB	SO
1987	Peoria	2-3	3.55	12	12	3	0	0	76.0	81	45	30	28	48
	Pittsfield	0-0	0.00	1	0	0	0	0	2.0	1	0	0	0	2
1988	Pittsfield	9-2	1.37	13	13	3	1	0	85.2	66	29	13	35	73
	Iowa	7-2	3.55	12	12	3	1	0	78.2	55	36	31	33	62
	CHICAGO-NL	0-3	2.60	5	5	0	0	0	34.2	33	14	10	15	18
1989	Iowa	2-7	4.43	12	12	0	0	0	63.0	67	37	31	25	37
1990	CHICAGO-NL	12-6	3.26	27	27	2	1	0	173.2	153	71	63	59	94
1991	CHICAGO-NL	0-2	5.30	4	4	0	0	0	18.2	21	11	11	6	15
1992	Peoria	1-0	3.00	2	2	0	0	0	12.0	15	6	4	3	17
	Iowa	0-1	5.56	4	4	0	0	0	22.2	21	15	14	13	6
	Charlotte	0-1	5.63	1	1	1	0	0	8.0	9	5	5	0	5
	CHICAGO-NL	4-0	1.89	7	7	0	0	0	38.0	34	13	8	15	21
1993	CHICAGO-NL	10-10	5.26	28	28	1	0	0	157.1	187	100	92	43	67
	Orlando	0-0	1.69	1	1	0	0	0	5.1	4	1	1	0	5
1994	COLORADO	1-6	5.79	24	13	0	0	0	91.2	125	61	59	35	39
	Colorado Springs	1-1	12.60	2	2	0	0	0	10.0	19	14	14	3	4
1995	OAKLAND	4-6	6.27	14	12	0	0	0	66.0	75	46	46	31	28
	CALIFORNIA	4-3	4.55	12	8	1	0	0	61.1	80	32	31	16	28
1996	Albuquerque	7-11	5.38	49	13	0	0	13	118.2	146	79	71	39	90
1997	LOS ANGELES-NL	1-0	4.30	10	0	0	0	0	14.2	12	8	7	5	6
Minor League Totals		**29-28**	**3.70**	**109**	**72**	**10**	**2**	**13**	**482.0**	**482**	**267**	**214**	**179**	**349**
AL Totals		**8-9**	**5.44**	**26**	**20**	**1**	**0**	**0**	**127.1**	**155**	**78**	**77**	**47**	**56**
NL Totals		**28-27**	**4.26**	**105**	**84**	**3**	**1**	**0**	**528.2**	**565**	**278**	**250**	**178**	**260**
Major League Totals		**36-36**	**4.49**	**131**	**104**	**4**	**1**	**0**	**656.0**	**720**	**356**	**327**	**225**	**316**

Mick Kelleher

50 First Base Coach
Opening Day Age: 62

Full Name
Michael Dennis Kelleher

Birthdate
July 25, 1947

Birthplace
Seattle, Wash.

Resides
Solvang, Calif.

Coaching Career
▶ Served his second season as Yankees first base coach and infield instructor in 2010…the Yankees led the Majors with a .988 fielding percentage, committing just 69 errors–the fewest for any Major League team in 2010…marked the Yankees' highest all-time fielding percentage and fewest errors for any non-abbreviated season…Yankees infielders combined for only 27E, fewest for any infield in the Majors, and SS Derek Jeter (.989) and 2B Robinson Cano (.996) became the first set of teammates to finish a season as the fielding leaders at SS and 2B (in either league) since SS Omar Vizquel and 2B Roberto Alomar for Cleveland in 2001 and the first Yankees since Phil Rizzuto/Jerry Coleman in 1949 (Credit: *Elias*).
▶ The Yankees have committed 155E over the last two years since Kelleher joined the staff, the second-fewest in the Majors…set an all-time Major League record with 18 consecutive errorless games in 2009 and featured two AL Gold Glove winners (SS Derek Jeter and 1B Mark Teixeira).
▶ Is his third tenure on a Major League coaching staff, having served three years as Detroit's first base coach from 2003-05 and as Jim Leyland's first base coach and infield instructor with Pittsburgh in 1986.
▶ Spent the previous three years as the Yankees' roving infield instructor (2006-08)…is in his second stint with the Yankees, having spent seven seasons (1996-2002) as the roving defensive coordinator and one year (1998) as a Major League scout for the club.
▶ Began his coaching career with the San Diego Padres as a roving minor league instructor from 1984-85…joined the Chicago Cubs as a roving minor league infield instructor from 1987-92, taking over as manager of the organization's Triple-A Iowa club in May 1991 for the remainder of the season…also spent two seasons (1994-95) as the roving minor league infield instructor with the Milwaukee Brewers.

Playing Career
▶ Played 15 seasons of professional baseball, including 11 at the Major League level with St. Louis (1972-73, '75), Houston (1974), Chicago-NL (1976-80), Detroit (1981-82) and California (1982)…finished his career with a .974 Major League fielding percentage, appearing in games at second base, third base and shortstop…since retiring in 1982, no position player has accrued as many career plate appearances without a homer.
▶ Was selected by St. Louis in the third round of the 1969 First-Year Player Draft.
▶ Paced league shortstops in fielding during four of his minor league seasons and won two Rawlings Silver Glove Awards (1972, '75) as the minors' best fielding shortstop…established an American Association record for shortstops with a .979 fielding percentage in 1972.
▶ Received his bachelor of science degree in political science from the University of Puget Sound in Tacoma, Wash…was an NCAA Division II All-American in 1969 and named to the NCAA Division II All-Tournament Team the same season…was also Division II All-Coast in 1968 and '69.

Personal
▶ He and his wife, Renee, have one daughter, Brittney, and two grandchildren…Renee is an accomplished painter and is represented at galleries throughout California…is an aficionado of the wine industry and grows his own grapes and olives…in offseason, works as a ranch hand tending to llamas and cows.

Kelleher's Career Playing Record

Year	Club	AVG.	G	AB	R	H	2B	3B	HR	RBI	BB	SO	SB
1972	ST. LOUIS	.159	23	63	5	10	2	1	0	1	6	15	0
1973	ST. LOUIS	.184	43	38	4	7	2	0	0	2	4	11	0
1974	HOUSTON	.158	19	57	4	9	0	0	0	2	5	10	1
1975	ST. LOUIS	.000	7	4	0	0	0	0	0	0	0	1	0
1976	CHICAGO-NL	.228	124	337	28	77	12	1	0	22	15	32	0
1977	CHICAGO-NL	.230	63	122	14	28	5	2	0	11	9	12	0
1978	CHICAGO-NL	.253	68	95	8	24	1	0	0	6	7	11	4
1979	CHICAGO-NL	.254	73	142	14	36	4	1	0	10	7	9	2
1980	CHICAGO-NL	.146	105	96	12	14	1	1	0	4	9	17	1
1981	DETROIT	.221	61	77	10	17	4	0	0	6	7	10	0
1982	DETROIT	.000	2	1	0	0	0	0	0	0	0	0	0
	CALIFORNIA	.163	34	49	9	8	1	0	0	1	5	5	1
Major League Totals		**.213**	**622**	**1081**	**108**	**230**	**32**	**6**	**0**	**65**	**74**	**133**	**9**

Kevin Long
54 Hitting Coach
Opening Day Age: 43

Full Name
Kevin Richard Long

Birthdate
December 30, 1966

Birthplace
Van Nuys, Calif.

Resides
Scottsdale, Ariz.

Coaching Career
▸ Completed his fourth season as Yankees hitting coach in 2010…the Yankees led the Majors with 859 runs and a .350 on-base percentage…ranked second in walks (662), third in home runs (201) and eighth in batting average (.267)…had seven players score at least 70 runs, one shy of the franchise record.

▸ Yankees batters led the Majors in 2009 with 915R, 244HR, a .478 slugging percentage, a .362 on-base percentage and 663BB, and ranked second with a .283 batting average…set a franchise record in homers, surpassing the previous mark of 242 (2004)…guided an offense that featured a franchise-record five players with at least 25HR and a franchise-record nine players with at least 65RBI…coached middle infielders Derek Jeter and Robinson Cano, who became the first shortstop/second baseman combination in Baseball history to each record 200H at their respective positions in a single season…also featured two Silver Slugger Award winners (1B Mark Teixeira and Jeter).

▸ The 2008 Yankees ranked third in the AL in OBP (.342), fourth in average (.271) and tied for fourth in HR (180)…guided a Yankees offense in 2007 that led the Majors in runs (968), hits (1,656), HR (201), RBI (929), team batting average (.290), slugging percentage (.463), OBP (.366) and total bases (2,649)…the 968R were the most for the franchise since 1937 (979)…his offense also featured the AL MVP (Rodriguez), three Silver Sluggers (Jeter, Posada and Rodriguez) and four of the American League's top-15 batting averages.

▸ Joined the Yankees at the Major League level after serving three years as the hitting coach with the Yankees' Triple-A affiliate in Columbus (2004-06)…before joining the Yankees organization, served as the hitting coach with the Triple-A Omaha Royals (2002-03) and with the Double-A Wichita Wranglers (2000-01)…was named the Northwest League's "co-Manager of the Year" after leading the Spokane Indians to the league title in 1999…made his professional coaching debut at Single-A Wilmington in 1997.

Playing Career
▸ Was originally selected by the Kansas City Royals in the 31st round of the 1989 First-Year Player Draft and played in their system for eight years from 1989-96 as an outfielder.

▸ Led Class-A Eugene in 1989 in almost all offensive categories, including games played, at-bats, runs scored, hits, doubles and RBI…ranked eighth among all Northwest League hitters with a .312 batting average in his rookie season.

▸ Missed most of the 1994 season after undergoing surgery on his left wrist.

Personal
▸ Named a second-team All-American and first-team PAC-10 in 1989 at the University of Arizona…a three-year letter-winner, Long graduated with the Arizona record for most extra-base hits in a game (five) and ranked in the top 10 in several single-season statistical categories: third in extra-base hits (41), tied for seventh in doubles (23), eighth in multi-hit games (30), ninth in total bases (162) and tied for ninth in runs (80).

▸ Resides in Scottsdale, Ariz., with his wife, Marcey, daughter, Britney, and sons, Tracy and Jaron.

Long's Career Playing Record

Year	Club	AVG	G	AB	R	H	2B	3B	HR	RBI	BB	SO	SB
1989	Eugene	.312	69	260	54	81	19	1	3	45	36	40	15
1990	Baseball City	.282	85	308	53	87	17	5	5	33	32	28	22
1991	Memphis	.275	106	407	60	112	18	2	3	35	45	63	27
1992	Omaha	.228	88	312	28	71	16	3	1	29	29	41	9
1993	Memphis	.272	79	301	47	82	14	6	1	20	37	56	7
	Omaha	.255	17	51	7	13	2	0	0	4	2	13	3
1994	Memphis	.208	10	24	5	5	3	0	0	1	5	2	2
1995	Omaha	.250	22	64	7	16	3	0	0	1	5	8	1
	Wichita	.292	67	250	38	73	14	1	1	26	41	29	9
1996	Wichita	.273	128	436	62	119	31	3	3	48	56	36	9
Minor League Totals		**.273**	**671**	**2413**	**361**	**659**	**137**	**21**	**17**	**242**	**288**	**316**	**104**

Tony Pena

56   Bench Coach
Opening Day Age: 52

Full Name
Antonio Francisco Pena

Birthdate
June 4, 1957

Birthplace
Monte Cristi, D.R.

Resides
Santiago, D.R.

Career Highlights
BBWAA
  A.L. Manager of the Year
  ▸ 2003

N.L. All-Star Team
  ▸ 1982, 1984, 1985,
    1986, 1989

N.L. Gold Glove Award
  ▸ 1983, 1984, 1985

A.L. Gold Glove Award
  ▸ 1991

Managerial/Coaching Career

▸ Served his second season as Yankees bench coach in 2010…was his fifth season on the Yankees' Major League coaching staff, serving as first base coach from 2006-08 and catching instructor over the entire span…since joining the staff, Yankees catchers have caught a Major League-best 185 potential base stealers.

▸ Previously spent parts of four seasons as manager of the Kansas City Royals from 2002-05.

▸ In his first full season as manager in 2003, led the Royals to an 83-79 record, the sixth-best turnaround in Major League history following a 100-loss season…the 2003 season marked Kansas City's first winning season since 1993, when they went 84-78.

▸ Was selected as the 2003 American League "Manager of the Year" by the Baseball Writers' Association of America, becoming the fourth manager since 1983 to win the award in his first full season as a Major League skipper (also Houston's Hal Lanier, 1986; San Francisco's Dusty Baker, 1993; and San Diego's Bruce Bochy, 1996)… also named the 2003 AL "Manager of the Year" by both *Sporting News* and *Sports Illustrated*.

▸ Became only the third Dominican-born manager in Major League history, joining Felipe Alou and Luis Pujols.

▸ Began his Major League coaching career in 2002 as the bench coach for the Houston Astros…was named Royals manager on 5/15/02.

▸ Also served as manager of Triple-A New Orleans from 1999-2001…began his coaching career as White Sox' Coordinator of Dominican Operations in 1998 and led the Aguilas Dominican team to the Caribbean Series title.

Playing Career

▸ A five-time National League All-Star catcher, Pena posted a .260 career batting average over an 18-year Major League career, appearing in 1,988 games for the Pittsburgh Pirates (1980-86), St. Louis Cardinals (1987-88), Boston Red Sox (1990-93), Cleveland Indians (1994-96), Chicago White Sox (1997) and Houston Astros (1997).

▸ Ranks fifth all-time among Major League catchers with 1,950 games behind the plate, trailing only Ivan Rodriguez (2,390), Carlton Fisk (2,226), Bob Boone (2,225) and Gary Carter (2,056).

▸ Won four Gold Glove Awards (1983-85, 1991) and recorded a .338 career postseason batting average…was named Topps' Rookie All-Star catcher in 1981 and was selected to the UPI Rookie All-Star Team…originally signed as a non-drafted free agent by the Pittsburgh Pirates on 7/22/75 and made his Major League debut on 9/1/80.

Personal

▸ Married (Amaris) with two sons: Tony, Jr. (a pitcher in the San Francisco system) and Francisco Antonio (a catcher in the New York Mets system)…also has a daughter, Jennifer Amaris, who won the Miss Dominican Republic-U.S.A. beauty pageant in 2007…his brother, Ramon, pitched with the Detroit Tigers organization.

▸ Tony did not play high school baseball…credits his mother, who was an outstanding softball player, with teaching him how to play the game.

▸ Took part in the Yankees' hurricane relief donation of $35,000 in cash and food to the Dominican Republic in October 2007.

▸ Joined the Yankees delegation and the World Series trophy on 1/7/10 to meet Dominican Republic President Dr. Leonel Fernandez at the National Palace in Santo Domingo.

TONY PENA

Pena's Career Playing Record

Year	Club	AVG	G	AB	R	H	2B	3B	HR	RBI	BB	SO	SB
1976	Bradenton	.209	33	110	10	23	2	2	1	11	4	17	5
	Charleston	.224	14	49	4	11	2	0	1	8	4	7	0
1977	Charleston	.238	29	101	10	24	4	0	3	16	7	21	2
	Salem	.276	84	319	36	88	15	3	7	46	14	60	3
1978	Shreveport	.230	104	348	34	80	14	0	8	42	15	96	3
1979	Buffalo	.313	134	515	89	161	16	4	34	97	39	83	5
1980	Portland	.329	124	450	57	148	23	13	9	77	29	75	5
1980	PITTSBURGH	.429	8	21	1	9	1	1	0	1	0	4	0
1981	PITTSBURGH	.300	66	210	16	63	9	1	2	17	8	23	1
1982	PITTSBURGH	.296	138	497	53	147	28	4	11	63	17	57	2
1983	PITTSBURGH	.301	151	542	51	163	22	3	15	70	31	73	6
1984	PITTSBURGH	.286	147	546	77	156	27	2	15	78	36	79	12
1985	PITTSBURGH	.249	147	546	53	136	27	2	10	59	29	67	12
1986	PITTSBURGH	.288	144	510	56	147	26	2	10	52	53	69	9
1987	ST. LOUIS	.214	116	384	40	82	13	4	5	44	36	54	6
1988	ST. LOUIS	.263	149	505	55	133	23	1	10	51	33	60	6
1989	ST. LOUIS	.259	141	424	36	110	17	2	4	37	35	33	5
1990	BOSTON	.263	143	491	62	129	19	1	7	56	43	71	8
1991	BOSTON	.231	141	464	45	107	23	2	5	48	37	53	8
1992	BOSTON	.241	133	410	39	99	21	1	1	38	24	61	3
1993	BOSTON	.181	126	304	20	55	11	0	4	19	25	46	1
1994	CLEVELAND	.295	40	112	18	33	8	1	2	10	9	11	0
1995	CLEVELAND	.262	91	263	25	69	15	0	5	28	14	44	1
1996	CLEVELAND	.195	67	174	14	34	4	0	1	27	15	25	0
1997	CHICAGO-AL	.164	31	67	4	11	1	0	0	8	8	13	0
	HOUSTON	.211	9	19	2	4	3	0	0	2	2	3	0
Minor League Totals		**.283**	**522**	**1892**	**240**	**535**	**76**	**22**	**63**	**297**	**112**	**359**	**23**
Major League Totals		**.260**	**1988**	**6489**	**667**	**1687**	**298**	**27**	**107**	**708**	**455**	**846**	**80**

Pena's Division Series Record

Year	Club/Opponent	AVG	G	AB	R	H	2B	3B	HR	RBI	BB	SO	SB
1995	CLE vs. BOS	.500	2	2	1	1	0	0	1	1	0	0	0
1996	CLE vs. BAL	.000	1	0	0	0	0	0	0	0	0	0	0
1997	HOU vs. ATL	.000	2	0	0	0	0	0	0	0	0	0	0
Division Series Totals		**.200**	**5**	**2**	**1**	**1**	**0**	**0**	**1**	**1**	**0**	**0**	**0**

Pena's League Championship Series Record

Year	Club/Opponent	AVG	G	AB	R	H	2B	3B	HR	RBI	BB	SO	SB
1987	STL vs. SF	.381	7	21	5	8	0	1	0	0	3	4	1
1990	BOS vs. OAK	.214	4	14	0	3	0	0	0	0	0	0	0
1995	CLE vs. SEA	.333	4	6	1	2	1	0	0	0	1	0	0
LCS TOTALS		**.317**	**15**	**41**	**6**	**13**	**1**	**1**	**0**	**0**	**4**	**4**	**1**

Pena's World Series Record

Year	Club/Opponent	AVG	G	AB	R	H	2B	3B	HR	RBI	BB	SO	SB
1987	STL vs. MIN	.409	7	22	2	9	1	0	0	4	3	2	1
1995	CLE vs. ATL	.167	2	6	0	1	0	0	0	0	0	0	0
World Series Totals		**.357**	**9**	**28**	**2**	**10**	**1**	**0**	**0**	**4**	**3**	**2**	**1**
POSTSEASON TOTALS		**.338**	**29**	**71**	**9**	**24**	**2**	**1**	**1**	**5**	**7**	**6**	**2**

Pena's All-Star Game Record

Year	Club, Site	AVG	G	AB	R	H	2B	3B	HR	RBI	BB	SO	SB
1982	PIT, Montreal	.000	1	1	0	0	0	0	0	0	0	0	1
1984	PIT, San Francisco	.000	1	0	0	0	0	0	0	0	0	0	0
1985	PIT, Minnesota	.000	1	1	0	0	0	0	0	0	0	1	0
1986	PIT, Houston	.000	1	0	0	0	0	0	0	0	0	0	0
1989	STL, Anaheim	.000	1	2	0	0	0	0	0	0	0	0	0
All-Star Game Totals		**.000**	**5**	**4**	**0**	**0**	**0**	**0**	**0**	**0**	**0**	**1**	**1**

Rob Thomson

59   Third Base Coach
Opening Day Age: 46

Full Name
Robert Thomson

Birthdate
August 16, 1963

Birthplace
Ontario, Canada

Resides
Odessa, Fla.

Coaching Career

▸ Completed his 21st season as a member of the Yankees organization in 2010, second as the Yankees' third base coach…served as the club's bench coach for the 2008 season.

▸ Instructed Yankees outfielders, who collected 32 outfield assists (sixth-most in the AL) and included a pair of 10-assist outfielders (Gardner-12 and Swisher-10) for the first time since 1975.

▸ Managed the Yankees for three games in 2008, going 1-2, becoming the first Canadian to manage a Major League game since George (Mooney) Gibson, a Londoner, with the Pittsburgh Pirates in 1934…was 0-2 from 4/4-5 vs. Tampa Bay when Joe Girardi missed two games with an upper respiratory infection…won on 5/23 vs. Baltimore while Girardi served a one-game suspension…also guided the Yankees to a "walk-off" victory on 5/22 vs. Baltimore when Joe Girardi was ejected in the sixth inning…went in the books as Girardi's 100th career managerial victory…again took over following a Girardi ejection on 7/5 vs. Boston, also recording a "walk-off" win.

▸ Served as the Yankees' Major League field coordinator in 2007 after spending the previous three seasons as a special assignment instructor…was named to the Yankees' Major League coaching staff on 11/4/03.

▸ Joined the Yankees organization in 1990 as a third-base coach for Single-A Fort Lauderdale.

▸ Coached in the Yankees system for five years before taking over as manager of Single-A Oneonta of the NY-Penn League in 1995.

▸ Served as the third base coach at Triple-A Columbus in 1996 and 1997 before moving to the Yankees front office as a field coordinator in 1998.

▸ Was promoted to director of player development in 2000 and named vice president of minor league development prior to the 2003 season.

Playing Career

▸ Attended the University of Kansas and was selected in the 32nd round of the 1985 draft by the Detroit Tigers.

▸ Was a catcher and a third baseman in the Tigers system from 1985-88 before joining the Tigers' minor league coaching staff in 1988.

Personal

▸ Resides in Odessa, Fla., with his wife, Michele and their daughters, Jacqueline and Christina.

Thomson's Career Playing Record

Year	Club	AVG	G	AB	R	H	2B	3B	HR	RBI	BB	SO	SB
1985	Bristol	.000	2	5	0	0	0	0	0	0	1	3	0
	Gastonia	.187	39	123	7	23	6	0	0	10	5	17	0
1986	Gastonia	.252	94	298	42	75	11	1	4	38	48	44	1
	Lakeland	.182	8	22	2	4	1	0	1	4	0	2	0
1987	Lakeland	.228	71	206	21	47	12	0	1	22	25	30	2
1988	Lakeland	.000	2	7	0	0	0	0	0	0	0	2	0
Minor League Totals		**.225**	**216**	**661**	**72**	**149**	**30**	**1**	**6**	**74**	**79**	**98**	**3**

Scoring Machine

The Yankees hold the Major League record for consecutive games without being shut out, scoring at least one run in 308 straight contests from 8/3/31-8/2/33…the streak was broken by a 7-0 shutout by Philadelphia's Lefty Grove.

How the Yankees Were Built

FIRST-YEAR PLAYER DRAFT: (9)

Andrew Brackman .... June 2007, 1st Round (30th overall)
Joba Chamberlain ... June 2006, Compensation Round A (41st overall)
Colin Curtis ....June 2006, 4th round
Brett Gardner ....June 2005, 3rd round
Phil Hughes.............. June 2004, 1st Round (23rd overall)
Derek Jeter .... June 1992, 1st Round (6th overall)
Jorge Posada ....June 1990, 24th round
David Robertson ....June 2006, 17th round
Kevin Russo..........................June 2006, 20th round

SIGNED AS A NON-DRAFTED FREE AGENT: (9)

Robinson Cano .... January 5, 2001
Francisco Cervelli .... March 1, 2003
Reegie Corona .... July 2, 2003
Juan Miranda ....December 22, 2006
Hector Noesi.............................December 3, 2004
Ivan Nova.....................................July 15, 2004
Eduardo Nunez .... February 25, 2004
Ramiro Pena .... February 18, 2005
Mariano Rivera...........................February 17, 1990

SIGNED AS A FREE AGENT: (13)

Alfredo Aceves* ....March 10, 2008
A.J. Burnett ....December 18, 2008
Chad Gaudin....................................May 26, 2010
Nick Johnson* ....December 23, 2009
Sergio Mitre .... January 14, 2009
Chad Moeller ....April 6, 2010
Dustin Moseley .... February 16, 2010
Andy Pettitte ....December 9, 2009
Royce Ring.. January 5, 2010
Alex Rodriguez.........................December 13, 2007
CC Sabathia...........................December 18, 2008
Mark Teixeira............................. January 6, 2009
Marcus Thames .... February 8, 2010

CLAIMED OFF WAIVERS: (1)

Steve Garrison, San Diego .... September 9, 2010

ACQUIRED BY TRADE: (11)

PLAYER	FROM	DATE	FOR
Jonathan Albaladejo	Washington	December 5, 2007	RHP Tyler Clippard
Lance Berkman	Houston	July 31, 2010	RHP Mark Melancon INF Jimmy Paredes
Greg Golson	Texas	January 26, 2010	INF Mitch Hilligoss
Curtis Granderson-a	Detroit	December 9, 2009	Three team, seven player deal
Austin Kearns	Cleveland	July 30, 2010	Player to be named later - RHP Zach McAllister
Boone Logan-b	Atlanta	December 21, 2009	OF Melky Cabrera LHP Mike Dunn RHP Arodys Vizcaino
Damaso Marte*-c	Pittsburgh	July 26, 2008	RHP Jeff Karstens RHP Dan McCutchen RHP Ross Ohlendorf OF Jose Tabata
Romulo Sanchez	Pittsburgh	May 16, 2009	RHP Eric Hacker
Nick Swisher-d	Chicago (AL)	November 13, 2008	INF Wilson Betemit RHP Jeff Marquez OF Jhonny Nunez
Javier Vazquez-e	Atlanta	December 21, 2009	OF Melky Cabrera LHP Mike Dunn RHP Arodys Vizcaino
Kerry Wood	Cleveland	July 31, 2010	Player to be named later or cash

a – Acquired from the Detroit Tigers in a three-team, seven-player deal in which the Yankees sent LHP Phil Coke and OF Austin Jackson to Detroit and RHP Ian Kennedy to Arizona.
b – Acquired from the Atlanta Braves along with RHP Javier Vazquez in exchange for OF Melky Cabrera, LHP Mike Dunn and RHP Arodys Vizcaino.
c – Acquired from Pittsburgh along with Xavier Nady.
d – Acquired from Chicago-AL along with RHP Kanekoa Texeira.
e – Acquired from the Atlanta Braves along with LHP Boone Logan in exchange for OF Melky Cabrera, LHP Mike Dunn and RHP Arodys Vizcaino.
*60-day disabled list

2010 Yankees Support Staff

Gene Monahan	Head Athletic Trainer
Steve Donohue	Assistant Athletic Trainer
Dr. Christopher Ahmad	Team Physician
Dana Cavalea	Strength and Conditioning Coordinator
Charlie Wonsowicz	Advance Scout/Head Video Coordinator
Roman Rodriguez	Bullpen Catcher
Rob Cucuzza	Home Clubhouse Manager
Lou Cucuzza, Jr.	Visiting Clubhouse Manager
Lou Cucuzza, Sr.	Assistant Visiting Clubhouse Manager
Lou Potter	Massage Therapist
Anthony Flynn	Major League Video Coordinator
Brett Weber	Baseball Operations/Coaching Assistant

Clubhouse Assistants: Cesar Caceres, Chris Cruz, Joe Lee, Chris Manzione, Steve Antonucci, Jake Ryan

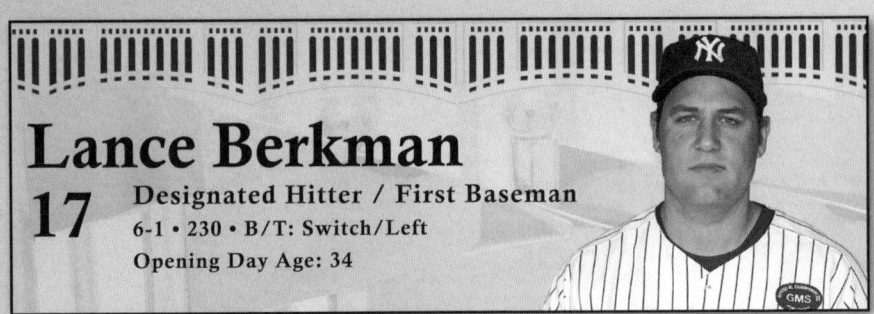

Lance Berkman

17

Designated Hitter / First Baseman
6-1 • 230 • B/T: Switch/Left
Opening Day Age: 34

Birthdate
February 10, 1976

Birthplace
Waco, Tex.

Resides
Houston, Tex.

M.L. Service
11 years, 52 days

College
Rice University

Career Highlights
N.L. All-Star Team
▸ 2001, 2002, 2004,
  2006, 2008

Status
▸ Acquired by the Yankees along with cash considerations from the Houston Astros on July 31, 2010 in exchange for RHP Mark Melancon and INF Jimmy Paredes…signed a six-year contract extension on April 8, 2005 (w/ Houston)…contract extends through the 2010 season.

Postseason Notes
▸ Owns a .321 (34-for-106) career postseason batting average, the fourth-highest mark among all active players…hit safely in 11 of his first 12 career postseason games, including a stretch of 10 straight from Game 3 of the 2001 NLDS to Game 4 of the 2004 NLCS…hit a grand slam in the eighth inning of the Astros' 18-inning win in Game 4 of the 2005 NLDS vs. Atlanta off Kyle Farnsworth…hit .385 (5-for-13) in his only World Series appearance in 2005 vs. Chicago-AL, leading the Astros with 6RBI in the Series.

Career Notes
▸ Ranks fifth all time in career homers by a switch-hitter (327)…is one of seven switch-hitters in Baseball history to reach the 300HR plateau.
▸ Collected 309HR from 2000-2009, hitting at least 20HR in each of the 10 seasons…is one of just 11 players in Major League history to hit at least 20HR in each year of a decade, joining Carlos Lee and now-teammate Alex Rodriguez as the only players to accomplish the feat from 2000-09.
▸ Originally selected by the Houston Astros in the first round of the 1997 First-Year Player Draft, departed the Astros ranking second in franchise history in home runs (326), third in runs scored (1,008), doubles (375) and RBI (1090), fourth in games played (1,592) and fifth in at-bats (5,560) and hits (1,648).

2010 Highs and Streaks

Hits	3 - 7 times
	Last: vs. BOS, 8/8/10
Runs	3 - vs. CHC, 7/28/10
2B	2 - vs. BOS, 8/8/10
3B	1 - at SD, 7/4/10
HR	2 - vs. PIT, 7/8/10
RBI	5 - vs. WAS, 6/1/10
BB	4 - at STL, 5/12/10
SO	3 - 3 times
	Last: at CHC, 7/21/10
SB	1 - 3 times
	Last: vs. SF, 6/24/10
Hit Streak	6g - 2 times
	Last: 6/1-6/10

Career Highs and Streaks

Hits	5 - vs. WAS, 5/6/08
Runs	4 - vs. WAS, 5/6/08
2B	2 - 38 times
	Last: vs. BOS, 8/8/10
3B	1 - 26 times
	Last: at SD, 7/4/10
HR	3 - at CIN, 4/16/02
RBI	6 - 2 times
	Last: vs. ATL, 5/1/03
BB	4 - 3 times
	Last: at STL, 5/12/10
SO	4 - 3 times
	Last: vs. CHC, 5/7/09
SB	2 - 4 times
	Last: at PIT, 7/9/08
Hit Streak	21g - 6/17-7/8/01

2010
▸ Combined to bat .248 (100-for-404) with 48R, 23 doubles, 14HR, 58RBI and 60BB in 122 games (91 starts at 1B and 21 at DH) with the Yankees and Astros in 2010…hit .267 (86-for-322) with 13HR as right-handed batter, and .171 (14-for-82) with 1HR as a left-hander.
▸ Averaged 6.25 PA/BB, ranking third in the Majors (min. 450PA).
▸ Was acquired by the Yankees from Houston on 7/31 after playing 1,592 games for the Astros…according to *Elias*, became the fifth player to join the Yankees after playing at least 1,500 games in the Majors all for one team (also Joe Sewell in 1931—1,513 games with the Indians; Enos Slaughter in 1954—1,820 games with the Cardinals; Paul Blair in 1977—1,700 games with the Orioles; and Wade Boggs in 1993—1,625

games for the Red Sox)...Sewell (1932), Slaughter (1956 and '58), Blair (1977-78) and Boggs (1996) all won World Series with the Yankees.

▸ Hit .248 (27-for-106) with 7 doubles, 1HR and 9RBI in 37 games (20 starts at DH and seven at 1B) with the Yankees in 2010...drew 17BB with only 15K...was 2-for-7 with 2BB as a pinch-hitter.

▸ Made his Yankees debut in 7/31 win at Tampa Bay, going 0-for-4...collected his first hit as a Yankee with a sixth-inning single in 8/1 loss at Tampa Bay, going 1-for-4.

▸ Batted seventh in the starting lineup in 8/2 loss vs. Toronto, going 1-for-3 with 1RBI and 1BB and drove in his first run as a Yankee with a sixth-inning RBI single...was his first time batting seventh since 7/4/00 vs. Arizona.

▸ Was placed on the 15-day disabled list on 8/19 (retroactive to 8/16) with a sprained right ankle...suffered the injury in the fifth inning of 8/15 win at Kansas City when he attempted to beat a throw at first base...had a two-game rehab assignment with Double-A Trenton, going 2-for-8 with 1R and 1BB.

▸ Was returned from rehab and reinstated from the 15-day D.L. prior to 9/1 win vs. Oakland...doubled as a pinch-hitter in the eighth on the first pitch he saw.

▸ Batted .299 (20-for-67) in 25 games following his return from the D.L., hitting safely in 11 of his 17 starts over the remainder of the season

▸ Hit his first home run as a Yankee and was 2-for-4 in 9/22 loss vs. Tampa Bay.

▸ Drew 3BB in his final start of the season in 10/2 Game 2 loss at Boston, going 0-for-1 with 1R and 1RBI.

▸ Batted .245 (73-for-298) with 39R, 16 doubles, 13HR and 49RBI in 85 games with the Astros this season prior to being acquired...played entirely at first base, committing just one error in 769 total chances.

▸ Opened the season on the 15-day disabled list, recovering from arthroscopic surgery on his left knee performed on 3/13...made two rehab appearances at Triple-A Round Rock, going 3-for-6 with 2 doubles, 1HR and 3RBI.

MOST CAREER HRs PRIOR TO BEING ACQUIRED BY THE YANKEES

440 – Jose Canseco	(2000)
379 – Gary Sheffield	(2003)
369 – Rocky Colavito	(1968)
345 – ALEX RODRIGUEZ	**(2004)**
328 – Chili Davis	(1998)
326 – LANCE BERKMAN	**(2010)**
315 – Johnny Mize	(1949)
305 – Richie Sexson	(2008)
294 – Darryl Strawberry	(1995)
293 – Ivan Rodriguez	(2008)
290 – Jimmy Wynn	(1977)
281 – Reggie Jackson	(1977)

HIGHEST OBP IN MAJORS SINCE 2000

1.	Barry Bonds	.517
2.	Todd Helton	.431
3.	Albert Pujols	.426
4.	Manny Ramirez	.418
5.	Jason Giambi	.416
6.	Chipper Jones	.411
7.	**LANCE BERKMAN**	**.410**
8.	Joe Mauer	.407
9.	Nick Johnson	.401
10.	Brian Giles	.400

MOST HR ALL TIME, SWITCH HITTERS

1.	Mickey Mantle	536
2.	Eddie Murray	504
3.	Chipper Jones	436
4.	Chili Davis	350
5.	**LANCE BERKMAN**	**327**

▸ Homered—and went 1-for-4 with 1R and 2RBI—in 4/28 loss vs. Cincinnati...was his 315th career home run, surpassing Reggie Smith (314) for sole possession of fifth place on the all-time list for switch hitters.

▸ Was 1-for-1 with 2R, 1HR and 4BB in 5/12 win at St. Louis...tied his career high for walks in a game (third time)...became the first player to collect 4BB and 1HR in five plate appearances in the same game since Barry Bonds on 7/27/07 vs. Florida.

▸ Went 3-for-5 with 1R, 1 double and 5RBI in the Astros' 6/1 win vs. Washington, providing the "walk-off" two-run single in the bottom of the ninth...marked his most RBI since 6/10/08 vs. Milwaukee...also committed his first and only error in that game, snapping a 90-game errorless streak that dated back to his last miscue on 7/7/09 vs. Pittsburgh.

▸ Homered and tripled in 7/4 loss at San Diego, the fifth time in his career he accomplished the feat...the home run came as a right-handed batter, his only such homer in 2010.

▸ Hit his fifth career grand slam—and went 1-for-3 with 1R and 4RBI—in 7/27 win at Chicago-AL...went 2-for-2 with 3R and 3BB in the next day's win vs. Chicago-NL, the third time in his career he collected at least 3R and 3BB in the same game (also 8/30/03 vs. San Diego; 8/9/06 vs. Pittsburgh).

▸ Reached base safely in each of his last 7PA with the Astros (3-for-3 with 1 double, 1HR and 4BB).

MOST CAREER GAMES WITH ONE TEAM, PRIOR TO BEING ACQUIRED BY THE YANKEES
(Credit: *Elias Sports Bureau***)**

Player (Acquired by NYY)	Games w/ Prior Team	Won World Series w/ NYY
1. Enos Slaughter (1954)*	1,820G w/St. Louis-NL	1956
2. Paul Blair (1977)	1,700G w/Baltimore	1977-78
3. Wade Boggs (1993)	1,625G w/Boston	1996
4. Lance Berkman (2010)	1,592G w/Houston	---
5. Joe Sewell (1931)	1,513G w/Cleveland	1932
* Was acquired via trade in 1954, traded away in 1955 and picked up on waivers in 1956.		

LANCE BERKMAN

Berkman's Career Hitting Record

Year	Team	AVG	G	AB	R	H	2B	3B	HR	RBI	SH	SF	HP	BB	SO	SB	CS	E	OBP	SLG
1997	Kissimme	.293	53	184	31	54	10	0	12	35	0	0	2	37	38	2	1	0	.417	.543
1998	Jackson	.306	122	425	82	130	34	0	24	89	0	3	4	85	82	6	4	4	.424	.555
	New Orleans	.271	17	59	14	16	4	0	6	13	0	0	2	12	16	0	0	0	.411	.644
1999	New Orleans	.323	64	226	42	73	20	0	8	49	0	2	0	39	47	7	1	4	.419	.518
	HOUSTON	.237	34	93	10	22	2	0	4	15	0	1	0	12	21	5	1	2	.321	.387
2000	New Orleans	.330	31	112	18	37	4	2	6	27	0	0	1	31	20	4	4	2	.479	.563
	HOUSTON	.297	114	353	76	105	28	1	21	67	0	7	1	56	73	6	2	6	.388	.561
2001	HOUSTON	.331	156	577	110	191	55	5	34	126	0	6	13	92	121	7	9	6	.430	.620
2002	HOUSTON	.292	158	578	106	169	35	2	42	128	0	3	4	107	118	8	4	7	.405	.578
2003	HOUSTON	.288	153	538	110	155	35	6	25	93	1	3	9	107	108	5	3	3	.412	.515
2004	HOUSTON	.316	160	544	104	172	40	3	30	106	0	6	10	127	101	9	7	2	.450	.566
2005	HOUSTON	.293	132	468	76	137	34	1	24	82	0	2	4	91	72	4	1	8	.411	.524
	Round Rock - a	.286	4	14	2	4	1	0	0	1	0	0	0	3	4	0	0	0	.412	.357
2006	HOUSTON	.315	152	536	95	169	29	0	45	136	0	8	4	98	106	3	2	9	.420	.621
2007	HOUSTON	.278	153	561	95	156	24	2	34	102	0	5	8	94	125	7	3	12	.386	.510
2008	HOUSTON	.312	159	554	114	173	46	4	29	106	0	5	7	99	108	18	4	5	.420	.567
2009	HOUSTON - b	.274	136	460	73	126	31	1	25	80	0	4	1	97	98	7	4	6	.399	.509
2010	Round Rock	.500	2	6	3	3	2	0	1	3	0	1	0	0	2	0	0	1	.4291	.333
	HOUSTON - c	.245	85	298	39	73	16	1	13	49	0	0	0	60	70	3	2	1	.372	.436
	YANKEES - d, e	.255	37	106	9	27	7	0	1	9	0	0	0	17	15	0	0	1	.358	.349
	Trenton	.250	2	8	1	2	0	0	0	0	0	0	0	1	3	0	0	0	.333	.250
Minor League Totals		**.309**	**295**	**1034**	**193**	**319**	**75**	**2**	**57**	**217**	**0**	**6**	**9**	**208**	**212**	**19**	**10**	**11**	**.426**	**.550**
AL Totals		**.255**	**37**	**106**	**9**	**27**	**7**	**0**	**1**	**9**	**0**	**0**	**0**	**17**	**15**	**0**	**0**	**1**	**.358**	**.349**
NL Totals		**.296**	**37**	**106**	**1008**	**1648**	**375**	**26**	**326**	**1090**	**1**	**50**	**61**	**1040**	**1121**	**82**	**42**	**67**	**.410**	**.549**
Major League Totals		**.296**	**1629**	**5666**	**1017**	**1675**	**382**	**26**	**327**	**1099**	**1**	**50**	**61**	**1057**	**1136**	**82**	**42**	**68**	**.409**	**.545**

Selected by Houston in the first round (16th pick overall) of the 1997 First-Year Player Draft.
a – Placed on the 15-day disabled list from March 25-May 6, 2005 after having right knee surgery.
b – Placed on the 15-day disabled list from July 23-August 12, 2009 with a left calf strain.
c – Placed on the 15-day disabled list from March 26-April 20, 2010 after having left knee surgery.
d – Acquired by the Yankees from Houston along with cash considerations on July 31, 2010 in exchange for RHP Mark Melancon and INF Jimmy Paredes.
e – Was placed on the 15-day disabled list from August 19 (retroactive to August 16)-31, 2010 with a sprained right ankle

	2010					CAREER				
	AVG	AB	H	HR	RBI	AVG	AB	H	HR	RBI
Overall	.248	404	100	14	58	.296	5666	1675	327	1099
Minnesota	-	-	-	-	-	.293	41	12	5	13
Tampa Bay	.290	31	9	2	4	.235	51	12	3	10
Texas	.226	31	7	1	4	.283	230	65	11	39
Atlanta	.000	5	0	0	1	.292	195	57	12	45
Cincinnati	.167	30	5	1	4	.318	525	167	49	137
Philadelphia	-	-	-	-	-	.292	219	64	10	46
San Francisco	.318	22	7	0	3	.250	216	54	11	35
March	-	-	-	-	-	.000	2	0	0	0
April	.242	33	8	2	6	.271	706	191	50	144
May	.221	95	21	3	11	.307	991	304	61	205
June	.278	97	27	2	18	.309	1000	309	61	213
July	.221	77	17	6	14	.301	967	291	51	181
August	.200	35	7	0	4	.283	982	278	46	167
September	.303	66	20	1	4	.292	954	279	57	179
October	.000	1	0	0	1	.359	64	23	1	10
Home	.286	220	63	10	36	.302	2824	854	154	539
Road	.201	184	37	4	22	.289	2842	821	173	560
vs. Left	.171	82	14	1	5	.260	1366	355	42	207
vs. Right	.267	322	86	13	53	.307	4300	1320	285	892

Berkman's Career by Ballpark

Park	AVG	AB	H	HR	RBI	Park	AVG	AB	H	HR	RBI
AT&T Park	.266	109	29	7	22	Target Field	-	-	-	-	-
Citizens Bank Park	.299	67	20	5	15	Tropicana Field	.125	24	3	0	1
Great American Ball Park	.339	183	62	21	55	Turner Field	.257	101	26	5	18
Rangers Ballpark	.289	121	35	7	21	Yankee Stadium	.250	64	16	1	5

LANCE BERKMAN

Berkman's Division Series Record

Year	Club vs. Opp.	AVG	G	AB	R	H	2B	3B	HR	RBI	SH	SF	HP	BB	SO	SB	CS	E	OBP	SLG
2001	HOU vs. ATL	.167	3	12	0	2	0	0	0	0	0	0	0	0	4	0	0	0	.167	.167
2004	HOU vs. ATL	.409	5	22	5	9	1	0	1	3	0	0	0	3	6	0	1	1	.480	.591
2005	HOU vs. ATL	.357	4	14	4	5	1	0	1	5	0	0	1	3	4	0	0	0	.500	.643
Division Series Totals		**.333**	**12**	**48**	**9**	**16**	**2**	**0**	**2**	**8**	**0**	**0**	**1**	**6**	**14**	**0**	**1**	**1**	**.418**	**.500**

Berkman's Championship Series Record

Year	Club vs. Opp.	AVG	G	AB	R	H	2B	3B	HR	RBI	SH	SF	HP	BB	SO	SB	CS	E	OBP	SLG
2004	HOU vs. STL	.292	7	24	7	7	2	0	3	9	0	1	0	5	4	1	0	0	.400	.750
2005	HOU vs. STL	.286	6	21	2	6	2	0	1	3	0	0	0	4	3	0	0	0	.400	.524
LCS Totals		**.289**	**13**	**45**	**9**	**13**	**4**	**0**	**4**	**12**	**0**	**1**	**0**	**9**	**7**	**1**	**0**	**0**	**.400**	**.644**

Berkman's World Series Record

Year	Club vs. Opp.	AVG	G	AB	R	H	2B	3B	HR	RBI	SH	SF	HP	BB	SO	SB	CS	E	OBP	SLG
2005	HOU vs. CHW	.385	4	13	0	5	2	0	0	6	0	1	0	5	5	1	0	0	.526	.538
World Series Totals		**.385**	**4**	**13**	**0**	**5**	**2**	**0**	**0**	**6**	**0**	**1**	**0**	**5**	**5**	**1**	**0**	**0**	**.526**	**.538**
POSTSEASON TOTALS		**.321**	**29**	**106**	**18**	**34**	**8**	**0**	**6**	**26**	**0**	**2**	**1**	**20**	**26**	**2**	**1**	**1**	**.426**	**.566**

Berkman's All-Star Game Record

Year	Club, Site	AVG	G	AB	R	H	2B	3B	HR	RBI	SH	SF	HP	BB	SO	SB	CS	E	OBP	SLG
2001	HOU, Seattle	.500	1	2	0	1	0	0	0	0	0	0	0	0	0	0	0	0	.500	.500
2002	HOU, Milwaukee	.333	1	3	0	1	0	0	0	2	0	0	0	0	1	0	0	0	.333	.333
2004	HOU, Houston	.000	1	2	0	0	0	0	0	0	0	0	0	0	0	0	0	0	.000	.000
2006	HOU, Pittsburgh	---	1	0	0	0	0	0	0	0	0	0	0	1	0	0	0	0	1.000	---
2008	HOU, New York (AL)	.000	1	2	0	0	0	0	0	1	0	1	0	0	1	0	0	0	.000	.000
All-Star Game Totals		**.222**	**5**	**9**	**0**	**2**	**0**	**0**	**0**	**3**	**0**	**1**	**0**	**1**	**1**	**1**	**0**	**0**	**.273**	**.222**

Berkman's Career Fielding Record

Position	PCT	G	PO	A	E	TC
Outfield	.978	841	1487	45	34	1566
First Base	.995	684	5856	547	34	6437

Berkman's Career Home Run Chart

MULTI-HOMER GAMES: 25. **TWO-HOMER GAMES:** 24, last on 7/8/10 vs. Pittsburgh. **THREE-HOMER GAMES:** 1, on 4/16/02 at Cincinnati. **GRAND SLAMS:** 5, last on 7/27/10 vs. Chicago-NL (Andrew Cashner). **PINCH-HIT HR:** 1, on 5/12/01 at Cincinnati (Danny Graves). **INSIDE-THE-PARK HR:** 1, on 6/17/02 at Milwaukee (Jose Cabrera). **WALK-OFF HR:** 1, on 8/29/08 vs. St. Louis (Russ Springer). **LEADOFF HR:** None.

A.J. Burnett

34
Right-handed Pitcher
6-4 • 230 • B/T: Right/Right
Opening Day Age: 33

Birthdate
January 3, 1977

Birthplace
North Little Rock, Ark.

Resides
Monkton, Md.

M.L. Service
11 years, 38 days

Career Highlights
No-hitter
▸ 5/12/01
   at San Diego

Status
▸ Signed as a free agent by the Yankees to a five-year contract on December 18, 2008…contract extends through the 2013 season.

Postseason Notes
▸ Made his postseason debut in 2009, going 1-1 with a 5.27 ERA in five starts…did not draw a decision in his first career postseason start in ALDS Game 2 vs. Minnesota on 10/9 /09 (6.0IP, 3H, 1ER, 5BB, 6K, 2HP)…marked the fewest hits allowed by a Yankee making his first career postseason start since Orlando Hernandez (7.0IP, 3H) in ALCS Game 4 at Cleveland on 10/10/98…earned the win in his first World Series start on 10/29/09 in Game 2, limiting the Phillies to 1ER on 4H in 7/0IP (2BB, 9K)…according to the *Elias Sports Bureau*, entered the 2009 playoffs tied with Brian Moehler for the fourth-most regular season starts among active pitchers without appearing in the postseason.

Career Notes
▸ Has recorded six consecutive seasons (2005-10) of 10-or-more wins and eight such seasons in his career (also 2001-02)…has a 61-50 record since joining the American League with Toronto in 2006, fourth in the AL in strikeouts (865) and tied for 10th in the AL in wins over the stretch.

2010
▸ Was 10-15 with a 5.26 ERA (186.2IP, 109ER) in 33 starts with the Yankees…set career highs in losses, runs allowed (118), earned runs, ERA and hit batsmen (19), and tied a career high with 25HR allowed…set the franchise mark for highest single-season ERA among pitchers with at least 30 starts or 180.0IP…opponents batted .285 (204-for-785, 25HR); LHH .286 (110-for-385, 11HR) and RHH .285 (94-for-330, 14HR)…the Yankees were 13-20 in his starts.
▸ Held opponents scoreless six times, tying for the fourth-most such games in the AL…also held opponents without an earned run seven times this season, tying for the sixth-most such starts in the AL in 2010.
▸ Is one of four Yankees to lose 15-or-more games in a single season in the last 34 years (since 1977), joining Tim Leary (9-19 in 1990), Melido Perez (13-16 in 1992) and Andy Hawkins (15-15 in 1989)…is the first pitcher in franchise history to lose 15-or-more games with an ERA above 5.00 and is just the fifth player in Baseball history to post such numbers for a team that made the postseason, joining Tampa Bay's James Shields (13-15, 5.18 ERA in 2010), St. Louis's Jason Marquis (14-16, 6.02 in 2006), Minnesota's Carlos Silva (11-15, 5.94 in 2006) and Baltimore's Dennis Martinez (7-16, 5.53 in 1983) according to the *Elias Sports Bureau*.
▸ Allowed six-or-more runs in a game a Major League-leading 10 times in 2010 (going 0-10 with a 13.70 ERA in those starts)…mark the most such games by a Yankee since David Cone had 12 in 2000…when allowing less than 6R in a start this season, was 10-5 with a 2.60 ERA (142.0IP, 41ER) in 23GS.
▸ Surrendered the first run of the game in 21 of his 33 starts this season.

2010 Highs and Streaks

Low hit CG	4 - at KC, 8/15/10
IP (start)	8.0 - 3 times
	Last: at KC, 8/15/10
IP (relief)	N/A
Hits	12 - vs. SEA, 8/20/10
Runs	9 - 2 times
	Last: at CWS, 8/27/10
BB	6 - at LAD, 6/26/10
SO	8 - 3 times
	Last: vs. OAK, 9/1/10
HR	3 - 2 times
	Last: at ARI, 6/21/10
Winning Streak	4g - 4/11-5/4/10
Losing Streak	5g - 6/4-26/10

Career Highs and Streaks

Low hit CG	0 - at SD, 5/12/01
IP (start)	9.0 - 16 times
	Last: vs. BAL, 5/16/07
IP (relief)	2.0 - at PHI, 10/3/04
Hits	12 - 5 times
	Last: vs. SEA, 8/20/10
Runs	9 - 3 times
	Last: at CWS, 8/27/10
BB	9 - at SD, 5/12/01
SO	14 - 2 times
	Last: vs. MIL, 7/6/05
HR	3 - 8 times
	Last: at ARI, 6/21/10
Winning Streak	7g - 7/19-8/19/05
Losing Streak	7g - 8/24/05-4/15/06

- Allowed opponents to bat .345 (48-for-139) with 27 runs scored in the first inning this season...opponents had a .272 BA (156-for-576) and 91R from the second inning on in 2010.

- Threw 16 wild pitches in 2010, tied for third in the Majors and second in the AL...including this season, now owns two of the four highest single-season wild pitch totals in Yankees franchise history (Tim Leary-23 in 1990; Burnett-17 in 2009; and Jason Grimsley-16 in 2000).

- Led the Major Leagues with 19HP, setting a single-season career high (previous was 12HP in 2007 w/ Toronto)...according to baseball-reference.com, marks the Yankees' second-highest single-season total since the franchise was established in New York in 1903 behind Jack Warhop's 26 in 1909.

- Allowed 37SB this season, the most in the Majors...was the highest total allowed by a Yankee since at least 1950, according to baseball-reference.com.

Burnett's 2010 Pitching Lines												
Date/Opp	Score	W/L	IP	H	R	ER	HR	BB	K	NP/K	ERA	Left game...
4/6 at BOS*	6-4	ND	5.0	7	4	3	1	1	5	94-58	5.40	Tied 4-4
4/11 at TB	7-3	W	7.0	6	2	2	0	3	1	92-49	3.75	Leading 7-2
4/17 vs. TEX	7-3	W	7.0	6	0	0	0	2	7	111-68	2.37	Leading 7-0
4/23 at LAA*	4-6	ND	6.1	4	4	0	2	3	103-59	3.20	Tied 4-4	
4/29 at BAL	4-0	W	8.0	3	0	0	0	1	4	116-77	2.43	Leading 4-0
5/4 vs. BAL	4-1	W	7.1	5	1	0	0	2	8	107-68	1.99	Leading 3-1
5/9 at BOS	3-9	L	4.1	9	9	8	1	3	4	97-54	3.40	Trailing 9-2
5/14 vs. MIN*	8-4	ND	6.2	7	3	2	1	4	4	100-51	3.31	Leading 3-2
5/19 vs. TB*	6-10	L	6.2	9	6	6	1	4	4	116-67	3.86	Trailing 6-2
5/25 at MIN*	1-0	W	5.0	3	0	0	0	2	5	75-46	3.55	Leading 1-0
5/30 vs. CLE*	7-3	W	8.0	5	3	1	0	0	8	115-71	3.28	Leading 7-3
6/4 at TOR	1-6	L	6.0	6	6	6	3	4	2	103-59	3.72	Trailing 6-1
6/10 at BAL	3-4	L	6.2	8	4	4	1	1	5	95-60	3.86	Trailing 4-3
6/16 vs. PHI	3-6	L	3.1	6	6	6	2	4	3	87-48	4.33	Trailing 6-0
6/21 at ARI	4-10	L	4.0	9	7	7	3	2	4	91-50	4.83	Trailing 7-1
6/26 at LAD	4-9	L	3.0	6	6	6	0	6	5	79-38	5.25	Trailing 6-4
7/2 vs. TOR	1-6	ND	6.2	4	0	0	0	3	6	106-68	4.90	Leading 1-0
7/7 at OAK	6-2	W	7.0	5	2	2	0	2	3	110-67	4.75	Leading 6-2
7/17 vs. TB	5-10	L	2.0	4	4	4	1	0	1	43-25	4.99	Trailing 4-2
7/23 vs. KC	7-1	W	5.0	4	0	0	0	1	3	58-36	4.77	Leading 4-0
7/28 at CLE*	8-0	W	6.1	7	0	0	0	3	7	114-75	4.52	Leading 8-0
8/2 vs. TOR*	6-8	L	4.2	8	8	8	2	2	4	95-58	4.93	Trailing 7-2
8/10 at TEX*	3-4 (10)	ND	7.0	6	3	3	1	2	4	112-68	4.87	Trailing 3-2
8/15 at KC	1-0	L	8.0	4	1	1	0	3	6	103-64	4.66	Trailing 1-0
8/20 vs. SEA	0-6	L	7.0	12	6	6	2	3	4	122-77	4.80	Trailing 6-0
8/27 at CWS*	4-9	L	3.1	8	9	8	0	3	3	81-47	5.17	Trailing 9-2
9/1 vs. OAK	4-3	W	6.0	6	3	3	1	2	8	91-59	5.15	Leading 4-3
9/6 vs. BAL*	3-4	L	7.0	7	4	4	0	4	5	104-63	5.15	Trailing 4-3
9/11 at TEX*	6-7	ND	4.0	4	2	2	0	3	6	88-51	5.13	Tied 2-2
917 at BAL*	4-3	ND	7.0	6	3	3	2	1	5	106-67	5.08	Trailing 3-1
9/22 vs. TB	2-7	L	3.0	2	1	1	0	2	2	51-33	5.05	Trailing 1-0
9/27 at TOR	5-7	L	2.1	7	7	7	2	1	1	48-28	5.33	Trailing 6-0
10/2 at BOS	6-7 (10)	ND	6.0	4	2	6	1	2	5	105-61	5.26	Leading 6-4
TOTALS	**10-15**		**186.2**	**204**	**118**	**109**	**25**	**78**	**145**	--	**5.26**	

*start came after a Yankees loss – **Bold**-season high – *italics*-relief appearance

- Posted a 3.33 ERA (48.2IP, 18ER) in seven day starts in 2010, tallying a 3-4 record.

- Started the season 4-0 with a 1.99 ERA over his first six starts, marking the first time he won his first four decisions of a season...his 1.99 ERA was his lowest mark after six starts since 2001 when he posted a 1.71 ERA through his first six starts.

- Made his 250th career appearance on 4/11 at Tampa Bay, recording the win in the 7-3 Yankees victory (7.0IP, 6H, 2ER, 3BB, 1K)...allowed the first two batters to hit safely and score, then allowed just one runner past second base over the remainder of his outing.

- Did not allow an earned run in his first 18.1 innings at Yankee Stadium...streak was snapped on 5/14 vs. Minnesota in his third start at home, when he surrendered a fifth-inning solo home run to Joe Mauer.

- Compiled a 21.0-inning stretch without allowing an earned run between 4/23 at Los Angeles-AL and 5/9 at Boston...was his longest such stretch without an earned run surrendered since a 21.1IP streak over three starts from 7/24-8/4/05.

- Tossed 8.0 scoreless innings and recorded the win in a 4-0 Yankees victory on 4/29 at Baltimore (3H, 1BB, 4K)...threw first-pitch strikes to 20 of his 28 batters faced...marked the first time since 9/13/06 w/ Toronto at Seattle (8.0IP, 0R) that he tossed at least 8.0 scoreless IP in a start.

- Made his 250th career start on 5/4 vs. Baltimore, recording the win on a 4-1 Yankees victory...limited to Orioles to one unearned run in 7.1IP, striking out a season-high-tying eight batters (5H, 2BB)...his strikeout of Luke Scott in the fourth inning marked his 1,500th K...came in his 1,621st career IP...among active pitchers, only Kerry Wood (1,303.0IP) and Johan Santana (1,447.0IP) have reached 1,500 strikeouts in fewer IP.

- Earned the win on 5/25 at Minnesota in a 1-0 Yankees victory, tossing 5.0 scoreless IP (3H, 2BB, 5K)...game was suspended tied 0-0 prior to the sixth (rain) and resumed the next day...got the win after the Yankees scored in the top of the sixth, despite not pitching the day the game was completed.

- Tossed a season-high-tying 8.0IP in 5/30 win vs. Cleveland (5H, 3R, 1ER, 0BB, 8K, 2HP)...was the fourth time in his career he has tossed at least 8.0 innings without allowing a walk (first time since 6/27/06 w/ Toronto vs. Washington).

- Lost each of his five June starts, going 0-5 with an 11.35 ERA...according to the *Elias Sports Bureau*, became the first Yankee to appear in at least five games and lose them all in a calendar month since Stan Bahnsen in April 1969...marked the fifth time Burnett went winless in a month in which he made at least five starts, second as a Yankee (also August 2009, 0-4, 6GS)...*Elias* also notes he became the first Yankee ever to have an ERA above 11.00 in a month in which he had at least 20.0IP...marked the second time in his career he had lost five consecutive starts (also 8/24-9/14/05 w/ Florida).

- Rebounded in July to go 3-1 with a 2.00 ERA (27.0IP, 6ER) in five starts during the month...earned the win on 7/7 at Oakland (7.0IP, 2ER), snapping a six-start winless streak.

- Exited his start on 7/17 vs. Tampa Bay after 2.0IP with lacerations on his right hand (4H, 4ER, 0BB, 1K, 1WP, 2HP, 1HR).

- Held opponents scoreless in consecutive starts on 7/28 at Cleveland (6.1 scoreless IP) and 7/23 vs. Kansas City (5.0 scoreless IP before a 1 hour, 25 minute rain delay)...marked the third time in his career holding his opponent scoreless in consecutive starts (also 6/15/02 vs. Tampa Bay and 6/20/02 vs. Cleveland; and 5/29/01 at Pittsburgh and 6/3/01 vs. Mets)

- Posted an 0-4 record with a 7.80 ERA (30.0IP, 26ER) in five August starts...according to *Elias*, is winless in his last 13 August starts dating to 8/24/08, going 0-9 with a 6.45 ERA (82.1IP, 59ER).

- Won just once over his final 12 starts (beginning 8/2), going 1-7 with a 6.61 (65.1IP, 48ER) in August, September and October.

- Recorded his 20th career complete game on 8/15 at Kansas City (8.0IP, 4H, 1ER, 3BB, 6K, 1HP) in a 1-0 Royals victory, opposing Bryan Bullington...was his fourth straight loss when throwing complete game.

- Suffered the loss on 8/20 vs. Seattle, allowing 6ER on a career-high-tying 12H (fifth time)...threw a season-high 122 pitches, his most since 5/17/09 vs. Minnesota (123)...allowed a career-high tying 9R on 8/27 at Chicago-AL (also 5/9/10 and 8/22/09 at Boston) and matched a season-high with 8ER (also 5/9/10 at Boston)...pitched 3.1IP (8H, 3BB, 3K, 2WP) and recorded the loss in a 9-4 Yankees defeat.

- Snapped a five-start winless streak on 9/1 vs. Oakland, allowing 3ER in 6.0IP (6H, 2BB, 8K, 1HR)...held left-handed hitters hitless in 12AB, marking the most LH hitters faced in a game without allowing a hit since 7/9/04 w/ Florida vs. Mets (held LHH to 0-for-13).

- Went winless over his final six starts from 9/6, going 0-3 with a 5.83 ERA (29.1IP, 19ER) over the stretch.

A TALE OF TWO SEASONS

STAT	THRU 6/3	AFTER 6/4
Starts	11	22
Record	6-2	4-13
ERA	3.28	6.48
Innings	71.1	115.1
Hits	69	135
ER	26	83
BB	24	54
K	53	92
HR	4	21

AMERICAL LEAGUE SINCE 2006
(When Burnett joined the AL w/ Toronto)

MOST STRIKEOUTS IN AL
1. Felix Hernandez 965
2. Justin Verlander 958
3. CC SABATHIA 898
4. **A.J. BURNETT** **865**
5. Josh Beckett .... .839

HIGHEST K/9.0IP IN AL
1. Erik Bedard 9.19
2. Francisco Liriano 9.15
3. Scott Kazmir 8.74
4. **A.J. BURNETT** **8.50**
5. Jon Lester 8.37

Burnett's Career Pitching Record

Year	Club	W	L	ERA	G	GS	CG	SHO	SV	IP	H	R	ER	HR	HP	BB	SO	WP	BK
1995	GCL Mets	2	3	4.28	9	8	1	0	0	33.2	27	16	16	2	2	23	26	7	4
1996	Kingsport	4	0	3.88	12	12	0	0	0	58.0	31	26	25	0	7	54	68	16	3
1997	GCL Mets	0	1	3.18	3	2	0	0	0	11.1	8	8	4	0	2	8	15	3	0
	Pittsfield	3	1	4.70	9	9	0	0	0	44.0	28	26	23	3	6	35	48	9	0
1998	Kane County - a	10	4	1.97	20	20	0	0	0	119.0	74	27	26	3	8	45	186	6	2
1999	Portland	6	12	5.52	26	23	0	0	0	120.2	132	91	74	15	5	71	121	16	2
	FLORIDA	4	2	3.48	7	7	0	0	0	41.1	37	23	16	3	0	25	33	0	0
2000	Brevard County	0	0	3.68	2	2	0	0	0	7.1	4	3	3	0	0	6	6	0	2
	Calgary	0	0	0.00	1	1	0	0	0	5.0	0	0	0	0	0	3	6	2	0
	FLORIDA - b	3	7	4.79	13	13	0	0	0	82.2	80	46	44	8	2	44	57	2	0
2001	FLORIDA - c	11	12	4.05	27	27	2	1	0	173.1	145	82	78	20	7	83	128	7	1
	Brevard County	0	0	1.93	2	2	0	0	0	9.1	4	2	2	0	0	4	10	0	0
2002	FLORIDA - d	12	9	3.30	31	29	7	5	0	204.1	153	84	75	12	9	90	203	14	0
2003	FLORIDA - e,f	0	2	4.70	4	4	0	0	0	23.0	18	13	12	2	2	18	21	2	0
2004	Jupiter	0	0	0.00	1	1	0	0	0	4.0	2	1	0	0	0	2	4	2	0
	Albuquerque	0	0	10.80	1	1	0	0	0	3.1	7	4	4	1	1	2	6	1	0
	FLORIDA - g	7	6	3.68	20	19	1	0	0	120.0	102	50	49	9	4	38	113	7	0
2005	FLORIDA - h	12	12	3.44	32	32	4	2	0	209.0	184	97	80	12	7	79	198	12	0
2006	Dunedin	0	0	3.38	2	2	0	0	0	8.0	9	3	3	0	1	2	6	0	0
	New Hampshire	1	0	1.50	1	1	0	0	0	6.0	2	2	1	1	0	3	9	0	0
	Syracuse	1	0	0.00	1	1	0	0	0	5.0	0	0	0	0	1	1	7	1	0
	TORONTO - i, j	10	8	3.98	21	21	2	1	0	135.2	138	67	60	14	8	39	118	6	1
2007	Syracuse	0	0	1.80	1	1	0	0	0	5.0	3	1	1	0	1	1	7	0	0
	TORONTO - k, l	10	8	3.75	25	25	2	0	0	165.2	131	74	69	23	12	66	176	5	0
2008	TORONTO - m	18	10	4.07	35	34	1	0	0	221.1	211	109	100	19	9	86	231	11	2
2009	YANKEES	13	9	4.04	33	33	1	0	0	207.0	193	99	93	25	10	97	195	17	1
2010	YANKEES	10	15	5.26	33	33	1	0	0	186.2	204	118	109	25	19	78	145	16	0
Minor League Totals		27	21	3.73	91	86	1	0	0	439.2	331	210	182	25	33	260	525	63	13
AL Totals		61	50	4.23	147	146	7	1	0	916.1	877	467	431	106	58	366	865	55	4
NL Totals		49	50	3.73	134	131	14	8	0	853.2	719	395	354	66	31	377	753	44	1
Major League Totals		110	100	3.99	281	277	21	9	0	1770.0	1596	862	785	172	89	743	1618	99	5
NYY Total		23	24	4.62	66	66	2	0	0	393.2	397	217	202	50	29	175	340	33	1

A.J. BURNETT

Selected by the Mets in the eighth round of the 1995 First-Year Player Draft.

a – Acquired by the Florida Marlins along with LHP Jesus Sanchez, RHP Brandon Villafuerte and a player to be named later (OF Cesar Crespo) in exchange for LHP Al Leiter and INF Ralph Milliard on February 6, 1998.
b – Placed on the 15-day disabled list from March 17 – July 20, 2000 with a ruptured ulnar collateral ligament in his right thumb.
c – Placed on the 15-day disabled list from March 23 – May 7, 2001 with a stress fracture to the fifth metatarsal in his right foot.
d – Placed on the 15-day disabled list from August 19 – September 14, 2002 with a right acute bone bruise.
e – Placed on the 15-day disabled list from March 21 –April 9, 2003 with a sore right elbow.
f – Placed on the 15-day disabled list on April 26, 2003 with a sore right elbow… was transferred to the 60-day disabled list on May 6, 2003 and reinstated on November 19, 2003.
g – Placed on the 15-day disabled list on April 3, 2004 with a sore right elbow… was transferred to the 60-day disabled list on June 2, 2004 and reinstated on June 3, 2004.
h – Signed by Toronto as a free agent on December 6, 2005.
i – Placed on the 15-day disabled list from April 1-14, 2006 with a sore right elbow.
j – Placed on the 15-day disabled list from April 22, 2006 with a sore right elbow… was transferred to the 60-day disabled list on May 29, 2006 and reinstated on June 21, 2006.
k – Placed on the 15-day disabled list from June 13-27, 2007 with a right shoulder strain.
l – Placed on the 15-day disabled list from June 29 – August 28, 2007 with a right shoulder strain.
m – Signed by the Yankees as a free agent on December 18, 2008.

Burnett's Division Series Record

Year	Club vs. Opp.	W	L	ERA	G	GS	CG	SHO	SV	IP	H	R	ER	HR	HP	BB	SO	WP	BK
2009	NYY vs. MIN	0	0	1.50	1	1	0	0	0	6.0	3	1	1	0	2	5	6	0	0
Division Series Totals		**0**	**0**	**1.50**	**1**	**1**	**0**	**0**	**0**	**6.0**	**3**	**1**	**1**	**0**	**2**	**5**	**6**	**0**	**0**

Burnett's League Championship Series Record

Year	Club vs. Opp.	W	L	ERA	G	GS	CG	SHO	SV	IP	H	R	ER	HR	HP	BB	SO	WP	BK
2009	NYY vs. LAA	0	0	5.84	2	2	0	0	0	12.1	11	8	8	0	2	5	7	2	0
LCS Totals		**0**	**0**	**5.84**	**2**	**2**	**0**	**0**	**0**	**12.1**	**11**	**8**	**8**	**0**	**2**	**5**	**7**	**2**	**0**

Burnett's World Series Record

Year	Club vs. Opp.	W	L	ERA	G	GS	CG	SHO	SV	IP	H	R	ER	HR	HP	BB	SO	WP	BK
2009	NYY vs. PHI	1	1	7.00	2	2	0	0	0	9.0	8	7	7	1	1	6	11	0	0
World Series Totals		**1**	**1**	**7.00**	**2**	**2**	**0**	**0**	**0**	**9.0**	**8**	**7**	**7**	**1**	**1**	**6**	**11**	**0**	**0**
POSTSEASON TOTALS		**1**	**1**	**5.27**	**5**	**5**	**0**	**0**	**0**	**27.1**	**22**	**16**	**16**	**1**	**5**	**16**	**24**	**2**	**0**

Burnett's Regular Season Batting Record

Year	Team	AVG	G	AB	R	H	2B	3B	HR	RBI	SH	SF	HP	BB	SO	SB	CS
2010	NYY	.000	33	1	0	0	0	0	0	0	2	0	0	0	1	0	0
Major League Totals		**.131**	**281**	**267**	**12**	**35**	**6**	**3**	**3**	**9**	**36**	**0**	**2**	**12**	**127**	**0**	**0**

Burnett's Career Fielding Record

Position	PCT	G	PO	A	E	TC	DP
Pitcher	.918	281	106	195	27	328	11

				2010										**Career**						
	W	L	SV	ERA	G	GS	IP	H	HR	ER	SO	W	L	SV	ERA	G	GS	IP	H	HR	ER	SO
Overall	10	15	0	5.26	33	33	186.2	204	25	109	145	110	100	0	3.99	281	277	1770.0	1596	172	785	1618
Minnesota	1	0	0	1.54	2	2	11.2	10	1	2	9	3	1	0	3.22	8	8	50.1	44	4	18	50
Tampa Bay	1	3	0	6.27	4	4	18.2	21	2	13	8	12	7	0	3.15	25	25	168.1	128	12	59	164
Texas	1	0	0	2.50	3	3	18.0	16	1	5	17	4	3	0	3.66	12	11	71.1	62	8	29	78
Atlanta	-	-	-	-	-	-	-	-	-	-	-	5	9	0	3.74	18	17	98.2	90	9	41	88
Cincinnati	-	-	-	-	-	-	-	-	-	-	-	2	3	0	5.75	7	7	40.2	44	2	26	47
Philadelphia	0	1	0	16.20	1	1	3.1	6	2	6	3	5	9	0	5.13	18	17	100.0	104	15	57	90
San Francisco	-	-	-	-	-	-	-	-	-	-	-	5	2	0	1.84	7	7	49.0	33	1	10	37
March	-	-	-	-	-	-	-	-	-	-	-	-	-	-	-	-	-	-	-	-	-	-
April	3	0	0	2.43	5	5	33.1	31	1	9	20	16	9	0	3.82	38	37	235.1	206	23	100	188
May	3	2	0	4.03	6	6	38.0	38	3	17	33	14	18	0	3.84	39	39	255.2	224	27	109	254
June	0	5	0	11.35	5	5	23.0	35	9	29	19	14	18	0	4.19	45	45	281.1	254	26	131	258
July	3	1	0	2.00	5	5	27.0	24	1	6	20	23	14	0	4.08	46	46	280.1	277	30	127	255
August	0	4	0	7.80	5	5	30.0	38	5	26	21	23	22	0	4.01	54	54	356.2	313	35	159	312
September	1	3	0	6.14	6	6	29.1	32	5	20	27	17	19	0	4.08	54	52	333.0	297	28	151	323
October	0	0	0	3.00	1	1	6.0	6	1	2	5	3	0	0	2.60	5	4	27.2	25	3	8	28
Home	5	7	0	4.59	14	14	80.1	85	10	41	67	59	35	0	3.56	133	130	861.0	729	76	341	878
Road	5	8	0	5.76	19	19	106.1	119	15	68	78	51	65	0	4.40	148	147	909.0	867	96	444	740

Burnett's Career By Ballpark

Park	W	L	SV	ERA	G	GS	IP	ER	Park	W	L	SV	ERA	G	GS	IP	ER
AT&T Park	2	2	0	2.77	4	4	26.0	8	Target Field	1	0	0	0.00	1	1	5.0	0
Citizens Bank Park	2	3	0	5.04	6	5	30.1	17	Tropicana Field	6	2	0	2.09	11	11	81.2	19
Great American BP	-	-	-	-	-	-	-	-	Turner Field	1	7	0	5.08	11	11	56.2	32
Rangers Ballpark	2	1	0	4.00	6	6	36.0	16	Yankee Stadium	10	10	0	3.98	30	30	185.1	82

Robinson Cano

24
Second Baseman
6-0 • 205 • B/T: Left/Right

Opening Day Age: 27

Birthdate
October 22, 1982

Birthplace
San Pedro de Macoris, D.R.

Resides
San Pedro de Macoris, D.R.

M.L. Service
5 years, 153 days

Career Highlights
A.L. All-Star Team
▸ 2006, 2010

A.L. Silver Slugger
▸ 2006

MLB All-Star Futures Game
▸ 2003, 2004

Status
▸ Signed as a non-drafted free agent on January 5, 2001…signed a four-year contract with two one-year club options on February 7, 2008…contract extends through 2011 with options for 2012 and 2013.

Postseason Notes
▸ Reached base in 11 of his 15 postseason games in 2009, batting .193 (11-for-57) with 5R, 1 double, 2 triples, 6RBI and 4BB.
▸ Hit a bases-clearing double in his first career postseason at-bat in 2005 ALDS Game 1 at Los Angeles-AL…hit safely in three of the four 2007 ALDS games vs. Cleveland, hitting a solo HR in Games 1 and 4.

Career Notes
▸ Has 1,060 hits as a second baseman since his debut on 5/3/05, most among all Major League second baseman over that span (Philadelphia's Chase Utley ranks second with 962)—credit: *Elias Sports Bureau*.
▸ Recorded 911 hits in the first five years of his Major League career (5/3/05-5/2/10), second-most in franchise history through a player's first five years in the Majors, trailing only Joe DiMaggio (995)—credit: *Elias*.
▸ Owns a .489 career slugging percentage, fourth-highest all-time among Major League second basemen (min. 3,000PA) – credit: Stats, LLC.
▸ Is one of just three Yankees second basemen to hit 100HR for the club, joining Tony Lazzeri-169 and Joe Gordon-153 (min. 50.0% of games played at 2B).
▸ Since 1961, ranks fifth among all Major Leaguers with a .337 (221-for-656) career average in September/October (reg. season only/min. 300PA).
▸ Over the last five seasons (2006-10), has posted a .987 fielding percentage, handling a Major League-high 3,722 chances at second base over the span.
▸ Has played in 755 games at second base over the last five seasons (2006-10), most in the AL and second-most in the Majors over the span behind Florida's Dan Uggla (769)…has played more games at second base (886) than any other left-handed batter in franchise history…his 637 games played since the start of the 2007 season are tied for the highest total in the Majors over the span for any position (also Adrian Gonzalez and Nick Markakis).
▸ Has reached 40 doubles in each of the last two seasons and four times in his career…ties Don Mattingly for the third-most 40-double seasons by a Yankee, behind Lou Gehrig (seven) and Bob Meusel (five).
▸ Is one of only three second basemen in franchise history to hit at least 25HR in more than one season – also Joe Gordon, 1938-40 and Alfonso Soriano, 2002-03.

2010 Highs and Streaks
Hits	4 - 2 times
	Last: vs. TB, 5/19/10
Runs	3 - 7 times
	Last: vs. OAK, 8/30/10
2B	2 - 4 times
	Last: at BOS, 10/2/10(G1)
3B	1 - 3 times
	Last: vs. TB, 7/18/10
HR	2 - 2 times
	Last: at BAL, 4/29/10
RBI	6 - vs. SEA, 8/22/10
BB	3 - at OAK, 4/20/10
SO	2 - 11 times
	Last: at TOR, 9/27/10
SB	1 - 3 times
	Last: at BOS, 10/2/10(G2)
Hit Streak	17g - 5/17-6/3/10

Career Highs and Streaks
Hits	4 - 17 times
	Last: vs. TB, 5/19/10
Runs	4 - at BAL, 4/9/09
2B	3 - 3 times
	Last: at SEA, 9/19/09
3B	1 - 20 times
	Last: vs. TB, 7/18/10
HR	2 - 6 times
	Last: at BAL, 4/29/10
RBI	6 - vs. SEA, 8/22/10
BB	3 - 4 times
	Last: at OAK, 4/20/10
SO	3 - 3 times
	Last: at OAK, 8/19/09
SB	1 - 20 times
	Last: at BOS, 10/2/10(G2)
Single Season Hit Strk	18g - 4/12-5/1/09
Hit Streak	18g - 2 times
	Last: 4/12-5/1/09

ROBINSON CANO

American Leaguers to record a .319 avg., 103R, 200H, 41 doubles, 29HR and 109RBI under the age of 28 in last 50 years									
Player	**Year**	**Team**	**Age**	**Avg.**	**R**	**H**	**2B**	**HR**	**RBI**
ROBINSON CANO	2010	NYY	27	.319	103	200	41	29	109
Alex Rodriguez	1996	SEA	20	.358	141	215	54	36	123
Don Mattingly	1986	NYY	25	.352	117	238	53	31	113
Don Mattingly*	1985	NYY	24	.324	107	211	48	35	145
Robin Yount*	1982	MIL	26	.331	129	210	46	29	114
Jim Rice	1979	BOS	26	.325	117	201	39	39	130

2010

▸ Hit .319 (200-for-626) with 103R, 41 doubles, 3 triples, 29HR and 109RBI in 160 games (157 starts at 2B, 2 starts at DH) with the Yankees in 2010.

▸ Collected the second-most hits in the Majors, trailing only Ichiro Suzuki (214)…among American Leaguers, ranked fifth in average, tied for sixth in runs, seventh in RBI and slugging pct. (.534), ninth in OBP (.420) and tied for ninth in doubles and home runs…reached safely in 141 of 160 games in 2010, starting all but four team games at 2B…led all AL second basemen in average, runs, hits, doubles, HR, RBI, slugging pct. and OBP.

▸ Established single-season career highs with 29RBI and 109RBI and tied his career high with 103R…the Yankees were 25-2 in games in which he homered…marked the most RBI by a Yankees second baseman since Joe Gordon (111) in 1939.

▸ Finished the season with 200 hits, reaching the plateau in his final at-bat of the season…became the first-ever Yankees second baseman to record back-to-back 200H seasons, and the first 2B in the Majors to accomplish the feat since Cleveland's Carlos Baerga in 1992-93 (205H and 200H, respectively).

▸ Hit .611 (11-for-18) with 26RBI with the bases loaded in 2010, the second-highest such average in the Majors and third-most RBI…batted .322 (55-for-171) with 77RBI with runners in scoring position.

▸ Hit .324 (33-for-102) with 4 doubles, 7HR and 28RBI in 26 games as the No. 4 hitter in the lineup…in 28 games without three-time MVP 3B Alex Rodriguez, Cano has hit .321 (35-for-109) with 28R, 5 doubles, 8HR, 31RBI as the Yankees went 21-7.

▸ Ranked third in the Majors with 60 multi-hit games, including a team-high 19 games of three-or-more hits.

▸ Drew a career-high 57BB (previous high was 39 in 2007), 27 more than his total from 2009 (30).

▸ Hit .285 (61-for-214) with 13HR off left-handed pitching, and .337 (139-for-412) with 16HR against righties…his 13HR and 43RBI off LH pitchers ranked third and first, respectively in the Majors…had 10HR off lefty pitchers in 2009…according to *Elias*, became the first Yankees left-handed batter with at least 10HR off left-handed pitching in two straight seasons since Reggie Jackson in 1979 (10) and '80 (19).

▸ Hit .324 (33-for-102) with 26R, 4 doubles, 7HR and 28RBI in 26 games when batting fourth in the starting lineup…the Yankees went 20-6 in those games.

▸ Led American League with a .996 fielding percentage at second base…with teammate Derek Jeter's Major League-leading .989 fielding percentage at SS, became the first teammates to finish a season as the fielding leaders at shortstop and second base (in either league) since Omar Vizquel and Roberto Alomar for the 2001 Cleveland Indians.

▸ Led all American League second basemen in fielding percentage (.996), committing just 3E in 776 total chances (most TC among all Major League second basemen)…was involved in 114 double plays, most for any Major League second basemen…played in 160 of the Yankees' 162 games, including 158 at second base…played in 1,393.0 innings, fifth-most among all Major Leaguers.

▸ Established a franchise-record with 81 consecutive errorless games at second base from 4/23-7/26…his error on 7/27 snapped a streak of 37 consecutive errorless games by Yankees middle infielders, the longest such streak in franchise history (credit: *Elias Sports Bureau*).

▸ Made his fifth career Opening Day roster in 2010.

▸ Was named MLB's April American League "Player of the Month," marking his second career monthly award (also September 2006)…finished the month of April with a Major League-leading .400 (34-for-85) batting average, 5 doubles, 1 triple, 8HR, 18RBI, 65 total bases, a .765 slugging percentage, 11 multi-hit games and 21 runs scored…ranked second in runs scored and slugging percentage, tied for second in the Majors in hits and tied for third in home runs.

▸ Became just the second American Leaguer to record a .400 average and 8HR in the month of April in the expansion era (since 1961), joining Manny Ramirez with Boston in 2001 (.408, 9HR)…became the fourth Yankee to finish April with a .400 batting average or better (min. 50PA) in the expansion era, joining Paul O'Neill in 1994 (.448) and 1996 (.400), Clete Boyer in 1962 (.429) and Willie Randolph in 1976 (.400)…according to *Elias*, the last Yankee to lead the Majors in April batting average was Paul O'Neill in 1994.

▸ Hit safely in each of the first 10 games of the season (4/4-16)…with Derek Jeter, became the first 2B-SS duo in the Modern Era (since 1900) to each hit safely in nine-or-more of their club's first games of the season: *Elias*…became the first Yankees tandem at any position to each hit safely in each of the team's first 10 games of a season…became the first combo in the Majors to accomplish the feat since Tampa Bay's Carl Crawford and Rocco Baldelli in 2003.

▶ Recorded six multi-hit games through the team's first nine games of the season, becoming the first Yankee to accomplish the feat since Alfonso Soriano in 2003.

▶ Hit safely in 27 straight April games from 4/12/09-4/16/10…according to the *Elias Sports Bureau*, was the longest such streak in AL history (previous was Washington's Goose Goslin-25 games) and one shy of the Major League Modern Era record held by the New York Giants' Dan McGann (28 straight April games from 1903-06)…owns a combined .382 (68-for-178) batting average over the last two Aprils with 39R, 10 doubles, 13HR and 34RBI…reached base safely in 42-of-44 contests over the span, hitting safely in 40 of those games…trails only Manny Ramirez (.387) in 2009-10 April batting average (min. 100AB).

▶ Hit .400 in April, .336 in May and .333 in June, joining Derek Jeter (1999: .378 in April, .367 in May and .378 in June) as the only Yankees in the last 60 years to hit at least .330 in each of the first three months of the season (min: 50AB each month)—credit: *Elias*.

▶ Collected his fifth career multi-homer game in 4/15 win vs. Los Angeles-AL…both homers came off LHP Scott Kazmir, the first time he hit two homers off a LHP in the same game…hit three of his first five home runs of the season overall off Kazmir.

▶ Went 17-for-34 (.500) with 11R, 1 double, 1 triple, 4HR, 7RBI, 4BB, 1HP and 1SB on the Yankees nine-game road trip from 4/20-29…marked the highest average by a Yankee on a road trip since Jim Leyritz from 4/27-5/4/94 (credit: *Elias*).

▶ Recorded 13H and 4HR over a five-game span from 4/24-29, becoming the first Yankee with that many hits and homers over a five-game stretch since Don Mattingly from 7/7-11/87 (13H, 5HR)—credit: *Elias Sports Bureau*.

▶ Was 0-for-2 with 1R and a career-high-tying 3BB in 4/20 win at Oakland (fourth time, first since 8/5/08 at Texas).

▶ Singled in his first AB in 4/21 win at Oakland, snapping an 0-for-29 stretch at the Oakland Coliseum – the longest streak for any Yankees player in the ballpark's history (credit: *Elias*).

▶ Hit safely in a season-high 17 straight games from 5/17-6/3, batting .465 (33-for-71) with 9 doubles, 3HR and 20RBI over the stretch…marked the longest hitting streak by a Yankee in 2010.

▶ Was named the AL "Player of the Week" for the period ending 5/30…marked his fourth weekly award, first since the first week of August 2007.

▶ Recorded eight straight multi-hit games from 5/26-6/2, marking the Majors' longest such streak this season and longest by a Yankee since Bernie Williams (10 straight from 8/9-20/02)…had a .576 average, 19H and 14RBI over the span, becoming the first Yankee to reach those hit and RBI totals over an eight-game stretch since Joe DiMaggio (.528, 19-for-36 with 4HR and 14RBI) over the first eight games of the 1941 season—credit: *Elias…Elias* also notes the last Yankee with at least 19H, 14RBI and a .576BA over 8G was Lou Gehrig in 1936 (6/8-18, .594, 19-for-32, 6HR and 14RBI).

▶ During the multi-hit game stretch, Derek Jeter also collected six straight multi-hit games (from 5/27-6/1)…according to *Elias*, became the first pair of Major League teammates to collect at least two hits apiece in each of six straight games since Atlanta's Chipper Jones and Brian McCann from 7/9-18/06…*Elias* also notes they became just the second pair of Yankees teammates to accomplish the feat in six straight games, joining Lou Gehrig and Jack Saltzgaver from 7/3-7/34.

▶ Hit grand slam and was 3-for-4 with 3R and 1BB in 5/28 win vs. Cleveland, snapping a 96AB homerless stretch…was his third career grand slam…batted fourth in the lineup for the first time in his career.

▶ Had 71 hits through his first 50 games of a season (through 5/30), which *Elias* notes was the most by a Yankee since Alfonso Soriano in 2002 (71H in 50G).

▶ Scored at least one run in a career-high eight straight games from 6/8-16, scoring 11 total runs over the span.

▶ Had 89 hits through his first 60 games of the season (through 6/10), most by a Yankee since Derek Jeter had 89H through 60G in 1999.

▶ Hit his 100th career home run in 6/13 win vs. Houston off Brian Moehler.

▶ Collected his 100th hit of the season on 6/21 at Arizona in the team's 70th game of the season…according to the *Elias Sports Bureau*, since 1936 when Lou Gehrig reached the century mark in the team's 63rd game (the

AL SECOND BASEMEN (2006-10)*

HITS

1. ROBINSON CANO	905
2. Chase Utley	828
3. Brandon Phillips	808
4. Dan Uggla	769
5. Brian Roberts	762

RUNS

1. Chase Utley	531
2. Dan Uggla	497
3. Ian Kinsler	437
4. Brian Roberts	431
5. ROBINSON CANO	424
Dustin Pedroia	424

DOUBLES

1. ROBINSON CANO	205
2. Brian Roberts	196
3. Chase Utley	176
4. Dan Uggla	168
5. Dustin Pedroia	165

HOME RUNS

1. Dan Uggla	154
2. Chas Utley	133
3. Brandon Phillips	104
4. ROBINSON CANO	99
5. Ian Kinsler	92

RBI

1. Chase Utley	465
2. Dan Uggla	464
3. ROBINSON CANO	434
4. Brandon Phillips	400
5. Ian Kinsler	318

GAMES

1. Dan Uggla	769
2. ROBINSON CANO	755
3. Brandon Phillips	741
4. Chase Utley	716
5. Orlando Hudson	668

*as a second basemen

BATTING AVERAGE (min. 1,200PA)

1. ROBINSON CANO .310 (905-for-2,922)
2. Placido Polanco .307 (698-for-2,278)
3. Dustin Pedroia .304 (658-for-2,166)
4. Chase Utley .300 (828-for-2,763)
5. Mark Grudzielanek .299 (426-for-1,423)

*as a second baseman

franchise record for the "quickest" to 100 hits), the only Yankees to collect 100 hits within the team's first 70 games of a season are Cano and Derek Jeter (69 games in 1999)…collected his 100th hit of the season in his 274th at-bat…only three players have reached the century mark in hits in less at-bats for the Yankees since 1973 (Paul O'Neill in 1994 – 264AB; Dave Winfield in 1984 – 266AB; and Derek Jeter in 1999 – 267AB).

▸ According to the *Elias Sports Bureau*, became the first player to accumulate 100 hits, 50 runs and 50RBI through his team's first 71 games of a season (through 6/22) since the Tigers' Magglio Ordonez in 2007, and the first Yankee since Derek Jeter in 1999.

▸ Was elected to start in his first All-Star Game (was also selected in 2006 but did not play due to injury)…went 0-for-1 with 1RBI and 1SF before being removed defensively (Ian Kinsler) in the sixth in the National League's 3-1 win, starting at 2B for the American League…according to *Elias*, Cano and SS Derek Jeter joined Bucky Dent and Willie Randolph as the only Yankees SS/2B combos to start an All-Star game together…also joined Jeter, Joe Mauer and Albert Pujols as the only Major League players to top four million fan votes in 2010.

▸ Recorded his 1,000th career hit with his eighth-inning, two-run double in 7/25 win vs. Kansas City…according to the *Elias Sports Bureau*, only two "homegrown" Yankees in the expansion era collected 1,000H in fewer at-bats than Cano (3,232) – Derek Jeter (3,112) and Don Mattingly (3,042)…became the sixth second baseman to collect 1,000H with the Yankees, first since Willie Randolph…*Elias* also notes that only six active players reached 1,000H in fewer at-bats than Cano (Ichiro Suzuki, Todd Helton, Albert Pujols, Derek Jeter, Vladimir Guerrero and Matt Holliday).

▸ Homered in three straight games for the first time in his career from 8/17-19 vs. Detroit.

▸ Hit grand slam—his fourth homer in six games—and drove in a career-high six runs in 8/22 win vs. Seattle, going 2-for-5…was his fourth career grand slam (second this season, also 5/28 vs. Cleveland off LHP Tony Sipp).

▸ Was named AL "co-Player of the Week" with Tampa Bay's Evan Longoria for the week ending 8/22…led the AL with 13RBI and tied for the lead with 4HR while batting .333 (9-for-27) with 7R, a .815 slugging percentage and a .438 OBP…was his fifth career AL weekly award and second of the season.

▸ Batted second in the starting lineup in 9/13 loss at Tampa Bay, for the first time since 5/21/09 vs. Baltimore.

▸ Collected five straight multi-hit games from 9/14-19, batting .571 (12-for-21) with 5R, 1 double, 2HR and 7RBI over the stretch.

▸ Collected his 500th career run batted in with an eighth-inning sacrifice fly in 9/28 postseason-clinching win at Toronto.

▸ Played all 20 innings in 10/2 doubleheader at Boston…reached base safely in all six plate appearances in Game 2 loss, going 3-for-3 with 1R, 2BB (1IBB), 1SB and 1HP…hit solo-HR and was 3-for-5 with 2 doubles and 2RBI in Game 1 win.

▸ Went 1-for-4 in the regular season finale on 10/3 at Boston, recording his 200th hit of the season in his final at-bat of the loss.

▸ In 18 spring training games, batted .377 (20-for-53) with 8R, 4 doubles, 2HR and 12RBI…led the team in hits and RBI.

MOST MULTI-HIT GAMES, 2009-10
1. Ichiro Suzuki 142
2. **ROBINSON CANO** 126
3. Ryan Braun 124
4. DEREK JETER 119
5. Miguel Cabrera 108

TOP ROAD BATTING AVERAGES, AL, 2006-10 (min. 750PA)
1. Joe Mauer .... .336 (432-for-1,286)
2. Ichiro Suzuki .... .319 (549-for-1,722)
3. Vladimir Guerrero .. .309 (408-for-1,320)
4. **ROBINSON CANO** .309 (466-for-1,508)
5. Carl Crawford .... .304 (443-for-1,459)

CONSECUTIVE 200H SEASONS BY 2B, LAST 50 YEARS
ROBINSON CANO 2009-10
Carlos Baerga 1992-93
Dave Cash 1974-75
Rod Carew 1973-74
Pete Rose 1965-66

Cano's Career Playing Record

Year	Club	AVG	G	AB	R	H	2B	3B	HR	RBI	SH	SF	HP	BB	SO	SB	CS	E	OBP	SLG
2001	GCL Yankees	.230	57	200	37	46	14	2	3	34	0	2	3	28	27	11	2	5	.330	.365
	Staten Island	.250	2	8	0	2	0	0	0	2	0	0	0	0	2	0	0	1	.250	.250
2002	Greensboro	.276	113	474	67	131	20	9	14	66	0	1	3	29	78	2	1	14	.321	.445
	Staten Island	.276	22	87	11	24	5	1	1	15	1	0	0	4	8	6	1	1	.308	.391
2003	Tampa	.276	90	366	50	101	16	3	5	50	0	3	4	17	49	1	1	13	.313	.377
	Trenton	.280	46	164	21	46	9	1	1	13	2	0	6	9	16	0	0	5	.341	.366
2004	Trenton	.301	74	292	43	88	20	8	7	44	0	4	3	24	40	2	4	11	.356	.497
	Columbus	.259	61	216	22	56	9	2	6	30	3	2	1	18	27	0	1	4	.316	.403
2005	Columbus	.333	24	108	19	36	8	3	4	24	0	0	0	6	13	0	0	4	.368	.574
	YANKEES	.297	132	522	78	155	34	4	14	62	7	3	3	16	68	1	3	17	.320	.458
2006	YANKEES - a	.342	122	482	62	165	41	1	15	78	1	5	2	18	54	5	2	9	.365	.525
	GCL Yankees	.400	1	5	0	2	0	0	0	1	0	0	0	0	0	0	0	0	.400	.400
	Trenton	.500	3	10	1	5	2	0	0	2	0	0	0	3	1	0	0	0	.615	.700
2007	YANKEES	.306	160	617	93	189	41	7	19	97	1	4	8	39	85	4	5	13	.353	.488
2008	YANKEES	.271	159	597	70	162	35	3	14	72	1	5	5	26	65	2	4	13	.305	.410
2009	YANKEES	.320	161	637	103	204	48	2	25	85	0	4	3	30	63	5	7	12	.352	.520
2010	YANKEES	.319	160	626	103	200	41	3	29	109	0	5		57	77	3	2	3	.381	.534
Minor League Totals		**.278**	**493**	**1930**	**271**	**537**	**103**	**29**	**41**	**281**	**6**	**12**	**20**	**138**	**261**	**22**	**10**	**90**	**.331**	**.425**
Major League Totals		**.309**	**894**	**3481**	**509**	**1075**	**240**	**20**	**116**	**503**	**10**	**26**	**29**	**186**	**412**	**20**	**23**	**67**	**.347**	**.489**

Signed by the Yankees as a non-drafted free agent on January 5, 2001.

a – Placed on the 15-day disabled list from June 27 – August 8, 2006 with a strained left hamstring.

ROBINSON CANO

	2010						CAREER				
	AVG	AB	H	HR	RBI		AVG	AB	H	HR	RBI
Overall	.319	626	200	29	109		.309	3481	1075	116	503
Minnesota	.348	23	8	0	3		.321	165	53	5	22
Tampa Bay	.378	74	28	4	14		.323	375	121	15	63
Texas	.233	30	7	0	1		.309	181	56	4	26
Atlanta	-	-	-	-	-		.143	7	1	0	0
Cincinnati	-	-	-	-	-		.222	9	2	0	2
Philadelphia	.385	13	5	1	2		.303	33	10	1	2
San Francisco	-	-	-	-	-		.286	14	4	0	1
March	-	-	-	-	-		-	-	-	-	-
April	.400	85	34	8	18		.294	452	133	18	58
May	.336	116	39	3	22		.283	621	176	12	86
June	.333	102	34	4	13		.310	590	183	16	70
July	.276	98	27	6	18		.328	527	173	21	86
August	.292	106	31	5	19		.298	635	189	26	93
September	.262	107	28	2	16		.332	624	207	22	106
October	.583	12	7	1	3		.438	32	14	1	4
Home	.298	309	92	16	67		.304	1689	514	61	271
Road	.341	317	108	13	42		.313	1792	561	55	232
vs. Left	.285	214	61	13	43		.297	1074	319	36	164
vs. Right	.337	412	139	16	66		.314	2407	756	80	339

Cano's Career by Ballpark

Park	AVG	AB	H	HR	RBI	Park	AVG	AB	H	HR	RBI
AT&T Park	.286	14	4	0	1	Target Field	.455	11	5	0	2
Citizens Bank Park	.250	8	2	0	0	Tropicana Field	.335	194	65	12	36
Great American Ball Park	-	-	-	-	-	Turner Field	.143	7	1	0	0
Rangers Ballpark	.360	89	32	3	12	Yankee Stadium	.318	623	198	30	114

Cano's Division Series Record

Year	Club vs. Opp.	AVG	G	AB	R	H	2B	3B	HR	RBI	SH	SF	HP	BB	SO	SB	CS	E	OBP	SLG
2005	NYY vs. LAA	.263	5	19	3	5	3	0	0	5	0	0	0	2	4	0	1	2	.333	.421
2006	NYY vs. DET	.133	4	15	0	2	0	0	0	0	0	0	0	0	1	0	0	0	.133	.133
2007	NYY vs. CLE	.333	4	15	3	5	1	0	2	3	0	0	0	1	1	0	1	1	.375	.800
2009	NYY vs. MIN	.167	3	12	1	2	0	0	0	1	0	0	0	1	1	0	0	0	.167	.167
Division Series Totals		**.230**	**16**	**61**	**7**	**14**	**4**	**0**	**2**	**9**	**0**	**0**	**0**	**3**	**7**	**0**	**2**	**3**	**.266**	**.393**

Cano's Championship Series Record

Year	Club vs. Opp.	AVG	G	AB	R	H	2B	3B	HR	RBI	SH	SF	HP	BB	SO	SB	CS	E	OBP	SLG
2009	NYY vs. LAA	.261	6	23	4	6	1	2	0	4	0	0	2	4	3	0	0	2	.414	.478
LCS Totals		**.261**	**6**	**23**	**4**	**6**	**1**	**2**	**0**	**4**	**0**	**0**	**2**	**4**	**3**	**0**	**0**	**2**	**.414**	**.478**

Cano's World Series Record

Year	Club vs. Opp.	AVG	G	AB	R	H	2B	3B	HR	RBI	SH	SF	HP	BB	SO	SB	CS	E	OBP	SLG
2009	NYY vs. PHI	.136	6	22	0	3	0	0	0	1	0	1	0	0	5	0	0	0	.130	.136
World Series Totals		**.136**	**6**	**22**	**0**	**3**	**0**	**0**	**0**	**1**	**0**	**1**	**0**	**0**	**5**	**0**	**0**	**0**	**.130**	**.136**
POSTSEASON TOTALS		**.217**	**28**	**106**	**11**	**23**	**5**	**2**	**2**	**14**	**0**	**1**	**2**	**7**	**15**	**0**	**2**	**5**	**.276**	**.358**

Cano's All-Star Game Record

Year	Club, Site	AVG	G	AB	R	H	2B	3B	HR	RBI	SH	SF	HP	BB	SO	SB	CS	E	OBP	SLG
2006	NYY, Pittsburgh					Did Not Play - Injured														
2010	NYY, Los Angeles (AL)	.000	1	1	0	0	0	0	0	1	0	1	0	0	0	0	0	0	.000	.000
All-Star Game Totals		**.000**	**1**	**1**	**0**	**0**	**0**	**0**	**0**	**1**	**0**	**1**	**0**	**0**	**0**	**0**	**0**	**0**	**.000**	**.000**

Cano's Career Home Run Chart

MULTI-HOMER GAMES: 6. **TWO-HOMER GAMES:** 6, last on 4/29/10 at Baltimore. **GRAND SLAMS:** 4, last on 8/22/10 vs. Seattle (Luke French). **PINCH-HIT HR:** 2, last on 4/14/08 at Tampa Bay (Al Reyes). **INSIDE-THE-PARK HR:** None. **WALK-OFF HR:** 1, on 8/28/09 vs. Chicago-AL (Randy Williams). **LEADOFF HR:** None.

Second Basemen since 1920 .315, 100R, 29HR, 100RBI			
Rogers Hornsby	1922	STL	.401 / 141 / 42 / 152
Rogers Hornsby*	1925	STL	.403 / 133 / 39 / 143
Rogers Hornsby*	1929	CHC	.380 / 156 / 39 / 149
Jeff Kent*	2000	SF	.334 / 114 / 33 / 125
Bret Boone	2001	SEA	.331 / 118 / 37 / 141
ROBINSON CANO	**2010**	**NYY**	**.319 / 103 / 29 / 109**
*Won MVP Award that season			

FEWEST TEAM GAMES BY A YANKEE TO REACH 100 HITS *Elias Sports Bureau*			
	Team	Year	Games
1.	Lou Gehrig	1936	63
2.	Earle Combs	1931	65
3.	Earle Combs	1929	67
4.	Lou Gehrig	1927	68
5.	DEREK JETER	1999	69
T6.	R. CANO	2010	70
	Lou Gehrig	1934	70
	Lou Gehrig	1930	70
	Earle Combs	1927	70
	Whitey Witt	1923	70

Francisco Cervelli

29
Catcher
6-1 • 210 • B/T: Right/Right
Opening Day Age: 24

Birthdate
March 6, 1986

Birthplace
Valencia, Venezuela

Resides
Valencia, Venezuela

M.L. Service
1 year, 113 days

Status
▸ Signed by the Yankees as a non-drafted free agent on March 1, 2003…signed through the 2010 season.

Postseason Notes
▸ Was named to the Yankees playoff roster in the 2009 ALDS and ALCS, appearing in two games and striking out in his only at bat.

Career Notes
▸ Has entered each of the last four seasons (2007-10) ranked by *Baseball America* as the "Best Defensive Catcher" in the Yankees organization.

2010
▸ Hit .271 (72-for-266) with 11 doubles, 3 triples and 38RBI in 93 games (80 starts at C) with the Yankees in 2010…the Yankees were 44-36 in his starts at catcher…marked the most hits and RBI by a Yankees catcher other than Jorge Posada since Joe Girardi in 1997 (105H and 50RBI)…his 3 triples were the most by a Yankees catcher since Girardi in 1998 (4).

▸ Hit .545 (6-for-11) with 17RBI with the bases loaded…batted .381 (16-for-42) with 24RBI and a .435OBP with RISP and two outs, ranking third in the Majors in batting average (min. 40PA).

▸ Caught 8-of-63 (12.7%) of runners attempting to steal…Yankees pitchers worked to a 4.04 ERA with him behind the plate.

▸ Made his first career Opening Day roster…hit safely in each of his first four starts, six of his first seven and 10 of his first 12…hit .360 (9-for-25) in April.

▸ Made his first start—and appearance—of the season, in 4/10 win at Tampa Bay, when Sabathia held the Rays hitless through the first 7.2 innings.

▸ Appeared at 3B as eighth-inning defensive replacement in 5/2 win vs. Chicago-AL, marking his first career appearance at a position other than C.

▸ Hit his first career triple, going 3-for-3 with 2R in 5/4 win vs. Baltimore…became the third Yankee in the last 15 years with a triple and bunt single in the same game (also Derek Jeter-1996 and 2009; and Alfonso Soriano-2002)—credit: *Elias*.

▸ Established a career high with 5RBI in 5/8 win at Boston, going 3-for-4 with 1BB…the 5RBI were the most by a Yankees catcher since Jorge Posada on 9/6/06 at Kansas City (6RBI)…were also the most RBI by a Yankees catcher in a game vs. Boston since Yogi Berra had 8RBI on 7/3/57 at Yankee Stadium and the most RBI by a Yankees catcher at Fenway Park since Berra on 5/29/54 (6RBI).

▸ Started 10-of-15 games between 5/20-6/1 when Jorge Posada was on the disabled list, including four straight games from 5/20-23.

▸ Went 23 consecutive games without an extra-base hit from 5/20-6/17…snapped the stretch with a seventh-inning double in 6/18 loss vs. the Mets.

▸ Established a career high in hits in 8/29 win at Chicago-AL, going 4-for-4 with 1R and 1 double.

2010 Highs and Streaks	
Hits	4 - at CWS, 8/29/10
Runs	3 - 2 times
	Last. vs. TB, 9/20/10
2B	2 - vs. TOR, 9/4/10
3B	1 - 3 times
	Last: vs. NYM, 6/20/10
HR	N/A
RBI	5 - at BOS, 5/8/10
BB	3 - 2 times
	Last: at TEX, 9/11/10
SO	2 - 3 times
	Last: vs. TB, 9/22/10
SB	1 - vs. TB, 7/17/10
Hit Streak	6g - 6/11-20/10

Career Highs and Streaks	
Hits	4 - at CWS, 8/29/10
Runs	3 - 2 times
	Last: vs. TB, 9/20/10
2B	2 - vs. TOR, 9/4/10
3B	1 - 3 times
	Last: vs. NYM, 6/20/10
HR	1 - at ATL, 6/24/09
RBI	5 - at BOS, 5/8/10
BB	3 - 2 times
	Last: at TEX, 9/11/10
SO	2 - 6 times
	Last: vs. TB, 9/22/10
SB	1 - vs. TB, 7/17/10
Hit Streak	6g - 6/11-20/10

- Hit a career-high 2 doubles in 9/4 win vs. Toronto, going 2-for-4 with 2R.
- Reached base safely in eight straight plate appearances (two singles, 6BB) over two games from 9/10-11 at Texas…established a career high with 3BB on 9/10 and tied the mark on 9/11.
- Was 3-for-4 with a career-high-tying 3R in 9/20 win vs. Tampa, becoming the first Yankees catcher with at least 3R and 3H in the same game since Jose Molina on 8/2/08 vs. Los Angeles-AL (3R and 3H).
- Reached base safely in all four of his plate appearances in 9/29 loss at Toronto, going 3-for-3 with 1RBI and 1BB.
- In 14 spring training games, hit .344 (11-for-32) with 3R, 2 doubles and 2RBI.

Cervelli's Career Playing Record

Year	Club	AVG	G	AB	R	H	2B	3B	HR	RBI	SH	SF	HB	BB	SO	SB	CS	E	SLUG	OBP
2003	DSL Yankees1	.239	52	155	14	37	4	1	0	14	2	0	11	24	25	0	0	-	.379	.277
2004	DSL Yankees1	.216	40	88	14	19	2	0	1	14	4	4	9	19	18	1	2	-	.392	.273
2005	GCL Yankees	.190	24	58	10	11	2	0	1	9	0	2	2	8	13	1	0	2	.300	.276
2006	Staten Island	.309	42	136	21	42	10	0	2	16	1	0	7	13	30	0	0	7	.397	.426
2007	Tampa	.279	89	290	34	81	24	2	2	32	4	2	16	36	59	4	3	2	.387	.397
2008	Tampa	.300	3	10	2	3	0	0	0	1	0	0	1	0	3	0	0	0	.364	.300
	GCL Yankees	.250	3	8	0	2	1	0	0	0	0	0	0	0	1	0	0	0	.250	.375
	Trenton	.315	21	73	8	23	5	0	0	8	0	0	4	11	14	0	0	1	.432	.384
	YANKEES	.000	3	5	0	0	0	0	0	0	0	0	0	0	3	0	0	0	.000	.000
2009	Trenton	.190	16	58	8	11	1	0	2	7	0	0	0	6	13	0	0	5	.266	.310
	YANKEES	.298	42	94	13	28	4	0	1	11	4	1	1	2	11	0	3	1	.309	.372
	Scranton/WB	.275	21	69	7	19	5	0	1	7	1	1	1	3	13	0	2	3	.311	.391
	GCL Yankees	.167	2	6	1	1	0	0	0	0	0	0	0	1	0	0	0	0	.286	.167
2010	YANKEES	.271	93	266	27	72	11	3	0	38	8	4	6	33	42	1	1	13	.694	.335
Minor League Totals		**.262**	**313**	**951**	**119**	**249**	**54**	**3**	**9**	**108**	**12**	**9**	**51**	**121**	**189**	**6**	**7**	**21**	**.372**	**.353**
Major League Totals		**.274**	**138**	**365**	**40**	**100**	**15**	**3**	**1**	**49**	**12**	**5**	**6**	**35**	**56**	**1**	**4**	**14**	**.343**	**.340**

Signed by the Yankees as a non-drafted free agent on March 1, 2003.

Cervelli's Division Series Record

Year	Club vs. Opp.	AVG	G	AB	R	H	2B	3B	HR	RBI	SH	SF	HP	BB	SO	SB	CS	E	OBP	SLG
2009	NYY vs. MIN							On Roster - Did Not Appear												

Cervelli's League Championship Series Record

Year	Club vs. Opp.	AVG	G	AB	R	H	2B	3B	HR	RBI	SH	SF	HP	BB	SO	SB	CS	E	OBP	SLG
2009	NYY vs. LAA	.000	1	1	0	0	0	0	0	0	0	0	0	0	1	0	0	0	.000	.000
LCS Totals		**.000**	**1**	**1**	**0**	**0**	**0**	**0**	**0**	**0**	**0**	**0**	**0**	**0**	**1**	**0**	**0**	**0**	**.000**	**.000**
POSTSEASON TOTALS		**.000**	**1**	**1**	**0**	**0**	**0**	**0**	**0**	**0**	**0**	**0**	**0**	**0**	**1**	**0**	**0**	**0**	**.000**	**.000**

Cervelli's Career Fielding Record

Position	PCT	G	PO	A	E	TC	PB
Catcher	.984	133	797	59	14	870	2
Third Base	1.000	2	1	0	0	1	-

	2010					CAREER				
	AVG	AB	H	HR	RBI	AVG	AB	H	HR	RBI
Overall	.271	266	72	0	38	.274	365	100	1	49
Minnesota	.188	16	3	0	1	.320	25	8	0	4
Tampa Bay	.250	24	6	0	5	.194	31	6	0	5
Texas	.556	9	5	0	4	.412	17	7	0	5
Atlanta	-	-	-	-	-	.333	3	1	1	1
Cincinnati	-	-	-	-	-	-	-	-	-	-
Philadelphia	.333	6	2	0	2	.273	11	3	0	2
San Francisco	-	-	-	-	-	-	-	-	-	-
Home	.262	122	32	0	14	.276	170	47	0	18
Road	.278	144	40	0	24	.272	195	53	1	31
vs. Left	.322	87	28	0	10	.328	116	38	0	14
vs. Right	.246	179	44	0	28	.249	249	62	1	35

Cervelli's Career by Ballpark

Park	AVG	AB	H	HR	RBI	Park	AVG	AB	H	HR	RBI
AT&T Park	-	-	-	-	-	Target Field	.111	9	1	0	2
Citizens Bank Park	-	-	-	-	-	Tropicana Field	.091	11	1	0	3
Great American Ball Park	-	-	-	-	-	Turner Field	.333	3	1	1	1
Rangers Ballpark	.400	10	4	0	4	Yankee Stadium	.276	170	47	0	18

Joba Chamberlain

62
Right-handed Pitcher
6-2 • 230 • B/T: Right/Right

Opening Day Age: 24

Birthdate
September 23, 1985

Birthplace
Lincoln, Neb.

Resides
Lincoln, Neb.

M.L. Service
3 years, 55 days

College
University of Nebraska

Career Highlights
MLB All-Star
  Futures Game
▸ 2007

Status
▸ Selected by the Yankees in Compensation Round A (41st overall) of the 2006 First-Year Player Draft…signed through the 2010 season.

Postseason Notes
▸ Made 10 relief appearances for the World Champion Yankees in the 2009 postseason, going 1-0 with a 2.84 ERA (6.1IP, 9H, 2ER, 1BB, 7K)…made two relief appearances in the 2007 ALDS vs. Cleveland…made his playoff debut in the Yankees' 2-1, 11-inning loss in Game 2, when he allowed the game-tying run to score in the eighth on 2BB, 2WP and 1HP while "midges" descended on the pitcher's mound.

Career Notes
▸ In his career, is 6-6 with a 3.08 ERA in 123 relief appearances (131.2IP, 110H, 45ER, 42BB, 156K, 8HR)…has made 43 career starts, going 12-7 with a 4.18 ERA (221.2IP, 103ER) with 206K.
▸ Over the last three seasons (2008-10), has averaged 8.96K/9.0IP (328K, 329.1IP), marking the best such ratio in the AL (min. 300.0IP).

2010
▸ Was 3-4 with three saves and a 4.40 ERA in a team-leading 73 relief appearances with the Yankees in 2010, working exclusively out of the bullpen for the entire season…opponents batted .253 (71-for-281, 6HR); LH .246 (31-for-126, 3HR), RH .258 (40-for-155, 3HR)…retired 48-of-73 first batters faced (65.8%)…prevented 28-of-37 inherited runners from scoring (75.7%)…appeared in consecutive games 18 times…the Yankees were 48-25 in games he appeared in.
▸ 56 of his relief outings were at least 1.0IP (76.7%)…held opponents scoreless in 52 of his appearances.
▸ Made his third consecutive Opening Day roster in 2010.
▸ Suffered his first loss of the season on 4/23 at Los Angeles-AL, allowing a go-ahead two-run HR to Morales in the eighth inning (1.0IP, 3H, 2ER)…was his third appearance in a four-day span.
▸ Did not allow a run in eight relief outings from 4/28-5/14, tossing 7.1 scoreless innings and going 1-0 with two saves over the stretch (2H, 2BB, 11K).
▸ Earned the save in back-to-back games on 5/3 vs. Baltimore and on 5/4 vs. Baltimore—his first save since 9/23/07 vs. Toronto…according to Elias, is one of just three pitchers to earn a save in consecutive games since Mariano Rivera became the Yankees' closer in 1997 (also Mike Stanton-April 11-12, 1998 and Juan Acevedo-April 25-26, 2003).

2010 Highs and Streaks	
Low hit CG	N/A
IP (start)	N/A
IP (relief)	2.0 - at TB, 7/30/10
Hits	4 - 2 times
	Last: vs. CLE, 5/29/10
Runs	4 - 3 times
	Last: at SEA, 7/10/10
BB	1 - 22 times
	Last: vs. BOS, 9/25/10
SO	3 - 8 times
	Last: at BOS, 10/3/10
HR	1 - 6 times
	Last: at BOS, 10/3/10
Winning Streak	2g - 9/4-8/10
Losing Streak	1g - 4 times
	Last: 7/10/10

Career Highs and Streaks	
Low hit CG	N/A
IP (start)	8.0 - 2 times
	Last: at TB, 7/29/09
IP (relief)	2.0 - 10 times
	Last: at TB, 7/30/10
Hits	9 - 6 times
	Last: vs. TEX, 8/25/09
Runs	8 - vs. TOR, 7/5/09
BB	7 - vs. BOS, 8/6/09
SO	12 - vs. BOS, 5/5/09
HR	2 - 4 times
	Last: vs. BOS, 9/25/09
Winning Streak	5g - 6/24-8/6/09
Losing Streak	4g - 8/16-9/20/09

- Struck out the side in a perfect eighth inning on 5/14 vs. Minnesota (1.0IP, 3K)…was credited with the win despite not being the pitcher of record when the Yankees took the lead.
- Allowed a relief-appearance career-high-tying 4ER in 0.1IP on 5/29 vs. Cleveland, recording his first blown save and third loss of the season (4H, 1BB, 1K)…also allowed 4ER in 1.0IP in 7/10 loss at Seattle.

MOST K/9.0IP IN THE AL, 2008-10 (min. 300.0IP)		
1.	JOBA CHAMBERLAIN	8.96 (329.1IP, 328K)
2.	Justin Verlander	8.81 (665.1IP, 651K)
3.	Jon Lester	8.72 (621.2IP, 602K)
4.	Francisco Liriano	8.68 (404.1IP, 390K)
5.	Josh Beckett	8.52 (514.1IP, 487K)

- Beginning 7/28, just prior to the acquisition of Kerry Wood on 7/31, through the end of the season, went 2-0 with a 2.15 ERA in 30 relief appearances (29.1IP, 20H, 5BB, 30K)…allowed no more than 2H in any of his outings…three of the seven runs allowed came via solo HRs.
- Went nine consecutive appearances without allowing a run from 7/28-8/14 (8.2IP, 2H, 3BB, 6K)…was the second-longest such streak in his career, trailing only an 11-game stretch from 8/7-9/7/07 to begin his Major League career.
- Tossed a season-high 2.0 perfect innings in 7/30 loss at Tampa Bay, striking out three.
- Recorded his third save of the season in 9/21 win vs. Tampa Bay.
- Posted one save and a 10.45 ERA without recording a decision in seven spring training appearances (one start), allowing 13H and 12ER in 10.1IP (8BB, 9K, 1HR)…was selected as a member of the Yankees bullpen on 3/25 when Phil Hughes was named the Yankees' fifth starter.

Chamberlain's Career Pitching Record

Year	Club	W	L	ERA	G	GS	CG	SHO	SV	IP	H	R	ER	HR	HP	BB	SO	WP	BK
2007	Tampa	4	0	2.03	7	7	0	0	0	40.0	25	10	9	0	1	11	51	2	0
	Trenton	4	2	3.35	8	7	0	0	0	40.1	32	15	15	4	2	15	66	3	0
	Scranton/WB	1	0	0.00	3	1	0	0	0	8.0	5	0	0	0	0	1	18	1	0
	YANKEES	2	0	0.38	19	0	0	0	1	24.0	12	2	1	1	1	6	34	1	0
2008	YANKEES - a	4	3	2.60	42	12	0	0	0	100.1	87	32	29	5	2	39	118	4	2
2009	YANKEES	9	6	4.75	32	31	0	0	0	157.1	167	94	83	21	12	76	133	5	2
2010	YANKEES	3	4	4.40	73	0	0	0	3	71.2	71	37	35	6	1	22	77	5	1
Minor League Totals		**9**	**2**	**2.45**	**18**	**15**	**0**	**0**	**0**	**88.1**	**62**	**25**	**24**	**4**	**3**	**27**	**135**	**6**	**0**
Major League Totals		**18**	**13**	**3.77**	**166**	**43**	**0**	**0**	**4**	**353.1**	**337**	**165**	**148**	**33**	**16**	**143**	**363**	**15**	**5**

Selected by the Yankees in Compensation Round A (41st overall) of the 2006 First-Year Player Draft

a – Placed on the 15-day disabled list from August 6 – September 2, 2008 with right shoulder tendinitis.

Chamberlain's Division Series Pitching Record

Year	Club vs. Opp.	W	L	ERA	G	GS	CG	SHO	SV	IP	H	R	ER	HR	HP	BB	SO	WP	BK
2007	NYY vs. CLE	0	0	4.91	2	0	0	0	0	3.2	3	2	2	0	1	3	4	2	0
2009	NYY vs. MIN	0	0	0.00	3	0	0	0	0	1.2	2	0	0	0	0	0	1	0	0
Division Series Totals		**0**	**0**	**3.37**	**5**	**0**	**0**	**0**	**0**	**5.1**	**5**	**2**	**2**	**0**	**1**	**3**	**5**	**2**	**0**

Chamberlain's League Championship Series Record

Year	Club vs. Opp.	W	L	ERA	G	GS	CG	SHO	SV	IP	H	R	ER	HR	HP	BB	SO	WP	BK
2009	NYY vs. LAA	0	0	5.40	4	0	0	0	0	1.2	5	1	1	0	0	0	2	0	0
LCS Totals		**0**	**0**	**5.40**	**4**	**0**	**0**	**0**	**0**	**1.2**	**5**	**1**	**1**	**0**	**0**	**0**	**2**	**0**	**0**

Chamberlain's World Series Record

Year	Club vs. Opp.	W	L	ERA	G	GS	CG	SHO	SV	IP	H	R	ER	HR	HP	BB	SO	WP	BK
2009	NYY vs. PHI	1	0	3.00	3	0	0	0	0	3.0	2	1	1	1	0	1	4	0	0
World Series Totals		**1**	**0**	**3.00**	**3**	**0**	**0**	**0**	**0**	**3.0**	**2**	**1**	**1**	**1**	**0**	**1**	**4**	**0**	**0**
POSTSEASON TOTALS		**1**	**0**	**3.60**	**12**	**0**	**0**	**0**	**0**	**10.0**	**12**	**4**	**4**	**1**	**1**	**4**	**11**	**2**	**0**

Chamberlain's Regular Season Batting Record

Year	Team	AVG	G	AB	R	H	2B	3B	HR	RBI	SH	SF	HP	BB	SO	SB	CS
2010	NYY					Did Not Bat											
Major League Totals		**.000**	**166**	**5**	**0**	**0**	**0**	**0**	**0**	**0**	**2**	**0**	**0**	**1**	**1**	**0**	**0**

Chamberlain's Career Fielding Record

Position	PCT	G	PO	A	E	TC	DP
Pitcher	.968	166	13	48	2	63	6

Brett Gardner

11

Outfielder

5-10 • 183 • B/T: Left/Left

Opening Day Age: 26

Birthdate
August 24, 1983

Birthplace
Holly Hill, S.C.

Resides
Holly Hill, S.C.

M.L. Service
2 years, 72 days

College
College of Charleston

Status

▸ Selected by the Yankees in the third round of the 2005 First-Year Player Draft…signed through the 2010 season.

Postseason Notes

▸ Appeared in 14 of the Yankees' 15 postseason games in 2009, going 2-for-13 with 3R and 1SB…started the final two games (World Series Games 5 and 6) in CF when Melky Cabrera was removed from the roster with a hamstring strain.

Career Notes

▸ Recorded his 50th career stolen base (in 57 career attempts) in 5/1/10 loss vs. Chicago-AL…reached the plateau in his 171st career game, becoming the first Major Leaguer to reach the total that quickly since Jacoby Ellsbury on 8/20/08 (147 games)…became the first Yankee to reach the total in as few games with the club since Rickey Henderson on 8/3/85 (88 games) and the first Yankee to reach 50SB in as few games from the start of his career since Fritz Maisel on 6/21/14 (102 games)—credit: *Elias Sports Bureau*.

▸ His 63SB within two years of his Major League debut (6/30/08-6/29/10) were the most for any Yankee since Snuffy Stirnweiss had 66SB from 4/22/43-4/21/45…has stolen 86 bases in 101 career attempts…his 85.1% success rate ranks fourth among active players with at least 100 stolen base attempts.

▸ Has hit eight home runs in his career, with the Yankees going 8-0 in those contests.

2010

▸ Hit .277 (132-for-477) with 97R, 20 doubles, 7 triples, 5HR, 47RBI and 47SB in 150 games (96 starts in LF, 38 in CF) with the Yankees in 2010…stole 47 bases in 56 attempts (83.9%)…led all Major Leaguers with 4.61 pitches seen per plate appearance…swung at only 7.6% of first pitches, the lowest such mark in the Majors…of the 14 times he swung at the first pitch, recorded 8H (.571BA) with 3 doubles and 1 triple…worked the count to 3-2 in 124 of his 569 plate appearances (21.79%), the third-highest mark among AL qualifiers (credit: *Elias*).

▸ Had 75 hits with two strikes, tied for seventh in the Majors…ranked 10th in the Majors with one walk every 7.20 plate appearances…ranked 10th in the AL with 79 walks.

▸ The Yankees were 56-16 when he scored a run and 20-3 when he scored multiple runs…batted .308 (4-for-13) with 3 singles, 1HR, 15RBI and 3BB with the bases loaded.

▸ Hit .290 (27-for-93) with 21R, 6 doubles, 1 triple and 11RBI in 25 games in the leadoff spot in the lineup…hit .243 (44-for-181) with 32R, 7 doubles, 3 triples, 2HR and 19RBI in 58 games when batting ninth…batted .342 (40-for-117) when leading off an inning.

2010 Highs and Streaks

Hits	4 - at ARI, 6/21/10
Runs	3 - 2 times
	Last: vs. TOR, 9/3/10
2B	1 - 20 times
	Last: at BOS, 10/3/10
3B	1 - 7 times
	Last: at TOR, 9/28/10
HR	1 - 5 times
	Last: vs. TOR, 7/4/10
RBI	4 - vs. TOR, 7/3/10
BB	3 - 2 times
	Last: at CLE, 7/29/10
SO	3 - 4 times
	Last: at TOR, 8/23/10
SB	3 - at BOS, 10/20/10(G2)
Hit Streak	11g - 4/28-5/9/10

Career Highs and Streaks

Hits	5 - at NYM, 6/26/09
Runs	3 - 4 times
	Last: vs. TOR, 9/3/10
2B	2 - at TB, 4/14/09
3B	1 - 13 times
	Last: vs. TOR, 9/3/10
HR	1 - 8 times
	Last: vs. TOR, 7/4/10
RBI	4 - 2 times
	Last: vs. TOR, 7/3/10
BB	3 - 2 times
	Last: at CLE, 7/29/10
SO	3 - 7 times
	Last: at TOR, 8/23/10
SB	3 - 2 times
	Last at BOS, 10/20/10(G2)
Hit Streak	11g - 2 times
	Last: 4/28-5/9/10

- Tied for fourth in the Majors with 47 stolen bases, becoming the seventh Yankee in the last 70 years to reach the 40-steal plateau in a season (also Rickey Henderson, Roberto Kelly, Mickey Rivers, Steve Sax, Alfonso Soriano and Snuffy Stirnweiss)…mark the most steals by a Yankee in a single season since Rickey Henderson in 1988 (93SB).

- Recorded 45.6% of the Yankees' 103 stolen bases this season, marking the highest percentage by a Yankee since Rickey Henderson in 1988 (63.7%, 93-of-147)—credit: *Elias Sports Bureau*.

- Tied for second in the Majors with 12 outfield assists…his nine assists as a leftfielder trailed only Minnesota's Delmon Young (12) for most in the Majors.

HIGHEST SB PERCENTAGE IN AL, 2008-10		
1.	Chris Getz	89.1 (41-for-46)
2.	Ian Kinsler	85.7 (72-for-84)
3.	Johnny Damon	85.2 (52-for-61)
4.	**BRETT GARDNER**	**85.1 (86-for-101)**
5.	Coco Crisp	84.4 (65-for-77)

MOST SB BY NYY, SINGLE SEASON, LAST 60 YEARS		
1.	Rickey Henderson	93 (1988)
2.	Rickey Henderson	87 (1986)
3.	Rickey Henderson	80 (1985)
4.	**BRETT GARDNER**	**47 (2010)**

- Made his second career Opening Day roster (also 2009)…went 2-for-4 with 1R, 1RBI and 1SB in Opening Day loss at Boston.

- Stole home on the back of a double steal in the fourth inning of 4/4 Opening Day loss at Boston…became the first Yankee to steal home since Alex Rodriguez on 7/31/04 vs. Baltimore (also as part of a double steal) and the first Major League player to steal home on Opening Day since Oakland's Mike Bordick on 4/6/92 vs. Kansas City (credit: *Elias*).

- Batted .323 (21-for-65) with 14 runs in April 2010, his most runs for any calendar month in his career…finished April tied with Oakland's Rajai Davis and Pittsburgh's Andrew McCutchen for the Major League lead in stolen bases (10)…marked the most SB by a Yankee in March/April since Chuck Knoblauch led the AL with 11 in 2001…Rickey Henderson is the only other Yankee to steal double-digit bases in March/April (3x: 1988-20; 1986-15; 1989-14).

- Had three infield hits—including two to the pitcher—in 4/17 win vs. Texas, marking the most infield hits by a Yankee since Don Mattingly on 8/19/92 vs. Oakland—credit: *Elias Sports Bureau*.

- Hit safely in a single-season career-high 11 straight games from 4/28-5/10, batting .410 (16-for-39) with 12R, 1 double, 1HR, 3RBI, 5BB and 5SB during the stretch.

- Homered off a left-handed pitcher (Mark Beuhrle) for the first time in his career in 5/2 win vs. Chicago-AL, going 2-for-4 with 2R, 2RBI and 1BB…snapped a 167AB homerless stretch vs. all pitchers, dating back to 6/26/09 at the Mets.

- Did not steal a base over a 13-game span from 5/16-29…was the second-longest such stretch of his career behind a 14-game span from 5/5-25/09.

- Was caught stealing twice in the game for the first time in his career in 5/31 win vs. Cleveland and became the first Yankees with 2CS in a game since Bobby Abreu on 9/23/07 vs. Toronto.

- Hit a team-high .383 (23-for-60) with 13R and a .472OBP in 21 June games, ranking fourth in the Majors in batting average for the month.

- Was removed from 6/8 win at Baltimore for PH (Thames) in the eighth with a sore left thumb and missed the following two games…underwent X-rays on 6/9, the results of which were negative.

- Collected a season-high 4H, going 4-for-4 with 2R and 1SB in 6/21 loss at Arizona.

- Missed 6/29-30 games vs. Seattle with a right wrist contusion.

- Hit his first career grand slam and was 2-for-3 with 2R and 1BB in 7/3 win vs. Toronto…tied his career high with 4RBI.

- Hit second career inside-the-park HR (also 5/15/09 vs. Minnesota)—his second homer in as many games—and was 2-for-4 with 2R and 1BB in 7/4 win vs. Toronto…became the first player with multiple inside-the-park HRs as a Yankee since Mickey Rivers (1976-79)—credit: *SABR's* David Vincent…according to *Elias*, became the first player to hit a grand slam and inside-the-park home run in back-to-back games since Scott Rolen on 7/2-3/99 w/ Philadelphia vs. Chicago-NL.

- Was ejected for the first time in his career in 7/21 win vs. Los Angeles-AL for arguing balls and strikes during his seventh-inning AB.

- Recorded two outfield assists in the same game for the first time in his career in 7/22 win vs. Kansas City…became the first Yankees left fielder with two assist in the same game since Melky Cabrera had two assists on 5/16/06 vs. Texas.

- Recorded at least one walk in 10 straight games from 8/25-9/5, marking the longest streak in the Majors in 2010 and the longest by a Yankee since Jorge Posada's 13-game stretch from 5/9-29/04—credit: *Elias*.

- Recorded his second multi-steal game of the season in 8/31 win vs. Oakland (also 4/18 vs. Texas), stealing second and third base in the first inning.

- Scored a career-high-tying 3R (fourth time, second in 2010—also 5/17 vs. Boston) in 9/3 win vs. Toronto, going 1-for-3 with 1 triple, 1RBI and 2BB.

- Did not start in four straight games from 9/12-15, missing time with a sore right wrist.

- Played all 20 innings in 10/2 doubleheader at Boston…stole two bases in Game 1 and a career-high-tying three bases in Game 2, becoming the first player in franchise history to steal five bases in a single day (credit: *Elias*).

BRETT GARDNER

Gardner's Career Playing Record

Year	Club	AVG	G	AB	R	H	2B	3B	HR	RBI	SH	SF	HP	BB	SO	SB	CS	E	OBP	SLG
2005	Staten Island	.284	73	282	62	80	9	1	5	32	3	5	6	39	49	19	3	0	.376	.377
2006	Tampa	.323	63	232	46	75	12	5	0	22	1	0	2	43	51	30	7	0	.418	.433
	Trenton	.272	55	217	41	59	4	3	0	13	1	4	2	27	39	28	5	0	.318	.352
2007	Trenton	.300	54	203	43	61	14	5	0	17	1	4	0	33	32	18	4	1	.419	.392
	Scranton/WB	.260	45	181	37	47	4	3	1	9	3	0	2	21	43	21	3	2	.331	.343
2008	Scranton/WB	.296	94	341	68	101	12	11	3	32	11	3	1	70	76	37	9	0	.414	.422
	YANKEES	.228	42	127	18	29	5	2	0	16	3	1	2	8	30	13	1	0	.283	.299
2009	YANKEES - a	.270	108	248	48	67	6	6	3	23	6	1	3	26	40	26	5	2	.345	.379
	Scranton/WB	.091	4	11	3	1	0	0	0	0	0	0	0	5	1	3	0	0	.375	.091
2010	YANKEES	.277	150	477	97	132	20	7	5	47	5	3	5	79	101	47	9	1	.383	.379
Minor League Totals		**.289**	**386**	**1467**	**300**	**424**	**55**	**28**	**9**	**125**	**20**	**16**	**13**	**238**	**291**	**156**	**31**	**3**	**.389**	**.383**
Major League Totals		**.268**	**300**	**852**	**163**	**228**	**31**	**15**	**8**	**86**	**14**	**5**	**10**	**113**	**171**	**86**	**15**	**3**	**.358**	**.367**

Selected by the Yankees in the third round of the 2005 First-Year Player Draft.
a – Placed on the 15-day disabled list from July 26– September 7, 2009 with a left thumb fracture.

Gardner's Division Series Record

Year	Club vs. Opp.	AVG	G	AB	R	H	2B	3B	HR	RBI	SH	SF	HP	BB	SO	SB	CS	E	OBP	SLG
2009	NYY vs. MIN	---	3	0	0	0	0	0	0	0	0	0	0	0	0	1	0	0	---	---
Division Series Totals		**---**	**3**	**0**	**0**	**0**	**0**	**0**	**0**	**0**	**0**	**0**	**0**	**0**	**0**	**1**	**0**	**0**	**---**	**---**

Gardner's Championship Series Record

Year	Club vs. Opp.	AVG	G	AB	R	H	2B	3B	HR	RBI	SH	SF	HP	BB	SO	SB	CS	E	OBP	SLG
2009	NYY vs. LAA	.667	6	3	2	2	0	0	0	0	1	0	0	0	0	0	2	0	.667	.667
LCS Totals		**.667**	**6**	**3**	**2**	**2**	**0**	**0**	**0**	**0**	**1**	**0**	**0**	**0**	**0**	**0**	**2**	**0**	**.667**	**.667**

Gardner's World Series Record

Year	Club vs. Opp.	AVG	G	AB	R	H	2B	3B	HR	RBI	SH	SF	HP	BB	SO	SB	CS	E	OBP	SLG
2009	NYY vs. PHI	.000	5	10	1	0	0	0	0	0	0	0	0	0	4	0	0	0	.000	.000
World Series Totals		**.000**	**5**	**10**	**1**	**0**	**0**	**0**	**0**	**0**	**0**	**0**	**0**	**0**	**4**	**0**	**0**	**0**	**.000**	**.000**
POSTSEASON TOTALS		**.154**	**14**	**13**	**3**	**2**	**0**	**0**	**0**	**0**	**0**	**0**	**0**	**0**	**4**	**1**	**2**	**0**	**.154**	**.154**

Gardner's Career Fielding Record

Position	PCT	G	PO	A	E	TC
Outfield	.995	288	551	20	3	574

	2010					CAREER				
	AVG	AB	H	HR	RBI	AVG	AB	H	HR	RBI
Overall	.277	477	132	5	47	.268	852	228	8	86
Minnesota	.240	25	6	1	2	.288	52	15	2	9
Tampa Bay	.195	41	8	0	4	.169	83	14	0	6
Texas	.333	21	7	0	2	.326	46	15	0	4
Atlanta	-	-	-	-	-	.250	12	3	0	0
Cincinnati	-	-	-	-	-	-	-	-	-	-
Philadelphia	.222	9	2	0	2	.286	14	4	0	2
San Francisco	-	-	-	-	-	-	-	-	-	-
Home	.274	237	65	5	29	.252	428	108	6	46
Road	.279	240	67	0	18	.283	424	120	2	40
vs. Left	.252	139	35	2	17	.248	218	54	2	25
vs. Right	.287	338	97	3	30	.274	634	174	6	61

Gardner's Career by Ballpark

Park	AVG	AB	H	HR	RBI	Park	AVG	AB	H	HR	RBI
AT&T Park	-	-	-	-	-	Target Field	.273	11	3	0	1
Citizens Bank Park	-	-	-	-	-	Tropicana Field	.212	33	7	0	3
Great American Ball Park	-	-	-	-	-	Turner Field	.250	12	3	0	0
Rangers Ballpark	.320	25	8	0	1	Yankee Stadium	.265	343	91	6	37

Gardner's Career Home Run Chart

MULTI-HOMER GAMES: None. **TWO-HOMER GAMES:** None. **GRAND SLAMS:** 1, 7/3/10 vs. Toronto (Ricky Romero). **PINCH-HIT HR:** None. **INSIDE-THE-PARK HR:** 2, last on 7/4/10 vs. Toronto (Brandon Morrow). **WALK-OFF HR:** None. **LEADOFF HR:** None.

Chad Gaudin

41

Right-handed Pitcher
5-10 • 190 • B/T: Right/Right
Opening Day Age: 27

Birthdate
March 24, 1983

Birthplace
River Ridge, La.

Resides
Harahan, La.

M.L. Service
5 years, 163 days

Status

▸ Signed by the Yankees as a free agent on May 26, 2010…was originally acquired by the Yankees from the San Diego Padres in exchange for cash considerations on August 6, 2009.

Postseason Notes

▸ Appeared on the Yankees' postseason roster in all three rounds of the 2009 playoffs…made one appearance in Game 4 of the ALCS at Los Angeles-AL, tossing 1.0 scoreless inning in the Yankees victory…also made two scoreless appearances with Oakland in the 2006 ALCS vs. Detroit (2.1IP).

2010

▸ Combined to go 1-4 with a 5.65 ERA in 42 relief appearances with the Yankees and Athletics in 2010…opponents batted .185 (73-for-256, 16HR); LH .283 (36-for-127, 9HR), RH .287 (37-for-129, 7HR)…appeared in consecutive games four times.

▸ Went 1-2 with a 4.50 ERA in 30 relief appearances with the Yankees in 2010…retired 24-of-30 first batters faced (80.0%)…prevented nine-of-30 inherited runners from scoring (70.0%)…made 15 appearances of more than 1.0IP…the Yankees went 11-19 in his appearances…17 of his outings were more than 1.0 IP and 13 were more than 2.0 IP.

▸ Attended 2010 spring training with the Yankees (0-3, 8.68 ERA, 4G, 2GS)…was released on 3/25 and signed with Oakland on 3/30.

▸ Was 0-2 with an 8.83 ERA in 12 relief appearances (17.1IP, 17ER) with Oakland before being designated for assignment on 5/16 and released on 5/21.

▸ Was re-signed by the Yankees to a Major League contract and added to the 25-man roster on 5/26.

▸ Allowed 7ER over his first five appearances with the Yankees (5/27-6/8, 7.88 ERA)…pitched to a 3.38 ERA over the remainder of the season beginning 6/12 (40.0IP, 17ER).

▸ Recorded his third loss of the season in the Yankees' 14th-inning "walk-off" loss on 6/5 at Toronto, allowing the game-winning single to Aaron Hill (0.1IP, 1H, 1BB).

▸ In 7/17 loss vs. Tampa Bay, tossed a season-high 4.0IP (4H, 2ER, 1BB, 5K, 1HR)…was his fifth career relief outing of at least 4.0 innings and first since 5/4/06 w/ Oakland vs. Cleveland (4.0IP)…recorded his 500th career strikeout (Evan Longoria to end the seventh inning).

▸ Surrendered just 2ER in eight August outings (1.38 ERA), holding opponents to a .170 batting average (8-for-47).

▸ Appeared in nine games in September, including five of the Yankees' nine games from 9/18-27, going 1-1 with a 7.45 ERA for the month (9.2IP, 8ER).

2010 Highs and Streaks

Low hit CG	N/A
IP (start)	N/A
IP (relief)	4.0 - vs. TB, 7/17/10
Hits	8 - at LAA, 5/15/10
Runs	6 - at LAA, 5/15/10
BB	2 - 7 times
	Last: at TB, 9/13/10
SO	5 - vs. TB, 7/17/10
HR	3 - at TEX, 5/12/10
Winning Streak	1g - 9/20/10
Losing Streak	4g - 4/14-9/10/10

Career Highs and Streaks

Low hit CG	4 - at SEA, 7/28/07
IP (start)	8.0 - 4 times
	Last: at TEX, 6/28/09
IP (relief)	5.0 - at BOS, 9/18/03
Hits	10 - 5 times
	Last: at LAA, 6/12/09
Runs	8 - 2 times
	Last: at LAA, 6/12/09
BB	7 - 2 times
	Last: at CHC, 5/14/09
SO	11 - 2 times
	Last at SEA, 6/23/09
HR	3 - 2 times
	Last: at TEX, 5/12/10
Winning Streak	5g - 2 times
	Last: 5/8-6/3/07
Losing Streak	5g - 2 times
	Last: 7/12-8/7/07

CHAD GAUDIN

▸ Allowed game-winning "walk-off" solo-HR to Nelson Cruz to lead off the 13th inning on 9/10 at Texas to suffer his fourth loss of the season (1.0IP, 1H, 1ER, 1HR).

▸ Earned the win on 9/20 vs. Tampa Bay, despite being charged with his only blown save of the season.

Gaudin's Career Pitching Record

Year	Club	W	L	ERA	G	GS	CG	SHO	SV	IP	H	R	ER	HR	HB	BB	SO	WP	BK
2003	Bakersfield	5	3	2.13	14	14	1	0	0	80.1	63	23	19	2	1	23	70	0	2
	Orlando	2	0	0.47	3	3	1	1	0	19.0	8	1	1	0	0	3	23	0	0
	TAMPA BAY	2	0	3.60	15	3	0	0	0	40.0	37	18	16	4	1	16	23	1	0
2004	Durham	1	3	4.72	17	7	0	0	2	47.2	48	26	25	8	2	17	52	0	1
	TAMPA BAY	1	2	4.85	26	4	0	0	0	42.2	59	27	23	4	4	16	30	0	0
2005	Syracuse - a	9	8	3.35	23	23	2	2	0	150.1	140	61	56	12	8	35	113	5	2
	TORONTO	1	3	13.15	5	3	0	0	0	13.0	31	19	19	6	1	6	12	0	0
2006	Sacramento - b	3	0	0.37	4	4	0	0	2	24.1	14	6	1	0	0	8	26	0	0
	OAKLAND	4	2	3.09	55	0	0	0	2	64.0	51	24	22	3	1	42	36	2	2
2007	OAKLAND	11	13	4.42	34	34	1	0	0	199.1	205	108	98	21	8	100	154	3	1
2008	OAKLAND	5	3	3.59	26	6	0	0	0	62.2	63	29	25	6	3	17	44	2	1
	CHICAGO-NL - c	4	2	6.26	24	0	0	0	0	27.1	29	21	19	5	0	10	27	0	1
2009	Portland - d	0	0	0.00	2	2	0	0	0	8.2	4	0	0	0	0	2	10	1	0
	SAN DIEGO	4	10	5.13	20	19	0	0	0	105.1	105	69	60	7	5	56	105	4	1
	YANKEES - e	2	0	3.43	11	6	0	0	0	42.0	41	16	16	7	3	20	34	3	0
2010	OAKLAND - f	0	2	8.83	12	0	0	0	0	17.1	27	18	17	5	3	5	20	0	0
	YANKEES - g	1	2	4.50	30	0	0	0	0	48.0	46	27	24	46	5	20	33	3	0
Minor League Totals		**24**	**20**	**2.64**	**89**	**70**	**4**	**3**	**3**	**449.2**	**383**	**160**	**132**	**27**	**22**	**125**	**400**	**10**	**8**
AL Totals		**27**	**27**	**4.42**	**214**	**56**	**1**	**0**	**2**	**529.0**	**560**	**286**	**260**	**67**	**29**	**242**	**386**	**14**	**4**
NL Totals		**8**	**12**	**5.36**	**44**	**19**	**0**	**0**	**0**	**132.2**	**134**	**90**	**79**	**12**	**5**	**66**	**132**	**4**	**2**
Major League Totals		**35**	**39**	**4.61**	**258**	**75**	**1**	**0**	**2**	**661.2**	**694**	**376**	**339**	**79**	**34**	**308**	**518**	**18**	**6**
NYY Total		**3**	**2**	**4.00**	**41**	**6**	**0**	**0**	**0**	**90.0**	**87**	**43**	**40**	**18**	**8**	**40**	**67**	**6**	**0**

Selected by Tampa Bay in the 34th round of the 2001 First-Year Player Draft.
a – Acquired by Toronto in exchange for C Kevin Cash on December 12, 2004.
b – Acquired by Oakland in exchange for a player to be named later (OF Dustin Majewski) on December 2, 2005.
c – Acquired by Chicago-NL along with RHP Rich Harden in exchange for LHP Sean Gallagher, C Josh Donaldson, OF Matt Murton and INF Eric Patterson on July 8, 2008.
d – Signed by San Diego as a minor league free agent on April 16, 2009.
e – Acquired by the Yankees in exchange for a player to be named later or cash on August 6, 2009.
f – Signed by Oakland as a free agent on March 30, 2010.
g – Signed by the Yankees as a free agent on May 26, 2010.

Gaudin's Division Series Record

Year	Club vs. Opp.	W	L	ERA	G	GS	CG	SHO	SV	IP	H	R	ER	HR	HP	BB	SO	WP	BK
2006	OAK vs. MIN							On Roster - Did Not Pitch											
2009	NYY vs. MIN							On Roster - Did Not Pitch											
Division Series Totals								**Has Not Pitched**											

Gaudin's League Championship Series Record

Year	Club vs. Opp.	W	L	ERA	G	GS	CG	SHO	SV	IP	H	R	ER	HR	HP	BB	SO	WP	BK
2006	OAK vs. DET	0	0	0.00	3	0	0	0	0	3.1	2	0	0	0	0	3	1	0	0
2009	NYY vs. LAA	0	0	0.00	1	0	0	0	0	1.0	0	0	0	0	0	0	0	0	0
LCS Totals		**0**	**0**	**0.00**	**4**	**0**	**0**	**0**	**0**	**4.1**	**2**	**0**	**0**	**0**	**0**	**3**	**1**	**0**	**0**

Gaudin's World Series Record

Year	Club vs. Opp.	W	L	ERA	G	GS	CG	SHO	SV	IP	H	R	ER	HR	HP	BB	SO	WP	BK
2009	NYY vs. PHI							On Roster - Did Not Pitch											
World Series Totals								**Has Not Pitched**											
POSTSEASON TOTALS		**0**	**0**	**0.00**	**4**	**0**	**0**	**0**	**0**	**4.1**	**2**	**0**	**0**	**0**	**0**	**3**	**1**	**0**	**0**

Gaudin's Regular Season Batting Record

Year	Team	AVG	G	AB	R	H	2B	3B	HR	RBI	SH	SF	HP	BB	SO	SB	CS
2010	OAK					Did Not Bat											
	NYY					Did Not Bat											
Major League Totals		**.031**	**258**	**32**	**1**	**1**	**0**	**0**	**0**	**0**	**3**	**0**	**0**	**2**	**16**	**0**	**0**

Gaudin's Career Fielding Record

Position	PCT	G	PO	A	E	TC	DP
Pitcher	.918	258	52	71	11	134	4

Curtis Granderson

14 Outfielder
6-1 • 185 • B/T: Left/Right
Opening Day Age: 29

Birthdate
March 16, 1981

Birthplace
Blue Island, Ill.

Resides
Chicago, Ill.

M.L. Service
5 years, 77 days

College
University of Illinois

Career Highlights
A.L. All-Star Team
▸ 2009

Status
▸ Acquired by the Yankees from the Detroit Tigers in a three-team, seven-player deal in which the Yankees sent LHP Phil Coke and OF Austin Jackson to Detroit and RHP Ian Kennedy to Arizona on December 9, 2009...is in the third year of a five-year contract that extends through 2012 with a club option for 2013.

Postseason Notes
▸ Saw his only postseason action in 2006 for the AL-champion Detroit Tigers, batting .226 (12-for-53) with 3 doubles, 1 triple, 3HR, 7RBI and 2SB...went 3-for-5 with 1HR and 1RBI in his first career playoff game at the original Yankee Stadium in Game 1 of the ALDS on 10/3/06.

Career Notes
▸ Became the first player in Major League history to be acquired during the offseason by the defending World Series champions after coming off a 30-homer season (hit 30HR in 2009 w/ Detroit)—credit: *Elias Sports Bureau*.
▸ Has hit at least 20 home runs in each of the last four seasons (2007-10).
▸ In his career, has hit .287 (650-for-2,268) with 57HR vs. right-handed pitchers...owns a .215 (167-for-777) batting average with 20HR off lefties.
▸ Named the Yankees' 2010 Roberto Clemente Award nominee, his third such selection (also 2007 and 2009 w/ Detroit).

2010
▸ Batted .247 (115-for-466) with 76R, 17 doubles, 7 triples, 24HR, 67RBI and 12SB in 136 games (134 starts in CF) with the Yankees in 2010...started at five different spots in the batting order (No. 2 and 6-9)...hit .234 (37-for-158) with 4HR vs. left-handed pitchers and .253 (78-for-308) with 20HR against righties.
▸ From 8/12 through the end of the season, hit .286 (16-for-56) with 3HR vs. left-handed pitching...batted just .206 (21-for-102) off lefties through 8/11 and had hit only 3HR against LH pitchers from Opening Day 2009 through 8/11/10.
▸ Hit a team-high 14HR in 157AB over his final 46 games of the season (from 8/14) after hitting just 10HR in 309AB over his first 90 games of the season...hit 9HR over his last 23 home games of the season.
▸ Made his fourth career Opening Day roster...hit solo HR in his first plate appearance as a Yankee in the second inning of 4/4 Opening Day loss at Boston, going 1-for-4 with 1BB...became the first player to homer in his first AB or PA as a Yankee since Cody Ransom on 8/17/08 vs. Kansas City...became the fourth

2010 Highs and Streaks		
Hits	3 - 6 times	
	Last: vs. BOS, 9/25/10	
Runs	3 - vs. KC, 7/25/10	
2B	2 - 2 times	
	Last: at TB, 9/14/10	
3B	2 - vs. LAA, 4/15/10	
HR	2 - 3 times	
	Last: vs. TB, 9/20/10	
RBI	5 - vs. TB, 9/20/10	
BB	2 - 7 times	
	Last: at BOS, 10/2/10 (G1)	
SO	4 - vs. TOR, 7/4/10	
SB	1 - 12 times	
	Last: vs. TB, 9/20/10	
Hit Streak	8g - 9/13-21/10	

Career Highs and Streaks		
Hits	5 - 2 times	
	Last: at CLE, 7/30/08	
Runs	4 - at KC, 7/21/08	
2B	2 - 7 times	
	Last: vs. TOR, 9/3/10	
3B	2 - 5 times	
	Last: vs. LAA, 4/15/10	
HR	2 - 7 times	
	Last: vs. TB, 9/20/10	
RBI	5 - 3 times	
	Last: vs. TB, 9/20/10	
BB	3 - 3 times	
	Last: vs. OAK, 5/17/09	
SO	4 - 4 times	
	Last: vs. TOR, 7/4/10	
SB	3 - at CWS, 9/30/07	
Hit Streak	15g - 6/10-27/08	

CURTIS GRANDERSON

Yankee to do so at Fenway Park (also John Miller-1966, Graig Nettles-1973 and Andy Phillips-2004)—credit: *Elias*…was his second straight year with an Opening Day homer…was the first Yankee to homer in his first at-bat as a Yankee on Opening Day since Jimmy Wynn on 4/7/77 vs. Milwaukee…was the second of back-to-back homers with Jorge Posada, becoming the first pair of Yankees to hit back-to-back home runs on Opening Day since Dave Winfield and Steve Kemp on 4/5/83 at Seattle (credit: *Elias*).

- Was 1-for-4 with 1R in 4/6 win at Boston, batting ninth in the starting batting order for the first time since 6/30/08 at Minnesota and 11th time in his career…marked the first time in franchise history the Yankees batted a 30-or-more HR hitter from the previous season in the ninth spot (credit: *Elias*).

- Hit a game-winning solo HR in the 10th inning of 4/7 win at Boston off Jonathan Papelbon…marked his second career extra-inning HR (also solo HR on 9/29/09 vs. Minnesota off Joe Nathan in a 3-2 Tigers loss) and his second career go-ahead HR in the ninth inning or later (also 9/26/05 vs. Chicago-AL off Cliff Politte).

- Was 2-for-4 with 1R, 2 triples and 1RBI in 4/15 win vs. Los Angeles-AL…tripled twice in the same game for the fifth time in his career and first since 8/18/08 at Texas…became the first Yankee to triple twice in the same contest since Bobby Abreu on 5/30/08 at Minnesota and the first Yankee to do so at home since Enrique Wilson on 7/3/02 vs. Cleveland…became the first Yankee to triple in consecutive at-bats in the same game since Clay Bellinger on 8/26/00 at Oakland…teammate Robinson Cano homered twice in the same game…according to *Elias*, marked the first game in which the Yankees had one player with 2HR and another with a pair of triples since 4/24/60, when Tony Kubek homered twice and Elston Howard had two triples in a 15-9 win vs. Baltimore at the original Yankee Stadium.

- Went hitless in 17 consecutive at-bats from 4/21-27…was the second-longest hitless stretch of his career behind a 21AB hitless streak from 8/15-23/06.

- Was placed on the 15-day disabled list with a Grade 2 strain of the left groin from 5/2-28…suffered the injury while running the bases in 5/1 loss vs. Chicago-AL…was taken to New York-Presbyterian Hospital for an MRI following the game.

- Began a rehab assignment on 5/22 with Triple-A Scranton/Wilkes-Barre, going 4-for-16 (.250) with 2RBI and 2BB/1IBB in 5G (3GS in CF, 2GS at DH).

- Was reinstated from the 15-day disabled list prior to 5/28 win vs. Cleveland and batted second in the starting lineup for just the third time in his career (also 7/23/05 Game 2 vs. Minnesota and 9/30/07 at Chicago-AL)—credit: *Elias*.

- Hit solo HR off Brian Matusz in 6/1 win vs. Baltimore, marking his first homer since 4/7 at Boston and his first home run off a left-hander since 4/22/09 at Los Angeles-AL off Joe Saunders.

- Hit grand slam and was 2-for-5 with 2R and 1SB in 6/8 win at Baltimore…was his second career grand slam (also 4/4/07 vs. Toronto) and his most RBI in a game since 9/28/08 vs. Tampa Bay (also 4RBI).

- Hit game-winning solo-HR in the 10th and was 3-for-5 with 2R, 1 double and 1SB in 6/23 win at Arizona…was his third career extra-inning HR and second this season (also 10th inning of 4/7 win at Boston off Jonathan Papelbon).

- Was 2-for-4 in 6/29 loss vs. Seattle…marked his first game with 2H off left-handed pitching since 9/16/09 vs. Kansas City.

- Collected his fifth career multi-HR game in 7/25 win vs. Kansas City—and first since 7/29/09 at Texas—hitting two solo HRs.

- Was 3-for-3 with 1 double and 1BB in 8/16 loss vs. Detroit…was caught stealing in the fifth, marking his first CS since 7/31/09 at Cleveland and snapping a streak of 13 straight successful stolen base attempts.

- Collected 9HR and 23RBI in September, each marking highs for any calendar month in his career.

- Recorded three straight multi-hit games from 9/1-3, going 6-for-10 with 4R, 2 doubles, 2HR and 6RBI as the Yankees went 3-0.

- Went 2-for-3, with his second multi-HR game this season in 9/2 win vs. Oakland, entering the game defensively in the second in CF when Swisher left with a left knee injury…became the third player in franchise history to collect a multi-homer game despite not being in the starting lineup, joining Steve Balboni (5/23/90 at Minnesota) and Cody Ransom (9/26/08 at Boston) – credit: *Elias Sports Bureau*.

- Collected his seventh career multi-HR game (all 2HR games) and third this season (also 7/25 vs. Kansas City and 9/2 vs. Oakland) in 9/20 win vs. Tampa Bay…hit a two-run HR and a three-run HR, tying his career high with 5RBI (also 4/4/07 vs. Toronto and 5/26/06 vs. Cleveland).

- Hit 4HR with 9RBI in seven games over the Yankees' final homestand of the season (9/20-26)…overall, homered seven times in his final 16 games from 9/15 through the end of the season, collecting 19RBI over the stretch.

- Played all 20 innings in the 10/2 doubleheader split at Boston in which both games went 10 innings.

- In 18 spring training games with the Yankees, hit .286 (14-for-49) with 4R, 3 doubles and 4BRI.

CURTIS GRANDERSON

Granderson's Career Batting Record

Year	Club	AVG	G	AB	R	H	2B	3B	HR	RBI	SH	SF	HP	BB	SO	SB	CS	E	OBP	SLG
2002	Oneonta	.344	52	212	45	73	15	4	3	34	0	1	7	20	35	9	2	1	.417	.495
2003	Lakeland	.286	127	476	71	136	29	10	11	51	5	3	12	49	91	10	7	5	.365	.458
2004	Erie	.303	123	462	89	140	19	8	21	93	3	4	4	80	95	14	8	3	.407	.515
	DETROIT - a	.240	9	25	2	6	1	1	0	0	0	0	0	3	8	0	0	0	.321	.360
2005	Toledo	.290	111	445	79	129	29	13	15	65	2	5	3	48	129	22	6	4	.359	.515
	DETROIT	.272	47	162	18	44	6	3	8	20	2	0	0	10	43	1	1	0	.314	.494
2006	DETROIT	.260	159	596	90	155	31	9	19	68	7	6	4	66	174	8	5	1	.335	.438
2007	DETROIT	.302	158	612	122	185	38	23	23	74	5	2	5	52	141	26	1	5	.361	.552
2008	Toledo	.333	2	9	1	3	1	0	0	0	0	0	0	0	1	0	0	0	.333	.444
	West Michigan	.364	3	11	1	4	0	2	0	1	0	0	0	1	2	0	0	0	.417	.727
	DETROIT - b	.280	141	553	112	155	26	13	22	66	1	1	3	71	111	12	4	4	.365	.494
2009	DETROIT - c	.249	160	631	91	157	23	8	30	71	3	2	2	72	141	20	6	3	.327	.453
2010	YANKEES - d	.247	136	466	76	115	17	7	24	67	4	3	2	53	116	12	2	2	.324	.468
	Scranton/WB	.250	5	16	0	4	0	0	0	2	0	0	0	2	2	0	0	0	.333	.250
Minor League Totals		**.300**	**423**	**1631**	**286**	**489**	**93**	**37**	**50**	**246**	**10**	**13**	**26**	**200**	**355**	**55**	**23**	**13**	**.382**	**.494**
Major League Totals		**.268**	**810**	**3045**	**511**	**817**	**142**	**64**	**126**	**366**	**22**	**14**	**16**	**327**	**734**	**79**	**19**	**15**	**.341**	**.481**

Selected by the Detroit Tigers in the third round of the 2002 First-Year Player Draft.

a – Placed on the disabled list from June 21-July 3, 2004 with a left ankle sprain.

b – Placed on the disabled list from March 23-April 23, 2008 with a non-displaced fracture of the third metacarpal in his right hand.

c – Traded to the Yankees from the Detroit Tigers in a three-team, seven-player deal in which the Yankees sent LHP Phil Coke and OF Austin Jackson to Detroit and RHP Ian Kennedy to the Arizona Diamondbacks.

d – Placed on the 15-day disabled list from May 2-27, 2010 with a grade 2 left groin strain.

Granderson's Division Series Record

Year	Club vs. Opp.	AVG	G	AB	R	H	2B	3B	HR	RBI	SH	SF	HP	BB	SO	SB	CS	E	OBP	SLG
2006	DET vs. NYY	.294	4	17	3	5	0	1	2	5	0	1	0	0	1	1	0	0	.278	.765
Division Series Totals		**.294**	**4**	**17**	**3**	**5**	**0**	**1**	**2**	**5**	**0**	**1**	**0**	**0**	**1**	**1**	**0**	**0**	**.278**	**.765**

Granderson's Championship Series Record

Year	Club vs. Opp.	AVG	G	AB	R	H	2B	3B	HR	RBI	SH	SF	HP	BB	SO	SB	CS	E	OBP	SLG
2006	DET vs. OAK	.333	4	15	4	5	2	0	1	2	0	0	0	4	2	1	0	0	.474	.667
LCS Totals		**.333**	**4**	**15**	**4**	**5**	**2**	**0**	**1**	**2**	**0**	**0**	**0**	**4**	**2**	**1**	**0**	**0**	**.474**	**.667**

Granderson's World Series Record

Year	Club vs. Opp.	AVG	G	AB	R	H	2B	3B	HR	RBI	SH	SF	HP	BB	SO	SB	CS	E	OBP	SLG
2006	DET vs. STL	.095	5	21	1	2	1	0	0	0	0	0	0	1	7	0	0	0	.136	.143
World Series Totals		**.095**	**5**	**21**	**1**	**2**	**1**	**0**	**0**	**0**	**0**	**0**	**0**	**1**	**7**	**0**	**0**	**0**	**.136**	**.143**
POSTSEASON TOTALS		**.226**	**13**	**53**	**8**	**12**	**3**	**1**	**3**	**7**	**0**	**1**	**0**	**5**	**10**	**2**	**0**	**0**	**.288**	**.491**

Granderson's All-Star Game Record

Year	Club, Site	AVG	G	AB	R	H	2B	3B	HR	RBI	SH	SF	HP	BB	SO	SB	CS	E	OBP	SLG
2009	DET, St. Louis	1.000	1	1	1	1	0	1	0	0	0	0	0	0	0	0	0	0	1.000	3.000
All-Star Game Totals		**1.000**	**1**	**1**	**1**	**1**	**0**	**1**	**0**	**0**	**0**	**0**	**0**	**0**	**0**	**0**	**0**	**0**	**1.000**	**3.000**

Granderson's World Baseball Classic Record

Year	Country, Site	AVG	G	AB	R	H	2B	3B	HR	RBI	SH	SF	HP	BB	SO	SB	CS	E	OBP	SLG
2009	USA, USA	.235	7	17	1	4	0	0	0	2	0	0	0	2	5	0	0	0	.316	.235
WBC Totals		**.235**	**7**	**17**	**1**	**4**	**0**	**0**	**0**	**2**	**0**	**0**	**0**	**2**	**5**	**0**	**0**	**0**	**.316**	**.235**

Granderson's Career Fielding Record

Position	PCT	G	PO	A	E	TC
Outfield	.993	801	2040	30	15	2085

Granderson's Career Home Run Chart

MULTI-HOMER GAMES: 7. **TWO-HOMER GAMES:** 7, last on 9/20/10 vs. Tampa Bay. **GRAND SLAMS:** 2, on 6/8/10 at Baltimore (Kevin Millwood). **PINCH-HIT HR:** None. **INSIDE-THE-PARK HR:** 2, last on 8/26/07 vs. New York-AL (Phil Hughes). **WALK-OFF HR:** 1, on 9/26/05 vs. Chicago-AL (Cliff Politte). **LEADOFF HR:** 15, last on 9/27/09 at Chicago-AL (Daniel Hudson).

Granderson's Postseason Home Run Chart

MULTI-HOME RUN GAMES: None. **TWO-HOMER GAMES:** None. **GRAND SLAMS:** None. **PINCH-HIT HOME RUNS:** None. **INSIDE-THE-PARK HOME RUNS:** None. **WALK-OFF HOME RUNS:** None. **LEADOFF:** None.

Phil Hughes

65

Right-handed Pitcher

6-5 • 240 • B/T: Right/Right

Opening Day Age: 23

Birthdate
June 24, 1986

Birthplace
Mission Viejo, Calif.

Resides
Tampa, Fla.

M.L. Service
3 years, 113 days

Career Highlights
Kevin Lawn Award
Yankees "Minor
League Pitcher
of the Year"
▸ 2006

A.L. All-Star Team
▸ 2010

All-Star Futures Game
▸ 2006

Status
▸ Selected by the Yankees in the first round (23rd overall) of the 2004 First-Year Player Draft…signed through the 2010 season.

Postseason Notes
▸ Worked exclusively out of the bullpen in the 2009 postseason, going 0-1 with an 8.53 ERA (6.1IP, 11H, 6ER, 4BB, 7K, 1HR) in nine appearances…pitched in all three 2009 ALDS games vs. Minnesota, allowing 2ER in 2.0 combined IP without recording a decision.

▸ Appeared in two Division Series games vs. Cleveland in 2007, allowing 1ER in 5.2IP of relief (1.59 ERA, 3H, 0BB, 6K)…at 21 years, 102 days old, became the youngest Yankees pitcher to appear in a postseason game since Bill Stafford (21 years, 58 days) in Game 5 of the 1960 World Series vs. Pittsburgh…tossed 3.2 scoreless innings and earned the win in the Yankees' Game 3 victory (2H, 4K).

Career Notes
▸ According to the *Elias Sports Bureau*, his 31 career wins are the most victories by a player the Yankees selected in the first round of the First-Year Player Draft (excluding Compensation rounds), surpassing the six career wins of Bill Burbach (Yankees 1965 first-round pick).

▸ Was 23-11 prior to turning 24 on 6/24/10, marking the most wins by a Yankee under 24 since 1965, when both Mel Stottlemyre (29 wins) and Al Downing (32 wins) both celebrated their 24th birthday.

▸ Is 25-17 with a 4.68 ERA (315.2IP, 164ER) in 57 career starts…is 6-1 with a 1.35 ERA (53.1IP, 8ER) in 46 career relief appearances.

▸ Is 9-0 in his last 12 starts immediately following a Yankees loss (since May 2009).

▸ Is 9-2 with a 3.27 ERA (85.1IP, 31ER) in 29G/11GS in day games over the last two years (2009-10), including relief appearances.

2010 Highs and Streaks		
Low hit CG	N/A	
IP (start)	7.1 - at OAK, 4/21/10	
IP (relief)	1.0 - 2 times	
	Last: at BOS, 10/2/10(G1)	
Hits	10 - vs. SEA, 6/29/10	
Runs	7 - vs. SEA, 6/29/10	
BB	5 - 4 times	
	Last: vs. TB, 9/21/10	
SO	10 - at OAK, 4/21/10	
HR	3 - 2 times	
	Last: vs. TOR, 9/5/10	
Winning Streak	5g - 5/28-6/19/10	
Losing Streak	2g - 9/5-15/10	

Career Highs and Streaks		
Low hit CG	Low hit CG N/A	
IP (start)	8.0 - 2 times	
	Last: at TEX, 5/25/09	
IP (relief)	3.2 - at BOS, 6/10/09	
Hits	10 - vs. SEA, 6/29/10	
Runs	8 - at BAL, 5/9/09	
BB	5 - 4 times	
	Last: vs. OAK, 8/31/10	
SO	10 - at OAK, 4/21/10	
HR	3 - 3 times	
	Last: vs. TOR, 9/5/10	
Winning Streak	9g - 8/14/09-5/12/10	
Losing Streak	4g - 4/8-29/08	

2010
▸ Went 18-8 with a 4.19 ERA (176.1IP, 82ER) and 146K in 31G/29GS with the Yankees in 2010, setting career highs wins, losses, IP and strikeouts…was tied for fourth in the AL and tied for seventh in the Majors in wins…was tied for fifth in the AL and tied for sixth in the Majors with a .692 winning percentage…lasted at least 5.0IP in 28 of his 29 starts in 2010 (only exception on 8/25 at Toronto, 3.2IP)…opponents batted .244 (162-for-665, 25HR); LHH .235 (81-for-345, 17HR) and RHH .253 (81-for-320, 8HR)…the Yankees went 20-9 in his starts.

▸ Became the second Yankees pitcher age 24 or younger in the last 45 years to win at least 18 games in a season (also Andy Pettitte in 1996 -21 wins) according to baseball-reference.com…was the youngest Yankees right-hander to win at least 18 games in a season since 23-year-old Mel Stottlemyre won 20 games in 1965.

▸ Joined CC Sabathia (21-7) as the first set of Yankees teammates with at least 18 wins each since 2002 (Mike Mussina 18-10; and Davis Wells 19-7)…is the first time a pair of 18-game winning Yankees were 30 years old or younger since 1978 (Ron Guidry 25-3 and Ed Figueroa 20-9)

▸ Allowed 20HR at home (including each of his first 15 total HR allowed), tying Scott Sanderson (20 in 1992) for the most HRs allowed at home in a single season in franchise history, according to the *Elias Sports Bureau*…tied Baltimore's Kevin Millwood and the Dodgers' Ted Lilly for

Hughes' 2010 Starting Pitching Lines

Date/Opp	Score	W/L	IP	H	R	ER	HR	BB	K	NP/K	ERA	Left game
4/15 vs. LAA*	6-2	W	5.0	3	2	2	1	**5**	6	108-66	3.60	Leading 6-1
4/21 at OAK	3-1	W	**7.1**	1	1	1	0	2	**10**	101-70	2.19	Leading 2-0
4/27 at BAL*	4-5	ND	5.2	2	1	1	0	4	2	109-68	2.00	Leading 2-1
5/2 vs. CWS	12-3	W	7.0	4	0	0	0	1	6	99-69	1.44	Leading 12-0
5/7 vs. BOS	10-3	W	7.0	7	2	2	0	1	7	101-70	1.69	Leading 10-2
5/12 vs. DET (G2)*	8-0	W	7.0	5	0	0	0	1	8	101-71	1.38	Leading 2-0
5/17 vs. BOS*	11-9	ND	5.0	6	5	5	2	1	3	104-71	2.25	Leading 6-5
5/22 at NYM	3-5	L	5.2	8	4	4	0	3	7	**117**-88	2.72	Trailing 4-1
5/28 vs. CLE*	8-2	W	7.0	5	2	2	1	1	8	109-76	2.70	Leading 8-2
6/2 vs. BAL	9-1	W	7.0	6	1	1	0	1	7	101-72	2.54	Leading 8-1
6/8 at BAL	12-7	W	6.0	9	3	3	0	0	4	102-70	2.71	Leading 12-3
6/13 vs. HOU	9-5	W	5.2	7	5	5	1	2	6	110-73	3.11	Leading 7-5
6/19 vs. NYM*	5-3	W	7.0	5	3	3	2	3	4	99-62	3.17	Leading 5-3
6/29 vs. SEA	4-7	L	5.2	**10**	**7**	6	1	2	3	94-63	3.58	Trailing 1-7
7/4 vs. TOR	7-6 (10)	ND	6.0	6	5	5	**3**	2	5	101-66	3.83	Tied 5-5
7/9 at SEA	6-1	W	7.0	6	1	1	0	0	5	109-79	3.65	Leading 5-1
7/20 vs. LAA	2-10	L	5.0	9	6	**6**	2	3	2	98-57	3.99	Trailing 6-2
7/25 vs. KC	12-6	W	5.1	6	3	3	2	0	3	95-61	4.04	Leading 5-3
7/30 at TB	2-3	L	6.0	4	3	3	1	2	6	104-61	4.07	Trailing 3-2
8/4 vs. TOR*	5-1	W	5.1	4	1	1	0	2	5	99-60	3.96	Leading 5-1
8/9 vs. BOS	1-2	L	6.0	6	2	2	0	1	3	114-74	3.92	Trailing 2-0
8/14 at KC*	8-3	W	6.0	9	3	3	1	1	0	99/71	3.94	Leading 4-3
8/19 at DET	11-5	W	6.0	4	2	2	1	0	6	84-61	3.90	Leading 11-2
8/25 at TOR	3-6	L	3.2	6	5	5	1	**5**	6	102-66	4.12	Trailing 5-2
8/31 vs. OAK	9-3	W	5.0	4	2	2	0	**5**	1	98-46	4.10	Leading 9-3
9/5 vs. TOR	3-7	L	6.0	7	6	6	**3**	1	5	100-69	4.29	Trailing 6-2
9/10 at TEX	*5-6 (13)*	*ND*	*1.0*	*0*	*0*	*0*	*0*	*0*	*1*	*11-7*	*4.26*	*Tied 5-5*
9/15 at TB	3-4	L	6.2	6	4	4	2	0	5	106-65	4.31	Trailing 4-3
9/21 vs. TB	8-3	W	6.1	4	3	3	1	**5**	6	112-67	4.31	Leading 5-2
9/26 vs. BOS*	4-3 (10)	ND	6.0	3	1	1	0	4	4	105-67	4.21	Trailing 1-0
10/2 at BOS (G1)	*6-5 (10)*	*ND*	*1.0*	*0*	*0*	*0*	*0*	*0*	*2*	*14-9*	*4.19*	*Leading 6-5*
Totals	**18-8**		176.1	162	83	82	25	58	146	--	4.19	

*start came after a Yankees loss – **Bold**-season high – *italics*-relief appearance

most homers allowed at home in the Majors this season…according to the *Elias Sports Bureau*, became the first pitcher to allow his first 15HR at home since Seattle's Gaylord Perry in 1982 (first 21HR were at the Kingdome)…allowed just 5HR in 70.0 road IP in 2010 (including 2HR on 9/15 at Tampa Bay).

▸ Surrendered 21HR over his final 20G/18GS from 6/13 to the end of the season after allowing just 4HR over his first 11 starts of 2010.

▸ Received 7.45R/9.0IP of support this season (7.49 in his starts), the highest marks among qualifying Major League pitchers.

▸ Appeared on his first All-Star roster, receiving his selection via the player ballot…according to the *Elias Sports Bureau*, became the third-youngest pitcher to represent the Yankees in an All-Star Game (1956-Johnny Kucks age 22; and 1965-Mel Stottlemyre age 23)…was charged with the loss in the 3-1 NL victory (0.1IP, 2H, 2ER), becoming the first Yankee to take the loss in the Midsummer Classic since Tommy John in 1980…faced three batters in the seventh inning, retiring Cincinnati's Joey Votto before allowing back-to-back singles to Cincinnati's Scott Rolen and St. Louis's Matt Holliday…the White Sox's Matt Thornton allowed both inherited runners to score on a bases-clearing double by All-Star Game MVP Brian McCann.

▸ Was named the Yankees' fifth starter to open the season by Manager Joe Girardi on 3/25…following spring training, pitched in extended spring training – while remaining on the Yankees' 25-man active roster…pitched in two intrasquad extended spring training games at the Yankees' minor league complex in Tampa.

▸ Made his season debut on 4/15 vs. Los Angeles-AL, starting and recording the win in the 6-2 Yankees victory…limited the Angels to 3H and 2ER in 5.0IP (5BB, 6K, 1HR, 1BK) in his first start since 5/31/09…struck out four of his first seven batters faced.

▸ Allowed just 10 combined hits in his first four starts of the season (25.0IP) and 17 combined hits in his first five starts (32.0IP) of 2010…according to the *Elias Sports Bureau*, became the first Major League pitcher since the Yankees' David Cone in 1999 to limit his opposition to as few hits with as many IP over his first four and first five starts of a season.

PHIL HUGHES

- Carried a no-hitter through 7.0 innings on 4/21 at Oakland in his 30th career start, recording the win in a 3-1 Yankees victory (7.1IP, 1H, 1ER, 2BB, 10K)...marked his first double-digit strikeout game, recording eight swinging Ks...also held the Rangers hitless for 6.1IP in his second Major League start on 5/1/07 at Texas before leaving the game with a strained left hamstring...according to the *Elias Sports Bureau*, is one of four active pitchers to have carried a no-hitter through six innings twice in their first 30 career starts along with Jamie Moyer, Derek Lowe and Hiroki Kuroda.

YANKEES TEAMMATES WITH 18 OR MORE WINS EACH OVER THE LAST 50 YEARS (since 1961)		
2010	Phil Hughes (18) and CC Sabathia (21)	
2002	Mike Mussina (18) and David Wells (19)	
1998	David Cone (20) and David Wells (18)	
1979	Ron Guidry (18) and Tommy John (21)	
1978	Ed Figueroa (20) and Ron Guidry (25)	
1974	Pat Dobson (19) and Doc Medich (19)	
1963	Jim Bouton (21) and Whitey Ford (24)	

- Retired 25 consecutive right-handed batters over three starts from 4/17-5/7 –including all 13 on 5/2 vs. Chicago-AL.

- Tossed 7.0 shutout IP on 5/12 at Detroit, recording the win in an 8-0 Yankees victory in Game 2 of a doubleheader (5H, 1BB)...was his fifth straight win to start the season, becoming the youngest Yankees starter to begin a season 5-0 since Whitey Ford in 1950 (9-0)...according to *Elias*, with a 1.38 ERA after his first six starts, became the first Yankee with at least five wins and a sub-1.50 ERA through his first six starts since 1958, when Bob Turley went 6-0 with 0.83 ERA in his first six starts in his Cy Young Award-winning season...the last Major League pitcher Hughes' age or younger to start a season 5-0 with an ERA under 1.50 was the Angels' Jered Weaver in 2006 (6-0 with a 1.12 ERA), according to the *Elias Sports Bureau*.

- Joined Andy Pettitte at 5-0 to start the season, marking just the fourth time in the last 50 years that two Yankees starters each won their first five decisions in the same season...also occurred in 2004 (Kevin Brown and Orlando Hernandez), 2003 (Mike Mussina and David Wells) and 1980 (Ron Guidry and Tommy John), according to the *Elias Sports Bureau*.

- Tossed a career-high 117 pitches on 5/22 at Citi Field, recording his first loss of the season in a 5-3 Mets victory (5.2IP, 8H, 4ER, 3BB, 7K)...allowed 41 foul balls, marking the most by one pitcher since Jon Garland on 9/16/05 w/Chicago-AL vs. Minnesota (credit: mlb.com)...the loss snapped an 11-start undefeated streak and a nine-game overall winning streak (including starts and relief apps.) since 8/2/09.

- Faced off against Mike Pelfrey (who entered 9-1) on 6/19 vs. the Mets and recorded his 10th win in a 5-3 Yankees victory (7.0IP, 5H, 3ER, 3BB, 4K, 2HR)...according to the *Elias Sports Bureau*, the game was only the second time in Major League history in which both starting pitchers came into the game with at least nine wins and a winning percentage of .900 or higher (also 6/22/1900 at Baker Bowl when Brooklyn's Joe McGinnity at 12-1 faced the Phillies' Bill Bernhard also at 12-1)...was Hughes' final win of a 10-game home winning streak from 5/15/09-6/19/10, stretching a span of 33G/9GS...was 7-0 with a 4.02 ERA (53.2IP, 24ER) as a starter over the stretch.

- Had 10-1 record and a 3.17 ERA through 6/19, becoming the 12th Yankees pitcher to win at least 10 of his first 11 decisions (all as a starter) to start a season...was the first such Yankee with an ERA at or below 3.17 since Jimmy Key in 1994 (10-1, 2.99 ERA) – credit: *Elias*.

- Took the loss on 6/29 vs. Seattle, snapping a 10-game winning streak at home that dated back to 5/20/09...had been tied for the longest home winning streak in the Majors with teammate CC Sabathia.

- Allowed a career high-tying 3HR (also 8/26/07 at Detroit) in a 7/4 loss vs. Toronto, recording a no-decision (6.0IP, 6H, 5ER, 2BB, 5K, 1WP, 3HR).

- Suffered the loss on 7/30 at Tampa Bay, allowing 3ER in 6.0IP (4H, 2BB, 6K, 1HR) in a 3-2 Yankees defeat...his home run allowed to Matt Joyce was his first homer surrendered on the road in 2010.

- Made his 50th career start on 8/14 at Kansas City, recording the win (6.0IP, 9H, 3ER, 1BB, 0K, 1HR) in an 8-3 Yankees victory...marked just his second career start without a strikeout (also 5/9/09 at Baltimore – 1.2IP)...became the youngest Yankee to record his 50th career start since Al Downing (at 24 years, 51days) in 1964, according to the *Elias Sports Bureau*.

- Recorded his 16th win of the season on 8/31 vs. Oakland...joined CC Sabathia (18-5) to give the Yankees two pitchers each with 16 wins prior to September 1 for the first time since 1998 (David Cone-18 and David Wells-16).

- Allowed a season-high 6ER on 9/5 vs. Toronto (also 7/20 vs. Los Angeles-AL and 6/29 vs. Seattle) and tied a career high with 3HR allowed (also 7/4/10 vs. Toronto and 8/26/07 at Detroit)...two of the HRs came on 0-2 counts (Wells and Hill) after Hughes had surrendered just two prior 0-2 HRs in his entire career (also 8/25/10 at Toronto vs. Vernon Wells; and 5/9/09 at Baltimore vs. Aubrey Huff)...marked his first career loss in September after winning his first six with six decisions...according to *Elias*, was the first Yankee since Ray Fontenot (1983-84) to win his first six Sept. decisions.

- Was skipped in the rotation from 9/6-14, going nine days without a start...made his first of two relief appearances of the season on 9/10 at Texas, tossing 1.0 perfect inning of relief (1K) in the Yankees' 6-5,

13-inning loss.

▸ Lost his second consecutive start on 9/15 at Tampa Bay, marking his only instance of losing consecutive starts in 2010…was perfect through his first 4.0IP before Evan Longoria led off the fifth with a single…surrendered two of his five road HRs this season while allowing 4ER in 6.2IP.

▸ Allowed 1ER in 6.0IP (3H, 4BB, 4K) in his final start of the season on 9/26 vs. Boston, recording a no-decision…marked his fewest hits allowed in a start since 4/27/10 at Baltimore (2H).

▸ Tossed a perfect ninth inning on 10/2 at Boston (Game 1), recording his only relief win of the season (1.0IP, 2K).

Hughes' Career Pitching Record

YEAR	CLUB	W	L	ERA	G	GS	CG	SHO	SV	IP	H	R	ER	HR	HB	BB	SO	WP	BK
2004	GCL Yankees	0	0	0.00	3	3	0	0	0	5.0	4	0	0	0	0	0	8	0	0
2005	Charleston	7	1	1.97	12	12	1	0	0	68.2	46	19	15	1	3	16	72	3	0
	Tampa	2	0	3.06	5	4	0	0	0	17.2	8	6	6	0	3	4	21	0	0
2006	Tampa	2	3	1.80	5	5	0	0	0	30.0	19	7	6	0	1	2	30	0	0
	Trenton	10	3	2.25	21	21	0	0	0	116.0	73	30	29	5	2	32	138	5	0
2007	Tampa	0	0	0.00	1	1	0	0	0	2.0	1	0	0	0	0	2	3	0	0
	Trenton	0	0	1.29	2	2	0	0	0	7.0	5	1	1	0	0	2	11	0	0
	Scranton/WB	4	1	2.20	5	5	0	0	0	28.2	16	7	7	0	1	8	28	2	0
	YANKEES - a	5	3	4.46	13	13	0	0	0	72.2	64	39	36	8	2	29	58	4	0
2008	YANKEES - b	0	4	6.62	8	8	0	0	0	34.0	43	26	25	3	1	15	23	2	0
	Charleston	2	0	0.00	2	0	0	0	0	6.2	3	0	0	0	0	2	6	2	0
	Scranton/WB	1	0	5.90	6	6	0	0	0	29.0	34	19	19	2	2	9	31	0	0
2009	Scranton/WB	3	0	1.86	3	3	0	0	0	19.1	17	4	4	2	0	3	19	0	0
	YANKEES	8	3	3.03	51	7	0	0	3	86.0	68	31	29	8	5	28	96	4	2
2010	YANKEES	18	8	4.19	31	29	0	0	0	176.1	162	83	82	25	0	58	146	9	1
Minor League Totals		**31**	**8**	**2.37**	**65**	**62**	**1**	**0**	**0**	**330.0**	**225**	**94**	**87**	**10**	**12**	**80**	**367**	**12**	**0**
Major League Totals		**31**	**18**	**4.20**	**103**	**29**	**0**	**0**	**3**	**369.0**	**337**	**83**	**172**	**44**	**8**	**130**	**323**	**19**	**3**

Selected by the Yankees in the first round (23rd overall) of the 2004 First-Year Player Draft.

a – Placed on the 15-day disabled list from May 3-August 4, 2007 with a strained left hamstring (transferred to 60-day D.L. on June 9).

b – Placed on the 15-day disabled list from May 1 – July 30, 2008 with a stress fracture in his ninth right rib (transferred to 60-day D.L. on July 18).

Hughes' Division Series Record

Year	Club vs. Opp.	W	L	ERA	G	GS	CG	SHO	SV	IP	H	R	ER	HR	HP	BB	SO	WP	BK
2007	NYY vs. CLE	1	0	1.59	2	0	0	0	0	5.2	3	1	1	1	0	0	6	1	0
2009	NYY vs. MIN	0	0	9.00	3	0	0	0	0	2.0	5	2	2	0	0	1	3	0	0
Division Series Totals		**1**	**0**	**3.52**	**5**	**0**	**0**	**0**	**0**	**7.2**	**8**	**3**	**3**	**1**	**0**	**1**	**9**	**1**	**0**

Hughes' League Championship Series Record

Year	Club vs. Opp.	W	L	ERA	G	GS	CG	SHO	SV	IP	H	R	ER	HR	HP	BB	SO	WP	BK
2009	NYY vs. LAA	0	1	3.38	3	0	0	0	0	2.2	4	1	1	0	0	1	3	0	0
LCS Totals		**0**	**1**	**3.38**	**3**	**0**	**0**	**0**	**0**	**2.2**	**4**	**1**	**1**	**0**	**0**	**1**	**3**	**0**	**0**

Hughes' World Series Record

Year	Club vs. Opp.	W	L	ERA	G	GS	CG	SHO	SV	IP	H	R	ER	HR	HP	BB	SO	WP	BK
2009	NYY vs. PHI	0	0	16.20	3	0	0	0	0	1.2	2	3	3	1	0	2	1	0	0
World Series Totals		**0**	**0**	**16.20**	**3**	**0**	**0**	**0**	**0**	**1.2**	**2**	**3**	**3**	**1**	**0**	**2**	**1**	**0**	**0**
POSTSEASON TOTALS		**1**	**1**	**5.25**	**11**	**0**	**0**	**0**	**0**	**12.0**	**14**	**7**	**7**	**2**	**0**	**4**	**13**	**1**	**0**

Hughes' All-Star Game Record

Year	Club, Site	W	L	ERA	G	GS	CG	SHO	SV	IP	H	R	ER	HR	HP	BB	SO	WP	BK
2010	NYY, Los Angeles (AL)	0	1	54.00	1	0	0	0	0	0.1	2	2	2	0	0	0	0	0	0
All-Star Game Totals		**0**	**1**	**54.00**	**1**	**0**	**0**	**0**	**0**	**0.1**	**2**	**2**	**2**	**0**	**0**	**0**	**0**	**0**	**0**

Hughes' Career Fielding Record

Position	PCT	G	PO	A	E	TC	DP
Pitcher	.979	103	17	30	1	48	2

Hughes' Regular Season Batting Record

Year	Team	AVG	G	AB	R	H	2B	3B	HR	RBI	SH	SF	HP	BB	SO	SB	CS
2010	NYY	.000	31	1	0	0	0	0	0	0	1	0	0	0	0	0	0
Major League Totals		**.000**	**103**	**1**	**0**	**0**	**0**	**0**	**0**	**0**	**1**	**0**	**0**	**0**	**0**	**0**	**0**

Derek Jeter

2

Shortstop

6-3• 195 • B/T: Right/Right

Opening Day Age: 35

Birthdate
June 26, 1974

Birthplace
Pequannock, N.J.

Resides
Tampa, Fla.

M.L. Service
15 years, 43 days

Career Highlights
World Series MVP
▸ 2000

All-Star Game MVP
▸ 2000

A.L. All-Star Team
▸ 1998, 1999, 2000,
2001, 2002, 2004,
2006, 2007, 2008,
2009, 2010

A.L. Gold Glove
▸ 2004, 2005, 2006,
2009

A.L. Silver Slugger
▸ 2006, 2007, 2008,
2009

A.L. Rookie of the Year
▸ 1996

Sports Illustrated
Sportsman of the Year
▸ 2009

Roberto Clemente Award
▸ 2009

Hank Aaron Award
▸ 2006, 2009

Status

▸ Selected in the first round (sixth pick overall) of the 1992 First-Year Player Draft…signed a 10-year contract on February 9, 2001…contract extends through the 2010 season.

Postseason Notes

▸ Ranks first on Major League Baseball's all-time postseason list with 175 career hits, 99 runs and 138 games played…also ranks second with 50 extra-base hits and third in home runs (20), with 12 of the homers tying the game or giving the Yankees the lead…owns three career leadoff home runs in postseason play (2009 ALCS Game 3 at Los Angeles-AL, 2004 ALDS Game 2 vs. Minnesota and 2000 World Series Game 4 at the Mets)…is the only player ever with a leadoff homer in each the three rounds of the playoffs…owns a .417 (53-for-127) career average against left-handed pitching in postseason play.

▸ Led the team in hits (22) for the World Champion Yankees in the 2009 postseason, reaching base safely in all 15 contests…trailed only Barry Bonds (17 straight in 2002) and Gary Sheffield (16 straight in 1997) for the longest streak of reaching base in a single postseason…reached base four times in ALDS Game 1 win (single, HR, 2BB)…according to the *Elias Sports Bureau*, became the third Yankee to have at least 4PA in a postseason game and reach base safely in each, score at least 3R with at least 2RBI and hit a HR (also Babe Ruth in 1926 World Series Game 4 and Reggie Jackson in Game 6 of the 1977 World Series)…batted .407 (11-for-27) in the World Series, hitting safely in all six games and marking his most hits in any postseason series.

▸ Is the all-time Division Series leader in hits (74), runs (37), singles (52) and games played (53)…reached base safely in a Division Series-record 21 straight games between 2000 and 2005…tied the Major League record for hits in a single postseason game with five in Game 1 of the 2006 ALDS vs. Detroit (sixth time in ML history), becoming only the second player ever to go 5-for-5 (also Atlanta's Marquis Grissom in Game 4 of the 1995 NLDS vs. Colorado)…hit the second of three consecutive home runs (between Raines and O'Neill) in Game 1 of the 1997 ALDS, the first time three consecutive home runs had been hit in postseason play.

▸ Ranks second all time with 47 Championship Series games played, is third in hits (51), tied for fourth in doubles (seven), tied for fifth in RBI (23) and tied for sixth in home runs (seven)…hit controversial home run in the eighth inning of Game 1 of the 1996 ALCS off Baltimore's Armando Benitez when a young fan reached over the wall (Yankees would win 5-4 in 11 innings).

▸ Has scored 32 runs in the World Series, fourth-most all time, while ranking fifth with 50 World Series hits…has carried at least a .300 average in five World Series (1998-2000, '03 and '09), matching Babe Ruth and Yogi Berra for the most such Series

2010 Highs and Streaks	
Hits	4 - vs. TOR, 8/4/10
Runs	3 - 6 times
	Last: at TOR, 9/28/10
2B	2 - vs. TOR, 8/4/10
3B	1 - 3 times
	Last: vs. DET, 8/19/10
HR	2 - vs. HOU, 6/12/10
RBI	4 - 2 times
	Last: vs. HOU, 6/12/10
BB	3 - vs. TOR, 7/3/10
SO	3 - at LAD, 6/26/10
SB	1 - 17 times
	Last: at BOS, 10/2/10 (G1)
Hit Streak	14g - 9/10-25/10

Career Highs and Streaks	
Hits	5 - 2 times
	Last: vs. TB, 6/21/05
Runs	5 - vs. TB, 6/21/05
2B	3 - at TOR, 5/28/99
3B	2 - at DET, 9/10/96
HR	2 - 9 times
	Last: vs. HOU, 6/12/10
RBI	5 - 3 times
	Last: vs. CHC, 6/18/05
BB	3 - 21 times
	Last: vs. TOR, 7/3/10
SO	4 - 2 times
	Last: at PHI, 9/1/97
SB	3 - 2 times
	Last: vs. BOS, 5/11/06
Hit Streak	25g - 8/20-9/16/06

all-time…hit safely in 14 consecutive World Series games from 10/26/96-10/26/00, tying Roberto Clemente for the third-longest streak all-time, trailing Hank Bauer (17G) and Marquis Grissom (15G)…hit game-winning "walk-off" home run in the 10th inning of Game 4 of the 2001 World Series vs. Arizona to earn the nickname "Mr. November"…named the MVP of the 2000 World Series (.409, 9-for-22, 6R, 2 doubles, 1 triple, 2HR, 2RBI).

Career Notes

▸ Leads all active Major Leaguers with 2,926 career hits…according to the *Elias Sports Bureau*, is the first Yankee to hold that distinction since Johnny Mize in 1952.

▸ Is one of just 10 players in Baseball history with at least 1,500R, 2,500H, 200HR and 300SB (also teammate Alex Rodriguez, Roberto Alomar, Craig Biggio, Barry Bonds, Johnny Damon, Rickey Henderson, Willie Mays, Paul Molitor and Joe Morgan)…is one of 16 players all time to collect 2,000H, 200HR and 300SB, joining Rodriguez, Bobby Abreu and Johnny Damon as the only active players to reach the totals…is one of four players since 1920 with at least 2,600H, 200HR and 1,000RBI within his first 15 seasons (also Hank Aaron, Stan Musial and Al Simmons)—credit: *Elias Sports Bureau*.

> **DID YOU KNOW?** Of the 2,295 games Derek Jeter has appeared in, in only one were the Yankees mathematically eliminated from postseason play (9/26/08).

▸ Over the last 10 seasons, (2001-10), ranks second in the Majors in hits (1,918), third in runs scored (1,080), fourth in at-bats (6,192) and ninth in games played (1,509).

▸ His 1,602 runs and 2,807 hits from 5/29/95-5/28/10 were the most for any player in Major League history through his first 15 years in the Majors.

▸ Has 15 consecutive seasons with at least 150 hits (since 1996), extending both the longest such streak among active players and the longest in franchise history.

▸ Has at least 150 hits against 11 Major League teams (every American League opponent except the White Sox and Twins)…among players who have debuted over the last 25 seasons, joins only Craig Biggio (12), Barry Bonds (11), Rafael Palmeiro (11) and Mark Grace (11) as the only players to have 150-or-more hits against at least 11 franchises—credit: *Elias*.

▸ Has 42 career hitting streaks of at least 10 games, the most among active players and most ever by a Yankee in franchise history…according to *Elias*, is tied for the fifth-highest total in Baseball since 1903, trailing Ty Cobb (66), Hank Aaron (48), Tris Speaker (47) and Al Simmons (44).

▸ Has reached the 100-run plateau 13 times in his career, tied with Lou Gehrig for most 100R seasons in franchise history…according to *Elias*, is tied with Gehrig, Rickey Henderson and teammate Alex Rodriguez for the second-most 100-run seasons in Major League history behind Hank Aaron (15).

▸ Has reached double digits in home runs in 15 consecutive seasons (since 1996)…is one of only five active players to record double-digit home run totals over 15 consecutive seasons at some point in their career, joining teammate Alex Rodriguez, Chipper Jones, Manny Ramirez and Ivan Rodriguez (credit: *Elias Sports Bureau*)…has collected at least 10HR and 10SB in each of his last 15 seasons (since 1996), the second-longest streak all time behind only Barry Bonds (16 straight from 1986-2001)—credit: *Elias*.

▸ Owns 24 career leadoff home runs (17 at home, seven on the road), tied with Rickey Henderson (24) for most in franchise history.

▸ Owns the most hits in Major League history from the shortstop position, surpassing Luis Aparicio (2,673) on 8/16/09 at Seattle…according to the *Elias Sports Bureau*, is one of four players all time to record 1,500R and 1,500 games played at shortstop (also Bill Dahlen, Honus Wagner and Cal Ripken, Jr.).

▸ Has played 2,274 games at shortstop for the Yankees…according to the *Elias Sports Bureau*, is second on Baseball's all-time list in games at shortstop for one club, trailing the Orioles' Cal Ripken (2,302)…marks the third-most among players who never played a game at any other fielding position, trailing only Luis Aparicio (2,583) and Ozzie Smith (2,511)—credit: *Elias Sports Bureau*.

▸ Among the Yankees' all-time leaders, ranks first in hits (2,926) and at-bats (9,322), second in games played (2,295), doubles (468) and stolen bases (323), third in runs (1,685), fifth in batting average (.314), sixth in walks (948) and extra-base hits (763), ninth in RBI (1,135) and 10th in home runs (234)…is the franchise leader in singles (2,163) and hit by pitches (152)…is one of four players who hold their current franchise's all-time hits record (also Colorado's Todd Helton, Texas' Michael Young and Tampa Bay's Carl Crawford).

▸ According to the *Elias Sports Bureau*, at 1,379-914-2, has the highest personal winning percentage (.601) among active players (min. 1,000G)…according to the *Elias Sports Bureau*, has played in 1,379 regular season victories, surpassing Mickey Mantle (1,376) for the most in franchise history…the only active player who has played in as many wins as Jeter is Omar Vizquel (1,482)…*Elias* also notes that only five players who made their Major League debuts since 1929 played in more winning games than Jeter (1,197) before reaching the 2000-game mark: Yogi Berra (1,221), Pee Wee Reese (1,221), Paul Blair (1,207), Mickey Mantle (1,206) and Gil Hodges (1,200).

- Along with Jorge Posada and Mariano Rivera, have become the first trio of teammates in MLB, NBA, NFL and NHL history to appear in a game together in each of 16 straight seasons (credit: *Elias Sports Bureau*).

- Earned his 11th trip to the All-Star Game, including his sixth fan-selected start (fifth consecutive start)…went 1-for-2 with 1BB before being removed for PR (Elvis Andrus) in the sixth in the 3-1 National League win on 7/13, starting at SS for the American League…according to the *Elias Sports Bureau*, Jeter and 2B Robinson Cano joined Bucky Dent and Willie Randolph as the only Yankees SS/2B combos to start an All-Star game together…also joined Cano, Joe Mauer and Albert Pujols as the only Major League players to top four million fan votes, finishing second behind Mauer…his 11 All-Star Game selections are tied with Bill Dickey and Mariano Rivera for the fifth-most in club history, trailing Mickey Mantle (20), Yogi Berra (19), Joe DiMaggio (13) and Elston Howard (12)…joins teammate Mariano Rivera as the only players to be named to the All-Star team with their current team at least 11 times, according to *Elias*.

2010

- Hit .270 (179-for-663) with 111R, 30 doubles, 3 triples, 10HR and 67RBI in 157 games (150 starts at SS, five at DH) with the Yankees in 2010…his 111R were his most since 2006 (118)…six of his 10HR tied the game or gave the Yankees the lead.

- Ranked second among Major League leadoff hitters with 104R and 60RBI when batting first in the lineup…ranked fifth with 167H as the leadoff batter.

- Batted .295 (95-for-322) with 17 doubles, 7HR and 38RBI at home…hit .246 (84-for-341) with 13 doubles, 4HR and 29RBI on the road.

- With 2B Robinson Cano (103R), and 1B Mark Teixeira (113R), became the fourth trio of infield teammates to each score at least 100R in consecutive seasons – also 1999-2000 Cleveland Indians (R. Alomar, J. Thome, O. Vizquel), 1936-38 Yankees (F. Crosetti, L. Gehrig, R. Rolfe) and 1929-30 Philadelphia A's (M. Bishop, M. Cochrane, J. Foxx).

- Recorded a career-best .989 fielding percentage at SS and made just six errors, the lowest full season total of his career and the fewest among all Major League shortstops this season (min. 110G at SS).

- Led the Majors in fielding percentage at SS…with teammate Robinson Cano leading the American League with a .996 fielding percentage at second base, became the first teammates to finish a season as the fielding leaders at shortstop and second base (in either league) since Omar Vizquel and Roberto Alomar for the 2001 Cleveland Indians.

- Made his 14th Opening Day start at SS for the Yankees on 4/4 at Boston, the most Opening Day starts by a Yankee at shortstop in franchise history…became the oldest shortstop (35 years, 282 days) to start for the Yankees in a season opener since Phil Rizzuto in 1955 (37 years, 200 days)—credit: *Elias*.

- According to *Elias*, is the only active player to make 14 Opening Day starts, all for the same team, at any single position…is the first shortstop to do so since Barry Larkin started 17 Opening Day games for the Reds (1987-2004)—credit: *Elias*…was his sixth Opening Day start at SS with Alex Rodriguez at 3B, matching Bucky Dent/Graig Nettles (six) and Frank Crosetti/Red Rolfe (six) for most such starts in franchise history.

MOST CAREER POSTSEASON HITS, ALL-TIME

1. **DEREK JETER**............................175
2. Bernie Williams........................... 128
3. Manny Ramirez............................117
4. Kenny Lofton............................. 97
5. Chipper Jones............................ 96

MOST CAREER POSTSEASON RUNS, ALL-TIME

1. **DEREK JETER**............................99
2. Bernie Williams........................... 83
3. Manny Ramirez............................ 67
4. Kenny Lofton............................. 65
5. Chipper Jones............................ 58

HIGHEST CAREER AVERAGES IN WORLD SERIES HISTORY (100 or more AB)

Player	AVG.
1. Lou Gehrig	.361 (43-for-119)
2. Eddie Collins	.328 (42-for-128)
3. Babe Ruth	.326 (42-for-129)
4. DEREK JETER	**.321 (50-for-156)**
5. Steve Garvey	.319 (36-for-113)

AMONG ACTIVE MAJOR LEAGUE PLAYERS RUNS SCORED

1. ALEX RODRIGUEZ 1,757
2. **DEREK JETER** **1,685**
3. Johnny Damon 1,564
4. Manny Ramirez......................... 1,544
5. Jim Thome.............................1,534

HITS

1. **DEREK JETER**........................**2,926**
2. Ivan Rodriguez.........................2,817
3. Omar Vizquel 2,799
4. ALEX RODRIGUEZ 2,672
5. Manny Ramirez......................... 2,573

MOST HITS IN FRANCHISE HISTORY

1. **DEREK JETER**........................**2,926**
2. Lou Gehrig 2,721
3. Babe Ruth..............................2,518
4. Mickey Mantle 2,415
5. Bernie Williams........................ 2,336

MOST 100-RUN SEASONS, ALL TIME

1. Hank Aaron 15
2. Lou Gehrig................................13
   Rickey Henderson..........................13
   DEREK JETER............................**13**
   ALEX RODRIGUEZ 13
6. Four tied.................................12

▸ Batted .330 (31-for-94) with 18RBI in April…marked his most RBI in a calendar month since May 2007 (20RBI) and his most in an April since an April-career-high 20RBI in 2006…recorded at least 30H in April for the seventh time in his career, one shy of Tony Gwynn's Major League record (credit: *Elias*)…hit 4HR in April for the second straight year after going homerless in April 2008.

▸ Hit safely in each of his first 11 games this season (4/4-17), the longest hitting streak to start a season of his career…according to *Elias*, with Robinson Cano, became the first 2B-SS duo in the Modern Era (since 1900) to each hit safely in nine-or-more of their club's first games of the season…became the first Yankees tandem at any position to each hit safely in each of the team's first 10 games of a season…became the first combo in the Majors to accomplish the feat since Tampa Bay's Carl Crawford and Rocco Baldelli in 2003.

▸ Hit solo-HR and was 2-for-5 with 2RBI in 4/13 home opening win vs. Los Angeles-AL…has hit safely in nine straight home openers (since 2002), marking the second-longest streak in franchise history, trailing Lou Gehrig (12 straight from 1926-37)—credit: *Elias*.

▸ Recorded 19 hits over his first 50 at-bats (.380)…according to the *Elias Sports Bureau*, marked his highest batting average through his first 50AB of a season since 1999, when he hit .440 (22-for-50).

▸ Hit two-run HR and was 3-for-4 with 2R, 1 triple and 4RBI in 4/30 win vs. Chicago-AL, marking his most RBI in a game since 9/10/06 at Baltimore (4RBI).

▸ Led off 5/4 win vs. Baltimore with a double—the 443rd of his career—to pass Don Mattingly (442) for sole possession of third place on the Yankees' all-time list.

▸ Appeared in his 2,165th game on 5/7 at Boston, surpassing Lou Gehrig (2,164) for sole possession of second place on the Yankees' all-time list.

▸ Hit game-winning solo-HR in the sixth inning to lead off the resumption 5/25 suspended-game win at Minnesota…was his first career RBI in a 1-0 Yankees win…became the first Yankee to homer in a 1-0 Yankees victory since Melky Cabrera on 4/28/07 at Cleveland.

▸ Recorded six straight multi-hit games from 5/27-6/1, one shy of his career high…overlapping the six-game multi-hit contest stretch, Robinson Cano collected eight straight multi-hit games (5/26-6/2)…according to *Elias*, became the first pair of Major League teammates to collect at least two hits apiece in each of six straight games since Atlanta's Chipper Jones and Brian McCann from 7/9-18/06…*Elias* also notes they are just the second pair of Yankees teammates to accomplish the feat in six straight games, joining Lou Gehrig and Jack Saltzgaver from 7/3-7/34.

▸ Hit his 450th career double in the third inning of 6/1 win vs. Baltimore, surpassing Bernie Williams (449) for sole possession of sixth place on the Yankees' all-time doubles list, trailing only Lou Gehrig (534).

▸ Hit two-run HR and in 6/5 loss at Toronto giving him 1,101 career RBI, surpassing Don Mattingly (1,099) for sole possession of ninth place on the Yankees' all-time RBI list.

▸ Hit leadoff HR and three-run HR and was 2-for-4 with 3R, 1BB and 1SB in 6/12 win vs. Houston…was his ninth career multi-homer game and first since 8/27/06 at Los Angeles-AL…was his first multi-homer game at home since 6/18/05 vs. the Cubs…three of his nine career multi-homer games have come in Interleague play…hit his 24th career leadoff HR, tying Rickey Henderson for most such homers in franchise history.

▸ Did not drive in a run in a career-high 19 consecutive games from 6/13-7/5 (previous was 13G from 7/16-30/04)—credit: *Elias Sports Bureau*.

▸ Scored at least three runs without recording a hit for the second time in his career in 6/23 win at Arizona, going 0-for-4 with 3R and 2BB (also 9/12/06 vs. Tampa Bay, 0-for-0, 3R, 3BB, 1HBP).

▸ Collected 2,834 career hits prior to his 36th birthday on 6/26…since 1961, the only players to accumulate more hits prior to turning 36 years old were Hank Aaron (2,956) and Robin Yount (2,868)—credit: *Elias Sports Bureau*.

▸ Hit inside-the-park HR and was 2-for-5 with 2R in 7/22 win vs. Kansas City…was his second career inside-the-park home run (also 8/2/96 at Kansas City off Jeff Montgomery, with Joe Girardi scoring on the play)…at 36 years, 26 days old, became the oldest Yankee to hit an inside-the-park home run since Earle Combs on 6/28/35 (36 years, 45 days)—credit: *Elias*…according to SABR's David Vincent, only three other players have had a longer stretch between inside-the-park homers: Luke Appling (16-plus years, 5/26/33-5/13/49); Nick Altrock (14-plus years, 5/26/1904-9/2/1918) and Tony Fernandez (14-plus years, 8/10/84-9/22/98).

▸ Hit .239 (28-for-117) in August, marking his lowest average in any calendar month (excluding regular season games in March and October) since batting .172 (15-for-87) in April 2004—credit: *Elias Sports Bureau*.

▸ Was 4-for-4 with 3R and 2 doubles in 8/4 win vs. Toronto, marking his most hits in a game since 7/10/09 at Los Angeles-AL (also 4H)…hit two doubles in the same game for the first time since 6/25/08 at Pittsburgh and the first time at home since 4/18/07 vs. Cleveland.

▸ Surpassed Babe Ruth (2,873) for sole possession of 39th place on Baseball's all-time hits list with a second-inning single in 8/8 win vs. Boston.

DEREK JETER

- Collected his 2,877th career hit with a first-inning single in 8/11 win at Texas, surpassing Mel Ott for 38th place on Baseball's all-time list…also surpassed Ott—who played his entire career with the New York Giants—for the most hits by a player while playing for a New York team (credit: *Elias*).

- Committed a throwing error in the fifth inning of 8/16 loss vs. Detroit, snapping a career-long 52-game stretch without a miscue at SS (from 6/12)…marked the longest errorless stretch in the Majors at that position in 2010—credit: *Elias*.

- Snapped a 131AB homerless streak with a solo HR in 8/24 win at Toronto.

- Hit safely in a season-high 14 straight games from 9/10-25, batting .322 (19-for-59) with 9R, 4 doubles and 5RBI.

- Over his final 20 games of the season (9/10-10/3), batted .326 (28-for-86) with 15R and a .416OBP, hitting safely in 19 of those contests.

- Scored his 1,678th career run in the sixth inning of 9/22 loss vs. Tampa Bay, surpassing Mickey Mantle (1,677) for sole possession of third place on the Yankees' all-time list…tied Mantle in 9/20 win vs. Tampa Bay.

- Played in his 1,377th regular season victory on 9/26 vs. Boston, surpassing Mickey Mantle (1,376) for the most in franchise history.

Jeter's Career Batting Record

Year	Club	AVG	G	AB	R	H	2B	3B	HR	RBI	SH	SF	HP	BB	SO	SB	CS	E	OBP	SLG
1992	GCL Yankees	.202	47	173	19	35	10	0	3	25	0	2	5	19	36	2	2	9	.296	.312
	Greensboro	.243	11	37	4	9	0	0	1	4	0	0	1	7	16	0	1	12	.378	.324
1993	Greensboro	.295	128	515	85	152	14	11	5	71	2	4	11	58	95	18	9	56	.376	.394
1994	Tampa	.329	69	292	61	96	13	8	0	39	3	3	3	23	30	28	2	6	.380	.428
	Albany	.377	34	122	17	46	7	2	2	13	3	1	1	15	16	12	2	12	.446	.516
	Columbus	.349	35	126	25	44	7	1	3	16	3	1	1	20	15	10	4	7	.439	.492
1995	Columbus	.317	123	486	96	154	27	9	2	45	2	5	4	61	56	20	12	29	.394	.422
	YANKEES	.250	15	48	5	12	4	1	0	7	0	0	0	3	11	0	0	2	.294	.375
1996	YANKEES	.314	157	582	104	183	25	6	10	78	6	9	9	48	102	14	7	22	.370	.430
1997	YANKEES	.291	159	654	116	190	31	7	10	70	8	2	10	74	125	23	12	18	.370	.405
1998	YANKEES - a	.324	149	626	*127	203	25	8	19	84	3	5	5	57	119	30	6	9	.384	.481
	Columbus	.400	1	5	2	2	2	0	0	0	0	0	0	0	2	0	0	1	.400	.800
1999	YANKEES	.349	158	627	134	*219	37	9	24	102	3	6	12	91	116	19	8	14	.438	.552
2000	YANKEES - b	.339	148	593	119	201	31	4	15	73	3	3	12	68	99	22	4	24	.416	.481
	Tampa	.667	1	3	2	2	1	0	0	0	0	0	0	0	0	0	0	0	.667	1.000
2001	YANKEES - c	.311	150	614	110	191	35	3	21	74	5	1	10	56	99	27	3	15	.377	.480
2002	YANKEES	.297	157	644	124	191	26	0	18	75	3	3	7	73	114	32	3	14	.373	.421
2003	YANKEES - d	.324	119	482	87	156	25	3	10	52	3	1	13	43	88	11	5	14	.393	.450
	Trenton	.444	5	18	2	8	1	1	0	5	0	0	1	3	0	0	0	1	.545	.611
2004	YANKEES	.292	154	643	111	188	44	1	23	78	16	2	14	46	99	23	4	13	.352	.471
2005	YANKEES	.309	159	654	122	202	25	5	19	70	7	3	11	77	117	14	5	15	.389	.450
2006	YANKEES	.343	154	623	118	214	39	3	14	97	7	4	12	69	102	34	5	15	.417	.483
2007	YANKEES	.322	156	639	102	206	39	4	12	73	3	2	14	56	100	15	8	18	.388	.452
2008	YANKEES	.300	150	596	88	179	25	3	11	69	7	4	9	52	85	11	5	12	.363	.408
2009	YANKEES	.334	153	634	107	212	27	1	18	66	4	1	5	72	90	30	5	8	.406	.465
2010	YANKEES	.270	157	663	111	179	30	3	10	67	1	3	9	63	106	18	5	6	.340	.370
Minor League Totals		.308	454	1777	313	548	82	32	16	218	13	16	27	206	266	90	32	133	.385	.418
Major League Totals		.314	2926	9322	1685	2926	468	61	234	1135	79	47	152	948	1572	323	85	219	.385	.452

* denotes league leader

Selected by New York (AL) in the first round (sixth pick overall) of the 1992 First-Year Player Draft.

a - Placed on the 15-day disabled list on June 6, 1998 with a strained abdominal muscle.
b - Placed on the 15-day disabled list from May 19-27, 2000 (retroactive to May 12) with a strained abdominal muscle.
c - Placed on the 15-day disabled list from March 31 - April 7, 2001 (retroactive to March 23) with a strained right quad.
d - Placed on the 15-day disabled list from April 1 - May 13, 2003 with a dislocated left shoulder.

DEREK JETER

	2010						CAREER				
	AVG	AB	H	HR	RBI		AVG	AB	H	HR	RBI
Overall	.270	663	179	10	67		.314	9322	2926	234	1135
Minnesota	.321	28	9	1	2		.322	451	145	11	52
Tampa Bay	.301	83	25	0	6		.311	855	266	19	115
Texas	.385	26	10	1	5		.318	532	169	22	84
Atlanta	-	-	-	-	-		.344	96	33	2	7
Cincinnati	-	-	-	-	-		.269	26	7	0	0
Philadelphia	.000	11	0	0	0		.296	98	15	0	3
San Diego	-	-	-	-	-		.324	37	12	0	4
San Francisco	-	-	-	-	-		.261	23	6	0	2
March	-	-	-	-	-		.222	9	2	0	1
April	.330	94	14	4	18		.307	1307	401	32	178
May	.281	128	36	1	13		.298	1580	471	37	200
June	.243	103	25	3	8		.307	1535	471	43	183
July	.245	106	26	1	9		.328	1596	523	33	182
August	.239	117	28	1	11		.318	1774	564	50	211
September	.276	105	29	0	7		.323	1457	471	38	170
October	.400	10	4	0	1		.359	64	23	1	10
Home	.295	322	95	7	38		.321	4592	1473	126	573
Road	.246	341	84	3	29		.307	4730	1453	108	562
vs. Left	.321	212	68	6	24		.335	2312	774	72	281
vs. Right	.246	451	111	4	43		.307	7010	2152	162	854

Jeter's Career by Ballpark

Park	AVG	AB	H	HR	RBI	Park	AVG	AB	H	HR	RBI
AT&T Park	.333	12	4	0	2	Target Field	.385	13	5	1	1
Citizens Bank Park	.333	12	4	0	2	Tropicana Field	.280	425	119	8	50
Great American Ball Park	.214	14	3	0	0	Turner Field	.432	37	16	0	3
PETCO Park	-	-	-	-	-	Yankee Stadium	.313	633	198	20	78
Rangers Ballpark	.306	278	85	8	36						

Jeter's Division Series Record

Year	Club vs. Opp.	AVG	G	AB	R	H	2B	3B	HR	RBI	SH	SF	HP	BB	SO	SB	CS	E	OBP	SLG
1996	NYY vs. TEX	.412	4	17	2	7	1	0	0	1	0	0	0	0	2	0	0	2	.412	.471
1997	NYY vs. CLE	.333	5	21	6	7	1	0	2	2	0	0	0	3	5	1	0	0	.417	.667
1998	NYY vs. TEX	.111	3	9	0	1	0	0	0	0	1	0	0	2	2	0	0	0	.273	.111
1999	NYY vs. TEX	.455	3	11	3	5	1	1	0	3	0	0	0	2	3	0	0	0	.538	.727
2000	NYY vs. OAK	.211	5	19	1	4	0	0	0	2	0	0	1	2	3	0	1	0	.318	.211
2001	NYY vs. OAK	.444	5	18	2	8	1	0	0	1	0	1	1	1	0	0	1	0	.476	.500
2002	NYY vs. ANA	.500	4	16	6	8	0	0	2	3	0	1	0	2	3	0	0	1	.526	.875
2003	NYY vs. MIN	.429	4	14	2	6	0	0	1	1	0	0	0	4	2	1	0	1	.556	.643
2004	NYY vs. MIN	.316	4	19	3	6	1	0	1	4	1	0	0	1	4	-1	0	1	.350	.526
2005	NYY vs. LAA	.333	5	21	4	7	0	0	2	5	0	1	0	1	5	1	0	0	.348	.619
2006	NYY vs. DET	.500	4	16	4	8	4	0	1	1	0	0	0	1	2	0	1	1	.529	.938
2007	NYY vs. CLE	.176	4	17	0	3	0	0	0	1	0	0	0	0	4	0	0	0	.176	.176
2009	NYY vs. MIN	.400	3	10	4	4	2	0	1	2	0	0	0	3	0	0	0	0	.538	.900
Division Series Totals		**.356**	**53**	**208**	**37**	**74**	**11**	**1**	**10**	**23**	**2**	**3**	**2**	**22**	**35**	**4**	**3**	**6**	**.417**	**.563**

Jeter's League Championship Series Record

Year	Club vs. Opp.	AVG	G	AB	R	H	2B	3B	HR	RBI	SH	SF	HP	BB	SO	SB	CS	E	OBP	SLG
1996	NYY vs. BAL	.417	5	24	5	10	2	0	1	1	0	0	0	0	5	2	0	0	.417	.625
1998	NYY vs. CLE	.200	6	25	3	5	1	1	0	2	2	0	0	2	5	3	0	0	.259	.320
1999	NYY vs. BOS	.350	5	20	3	7	1	0	1	3	0	0	0	2	3	0	0	2	.409	.550
2000	NYY vs. SEA	.318	6	22	6	7	0	0	2	5	0	0	0	6	7	1	0	0	.464	.591
2001	NYY vs. SEA	.118	5	17	0	2	0	0	0	2	1	1	0	2	2	0	0	0	.200	.118
2003	NYY vs. BOS	.233	7	30	3	7	2	0	1	2	0	0	0	2	4	1	0	0	.281	.400
2004	NYY vs. BOS	.200	7	30	5	6	1	0	0	5	2	0	0	6	2	1	0	2	.333	.233
2009	NYY vs. LAA	.259	6	27	5	7	0	0	2	3	0	0	0	6	5	0	1	1	.394	.481
LCS Totals		**.262**	**47**	**195**	**30**	**51**	**7**	**1**	**7**	**23**	**5**	**1**	**0**	**26**	**33**	**8**	**1**	**5**	**.347**	**.415**

Jeter's World Series Record

Year	Club vs. Opp.	AVG	G	AB	R	H	2B	3B	HR	RBI	SH	SF	HP	BB	SO	SB	CS	E	OBP	SLG
1996	NYY vs. ATL	.250	6	20	5	5	0	0	0	1	1	0	1	4	6	1	0	2	.400	.250
1998	NYY vs. SD	.353	4	17	4	6	0	0	0	1	0	0	0	3	3	0	0	0	.450	.353
1999	NYY vs. ATL	.353	4	17	4	6	1	0	0	1	0	0	0	1	3	3	1	0	.389	.412
2000	NYY vs. NYM	.409	5	22	6	9	2	1	2	2	0	0	0	3	8	0	0	0	.480	.864
2001	NYY vs. ARI	.148	7	27	3	4	0	0	1	1	0	0	1	0	6	0	0	0	.179	.259
2003	NYY vs. FLA	.346	6	26	5	9	3	0	0	2	0	0	1	1	7	0	0	1	.393	.462
2009	NYY vs. PHI	.407	6	27	5	11	3	0	0	1	0	0	0	1	6	0	0	0	.429	.519
World Series Totals		**.321**	**38**	**156**	**32**	**50**	**9**	**1**	**3**	**9**	**1**	**0**	**3**	**13**	**39**	**4**	**1**	**3**	**.384**	**.449**
POSTSEASON TOTALS		**.313**	**138**	**559**	**99**	**175**	**27**	**3**	**20**	**55**	**8**	**4**	**5**	**61**	**107**	**16**	**5**	**14**	**.383**	**.479**

Jeter's All-Star Game Record

Year	Club, Site	AVG	G	AB	R	H	2B	3B	HR	RBI	SH	SF	HP	BB	SO	SB	CS	E	OBP	SLG
1998	NYY, Colorado	.000	1	1	0	0	0	0	0	0	0	0	0	0	1	0	0	0	.000	.000
1999	NYY, Boston	.000	1	1	0	0	0	0	0	0	0	0	0	0	1	0	0	0	.000	.000
2000	NYY, Atlanta	1.000	1	3	1	3	1	0	0	2	0	0	0	0	0	0	0	0	1.000	1.333
2001	NYY, Seattle	1.000	1	1	1	1	0	0	1	1	0	0	0	0	0	0	0	0	1.000	4.000
2002	NYY, Milwaukee	.000	1	1	0	0	0	0	0	0	0	0	0	0	1	0	0	0	.000	.000
2004	NYY, Houston	1.000	1	3	1	3	0	0	0	0	0	0	0	0	0	0	0	0	1.000	1.000
2006	NYY, Pittsburgh	.000	1	3	0	0	0	0	0	0	0	0	0	0	2	0	0	0	.000	.000
2007	NYY, San Francisco	.333	1	3	0	1	0	0	0	0	0	0	0	0	0	0	0	0	.333	.333
2008	NYY, New York (AL)	.333	1	3	0	1	0	0	0	0	0	0	0	0	0	1	0	0	.333	.333
2009	NYY, St. Louis	.000	1	2	2	0	0	0	0	0	0	0	1	0	0	0	0	0	.333	.000
2010	NYY, Los Angeles (AL)	.500	1	2	0	1	0	0	0	0	0	0	0	1	1	0	0	0	.667	.500
All-Star Game Totals		**.435**	**11**	**23**	**5**	**10**	**1**	**0**	**1**	**3**	**0**	**0**	**1**	**1**	**6**	**1**	**0**	**0**	**.480**	**.609**

Jeter's World Baseball Classic Record

Year	Country, Site	AVG	G	AB	R	H	2B	3B	HR	RBI	SH	SF	HP	BB	SO	SB	CS	E	OBP	SLG
2006	USA, USA	.450	6	20	5	9	0	1	0	1	1	0	1	2	1	0	0	2	.522	.550
2009	USA, USA	.276	8	29	2	8	2	0	0	0	0	0	1	4	1	0	1	1	.382	.345
WBC Totals		**.347**	**14**	**49**	**7**	**17**	**2**	**1**	**0**	**1**	**1**	**0**	**2**	**6**	**2**	**0**	**1**	**3**	**.439**	**.429**

Jeter's Career Fielding Record

Position	PCT	G	PO	A	E	TC	DP
Shortstop	.976	2295	3341	5718	219	9278	1227

Jeter's Career Home Run Chart

MULTI-HOMER GAMES: 9. **TWO-HOMER GAMES:** 9, last on 6/12/10 vs. Houston. **GRAND SLAMS:** 1, 6/18/05 vs. Chicago-NL (Joe Borowski). **PINCH-HIT HR:** None. **INSIDE-THE-PARK HR:** 2, last on 7/22/10 vs. Kansas City (Bruce Chen). **WALK-OFF HR:** 1, on 4/5/05 vs. Boston (Keith Foulke). **LEADOFF HR:** 24, last on 6/12/10 vs. Houston (Wandy Rodriguez).

Jeter's Career Postseason Home Run Chart

MULTI-HOMER GAMES: None. **TWO-HOMER GAMES:** None. **GRAND SLAMS:** None. **PINCH-HIT HOME RUNS:** None. **INSIDE-THE-PARK HOME RUNS:** None. **WALK-OFF HOME RUNS:** 1, 10/31/01 (WS Game 4) vs. Arizona off Byung-Hyun Kim. **LEADOFF:** 3, 10/25/00 (WS Game 4) at New York (NL) off Bobby Jones; 10/6/04 (ALDS Game 2) vs. Minnesota off Brad Radke; 10/19/09 (ALCS Game 3) at Los Angeles-AL off Jered Weaver.

12 of Jeter's 20 career postseason HR have tied the game or given the Yankees the lead

Prior to the Yankees-Rays game on 7/16, the New York Yankees held a tribute to commemorate the lives and recognize the passings of former Principal Owner / Chairperson George M. Steinbrenner III and longtime Yankees public address announcer Bob Sheppard.

A moment of silence was held for both Yankees icons, led by Yankees captain Derek Jeter who said the following:

"We gather here tonight to honor two men who were both shining stars in the Yankee universe. Both men, Mr. George Steinbrenner and Mr. Bob Sheppard, cared deeply about their responsibilities to this organization and to our fans, and for that, will forever be remembered in baseball history and in our hearts.

"Simply put, Mr. Steinbrenner and Mr. Sheppard both left this organization in a much better place than when they first arrived. They've set the example for all employees of the New York Yankees to strive to follow.

"So now I ask everyone to join us in a moment of silence."

Austin Kearns

26 Outfielder
6-3 • 240 • B/T: Right/Right
Opening Day Age: 29

Birthdate
May 20, 1980

Birthplace
Lexington, Ky.

Resides
Sarasota, Fla.

M.L. Service
8 years, 145 days

Status
▸ Acquired by the Yankees along from the Cleveland Indians on July 30, 2010, in exchange for a player to be named later (RHP Zach McAllister)…contract extends through the 2010 season.

Postseason Notes
▸ Will be making his postseason debut.

2010
▸ Combined to bat .263 (106-for-403) with 55R, 21 doubles, 10HR and 49RBI in 120 games (83 starts in LF, 20 in RF, four in CF and one at DH) with the Yankees and Indians in 2010.
▸ Hit .235 (24-for-102) with 13R, 3 doubles, 2HR and 7RBI in 36 games with the Yankees in 2010 after being acquired from Cleveland on 7/30.
▸ Made his Yankees debut in 8/1 loss at Tampa Bay, starting in LF and going 0-for-2 before being removed for pinch-hitter (Rodriguez) in the seventh…collected his first hit as a Yankee with a fifth-inning single in 8/9 loss vs. Boston.
▸ Compiled a season-high 11-game hitting streak from 8/9-22, batting .400 (14-for-35) over the stretch…was his longest hitting streak since going a career-high 16 games with a hit from 5/4-23/03 w/ Cincinnati.
▸ Immediately followed hitting streak by going hitless in 19 consecutive at-bats until singling in 9/1 win vs. Oakland…marked the second-longest hitless stretch of his career (went 0-for-21 from 5/26-6/1/05)—credit: *Elias*.
▸ Struck out a career-high-tying four times in 9/21 win at Tampa Bay…was his fourth career 4K game and first since 9/28/05 w/ Cincinnati at Milwaukee.
▸ Began the season with Cleveland, batting .272 (82-for-301) with 18 doubles, 8HR, 42RBI and 34BB in 84 games prior to being traded…appeared in LF (68G), RF (14G) and CF (5G).
▸ Hit safely in each of his first seven games of the season, going 8-for-25 (.320) with 4 doubles…collected at least one hit in 23 of his first 26 games with an at-bat, hitting .327 (32-for-98) through May 17…closed out the stretch by hitting in nine straight games from May 5-17.
▸ Recorded a season-high 5RBI in 4/27 win at Los Angeles-AL, going 3-for-6 with 2 doubles and 1HR…marked his most RBI since 8/19/05 vs. Arizona (6RBI).
▸ Collected his fourth career multi-homer game in 6/11 win vs. Washington, going 2-for-4 with 2HR and 4RBI.
▸ Was hit by a pitch three times in the Indians' win on 7/5 at Texas, setting a Cleveland record and tying a Major League record (done many times)…was the first player since Manny Ramirez w/ Boston was plunked three times by Yankees pitchers on 7/5/08.
▸ Hit "walk-off" RBI single in the 11th inning of 7/17 Game 2 win vs. Detroit…was the third "walk-off" hit of his career (also 7/26/09 w/ Washington vs. San Diego and 4/11/03 w/ Cincinnati vs. Philadelphia).
▸ Signed a minor league contract with Cleveland on 1/5/10 and attended spring training with the Indians as a non-roster invitee.

2010 Highs and Streaks
Hits	3 - 6 times
	Last: at CWS, 6/6/10
Runs	3 - 2 times
	Last: at CWS, 6/4/10
2B	2 - 3 times
	Last: at CWS, 6/6/10
3B	1 - vs. NYY, 7/27/10
HR	2 - vs. WAS, 6/11/10
RBI	5 - at LAA, 4/27/10
BB	3 - vs. BOS, 6/10/10
SO	4 - at TB, 9/14/10
SB	2 - at CWS, 6/6/10
Hit Streak	11g - 8/9-22/10

Career Highs and Streaks
Hits	4 - 3 times
	Last: vs. WAS, 5/10/06
Runs	5 - at ATL, 7/20/08
2B	2 - 15 times
	Last: at CWS, 6/6/10
3B	1 - 12 times
	Last: vs. NYY, 7/27/10
HR	2 - 4 times
	Last: vs. WAS, 6/11/10
RBI	6 - vs. ARI, 8/19/05
BB	4 - at CHC, 4/16/03
SO	4 - 4 times
	Last: at TB, 9/15/10
SB	2 - at CWS, 6/6/10
Hit Streak	16g - 5/4-23/03

AUSTIN KEARNS

Kearns' Career Playing Record

Year	Team	AVG	G	AB	R	H	2B	3B	HR	RBI	SH	SF	HP	BB	SO	SB	CS	E	OBP	SLG
1998	Billings	.315	30	108	17	34	9	0	1	14	0	2	1	23	22	1	1	4	.433	.426
1999	Rockford	.258	124	426	72	110	36	5	13	48	0	3	9	50	120	21	8	13	.346	.458
2000	Dayton	.306	136	484	110	148	37	2	27	104	0	9	7	90	93	18	5	12	.415	.558
2001	Chattanooga	.268	59	205	30	55	11	2	6	36	2	2	6	26	43	7	5	2	.364	.429
	GCL Reds	.176	6	17	2	3	2	0	0	4	0	3	0	2	7	0	0	0	.227	.294
2002	Louisville	.750	1	4	3	3	2	0	0	2	0	0	0	1	0	0	0	0	.800	1.250
	Chattanooga	.268	12	41	10	11	2	0	5	13	0	0	3	9	9	1	0	0	.434	.683
	CINCINNATI - a	.315	107	372	66	117	24	3	13	56	0	3	6	54	81	6	3	-	.407	.500
2003	Chattanooga	.200	3	5	2	1	0	0	0	1	0	0	1	2	2	0	0	0	.500	.200
	CINCINNATI - b	.264	82	292	39	77	11	0	15	58	0	0	5	41	68	5	2	-	.364	.455
2004	Louisville	.337	25	83	19	28	7	1	2	15	0	0	2	19	16	3	1	3	.471	.518
	CINCINNATI - c, d	.230	64	217	28	50	10	2	9	32	0	0	1	28	71	2	1	-	.321	.419
2005	Louisville	.342	28	111	24	38	15	1	7	21	0	0	1	11	30	0	0	0	.407	.685
	CINCINNATI	.240	112	387	62	93	26	1	18	67	0	5	8	48	107	0	0	3	.333	.452
2006	CINCINNATI	.274	87	325	53	89	21	1	16	50	0	3	5	35	85	7	1	2	.351	.492
	WASHINGTON - e	.250	63	212	33	53	12	1	8	36	1	2	5	41	50	2	3	5	.381	.429
2007	WASHINGTON	.266	161	587	84	156	35	1	16	74	0	4	12	71	106	2	2	2	.355	.411
2008	WASHINGTON - f, g	.217	86	313	40	68	10	0	7	32	0	1	8	35	63	2	2	4	.311	.316
	Hagerstown	.333	2	3	2	1	0	0	0	1	0	0	0	3	1	0	0	-	.667	.333
	Columbus	.429	5	14	2	6	1	1	1	6	0	1	1	3	2	0	0	0	.526	.857
2009	WASHINGTON - h	.195	80	174	20	34	6	2	3	17	0	0	5	32	51	1	1	0	.336	.305
2010	CLEVELAND - i	.272	84	301	42	82	18	1	8	42	0	2	5	34	78	4	1	8	.354	.419
	YANKEES - j	.235	36	102	13	24	3	0	2	7	0	0	5	12	38	0	0	0	.345	.324
Minor League Totals		**.292**	**431**	**1501**	**293**	**438**	**122**	**12**	**62**	**265**	**2**	**20**	**31**	**239**	**345**	**51**	**20**	**34**	**.395**	**.513**
AL Totals		**.263**	**120**	**403**	**55**	**106**	**21**	**1**	**10**	**49**	**0**	**2**	**10**	**46**	**116**	**4**	**1**	**4**	**.351**	**.395**
NL Totals		**.256**	**842**	**2879**	**425**	**737**	**155**	**11**	**105**	**422**	**1**	**18**	**55**	**385**	**682**	**27**	**15**	**25**	**.353**	**.427**
Major League Totals		**.257**	**962**	**3282**	**480**	**843**	**176**	**12**	**115**	**471**	**1**	**20**	**65**	**431**	**798**	**31**	**16**	**29**	**.257**	**.423**

Selected by the Cincinnati Reds in the first round (seventh overall pick) of the 1998 First-Year Player Draft.

a – Placed on the 15-day disabled list from August 27, 2002 through the end of the season with a strained left hamstring.
b – Placed on the 15-day disabled list on July 9, 2003 with an inflamed right rotator cuff…was transferred to the 60-day disabled list from August 18, 2003 through the end of the season.
c – Placed on the 15-day disabled list from April 27-May 19, 2004 with a fractured left forearm.
d – Placed on the 15-day disabled list on June 2, 2004…was transferred to the 60-day disabled list from July 11-August 24, 2004 with a bone spur in his right thumb.
e – Acquired by the Washington Nationals with INF Felipe Lopez and RHP Ryan Wagner from Cincinnati on July 13, 2006 in exchange for RHPs Gary Majewski and Daryl Thompson, LHP Bill Bray, and INFs Royce Clayton and Brendan Harris.
f – Placed on the 15-day disabled list from May 22-July 3, 2008 after having right elbow surgery.
g – Placed on the 15-day disabled list from August 25, 2008 through the end of the season with a left foot stress fracture.
h – Placed on the 15-day disabled list from August 4, 2009 through the end of the season after having right thumb surgery.
i – Signed by Cleveland as a free agent on January 5, 2010.
j – Acquired by the Yankees from Cleveland on July 30, 2010 in exchange for a player to be named later (RHP Zach McAllister).

	2010					CAREER				
	AVG	AB	H	HR	RBI	AVG	AB	H	HR	RBI
Overall	.263	403	106	10	49	.257	3282	843	115	471
Minnesota	.286	21	6	0	2	.273	33	9	0	2
Tampa Bay	.244	45	11	0	3	.267	60	16	2	6
Texas	.231	26	6	0	0	.250	36	9	0	1
Atlanta	-	-	-	-	-	.219	242	53	4	35
Cincinnati	.286	21	6	0	1	.310	84	26	2	10
Philadelphia	.000	8	0	0	0	.270	215	58	5	23
San Francisco	-	-	-	-	-	.226	115	26	4	16
Home	.251	179	45	5	24	.255	1578	403	54	235
Road	.272	224	61	5	25	.258	1704	440	61	236
vs. Left	.252	147	37	4	12	.261	890	232	28	105
vs. Right	.270	256	69	6	37	.255	2392	611	87	366

Kearns' Career by Ballpark

Park	AVG	AB	H	HR	RBI	Park	AVG	AB	H	HR	RBI
AT&T Park	.200	70	14	1	6	Target Field	.222	9	2	0	0
Citizens Bank Park	.294	102	30	0	11	Tropicana Field	.273	55	15	2	6
Great American Ball Park	.257	658	169	29	108	Turner Field	.231	134	31	4	17
PETCO Park	.207	29	6	0	4	Yankee Stadium	.230	61	14	1	8
Rangers Ballpark	.241	29	7	0	1						

Kearns' Career Fielding Record

Position	PCT	G	PO	A	E	TC
Outfield	.986	962	2011	49	29	2089

Kearns' Career Home Run Chart

MULTI-HOMER GAMES: 4. **TWO-HOMER GAMES:** 4, last on 6/11/09 vs. Washington. **GRAND SLAMS:** 2, last on 4/18/09 vs. Florida (Josh Johnson). **PINCH-HIT HR:** 2, last on 5/6/05 vs. Los Angeles-NL (D.J. Houlton). **INSIDE-THE-PARK HR:** 1, on 5/12/07 vs. Florida (Renyel Pinto). **WALK-OFF HR:** 1, on 4/11/03 vs. Philadelphia (Jose Mesa). **LEADOFF HR:** None.

Boone Logan

48
Left-handed Pitcher
6-5 • 215 • B/T: Right/Left

Opening Day Age: 25

Birthdate
August 13, 1984

Birthplace
San Antonio, Texas

Resides
Helotes, Texas

M.L. Service
3 years, 140 days

College
Temple College (Tex.)

Status
▸ Acquired by the Yankees along with RHP Javier Vazquez in exchange for OF Melky Cabrera, LHP Mike Dunn and RHP Arodys Vizcaino on December 22, 2009…signed through the 2010 season.

Postseason Notes
▸ Will be making his postseason debut.

2010
▸ Was 2-0 with a 2.93 ERA in 51 relief appearances over three stints with the Yankees in 2010 (4/16-5/26, 6/15-7/2, 7/17-10/3)…opponents batted .231 (34-for-147, 3HR)…LH .190 (15-for-79, 0HR), RH .279 (19-for-68, 3HR)…retired 38-of-51 first batters faced (74.5%)…prevented 24-of-31 inherited runners from scoring (77.4%)…appeared in consecutive games nine times and three straight games three times.

▸ Tossed less than 1.0 inning in 31 of his 51 relief outings (60.8%)…held opponents scoreless in 39 of the appearances…faced just one batter 13 times.

▸ Began the season allowing 22H and 9ER in 20.0IP (4.05 ERA) over his first 18 relief appearances (4/20-7/18)…over his final 33 outings (beginning 7/19), pitched to a 1.80 ERA (20.0IP, 4ER), after taking over as the primary left-hander in the bullpen when Marte went on the disabled list.

▸ Was recalled from Triple-A Scranton/Wilkes-Barre prior to 4/16 win vs. Texas when RHP Chan Ho Park was placed on the 15-day disabled list.

▸ Made his Yankees debut in 4/20 win at Oakland, tossing 1.1 scoreless innings (2H, 1BB, 1K).

▸ Did not record a decision in 13 relief appearances with the Yankees (5.06 ERA, 10.2IP, 6ER) before being optioned to Scranton/WB on 5/26…left-handed batters hit .357 (5-for-14) with 5BB.

▸ Recalled for a second time on 6/15 when Sergio Mitre was placed on the 15-day disabled list…allowed 2ER in four outings (7.2IP) before being optioned to Scranton/WB on 7/2 when RHP Dustin Moseley joined the Major League staff.

▸ Tossed 2.2 scoreless innings (1BB, 3K) in 6/16 loss vs. Philadelphia…was his longest outing since 4/25/07 w/ Chicago-AL vs. Detroit (3.0IP) and the longest scoreless outing of his career.

▸ Recalled for a third time on 7/17 when Damaso Marte went on the disabled list, remaining with the Yankees for the remainder of the season…went 2-0 with a 1.80 ERA (20.0IP, 4ER) over the rest of the season, holding left-handers to a .148 average (8-for-54).

▸ Held left-handers hitless in 20 consecutive at-bats against him from 6/29-8/14…had the streak snapped with Kila Ka'aihua's single in 8/14 win at Kansas City…had last

2010 Highs and Streaks	
Low hit CG	N/A
IP (start)	N/A
IP (relief)	2.2 - vs. PHI, 6/16/10
Hits	4 - vs. MIN, 5/15/10
Runs	2 - vs. TB, 5/19/10
BB	2 - 4 times
	Last: at LAD, 6/26/10
SO	3 - vs. PHI, 6/16/10
HR	1 - 3 times
	Last: at TB, 9/14/10
Winning Streak	2g - 8/21-9/26/10
Losing Streak	N/A

Career Highs and Streaks	
Low hit CG	Low hit CG N/A
IP (start)	N/A
IP (relief)	3.0 - 2 times
	Last: vs. DET, 4/25/07
Hits	6 - at TB, 5/16/06
Runs	5 - 2 times
	Last: vs. MIN, 7/6/07
BB	2 - 15 times
	Last: at LAD, 6/26/10
SO	5 - at CLE, 5/2/06
HR	2 - 2 times
	Last: at MIN 9/23/08
Winning Streak	2g - 2 times
	Last: 8/21-9/26/10
Losing Streak	2g - 7/13-8/9/08

allowed a hit to a lefty batter on 6/29 vs. Seattle (Ichiro Suzuki single).

▶ Compiled a streak of 25 consecutive scoreless outings from 7/21-9/13…was the second-longest streak by a Yankees hurler since 1920, trailing only a 28-game scoreless stretch for Mariano Rivera from 7/22-10/2/99…had the streak snapped after surrendering a three-run pinch-hit HR to Willy Aybar in 9/14 win at Tampa Bay…during the stretch, allowed just 8H and 6BB with 18K in 15.1IP…held opponents hitless in 11 straight outings from 7/25-8/13.

▶ Tossed a perfect seventh inning for his first win of the season on 8/21 vs. Seattle (1.0IP).

▶ Appeared in five of the Yankees' six games from 9/8-14, retiring eight of 11 batters faced and seven of eight lefthanders.

▶ Earned win No. 2 on 9/26 vs. Boston, retiring his only batter faced (Ortiz) to end the 10th, before Yankees won it in the bottom of the frame.

▶ Held opposing left-handed batters to 3H in their final 17AB against him, holding them hitless over his final five appearances (6AB).

▶ Began the season with Scranton/WB, going 0-1 with a 2.11 ERA in 14 relief appearances (21.1IP, 5ER)…held left-handed batters to a .162 (6-for-37) batting average.

▶ Struck out a season-high four batters in his season debut in 4/8 win vs. Buffalo.

▶ Went 0-1 with one save and a 1.7 ERA in a team-high 10 spring training relief appearances with the Yankees (10.1IP, 4H, 3R, 2ER, 2BB, 8K).

Logan's Career Playing Record

Year	Team	W	L	ERA	G	GS	CG	SHO	SV	IP	H	R	ER	HR	HB	BB	SO	WP	BK
2003	Great Falls	3	3	6.58	16	14	0	0	0	67.0	76	60	49	4	11	31	48	8	1
2004	Great Falls	3	7	5.6	18	9	0	0	1	64.1	74	48	40	7	4	31	48	8	2
2005	Great Falls	1	1	3.31	21	0	0	0	2	35.1	34	15	13	1	3	4	29	4	0
	Winston-Salem	0	0	5.06	4	0	0	0	0	5.1	7	3	3	2	0	4	5	0	0
2006	Charlotte	3	1	3.38	38	0	0	0	11	42.2	35	18	16	1	9	12	57	3	0
	CHICAGO-AL	0	0	8.31	21	0	0	0	0	17.1	21	18	16	2	3	15	15	1	0
2007	Charlotte	0	1	2.16	4	0	0	0	1	8.1	8	2	2	1	0	4	11	0	0
	CHICAGO-AL	2	1	4.97	68	0	0	0	0	50.2	59	30	28	7	0	20	35	2	0
2008	CHICAGO-AL	2	3	5.95	55	0	0	0	0	42.1	57	31	28	7	1	14	42	1	0
	Charlotte	0	0	6	5	0	0	0	0	9.0	10	8	6	2	3	6	7	1	0
2009	Gwinnett - a	4	2	3.28	29	0	0	0	2	35.2	26	15	13	2	6	17	39	4	0
2009	ATLANTA - b	1	1	5.19	20	0	0	0	0	17.1	21	12	10	1	1	9	10	0	0
2010	YANKEES	2	0	2.93	51	0	0	0	1	40.0	34	13	13	3	1	20	38	1	0
Minor League Totals		**14**	**16**	**4.77**	**135**	**23**	**0**	**0**	**17**	**267.2**	**270**	**169**	**142**	**20**	**36**	**109**	**244**	**28**	**3**
AL Totals		**6**	**4**	**5.11**	**194**	**0**	**0**	**0**	**1**	**149.2**	**171**	**92**	**85**	**19**	**5**	**69**	**129**	**5**	**0**
NL Totals		**1**	**1**	**5.19**	**20**	**0**	**0**	**0**	**0**	**17.1**	**21**	**12**	**10**	**1**	**1**	**9**	**10**	**0**	**0**
Major League Totals		**7**	**5**	**5.1**	**215**	**0**	**0**	**0**	**1**	**167.2**	**192**	**104**	**95**	**20**	**6**	**78**	**139**	**5**	**0**

Selected by the Chicago White Sox in the 20th round of the 2002 First-Year Player Draft.

a – Acquired by the Atlanta Braves along with RHP Javier Vazquez in exchange for INFs Jon Gilmore and Brent Lillibridge, C Tyler Flowers and LHP Santos Rodriguez on December 4, 2008.

b – Acquired by the Yankees along with RHP Javier Vazquez in exchange for OF Melky Cabrera, LHP Mike Dunn and RHP Arodys Vizcaino on December 22, 2009.

	2010										Career								
	W	L	SV	ERA	G	GS	IP	H	HR	ER	SO	W	L	SV	ERA	G	GS	IP	H	HR	ER	SO
Overall	2	0	0	2.93	51	0	40.0	34	3	13	38	7	5	1	5.10	215	0	167.2	192	20	95	140
Minnesota	0	0	0	4.50	1	0	2.0	4	0	1	1	0	0	0	9.64	17	0	14.0	25	5	15	10
Tampa Bay	0	0	0	10.38	6	0	4.1	6	2	5	5	0	0	0	7.36	12	0	11.0	13	2	9	10
Texas	0	0	0	0.00	3	0	0.2	0	0	0	2	0	2	0	14.29	10	0	5.2	15	1	9	5
Atlanta	-	-	-	-	-	-	-	-	-	-	-	-	-	-	-	-	-	-	-	-	-	-
Cincinnati	-	-	-	-	-	-	-	-	-	-	-	-	-	-	-	-	-	-	-	-	-	-
Philadelphia	0	0	0	0.00	1	0	2.2	0	0	0	3	0	0	0	0.00	5	0	4.2	2	0	0	6
San Francisco	-	-	-	-	-	-	-	-	-	-	-	0	0	0	0.00	2	0	0.2	1	0	0	2
March	-	-	-	-	-	-	-	-	-	-	-	0	0	0	0.00	1	0	1.0	0	0	0	2
April	0	0	0	3.86	3	0	2.1	3	0	1	2	2	1	1	3.51	27	0	25.2	29	1	10	17
May	0	0	0	5.40	10	0	8.1	10	1	5	4	1	0	0	4.35	38	0	31.0	36	2	16	24
June	0	0	0	2.35	4	0	7.2	7	0	2	7	0	0	0	3.55	28	0	25.1	21	2	10	23
July	0	0	0	1.80	5	0	5.0	3	1	1	5	1	1	1	6.14	37	0	29.1	36	6	26	21
August	1	0	0	0.00	13	0	8.0	5	0	0	8	2	2	2	4.70	40	0	30.2	40	2	17	23
September	1	0	0	3.68	14	0	7.1	6	1	3	11	1	0	0	8.87	41	0	22.1	28	7	22	27
October	0	0	0	6.75	2	0	1.1	0	0	1	1	0	1	0	7.71	3	0	2.1	2	0	2	3
Home	2	0	0	2.74	26	0	23.0	21	2	7	21	2	2	0	6.67	106	0	81.0	103	11	60	68
Road	0	0	0	3.18	25	0	17.0	13	1	6	17	5	3	1	3.63	109	0	86.2	89	9	35	72

Sergio Mitre

45

Right-handed Pitcher
6-3 • 225 • B/T: Right/Right
Opening Day Age: 29

Birthdate
February 16, 1981

Birthplace
Los Angeles, Calif.

Resides
Chula Vista, Calif.

M.L. Service
5 years, 132 days

College
San Diego City College

Status
▸ Signed by the Yankees as a free agent on January 14, 2009…signed through the 2009 season.

2010
▸ Was 0-3 with one save and a 3.33 ERA in 27 appearances (three starts) with the Yankees in 2010…opponents batted .223 (43-for-193, 7HR); LH .226 (24-for-106, 3HR), RH .218 (19-for-87, 4HR)…retired 17-of-24 first batters faced (70.8%)…prevented five-of-nine inherited runners from scoring (55.6%)…appeared in consecutive games four times.

▸ Was 0-1 with a 2.45 ERA in 24 relief appearances…11 of his 24 relief outings were at least 2.0IP…17 of his 24 outings were scoreless…the Yankees were 7-17 in his relief outings.

▸ In three starts, was 0-2 with a 5.93 ERA (13.2IP, 9ER), throwing no more than 5.0 innings in a start.

▸ Made his third career Opening Day roster in 2010, first with the Yankees.

▸ Began the season in the bullpen, holding opponents scoreless in three of his first six outings (2.79 ERA, 9.2IP, 3ER).

▸ Made consecutive starts on 5/10 at Detroit and 5/16 vs. Minnesota…suffered the loss in 5/10 start, allowing 3ER in 4.1IP…on 5/16, allowed just 4H and 1ER in 5.0IP in a no-decision (1HR, 1BB, 3K).

▸ Returned to the bullpen from 5/22-6/4, allowing just 2H and 1ER in 6.0IP over five outings (2BB, 5K, 1HBP)…appeared on consecutive days in 5/22 and 5/23 losses at the Mets, marking the first time in his career he pitched on back-to-back days.

▸ Was placed on the disabled list from 6/15-7/24 with a strained left oblique (suffered during batting practice), missing 32 team games.

▸ Made five rehab appearances (four starts), combining to go 0-2 with a 4.61 ERA (13.2IP, 11H, 7ER, 2BB, 1HR, 16K) with Single-A Tampa, the GCL Yankees and Triple-A Scranton/Wilkes-Barre.

▸ Was returned from rehab and reinstated from the D.L. on 7/24…made his third and final start of the season that night vs. Kansas City, allowing 7H and 5ER in 4.1IP to record his second loss (7R, 1BB, 1K, 1HR, 1HBP)…marked his most runs and earned runs allowed since 9/15/09 vs. Toronto (7R/7ER).

▸ Returned to the bullpen on 7/28 for the remainder of the year, going 0-1 with a 2.55 ERA (24.2IP, 7ER)…surrendered just 2ER in 9.2IP over six appearances from 7/28-8/16 (both coming on 8/3 vs. Toronto).

▸ Earned his first career save in 8/19 win vs. Detroit, pitching the final 3.0 innings of the Yankees' victory (6H, 3ER, 1BB, 3K, 1HR).

▸ Tossed 4.2 scoreless innings in 8/28 loss at Chicago-AL (1H, 1BB), tying Dustin Moseley (7/24 vs. Kansas City) and Javier Vazquez (8/30 vs. Oakland) for the longest outing by a Yankees reliever in 2010.

▸ Suffered his third loss of the season on 9/13 at Tampa Bay, throwing one pitch and allowing a "walk-off" home run in the bottom of the 11th inning of a 1-0 Yankees

2010 Highs and Streaks	
Low hit CG	N/A
IP (start)	5.0 - vs. MIN, 5/16/10
IP (relief)	4.2 - at CWS, 8/27/10
Hits	6 - vs. DET, 8/19/10
Runs	3 - vs. DET, 8/19/10
BB	2 - 3 times
	Last: vs. TOR, 9/5/10
SO	3 - 3 times
	Last: at TOR, 9/29/10
HR	1 - 4 times
	Last: at TB, 9/13/10
Winning Streak	N/A
Losing Streak	3g - 5/10-9/13/10

Career Highs and Streaks	
Low hit CG	5 - vs. FLA, 6/14/05
IP (start)	9.0 - vs. FLA, 6/14/05
IP (relief)	5.0 - at SEA, 9/20/09
Hits	12 - at KC, 6/15/07
Runs	11 - at TOR, 9/6/09
BB	4 - 5 times
	Last: at COL, 9/15/07
SO	8 - vs. NYM, 5/25/07
HR	4 - vs. TOR, 9/15/09
Winning Streak	2g - 4 times
	Last: 8/15-29/09
Losing Streak	7g - 4/11/06-4/11/07

loss…was the first game-ending homer allowed in his career…became the first Yankee to surrender a "walk-off" homer in an extra-inning, 1-0 loss since Paul Quantrill on 5/18/04 at the Angels (Adam Riggs 11th-inning RBI single).

▸ Did not allow a run over his last four outings (4.2IP), holding opponents hitless over his final three appearances (0-for-8).

▸ Went 1-0 with a 3.27 ERA in six spring training appearances (three starts), allowing 14H and 8ER in 22.0IP (1HP, 4BB, 19K, 2HR)…ranked second on the team in strikeouts.

Mitre's 2010 Pitching Record

Year	Club	W	L	ERA	G	GS	CG	SHO	SV	IP	H	R	ER	HR	HB	BB	SO	WP	BK
2001	Boise	8	4	3.07	15	15	1	1	0	91.0	85	37	31	2	3	18	71	3	3
2002	Lansing	8	10	2.83	27	27	2	0	0	168.2	166	72	53	7	10	27	96	10	0
2003	West Tenn	7	9	3.34	25	24	0	0	0	145.2	162	75	54	6	12	41	128	6	0
	CHICAGO-NL	0	1	8.31	3	2	0	0	0	8.2	15	8	8	1	0	4	3	0	0
2004	Iowa	6	3	2.98	18	15	1	1	1	102.2	97	38	34	9	6	39	95	7	1
	CHICAGO-NL	2	4	6.62	12	9	0	0	0	51.2	71	38	38	6	4	20	37	5	1
2005	Iowa	5	6	4.33	13	13	1	0	0	70.2	72	34	34	5	1	22	55	4	2
	CHICAGO-NL - a	2	5	5.37	21	7	1	1	0	60.1	62	37	36	11	3	23	37	5	0
2006	FLORIDA - b	1	5	5.71	15	7	0	0	0	41.0	44	28	26	7	6	20	31	1	0
	GCL Marlins	0	0	0	1	1	0	0	0	1.0	0	0	0	0	0	1	0	0	0
2007	FLORIDA - c	5	8	4.65	27	27	0	0	0	149.0	180	88	77	9	10	41	80	6	0
	Jupiter	2	0	1	2	1	0	0	0	9.0	5	1	1	0	0	0	4	0	0
2008								Injured - Did Not Pitch - d											
2009	Tampa - e, f	1	0	1.93	2	2	0	0	0	9.1	10	6	2	0	1	2	8	1	0
	Scranton/WB	3	1	2.4	7	7	0	0	0	45.0	40	13	12	3	3	5	35	1	0
	YANKEES - f	3	3	6.79	12	9	0	0	0	51.2	71	45	39	10	3	13	32	3	0
2010	YANKEES - g	0	3	3.33	27	3	0	0	1	54.0	43	23	20	7	2	16	29	1	0
Minor League Totals		**40**	**33**		**110**	**105**	**5**	**2**	**1**	**643.0**	**637**	**276**	**221**	**32**	**36**	**155**	**492**	**32**	**6**
AL Totals		**3**	**6**	**5.07**	**38**	**12**	**0**	**0**	**1**	**104.2**	**114**	**68**	**59**	**17**	**5**	**29**	**61**	**4**	**0**
NL Totals		**10**	**23**	**5.36**	**78**	**52**	**1**	**1**	**0**	**310.2**	**372**	**199**	**185**	**34**	**23**	**108**	**188**	**17**	**1**
Major League Totals		**13**	**29**	**5.27**	**117**	**64**	**1**	**1**	**1**	**416.1**	**486**	**267**	**244**	**51**	**28**	**137**	**249**	**21**	**1**

Selected by Chicago-NL in the seventh round of the 2001 First-Year Player Draft.
a - Traded to Florida from Chicago-NL with RHP Carlos Nolasco and LHP Renyel Pinto in exchange for OF Juan Pierre on December 7, 2005.
b - Placed on the 15-day disabled list from May 13 - August 9, 2006 with right shoulder tendinitis(transferred to 60-day disabled list on May 26).
c - Placed on the 15-day disabled list from April 18 - May 5, 2007 with a blister on his right middle finger.
d - Placed on the 15-day disabled list on March 21, 2008 with a right elbow strain (transferred to the 60-day disabled list on April 18)…was released on September 29, 2008.
e - Signed by New York-AL as a free agent on November 16, 2008.
f - Served a 50-game suspension from April 9 - June 1, 2009 for violating Major League Baseball's Drug Prevention and Treatment Program.
g – Placed on the 15-day disabled list from June 15-July 23, 2010 with a strained left oblique.

	2010										Career								
	W	L	SV	ERA	G	GS	IP	H	HR	ER	SO	W	L	SV	ERA	G	GS	IP	H	HR	ER	SO
Overall	0	3	1	3.33	27	3	54.0	43	7	20	29	13	29	1	5.27	117	64	416.1	486	51	244	249
Minnesota	0	0	0	1.80	1	1	5.0	4	1	1	3	0	0	0	1.80	1	1	5.0	4	1	1	3
Tampa Bay	0	1	0	7.71	2	0	2.1	3	1	2	1	1	1	0	3.86	3	1	9.1	8	2	4	4
Texas	0	0	0	0.00	1	0	1.2	0	0	0	1	0	0	0	0.00	1	0	1.2	0	0	0	1
Atlanta	-	-	-	-	-	-	-	-	-	-	-	0	1	0	4.58	5	3	19.2	22	1	10	9
Cincinnati	-	-	-	-	-	-	-	-	-	-	-	0	1	0	6.14	8	3	22.0	30	3	15	16
Philadelphia	-	-	-	-	-	-	-	-	-	-	-	0	3	0	5.75	4	4	20.1	24	3	13	16
San Francisco	-	-	-	-	-	-	-	-	-	-	-	1	0	0	7.30	3	2	12.1	18	0	10	2
Home	0	1	1	4.76	12	2	28.1	31	5	15	10	5	13	1	4.87	58	32	223.2	260	33	121	140
Road	0	2	0	1.75	15	1	25.2	12	2	5	19	8	16	0	5.75	59	32	192.2	226	18	123	109

Mitre's Career By Ballpark

Park	W	L	SV	ERA	G	GS	IP	ER	Park	W	L	SV	ERA	G	GS	IP	ER
AT&T Park	1	0	0	6.75	1	1	6.2	5	Target Field	-	-	-	-	-	-	-	-
Citizens Bank Park	0	1	0	4.50	2	2	12.0	6	Tropicana Field	1	1	0	3.86	3	1	9.1	4
Great American BP	0	1	0	9.00	3	1	8.0	8	Turner Field	0	1	0	4.82	4	3	18.2	10
Rangers Ballpark	0	0	0	0.00	1	0	1.2	0	Yankee Stadium	2	3	1	5.14	18	7	56	32

Mitre's Career Fielding Record

Position	PCT	G	PO	A	E	TC	DP
Pitcher	.953	117	43	80	6	129	3

Mitre's Regular Season Batting Record

Year	Team	AVG	G	AB	R	H	2B	3B	HR	RBI	SH	SF	HP	BB	SO	SB	CS
2010	NYY					Did Not Bat											
Major League Totals		**.141**	**117**	**78**	**5**	**11**	**4**	**0**	**0**	**2**	**13**	**0**	**0**	**3**	**33**	**0**	**0**

Dustin Moseley

40

Right-handed Pitcher
6-4 • 215 • B/T: Right/Right
Opening Day Age: 28

Birthdate
December 26, 1981

Birthplace
Texarkana, Tex.

Resides
Texarkana, Tex.

M.L. Service
3 years, 30 days

Status
▸ Signed by the Yankees as a free agent on February 16, 2010.

2010
▸ Was 4-4 with a 4.96 ERA in 16 games (nine starts) with the Yankees in 2010…opponents batted 269 (66-for-245, 13HR); LH .281 (36-for-128, 8HR), RH .256 (30-for-117, 5HR).
▸ Made nine starts, going 4-4 with a 5.29 ERA (51.0IP, 30ER) and a .272 (52-for-191, 10HR) opponents batting average…did not record a decision in seven relief outings, posting a 3.77 ERA (14.1IP, 6ER) and holding opponents to a .259 batting average (14-for-54).
▸ Was signed to a Major League contract and selected to the 25-man roster on 7/2 from Triple-A Scranton/Wilkes-Barre.
▸ Tossed 2.0 scoreless IP of relief in his Yankees debut in 7/3 win vs. Toronto (2K).
▸ Threw 75 pitches in 7/17 loss vs. Tampa Bay (3.0IP, 5H, 4ER, 3BB, 2K, 1HR), his most ever in a relief appearance (previous was 54 pitches, also on 8/28/07).
▸ Tossed 4.2 scoreless innings in relief in 7/24 loss vs. Kansas City (1H, 1BB, 1K)…marked his longest scoreless outing—and longest career relief outing—since tossing 5.1 scoreless innings on 8/28/07 w/ Los Angeles-AL at Seattle…was tied for the Yankees' longest relief outing of the season (also Javier Vazquez on 8/30 vs. Oakland and Sergio Mitre on 8/27 at Chicago-AL).
▸ Joined the rotation when Andy Pettitte went on the disabled list, making seven starts from 7/29-8/30…posted a 4-2 record with a 5.03 ERA (39.1IP, 22) over the stretch.
▸ Made his first start on 7/29 at Cleveland, limiting the Indians to 1ER in 6.0IP to record the win (4H, 2BB, 4K, 1HP)…tossed 31 pitches in the first, allowing his lone run…needed just 52 pitches to get through the second through sixth innings.
▸ Tossed a career-high 7.1IP and recorded the loss in his second start on 8/3 vs. Toronto (9H, 5ER, 1BB, 2K, 2HR, 1HP).
▸ Earned the win in back-to-back starts on 8/18 vs. Detroit and 8/24 at Toronto.
▸ Made a spot start on 9/12 at Texas when Phil Hughes was skipped in the rotation…suffered the loss, allowing 4ER on 5H in 6.2IP (2BB, 1K).
▸ Had two outings out of the bullpen on 9/22 vs. Tampa Bay (1.1IP, 5H, 1ER, 1HR) and 9/27 at Toronto (2.0IP, 1H, 1BB, 2K).
▸ Started and recorded the loss in the Yankees' final regular season game on 10/3 at Boston, allowing 4ER on 5H in 5.0IP (2BB, 3K, 2HR).
▸ Began the season at Scranton/WB, going 4-4 with a 4.21 ERA in 12 starts…held his opponents to 3ER or less in nine of his outings…ranked third on the team in strikeouts at the time of his recall.
▸ Recorded a season-high 10K in back-to-back games—6/12 vs. Indianapolis (7.0IP) and 6/18 at Lehigh Valley (7.0IP).
▸ Signed by the Yankees as a free agent on 2/16/10…made five relief appearances in spring training, going 0-0 with a 9.95 ERA(6.1IP, 7ER).

2010 Highs and Streaks	
Low hit CG	N/A
IP (start)	7.1 - vs. TOR, 8/3/10
IP (relief)	4.2 - vs. KC, 7/24/10
Hits	9 - vs. TOR, 8/3/10
Runs	5 - vs. TOR, 8/3/10
BB	4 - 2 times
	Last: vs. OAK, 8/30/10
SO	5 - vs. BOS, 8/8/10
HR	3 - vs. DET, 8/18/10
Winning Streak	2g - 8/18-24/10
Losing Streak	2g - 8/3-13/10

Career Highs and Streaks	
Low hit CG	N/A
IP (start)	7.1 - vs. TOR, 8/3/10
IP (relief)	5.1 - at SEA, 8/28/07
Hits	10 - 3 times
	Last: vs. BOS, 8/8/07
Runs	7 - vs. OAK, 10/1/06
BB	5 - at TEX, 4/15/08
SO	6 - vs. NYY, 9/10/08
HR	3 - vs. DET, 8/18/10
Winning Streak	5g - 7/17/06-5/30/07
Losing Streak	4g - 6/12/07-4/4/08

DUSTIN MOSELEY

Moseley's Career Pitching Record

Year	Team	W	L	ERA	G	GS	CG	SHO	SV	IP	H	R	ER	HR	HP	BB	SO	WP	BK
2001	Dayton	10	8	4.20	25	25	0	0	0	148.0	158	83	69	10	8	42	108	3	2
2002	Stockton	6	3	2.74	14	14	2	2	0	88.2	60	28	27	3	8	21	80	2	3
	Chattanooga	5	6	4.13	13	13	0	0	0	80.2	91	47	37	5	4	37	52	2	0
2003	Chattanooga	5	6	3.83	18	18	0	0	0	112.2	116	55	48	10	7	28	73	2	0
	Louisville	2	3	2.70	8	8	0	0	0	50.0	46	19	15	5	1	14	27	2	1
2004	Chattanooga	3	2	2.66	8	8	0	0	0	47.1	33	16	14	4	2	10	40	0	3
	Louisville	2	4	4.65	12	12	0	0	0	71.2	78	38	37	7	4	34	48	2	0
2005	Salt Lake	4	6	5.03	17	17	0	0	0	82.1	102	51	46	11	5	30	38	1	2
2006	Salt Lake	13	8	4.69	26	26	3	0	0	149.2	164	89	78	18	8	51	114	7	2
	LOS ANGELES-AL	1	0	9.00	3	2	0	0	0	11.0	22	11	11	3	0	2	3	0	0
2007	LOS ANGELES-AL	4	4	4.40	46	8	0	0	0	92.0	97	45	45	7	3	27	50	6	1
2008	LOS ANGELES-AL - a	2	4	6.79	12	10	0	0	0	50.1	70	38	38	6	2	20	37	3	1
	Rancho Cucamonga	0	0	0.00	1	1	0	0	0	3.2	3	0	0	0	0	2	6	0	0
	Salt Lake	7	10	6.94	20	20	0	0	0	116.2	150	93	90	23	5	34	83	5	2
2009	LOS ANGELES-AL - b	1	0	4.30	3	3	0	0	0	14.2	20	8	7	3	0	3	8	0	0
2010	YANKEES - c	4	4	4.96	16	9	0	0	0	65.1	66	36	36	13	2	27	33	0	0
Minor League Totals		57	56	4.36	162	162	5	2	0	951.1	1001	519	461	96	52	303	669	26	15
Major League Totals		12	11	5.28	80	32	0	0	0	233.1	275	138	137	32	7	79	131	9	2

Selected by the Reds in the first round (34th overall) of the 2000 First-Year Player Draft.
a – Placed on the 15-day disabled list from May 2-26, 2008 with right forearm tightness.
b – Placed on the 15-day disabled list on April 18, 2009 with right forearm tightness…was transferred to the 60-day disabled list from June 6 through the end of the season.
c – Signed by the Yankees as a minor league free agent on March 23, 2010.

	2010											Career										
	W	L	SV	ERA	G	GS	IP	H	HR	ER	SO	W	L	SV	ERA	G	GS	IP	H	HR	ER	SO
Overall	4	4	0	4.96	16	9	65.1	66	13	36	33	12	11	0	5.28	80	32	233.1	275	32	137	131
Minnesota	-	-	-	-	-	-	-	-	-	-	-	0	0	0	5.68	4	1	6.1	9	2	4	5
Tampa Bay	0	0	0	10.38	2	0	4.1	10	2	5	2	0	0	0	16.20	3	0	5.0	12	3	9	2
Texas	0	1	0	5.40	1	1	6.2	5	0	4	1	0	2	0	5.46	10	5	31.1	39	2	19	16
Atlanta	-	-	-	-	-	-	-	-	-	-	-	-	-	-	-	-	-	-	-	-	-	-
Cincinnati	-	-	-	-	-	-	-	-	-	-	-	0	1	0	27.00	1	0	0.1	2	0	1	0
Philadelphia	-	-	-	-	-	-	-	-	-	-	-	-	-	-	-	-	-	-	-	-	-	-
San Francisco	-	-	-	-	-	-	-	-	-	-	-	-	-	-	-	-	-	-	-	-	-	-
March	-	-	-	-	-	-	-	-	-	-	-	-	-	-	-	-	-	-	-	-	-	-
April	-	-	-	-	-	-	-	-	-	-	-	4	2	0	4.61	14	10	56.2	67	8	29	34
May	-	-	-	-	-	-	-	-	-	-	-	2	1	0	4.60	10	0	15.2	16	1	8	7
June	-	-	-	-	-	-	-	-	-	-	-	0	1	0	4.15	12	0	13.0	16	1	6	3
July	1	0	0	3.24	5	1	16.2	11	2	6	9	2	0	0	6.20	4	0	40.2	43	7	28	28
August	3	2	0	5.67	6	6	33.1	38	8	21	18	3	3	0	5.13	12	10	59.2	69	8	34	31
September	0	1	0	4.35	4	1	10.1	12	1	5	3	1	3	0	4.89	15	6	38.2	49	4	21	24
October	0	1	0	7.20	1	1	5.0	5	2	4	3	0	1	0	11.00	2	2	9.0	15	3	11	4
Home	2	1	0	5.24	9	4	34.1	37	9	20	18	10	4	0	6.09	38	16	122.2	152	23	83	77
Road	2	3	0	4.65	7	5	31.0	29	4	16	15	2	7	0	4.39	42	16	110.2	123	9	54	54

Moseley's Career By Ballpark

Park	W	L	SV	ERA	G	GS	IP	ER	Park	W	L	SV	ERA	G	GS	IP	ER
AT&T Park	-	-	-	-	-	-	-	-	Target Field	-	-	-	-	-	-	-	-
Citizens Bank Park	-	-	-	-	-	-	-	-	Tropicana Field	0	0	0	54.00	1	0	0.2	4
Great American BP	0	1	0	27.00	1	0	0.1	1	Turner Field	-	-	-	-	-	-	-	-
Rangers Ballpark	0	1	0	4.30	7	4	23.0	11	Yankee Stadium	2	1	0	5.24	9	4	34.1	20

Moseley's Career Fielding Record

Position	PCT	G	PO	A	E	TC	DP
Pitcher	.977	80	17	25	1	43	2

Moseley's Regular Season Batting Record

Year	Team	AVG	G	AB	R	H	2B	3B	HR	RBI	SH	SF	HP	BB	SO	SB	CS
2010	NYY					Did Not Bat											
Major League Totals		-	80	-	-	-	-	-	-	-	-	-	-	-	-	-	-

Moseley's Division Series Record

Year	Club vs. Opp.	W	L	ERA	G	GS	CG	SHO	SV	IP	H	R	ER	HR	HP	BB	SO	WP	BK
2007	LAA vs. BOS	0	0	0.00	1	0	0	0	0	1.0	1	0	0	0	0	0	0	1	0	0
Division Series Totals		0	0	0.00	1	0	0	0	0	1.0	1	0	0	0	0	0	0	1	0	0

Ramiro Pena

19 Infielder

5-11 • 165 • B/T: Switch/Right

Opening Day Age: 24

Birthdate
July 18, 1985

Birthplace
Monterrey, Mexico

Resides
San Nicolas de los Garza, Mexico

M.L. Service
1 year, 137 days

Status
▸ Signed as a non-drafted free agent on February 18, 2005…signed through the 2010 season.

Postseason Notes
▸ Did not appear on the Yankees' 2009 ALDS or ALCS rosters…was added to the Yankees' World Series roster prior to Game 5 after Melky Cabrera sustained an injury (did not appear).

2010
▸ Hit .227 (35-for-154) with 18R, 1 double, 1 triple and 18RBI in 85 games (27 starts at 3B, nine at SS and five at 2B) with the Yankees in 2010…combined for a .970 fielding percentage at 2B, SS, 3B and RF (5E, 165TC)…made his second career Opening Day roster.
▸ Hit .264 (19-for-72) in 44 games following the All-Star break…in 41 games before the break, hit just .195 (16-for-82).
▸ Had 3H in 7AB with the bases loaded (.429 average), driving in seven runs…hit .333 (17-for-51) in 34 games against the AL East.
▸ Entered the game as a pinch-runner 14 times, scoring four times and stealing two bases.
▸ Made his first start of the season in 4/18 win vs. Texas, starting at SS and going 1-for-4 with 2RBI.
▸ Made his first career appearance in the outfield in 5/16 loss vs. Minnesota, starting at SS and moving to RF in the ninth.
▸ Hit safely in 12 of his 19 starts from 8/1 through the end of the season, batting .250 (15-for-60) with 6RBI and five multi-hit games over the stretch.
▸ Became the 10th Yankee to triple this season in 8/18 win vs. Detroit, going 1-for-3 with 1R, 1RBI and 1BB.
▸ Hit safely in a career-high seven straight games from 8/22-9/5…batting .476 (10-for-21) during the streak.
▸ In 20 spring training games, batted .260 (13-for-50) with 6R, 3 doubles, 1 triple, 1HR and 4RBI.

2010 Highs and Streaks
Hits	2 - 6 times
	Last: vs. TOR, 9/5/10
Runs	2 - vs. CLE, 5/31/10
2B	1 - at BOS, 5/8/10
3B	1 - vs. DET, 8/18/10
HR	N/A
RBI	2 - 5 times
	Last: vs. BOS, 8/7/10
BB	1 - 6 times
	Last: vs. TOR, 9/4/10
SO	2 - 2 times
	Last: at SEA, 7/10/10
SB	1 - 7 times
	Last: at BOS, 10/2/10 (G1)
Hit Streak	7g - 8/22-9/5/10

Career Highs and Streaks
Hits	3 - 2 times
	Last: at NYM, 6/26/09
Runs	2 - 3 times
	Last: vs. CLE, 5/31/10
2B	2 - at NYM, 6/26/09
3B	1 - 2 times
	Last: 8/18/10 vs. DET
HR	1 - vs. KC, 9/28/09
RBI	2 - 8 times
	Last: vs. BOS, 8/7/10
BB	1 - 11 times
	Last: vs. TOR, 9/4/10
SO	2 - 5 times
	Last: at SEA, 7/10/10
SB	1 - 11 times
	Last: at BOS, 10/2/10 (G1)
Hit Streak	7g - 8/22-9/5/10

Pena's Career Batting Record

YEAR	CLUB	AVG	G	AB	R	H	2B	3B	HR	RBI	SH	SF	HP	BB	SO	SB	CS	E	OBP	SLG
2005	Tampa	.247	23	73	11	18	4	1	1	6	2	2	0	9	12	1	0	4	.321	.370
	Trenton	.250	68	236	28	59	5	2	0	12	8	1	0	10	48	4	1	15	.279	.288
2006	Trenton	.198	26	86	6	17	2	0	0	6	5	1	1	5	19	0	1	2	.247	.221
	Tampa	.280	54	218	31	61	4	2	0	23	4	4	4	16	26	8	4	12	.335	.317
2007	Trenton	.252	52	202	23	51	7	1	0	10	7	0	2	22	33	7	3	4	.332	.297
2008	Trenton	.266	111	443	57	118	20	7	2	45	12	6	4	41	86	8	6	21	.330	.357
2009	YANKEES	.287	69	115	17	33	6	1	1	10	1	0	0	5	20	4	1	5	.317	.383
	Scranton/WB	.231	43	156	18	36	9	0	2	9	6	0	0	18	28	5	1	2	.310	.327
2010	YANKEES	.227	85	154	18	35	1	1	0	18	4	2	1	6	27	7	1	5	.258	.247
Minor League Totals		.255	377	1414	174	360	51	13	5	111	44	14	11	121	252	33	16	60	.315	.320
Major League Totals		.253	154	269	35	68	7	2	1	28	5	2	1	11	47	11	2	10	.283	.305

Signed by the Yankees as a non-drafted free agent on February 18, 2005.

Andy Pettitte

46

Left-handed Pitcher

6-5 • 225 • B/T: Left/Left

Opening Day Age: 37

Birthdate
June 15, 1972

Birthplace
Baton Rouge, La.

Resides
Deer Park, Tex.

M.L. Service
16 years

College
San Jacinto JC (Tex.)

Career Highlights
ALCS MVP
▸ 2001

A.L. All-Star Team
▸ 1996, 2001, 2010

Sporting News **A.L.**
All-Star Team
▸ 1996, 2003

Status

▸ Signed as a free agent on December 9, 2009 to a one-year contract…contract extends through the 2010 season.

Postseason Notes

▸ Is 18-9 with a 3.90 ERA in 40 career postseason starts, ranking first all time in wins, starts and innings pitched (249.0), and third in strikeouts (164)…24 of his starts have been "quality" (6.0-or-more IP, 3ER or less)…is 6-2 with a 3.95 ERA (70.2IP, 31ER) in 12 starts in possible series clinchers, recording the most series-clinching wins all time.

▸ Is undefeated in his last eight postseason starts, marking the longest current undefeated streak of postseason starts among active Major League pitchers…has appeared in eight World Series, second only to Whitey Ford who pitched in 11.

▸ As a Yankee, is 17-8 with a 3.86 ERA in 36 career postseason starts (223.2IP, 96ER)…is the Yankees' all-time postseason leader in wins, starts, innings pitched and strikeouts (148).

▸ Was a member of his fifth World Championship team in 2009, going 4-0 with a 3.52 ERA (30.2IP, 12ER) in five postseason starts…became the second Yankees pitcher (also David Wells, 4-0 in 1998) and the 14th pitcher in Major League history to win four-or-more games in a single postseason…became the first pitcher ever to start and win all three clinching games in a single postseason (ALDS, ALCS and WS)…following the playoffs, donated his postseason hat to the Baseball Hall of Fame.

2010 Highs and Streaks	
Low hit CG	N/A
IP (start)	8.0 - 4 times
	Last: at SEA, 7/8/10
IP (relief)	N/A
Hits	10 - vs. BOS, 9/24/10
Runs	7 - 2 times
	Last: vs. BOS, 9/24/10
BB	4 - at SEA, 7/8/10
SO	10 - at TOR, 6/5/10
HR	3 - vs. TB, 5/20/10
Winning Streak	5g - 4/13-5/15/10
Losing Streak	1g - 3 times
	Last: vs. BOS, 9/24/10

Career Highs and Streaks	
Low hit CG	2 - vs. OAK, 5/29/00
IP (start)	9.0 - 11 times
	Last: vs. CHC, 8/16/06
IP (relief)	3.1 - at BOS, 5/13/95
Hits	14 - at BOS, 4/15/01
Runs	10 - 3 times
	Last: vs. KC, 6/7/08
BB	7 - 2 times
	Last: at TOR, 7/19/98
SO	12 - 2 times
	Last: at TB, 7/28/02
HR	4 - vs. TB, 5/7/09
Winning Streak	8g - 2 times
	Last: 6/14-7/29/03
Losing Streak	5g - 8/26-9/16/08

▸ Went 2-0 with a 5.40 ERA in two World Series starts in Game 3 and 6…won the Game 6 clincher on 11/4/09 vs. Philadelphia, marking his second career World Series-clinching victory and making him one of 10 pitchers all time to own two such wins…start came on three days' rest, marking his first start on short rest since September 2006 and his third career World Series start on short rest (also 1996 and 2003)…became the oldest pitcher to start and win on three-days' rest in the World Series since Early Wynn in 1956 w/ Cleveland…improved to 3-0 with a 1.19 ERA (22.2IP, 3ER) in World Series starts on short rest…the three wins match the total of all the other World Series starters, pitching on short rest combined since 1993…became the first Yankees pitcher to start and win two games in a single World Series since Mike Torrez in 1977.

Career Notes

▸ Has posted a record of .500 or better and made at least 15 starts in 16 consecutive seasons since the start of his Major League career in 1995, surpassing Cy Young (15 seasons, 1890-1904) and Tom Seaver (15, 1967-81) for the longest such streak to begin a Major League career in Baseball history, according to the *Elias Sports Bureau*…posted a winning record in each of his first 13 Major League seasons (1995-2007), marking the third-longest streak of consecutive winning seasons to start a Major league career behind Grover Alexander (17) and Cy Young (15).

- Among active Major League pitchers, ranks second in wins (240), starts (479) and third in IP (3,055.1), and strikeouts (2,251)…among active lefthanders, is second in wins, starts, IP and strikeouts – trailing Jamie Moyer in each category…over the previous decade (2000-2009), led the Majors in wins (148), ranked ninth in starts (300), and 10th in strikeouts (1,441).

- Owns a .635 (240-138) career winning percentage, eighth-best among all lefthanders who began their careers in 1950 or later (min: 140 decisions).

- Has recorded 203 wins *as a Yankee*, third-most in franchise history and the most for any pitcher with his current club (credit: *Elias Sports Bureau*)…ranks second in strikeouts (1,823), second in games started (396), fourth in IP (2,535.2), and eighth in appearances (405)…is the first pitcher drafted by the Yankees to win 200 games in the Majors.

- Has made at least one start in 13 different seasons with the Yankees (1995-2003, '07-10), becoming just the sixth pitcher in franchise history to accomplish the feat…joined Whitey Ford (16 seasons), Red Ruffing (15), Ron Guidry (13), Lefty Gomez (13) and Bob Shawkey (13).

- As a Yankee, is 85-47 (.644) in regular season starts immediately following a Yankees loss (credit: *Elias*), including a 4-3 record with four no-decisions and a 4.88 ERA (62.2IP, 34ER) in 11 such starts in 2010.

Pettitte's 2010 Pitching Lines												
Date/Opp	Score	W/L	IP	H	R	ER	HR	BB	K	NP/K	ERA	Left game...
4/7 at BOS	3-1	ND	6.0	6	1	1	0	3	4	94-54	1.50	Tied 1-1
4/13 vs. LAA	7-5	W	6.0	5	0	0	0	3	6	100-59	0.75	Leading 5-0
4/18 vs. TEX	5-2	W	8.0	4	2	2	0	3	4	107-67	1.35	Leading 5-2
4/24 at LAA*	7-1	W	8.0	6	1	1	0	0	8	114-75	1.29	Leading 7-1
4/30 vs. CWS	6-4	ND	6.0	7	4	4	1	2	3	97-66	2.12	Tied 4-4
5/5 vs. BAL	7-5	W	5.0	6	1	1	0	2	2	77-46	2.08	Leading 6-1
5/15 vs. MIN	7-1	W	6.1	2	0	0	0	3	2	95-53	1.79	Leading 3-0
5/20 vs. TB*	6-8	L	5.0	9	7	6	3	2	1	103-65	2.68	Trailing 7-4
5/26 at MIN	3-2	W	8.0	8	2	2	0	0	4	94-72	2.62	Leading 3-2
5/31 vs. CLE	11-2	W	7.0	4	1	1	1	0	5	90-58	2.48	Leading 8-1
6/5 at TOR*	2-3 (14)	ND	7.2	5	2	2	2	3	10	107-74	2.47	Tied 2-2
6/11 vs. HOU*	4-3	W	7.1	4	3	2	0	1	4	98-68	2.46	Leading 4-2
6/17 vs. PHI*	1-7	L	7.0	6	3	2	1	3	7	108-68	2.47	Trailing 3-1
6/22 at ARI*	9-3	W	7.0	7	2	2	0	2	7	113-73	2.48	Leading 9-2
6/27 at LAD*	8-6 (10)	ND	5.0	6	5	4	1	3	5	93-61	2.72	Trailing 5-2
7/3 vs. TOR*	11-3	W	6.0	5	3	3	2	1	4	97-62	2.82	Leading 11-3
7/8 at SEA	3-1	W	8.0	5	1	1	0	4	9	107-67	2.70	Leading 3-1
7/18 vs. TB*	9-5	ND	2.1	6	3	3	1	3	3	64-38	2.88	Trailing 3-2
9/19 at BAL	3-4 (11)	ND	6.0	3	1	1	0	1	2	79-52	2.81	Leading 3-1
9/24 vs. BOS*	8-10	L	3.1	10	7	6	1	0	1	75-46	3.17	Trailing 7-1
10/2 at BOS*	6-5 (10)	ND	4.0	9	3	3	0	2	8	88-52	3.28	Leading 5-3
Totals		**11-3**	**129.0**	**123**	**52**	**47**	**13**	**41**	**101**	--	**3.28**	

*start came after a Yankees loss – Bold-season high

- Over the last 10 years (2001-10), has posted a 140-83 (.628) record with a 3.80 ERA (1806.1IP, 763ER), ranking sixth in wins among all Major League pitchers over the span.

- Is currently 102 games over .500 (240-138)…is the only pitcher currently on a Major League 40-man roster and one of 26 pitchers all-time at least 100 games over .500…of those other pitchers, 18 are in the Hall of Fame (Grover Alexander, Three-Fingered Brown, John Clarkson, Bob Feller, Whitey Ford, Lefty Grove, Walter Johnson, Tim Keefe, Juan Marichal, Christy Mathewson, Joe McGinnity, Kid Nichols, Jim Palmer, Eddie Plank, Old Hoss Radbourn, Tom Seaver, Warren Spahn and Cy Young)…six are not yet eligible (Roger Clemens, Tom Glavine, Randy Johnson, Greg Maddux, Pedro Martinez and Mike Mussina)…and one remains eligible for the HOF ("Parisian Bob" Caruthers, who went 218-99 from 1884-92).

- Has won 49.9% of his 479 career starts (is 239-137 in his starts), marking the second-best percentage among active pitchers with at least 250 career games started (Roy Halladay-51.9%)

- Has a .682 (118-55) career winning percentage and a 3.66 ERA (1420.1IP, 578ER) after the All-Star break compared to a .595 (122-83) career mark and a 4.07 ERA (1635.0IP, 739ER) before the break.

- Owns the best all-time career winning pct. vs. the AL East (84-37, .694) among the 208 pitchers with at least 50 decisions vs. AL East opposition.

- With 240 career wins, trails only Ted Lyons (260) all time among Louisiana-born pitchers…former Yankees lefty Ron "Louisiana Lightning" Guidry finished with 170 wins.

- Has recorded the most pickoffs (99) in the Majors since they became an official stat in 1974.

- Has made an all-time franchise high 129 consecutive starts as a Yankee without throwing a complete game, according to the *Elias Sports Bureau*…last completed a game *as a Yankee* on 8/9/03 vs. Seattle in a 2-1 Mariners victory…also has made 128 consecutive career starts without a complete game (last CG on 8/16/06 w/ Houston vs. Chicago-NL in a 1-0 Cubs victory), marking the longest active stretch in the Majors and the 13th longest since 1920 according to www.baseball-reference.com.

2010

▸ Went 11-3 with a 3.28 ERA (129.0IP, 47ER) in 21 starts with the Yankees in 2010…his .786 winning percentage was the best in the AL and third-best in the Majors among pitchers with 10-or-more decisions (Milwaukee's John Axford and Arizona's Daniel Hudson both were 8-2, .800)…was the best winning percentage of his career, surpassing a pair of .724 (21-8) seasons with the Yankees in 2003 and 1996…marked his fourth-best single-season ERA (2.39 w/ Houston in 2005, 2.88 w/ NYY in 1997 and 3.27 w/ NYY in 2002)…opponents batted .257 (123-for-479, 13HR); LHH .186 (24-for-129, 2HR) and RHH .283 (99-for-350, 11HR)…the Yankees went 16-5 in his starts.

▸ Tossed at least 8.0IP four times after reaching the mark only once in 2009 (8/31/09 at Baltimore)…marked his most starts of at least 8.0IP since 2005 w/ Houston (five such starts).

▸ Was undefeated in 11 daytime starts, going 7-0 with a 2.31 ERA (66.1IP, 17ER), marking his first winning record in day games since 2005 w/ Houston (3-2, 1.97 ERA in 9GS).

▸ Held opponents to a .219 (21-for-96) batting average *with runners in scoring position* and a .167 (7-for-42) *with RISP and 2 out*…held opponents to 2-for-10 (.200) with 1BB and 5RBI *with the bases loaded.*

▸ Induced 17GIDP in just 129.0IP, marking his highest total in the last three seasons (2009: 16GIDP in 194.2IP; 2008: 15GIDP in 204.0IP in 2008).

▸ Held left-handed hitters to a .186 (24-for-129) batting average, the sixth-lowest mark in the AL (permitted a .282, 62-for-220, mark in 2009)…allowed just 2HR to LHH (both by Carlos Pena)…allowed more than 3H to LHH just once in 2010 (9/24 vs. Boston – 4H)…had a seven-start stretch of allowing no more than 1H to LHH from 5/31-7/3.

▸ Allowed a .325 (55-for-169) opp. batting average with 16BB and 7HR his first trip through the lineup and limited opponents to a .212 (68-for-310) mark with 6HR thereafter.

▸ Opponents had just 2SB in three attempts with Pettitte on the mound in 2010 (SBs: Brian Roberts on 9/19 at Baltimore and Denard Span on 5/26 at Minnesota; CS: Justin Upton on 6/22 at Arizona).

▸ Was named to the 2010 All-Star team after Boston's Clay Buchholz withdrew due to injury…because Buchholz was elected via the "Player Ballot," Pettitte received the nod as he was the next-highest ranking pitcher who had not yet been named…tossed a scoreless third inning in the NL victory…marked his third All-Star appearance (also 1996 and 2001), all coming as a Yankee…became just the third player ever to go at least nine years between All-Star selections, joining Bert Blyleven (1973 to '85) and Claudell Washington (1975 to '84).

▸ Made his first start of the season on 4/7 at Boston, limiting the Red Sox to 1ER in 6.0IP (6H, 3BB, 4K, 1HP) and exiting without a decision in the Yankees' 3-1 extra-innings win.

▸ Started the Yankees' home opener on 4/13 vs. Los Angeles-AL, tossing 6.0 shutout innings and recording the win in the 7-5 Yankees victory (5H, 3BB, 6K)…improved to 4-0 with a 2.25 ERA (24.0IP, 6ER) in four career home opener starts as a Yankee (also wins vs. KC in 1996, vs. TB in 2002 and vs. MIN in 2003)…according the *Elias Sports Bureau,* only Whitey Ford (five) and Red Ruffing (four) have won as many home openers for the Yankees…*Elias* also notes that only two other active pitchers have four (or more) wins in his team's home opener: Josh Beckett (four total—three for Boston, one for Florida) and Livan Hernandez (four, one each for Florida, Minnesota, San Francisco and Washington).

▸ Surrendered a first-inning three-run HR to Paul Konerko on 4/30 vs. Chicago-AL…marked his first HR allowed in 2010 after starting the year with a 28.1IP homerless stretch…marked the longest such stretch to start a season in his career…had also tossed 8.1 homerless IP in spring training.

MOST WINS-SAVE COMBINATIONS
Since saves became an official statistic in 1969
Courtesy of the *Elias Sports Bureau*

1.	**ANDY PETTITTE/MARIANO RIVERA (NYY)**	**...68**
2.	Bob Welch/Dennis Eckersley (OAK)	.57
3.	Mike Mussina/MARIANO RIVERA (NYY)	.49
4.	Dave Stewart/Dennis Eckersley (OAK)	.43
5.	Jimmy Key/Tom Henke (TOR)	.37
	Kevin Tapani/Rick Aguilera (MIN)	.37

ALL-TIME WINS LIST

50.	Jack Powell	244
51.	Juan Marichal	243
52.	Herb Pennock	241
53.	Frank Tanana	240
	ANDY PETTITTE	**240**
55.	Three-Fingered Brown	239
	Clark Griffith	239
	David Wells	239
58.	Waite Hoyt	237
59.	Whitey Ford	236

MOST WINS
LAST 10 YEARS (2001-10)

1.	CC Sabathia	157
2.	Roy Halladay	156
3.	Roy Oswalt	150
4.	Mark Buehrle	144
5.	Derek Lowe	142
6.	**ANDY PETTITTE**	**140**

MOST WINS, ACTIVE PITCHERS

1.	Jamie Moyer	267
2.	**ANDY PETTITTE**	**240**
3.	Tim Wakefield	193
4.	Roy Halladay	169
5.	Livan Hernandez	166

MOST WINS, YANKEES FRANCHISE HISTORY

1.	Whitey Ford	236
2.	Red Ruffing	231
3.	**ANDY PETTITTE**	**203**
4.	Lefty Gomez	189
5.	Ron Guidry	170

MOST POSTSEASON WINS ALL-TIME

1.	**ANDY PETTITTE**	**18**
2.	John Smoltz	15
3.	Tom Glavine	14
4.	Roger Clemens	12
T5.	Greg Maddux	11
	Curt Schilling	11

MOST POSTSEASON STARTS ALL-TIME

1.	**ANDY PETTITTE**	**40**
2.	Tom Glavine	35
3.	Roger Clemens	34
4.	Greg Maddux	30
5.	John Smoltz	27

ANDY PETTITTE

- Finished April 3-0 with a 2.12 ERA, marking his lowest ERA ever for the first month of the season...went undefeated in the month for just the second time in his career: 5-0 with a 2.32 ERA (42.2IP, 11ER) in April 1997

- Left his start on 5/5 vs. Baltimore after the fifth inning with soreness in his left arm...still earned the win in a 7-5 Yankees victory (6H, 1ER, 2BB, 2K)...underwent an MRI that day at New York-Presbyterian Hospital that revealed mild inflammation of his left elbow...was held out of his next scheduled start on 5/10.

- Won his first five decisions of a season for just the second time in his career (started 1997, 5-0)...joined Phil Hughes in beginning the season 5-0...according to the *Elias Sports Bureau*, marked just the fourth time in the last 50 years that two Yankees starters each won their first five decisions in the same season (also 2004 with Kevin Brown and Orlando Hernandez; 2003 with Mike Mussina and David Wells; and 1980 with Ron Guidry and Tommy John.

- Tied season highs with 7R and 6ER on 5/20 vs. Tampa Bay, recording his first loss of the season in an 8-6 Rays victory (5.0IP, 9H, 2BB, 3K)...also allowed 3HR, his most since 5/7/09 vs. Tampa Bay, when he allowed a career-high 4HR.

- Tossed at least 7.0IP in six straight starts from 5/26-6/22, marking his longest such stretch since 7/15-8/31/05 (10 consecutive 7.0-or-more IP outings).

- Allowed just 2ER over a season-high-tying 8.0IP on 5/26 vs. Minnesota (8H, 0BB, 4K), recording the win in a 3-2 Yankees victory...marked his second start with at least 8.0IP and 0BB this season (also 4/24 at Los Angeles-AL) and the 14th such start of his career.

- Recorded his 200th career win as a Yankee on 6/11 vs. Houston in a 4-3 Yankees victory (7.1IP, 4H, 3R, 2ER, 1BB, 5K, 1HR)...became the third player to reach the plateau with the franchise (also Whitey Ford-236 and Red Ruffing-231)...became the 35th pitcher all time to win at least 200 games for one franchise (credit: *Elias*)...was his 237th career win, breaking a tie with Whitey Ford (236) and tying Hall of Famer Waite Hoyt for 57th place on baseball's all-time list.

- Also surpassed 3,000.0IP in 6/11 win vs. Houston...became the the the 105th pitcher all time to reach the plateau, and one of just three active pitcher to reach the mark (joining Jamie Moyer and Tim Wakefield)...according to the *Elias Sports Bureau*, became the fifth pitcher in the Expansion Era to reach the 3,000.0IP milestone as a Yankee (also Whitey Ford-1965, Catfish Hunter-1976, Tommy John-1979 and Mike Mussina-2005).

- Celebrated his 38th birthday on 6/15...as a 37-year-old (from 6/15/09-6/14/10), went 20-6 with a 3.35 ERA (226.0IP, 84ER), 76BB and 178K in 36 starts – including the postseason.

- In 6/17 loss vs. Philadelphia, surpassed Ron Guidry (1,778K) for sole possession of second place on the franchise's all-time strikeouts list and surpassed Bob Shawkey (2,493.0IP) for sole possession of fifth place on the Yankees' all-time innings pitched list...surpassed Lefty Gomez (2,497.0IP) for sole possession of fourth place on the Yankees' all-time list in his next start in 6/22 win at Arizona.

- Notched his final win of the season on 7/8 at Seattle, allowing just 1ER in 8.0IP (5H, 4BB, 9K)...marked a season-high in walks...earned the win to improve to 11-2, his most pre-All Star break wins since 2003 (11-6)...was his 392nd career start as a Yankee, surpassing Red Ruffing (391) for sole possession of second place on the Yankees' all-time list.

- Exited his 7/18 start vs. Tampa Bay in the third inning (with a 3-1 count against Shoppach) with a strained left groin...was taken to New York-Presbyterian Hospital to undergo an MRI which revealed a Grade 1 left groin strain.

- Was placed on the 15-day disabled list from 7/20/10 (retroactive to 7/19-9/18) with a strained left groin (missed 57 team games)...made two rehab starts with Double-A Trenton, both in postseason play...on 9/9 in Game 2 of the first round of the Eastern League playoffs, tossed 4.0 scoreless IP (2H, 4K, 2WP) with no decision in a 3-2 Thunder win in 10 innings...on 9/14 at Altoona in Game 1 of the Eastern League Finals, allowed 2ER in 5.0IP (6H,1BB, 4K, 1HR, 1WP) with no decision in a 12-inning, 1-0 Thunder victory.

- Made three starts after being returned from rehab and reinstated from the disabled list on 9/19, going 0-1 with a 6.75 ERA (13.1IP, 10ER)...was winless in his last four Major League starts in 2010 (including his start on 7/18 vs. Tampa Bay), his longest such stretch this season.

- Made his first post-D.L. start on 9/19, allowing just 3H in 6.0IP (1ER, 1BB, 2K, 79 pitches) in a no-decision...was his second-fewest hits allowed in a start in 2010 (2H on 5/15 vs. Minnesota)...exited with a 3-1 lead, which the bullpen relinquished.

- Allowed a season-high 10H and tied season highs with 7R and 6ER allowed on 9/24 vs. Boston (3.1IP, 0BB, 1K, 1HR)...left-handed hitters went 4-for-5 off Pettitte (single and double to Ortiz and 2 singles to Drew), marking the most hits he allowed to LHH in a game this season.

- Made his final start on 10/2 (G1) at Fenway Park, allowing 3ER in 4.0IP (9H, 2BB, 8K).

- Was limited to only two official spring outings due to rainouts, going 0-0 with a 2.16 ERA (8.1IP, 12H, 2ER, 2BB, 5K, 0HR)...had two starts cancelled due to rain (3/12 and 3/21)...tossed a 50-pitch bullpen session on 3/12...faced 25 batters in an intrasquad game at GMS Field on 3/22, allowing 12H and 3ER in 5.0IP and tossing 80 pitches, 54 strikes (0BB, 6K).

Pettitte's Career Pitching Record

Year	Club	W	L	ERA	G	GS	CG	SHO	SV	IP	H	R	ER	HR	HP	BB	SO	WP	BK
1991	GCL Yankees	4	1	0.98	6	6	0	0	0	36.2	16	6	4	0	1	8	51	4	6
	Oneonta	2	2	2.18	6	6	1	0	0	33.0	33	18	8	1	0	16	32	4	0
1992	Greensboro	10	4	2.20	27	27	2	1	0	168.0	141	53	41	4	5	55	130	11	2
1993	Prince William	11	9	3.04	26	26	2	1	0	159.2	146	68	54	7	5	47	129	8	1
	Albany	1	0	3.60	1	1	0	0	0	5.0	5	4	2	0	0	2	6	0	0
1994	Albany	7	2	2.71	11	11	0	0	0	73.0	60	32	22	5	1	18	50	5	1
	Columbus	7	2	2.98	16	16	3	0	0	96.2	101	40	32	3	2	21	61	5	0
1995	YANKEES	12	9	4.17	31	26	3	0	0	175.0	183	86	81	15	1	63	114	8	1
	Columbus	0	0	0.00	2	2	0	0	0	11.2	7	0	0	0	0	0	8	1	0
1996	YANKEES	*21	8	3.87	35	34	2	0	0	221.0	229	105	95	23	3	72	162	6	1
1997	YANKEES	18	7	2.88	35	#35	4	1	0	240.1	233	86	77	7	3	65	166	7	0
1998	YANKEES	16	11	4.24	33	32	5	0	0	216.1	226	110	102	20	6	87	146	5	0
1999	Tampa	1	0	0.00	1	1	0	0	0	5.0	4	0	0	0	0	2	8	0	0
	YANKEES - a	14	11	4.70	31	31	0	0	0	191.2	216	105	100	20	3	89	121	3	1
2000	YANKEES - b	19	9	4.35	32	32	3	1	0	204.2	219	111	99	17	4	80	125	2	3
2001	YANKEES - c	15	10	3.99	31	31	2	0	0	200.2	224	103	89	14	6	41	164	2	2
2002	YANKEES - d	13	5	3.27	22	22	3	1	0	134.2	144	58	49	6	4	32	97	2	1
	Tampa	0	0	0.00	2	2	0	0	0	5.0	3	0	0	0	0	0	4	0	0
	Norwich	0	0	1.42	1	1	0	0	0	6.1	2	1	1	0	0	0	5	0	0
2003	YANKEES	21	8	4.02	33	33	1	0	0	208.1	227	109	93	21	1	50	180	5	0
2004	HOUSTON - e,f,g,h	6	4	3.90	15	15	0	0	0	83.0	71	37	36	8	0	31	79	4	0
	Round Rock	0	0	2.25	2	2	0	0	0	8.0	4	2	2	1	0	2	9	0	0
2005	HOUSTON	17	9	2.39	33	33	0	0	0	222.1	188	66	59	17	3	41	171	2	0
2006	HOUSTON	14	13	4.20	36	#35	2	1	0	214.1	238	114	100	27	2	70	178	2	1
2007	YANKEES - i	15	9	4.05	36	#34	0	0	0	215.1	238	106	97	16	1	69	141	3	0
2008	YANKEES - j	14	14	4.54	33	33	0	0	0	204.0	233	112	103	19	7	55	158	6	1
2009	YANKEES	14	8	4.16	32	32	0	0	0	194.2	193	101	90	20	4	76	148	3	0
2010	YANKEES - k	11	3	3.28	21	21	0	0	0	129.0	123	52	47	13	3	41	101	2	0
	Trenton	0	0	2.00	2	2	0	0	0	9.0	8	2	2	1	0	1	8	3	0
Minor League Totals		**43**	**20**	**2.45**	**103**	**103**	**8**	**2**	**0**	**617.0**	**530**	**226**	**168**	**22**	**14**	**172**	**501**	**41**	**10**
AL Totals		**203**	**112**	**3.98**	**405**	**396**	**23**	**3**	**0**	**2535.2**	**2688**	**1244**	**1122**	**211**	**46**	**820**	**1823**	**54**	**10**
NL Totals		**37**	**26**	**3.38**	**84**	**83**	**2**	**1**	**0**	**519.2**	**497**	**217**	**195**	**52**	**5**	**142**	**428**	**8**	**1**
Major League Totals		**240**	**138**	**3.88**	**489**	**21**	**25**	**4**	**0**	**3055.1**	**3185**	**1461**	**1317**	**263**	**51**	**962**	**2251**	**62**	**11**

*Denotes league leader   #Tied for league lead

Selected by the New York Yankees in the 22nd round of the June 1990 free-agent draft; signed on May 25, 1991.

a - Placed on disabled list, April 4-17, 1999 with a strained left elbow.
b - Placed on disabled list, April 13-26, 2000 with a back strain.
c - Placed on disabled list, June 16-July 1, 2001 with a strained left groin.
d - Placed on disabled list, April 21-June 14, 2002 with left elbow tendinitis.
e - Signed by Houston as a free agent on Dec. 12, 2003.
f - Placed on disabled list, April 10-29, 2004 with a strained left elbow.
g - Placed on disabled list, May 31-June 29, 2004 with a strained left forearm.
h - Placed on disabled list, August 18, 2004 through remainder of season with left elbow surgery.
i - Signed by New York (AL) as a free agent on December 21, 2006.
j - Placed on the disabled list from March 31 - April 5, 2008 with lower back spasms.
k – Placed on the 15-day disabled list from July 20 (retroactive to July 19)-September 18, 2010 with a strained left groin.

	2010											Career									
	W	L	SV	ERA	G	GS	IP	H	HR	ER	SO	W	L	SV	ERA	G	GS	IP	H	HR	ER	SO
Overall	11	3	0	3.28	21	21	129.0	123	13	47	101	240	138	0	3.88	489	479	3055.1	3185	263	1317	2251
Minnesota	2	0	0	1.26	2	2	14.1	10	0	2	6	11	5	0	3.46	21	21	145.2	148	8	56	110
Tampa Bay	0	1	0	11.05	2	2	7.1	15	4	9	6	16	6	0	4.11	31	30	177.1	203	19	81	144
Texas	1	0	0	2.25	1	1	8.0	4	0	2	4	11	9	0	5.24	23	23	146.0	178	11	85	105
Atlanta	-	-	-	-	-	-	-	-	-	-	-	5	1	0	3.39	10	10	58.1	60	5	22	45
Cincinnati	-	-	-	-	-	-	-	-	-	-	-	4	3	0	3.64	10	10	59.1	72	3	24	55
Philadelphia	0	1	0	2.57	1	1	7.0	6	1	2	7	2	3	0	3.51	8	8	48.2	51	7	19	35
San Francisco	-	-	-	-	-	-	-	-	-	-	-	0	3	0	5.40	3	3	18.1	23	1	11	17
March	-	-	-	-	-	-	-	-	-	-	-											
April	3	0	0	2.12	5	5	34.0	28	1	8	25	32	22	0	3.55	75	71	446.0	475	35	176	301
May	4	1	0	2.87	5	5	31.1	29	4	10	16	38	26	0	4.22	81	77	491.0	522	50	230	357
June	2	1	0	3.18	5	5	34.0	28	4	12	33	36	24	0	4.05	81	81	515.2	532	54	232	368
July	2	0	0	3.86	3	3	16.1	16	3	7	16	48	27	0	4.02	87	86	546.0	592	44	244	431
August	-	-	-	-	-	-	-	-	-	-	-	50	19	0	3.43	87	87	598.2	588	45	228	462
September	0	1	0	6.75	2	2	9.1	13	1	7	3	36	19	0	3.98	74	73	440.2	450	33	195	318
October	0	0	0	6.75	1	1	4.0	9	0	3	8	0	1	0	6.23	4	4	17.1	26	2	6.23	14
Home	7	3	0	3.89	12	12	69.1	68	10	30	44	128	63	0	3.71	241	237	1561.0	1574	137	643	1157
Road	4	0	0	2.56	9	9	59.2	55	3	17	57	112	75	0	4.06	248	242	1494.1	1611	126	674	1094

Pettitte's Career By Ballpark

Park	W	L	SV	ERA	G	GS	IP	ER	Park	W	L	SV	ERA	G	GS	IP	ER
AT&T Park	0	1	0	3.86	1	1	7.0	3	Target Field	1	0	0	2.25	1	1	8.0	2
Citizens Bank Park	1	0	0	0.75	2	2	12.0	1	Tropicana Field	8	3	0	3.84	14	14	86.2	37
Great American BP	1	2	0	3.31	6	6	35.1	13	Turner Field	2	1	0	4.25	5	5	29.2	14
PETCO Park	1	0	0	0.00	1	1	6.0	0	Yankee Stadium	13	7	0	4.31	28	28	169.1	81
Rangers Ballpark	2	4	0	8.22	7	7	38.1	35									

Pettitte's Division Series Record

Year	Club vs. Opp.	W	L	ERA	G	GS	CG	SHO	SV	IP	H	R	ER	HR	HP	BB	SO	WP	BK
1995	NYY vs. SEA	0	0	5.14	1	1	0	0	0	7.0	9	4	4	1	0	3	0	0	0
1996	NYY vs. TEX	0	0	5.68	1	1	0	0	0	6.1	4	4	4	2	0	6	3	1	0
1997	NYY vs. CLE	0	2	8.49	2	2	0	0	0	11.2	15	11	11	1	0	1	5	0	0
1998	NYY vs. TEX	1	0	1.29	1	1	0	0	0	7.0	3	1	1	0	0	0	8	0	0
1999	NYY vs. TEX	1	0	1.23	1	1	0	0	0	7.1	7	1	1	1	0	0	5	0	0
2000	NYY vs. OAK	1	0	3.97	2	2	0	0	0	11.1	15	5	5	0	0	3	7	0	0
2001	NYY vs. OAK	0	1	1.42	1	1	0	0	0	6.1	7	1	1	1	0	2	4	0	0
2002	NYY vs. ANA	0	0	12.00	1	1	0	0	0	3.0	8	4	4	2	0	1	0	0	0
2003	NYY vs. MIN	1	0	1.29	1	1	0	0	0	7.0	4	1	1	1	0	3	10	1	0
2005	HOU vs. ATL	1	0	3.86	1	1	0	0	0	7.0	4	3	3	2	0	2	6	0	0
2007	NYY vs. CLE	0	0	0.00	1	1	0	0	0	6.1	7	0	0	0	0	2	5	0	0
2009	NYY vs. MIN	1	0	1.42	1	1	0	0	0	6.1	3	1	1	0	0	1	7	0	0
Division Series Totals		**6**	**3**	**3.74**	**14**	**14**	**0**	**0**	**0**	**86.2**	**86**	**36**	**36**	**11**	**0**	**23**	**61**	**2**	**0**

Pettitte's League Championship Series Record

Year	Club vs. Opp.	W	L	ERA	G	GS	CG	SHO	SV	IP	H	R	ER	HR	HP	BB	SO	WP	BK
1996	NYY vs. BAL	1	0	3.60	2	2	0	0	0	15.0	10	6	6	4	0	5	7	0	1
1998	NYY vs. CLE	0	1	11.57	1	1	0	0	0	4.2	8	6	6	4	0	3	1	0	0
1999	NYY vs. BOS	1	0	2.45	1	1	0	0	0	7.1	8	2	2	0	0	1	5	0	0
2000	NYY vs. SEA	1	0	2.70	1	1	0	0	0	6.2	9	2	2	0	0	1	2	0	0
2001	NYY vs. SEA	2	0	2.51	2	2	0	0	0	14.1	11	4	4	0	0	2	8	0	0
2003	NYY vs. BOS	1	0	4.63	2	2	0	0	0	11.2	17	6	6	2	0	4	10	0	0
2005	HOU vs. STL	0	1	5.11	2	2	0	0	0	12.1	15	7	7	1	1	4	6	0	0
2009	NYY vs. LAA	1	0	2.84	2	2	0	0	0	12.2	14	4	4	2	0	2	8	0	0
LCS Totals		**7**	**2**	**3.93**	**13**	**13**	**0**	**0**	**0**	**84.2**	**92**	**37**	**37**	**13**	**1**	**22**	**47**	**0**	**1**

Pettitte's World Series Record

Year	Club vs. Opp.	W	L	ERA	G	GS	CG	SHO	SV	IP	H	R	ER	HR	HP	BB	SO	WP	BK
1996	NYY vs. ATL	1	1	5.91	2	2	0	0	0	10.2	11	7	7	1	0	4	5	0	0
1998	NYY vs. SD	1	0	0.00	1	1	0	0	0	7.1	5	0	0	0	0	3	4	0	0
1999	NYY vs. ATL	0	0	12.27	1	1	0	0	0	3.2	10	5	5	0	0	1	1	1	0
2000	NYY vs. NYM	0	0	1.98	2	2	0	0	0	13.2	16	5	3	0	1	4	9	0	0
2001	NYY vs. ARI	0	2	10.00	2	2	0	0	0	9.0	12	10	10	1	1	2	9	0	0
2003	NYY vs. FLA	1	1	0.57	2	2	0	0	0	15.2	12	3	1	0	0	4	14	0	0
2005	HOU vs. CWS	0	0	3.00	1	1	0	0	0	6.0	8	2	2	0	0	0	4	0	0
2009	NYY vs. PHI	2	0	5.40	2	2	0	0	0	11.2	9	7	7	3	0	8	10	1	0
World Series Totals		**5**	**4**	**4.06**	**13**	**13**	**0**	**0**	**0**	**77.2**	**83**	**39**	**35**	**5**	**2**	**26**	**56**	**2**	**0**
POSTSEASON TOTALS		**18**	**9**	**3.90**	**40**	**40**	**0**	**0**	**0**	**249.0**	**261**	**112**	**108**	**29**	**3**	**71**	**164**	**4**	**1**

Pettitte's All-Star Game Record

Year	Club, Site	W	L	ERA	G	GS	CG	SHO	SV	IP	H	R	ER	HR	HP	BB	SO	WP	BK
1996	NYY, Philadelphia							Selected - Did Not Pitch											
2001	NYY, Seattle	0	0	0.00	1	0	0	0	0	1.0	1	0	0	0	0	0	1	0	0
2010	NYY, Los Angeles (AL)	0	0	0.00	1	0	0	0	0	1.0	1	0	0	0	0	0	2	0	0
All-Star Game Totals		**0**	**0**	**0.00**	**2**	**0**	**0**	**0**	**0**	**2.0**	**2**	**0**	**0**	**0**	**0**	**0**	**3**	**0**	**0**

Pettitte's Regular Season Batting Record

Year	Team	AVG	G	AB	R	H	2B	3B	HR	RBI	SH	SF	HP	BB	SO	SB	CS
2010	NYY	.250	21	4	0	1	0	0	0	0	1	0	0	0	3	0	0
Major League Totals		**.137**	**489**	**190**	**6**	**26**	**6**	**0**	**1**	**13**	**33**	**1**	**0**	**6**	**63**	**0**	**0**

Pettitte's Career Fielding Record

Position	PCT	G	PO	A	E	TC	DP
Pitcher	.951	489	122	501	32	655	31

Jorge Posada

20 Catcher
6-2 • 215 • B/T: Switch/Right
Opening Day Age: 38

Birthdate
August 17, 1971

Birthplace
Santurce, P.R.

Resides
Miami, Fla.

M.L. Service
14 years, 85 days

College
Calhoun Community
College

Career Highlights
A.L. All-Star Team
▸ 2000, 2001, 2002,
2003, 2007

**A.L. Silver Slugger
Award**
▸ 2000, 2001, 2002, 2003
2007

Status
▸ Selected in the 24th round of the 1990 First-Year Player Draft…signed a four-year contract on November 29, 2007…contract extends through the 2011 season.

Postseason Notes
▸ Started 68 consecutive postseason games from 10/27/99 (World Series Game 4) – 10/5/05 (Division Series Game 2)…is tied for fourth on Baseball's all-time list with 111 career postseason games played, including 110 postseason contests at catcher (Yogi Berra is second with 63)…has recorded 21 postseason doubles, third-most all-time.
▸ Collected his fifth World Championship in 2009, appearing in all 15 Yankees postseason games (10 starts) and batting .260 (13-for-50) with 5R, 2 doubles, 2HR and 8RBI…reached base in 14 of the contests…hit go-ahead solo home run in ALDS Game 3 clincher at Minnesota.
▸ In Game 3 of the 2001 ALDS at Oakland, became only the 10th player in postseason history—and second Yankee (also Tommy Henrich)—to hit a home run in a 1-0 game (off Barry Zito)…his 43 Division Series games are the third-most in Baseball history.
▸ Has caught at least one game in six different World Series, tied for third-most all-time with Elston Howard and Wally Schang, trailing only Yogi Berra (12) and Bill Dickey (8).

Career Notes
▸ Ranks seventh on the Yankees' all-time list with 365 doubles, eighth with 261HR and 897BB, and 11th with 1,021RBI.
▸ Among active Major League catchers, ranks second in home runs (261) and RBI (1,021), third in runs scored (866), hits (1,583) and doubles (365) and fourth in games played (1,714).
▸ According to the *Elias Sports Bureau*, has homered in more ballparks (28) than any player in Yankees history… his 246HR as a catcher rank second on the Yankees' all-time list behind only Yogi Berra (306).
▸ Has caught 1,573 games for the Yankees…only Bill Dickey (1,708) and Yogi Berra (1,695) have caught more games in pinstripes.
▸ Is the first Major Leaguer to catch at least one game with the same team in 16 straight seasons since Cincinnati's Johnny Bench (17 consecutive seasons, 1967-83)—credit: *Elias Sports Bureau*.
▸ Along with Derek Jeter and Mariano Rivera, have become the first trio of teammates in MLB, NBA, NFL and NHL history to appear in a game together in each of 16 straight seasons (credit: *Elias Sports Bureau*).
▸ Owns a .275 career batting average, 261HR and 1,021RBI…of the 13 former Major League catchers in the Hall of Fame (Johnny Bench, Yogi Berra, Roger Bresnahan, Roy

2010 Highs and Streaks	
Low hit CG	N/A
Hits	4 - at TOR, 8/24/10
Runs	2 - 8 times
	Last: vs. OAK, 8/30/10
2B	2 - 2 times
	Last: at CWS, 8/28/10
3B	1 - vs. OAK, 8/31/10
HR	1 - 18 times
	Last: at TB, 9/14/10
RBI	4 - 2 times
	Last: vs. HOU, 6/13/10
BB	2 - 10 times
	Last: at TB, 9/15/10
SO	3 - 5 times
	Last: at BOS, 10/2/10(G1)
SB	1 - 3 times
	Last: vs. DET, 8/17/10
Hit Streak	7g - 5/10-6/3/10

Career Highs and Streaks	
Hits	4 - 17 times
	Last: at TOR, 8/24/10
Runs	4 - 3 times
	Last: vs. SEA, 9/4/07
2B	3 - at CWS, 4/23/08
3B	1 - 10 times
	Last: vs. OAK, 8/31/10
HR	2 - 16 times
	Last: at BAL, 9/1/09
RBI	7 - vs. DET, 9/10/03
BB	4 - 2 times
	Last: at CLE, 7/9/03
SO	4 - 5 times
	Last: at ATL, 6/23/09
SB	1 - 20 times
	Last: vs. DET, 8/17/10
Hit Streak	15g - 5/3-20/07

Campanella, Gary Carter, Mickey Cochrane, Bill Dickey, Buck Ewing, Rick Ferrell, Carlton Fisk, Gabby Hartnett, Ernie Lombardi and Ray Schalk), only Berra (.285BA, 358HR, 1,430RBI) has better numbers in all three categories…is eighth all-time in HR among players who played at least 50.0% of their games at catcher.

- Is one of five players all time to record at least 1,500H, 350 doubles, 250HR and 1,000RBI while playing at least 50.0% of his games at catcher (also the Nationals' Ivan Rodriguez and Hall of Famers Johnny Bench, Gary Carter and Carlton Fisk).

- Is one of eight players to hit at least 250 home runs for his current team, joining teammate Alex Rodriguez, Chipper Jones, Albert Pujols, Paul Konerko, Todd Helton, David Ortiz and Ryan Howard—credit: Elias Sports Bureau.

- Has 261 career home runs, for eighth place on the Yankees' all-time list (teammate Alex Rodriguez is seventh with 268HR).

2010

- Hit .248 (95-for-383) with 49R, 23 doubles, 1 triple, 18HR and 57RBI in 120 games (78 starts at C, 28 at 1B) with the Yankees in 2010…the Yankees were 49-29 in his starts at catcher…caught 10-of-78 (11.4%) of potential base stealers…pitchers owned a 4.07 ERA with him behind the plate.

- Had 3SB, tying his career high (also 3SB in 2006)…all 3SB came in a nine-game stretch from 8/7-17 after having just 1SB in his previous 297G (7/15/07-8/6/10).

- Made his 11th career Opening Day start at catcher (since 2000), trailing only Bill Dickey (14, 1930-43) for most consecutive starts behind the plate for the Yankees on Opening Day in franchise history…became the oldest catcher (38 years, 230 days) to start an opener for the Yankees since Dickey in 1946 (38 years, 314 days).

- Hit solo HR in his first AB of the season in the second inning of 4/4 Opening Day loss at Boston, going 3-for-4 with 2RBI and 1BB…was his fourth career Opening Day home run, tied with Mickey Mantle and Yogi Berra for second-most Opening Day home runs in franchise history behind Babe Ruth (five)…was the first of back-to-back homers with Curtis Granderson, becoming the first pair of Yankees to hit back-to-back home runs on Opening Day since Dave Winfield and Steve Kemp on 4/5/83 at Seattle (credit: Elias).

- Hit his 345th career double in the seventh inning of 4/13 home opening win vs. Los Angeles-AL, surpassing Mickey Mantle (344) for sole possession of seventh place in franchise history…was 3-for-4 with 2 doubles, 1RBI and 1BB in the game overall…is a .444 (16-for-36) hitter in 11 career home openers with 8R, 6 doubles, 4HR, 7RBI and 9BB.

- Recorded his 1,500th career hit in 4/17 win vs. Texas…became the 19th overall Yankee and fourth Yankee whose primary position was catcher to reach the plateau (also Yogi Berra , Bill Dickey and Thurman Munson).

- Left 4/28 win at Baltimore in the bottom of the second inning after being hit by a pitch by Baltimore starter Jeremy Guthrie in the top of the inning…suffered a right knee contusion and missed 4/29 game with the injury.

- Missed four games with a strained right calf from 5/4-8.

- Was placed on the 15-day disabled list on 5/20 (retroactive to 5/17) with a hairline fracture of the bottom of his right foot…was reinstated from the disabled list on 6/2 (missed 15 team games).

- Hit grand slams in consecutive games on 6/12 and 6/13 vs. Houston, becoming the first Yankee to hit a grand slam in back-to-back games since Bill Dickey on 8/3 (G2) and 8/4/37…according to Elias, the only other Yankee to accomplish the feat was Babe Ruth who did so in 1927 and 1929…prior to his grand slam on 6/12, had hit 102HR since his last slam on 7/26/04 at Toronto (off Sean Douglass)…his grand slam on 6/13 was the 251st of his career, surpassing Graig Nettles for sole possession of seventh place on the Yankees' all-time list.

- Had 8RBI over the two game stretch, marking his most over a two-game span since 9/10-11/03 (9RBI).

- Drove in at least one run in a career-high eight straight games (10RBI total) from 7/11-24…was the longest such streak by a Yankee since Jason Giambi drove in a run in eight straight from 8/27-9/3/08 and tied for the second-longest streak in the Majors this season, trailing only Florida's Jorge Cantu (10 straight from 4/5-15).

MAJOR LEAGUE CATCHERS (SINCE 2000*)

MOST HITS

1.	Jason Kendall	1,628
2.	Ivan Rodriguez	1,431
3.	A.J. Pierzynski	1,351
4.	**JORGE POSADA**	**1,246**
5.	Bengie Molina	1,243

MOST HOME RUNS

1.	**JORGE POSADA**	**212**
2.	Ivan Rodriguez	160
3.	Mike Piazza	159
4.	Jason Varitek	153
5.	Ramon Hernandez	141

MOST RBI

1.	**JORGE POSADA**	**816**
2.	Ivan Rodriguez	669
3.	Bengie Molina	667
4.	Ramon Hernandez	635
5.	Jason Varitek	598

MOST GAMES STARTED

1.	Jason Kendall	1,517
2.	A.J. Pierzynski	1,235
3.	Ivan Rodriguez	1,216
4.	**JORGE POSADA**	**1,213**
5.	Benjie Molina	1,204

WALKS

1.	**JORGE POSADA**	**695**
2.	Jason Kendall	538
3.	Jason Varitek	518
4.	Brad Ausmus	384
5.	Joe Mauer	366

DOUBLES

1.	**JORGE POSADA**	**292**
2.	Ivan Rodriguez	288
3.	A.J. Pierzynski	279
4.	Jason Kendall	275
5.	Jason Varitek	238

*as a catcher

MOST GAMES CAUGHT IN YANKEES FRANCHISE HISTORY

1.	Bill Dickey	1,708
2.	Yogi Berra	1,695
3.	**JORGE POSADA**	**1,573**
4.	Thurman Munson	1,278
5.	Elston Howard	1,030

▶ Hit solo HR—the second of back-to-back HR with Cano—and was 1-for-3 with 1BB in 7/16 win vs. Tampa Bay…marked his first career home run on a 3-0 pitch.

▶ In 7/20 loss vs. Los Angeles-AL, caught Bobby Abreu stealing 2B in the fifth and the seventh innings, the first time he caught the same runner stealing twice in the same game since 7/29/04 vs. Baltimore (Jerry Hairston, Jr.).

CATCHERS* w/ 1,500H, 350 doubles, 250HR & 1,000RBI
JORGE POSADA 1,714G-1,583H-365 dbl-261HR-1,021RBI
Ivan Rodriguez 2,499G-2,817H-565 dbl-309HR-1,313RBI
Carlton Fisk# 2,499G-2,356H-421 dbl-376HR-1,330RBI
Gary Carter# 2,296G-2,092H-371 dbl-324HR-1,225RBI
Johnny Bench# 2,158G-2,048H-381 dbl-389HR-1,376RBI
*Played at least 50% of gms at C / #Hall of Famer

▶ Collected his 1,000th career RBI with his run-scoring double in the first inning of 7/23 win vs. Kansas City, going 2-for-3 with 1R, 1 double, 2RBI and 1BB…became the 12th Yankee and 11th player in Major League history whose primary position was catcher to reach the plateau…marked his seventh straight game with an RBI, becoming the third Major Leaguer to reach the 1,000RBI mark while on a streak of seven or more games – also Yogi Berra in 1956 (nine games) and B.J. Surhoff in 2001 (seven games)—credit: *Elias*.

▶ His sixth-inning single in 8/19 win vs. Detroit was the 1,559th hit of his career, surpassing Thurman Munson (1,558) for sole possession of 17th place on the Yankees' all-time hits list.

▶ Tied a career high with four hits in 8/24 win at Toronto, going 4-for-5 with 2R and 2RBI…was his 17th career four-hit game (first since 9/3/09).

▶ Collected his 10th career triple in the first inning of 8/31 win vs. Oakland…was his first triple since 4/26/08 at Cleveland…became the oldest Yankee to triple in a game since Chili Davis on 9/1/99 at age 39…drove in one run on the triple for his 1,014th career RBI, surpassing Bob Meusel (1,013) for sole possession of 11th place on the Yankees' all-time list.

▶ Was ejected on 9/1 vs. Oakland by HP Umpire Dana DeMuth for arguing balls and strikes…was his sixth career ejection, first since 9/15/09 vs. Toronto.

▶ Played in his 1,695th career game on 9/6 vs. Baltimore, surpassing Willie Randolph (1,694) for sole possession of 11th place on the Yankees' all-time list.

▶ Suffered a mild concussion after being hit with foul tip while catching on 9/7 vs. Baltimore and did not start the Yankees' first two games at Texas on 9/10 and 9/11.

▶ Hit game-winning, pinch-hit HR in the 10th inning on 9/14 at Tampa Bay…was his fifth career pinch-hit home run and first since 9/9/09 vs. Tampa Bay…had been hitless in his previous 10AB as a pinch-hitter in 2010.

▶ Had 1H in his final 25AB of the season…snapped an 0-for-14 stretch with a fourth-inning infield single in 9/28 win at Toronto.

Posada's Career Hitting Record

Year	Team	AVG	G	AB	R	H	2B	3B	HR	RBI	SH	SF	HP	BB	SO	SB	CS	E	OBP	SLG
1991	Oneonta	.235	71	217	34	51	5	5	4	33	7	1	4	51	51	6	5	21	.388	.359
1992	Greensboro	.277	101	339	60	94	22	4	12	58	0	3	6	58	87	11	6	11	.389	.472
1993	Prince William	.259	118	410	71	106	27	2	17	61	1	6	6	67	90	17	5	15	.366	.459
	Albany	.280	7	25	3	7	0	0	0	0	0	0	0	2	7	0	0	2	.333	.280
1994	Columbus	.240	92	313	46	75	13	3	11	48	4	5	1	32	81	5	5	11	.308	.406
1995	Columbus	.255	108	368	60	94	32	5	8	51	6	3	1	54	101	4	4	4	.350	.435
	YANKEES	.000	1	0	0	0	0	0	0	0	0	0	0	0	0	0	0	0	.000	.000
1996	Columbus	.271	106	354	76	96	22	6	11	62	1	3	3	79	86	3	3	10	.405	.460
	YANKEES	.071	8	14	1	1	0	0	0	0	0	0	0	1	6	0	0	0	.133	.071
1997	YANKEES	.250	60	188	29	47	12	0	6	25	1	2	3	30	33	1	2	3	.359	.410
1998	YANKEES	.268	111	358	56	96	23	0	17	63	0	4	0	47	92	0	1	4	.350	.475
1999	YANKEES	.245	112	379	50	93	19	2	12	57	0	2	3	53	91	1	0	5	.341	.401
2000	YANKEES	.287	151	505	92	145	35	1	28	86	0	4	8	107	151	2	2	8	.417	.527
2001	YANKEES	.277	138	484	59	134	28	1	22	95	0	5	6	62	132	2	6	11	.363	.475
2002	YANKEES	.268	143	511	79	137	40	1	20	99	0	3	3	81	143	1	0	12	.370	.468
2003	YANKEES	.281	142	481	83	135	24	0	30	101	0	4	10	93	110	2	4	6	.405	.518
2004	YANKEES	.272	137	449	72	122	31	0	21	81	0	1	9	88	92	1	3	9	.400	.481
2005	YANKEES	.262	142	474	67	124	23	0	19	71	0	4	2	66	94	1	0	3	.352	.430
2006	YANKEES	.277	143	465	65	129	27	2	23	93	0	5	11	64	97	3	0	9	.374	.492
2007	YANKEES	.338	144	506	91	171	42	1	20	90	0	3	6	74	98	2	0	5	.426	.543
2008	YANKEES - a, b	.268	51	168	18	45	13	1	3	22	0	1	2	24	38	0	0	1	.364	.411
2009	YANKEES - c	.285	111	383	55	109	25	0	22	81	0	5	2	48	101	1	0	7	.363	.522
2010	YANKEES - d	.248	120	383	49	95	23	1	18	57	0	2	7	59	99	3	1	8	.357	.454
Minor League Totals		**.258**	**603**	**2026**	**350**	**523**	**121**	**25**	**63**	**313**	**19**	**21**	**21**	**343**	**503**	**46**	**28**	**74**	**.368**	**.436**
Major League Totals		**.275**	**1714**	**5748**	**866**	**1583**	**365**	**10**	**261**	**1021**	**1**	**45**	**72**	**897**	**1377**	**20**	**19**	**91**	**.377**	**.479**

Selected by the Yankees in the 24th round of the 1990 First-Year Player Draft.
a – Placed on the 15-day disabled list from April 28 – June 3, 2008 with a right shoulder strain.
b – Placed on the 15-day disabled list from July 21 – September 28, 2008 with a right shoulder strain.
c – Placed on the 15-day disabled list from May 5-27, 2009 with a Grade 2 right hamstring strain.
d – Placed on the 15-day disabled list from May 20 (retroactive to May 17) - June 1, 2010 with a fractured right foot.

Posada's Division Series Record

Year	Club vs. Opp.	AVG	G	AB	R	H	2B	3B	HR	RBI	SH	SF	HP	BB	SO	SB	CS	E	OBP	SLG
1995	NYY vs. SEA	---	1	0	1	0	0	0	0	0	0	0	0	0	0	0	0	0	---	---
1997	NYY vs. CLE	.000	2	2	0	0	0	0	0	0	0	0	0	0	1	0	0	0	.000	.000
1998	NYY vs. TEX	.000	1	2	1	0	0	0	0	0	0	0	0	1	2	0	0	0	.333	.000
1999	NYY vs. TEX	.250	1	4	0	1	1	0	0	0	0	0	0	0	0	0	0	0	.250	.500
2000	NYY vs. OAK	.235	5	17	2	4	2	0	0	1	0	0	0	3	5	0	0	0	.350	.353
2001	NYY vs. OAK	.444	5	18	3	8	1	0	1	2	0	0	0	2	2	1	0	0	.500	.667
2002	NYY vs. ANA	.235	4	17	2	4	0	0	1	3	0	1	0	3	0	0	0	1	.222	.412
2003	NYY vs. MIN	.176	4	17	1	3	1	0	0	0	0	0	0	0	6	0	0	0	.176	.235
2004	NYY vs. MIN	.222	4	18	2	4	0	0	0	0	0	0	0	6	0	0	0	0	.222	.222
2005	NYY vs. LAA	.231	5	13	3	3	1	0	1	2	0	0	0	6	2	0	0	0	.474	.538
2006	NYY vs. DET	.500	4	14	2	7	1	0	1	2	0	0	0	2	2	0	0	0	.563	.786
2007	NYY vs. CLE	.133	4	15	1	2	1	0	0	0	0	0	0	2	3	0	0	0	.235	.200
2009	NYY vs. MIN	.364	3	11	1	4	0	0	1	2	0	0	0	0	2	0	0	0	.364	.636
Division Series Totals		**.270**	**43**	**148**	**19**	**40**	**8**	**0**	**5**	**12**	**0**	**1**	**0**	**16**	**34**	**1**	**0**	**1**	**.339**	**.426**

Posada's League Championship Series Record

Year	Club vs. Opp.	AVG	G	AB	R	H	2B	3B	HR	RBI	SH	SF	HP	BB	SO	SB	CS	E	OBP	SLG
1998	NYY vs. CLE	.182	5	11	1	2	0	0	1	2	0	0	0	4	2	0	1	0	.400	.455
1999	NYY vs. BOS	.100	3	10	1	1	0	0	1	2	0	0	0	1	2	0	0	1	.182	.400
2000	NYY vs. SEA	.158	6	19	2	3	1	0	0	3	0	0	1	5	5	0	1	0	.360	.211
2001	NYY vs. SEA	.214	5	14	4	3	1	0	0	0	0	0	0	6	7	0	0	0	.450	.286
2003	NYY vs. BOS	.296	7	27	5	8	4	0	1	6	0	0	3	4	0	0	0	0	.367	.556
2004	NYY vs. BOS	.259	7	27	4	7	1	0	0	2	0	1	1	7	1	0	0	0	.417	.296
2009	NYY vs. LAA	.200	6	20	3	4	1	0	1	1	0	0	0	5	5	1	0	0	.360	.400
LCS Totals		**.219**	**39**	**128**	**20**	**28**	**8**	**0**	**4**	**16**	**0**	**1**	**2**	**31**	**26**	**1**	**2**	**1**	**.377**	**.375**

Posada's World Series Record

Year	Club vs. Opp.	AVG	G	AB	R	H	2B	3B	HR	RBI	SH	SF	HP	BB	SO	SB	CS	E	OBP	SLG
1998	NYY vs. SD	.333	3	9	2	3	0	0	1	2	0	0	0	2	2	0	0	0	.455	.667
1999	NYY vs. ATL	.250	2	8	0	2	1	0	0	1	0	0	0	0	3	0	0	0	.250	.375
2000	NYY vs. NYM	.222	5	18	2	4	1	0	0	1	0	0	0	5	4	0	0	0	.391	.278
2001	NYY vs. AZ	.174	7	23	2	4	1	0	1	1	0	0	0	3	8	0	0	1	.269	.348
2003	NYY vs. FLA	.158	6	19	0	3	1	0	0	1	0	0	0	5	7	1	1	0	.333	.211
2009	NYY vs. PHI	.263	6	19	1	5	1	0	0	5	0	1	0	2	7	0	0	1	.318	.316
World Series Totals		**.219**	**29**	**96**	**7**	**21**	**5**	**0**	**2**	**11**	**0**	**1**	**0**	**17**	**31**	**1**	**1**	**2**	**.333**	**.333**
POSTSEASON TOTALS		**.239**	**111**	**372**	**46**	**89**	**21**	**0**	**11**	**39**	**0**	**3**	**2**	**64**	**91**	**3**	**3**	**4**	**.351**	**.384**

Posada's All-Star Game Record

Year	Club, Site	AVG	G	AB	R	H	2B	3B	HR	RBI	SH	SF	HP	BB	SO	SB	CS	E	OBP	SLG
2000	NYY, Atlanta	.000	1	2	0	0	0	0	0	0	0	0	0	0	1	0	0	0	.000	.000
2001	NYY, Seattle	1.000	1	1	0	1	1	0	0	0	0	0	0	0	0	0	0	0	1.000	2.000
2002	NYY, Milwaukee	.000	1	3	0	0	0	0	0	0	0	0	0	0	2	0	0	0	.000	.000
2003	NYY, Chicago (AL)	.000	1	2	0	0	0	0	0	0	0	0	0	0	2	0	0	0	.000	.000
2007	NYY, San Francisco	.333	1	3	0	1	1	0	0	0	0	0	0	0	0	0	0	0	.333	.333
All-Star Game Totals		**.182**	**5**	**11**	**0**	**2**	**2**	**0**	**0**	**0**	**0**	**0**	**0**	**0**	**5**	**0**	**0**	**0**	**.182**	**.364**

Posada's Career Fielding Record

Position	PCT	G	PO	A	E	TC	PB
Catcher	.992	1573	10009	694	90	10793	142
First Base	.992	28	117	12	1	130	--

JORGE POSADA

	2010					CAREER				
	AVG	AB	H	HR	RBI	AVG	AB	H	HR	RBI
Overall	.248	383	95	18	57	.275	5748	1583	261	1021
Minnesota	.714	7	5	1	2	.299	241	72	8	31
Tampa Bay	.250	36	9	4	8	.261	587	153	22	107
Texas	.250	16	4	1	1	.308	302	93	18	71
Atlanta	-	-	-	-	-	.213	47	10	1	4
Cincinnati	-	-	-	-	-	.188	16	3	0	2
Philadelphia	.333	6	2	1	1	.264	53	14	4	11
San Francisco	-	-	-	-	-	.238	21	5	0	2
March	-	-	-	-	-	.308	13	4	2	7
April	.310	58	18	5	12	.282	920	259	48	178
May	.355	31	11	1	2	.298	867	258	42	151
June	.203	74	15	3	14	.256	962	246	39	161
July	.247	73	18	3	10	.275	958	263	44	162
August	.259	81	21	4	12	.272	1021	278	44	185
September	.207	58	12	2	7	.274	959	263	40	172
October	.000	8	0	0	0	.250	48	12	2	5
Home	.288	198	57	11	33	.284	2729	774	141	512
Road	.205	185	38	7	24	.268	3019	809	120	509
vs. Left	.257	136	35	8	25	.295	1727	510	72	304
vs. Right	.243	247	60	10	32	.267	4021	1073	189	717

Posada's Career by Ballpark

Park	AVG	AB	H	HR	RBI	Park	AVG	AB	H	HR	RBI
AT&T Park	.273	11	3	0	1	Target Field	-	-	-	-	-
Citizens Bank Park	.231	13	3	1	2	Tropicana Field	.255	302	77	9	52
Great American BP	.125	8	1	0	1	Turner Field	.182	11	2	0	0
Rangers Ballpark	.264	140	37	9	25	Yankee Stadium	.306	389	119	25	77

POSADA'S CAREER HOME RUN CHART

MULTI-HOMER GAMES: 16. **TWO-HOMER GAMES:** 16, last 9/1/09 at Baltimore. **GRAND SLAMS:** 9, last on 6/13/10 vs. Houston (Casey Daigle). **PINCH-HIT HR:** 5, last on 9/14/10 at Tampa Bay (Dan Wheeler). **INSIDE-THE-PARK HR:** None. **WALK-OFF HR:** 2, last on 5/16/06 vs. Texas (Akinori Otsuka). **LEADOFF HR:** None.

Mariano Rivera

42
Right-handed Pitcher
6-2 • 185 • B/T: Right/Right
Opening Day Age: 40

Birthdate
November 29, 1969

Birthplace
Panama City, Panama

Resides
La Chorrera, Panama

M.L. Service
14 years, 105 days

Career Highlights
A.L. All-Star Team
▸ 1997, 1999, 2000,
2001, 2002, 2004,
2005, 2006, 2008,
2009

**League Championship
Series MVP**
▸ 2003

World Series MVP
▸ 1999

**Sporting News Pro
Athlete of the Year**
▸ 2009

**Sporting News A.L.
Reliver of the Year**
▸ 1997, 1999, 2009

**A.L. Rolaids Relief
Man Award**
▸ 1999, 2001, 2004,
2005, 2006, 2009

**MLB Delivery Man of
the Year**
▸ 2005, 2006, 2009

Status
▸ Signed as a non-drafted free agent on February 17, 1990…signed a three-year contract on December 17, 2007 that extends through the 2010 season.

Postseason Notes
▸ Has 39 career postseason saves—including 11 in the World Series—both Major League records…his 24 World Series appearances are the most all time…owns a 0.74 ERA (133.1IP, 11ER) in 88 postseason games, the lowest ERA all-time (min. 30.0IP) and the most postseason appearances for any pitcher in Major League history…owns 14 career 2.0-inning saves in the postseason.
▸ Leads all Major Leaguers with 34 appearances and 16 saves during the ALDS…has also pitched in a Major League-high 30 ALCS games, collecting an all-time-record 12 saves.
▸ Was a part of his fifth World Championship team in 2009, making 12 postseason appearances, recording five saves (in five opportunities) and allowing just 1ER in 16.0IP (0.56 ERA)…six of the outings were more than 1.0 inning, including two 2.0-inning saves (Game 6 of ALCS and Game 2 of WS)…was on the mound for the clinching game in each of the three rounds for the fourth time in his career…with two World Series saves, became the second-oldest pitcher to earn a save in a World Series game behind Baltimore's Dick Hall (age 40 in 1971)…has been the Yankees final pitcher in each of their last four World Series wins (1998, '99, 2000 and '09).

2010 Highs and Streaks	
Low hit CG	N/A
IP (start)	N/A
IP (relief)	2.0 - 3 times
	Last: at TEX, 9/10/10
Hits	3 - 2 times
	Last: at TEX, 8/10/10
Runs	2 - 2 times
	Last: vs. BOS, 9/26/10
BB	2 - at TEX, 9/11/10
SO	3 - 2 times
	Last: at LAD, 6/27/10
HR	1 - 2 times
	Last: at BAL, 9/19/10
Winning Streak	3g - 6/23-7/16/10
Losing Streak	2g - 8/10-9/11/10
Consec. Saves	11 - 2 times
	Last: 7/5-9/4/10

Career Highs and Streaks	
Low hit CG	N/A
IP (start)	8.0 - at CWS, 7/4/95
IP (relief)	5.1 - at SEA, 8/25/95
Hits	8 - at CAL, 5/23/95
Runs	7 - vs. OAK, 6/6/95
BB	4 - 2 times
	Last: at SEA, 8/23/97
SO	11 - at CWS, 7/4/95
HR	2 - 4 times
	Last: vs. TB, 5/7/09
Winning Streak	5g - 3 times
	Last: 5/28-7/25/03
Losing Streak	3g - 3 times
	Last: 4/15-5/7/07
Consec. Saves	36 - 4/30-9/14/09

Career Notes
▸ Owns 559 career saves, the most ever in AL history and second-most all time behind Trevor Hoffman (601)…has converted 559-of-626 save opportunities in his career (89.3%).
▸ Has a career ERA of 2.23, the second-lowest all time among pitchers with at least 1,000.0IP since earned runs became an official statistic (1912-NK, 1913-AL), behind Eddie Cicotte (2.20), and just ahead of Jim Scott (2.26) and Babe Ruth (2.28)—credit: *Elias Sports Bureau*.
▸ With Derek Jeter and Jorge Posada, have become the first trip of teammates in MLB, NBA, NFL and NHL history to play together in each of 16 straight seasons (credit: *Elias Sports Bureau*).
▸ Has recorded at least one save in 15 consecutive seasons (since 1996)…according to the *Elias Sports Bureau*, ties Tom Burgmeier's AL record (1970-84) and is tied for the sixth-longest streak all time.
▸ Has reached the 30-save plateau 13 times in his career, including each of his last

eight seasons (2002-10)…joins Trevor Hoffman (1995-2002) as the only Major Leaguers to register 30 saves in eight straight seasons…has at least 25 saves in 14 straight seasons (since 1997), surpassing Lee Smith (13) for the longest such streak since saves became an official stat in 1969.

▸ Converted 51 straight saves at home from 8/18/07-4/30/10, tied for the longest streak all time (Eric Gagne–51 from 8/28/02-7/1/04)—credit: *Elias*.

▸ Has made 978 career appearances, 455 more than any other pitcher in Yankees history (Dave Righetti is second with 523)…ranks second among all active pitchers in career appearances, trailing only Trevor Hoffman (1,035).

▸ Has appeared in at least 60 games 13 times in his career, tied with Mike Stanton (13) for most all time.

▸ Has made at least 60 appearances with a sub-2.00 ERA in each of the last three seasons…is the only pitcher in Baseball history to record three such seasons in consecutive years after the age of 35…has accomplished the feat in seven of his last eight seasons.

▸ Was named to his 11th All-Star team in 2010, joining Derek Jeter as the only players to be named to the All-Star team with their current team at least 11 times…both players now tie Bill Dickey (11) for fifth-most in franchise history, trailing Mickey Mantle (20), Yogi Berra (19), Joe DiMaggio (13) and Elston Howard (12)…did not attend the game to rest sore right knee and left side.

2010

▸ Was 3-3 with 33 saves (in 38 chances) and a 1.80 ERA in 61 relief appearances with the Yankees in 2010…opponents batted .183 (39-for-213, 2HR); LH .214 (22-for-103, 2HR), RH .155 (17-for-110, 0HR)…retired 49-of-61 first batters faced (80.3%)…prevented 13-of-16 inherited runners from scoring (81.3%)…appeared in consecutive games 15 times and three straight games once…his five blown saves were his most since 2003 (six).

▸ Just five of his 61 relief outings—and one of his 33 saves—were more than 1.0IP…51 of his 61 outings were scoreless.

▸ Made his 15th career Opening Day roster in 2010, most among all current Yankees.

▸ Did not allow a run in his first 11.0IP of the season…according to the *Elias Sports Bureau*, matched his second-longest scoreless streak to begin a season (also 11.0IP in 1998 and 16.0 in 2008).

▸ With his save on 4/6 at Boston, became the second pitcher in franchise history to record a save after turning 40 (40 years, 129 days), joining Jim Kaat, who earned two saves as a 40-year-old in 1979 (40 years, 312 days when he notched the second such save)—credit: *Elias Sports Bureau*.

▸ Collected his 1,014th and 1,015th career strikeouts in 4/30 save vs. Chicago-AL, tying and surpassing Roger Clemens (1,014) for sole possession of 10th place on the Yankees' all-time strikeouts list (1.0IP, 2K).

▸ Went 11 days between appearances from 4/30-5/11…was the second-longest gap between appearances in his 15 seasons as a reliever (not including D.L. stints)…went 21 days between outings from 8/31-9/22/06.

▸ In 5/16 loss vs. Minnesota, registered first blown save since 9/18/09 at Seattle after entering the game with the bases loaded and two outs in the eighth inning…walked in a run and allowed a grand slam to his next batter (Kubel) before recording his first and only out (0.1IP, 1H, 2ER, 1BB, 1K, 1HR)…was his fourth career grand slam surrendered and third as a reliever (also Bill Selby "walk-off" GS on 7/14/02 at Cleveland – ninth inning; Bobby Bonilla on 9/15/95 at Baltimore – sixth inning; and Geronimo Berroa on 6/6/95 vs. Oakland – third inning)…was the fourth bases-loaded walk issued in his career and first since 5/6/05 vs. Oakland (Keith Ginter).

▸ Recorded two saves in the same day for the sixth time in his career on 5/26 at Minnesota (also 5/3/07 at Texas; 9/16/97 vs. Boston, 7/8/00 in a split-stadium doubleheader vs. the Mets; 9/13/03 vs. Tampa Bay and 9/29/04 vs. Minnesota)…the first of the two saves came in the completion of 5/25 win at Minnesota and was credited to that day.

▸ Did not allow a run over a 16-appearance stretch from 5/25-7/2, holding opponents to just 5H and 3BB (1IBB) in 18.0IP while converting each of his 10 save opportunities (1HP, 20K)…allowed just 1ER over a 27-appearance stretch (27.2IP) from 5/25-8/8.

▸ Was voted as the winner of June's "Major League Baseball Clutch Performer of the Month Award Presented by Pepsi"…went 2-0 in 11 relief appearances in June, converting each of his seven save opportunities without allowing a run in 13.0IP (4H, 2BB, 16K).

▸ Held opponents hitless in 25 straight at-bats from 6/1-23 between a Luke Scott single on 6/1 at Baltimore and Stephen Drew's single on 6/23 at Arizona…also held right-handed batters hitless in 21 consecutive AB against him prior to Justin Upton's double on 6/23 at Arizona (streak started after Jason Bay double on 5/21 at New York-NL)—credit: *Elias*.

▸ Tossed 2.0 scoreless innings to earn his first win on 6/23 at Arizona…pitched out of a bases-loaded, no-out situation in the bottom of the 10th without allowing the tying run to score…recorded the 1,028th and 1,029th strikeouts of his career, tying and surpassing Al Downing (1,028) for sole possession of ninth place on the Yankees' all-time list…was the 944th appearance of his career, tying Rollie Fingers for 18th place on Baseball's all-time list…also had his third career at-bat (and fourth plate appearance) in the game, grounding out to first in the 10th inning.

▸ Made his second 2.0-inning outing in a five-day span on 6/27 at Los Angeles-NL – recording the win in both games…marked the first time he tossed at least 2.0IP twice in a five-day stretch since 7/6/08 vs. Boston and 7/9/08 vs. Tampa Bay, when he also recorded the win in both games.

▸ Earned the 550th save of his career in 8/11 win at Texas, tossing a scoreless ninth (1.0IP, 1H)…allowed a lead-off triple that he left stranded there.

▸ Earned his first save of the season of more than 1.0 inning in 8/21 win vs. Seattle, allowing 1ER in 1.1IP (2H, 1K) for his 25th save.

MOST POSTSEASON SAVES SINCE 1969

1.	**MARIANO RIVERA**	**39**
2.	Brad Lidge	16
3.	Dennis Eckersley	15
4.	Jason Isringhausen	11
	Robb Nen	11

MOST CONSECUTIVE SEASONS WITH AT LEAST ONE SAVE (ALL TIME)
List courtesy of the *Elias Sports Bureau*

1.	John Franco (1984-2001)	18
2.	Lee Smith (1981-1997)	17
T3.	Gene Garber (1973-1988)	16
	Goose Gossage (1974-1989)	16
	Jeff Reardon (1979-1994)	16
T6.	**MARIANO RIVERA (1996-2010)**	**15**
	Tom Burgmeier (1970-1984)	15
	Doug Jones (1986-2000)	15
	Kent Tekulve (1975-1989)	15

▸ Had three blown saves in September, his most in a calendar month since August 2003 (four)—credit: *Elias*…allowed 9H and 6ER in 5.2IP (9.53 ERA) in a six-game stretch from 9/11-26, going 0-1 with three saves in six opportunities…had allowed just 30H and 6ER in 52.2IP (1.03 ERA) over his first 53 appearances of the season, going 3-2 with 29 saves in 31 chances.

▸ Suffered his third loss and third blown save of the season on 9/11 at Texas, allowing 2H, 2ER and 2BB/1IBB in 0.1IP (1HBP)…was his first blown save on the road since 9/18/09 at Seattle.

▸ Allowed solo HR to Luke Scott to lead off the ninth in 9/19 loss at Baltimore to record his fourth blown save of the season and second on the road trip (also 9/11 at Texas)…was just his second home run allowed in 2010 (also Jason Kubel on 5/16 at Minnesota).

▸ Suffered his fifth blown save of the season and third in eight opportunities in September in 9/26 win vs. Boston, allowing 2H and 2ER in 1.1IP…was his first blown save at home against Boston since back-to-back blown saves on 4/5 and 4/6/05…allowed four stolen bases in the ninth inning, marking the first time a Yankees reliever allowed 4SB in a single inning since Lindy McDaniel in 1969—credit: *Elias*.

▸ Earned the save in the Yankees' final regular season win on 10/2 at Boston in Game 1 of a doubleheader (1.0IP, 1K).

RIVERA SAVE COMBINATIONS

Category	2010	Career	Postseason Career
0.1IP	1	22 (last, 4/15/10 vs. LAA)	None
0.2IP	1	14 (last, 4/13/10 vs. LAA)	None
1.0IP	30	408 (last, 10/2/10 at BOS)	9 (last on 11/1/09 at PHI in WS Game 4)
1.1IP	1	70 (last, 8/21/10 vs. SEA)	10 (last on 10/11/09 at MIN in ALDS Game 3)
1.2IP	0	34 (last, 8/29/08 vs. TOR)	6 (last on 10/18/01 at SEA in ALCS Game 2)
2.0IP	0	10 (last, 7/16/06 vs. CWS)	14 (last on 10/29/09 vs. PHI in WS Game 2)
2.1IP	0	1 (8/23/96 vs. OAK)	None

**Saved each win of a postseason series: Once (2000 ALDS vs. Oakland)

Rivera's Career Pitching Record

Year	Club	W	L	ERA	G	GS	CG	SHO	SV	IP	H	R	ER	HR	HP	BB	SO	WP	BK
1990	GCL Yankees	5	1	0.17	22	1	1	1	1	52.0	17	3	1	0	2	7	58	2	0
1991	Greensboro	4	9	2.75	29	15	1	0	0	114.2	103	48	35	2	3	36	123	3	0
1992	Ft. Lauderdale	5	3	2.28	10	10	3	1	0	59.1	40	17	15	5	0	5	42	0	0
1993	GCL Yankees	0	1	2.25	2	2	0	0	0	4.0	2	1	1	0	0	1	6	1	0
	Greensboro	1	0	2.06	10	10	0	0	0	39.1	31	12	9	0	0	15	32	2	0
1994	Tampa	3	0	2.21	7	7	0	0	0	36.2	34	12	9	2	2	12	27	0	0
	Albany	3	0	2.27	9	9	0	0	0	63.1	58	20	16	5	0	8	39	1	1
	Columbus	4	2	5.81	6	6	1	1	0	31.0	34	22	20	5	0	10	23	0	1
1995	Columbus	2	2	2.1	7	7	1	1	0	30.0	25	10	7	2	0	3	30	0	0
	YANKEES	5	3	5.51	19	10	0	0	0	67.0	71	43	41	11	2	30	51	0	1
1996	YANKEES	8	3	2.09	61	0	0	0	5	107.2	73	25	25	1	2	34	130	1	0
1997	YANKEES	6	4	1.88	66	0	0	0	43	71.2	65	17	15	5	0	20	68	2	0
1998	YANKEES - a	3	0	1.91	54	0	0	0	36	61.1	48	13	13	3	1	17	36	0	0
1999	YANKEES	4	3	1.83	66	0	0	0	45	69.0	43	15	14	2	3	18	52	2	1
2000	YANKEES	7	4	2.85	66	0	0	0	36	75.2	58	26	24	4	0	25	58	2	0
2001	YANKEES	4	6	2.34	71	0	0	0	50	80.2	61	24	21	5	1	12	83	1	0
2002	YANKEES - b, c, d	1	4	2.74	45	0	0	0	28	46.0	35	16	14	3	2	11	41	1	1
	GCL Yankees	0	0	0.00	1	1	0	0	0	2.0	2	0	0	0	0	1	2	0	0
2003	YANKEES - e	5	2	1.66	64	0	0	0	40	70.2	61	15	13	3	4	10	63	0	0
2004	YANKEES	4	2	1.94	74	0	0	0	53	78.2	65	17	17	3	5	20	66	0	0
2005	YANKEES	7	4	1.38	71	0	0	0	43	78.1	50	18	12	2	4	18	80	0	0
2006	YANKEES	5	5	1.80	63	0	0	0	34	75.0	61	16	15	3	5	11	55	0	0
2007	YANKEES	3	4	3.15	67	0	0	0	30	71.1	68	25	25	4	6	12	74	1	0
2008	YANKEES	6	5	1.40	64	0	0	0	39	70.2	41	11	11	4	2	6	77	1	0
2009	YANKEES	3	3	1.76	66	0	0	0	44	66.1	48	14	13	7	1	12	72	1	0
2010	YANKEES	3	3	1.80	61	0	0	0	33	60.0	39	14	12	2	5	11	45	0	0
Minor League Totals		27	18	2.35	103	68	7	3	1	432.1	346	145	113	21	7	98	382	9	2
Major League Totals		74	55	2.23	978	10	0	0	559	1150.0	887	309	285	62	43	267	1051	12	3

*Denotes league leader

Signed by New York (AL) as a non-drafted free agent on February 17, 1990.

a - Was placed on the 15-day disabled list with a strained right groin on April 6 - 24, 1998.
b - Was placed on the 15-day disabled list with a strained groin from June 9 - 25, 2002.
c - Was placed on the 15-day disabled list with a right shoulder muscle strain from July 21 - August 8, 2002.
d - Was placed on the 15-day disabled list with a right shoulder muscle strain from August 19 - September 21, 2002.
e - Was placed on the 15-day disabled list from March 30 - April 29, 2003 with a strained right groin.

	2010											Career										
	W	L	SV	ERA	G	GS	IP	H	HR	ER	SO	W	L	SV	ERA	G	GS	IP	H	HR	ER	SO
Overall	3	3	33	1.80	61	0	60.0	39	2	12	45	74	55	559	2.23	978	10	1150.0	887	62	285	1051
Minnesota	0	0	2	5.40	4	0	3.1	1	1	2	1	4	3	28	1.42	47	1	63.1	41	2	10	60
Tampa Bay	1	0	3	1.69	6	0	5.1	6	0	1	3	5	5	57	1.63	89	0	94.0	68	3	17	103
Texas	0	2	2	5.79	5	0	4.2	7	0	3	4	5	4	34	2.49	64	1	79.2	82	3	22	56
Atlanta	-	-	-	-	-	-	-	-	-	-	-	0	1	8	3.27	10	0	11.0	7	1	4	14
Cincinnati	-	-	-	-	-	-	-	-	-	-	-	0	0	1	0.00	2	0	2.1	3	0	0	3
Philadelphia	-	-	-	-	-	-	-	-	-	-	-	1	0	5	1.69	9	0	10.2	6	1	2	11
San Diego	-	-	-	-	-	-	-	-	-	-	-	0	0	3	0.00	4	0	4.0	1	0	0	9
San Francisco	-	-	-	-	-	-	-	-	-	-	-	0	1	2	0.00	3	0	3.2	2	0	0	4
March	-	-	-	-	-	-	-	-	-	-	-	0	0	0	0.00	1	0	1.0	0	0	0	2
April	0	0	7	0.00	10	0	9.0	3	0	0	9	10	9	74	2.29	136	0	157.0	124	9	40	146
May	0	1	3	3.68	8	0	7.1	5	1	3	4	9	10	94	1.93	159	2	187.0	145	10	40	154
June	2	0	7	0.00	11	0	13.0	4	0	0	16	11	10	109	2.15	168	2	200.2	140	10	48	206
July	1	0	5	0.96	10	0	9.1	7	0	1	7	17	9	96	2.24	168	4	208.2	161	12	52	196
August	0	1	5	2.00	10	0	9.0	8	0	2	2	14	9	104	2.27	181	1	214.0	179	14	54	179
September	0	1	5	4.76	11	0	11.1	12	1	6	6	13	8	76	2.69	154	1	170.1	134	7	51	158
October	0	0	1	0.00	1	0	1.0	0	0	0	1	0	0	6	0.00	11	0	11.1	4	0	0	10
Home	1	1	14	2.20	31	0	28.2	18	1	7	25	53	33	268	2.54	505	5	585.0	469	34	165	538
Road	2	2	19	1.44	30	0	31.1	21	1	5	20	21	22	291	1.91	473	5	565.0	418	28	120	513

Rivera's Career By Ballpark

Park	W	L	SV	ERA	G	GS	IP	ER	Park	W	L	SV	ERA	G	GS	IP	ER
AT&T Park	0	0	1	0.00	1	0	1.2	0	Target Field	0	0	2	0.00	2	0	2.0	0
Citizens Bank Park	0	0	1	0.00	2	0	3.0	0	Tropicana Field	0	1	33	0.76	44	0	47.1	4
Great American BP	0	0	0	0.00	1	0	1.0	0	Turner Field	0	0	5	0.00	5	0	6.0	0
Rangers Ballpark	2	2	17	2.59	32	1	41.2	12	Yankee Stadium	4	3	38	1.98	70	0	68.1	15

Rivera's Division Series Record

Year	Club vs. Opp.	W	L	ERA	G	GS	CG	SHO	SV	IP	H	R	ER	HR	HP	BB	SO	WP	BK
1995	NYY vs. SEA	1	0	0.00	3	0	0	0	0	5.1	3	0	0	0	0	1	8	0	0
1996	NYY vs. TEX	0	0	0.00	2	0	0	0	0	4.2	0	0	0	0	0	1	1	0	0
1997	NYY vs. CLE	0	0	4.50	2	0	0	0	1	2.0	2	1	1	1	0	0	1	0	0
1998	NYY vs. TEX	0	0	0.00	3	0	0	0	2	3.1	1	0	0	0	0	1	2	0	0
1999	NYY vs. TEX	0	0	0.00	2	0	0	0	2	3.0	1	0	0	0	0	0	3	1	0
2000	NYY vs. OAK	0	0	0.00	3	0	0	0	3	5.0	2	0	0	0	0	0	2	0	0
2001	NYY vs. OAK	0	0	0.00	3	0	0	0	2	5.0	4	1	0	0	0	0	4	0	0
2002	NYY vs. ANA	0	0	0.00	1	0	0	0	1	1.0	1	0	0	0	0	0	0	0	0
2003	NYY vs. MIN	0	0	0.00	2	0	0	0	2	4.0	0	0	0	0	0	0	4	0	0
2004	NYY vs. MIN	1	0	0.00	4	0	0	0	0	5.2	2	0	0	0	0	0	2	0	0
2005	NYY vs. LAA	0	0	3.00	2	0	0	0	2	3.0	1	1	1	1	0	0	2	0	0
2006	NYY vs. DET	0	0	0.00	1	0	0	0	0	1.0	1	0	0	0	0	0	0	0	0
2007	NYY vs. CLE	0	0	0.00	3	0	0	0	0	4.2	2	0	0	0	0	1	6	0	0
2009	NYY vs. MIN	0	0	0.00	3	0	0	0	1	3.2	4	0	0	0	0	1	7	0	0
Division Series Totals		**2**	**0**	**0.35**	**34**	**0**	**0**	**0**	**16**	**51.1**	**24**	**3**	**2**	**1**	**1**	**6**	**42**	**1**	**0**

Rivera's League Championship Series Record

Year	Club vs. Opp.	W	L	ERA	G	GS	CG	SHO	SV	IP	H	R	ER	HR	HP	BB	SO	WP	BK
1996	NYY vs. BAL	1	0	0.00	2	0	0	0	0	4.0	6	0	0	0	0	1	5	0	0
1998	NYY vs. CLE	0	0	0.00	4	0	0	0	1	5.2	0	0	0	0	0	1	5	0	0
1999	NYY vs. BOS	1	0	0.00	3	0	0	0	2	4.2	5	0	0	0	0	0	3	0	0
2000	NYY vs. SEA	0	0	1.93	3	0	0	0	1	4.2	4	1	1	0	0	0	1	0	0
2001	NYY vs. SEA	1	0	1.93	4	0	0	0	2	4.2	2	1	1	0	0	1	3	2	0
2003	NYY vs. BOS	1	0	1.13	4	0	0	0	2	8.0	5	1	1	0	0	0	6	0	0
2004	NYY vs. BOS	0	0	1.29	5	0	0	0	2	7.0	6	1	1	0	0	2	6	0	0
2009	NYY vs. LAA	0	0	1.29	5	0	0	0	2	7.0	3	1	1	0	0	2	4	0	0
LCS Totals		**4**	**0**	**0.99**	**30**	**0**	**0**	**0**	**12**	**45.2**	**31**	**5**	**5**	**0**	**0**	**7**	**33**	**2**	**0**

Rivera's World Series Record

Year	Club vs. Opp.	W	L	ERA	G	GS	CG	SHO	SV	IP	H	R	ER	HR	HP	BB	SO	WP	BK
1996	NYY vs. ATL	0	0	1.59	4	0	0	0	0	5.2	4	1	1	0	0	3	4	0	0
1998	NYY vs. SD	0	0	0.00	3	0	0	0	3	4.1	5	0	0	0	0	0	4	0	0
1999	NYY vs. ATL	1	0	0.00	3	0	0	0	2	4.2	3	0	0	0	0	1	3	0	0
2000	NYY vs. NYM	0	0	3.00	4	0	0	0	2	6.0	4	2	2	1	1	1	7	0	0
2001	NYY vs. ARI	1	1	1.42	4	0	0	0	1	6.1	6	2	1	0	1	1	7	0	0
2003	NYY vs. FLA	0	0	0.00	2	0	0	0	1	4.0	2	0	0	0	0	0	4	0	0
2009	NYY vs. PHI	0	0	0.00	4	0	0	0	2	5.1	3	0	0	0	0	2	3	0	0
World Series Totals		**2**	**1**	**0.99**	**24**	**0**	**0**	**0**	**11**	**36.1**	**27**	**5**	**4**	**1**	**2**	**8**	**32**	**0**	**0**
POSTSEASON TOTALS		**8**	**1**	**0.74**	**88**	**0**	**0**	**0**	**39**	**133.1**	**82**	**13**	**11**	**2**	**3**	**21**	**107**	**3**	**0**

Rivera's All-Star Game Record

Year	Club, Site	W	L	ERA	G	GS	CG	SHO	SV	IP	H	R	ER	HR	HP	BB	SO	WP	BK
1997	NYY, Cleveland	0	0	0.00	1	0	0	0	1	1.0	0	0	0	0	0	0	1	0	0
1999	NYY, Boston								Selected - Did Not Pitch											
2000	NYY, Atlanta	0	0	0.00	1	0	0	0	0	1.0	2	1	0	0	0	0	0	0	0
2001	NYY, Seattle								Selected - Did Not Pitch											
2002	NYY, Milwaukee	0	0	0.00	1	0	0	0	0	1.0	1	0	0	0	0	0	0	0	0
2004	NYY, Houston	0	0	0.00	1	0	0	0	0	1.0	0	0	0	0	0	0	0	0	0
2005	NYY, Detroit	0	0	0.00	1	0	0	0	1	0.1	0	0	0	0	0	0	1	0	0
2006	NYY, Pittsburgh	0	0	0.00	1	0	0	0	1	1.0	0	0	0	0	0	0	0	0	0
2008	NYY, New York (AL)	0	0	0.00	1	0	0	0	0	1.2	2	0	0	0	0	0	2	0	0
2009	NYY, St. Louis	0	0	0.00	1	0	0	0	1	1.0	0	0	0	0	0	0	1	0	0
2010	NYY, Los Angeles								Selected - Did Not Pitch											
All-Star Game Totals		**0**	**0**	**0.00**	**8**	**0**	**0**	**0**	**4**	**8.0**	**5**	**1**	**0**	**0**	**0**	**0**	**5**	**0**	**0**

Rivera's Regular Season Batting Record

Year	Team	AVG	G	AB	R	H	2B	3B	HR	RBI	SH	SF	HP	BB	SO	SB	CS
2010	NYY	.000	61	1	0	0	0	0	0	0	0	0	0	0	0	0	0
Major League Totals		.000	978	3	0	0	0	0	1	0	0	0	1	1	0	0	

Rivera's Career Fielding Record

Position	PCT	G	PO	A	E	TC	DP
Pitcher	.982	978	103	232	6	341	11

David Robertson

30   Right-handed Pitcher
5-11 • 190 • B/T: Right/Right
Opening Day Age: 24

Birthdate
April 9, 1985

Birthplace
Birmingham, Ala.

Resides
Tampa, Fla.

M.L. Service
2 years, 70 days

College
University of Alabama

Status
▸ Selected by the Yankees in the 17th round of the 2006 First-Year Player Draft…signed through the 2010 season.

Postseason Notes
▸ Did not allow a run in five appearances during the 2009 postseason, tossing 5.1 scoreless innings (4H, 3BB, 3K)…earned the win in each of his first two postseason appearances (ALDS Game 2 vs. Minnesota and ALCS Game 2 vs. Los Angeles-AL), as the Yankees recorded "walk-off" wins in each contest.

2010
▸ Was 4-5 with one save and a 3.82 ERA in 64 relief appearances with the Yankees in 2010…opponents batted .258 (59-for-229, 5HR); LH .268 (26-for-97, 2HR), RH .250 (33-for-132, 3HR)…retired 43-of-64 first batters faced (67.2%)…prevented 23-of-33 inherited runners from scoring (69.7%)…appeared in consecutive games 10 times and three straight games twice.
▸ Of his 64 relief outings, 48 were 1.0 inning or less (75.0%)…50 of his 64 outings were scoreless.
▸ Ranked seventh among all AL relievers with 10.42K/9.0IP.
▸ Made his first career Opening Day roster in 2010.
▸ Allowed 11ER over his first 10 appearances of the season from 4/4-5/7 (7.1IP)…in 54 appearances from 5/8 through the end of the season, posted a 2.50 ERA (54.0IP, 15ER)…held opponents scoreless in 45 of those 54 outings.
▸ Made his second appearance in as many days in 5/16 loss vs. Minnesota, tossing a season-high 2.0 scoreless IP (2BB, 2K, 1BK)…was his longest outing since 7/31/09 at Chicago-AL (also 2.0IP).
▸ Faced three batters before being removed from 5/29 loss vs. Cleveland with a mild lower back strain (0.1IP, 1H, 2ER, 1HBP)…did not pitch for six days.
▸ Allowed just 1ER in 9.0IP over nine relief appearances from 6/5-27.
▸ Surrendered a season-high-tying 4ER and was charged with the loss on 7/2 vs. Toronto, allowing all 4R in the 11th inning…following that outing, pitched to a 2.06 ERA over the remainder of the season.
▸ Earned his first win of the season on 7/4 vs. Toronto, tossing a scoreless 10th inning (1.0IP, 1H, 1BB, 1IBB, 1K).
▸ Pitched to a 2.27 ERA (31.2IP, 8ER) in 33 appearances after the All-Star break with 39 strikeouts.
▸ Did not allow a run in 19 consecutive appearances from 7/4-8/21 (18.1IP, 9H, 8BB, 24K)…according to *Elias*, held opponents hitless in 23 consecutive at-bats prior to Willie Bloomquist's ninth-inning double on 8/12 at Kansas City, the longest such streak of his career.
▸ Earned his second career save in 8/12 win at Kansas City (also 7/27/09 at Tampa Bay), allowing 2H in 0.1IP (1K).

2010 Highs and Streaks

Low hit CG	N/A
IP (start)	N/A
IP (relief)	2.0 - 2 times
	Last: vs. TB, 5/20/10
Hits	4 - vs. LAA, 4/13/10
Runs	4 - 2 times
	Last: vs. TOR, 7/2/10
BB	3 - vs. TOR, 9/3/10
SO	4 - vs. TB, 5/20/10
HR	2 - vs. BAL, 5/5/10
Winning Streak	2g - 7/4-31/10
Losing Streak	3g - 4/27-7/2/10

Career Highs and Streaks

Low hit CG	N/A
IP (start)	N/A
IP (relief)	2.0 - 10 times
	Last: vs. TB, 5/20/10
Hits	4 - 4 times
	Last: vs. LAA, 4/13/10
Runs	5 - vs. BAL, 7/28/08
BB	3 - 3 times
	Last: vs. TOR, 9/3/10
SO	4 - 3 times
	Last: vs. TB, 5/20/10
HR	2 - vs. BAL, 5/5/10
Winning Streak	5g - 7/19/08-6/4/09
Losing Streak	3g - 4/27-7/2/10

DAVID ROBERTSON

▸ Entered 8/18 win vs. Detroit with the bases loaded and no outs in the eighth and retired each of his three batters faced (1.0IP)…allowed just one inherited runner to score on Brandon Inge's sacrifice fly.

▸ Allowed solo-HR to Bautista in the eighth on 8/23 at Toronto to suffer his fourth loss (1.0IP, 1H, 1ER, 1BB, 3K)…was his first run allowed since 7/4.

▸ Appeared in 14 of the Yankees' final 28 games of the season…earned the win in back-to-back outings on 9/14 at Tampa Bay and 9/17 at Baltimore.

▸ Went 1-0 with one save and a 4.50 ERA in nine spring training relief outings with the Yankees (8.0IP, 10H, 4ER, 5BB, 8K, 1HR).

Robertson's Career Pitching Record

YEAR	Club	W	L	ERA	G	GS	CG	SHO	SV	IP	H	R	ER	HR	HB	BB	SO	WP	BK
2007	Charleston	5	2	0.77	24	0	0	0	3	47.0	25	5	4	0	0	15	67	5	0
	Tampa	3	1	1.08	18	0	0	0	1	33.1	18	6	4	0	0	15	37	2	0
	Trenton	0	0	2.25	2	0	0	0	0	4.0	2	1	1	0	0	2	9	1	0
2008	Trenton	0	0	0.96	9	0	0	0	2	18.2	8	2	2	0	1	6	26	1	0
	Scranton/WB	4	0	2.06	21	0	0	0	1	35.0	20	11	8	1	1	17	51	1	0
	YANKEES	4	0	5.34	25	0	0	0	1	30.1	29	18	18	3	0	15	36	6	0
2009	Scranton/WB	0	3	1.84	8	0	0	0	2	14.2	10	7	3	0	0	6	25	0	0
	YANKEES	2	1	3.30	45	0	0	0	1	43.2	36	19	16	4	1	23	63	6	0
2010	YANKEES	4	5	3.82	64	0	0	0	1	61.1	59	26	26	5	3	33	71	7	2
Minor League Totals		12	6	1.30	82	0	0	0	9	152.2	83	32	22	1	2	61	215	10	0
Major League Totals		10	6	3.99	134	0	0	0	2	135.1	124	63	60	12	4	71	170	19	2

Selected by the Yankees in the 17th round of the 2006 First-Year Player Draft.

	2010											Career									
	W	L	SV	ERA	G	GS	IP	H	HR	ER	SO	W	L	SV	ERA	G	GS	IP	H	HR	ER	SO
Overall	4	5	1	3.82	64	0	61.1	59	5	26	71	10	6	2	3.99	134	0	135.1	124	12	60	170
Minnesota	0	0	0	0.00	3	0	4.0	3	0	0	2	1	0	0	0.00	7	0	8.1	4	0	0	6
Tampa Bay	2	0	0	1.04	7	0	8.2	4	0	1	13	2	0	1	2.19	11	0	12.1	8	1	3	15
Texas	0	0	0	2.25	3	0	4.0	3	0	1	2	1	0	0	3.00	10	0	12.0	5	1	4	14
Atlanta	-	-	-	-	-	-	-	-	-	-	-	0	0	0	10.80	2	0	1.2	3	2	2	3
Cincinnati	-	-	-	-	-	-	-	-	-	-	-	-	-	-	-	-	-	-	-	-	-	-
Philadelphia	0	0	0	0.00	2	0	2.0	0	0	0	2	0	0	0	0.00	2	0	2.0	0	0	0	2
San Francisco	-	-	-	-	-	-	-	-	-	-	-	-	-	-	-	-	-	-	-	-	-	-
Home	1	2	0	4.60	29	0	29.1	23	3	15	34	6	2	0	4.10	63	0	63.2	48	7	29	79
Road	3	3	1	3.09	35	0	32.0	36	2	11	37	4	4	2	3.89	71	0	71.2	76	5	31	91

Robertson's Career By Ballpark

Park	W	L	SV	ERA	G	GS	IP	ER	Park	W	L	SV	ERA	G	GS	IP	ER
AT&T Park	-	-	-	-	-	-	-	-	Target Field	0	0	0	0.00	1	0	1.2	0
Citizens Bank Park	-	-	-	-	-	-	-	-	Tropicana Field	2	0	1	2.70	6	0	6.2	2
Great American BP	-	-	-	-	-	-	-	-	Turner Field	0	0	0	10.80	2	0	1.2	2
Rangers Ballpark	0	0	0	3.68	6	0	7.1	3	Yankee Stadium	3	2	0	3.65	50	0	49.1	20

Robertson's Division Series Record

Year	Club vs. Opp.	W	L	ERA	G	GS	CG	SHO	SV	IP	H	R	ER	HR	HP	BB	SO	WP	BK
2009	NYY vs. MIN	1	0	0.00	1	0	0	0	0	1.0	1	0	0	0	0	0	0	0	0
Division Series Totals		1	0	0.00	1	0	0	0	0	1.0	1	0	0	0	0	0	0	0	0

Robertson's League Championship Series Record

Year	Club vs. Opp.	W	L	ERA	G	GS	CG	SHO	SV	IP	H	R	ER	HR	HP	BB	SO	WP	BK
2009	NYY vs. LAA	1	0	0.00	2	0	0	0	0	2.0	1	0	0	0	0	2	1	0	0
LCS Totals		1	0	0.00	2	0	0	0	0	2.0	1	0	0	0	0	2	1	0	0

Robertson's World Series Record

Year	Club vs. Opp.	W	L	ERA	G	GS	CG	SHO	SV	IP	H	R	ER	HR	HP	BB	SO	WP	BK
2009	NYY vs. PHI	0	0	0.00	2	0	0	0	0	2.1	2	0	0	0	0	1	2	0	0
World Series Totals		0	0	0.00	2	0	0	0	0	2.1	2	0	0	0	0	1	2	0	0
POSTSEASON TOTALS		2	0	0.00	5	0	0	0	0	5.1	4	0	0	0	0	3	3	0	0

Robertson's Regular Season Batting Record

Year	Team	AVG	G	AB	R	H	2B	3B	HR	RBI	SH	SF	HP	BB	SO	SB	CS
2010	NYY					Did Not Bat											
Major League Totals		-	134	-	-	-	-	-	-	-	-	-	-	-	-	-	-

Robertson's Career Fielding Record

Position	PCT	G	PO	A	E	TC	DP
Pitcher	1.000	134	1	11	0	12	0

Alex Rodriguez

13

Third Baseman

6-3 • 228 • B/T: Right/Right

Opening Day Age: 34

Birthdate
July 27, 1975

Birthplace
New York, N.Y.

Resides
Miami, Fla.

M.L. Service
16 years, 11 days

Career Highlights
A.L. Most Valuable Player
▸ 2003, 2005, 2007

A.L. All-Star Team
▸ 1996, 1997, 1998, 2000, 2001, 2002, 2003, 2004, 2005, 2006, 2007, 2008, 2010

A.L. Silver Slugger Award
▸ 1996, 1998, 1999, 2000, 2001, 2002, 2003, 2005, 2007, 2008

Gold Glove Award
▸ 2002, 2003

Baseball America Player of the Year
▸ 2000, 2002, 2007

Sporting News Player of the Year
▸ 1996, 2002, 2007

Status

▸ Acquired from the Texas Rangers with cash in exchange for 2B Alfonso Soriano and a player to be named later (INF Joaquin Arias) on February 16, 2004…signed a seven-year contract with player options for three additional years on December 11, 2000…opted out of the contract on October 28, 2007…was re-signed by the Yankees to a 10-year contract on December 17, 2007…contract extends through the 2017 season.

Postseason Notes

▸ Owns a .302 (60-for-199) career batting average with 36R, 14 doubles, 13HR and 35RBI in 54 career postseason games…is tied for fourth among active Major Leaguers in postseason home runs, ranks sixth with a .568 slugging percentage, is eighth with a .409 on-base percentage, is tied for ninth in runs scored and ranks 10th in RBI.

▸ Hit .365 (19-for-52) with 15R, 5 doubles, 6HR and 18RBI in the 2009 postseason, leading the Yankees in batting average, runs, home runs and RBI and tying for tops in doubles…hit three game-tying HR in the seventh inning or later, the most such HR ever for a player in their postseason career (credit: *Elias Sports Bureau*)…hit ninth-inning, two-run home run (off Joe Nathan) to tie ALDS Game 2 win vs. Minnesota and seventh-inning solo HR (off Carl Pavano) to tie ALDS Game 3 clincher at Minnesota…tied the game with a solo HR (off Brian Fuentes) in the 11th inning of ALCS Game 2 win vs. Los Angeles-AL…matched Bernie Williams (6HR in 1996) for the most home runs in a single postseason in franchise history, and was 1HR shy of tying the AL record (Anaheim's Troy Glaus–7HR in 2002 and Tampa Bay's B.J. Upton–7HR in 2008)…his solo HR on 10/31/09 in Game 4 of the World Series at Philadelphia became the first playoff homer to be reviewed by video replay.

▸ Drove in a run in 11 of 15 postseason games in 2009 and set a franchise record with 18RBI, falling 1RBI shy of the all-time postseason record shared by Cleveland's Sandy Alomar, Jr. (1997), Anaheim's Scott Spiezio (2002) and Boston's David Ortiz (2004)…eight of his RBI tied the game or put the Yankees ahead…drove in at least one run in eight straight playoff games from 10/8/07 (ALDS Game 4) to 10/20/09 (ALCS Game 4), matching the all-time record (also Lou Gehrig and Philadelphia's Ryan Howard)…joined Boston's David Ortiz (2004) as the only two players to record three game-tying or go-ahead RBI hits in the ninth inning or later in a single postseason.

2010 Highs and Streaks

Hits	4 - at KC, 8/14/10
Runs	3 - 4 times
	Last: at KC, 8/14/10
2B	2 - 2 times
	Last: vs. KC, 7/22/10
3B	1 - 2 times
	Last: at OAK, 4/21/10
HR	3 - at KC, 8/14/10
RBI	6 - vs. KC, 5/31/10
BB	3 - 4 times
	Last: at ARI, 6/23/10
SO	3 - 4 times
	Last: at TEX, 8/11/10
SB	1 - 4 times
	Last: at KC, 8/14/10
Hit Streak	7g - 2 times
	Last: 5/31-6/6/10

Career Highs and Streaks

Hits	5 - 5 times
	Last: at TEX, 5/25/09
Runs	5 - 2 times
	Last: vs. TB, 4/18/05
2B	3 - vs. SEA, 4/7/01
3B	1 - 29 times
	Last: at OAK, 4/21/10
HR	3 - 4 times
	Last: at KC, 8/14/10
RBI	10 - vs. LAA, 4/26/05
BB	5 - vs. KC, 4/23/00
SO	4 - 4 times
	Last: at KC, 4/8/08
SB	3 - 2 times
	Last: vs. BOS, 9/25/09
Single-Season Hit Streak	20g - 8/16-9/4/96
Hit Streak	23g - 9/25/06-4/23/07

ALEX RODRIGUEZ

- Collected 11 extra-base hits in the 2009 playoffs, tying six others—including Hideki Matsui (2004)—for most in a single postseason (credit: *Elias*)…was hit by a pitch three times in the World Series, tying Pittsburgh's Max Carey (1925) and teammate Mark Teixeira (2009) for the all-time record.
- Snapped a 19AB hitless streak with runners in scoring position with his fifth-inning RBI single (driving in Derek Jeter) in 2009 ALDS Game 1 win vs. Minnesota…the single also snapped an 0-for-18 career postseason mark with runners in scoring position and two outs…was 2-for-3 with RISP in the game, all with two outs (also RBI single in the seventh, driving in Jeter).
- Won the Babe Ruth Award from the New York Chapter of the Baseball Writers Association of America as the 2009 postseason MVP.
- Went 4-for-6 with 3RBI in 2004 ALDS Game 2 vs. Minnesota, driving in the game-tying run with a 12th-inning double…with 5R in 2004 ALCS Game 3 at Boston, matched the single-game postseason record for runs scored (also Hideki Matsui in the same game)…homered in back-to-back games in the 2004 ALCS vs. Boston, driving in the game-tying run in Game 3 and a go-ahead run in Game 4.

> **Century City**
> Has driven in at least 100 runs while playing fewer than 140 games in each of the last three seasons…the only other players ever to have three such consecutive seasons were Joe DiMaggio (1939-41) and Chick Hafey (1928-30)…joins DiMaggio as the only players to also have at least 30HR in each of those three seasons—credit: *Elias*.

Career Notes

- Ranks sixth on Baseball's all-time list with 613 career home runs…in 2010, passed Hall of Famer Frank Robinson (586), Mark McGwire (583) and Sammy Sosa (609)…ranks seventh on the Yankees' all-time list with 268 HR.
- Is the only player in Baseball history to collect at least 30HR and 100RBI at least 14 times in his career…has accomplished the feat in each of the last 13 seasons (1998-2010), surpassing Jimmie Foxx (12) for the longest such streak all time.
- Has reached 30HR in 13 consecutive seasons and 14 times in his career…only one player has hit at least 30HR in as many consecutive seasons: Barry Bonds (13)…is tied with Bonds (14) for second-most 30-homer seasons all-time behind Hank Aaron (15)…his 13 consecutive seasons with at least 25HR are tied with Willie Mays (13) for third-longest in Major League history behind Babe Ruth and Barry Bonds (each 15 straight)…his 14 overall seasons with at least 25HR are tied with Jim Thome for most among active players…his 15 consecutive seasons of at least 20HR are tied with Bonds for the third-longest in Major League history behind Hank Aaron (20) and Babe Ruth (16)—credit: *Elias Sports Bureau*.
- Owns 58 career multi-homer games (four in 2010), marking the seventh-most multi-homer games all-time.
- According to the *Elias Sports Bureau*, his 599HR were the most for any player prior to turning 35 years old (on 7/27/10)…collected the most hits (2,629) and games played (2,259) for any player prior to turning 35 since Robin Yount (2,733H and 2,436G)…recorded the third-most RBI (1,787) for any player prior to turning 35 behind only Lou Gehrig (1,910) and Jimmie Foxx (1,884)–credit: *Elias*.
- Has hit 21 career grand slams, tying Manny Ramirez (21) for second place all-time behind Lou Gehrig (23)…in his career, is 5-for-6 with 1BB, 3HR, 1SF and 18RBI in 8PA after Mark Teixeira has been intentionally walked to load the bases in front of him (credit: STATS, Inc.).
- 21 of his career home runs have come in the ninth inning or later and tied the game or given his team the lead…has nine "walk-off" home runs in his career, tied with Vladimir Guerrero for third-most among active players behind Jim Thome (12) and David Ortiz (10).
- Has collected 100RBI in 13 consecutive seasons and 14 times in his career…marks the most 100RBI seasons all time…his current streak of 13 straight seasons with at least 100RBI matches Lou Gehrig (1926-38) and Jimmie Foxx (1929-41) for the longest such stretch all time.
- Is one of six players all time to collect at least 600HR and 2,500H (also Hank Aaron, Barry Bonds, Ken Griffey Jr., Willie Mays and Babe Ruth).
- Is one of three players all time with 400 doubles, 600HR and 300SB, joining Barry Bonds (601/762/514) and Willie Mays (523/660/338).
- Over the last 10 seasons (2001-10), leads the Majors in home runs (424) and RBI (1,236).
- Has hit 268HR with the Yankees after hitting 189HR with Seattle and 156HR with Texas…according to the *Elias Sports Bureau*, joins Paul Konerko as the only active players with at least 300HR for teams other than the one for which they made their Major League debut.
- Is one of eight players to hit at least 250 HR for his current team, joining teammate Jorge Posada, Chipper Jones, Albert Pujols, Paul Konerko, Todd Helton, David Ortiz and Ryan Howard—credit: *Elias Sports Bureau*.
- Has compiled over 3,000AB with the Yankees and Mariners, joining Manny Ramirez (Indians and Red Sox) and Ken Griffey, Jr. (Seattle and Cincinnati) as the only current Major Leaguers with at least 3,000AB for each of two different teams…joins Dave Winfield (3,997AB with San Diego) as the only players to accumulate 3,000 at-bats with the Yankees and at least that many for another team (credit: *Elias*).

ALEX RODRIGUEZ

- Is the all-time leader with 174 Interleague RBI and ranks second in Interleague hits (267) and third in runs (161).
- Was selected to his 13th All-Star team in 2010—the most among active Major League players—by American League All-Star Manager Joe Girardi (did not play).

2010

- Hit .270 (141-for-522) with 74R, 29 doubles, 30HR and 125RBI in 137 games (122 starts at 3B, 12 at DH) with the Yankees in 2010…ranked second in the Majors in RBI…had 16 game-winning RBI this season, tied with Chicago-AL's Paul Konerko and Toronto's Vernon Wells for most such RBI by an AL player…13 of his 30HR (43.3%) tied the game or gave the Yankees the lead…led the Majors with 4.18 AB/RBI…58 of his 125RBI (46.4%) either tied the game or gave the Yankees the lead.
- Had a Major League-leading 48RBI in the seventh inning or later in 2010, 20 of which tied the game or put the team ahead…hit four go-ahead home runs in the seventh inning or later in 2010 and had nine such homers since the start of 2009…according to *Elias*, had just seven go-ahead homers in the seventh inning or later from 2004-08.

LAST 10 SEASONS, MAJORS (2001-2010)		
MOST HOME RUNS		
1.	ALEX RODRIGUEZ	**424**
2.	Albert Pujols	408
3.	Jim Thome	356
4.	Adam Dunn	354
5.	David Ortiz	329
MOST RUNS SCORED		
1.	Albert Pujols	1,186
2.	ALEX RODRIGUEZ	**1,130**
3.	DEREK JETER	1,080
4.	Johnny Damon	1,060
5.	Ichiro Suzuki	1,047
MOST RBI		
1.	ALEX RODRIGUEZ	**1,236**
2.	Albert Pujols	1,230
3.	David Ortiz	1,055
4.	Vladimir Guerrero	1,029
5.	Manny Ramirez	1,026

- Played in 137 games and drove in 125 runs in 2010…since RBI became an official statistic in 1920, only nine different players (12 occasions) have recorded more RBI than Rodriguez while playing 137G or fewer, including just two Yankees–Babe Ruth in 1929 (154RBI) and '32 (137) and Joe DiMaggio in 1939 (126) and '40 (133).
- Hit 11 sacrifice flies in 2010, matching his single-season career high (also 11 in 2000 w/ Seattle)…according to *Elias*, combined for just eight sacrifice flies in 2008 and '09.
- Was 9-for-20 (.450) with 3HR (tied for most in the Majors) and a Major League-leading 34RBI this season with the bases loaded.
- Hit three grand slams in 2010, marking the fourth time in his career he hit at least three grand slams in a season (also 1996, '99 and 2007)…according to *Elias*, the only other player with at least four seasons with three-or-more grand slams is Jimmie Foxx (1932, '34, '38 and '40)…became the third Yankee to hit three grand slams before the All-Star break (also Lou Gehrig – four in 1934; and Don Mattingly – three in 1987).
- Since the start of 2009, has been involved in driving in the game-winning or tying run in seven of the Yankees' 20 "walk-off" innings (two game-ending HRs, two game-tying HRs, two game-winning runs scored and hit the pop-up resulting in a two-run "walk-off" error vs. the Mets).
- Committed just two errors over his final 81 games (80 starts) at 3B beginning on 5/27…made 5E in his first 43 games of the season (4/4-5/26)…went 45 straight games (44 starts) at third base without making an error from 7/17-9/28, marking his third-longest errorless stretch at 3B in his career (46 games from 5/30-7/23/07 and 61 games from 6/23-9/1/05)…ranked fourth among all Major League third basemen with a .976 fielding percentage…only Jhonny Peralta (5E) and Placido Polanco (5E) committed fewer errors than Rodriguez (7E) among players with at least 100G at 3B.

MOST RBI, SINGLE POSTSEASON, ALL TIME		
1.	Sandy Alomar, Jr.	19 (1997, CLE)
	David Ortiz	19 (2004, BOS)
	Scott Spiezio	19 (2002, ANA)
4.	**ALEX RODRIGUEZ**	**18 (2009, NYY)**

- Made his 14th career Opening Day roster…was his sixth Opening Day start at 3B after making eight Opening Day starts at SS…joined Manny Ramirez (seven Opening Day starts in RF and eight in LF) as the only active players to make at least six Opening Day starts at two different positions in their career…the last player to do so at both SS and 3B was Cal Ripken Jr. (credit: *Elias Sports Bureau*)…also made his sixth Opening Day start at 3B with Derek Jeter at SS, matching Bucky Dent and Graig Nettles (six) and Frank Crosetti and Red Rolfe (six) for most such starts in franchise history.
- Hit just 2HR in April, his lowest home run total of his career for a calendar month (min. 70AB)—credit: *Elias*.
- Reached the 1,000-hit plateau as a Yankee with his second-inning single off Wade Davis in 4/10 win at Tampa Bay…became the 39th player to reach the plateau with the Yankees and first since Jorge Posada on 8/20/05 at the White Sox…had 966H with Seattle (1994-2000) and 569 with Texas (2001-03)…the *Elias Sports Bureau* notes he became the second player to have 1,000H with other team(s) prior to getting 1,000 with the Yankees, joining Dave Winfield (1,134 w/ San Diego from 1973-80; and 1,300 w/ the Yankees from 1981-88, '90).
- Hit his 584th career home run on 4/17 vs. Texas, surpassing Mark McGwire for sole possession of eighth place on Baseball's all-time list…the home run also snapped a 41AB homerless stretch to begin the season, his longest such stretch to begin a campaign since 1995 when he homered in his 49th at-bat and third-longest of his career (did not homer in 54AB in 1994 rookie season).

- Snapped an 0-for-19 stretch with a first-inning double in 4/30 win vs. Chicago-AL, his longest hitless stretch since a career-high-tying 0-for-21 from 7/25-8/2/07.

- Batted .330 (34-for-103) with 18R, 5 doubles, 5HR, 27RBI and 14BB in 27 games in May.

- Snapped a 61AB homerless stretch in 5/9 loss at Boston, hitting his 586th career home run to tie Frank Robinson for seventh place on Baseball's all-time list.

- Hit game-winning grand slam and was 2-for-3 with 1BB in 5/14 win vs. Minnesota...was also his 587th career home run, breaking a tie with Frank Robinson for sole possession of seventh place on Baseball's all-time list...the Twins intentionally walked Mark Teixeira prior to the grand slam.

- Did not record an RBI over a seven-game stretch from 5/20-27, marking his longest drought without driving in a run since a nine-game span from 5/9-18/07.

- Hit his 20th career grand slam—the first of back-to-back homers with Cano—and was 3-for-4 with 6RBI in 5/31 win vs. Cleveland...surpassed Eddie Murray for sole possession of third place on Baseball's all-time grand slams list...became the fifth Yankee to hit two grand slams in a season before the end of May, joining Gehrig (1934), Tony Lazzeri (1936), Russ Derry (1945) and Alfonso Soriano (2003)—credit: *Elias Sports Bureau*.

- Did not play in four games from 6/11-15 (hip flexor tendinitis).

- Hit game-winning two-run HR in the eighth in 7/1 win vs. Seattle...was his 250th as a Yankee, tying Graig Nettles for eighth place on the team's all-time list...came in his 963rd game with the Yankees...according to *Elias*, the only player to reach the 250-homer plateau with the Yankees in fewer games was Babe Ruth in 1925 (774th game).

- Hit grand slam and solo HR in 7/6 win at Oakland...was his 21st career grand slam and third in 2010...was his 55th career multi-HR game (first of 2010), surpassing Manny Ramirez (54) for most among active players.

- Had 70RBI prior to the All-Star break for the seventh time in his career, tying Ted Williams for the most such seasons in Major League history...no other player has done it six times (credit: *Elias*).

- Collected a Major League-best 31RBI in July, marking his most RBI in a calendar month since September 2007 (also 31RBI)...was his fourth 30RBI month as a Yankee (also April and June 2007-both 34RBI)...are the most such months by a Yankee since Mickey Mantle (July 1952, May 1956, June 1957 and June 1961).

- With 5HR and 31RBI in July, became the first Yankee to drive in at least 30 runs in a calendar month with fewer than 7HR in that month since Paul O'Neill in September 1999 (5HR, 31RBI)—credit: *Elias Sports Bureau*.

- Hit first-inning, two-run HR—the 600th HR of his career—in 8/4 win vs. Toronto, becoming the seventh player in Major League history to accomplish the feat...at 35 years, 8 days old, became the youngest player ever to hit his 600th career home run, surpassing Babe Ruth (36 years, 196 days)...the home run came in his 2,267th career game, trailing only Ruth (2,044) for fewest games needed to reach the mark...joined Ruth (600th HR on 8/21/31 at St. Louis) as the only players to hit his 600th career homer as a Yankee...came exactly three years to the day after he hit his 500th home run (8/4/07 vs. Kansas City, off Kyle Davies)...snapped a 46 at-bat homerless stretch and an 0-for-17 stretch overall with the home run...hit .196 (9-for-46) with 3 doubles and 8RBI between his 599th and 600th home runs (7/22-8/3).

- Stole his 300th career base in the sixth inning of 8/8 win at Boston.

- Hit three home runs—solo-HR and two two-run HRs—and established a season-high with four hits in 8/14 win at Kansas City, going 4-for-5...hit the three homers in consecutive plate appearances off three different pitchers (a span of five pitches)...was his fourth career three-homer game and first sicne 4/26/05 vs. Los

MOST GRAND SLAMS, ALL TIME

1.	Lou Gehrig	23
2.	Manny Ramirez	21
	ALEX RODRIGUEZ	**21**
4.	Eddie Murray	1t9
5.	Willie McCovey	18
	Robin Ventura	18

MOST "WALK-OFF" HOME RUNS AMONG ACTIVE PLAYERS

1.	Jim Thome	12
2.	David Ortiz	10
3.	**ALEX RODRIGUEZ**	**9**
	Vladimir Guerrero	9

credit: *Elias Sports Bureau*

MOST HOME RUNS, ALL-TIME

1.	Barry Bonds	762
2.	Hank Aaron	755
3.	Babe Ruth	714
4.	Willie Mays	660
5.	Ken Griffey, Jr.	630
6.	**ALEX RODRIGUEZ**	**613**
7.	Sammy Sosa	609
8.	Jim Thome	589
9.	Frank Robinson	586
10.	Mark McGwire	583

AMONG ACTIVE PLAYERS

GAMES PLAYED

1.	Omar Vizquel	2,850
2.	Ivan Rodriguez	2,499
3.	Jim Thome	2,391
4.	**ALEX RODRIGUEZ**	**2,303**
5.	Manny Ramirez	2,297

RUNS SCORED

1.	**ALEX RODRIGUEZ**	**1,757**
2.	DEREK JETER	1,685
3.	Johnny Damon	1,564
4.	Manny Ramirez	1,544
5.	Jim Thome	1,534

HITS

1.	DEREK JETER	2,926
2.	Ivan Rodriguez	2,817
3.	Omar Vizquel	2,799
4.	**ALEX RODRIGUEZ**	**2,672**
5.	Manny Ramirez	2,573

RBI

1.	**ALEX RODRIGUEZ**	**1,831**
2.	Manny Ramirez	1,830
3.	Jim Thome	1,624
4.	Chipper Jones	1,491
5.	Vladimir Guerrero	1,433

ALEX RODRIGUEZ

Angeles-AL.

▸ Missed three games from 8/17-19 with tightness in his left calf…was 0-for-1 in 8/20 loss vs. Seattle before being removed for PH (Kearns) in the fourth with the same injury…was placed on the 15-day disabled list the next day through 9/5 with the injury (missed 14 team games).

▸ Hit 9HR with 28RBI in 25 games over the remainder of the season after being reinstated from the disabled list on 9/5, ranking third in the Majors in home runs and second in RBI.

▸ Was named the MLB "AL Player of the Month" for September (.309, 25-for-81) with 15R, 9HR and 26RBI in 22 games during the month.

▸ Hit second-inning solo HR and ninth-inning, game-winning three-run HR and was 2-for-5 with 2R and 4RBI in 9/17 win at Baltimore…drove in all four of the Yankees' runs…marked the third time in his career he drove in all of his team's runs in a one-run victory (also 4/27/97 w/ Seattle at Toronto, 2-1 win and 7/30/04 vs. Baltimore, 2-1 win)—credit: *Elias*.

▸ Hit 4HR in the Yankees' three-game series vs. Boston from 9/24-26.

▸ Hit solo HR in the sixth and two-run HR in the seventh and was 2-for-4 with 1BB in 9/24 loss vs. Boston…were his 609th and 610th career home runs, tying and surpassing Sammy Sosa (609) for sole possession of sixth place all-time…was his 58th career multi-HR game (54th two-homer game) and fourth this season.

Rodriguez' Career Playing Record

Year	Club	AVG	G	AB	R	H	2B	3B	HR	RBI	SH	SF	HP	BB	SO	SB	CS	E	OBP	SLG
1994	Appleton	.319	65	248	49	79	17	6	14	55	1	3	2	24	44	16	5	19	.379	.605
	Jacksonville	.288	17	59	7	17	4	1	1	8	0	0	0	10	13	2	1	3	.391	.441
	SEATTLE	.204	17	54	4	11	0	0	0	2	1	1	0	3	20	1	0	6	.241	.204
	Calgary	.311	32	119	22	37	7	4	6	21	0	0	1	8	25	2	4	3	.359	.588
1995	Tacoma	.360	54	214	37	77	12	3	15	45	1	2	2	18	44	2	4	10	.411	.654
	SEATTLE	.232	48	142	15	33	6	2	5	19	1	0	0	6	42	4	2	8	.264	.408
1996	SEATTLE - a	.358	146	601	141	215	54	1	36	123	6	7	4	59	104	15	4	15	.414	.631
	Tacoma	.200	2	5	0	1	0	0	0	0	0	0	0	2	1	0	0	1	.429	.200
1997	SEATTLE - b	.300	141	587	100	176	40	3	23	84	4	1	5	41	99	29	6	24	.350	.496
1998	SEATTLE	.310	161	686	123	213	35	5	42	124	3	4	10	45	121	46	13	18	.360	.560
1999	SEATTLE - c	.285	129	502	110	143	25	0	42	111	1	8	5	56	109	21	7	14	.357	.586
2000	SEATTLE - d	.316	148	554	134	175	34	2	41	132	0	11	7	100	121	15	4	10	.420	.606
2001	TEXAS - e	.318	162	632	133	201	34	1	52	135	0	9	16	75	131	18	3	18	.399	.622
2002	TEXAS	.300	162	624	125	187	27	2	57	142	0	4	10	87	122	9	4	10	.392	.623
2003	TEXAS	.298	161	607	124	181	30	6	47	118	0	6	15	87	126	17	3	8	.396	.600
2004	YANKEES - f	.286	155	601	112	172	24	2	36	106	0	7	10	80	131	28	4	13	.375	.512
2005	YANKEES	.321	162	605	124	194	29	1	48	130	0	3	16	91	139	21	6	12	.421	.610
2006	YANKEES	.290	154	572	113	166	26	1	35	121	0	4	8	90	139	15	4	24	.392	.523
2007	YANKEES	.314	158	583	143	183	31	0	54	156	0	9	21	95	120	24	4	13	.422	.645
2008	YANKEES - g	.302	138	510	104	154	33	0	35	103	0	5	14	65	117	18	3	10	.392	.573
2009	YANKEES - h	.286	124	444	78	127	17	1	30	100	0	3	8	80	97	14	2	9	.402	.532
2010	YANKEES - i	.270	137	522	74	141	29	2	30	125	0	11	3	59	98	4	3	7	.341	.506
Minor League Totals		**.327**	**170**	**645**	**115**	**211**	**40**	**14**	**36**	**129**	**2**	**5**	**5**	**62**	**127**	**22**	**14**	**36**	**.388**	**.600**
Major League Totals		**.303**	**2303**	**8826**	**1757**	**2672**	**474**	**29**	**613**	**1831**	**16**	**93**	**152**	**1119**	**1836**	**301**	**72**	**219**	**.387**	**.571**
NYY Total		**.296**	**1027**	**3833**	**748**	**1136**	**189**	**7**	**268**	**840**	**0**	**42**	**80**	**559**	**839**	**124**	**26**	**88**	**.393**	**.559**

* League leader   # Tied for league lead

Selected by Seattle in the first round (first pick overall) of the 1993 First-Year Player Draft.

a - Placed on the 15-day disabled list from April 22 - May 7, 1996 with a pulled left hamstring.
b - Placed on the 15-day disabled list from June 12-27, 1997 with a deep chest bruise.
c - Placed on the 15-day disabled list from April 7 - May 14, 1999 with torn cartilage in his left knee.
d - Placed on the 15-day disabled list from July 8-24, 2000 with a right knee strain.
e - Signed by Texas as a free agent on December 11, 2000.
f - Traded to New York (AL) on February 16, 2004 with cash in exchange for 2B Alfonso Soriano and player to be named later (INF Joaquin Arias).
g - Placed on the 15-day disabled list from April 30 - May 20, 2008 with a strained right quadriceps.
h – Placed on the 15-day disabled list on April 4 (retroactive to March 27) – May 8, 2009 with a right hip labral tear.
i – Placed on the 15-day disabled list from August 21-September 4, 2010 with a strained left calf.

ALEX RODRIGUEZ

	2010					CAREER				
	AVG	AB	H	HR	RBI	AVG	AB	H	HR	RBI
Overall	.270	522	141	30	125	.303	8826	2672	613	1831
Minnesota	.273	22	6	1	5	.328	488	160	45	115
Tampa Bay	.250	68	17	3	11	.277	676	187	44	133
Texas	.360	25	9	2	8	.316	412	130	18	76
Atlanta	-	-	-	-	-	.300	50	15	2	9
Cincinnati	-	-	-	-	-	.182	22	4	0	0
Philadelphia	.286	7	2	0	1	.250	28	7	2	5
San Francisco	-	-	-	-	-	.478	69	33	6	24
March	-	-	-	-	-	.120	25	3	1	2
April	.250	84	21	2	14	.311	1203	374	86	258
May	.330	103	34	5	27	.311	1456	453	104	302
June	.244	82	20	4	13	.302	1496	452	86	283
July	.248	195	26	5	31	.295	1576	465	106	321
August	.226	53	12	5	12	.313	1600	501	126	329
September	.309	81	25	9	26	.290	1401	406	98	319
October	.214	14	3	0	2	.261	69	18	6	17
Home	.294	228	67	15	62	.310	4343	1346	315	938
Road	.252	294	74	15	63	.296	4483	1326	298	893
vs. Left	.217	143	31	6	35	.290	2150	623	149	430
vs. Right	.290	379	110	24	90	.307	6676	2049	464	1401

Rodriguez' Career by Ballpark

Park	AVG	AB	H	HR	RBI	Park	AVG	AB	H	HR	RBI
AT&T Park	.625	24	15	2	9	Target Field	.182	11	2	0	0
Citizens Bank Park	.222	9	2	0	1	Tropicana Field	.263	323	85	22	59
Great American Ball Park	-	-	-	-	-	Turner Field	.308	26	8	1	6
Rangers Ballpark	.331	1154	382	97	267	Yankee Stadium	.277	455	126	33	102

Rodriguez' Division Series Record

YEAR	TEAM	AVG	G	AB	R	H	2B	3B	HR	RBI	SH	SF	HP	BB	SO	SB	CS	E	OBP	SLG
1995	SEA vs. NYY	.000	1	1	1	0	0	0	0	0	0	0	0	0	0	0	0	0	.000	.000
1997	SEA vs. BAL	.313	4	16	1	5	1	0	1	1	0	0	0	0	5	0	0	0	.313	.563
2000	SEA vs. CWS	.308	3	13	0	4	0	0	0	2	1	0	0	0	2	0	1	0	.308	.308
2004	NYY vs. MIN	.421	4	19	3	8	3	0	1	3	0	0	0	2	1	2	1	0	.476	.737
2005	NYY vs. LAA	.133	5	15	2	2	1	0	0	0	0	0	2	6	5	1	1	1	.435	.200
2006	NYY vs. DET	.071	4	14	0	1	0	0	0	0	0	0	1	0	4	0	0	1	.133	.071
2007	NYY vs. CLE	.267	4	15	2	4	0	0	1	1	0	0	0	2	6	0	0	0	.353	.467
2009	NYY vs. MIN	.455	3	11	4	5	0	0	2	6	0	0	0	1	2	0	0	0	.500	1.000
Division Series Totals		**.279**	**28**	**104**	**13**	**29**	**5**	**0**	**5**	**13**	**1**	**0**	**3**	**11**	**25**	**3**	**3**	**2**	**.364**	**.471**

Rodriguez' League Championship Series Record

Year	Club vs. Opp.	AVG	G	AB	R	H	2B	3B	HR	RBI	SH	SF	HP	BB	SO	SB	CS	E	OBP	SLG
1995	SEA vs. CLE	.000	1	1	0	0	0	0	0	0	0	0	0	0	1	0	0	0	.000	.000
2000	SEA vs. NYY	.409	6	22	4	9	2	0	2	5	0	0	0	3	8	1	0	0	.480	.773
2004	NYY vs. BOS	.258	7	31	8	8	2	0	2	5	0	0	2	4	6	0	0	0	.378	.516
2009	NYY vs. LAA	.429	6	21	6	9	2	0	3	6	0	1	0	8	3	1	0	0	.567	.952
LCS Totals		**.347**	**20**	**75**	**18**	**26**	**6**	**0**	**7**	**16**	**0**	**1**	**2**	**15**	**18**	**2**	**0**	**0**	**.462**	**.707**

Rodriguez' World Series Record

Year	Club vs. Opp.	AVG	G	AB	R	H	2B	3B	HR	RBI	SH	SF	HP	BB	SO	SB	CS	E	OBP	SLG
2009	NYY vs. PHI	.250	6	20	5	5	3	0	1	6	0	0	3	3	8	1	0	1	.423	.550
World Series Totals		**.250**	**6**	**20**	**5**	**5**	**3**	**0**	**1**	**6**	**0**	**0**	**3**	**3**	**8**	**1**	**0**	**1**	**.423**	**.550**
POSTSEASON TOTALS		**.302**	**54**	**199**	**36**	**60**	**14**	**0**	**13**	**35**	**1**	**1**	**8**	**29**	**51**	**6**	**3**	**3**	**.409**	**.568**

ALEX RODRIGUEZ

Rodriguez' All-Star Game Record

Year	Club, Site	AVG	G	AB	R	H	2B	3B	HR	RBI	SH	SF	HP	BB	SO	SB	CS	E	OBP	SLG
1996	SEA, Philadelphia	.000	1	1	0	0	0	0	0	0	0	0	0	0	0	0	0	0	.000	.000
1997	SEA, Cleveland	.333	1	3	0	1	0	0	0	0	0	0	0	0	2	0	0	0	.333	.333
1998	SEA, Colorado	.667	1	3	2	2	0	0	1	1	0	0	0	0	1	0	0	0	.667	1.667
2000	SEA, Atlanta								Injured - Did Not Play											
2001	TEX, Seattle	.000	1	2	0	0	0	0	0	0	0	0	0	0	2	0	0	0	.000	.000
2002	TEX, Milwaukee	.000	1	2	0	0	0	0	0	0	0	0	0	0	2	0	0	0	.000	.000
2003	TEX, Chicago (AL)	.333	1	3	1	1	0	0	0	0	0	0	0	0	1	0	0	0	.333	.333
2004	NYY, Houston	.333	1	3	0	1	0	1	0	1	0	0	0	0	1	0	0	0	.333	1.000
2005	NYY, Detroit	.500	1	2	1	1	0	0	0	0	0	0	0	1	0	0	0	0	.667	.500
2006	NYY, Pittsburgh	.000	1	2	0	0	0	0	0	0	0	0	0	0	0	0	0	0	.000	.000
2007	NYY, San Francisco	.333	1	3	0	1	0	0	0	0	0	0	0	0	0	0	0	0	.333	.333
2008	NYY, New York (AL)	.000	1	2	0	0	0	0	0	0	0	0	0	0	1	0	0	0	.000	.000
2010	NYY, Los Angeles (AL)								Selected - Did Not Play											
All-Star Game Totals		**.269**	**11**	**26**	**4**	**7**	**0**	**1**	**1**	**2**	**0**	**0**	**1**	**10**	**1**	**0**	**0**	**.296**	**.462**

Rodriguez' World Baseball Classic Record

Year	Country, Site	AVG	G	AB	R	H	2B	3B	HR	RBI	SH	SF	HP	BB	SO	SB	CS	E	OBP	SLG
2006	USA, USA	.333	6	21	3	7	1	0	0	3	0	0	0	2	7	0	0	0	.391	.381

Rodriguez' Career Fielding Record

Position	PCT	G	PO	A	E	TC
Third Base	.964	992	617	1738	88	2443
Shortstop	.977	1272	2015	3605	131	5751

Rodriguez' Home Run Chart

MULTI-HOMER GAMES: 58. **TWO-HOMER GAMES:** 54, last on 9/24/10 vs. Boston. **THREE-HOMER GAMES:** 4, last on 8/14/10 at Kansas City. **GRAND SLAMS:** 21, last on 7/6/10 at Oakland (Trevor Cahill). **PINCH-HIT HR:** None. **INSIDE-THE-PARK HR:** None. **WALK-OFF HR:** 9 (six as a Yankee), last on 8/7/09 vs. Boston (Junichi Tazawa). **LEADOFF HR:** None.

Rodriguez' Career Postseason Home Run Chart

MULTI-HOME RUN GAMES: None. **TWO-HOMER GAMES:** None. **GRAND SLAMS:** None. **PINCH-HIT HOME RUNS:** None. **INSIDE-THE-PARK HOME RUNS:** None. **WALK-OFF HOME RUNS:** None. **LEADOFF:** None.

Consecutive World Championships

NEW YORK YANKEES (5)	**1949-1953**
NEW YORK YANKEES (4)	**1936-1939**
Oakland A's (3)	1972-1975
NEW YORK YANKEES (3)	**1998-2000**
Chicago Cubs (2)	1907-1908
Philadelphia A's (2)	1910-1911
Boston Red Sox (2)	1915-1916
New York Giants (2)	1921-1922
NEW YORK YANKEES (2)	**1927-1928**
Philadelphia A's (2)	1929-1930
NEW YORK YANKEES (2)	**1961-1962**
Cincinnati Reds (2)	1975-1976
New York Yankees (2)	1977-1978
Toronto Blue Jays (2)	1992-1993

CC Sabathia

52
Left-handed Pitcher
6-7 • 290 • B/T: Left/Left
Opening Day Age: 29

Birthdate
July 21, 1980

Birthplace
Vallejo, Calif.

Resides
Alpine, N.J.

M.L. Service
10 years

Career Highlights
A.L. Cy Young Award
▶ 2007

A.L. All-Star Team
▶ 2003, 2004, 2007, 2010

ALCS MVP
▶ 2009

Status
▶ Signed as a free agent to a seven-year contract on December 18, 2008…contract extends through the 2015 season.

Postseason Notes
▶ Will be taking part in his fourth straight postseason, the previous three coming with three different clubs (2009 w/ the Yankees, 2008 w/ Milwaukee and 2007 w/ Cleveland)…is 5-4 with a 4.40 ERA (61.1IP, 30ER) in 10 career postseason starts.

▶ Made five postseason starts for the World Champion Yankees in 2009, going 3-1 with a 1.98 ERA (36.1IP, 28H, 9R, 8ER, 9BB, 32K, 4HR, 1HP) and limiting opponents to 3ER or less in each outing…started Game 1 in all three rounds, making his other two starts on three-days' rest…earned 2009 ALCS MVP after winning both starts with a 1.13 combined ERA (16.0IP, 2ER)…won his Yankees postseason debut on 10/7 in Game 1 of the ALDS vs. Minnesota (6.2IP, 8H, 2R, 1ER, 0BB, 8K, 1HP)…became the third African-American Yankees pitcher to start a World Series game, joining Dock Ellis and Al Downing…became the seventh Yankee to record three-or-more wins in a single postseason, joining David Wells (1998), Andy Pettitte (2003 and '09), Mike Stanton (2000), Orlando Hernandez (1999 and 2000), Dave Righetti (1981) and Sparky Lyle (1977).

▶ Made two 2009 postseason starts on three days' rest (World Series Game 4 at Philadelphia and ALCS Game 4 at Los Angeles-AL), going 1-0 with a 2.45 ERA (14.2IP, 4ER)…made one other career postseason start on three-days' rest, taking the loss in 2008 NLDS Game 2 w/ Milwaukee vs. Philadelphia (3.2IP, 5ER).

▶ Won his first career postseason start in ALDS Game 3 on 10/13/01 vs. Seattle (w/ Cleveland)…at the time, was the second-youngest pitcher to win a Division Series game behind only Fernando Valenzuela (defeated Houston in 1981)…also became the third-youngest pitcher in Division Series history (youngest in ALDS history) to start a game behind Valenzuela (1981, 20 years, 339 days) and Rick Ankiel (2000, 21 years, 77 days).

2010 Highs and Streaks
Low hit CG	3 - vs. TEX, 4/16/10
IP (start)	8.2 - at KC, 8/12/10
IP (relief)	N/A
Hits	11 - 2 times
	Last: vs. KC, 7/22/10
Runs	7 - vs. TB, 9/23/10
BB	6 - at OAK, 4/22/10
SO	10 - at OAK, 7/6/10
HR	2 - 6 times
	Last: at CWS, 8/28/10
Winning Streak	9g - 6/3-7/22/10
Losing Streak	2g - 2 times
	Last: 7/27-8/1

Career Highs and Streaks
Low hit CG	1 - at PIT, 8/31/08
IP (start)	9.0 - 23 times
	Last: at BAL, 5/8/09
IP (relief)	N/A
Hits	13 - at MIN, 7/15/06
Runs	9 - 5 times
	Last: at TB, 10/2/09
BB	6 - 3 times
	Last: at OAK, 4/22/10
SO	13 - vs. KC, 9/14/07
HR	3 - 6 times
	Last: at DET, 7/5/07
Winning Streak	12g - 6/10-8/31/08
Losing Streak	5g - 7/6-30/05

Career Notes
▶ Since his debut in 2001, has a 157-88 (.641) record, marking the most wins in the Majors…is second in shutouts (11), third in complete games (30) and IP (2127.0), fourth in strikeouts (1,787) and fourth in GS (322) over the span…owns the fifth-highest winning percentage among active pitchers.

▶ Has gone 88-43 (.672) over the last five seasons (2006-10), ranking first in the Majors in strikeouts, second in wins, innings pitched (1154.1) and shutouts (9), and tied for fourth in starts (165) over the stretch.

▶ Among active Major League lefthanders (min 1,000.0IP), ranks second in ERA (3.57) and winning percentage (.641), third in wins (157), fourth in strikeouts (1,787), and sixth in IP (2127.0) and starts (322)…his career winning percentage is seventh-best among all lefthanders who began their careers in 1950 or later (min: 140 decisions).

▸ Turned 30 years old on 7/21/10…prior to his birthday, led all active Major League pitchers under 30 in wins (148), strikeouts (1,700) and IP (2027.1)…were the most wins prior to turning 30 since Greg Maddux had 151 wins before turning 30 on 4/14/96).

▸ Recorded 40 wins from 2009-10, marking the most by a Yankee over a two-season stretch since Tommy John's 43 wins from 1979 (21-9) to 1980 (22-9)…is also the first Yankee with at least 230.0IP in two consecutive seasons since Tommy John (1979-276.1IP and 1980-265.1IP)…according to the *Elias Sports Bureau*, is one of three Yankees since 1923 to win at least 19 games in each of his first two seasons with the club, joining Tommy John (1979-80) and Herb Pennock (19-6 in 1923 and 21-9 in 1924).

Date/Opp	Score	W/L	IP	H	R	ER	HR	BB	K	NP/K	ERA	Left game
4/4 at BOS	7-9	ND	5.1	6	5	5	0	2	4	104-58	8.44	Leading 5-4
4/10 at TB	10-0	W	7.2	1	0	0	0	2	5	111-69	3.46	Leading 8-0
4/16 vs. TEX	5-1	W	6.0^	3	1	1	0	0	9	73-58	2.84	Leading 5-1
4/22 at OAK	2-4	L	8.0^	4	4	3	1	6	5	97-51	3.00	Trailing 4-2
4/28 at BAL*	8-3	W	7.2	11	3	3	1	2	5	111-72	3.12	Leading 8-3
5/3 vs. BAL	4-1	W	8.0	6	1	1	1	2	2	106-67	2.74	Leading 4-1
5/8 at BOS	14-3	ND	4.2	4	3	3	2	2	4	89-52	3.04	Leading 6-3
5/13 at DET	0-6	L	6.0	9	6	6	2	0	4	79-55	3.71	Trailing 6-0
5/18 vs. BOS	6-7	ND	7.0	4	1	1	1	3	5	112-66	3.43	Leading 5-1
5/23 at NYM*	4-6	L	5.0	10	6	5	2	2	6	93-61	3.86	Trailing 6-0
5/29 vs. CLE	11-13	ND	6.0	7	5	5	0	2	5	113-78	4.16	Leading 10-5
6/3 vs. BAL	6-3	W	7.0	3	3	3	2	1	7	94-60	4.14	Leading 6-3
6/9 at BAL	4-2	W	7.0	9	2	2	0	3	8	114-72	4.01	Leading 4-2
6/15 vs. PHI	8-3	W	7.0	5	3	3	0	3	7	113-68	4.00	Leading 8-3
6/20 vs. NYM	4-0	W	8.0	4	0	0	0	2	6	100-66	3.68	Leading 4-0
6/25 at LAD	2-1	W	8.0	4	1	1	0	3	7	115-75	3.49	Leading 2-1
7/1 vs. SEA*	4-2	W	8.0	5	2	1	0	2	4	117-71	3.33	Leading 4-2
7/6 at OAK	6-1	W	7.2	7	1	1	0	3	10	118-74	3.19	Leading 6-1
7/11 at SEA	8-2	W	7.0	6	1	1	0	1	1	96-61	3.09	Leading 8-1
7/16 vs. TB	5-4	ND	7.0	8	4	3	0	4	6	113-66	3.13	Trailing 4-3
7/22 vs. KC	10-4	W	6.1	11	4	3	0	4	9	120-78	3.18	Leading 5-4
7/27 at CLE	4-1	L	7.0	4	4	2	0	3	5	123-79	3.15	Trailing 4-0
8/1 at TB	0-3	L	6.2	8	3	3	0	3	3	112-67	3.19	Trailing 3-0
8/7 vs. BOS*	5-2	W	8.0	6	2	2	1	1	4	101-62	3.14	Leading 5-2
8/12 at KC	4-3	W	8.2	10	3	3	0	2	3	110-67	3.14	Leading 4-1
8/17 vs. DET*	7-2	W	7.0	5	2	2	2	3	9	115-71	3.12	Leading 6-2
8/22 vs. SEA	10-0	W	6.0	3	0	0	0	0	8	76-54	3.02	Leading 8-0
8/28 at CWS	12-9	W	7.0	9	5	5	2	1	9	113-78	3.14	Leading10-5
9/2 vs. OAK	5-0	W	8.0	1	0	0	0	3	5	95-58	3.02	Leading 5-0
9/7 vs. BAL	2-6	L	6.1	9	6	5	1	1	5	109-74	3.14	Trailing 6-2
9/13 at TB*	0-1 (11)	ND	8.0	2	0	0	0	2	9	119-77	3.03	Tied 0-0
9/18 at BAL	11-3	W	7.0	7	3	3	1	1	4	104-68	3.05	Leading 8-3
9/23 vs. TB*	3-10	L	5.1	10	7	7	0	3	6	111-71	3.26	Trailing 4-3
9/28 at TOR*	6-1	W	8.1	3	1	1	1	2	8	111-67	3.18	Leading 6-1
Totals		21-7	237.2	209	92	84	20	74	197	--	3.18	

(*) Denotes start following a team loss – **Bold indicates season highs**

▸ Became the first pitcher to win at least 17 games in four consecutive years (2010: 21-7 w/ NYY; 2009: 19-8 w/ NYY; 2008: 17-10 w/ Cleveland and Milwaukee; and 2007: 19-7 w/ Cleveland), since Randy Johnson accomplished the feat in six straight years from 1997-2002.

▸ Has recorded at least 11 wins in each of his first 10 seasons to begin his Major League career, marking the longest such current streak among active pitchers.

▸ According to the *Elias Sports Bureau*, is the first pitcher to start at least 34 games in four consecutive years (2007-10) since San Francisco's Barry Zito accomplished the feat over a six-season stretch from 2001-06.

▸ Is 20-5 with a 2.95 ERA (237.2IP, 78ER) and a .220 opp. batting average against in 34 overall career starts at Yankee Stadium including the postseason.

▸ Is 4-2 with a 2.40 ERA (45.0IP, 12ER) in seven career starts on three-days' rest including regular season and postseason games (11/1/09 at Philadelphia in World Series Game 4; 10/20/09 at Los Angeles-AL in ALCS Game 4; each of his final four starts w/ Milwaukee from 9/20-10/2/08-including one postseason start, and on 10/7/01w/ Cleveland at Toronto).

2010

▸ Was 21-7 (.750) with a 3.18 ERA (237.2IP, 84ER) and 197K in 34 starts with the Yankees in 2010, marking his first career 20-win season…left with a lead in 25 of 34 starts this season…the Yankees bullpen blew three potential wins (4/4 at Boston, 5/18 vs. Boston and 5/29 vs. Cleveland) and he was removed from his 5/8 start at Boston due to a rain delay (Yankees led, 6-3, after 4.2IP)…opponents batted .239 (209-for-876, 20HR); LHH .261 (53-for-203, 4HR) and RHH .232 (156-for-673, 16HR)…the Yankees went 23-11 in his starts.

▸ Became the first American Leaguer to win 21 games since Cleveland's Cliff Lee in 2008 and is just the second Yankee in the last 25 years (since 1986) to reach the total (Andy Pettitte went 21-8 in 2003 and 1996).

▸ Is the first Yankee to have at least a share of the American League lead in wins in consecutive seasons (also led the AL with 19 wins in 2009, tied with Felix Hernandez and Justin Verlander).

- Ranked among the leaders in wins (first in AL, tied for first in Majors), IP (second in AL, third in Majors), winning percentage (third in Majors and AL), starts (tied for first in AL, tied for third in Majors), strikeouts (sixth in AL) and ERA (seventh in AL).

- Made 22 starts this season against pitchers who finished 2010 with 10-or-more wins, going 14-5 in those outings...defeated two pitchers who threw no-hitters earlier in 2010 (Roy Halladay on 6/15 and Dallas Braden on 9/2) and two former Cy Young Award winners (Halladay and Johan Santana on 6/20).

- Became the 34th different Yankee to record a 20-win season, marking the 59th 20-win season in franchise history...became the ninth Yankees lefthander all time to collect at least 20 wins in a season...marked the most single-season wins by an African-American pitcher in Yankees franchise history...was the Majors' first African-American 20-game winner since Florida's Dontrelle Willis in 2005 (22-10) and the AL's first since Oakland's Dave Stewart in 1990 (21-12).

- Is the 26th different Yankee to record a 21-win season, marking the 43rd 21-win season in franchise history...became the eighth Yankees lefthander all time to collect at least 21 wins in a season.

- Is one of 14 pitchers to win 40 of his first 68 starts with the Yankees and the first since Tommy John (41-16 through his first 68 starts in 1979-1980).

- Went 11-2 with a 3.00 ERA (111.0IP, 37ER) at Yankee Stadium...became the first Yankee to win his first 11 home decisions to begin a season since David Cone and David Wells in 1998 (credit: *Elias Sports Bureau*).

- According to ESPN, became the fourth Yankee to be the first in the Majors to 20 wins in a season since the Cy Young Award was first given out in 1956...the previous three Yankees to accomplish the feat (Bob Turley in 1958; Whitey Ford in 1961; and Ron Guidry in 1978), all won the Cy Young that same year with the Yankees winning the World Series.

- Compiled 22 starts this season in which he held his opponent to 3ER less and threw at least 7.0IP, the third-highest total in the Majors behind Felix Hernandez (25) and Roy Halladay (23).

- Did not allow a HR over a career-long 80.2IP stretch between Luke Scott's HR on 6/3 vs. Baltimore and Victor Martinez's second-inning HR on 8/7 vs Boston.

- Went 10-5 (.667) with a 3.34 ERA (126.2IP, 47ER) in 18 starts away from the Bronx in 2010, tying for the second-most road wins in the Majors.

- Lasted at least 8.0IP in 10 starts in 2010 (including five of his last 11 GS), surpassing his total from 2009 (seven)...is one of just three Yankees with 10-or-more starts of at least 8.0IP in a season in the last decade (2001-10), joining Mike Mussina (11 in '03; nine in '01).

- In his final 22 starts of the season (beginning on 6/3), went 17-4 with a 2.76 ERA (166.1IP, 144H, 51ER, 51BB, 143K), leading the Majors in wins over the stretch.

- Was named to his fourth career All-Star team in 2010 (also 2003-04, '07 w/ Cleveland) and was in uniform for the contest in Anaheim, Calif...was not allowed to participate in the game due to the MLB rule forbidding starting pitchers who pitched on the Sunday prior to the ASG from playing.

- Made his seventh career Opening Day start, second with the Yankees, on 4/4 at Boston, recording a no-decision in the 9-7 Red Sox victory (5.1IP, 6H, 5ER, 2BB, 4K)...became the 22nd pitcher in franchise history to make multiple Opening Day starts, first since Randy Johnson in 2005 and 2006.

- Started and carried a no-hitter through two outs in the eighth inning of a 10-0 win on 4/10 at Tampa Bay until Kelly Shoppach singled to left field (7.2IP, 1H, 2BB, 5K, 111/69)...was removed immediately following the single...was the furthest he had ever gone in a game without allowing a hit (previous best was on 4/7/02 w/ Cleveland at Detroit, 7.0 no-hit IP before eighth-inning leadoff single by Randall Simon)...was the deepest a Yankee had taken a no-hitter since Mike Mussina took a perfect game 8.2IP on 9/2/01 at Boston (Carl Everett single)...according to the *Elias Sports Bureau*, was the first pitcher to lose a no-hitter in the eighth inning or later on a base hit by a former battery-mate since Texas' Nolan Ryan on 9/30/89 at Anaheim Stadium, when California's Brian Downing singled with one out in the eighth inning.

SABATHIA ON THE MAJOR LEAGUE AND AL LEADERBOARD IN 2010

Statistic	AL Rank	ML Rank
Wins	21 1	T1
Win Pct.	.750 3	3
Innings	237.2 2	3
Starts	34 ...... T1	T3
Strikeouts	197 6	T17
ERA	3.18 7	22

YANKEES 20-GAME WINNERS
(Last 25 years – since 1986)

Player	Record	Year
CC SABATHIA	(21-7)	2010
Mike Mussina	(20-9)	2008
*ANDY PETTITTE	(21-8)	2003
Roger Clemens	(20-3)	2001
David Cone	(20-7)	1998
*ANDY PETTITTE	(21-8)	1996

*Left-handed pitcher

YANKEES LEFTHANDED 20-GAME WINNERS (All time)

Player	No. (Years)
Lefty Gomez	4 (1931-32, '34, '37)
Ron Guidry	3 (1978, '83, '85)
ANDY PETTITTE	2 (1996, 2003)
Tommy John	2 (1979-80)
Whitey Ford	2 (1961, '63)
Herb Pennock	2 (1924, '26)
CC SABATHIA	1 (2010)
Fritz Peterson	1 (1970)
Ed Lopat	1 (1951)

OTHER NYY 20 WIN NOTES

* Sabathia is the Yankees first 20-game winner since Mike Mussina (20-9 in 2008).
* 34 different Yankees have had a total of 59 20-win seasons since the franchise was established in New York in 1903.
* Red Ruffing, Lefty Gomez and Bob Shawkey have had the most 20-win seasons by a Yankee (four each).
* The Yanks' first 20-win season was 1903, when Jack Chesboro set the still-standing all-time single-season win mark (41-12).

CC SABATHIA

- Recorded complete games in two straight starts, despite not throwing 9.0 innings in either start (6.0IP win on 4/16 vs. Texas and 8.0IP loss on 4/22 at Oakland)...became the first Yankee credited with back-to-back complete games since David Wells in Sept. 1998.

- Struck out six straight batters on 4/16 vs. Texas in a rain-shortened complete-game game...marked the most consecutive K's in a game by a Yankee since 8/8/99 when David Cone fanned six in-a-row at Seattle – credit: *Elias Sports Bureau.*

- Went winless in five straight starts from 5/8-29, his longest such stretch w/the Yankees and one start shy of his career-long (six: 3/31-4/27/03 and 7/3-8/1/02).

- Followed the stretch by winning a career-high eight consecutive starts from 6/3-7/11, compiling a 1.81 ERA (59.2IP, 43H, 12ER, 18BB, 50K, 2HR)...surpassed his previous career high seven-start winning streak w/ Cleveland from 8/5-9/7/05...became the first Yankee to win eight consecutive starts since Roger Clemens in 2001 (5/26-7/4/01: also 8GS).

- Made his 300th career start on 6/3 vs. Baltimore, recording the win in a 6-3 Yankees victory...retired 19 of his first 21 batters faced (1H, 1E)...allowed a seventh-inning HR to Luke Scott, the only regular season HR he has surrendered to a left-handed batter at the current Yankee Stadium (allowed 2HR to Philadelphia's Chase Utley in Game 1 of the 2009 World Series)...snapped a streak of 37 consecutive home starts without allowing a homer to an LH batter, dating back to 4/5/08.

- Became the youngest pitcher at the time of his 300th start since Dwight Gooden (age 29 years, 205 days on 6/9/94) and the youngest lefty since Fernando Valenzuela (age 29 years, 226 days on 6/15/90) – credit: *Elias*...became the eighth pitcher to make his 300th career start with the Yankees since 1955, just the second such pitcher to win (also Jimmy Key in 1994) – credit: *Elias*...his career .627 (141-84) winning pct. was the third-highest among active pitchers through their first 300 career starts behind Tim Hudson (.655, 144-76) and teammate Andy Pettitte (.642, 156-87).

- Defeated former Cy Young Award winners Roy Halladay (2003) on 6/15 and Johan Santana (2004, '06) on 6/20 in back-to-back starts, a feat last accomplished by a Yankee in 2001 when Mike Mussina defeated David Cone in consecutive starts on 9/2/01 and 9/8/01.

- Was the winning pitcher in the Yankees' 9,500th all-time victory on 6/20 vs. the Mets...tossed 8.0 scoreless IP, allowing just 4H and 2BB with 6K.

- Tossed 8.0 innings in three straight starts from 6/20-7/1, becoming the first Yankee to accomplish the feat since Randy Johnson in 2005.

- Allowed 1ER or less in each of his five starts from 6/20-7/11, setting a career high...according to the *Elias Sports Bureau*, it marked the longest such stretch by a Yankee since David Cone in 1999.

- Made his 50th start as a Yankee on 6/25 at Los Angeles-NL, recording the win to improve his record to 28-11 with 286K as a Yankee...according to the *Elias Sports Bureau*, only two other pitchers posted as many wins and as many Ks over their first 50 starts with the Yankees: Ron Guidry (31-10, 347K) and David Cone (28-10, 374K).

- Surpassed 2,000.0 career IP in 7/1 win, becoming the youngest pitcher to reach the mark since Greg Maddux in 1995 and the youngest lefthander since Fernando Valenzuela in 1990.

- Struck out a season-high10 batters on 7/6 at Oakland, allowing just 1ER on 7H in 7.2IP (3BB, 10K)...marked his 23rd career game with 10-or-more K.

- Reached the All-Star break with a 12-3 record and a 3.09 ERA...became just the sixth Yankee since 1990 to win at least 12 games prior to the All-Star break (also Jimmy Key, 13-2 in 1994; Andy Pettitte 13-4 in 1996; David Cone, 12-2 in 1998; Roger Clemens, 12-1 in 2001; and Mike Mussina, 12-3 in 2002)...recorded at least 10 wins prior to the All-Star Break for just the second time in his career (also 12-3 pre-ASG in 2007).

- Threw 120 and 123 pitches in consecutive starts on 7/22 vs. Kansas City and 7/27 vs. Cleveland, respectively...according to the *Elias Sports Bureau*, became the first Yankee to toss at least 120 pitches in consecutive starts since Jeff Weaver in April 2003.

- Was undefeated in 11 starts from 5/29-7/22, going 9-0 with two no-decisions and a 2.62 ERA (79.0IP, 69H, 23ER, 28BB, 70K, 2HR).

- Followed the stretch by recording the loss in consecutive starts on 7/27 at Cleveland and 8/1 at Tampa Bay...marked just the second time he dropped back-to-back starts as a Yankee (also 4/27/09 at Detroit and 5/2/09 vs. Los Angeles-AL)...the 8/1 loss snapped an 11-game winning streak in August starts.

- Recorded his 150th career victory on 8/7 vs. Boston...reached the plateau with just 86 losses (a .636 winning pct.)...according to the *Elias Sports Bureau*, only three active pitchers reached the plateau with fewer losses (Roy Halladay was 150-76, Tim Hudson was 150-79, and Andy Pettitte was 150-79).

- With his victory on 8/28 at the Chicago White Sox, became the first Yankees pitcher to win 18 games in a season before 9/1 since Roger Clemens ran his record to 18-1 on 8/31/01, according to the *Elias Sports Bureau*...was the earliest a Yankee recorded his 18th win since David Cone in 1998 (8/17).

- Limited the A's to 1H in 8.0 shutout innings on 9/2 vs. Oakland (3BB, 5K and 1HP)…was his fourth scoreless start in 2010…matched his fewest hits allowed in a game (seventh time, second this season – 4/10 at Tampa Bay).

- Failed in his first two attempts at winning his 20th game, recording the loss on 9/7 vs. Baltimore and a no-decision on 9/13 at Tampa Bay.

- Suffered the loss on 9/7 vs. Baltimore, marking his first loss at Yankee Stadium since 7/2/09 and snapping a 21-start undefeated streak at home…over the stretch, went 16-0 with a 2.05 ERA (149.0IP, 34ER) as the Yankees went 19-2 in those starts…according to the *Elias Sports Bureau*, the streak tied Whitey Ford (8/8/64-8/18/65) for the longest undefeated streak of starts by a Yankee at ANY Stadium (home or away)…it was the longest undefeated streak of starts by any pitcher at any stadium since Johan Santana's 24-start undefeated streak at the Metrodome from 8/6/05-4/2/07…*Elias* also notes that Sabathia's 16-game home winning streak matched Johnny Allen (1932-33) and Ron Guidry (1985-86) for the longest in franchise history.

- Tossed 8.0 scoreless IP on 9/13 vs. Tampa Bay, limiting the Rays to 2H with 2BB and 9K…opposed David Price (17-6), marking the first game in which each starting pitcher came in with at least 17 wins and went at least eight scoreless IP since 9/11/85 when St. Louis's John Tudor (17-8) threw a 10.0-inning shutout at the Mets against Dwight Gooden (20-4) – credit: *Elias Sports Bureau*.

- Recorded his 20th win on 9/18 at Baltimore in an 11-3 Yankees victory (7.0IP, 7H, 3ER, 1BB, 4K, 1HR), becoming the first Yankee to reach the plateau since Mike Mussina went 20-9 in 2008.

- Won his 21st game of the season on 9/28 at Toronto, limiting the Jays to 3H and 1ER in 8.1IP (2BB, 8K, 1HR), becoming the first Yankee to reach the 21-win plateau since Andy Pettitte (21-8) in 2003.

- Threw out the first pitch at the North Vallejo Little League Spring Classic on 4/19…following the 2009 season, underwrote the rebuilding of North Vallejo Little League's Thurmon Field through his PitCCh In Foundation, including the irrigation system, infield dirt, bases and home plate, pitching rubber, dugouts, fencing, and 37,000 square feet of sod…also handed out loaded backpacks to 1,000 students, along with his wife Amber, on 9/8 at P.S. 152 in the Bronx.

Sabathia's Career Pitching Record

Year	Club	W	L	ERA	G	GS	CG	SHO	SV	IP	H	R	ER	HR	HP	BB	SO	WP	BK
1998	Burlington	1	0	4.50	5	5	0	0	0	18.0	20	14	9	1	1	8	35	1	1
1999	Mahoning Valley	0	0	1.83	6	6	0	0	0	19.2	9	5	4	0	0	12	27	0	0
	Columbus	2	0	1.08	3	3	0	0	0	16.2	8	2	2	1	1	5	20	1	0
	Kinston	3	3	5.34	7	7	0	0	0	32.0	30	22	19	3	1	19	29	6	0
2000	Kinston	3	2	3.54	10	10	2	2	0	56.0	48	23	22	4	2	24	69	2	1
	Akron	3	7	3.59	17	17	0	0	0	90.1	75	41	36	6	7	48	90	2	1
2001	CLEVELAND	17	5	4.39	33	33	0	0	0	180.1	149	93	88	19	7	95	171	7	3
2002	CLEVELAND	13	11	4.37	33	33	2	0	0	210.0	198	109	102	17	7	88	149	6	*3
2003	CLEVELAND	13	9	3.60	30	30	2	1	0	197.2	190	85	79	19	6	66	141	4	2
2004	CLEVELAND	11	10	4.12	30	30	1	0	0	188.0	176	90	86	20	7	72	139	1	1
2005	Akron	0	1	1.00	2	2	0	0	0	9.0	4	3	1	0	1	2	9	1	0
	CLEVELAND - a	15	10	4.03	31	31	1	0	0	196.2	185	92	88	19	7	62	161	7	0
2006	CLEVELAND - b	12	11	3.22	28	28	*6	*2	0	192.2	182	83	69	17	7	44	172	3	0
	Buffalo	1	0	1.80	1	1	0	0	0	5.0	6	2	1	0	0	1	5	1	0
2007	CLEVELAND	19	7	3.21	34	*34	4	1	0	*241.0	238	94	86	20	8	37	209	1	0
2008	CLEVELAND	6	8	3.83	18	18	3	2	0	122.1	117	54	52	13	3	34	123	1	2
	MILWAUKEE - c	11	2	1.65	17	17	*7	#3	0	130.2	106	31	24	6	4	25	128	1	0
2009	YANKEES - d	#19	8	3.37	34	34	2	1	0	230.0	197	96	86	18	9	67	197	5	0
2010	YANKEES	*21	7	3.18	34	#34	2	0	0	237.2	209	92	84	20	7	74	197	8	1
Minor League Totals		13	13	3.43	51	51	2	2	0	246.2	200	112	94	15	13	119	284	14	3
AL Totals		146	86	3.70	305	305	23	8	0	1996.1	1841	888	820	182	62	639	1659	43	12
NL Totals		11	2	1.65	17	17	7	3	0	130.2	106	31	24	6	4	25	128	1	4
Major League Totals		157	88	3.57	322	322	30	11	0	2127.0	1947	919	844	188	66	664	1787	44	12
NYY Total		40	15	3.27	68	68	4	1	0	467.2	406	188	170	38	16	141	394	13	1

* League leader # Tied for league lead

Selected by Cleveland in the first round (20th overall) of the 1998 First-Year Player Draft.

a – Placed on the 15-day disabled list from March 25 – April 15, 2005 with a right oblique strain.

b – Placed on the 15-day disabled list from April 3 – May 2, 2006 with a right oblique strain.

c – Acquired by Milwaukee from Cleveland on July 7, 2008 in exchange for OF Matt LaPorta, LHP Zach Jackson, RHP Rob Bryson and a player to be named later.

d – Signed by New York (AL) as a free agent on December 18, 2008.

CC SABATHIA

Sabathia's Division Series Record

Year	Club vs. Opp.	W	L	ERA	G	GS	CG	SHO	SV	IP	H	R	ER	HR	HP	BB	SO	WP	BK
2001	CLE vs. SEA	1	0	3.00	1	1	0	0	0	6.0	6	2	2	0	0	5	5	0	0
2007	CLE vs. NYY	1	0	5.40	1	1	0	0	0	5.0	4	3	3	2	0	6	5	0	0
2008	MIL vs. PHI	0	1	12.27	1	1	0	0	0	3.2	6	5	5	1	0	4	5	0	0
2009	NYY vs. MIN	1	0	1.35	1	1	0	0	0	6.2	8	2	1	0	1	0	8	1	0
Division Series Totals		**3**	**1**	**4.64**	**4**	**4**	**0**	**0**	**0**	**21.1**	**24**	**12**	**11**	**3**	**1**	**15**	**23**	**1**	**0**

Sabathia's League Championship Series Record

Year	Club vs. Opp.	W	L	ERA	G	GS	CG	SHO	SV	IP	H	R	ER	HR	HP	BB	SO	WP	BK
2007	CLE vs. BOS	0	2	10.45	2	2	0	0	0	10.1	17	12	12	1	3	7	9	1	0
2009	NYY vs. LAA	2	0	1.13	2	2	0	0	0	16.0	9	2	2	1	0	3	12	0	0
LCS Totals		**2**	**2**	**4.78**	**4**	**4**	**0**	**0**	**0**	**26.1**	**26**	**14**	**14**	**2**	**3**	**10**	**21**	**1**	**0**

Sabathia's World Series Record

Year	Club vs. Opp.	W	L	ERA	G	GS	CG	SHO	SV	IP	H	R	ER	HR	HP	BB	SO	WP	BK
2009	NYY vs. PHI	0	1	3.29	2	2	0	0	0	13.2	11	5	5	3	0	6	12	0	0
World Series Totals		**0**	**1**	**3.29**	**2**	**2**	**0**	**0**	**0**	**13.2**	**11**	**5**	**5**	**3**	**0**	**6**	**12**	**0**	**0**
POSTSEASON TOTALS		**5**	**4**	**4.40**	**10**	**10**	**0**	**0**	**0**	**61.1**	**61**	**31**	**30**	**8**	**4**	**31**	**56**	**2**	**0**

Sabathia's All-Star Game Record

Year	Club, Site	W	L	ERA	G	GS	CG	SHO	SV	IP	H	R	ER	HR	HP	BB	SO	WP	BK
2003	CLE, Chicago (AL)						Selected - Did Not Pitch												
2004	CLE, Houston	0	0	27.00	1	0	0.0	0	0	1.0	4	3	3	0	0	0	0	0	0
2007	CLE, San Francisco	0	0	0.00	1	0	0	0	0	1.0	1	0	0	0	0	0	0	0	0
2010	NYY, Los Angeles (AL)						Selected - Did Not Pitch												
All-Star Game Totals		**0**	**0**	**13.50**	**2**	**0**	**0**	**0**	**0**	**2.0**	**5**	**3**	**3**	**0**	**0**	**0**	**0**	**0**	**0**

Sabathia's Regular Season Batting Record

Year	Team	AVG	G	AB	R	H	2B	3B	HR	RBI	SH	SF	HP	BB	SO	SB	CS
2010	NYY	.200	34	5	0	1	0	0	0	0	0	0	0	0	3	0	0
Major League Totals		**.258**	***322**	**97**	**7**	**25**	**3**	**0**	**3**	**14**	**3**	**0**	**0**	**1**	**26**	**0**	**0**

*one game as pinch-hitter

Sabathia's Career Fielding Record

Position	PCT	G	PO	A	E	TC	DP
Pitcher	.955	322	35	218	12	265	17

	2010										Career									
	W	L	SV	ERA	G	GS	IP	H	HR	ER	SO	W	L	SV	ERA	G	GS	IP	H	HR	ER	SO
Overall	21	7	0	3.18	34	34	237.2	209	20	84	197	157	88	0	3.57	322	322	2127.0	1947	188	844	1787
Minnesota	-	-	-	-	-	-	-	-	-	-	-	13	8	0	3.05	28	28	191.2	173	13	65	143
Tampa Bay	1	2	0	3.38	5	5	34.2	29	0	13	29	8	5	0	3.24	20	20	139.0	121	12	50	126
Texas	1	0	0	1.50	1	1	6.0	3	0	1	9	8	3	0	4.29	14	14	86.0	89	7	41	77
Atlanta	-	-	-	-	-	-	-	-	-	-	-	1	1	0	3.24	2	2	16.2	18	0	6	16
Cincinnati	-	-	-	-	-	-	-	-	-	-	-	4	1	0	2.33	11	11	73.1	62	4	19	75
Philadelphia	1	0	0	3.86	1	1	7.0	5	0	3	7	2	1	0	4.23	4	4	27.2	27	1	13	19
San Francisco	-	-	-	-	-	-	-	-	-	-	-	2	0	0	1.59	2	2	17.0	9	2	3	16
March	-	-	-	-	-	-	-	-	-	-	-	0	0	0	5.11	2	2	12.1	14	2	7	10
April	3	1	0	3.12	5	5	34.2	25	2	12	28	15	13	0	4.32	42	42	256.1	244	19	123	200
May	1	2	0	5.15	6	6	36.2	40	8	21	26	29	16	0	3.46	58	58	388.0	369	44	149	289
June	5	0	0	2.19	5	5	37.0	25	2	9	35	26	11	0	3.65	53	53	340.0	291	23	138	285
July	4	1	0	2.30	6	6	43.0	46	0	11	35	21	24	0	4.33	55	55	353.1	369	34	170	299
August	5	1	0	3.12	6	6	43.1	41	5	15	36	38	10	0	3.14	58	58	404.0	364	38	141	373
September	3	2	0	3.35	6	6	43.0	32	3	16	37	26	13	0	2.75	51	51	360.1	285	28	110	318
October	-	-	-	-	-	-	-	-	-	-	-	2	1	0	4.26	3	3	12.2	11	0	6	13
Home	11	2	0	3.00	16	16	111.0	90	8	37	97	73	43	0	3.52	159	159	1045.2	957	86	409	931
Road	10	5	0	3.34	18	18	126.2	119	12	47	100	84	45	0	3.62	163	163	1081.1	990	102	435	856

Sabathia's Career By Ballpark

Park	W	L	SV	ERA	G	GS	IP	ER	Park	W	L	SV	ERA	G	GS	IP	ER
AT&T Park	2	0	0	1.59	2	2	17.0	3	Target Field	-	-	-	-	-	-	-	-
Citizens Bank Park	-	-	-	-	-	-	-	-	Tropicana Field	3	4	0	3.79	11	11	73.2	31
Great American BP	1	1	0	2.03	4	4	26.2	6	Turner Field	1	0	0	2.16	1	1	8.1	2
Rangers Ballpark	4	2	0	4.71	6	6	36.1	19	Yankee Stadium	18	4	0	3.08	31	31	216	74

Nick Swisher

33

Outfielder/Infielder

5-11 • 210 • B/T: Switch/Left

Opening Day Age: 29

Birthdate
November 25, 1980

Birthplace
Columbus, Ohio

Resides
Parkersburg, W. Va.

M.L. Service
6 years, 31 days

College
Ohio State University

Career Highlights
A.L. All-Star Team
▸ 2010

Status
▸ Acquired by the Yankees along with RHP Kanekoa Texeira from the Chicago White Sox on November 13, 2008, in exchange for INF Wilson Betemit and RHPs Jeff Marquez and Jhonny Nunez…signed a five-year contract on May 11, 2007 (w/ Oakland)…contract extends through the 2011 season.

Postseason Notes
▸ Appeared in 14 of the Yankees' 15 postseason games in 2009, batting .128 (6-for-47) with 5R, 2 doubles, 1HR, 2RBI and 7BB…hit his first career postseason homer in Game 3 of the World Series at Philadelphia.

Career Notes
▸ Has hit at least 20HR in six straight seasons (2005-10).
▸ His 139HR since 2006 are the third-most among Major League switch-hitters over the last five seasons, trailing only teammates Mark Teixeira (168) and Lance Berkman (147).
▸ Has homered from both sides of the plate 10 times in his career…according to SABR's David Vincent, the 10 career switch-hit homers are tied with teammate Mark Teixeira for the most among active players and tied with Teixeira, Ken Caminiti, Tony Clark and Mickey Mantle for the second-most all-time behind Chili Davis and Eddie Murray (11 each).

2010
▸ Hit .288 (163-for-566) with 91R, 33 doubles, 3 triples, 29HR and 89RBI in 150 games (131 starts in RF, 11 at DH) with the Yankees in 2010, setting career highs in batting average, at-bats, hits and triples…made his sixth career Opening Day roster, second as a Yankee….hit .286 (110-for-384) with 25HR as a left-handed batter and .291 (53-for-182) with 4HR as a righty batter…17 of his 29 homers tied the game or gave the Yankees the lead.
▸ Among Major League switch-hitters, ranked second in runs scored (91), home runs (29) and RBI (89), trailing only teammate Mark Teixeira in each of the three categories (113R, 33HR and 108RBI)…ranked third in batting average (.288).
▸ Hit .345 (88-for-255) with 15 doubles, 3 triples, 13HR, 73RBI and 29BB with runners on base, fourth-best in the American League.
▸ Hit in seven different spots in the starting lineup (two through eight), homering in five of those spots (two, four, five, six and eight).
▸ Had 10 outfield assists in 2010, eight more than his total from 2009 (two) and surpassing his previous career high (six in 2005 w/ Oakland).
▸ Hit 15HR at home this season, nearly doubling his home run total at Yankee Stadium from 2009 (8HR).
▸ Had at least three hits in a game 14 times in 2010, the most such games in any season in his career (previous was 10 in 2007)…only Robinson Cano (19) had more three-hit games among Yankees players in 2010.
▸ Won the 2010 All-Star Final Vote, earning the final spot on the AL's All-Star roster…pinch-hit for Ty Wigginton in the seventh, going 0-for-1…with his dad, Steve, a 1976 NL All-Star for the Chicago Cubs, the Swishers became the 12th family to have both a father and son named to an MLB All-Star team.

2010 Highs and Streaks		
Hits	4 - at SEA, 7/8/10	
Runs	2 - 19 times	
	Last: vs. OAK, 8/31/10	
2B	2 - 4 times	
	Last: vs. OAK, 8/30/10	
3B	1 - 3 times	
	Last: at ARI, 6/21/10	
HR	2 - 2 times	
	Last: vs. TOR, 8/2/10	
RBI	5 - at BAL, 6/8/10	
BB	3 - vs. LAA, 4/13/10	
SO	4 - at TEX, 8/11/10	
SB	1 - vs. TOR, 7/2/10	
Hit Streak	9g - 7/25-8/2/10	

Career Highs and Streaks		
Hits	4 - 2 times	
	Last: at SEA, 7/8/10	
Runs	3 - 17 times	
	Last: at DET, 4/28/09	
2B	2 - 14 times	
	Last: vs. OAK, 8/30/10	
3B	1 - 9 times	
	Last: at ARI, 6/21/10	
HR	2 - 16 times	
	Last: vs. TOR, 8/2/10	
RBI	5 - 4 times	
	Last: at BAL, 6/8/10	
BB	3 - 18 times	
	Last: vs. LAA, 4/13/10	
SO	5 - at SD, 6/29/06	
SB	1 - 8 times	
	Last: vs. TOR, 7/2/10	
Hit Streak	11g - 4/30-5/11/06	

NICK SWISHER

- Hit safely in each of his first six games of the season with an official at-bat for the second time in his career (first nine games in 2009).

- Batted .374 (34-for-91) with 7HR and 17RBI in May, marking his most hits in any calendar month of his career (previous best was 32H in May 2007 and May 2006).

- Snapped a 22AB hitless stretch at home with a fifth-inning single in 5/1 loss vs. Chicago-AL…had just 1H at Yankee Stadium in 2010 entering the game (triple on 4/14 vs. Los Angeles-AL).

- Hit three home runs in a four-game stretch (5/5-9) and five HR in an eight-game span from 5/1-9.

- Missed four games with a sore left biceps (5/13 and 5/17-19)…underwent an MRI at New York-Presbyterian Hospital on 5/14 and was diagnosed with a slight strain of the left biceps.

- Hit game-winning solo-HR in the ninth and was 2-for-5 with 1 double in 5/26 win at Minnesota.

- Hit two-run HR and was 3-for-6 with 2R, 1 double and 5RBI in 6/8 win at Baltimore…tied his career high in RBI (last 4/9/09 at Baltimore).

- Recorded two outfield assists in 6/23 win at Arizona, both coming in the first inning (Johnson at home, Montero at third)…marked his first career multi-assist game as an outfielder.

- Recorded his 15th career multi-HR game in 6/29 loss vs. Seattle, homering twice off LHP Cliff Lee…was his first multi-HR game—and his first homers off a left-handed pitcher—since 9/8/09 vs. Tampa Bay (David Price)…marked the second time in his career he hit 2HR off left-handed pitching in the same game (also 5/11/06 w/ Oakland at Toronto – both off Ted Lilly).

- Was 4-for-4 with 1R, 2 doubles and 1BB, reaching base five times in 7/8 win at Seattle…tied his career high in hits (also 9/8/06 w/ Oakland at Tampa Bay).

- Scored at least one run in 10 consecutive starts from 7/10-26, tying a career high (also 9/5-15/07).

- Hit ninth-inning "walk-off" RBI single and was 3-for-5 with 1R, 1HR and 3RBI in 7/16 win vs. Tampa Bay…was his third career "walk-off" hit and second with the Yankees (also 9/8/09 vs. Tampa Bay)…was also his eighth home run at Yankee Stadium in 2010, coming in his 39th home game of the season…did not hit his eighth HR at Yankee Stadium in 2009 until his 75th—and final—home game of the year.

- Collected his 16th career multi-HR game and second of 2010 (also 6/29 vs. Seattle) in 8/2 loss vs. Toronto, going 2-for-5 with a two-run HR and solo HR…moved to CF at the start of the ninth inning, playing the position for the first time since 9/1/08 w/ Chicago-AL at Cleveland.

- Fouled a ball off his left knee in 8/24 win at Toronto and was removed from the game with a 2-2 count in the seventh…missed the game on 8/25 at Toronto with soreness in the knee…also missed two games (9/3-4) with left knee stiffness.

- Hit ninth-inning, two-run "walk-off" HR and was 2-for-4 in 9/8 win vs. Baltimore…was his fourth career "walk-off" hit (second this season) and third such HR…came one year to the day after his last "walk-off" homer (9/8/09 vs. Tampa Bay off Dan Wheeler)…became the fourth player in Baseball history ever to hit "walk-off" home runs exactly a year apart and first since the Giants' Jack Clark on 9/4/81 and 9/4/82.

- Did not start in four straight games (9/13-15 at Tampa Bay and 9/17 at Baltimore) due to left knee inflammation.

- Hit safely in 11 of his final 12 starts of the season with 3HR.

Swisher's Career Playing Record

Year	Club	AVG	G	AB	R	H	2B	3B	HR	RBI	SH	SF	HP	BB	SO	SB	CS	E	OBP	SLG
2002	Vancouver	.250	13	44	10	11	3	0	2	12	0	1	2	13	11	3	0	0	.433	.455
	Visalia	.240	49	183	22	44	13	2	4	23	2	1	2	26	48	3	1	4	.340	.399
2003	Modesto	.296	51	189	38	56	14	2	10	43	0	5	2	41	49	0	2	4	.418	.550
	Midland	.230	76	287	36	66	24	2	5	43	0	6	6	37	76	0	1	5	.324	.380
2004	Sacramento	.269	125	443	109	119	28	2	29	92	0	5	3	103	109	3	3	7	.406	.537
	OAKLAND	.250	20	60	11	15	4	0	2	8	0	1	2	8	11	0	0	3	.352	.417
2005	OAKLAND - a	.236	131	462	66	109	32	1	21	74	0	1	4	55	110	0	1	2	.322	.446
	Sacramento	.391	6	23	4	9	3	0	0	1	0	0	1	2	7	0	1	0	.462	.522
2006	OAKLAND	.254	157	556	106	141	24	2	35	95	2	6	11	97	152	1	2	8	.372	.493
2007	OAKLAND	.262	150	539	84	141	36	1	22	78	1	9	10	100	131	3	2	5	.381	.455
2008	CHICAGO-AL - b	.219	153	497	86	109	21	1	24	69	1	4	4	82	135	3	3	7	.332	.410
2009	YANKEES - c	.249	150	498	84	124	35	1	29	82	3	6	3	97	126	0	0	6	.371	.498
2010	YANKEES	.288	150	566	91	163	33	3	29	89	3	2	6	58	139	1	2	4	.359	.511
Minor League Totals		**.261**	**320**	**1169**	**219**	**305**	**85**	**8**	**50**	**214**	**2**	**18**	**16**	**222**	**300**	**9**	**8**	**20**	**.381**	**.476**
Major League Totals		**.252**	**911**	**3178**	**528**	**802**	**185**	**9**	**162**	**495**	**10**	**29**	**40**	**497**	**804**	**8**	**10**	**35**	**.358**	**.469**
NYY Total		**.270**	**300**	**1064**	**175**	**287**	**68**	**4**	**58**	**171**	**6**	**8**	**9**	**155**	**265**	**1**	**2**	**10**	**.365**	**.505**

Selected by Oakland in the first round (16th overall) of the 2002 First-Year Player Draft.

a – Placed on the 15-day disabled list from May 2-25, 2005 with a right shoulder sprain.

b – Acquired by Chicago-AL on January 3, 2008 in exchange for RHP Fautino De Los Santos, LHP Giovany Gonzalez and OF Ryan Sweeney.

c – Acquired by the Yankees along with RHP Kanekoa Texeira on November 13, 2008 in exchange for INF Wilson Betemit and RHPs Jeff Marquez and Jhonny Nunez.

NICK SWISHER

	2010					CAREER				
	AVG	AB	H	HR	RBI	AVG	AB	H	HR	RBI
Overall	.288	566	163	29	89	.252	3178	802	162	495
Minnesota	.235	17	4	1	1	.254	181	46	10	28
Tampa Bay	.364	55	20	5	11	.306	235	72	18	42
Texas	.103	29	3	0	1	.246	289	71	16	49
Atlanta	-	-	-	-	-	.160	25	4	1	2
Cincinnati	-	-	-	-	-	.444	4	9	0	2
Philadelphia	.167	12	2	1	2	.074	27	2	1	3
San Francisco	-	-	-	-	-	.231	65	15	3	14
March	-	-	-	-	-	.500	4	2	0	0
April	.250	76	19	2	11	.260	469	122	29	79
May	.374	91	34	7	17	.267	491	131	22	79
June	.240	104	25	4	19	.248	569	141	25	90
July	.324	102	33	7	16	.243	518	126	27	83
August	.296	108	32	5	17	.260	566	147	28	88
September	.237	76	18	3	8	.236	525	124	30	74
October	.222	9	2	1	1	.250	36	9	1	2
Home	.287	279	80	15	47	.248	1546	384	79	244
Road	.289	287	83	14	42	.256	1632	418	83	251
vs. Left	.294	180	53	4	16	.260	897	233	36	128
vs. Right	.285	386	110	25	73	.249	2281	569	126	367

Swisher's Career by Ballpark

Park	AVG	AB	H	HR	RBI	Park	AVG	AB	H	HR	RBI
AT&T Park	.250	28	7	0	5	Target Field	.250	12	3	1	1
Citizens Bank Park	-	-	-	-	-	Tropicana Field	.313	131	41	11	22
Great American Ball Park	-	-	-	-	-	Turner Field	.160	25	4	1	2
Rangers Ballpark	.244	156	38	8	28	Yankee Stadium	.259	505	131	23	74

Swisher's Division Series Record

Year	Club vs. Opp.	AVG	G	AB	R	H	2B	3B	HR	RBI	SH	SF	HP	BB	SO	SB	CS	E	OBP	SLG
2006	OAK vs. MIN	.300	3	10	3	3	2	0	0	1	0	0	0	2	2	0	0	0	.417	.500
2008	CWS vs. TB	.250	3	4	1	1	0	0	0	0	0	0	0	2	1	0	0	0	.500	.250
2009	NYY vs. MIN	.083	3	12	0	1	1	0	0	1	0	0	0	4	0	0	0	0	.083	.167
Division Series Totals		**.192**	**9**	**26**	**4**	**5**	**3**	**0**	**0**	**2**	**0**	**0**	**0**	**4**	**7**	**0**	**0**	**0**	**.300**	**.308**

Swisher's Championship Series Record

Year	Club vs. Opp.	AVG	G	AB	R	H	2B	3B	HR	RBI	SH	SF	HP	BB	SO	SB	CS	E	OBP	SLG
2006	OAK vs. DET	.100	4	10	0	1	0	0	0	0	0	0	0	5	5	0	0	0	.400	.100
2009	NYY vs. LAA	.150	6	20	2	3	0	0	0	0	1	0	1	3	7	0	0	0	.292	.150
LCS Totals		**.133**	**10**	**30**	**2**	**4**	**0**	**0**	**0**	**0**	**1**	**0**	**1**	**8**	**12**	**0**	**0**	**0**	**.333**	**.133**

Swisher's World Series Record

Year	Club vs. Opp.	AVG	G	AB	R	H	2B	3B	HR	RBI	SH	SF	HP	BB	SO	SB	CS	E	OBP	SLG
2009	NYY vs. PHI	.133	5	15	3	2	1	0	1	1	0	0	0	4	4	0	0	0	.316	.400
World Series Totals		**.133**	**5**	**15**	**3**	**2**	**1**	**0**	**1**	**1**	**0**	**0**	**0**	**4**	**4**	**0**	**0**	**0**	**.316**	**.400**
POSTSEASON TOTALS		**.155**	**24**	**71**	**9**	**11**	**4**	**0**	**1**	**3**	**1**	**0**	**1**	**16**	**23**	**0**	**0**	**0**	**.318**	**.254**

Swisher's All-Star Game Record

Year	Club, Site	AVG	G	AB	R	H	2B	3B	HR	RBI	SH	SF	HP	BB	SO	SB	CS	E	OBP	SLG
2010	NYY, Los Angeles (AL)	.000	1	1	0	0	0	0	0	0	0	0	0	0	1	0	0	0	.000	.000
All-Star Game Totals		**.000**	**1**	**1**	**0**	**0**	**0**	**0**	**0**	**0**	**0**	**0**	**0**	**0**	**1**	**0**	**0**	**0**	**.000**	**.000**

Swisher's Career Fielding Record

Position	PCT	G	PO	A	E	TC
Pitcher	-	1	0	0	0	0
First Base	.994	255	1740	116	11	1867
Outfield	.983	687	1348	29	24	1401

Swisher's Career Home Run Chart

MULTI-HOMER GAMES: 16. **TWO-HOMER GAMES:** 16, last on 8/2/10 vs. Toronto. **GRAND SLAMS:** 4, last on 6/30/08 vs. Cleveland (Jeremy Sowers). **PINCH-HIT HR:** None. **INSIDE-THE-PARK HR:** 1, on 6/11/06 at New York-AL (Shawn Chacon). **WALK-OFF HR:** 3, last on 9/9/10 vs. Baltimore (Koji Uehara). **LEADOFF HR:** 1, on 4/6/08 at Detroit (Justin Verlander).

Mark Teixeira

25 First Baseman
6-3 • 220 • B/T: Switch/Right
Opening Day Age: 29

Birthdate
April 11, 1980

Birthplace
Annapolis, Md.

Resides
Greenwich, Conn.

M.L. Service
8 years

College
Georgia Tech

Career Highlights
A.L. All-Star Team
▸ 2005, 2009

A.L. Gold Glove
▸ 2005, 2006, 2009

A.L. Silver Slugger
▸ 2004, 2005, 2009

Status
▸ Signed as a free agent to an eight-year contract on January 6, 2009…contract extends through the 2016 season.

Postseason Notes
▸ Batted .180 (11-for-61) with 2 doubles, 2HR and 8RBI for the Yankees in the 2009 postseason, as part of his first World Championship…hit "walk-off" solo home run off Jose Mijares in the 11th inning of ALDS Game 2 vs. Minnesota, marking his first career postseason home run and first career "walk-off" homer (regular and postseason)…was the Yankees' second "walk-off" HR in ALDS play (also Jim Leyritz in 1995 vs. Seattle)…scored a run in five of the Yankees' six World Series games…was hit by a pitch three times in the 2009 World Series, joining teammate Alex Rodriguez (also 2009) and Pittsburgh's Max Carey (1925) as the only players to have 3HBP in a single Series.

▸ Made his first career postseason appearance in 2008 with the Angels, batting .467 (7-for-15) with 4R, 1RBI and 4BB in four games against the Red Sox.

Career Notes
▸ Is one of only three Major Leaguers to reach 30HR and 100RBI in each of the last seven seasons (2004-10), joining Albert Pujols and teammate Alex Rodriguez…according to *Elias*, is one of three first basemen all time to surpass 30HR and 100RBI in seven straight years by age 30 (also Jimmie Foxx and Pujols).

▸ Is one of just three Yankees first basemen in franchise history to record at least 100R, 30HR and 100RBI in multiple seasons with the club, joining Lou Gehrig (10 times, 1927 and '29-37) and Don Mattingly (twice, 1985-86)…is the only player to accomplish the feat in his first two seasons with the club.

▸ Is the sixth Yankee all time to hit at least 30HR in each of his first two seasons with the club (also Babe Ruth, Roger Maris, Jason Giambi, Alex Rodriguez and Gary Sheffield).

▸ Is one of 13 players all-time to hit 250 home runs within the first eight years of their Major League career and one of just four active players to accomplish the feat, joining Albert Pujols (319 from 2001-08), Adam Dunn (278 from 2001-08) and Todd Helton (251 from 1997-2004)…his 275 career home runs are the most ever by a switch-hitter in his first eight seasons.

▸ Has reached the 25HR plateau in each of his first eight Major League seasons…according to *Elias*, became just the fourth player in Baseball history to accomplish the feat, joining Eddie Mathews (11 seasons), Albert Pujols (10) and Darryl Strawberry (nine).

2010 Highs and Streaks
Hits	4 - 4 times
	Last: at TOR, 8/24/10
Runs	3 - 4 times
	Last: vs. BOS, 9/25/10
2B	2 - 4 times
	Last: vs. LAA, 7/21/10
3B	N/A
HR	3 - at BOS, 5/8/10
RBI	5 - at BOS, 5/8/10
BB	3 - 4 times
	Last: vs. TOR, 9/5/10
SO	5 - at TOR, 6/5/10
SB	N/A
Hit Streak	12g - 6/18-7/1/10

Career Highs and Streaks
Hits	4 - 21 times
	Last: at TOR, 8/24/10
Runs	4 - 2 times
	Last: at CIN, 8/20/07
2B	3 - at NYY, 5/10/07
3B	1 - 16 times
	Last at SEA, 9/19/09
HR	3 - 3 times
	Last: at BOS, 5/8/10
RBI	7 - 2 times
	Last: at BAL, 7/13/06
BB	5 - 2 times
	Last: at BOS, 4/25/09
SO	5 - 2 times
	Last: at TOR, 6/5/10
SB	1 - 15 times
	Last: at CWS, 8/2/09
Hit Streak	14g - 5/18-6/1/09

- Has homered from both sides of the plate in the same game 10 times in his career (tied with teammate Nick Swisher for most among actives)…is tied with Swisher, Ken Caminiti, Tony Clark and Mickey Mantle for the second-most all-time behind Chili Davis and Eddie Murray (11 each).
- Since returning to the AL on 7/29/08 when he was acquired by Los Angeles-AL from Atlanta, ranks second in RBI (273) and home runs (85) among American Leaguers.
- Leads all active first basemen with a .99643 career fielding percentage at 1B.

2010

- Hit .256 (154-for-601) with 113R, 36 doubles, 33HR and 108RBI in 158 games (148 starts at 1B, nine at DH) with the Yankees in 2010…was one of nine Major Leaguers with at least 100R and 100RBI this season…led the AL and ranked second in the Majors in runs scored, trailing only the Cardinals' Albert Pujols (115).
- Hit .245 (102-for-417) with 23HR as a left-handed batter and .283 (52-for-184) with 10HR as a right-handed batter…owned a .533 batting average (8-for-15) with 1 double, 1HR and 22RBI with the bases loaded.
- Over his final 101 games of the season (from 6/8), batted .283 (107-for-378) with 25HR and 74RBI…ranked second in the AL in home runs and tied for fourth in RBI over the stretch…over his first 57 games of the season (4/4-6/7), hit just .211 (47-for-223) with 8HR and 34RBI.
- Committed just 3E in 1,310 chances in 2010, a .998 fielding percentage…marked the second-fewest errors and second-highest fielding percentage among Major League first basemen, behind only Seattle's Casey Kotchman.

MOST HOME RUNS AMONG ACTIVE SWITCH-HITTERS	
1. Chipper Jones	436
2. LANCE BERKMAN	327
3. Carlos Beltran	280
4. MARK TEIXEIRA	275
5. JORGE POSADA	261

MOST HOME RUNS, FIRST TWO YEARS W/NYY	
1. Babe Ruth	113 (1920-21)
2. Roger Maris	100 (1960-61)
3. ALEX RODRIGUEZ	84 (2004-05)
4. Jason Giambi	82 (2002-03)
5. Joe DiMaggio	75 (1936-37)
6. MARK TEIXEIRA	72 (2009-10)

- Recorded 54 putouts on foul balls, the most for any fielder in the Majors in 2010—credit: *Elias*.
- Started 100 games at 1B with Alex Rodriguez at 3B, Derek Jeter at SS and Robinson Cano at 2B, marking the most starts for any set of infielders for a single team in the AL this season—credit: *Elias*.
- Made his eighth career Opening Day roster (second as a Yankee) and seventh Opening Day start at 1B.
- Was hitless in his first 17 at-bats to start the season… snapped streak with a fifth-inning RBI double in 4/10 win at Tampa Bay…marked the longest hitless streak to begin a season of his career (was 0-for-16 to begin 2003 w/ Texas)…was 3-for-4 with 2R, 1 double, 1RBI and 1BB in the game…following the 4/10 game, again went hitless in his next 17AB before snapping the stretch with a second-inning single in 4/17 win vs. Texas.
- Hit his first home run of the season in 4/18 win vs. Texas, snapping a 40AB homerless stretch to start the year…marked the second-longest such stretch of his career behind a 76AB homerless span to start the 2007 season.
- Collected 33H and 25RBI in 29 games in May after having 11H and 9RBI in 22 games in April.
- Recorded his 26th career multi-HR game and third 3HR game in 5/8 win at Boston, hitting solo home runs in the fifth and seventh and a two-run HR in the ninth…became the fourth player in Major League history to have 3HR games with three different teams, (also Johnny Mize-Cardinals, Giants, Yankees; Dave Kingman-Mets, Cubs, Athletics; and Alex Rodriguez-Mariners, Rangers, Yankees)…became just the second Yankee in franchise history to hit 3HR in a game vs. Boston (also Lou Gehrig on 6/23/27 at Boston)…became the first Yankee to hit three home runs in a game since Alex Rodriguez on 4/26/05 vs. Los Angeles-AL.
- Drove in a run with a fourth-inning RBI on a bases-loaded hit-by-pitch in 5/29 loss vs. Cleveland, snapping a 10-game streak without an RBI from 5/18-28…was one game shy of a career-high 11-game span without driving in a run from 5/7-21/04.
- Hit his 250th career home run in 5/31 win vs. Cleveland, snapping a 56AB homerless stretch.
- Was removed from 6/1 win vs. Baltimore in the top of the fourth inning with a bruised left foot, suffered on a foul ball in his first-inning at-bat…did not miss a game.

Big Heart

In May 2010, Mark and his wife, Leigh, partnered up with Harlem RBI, making a $100,000 donation to the Harlem RBI Futures Fund to support Harlem RBI's college-bound seniors…in addition, Mark signed up as a member of the Harlem RBI Board of Directors and will serve as an Honorary Chair of Harlem RBI's Capital Campaign.

MARK TEIXEIRA

▸ Struck out five times in 6/5 loss at Toronto, tying his career high (second time, also 8/18/03 at Detroit)…became just the sixth Yankee all time to strike out five times in a game and first since Melky Cabrera on 7/7/07 vs. Los Angeles-AL.

▸ Reached base safely (via hit, walk or hit-by-pitch) in a career-high 42 straight games from 6/6-7/26…marked the longest such streak by a Yankee since Alex Rodriguez reached safely in 53 straight from 4/18-6/17/04.

▸ Reached base safely five times in 6/8 win at Baltimore (3-for-4, 2BB), doing so for the first time since 5/16/09 vs. Minnesota (4-for-4, 1BB).

▸ Made his first error of the season—and first since 10/2/09—in 6/13 win vs. Houston, snapping a 64-game errorless stretch.

▸ Hit his fifth career grand slam and was 1-for-3 with 1BB in 6/20 win vs. the Mets…was his first grand slam since 8/3/08 w/ Los Angeles-AL at Yankee Stadium (off Edwar Ramirez).

▸ Hit safely in a season-high 12 straight games from 6/18-7/1, batting .292 (14-for-48) with 8R, 3HR and 11RBI.

▸ Batted .344 (33-for-96) with 26RBI and 20BB in 26 games in July, collecting 11 multi-hit contests…18 of his 33H (54.5%) went for extra bases (10 doubles, 8HR).

▸ Homered from both sides of the plate for the 10th time in his career—and second in 2010—in 7/9 win at Seattle…homered six times in a nine-game stretch from 7/31-8/9.

▸ Missed two-game series in Texas on 8/10 and 8/11 for the birth of his son, William Charles.

▸ Matched his career high with 4H in 8/24 win at Toronto.

▸ Missed 8/29 win at Chicago-AL with a bruised right thumb.

▸ Hit solo HR—the first of back-to-back HRs with Cano—and was 3-for-3 with 3R, 1 double and 1BB in 8/30 win vs. Oakland before being removed for PH (Kearns) in the eighth.

▸ Was named AL "Player of the Week" for the period ending 9/5…hit .476 (10-for-21) with 3 doubles, 2HR and 8RBI during the week…marked his fifth career weekly award and first since 2007 with Texas.

▸ Became the first player to record both 100R and 100RBI in 2010, reaching the totals in 9/10 loss at Texas.

▸ Went hitless in a season-high 19 straight at-bats from 9/15-23…snapped the hitless stretch with his third-inning double in 9/23 loss vs. Tampa Bay.

▸ Recorded his 29th career multi-HR game—and fourth of 2010—in 9/24 loss vs. Boston, hitting two solo homers and going 2-for-4 with 3R and 1BB…snapped a 75AB homerless stretch with his sixth-inning homer.

Teixeira's Career Hitting Record

Year	Team	AVG	G	AB	R	H	2B	3B	HR	RBI	SH	SF	HP	BB	SO	SB	CS	E	OBP	SLG
2002	Charlotte	.320	38	150	32	48	10	2	9	41	0	1	3	21	24	2	0	9	.411	.593
	Tulsa	.316	48	171	31	54	11	3	10	28	0	0	4	25	36	3	2	12	.415	.591
2003	TEXAS	.259	146	529	66	137	29	5	26	84	0	2	14	44	120	1	2	4	.331	.480
2004	TEXAS - a	.281	145	545	101	153	34	2	38	112	0	2	10	68	117	4	1	10	.370	.560
	Frisco	.000	1	3	0	0	0	0	0	0	0	0	0	1	0	1	0	0	0	.250	.000
2005	TEXAS	.301	#162	644	112	194	41	3	43	144	0	3	11	72	124	4	0	3	.379	.575
2006	TEXAS	.282	#162	628	99	177	45	1	33	110	0	6	4	89	128	2	0	4	.371	.514
2007	TEXAS - b	.297	78	286	48	85	24	1	13	49	0	1	3	45	66	0	0	1	.397	.524
	Frisco	.000	1	2	0	0	0	0	0	0	0	0	0	2	0	0	0	0	.500	.000
	ATLANTA - c	.317	54	208	38	66	9	1	17	56	0	1	4	27	46	0	0	4	.404	.615
2008	ATLANTA	.283	103	381	63	108	27	0	20	78	0	2	3	65	70	0	0	2	.390	.512
	LOS ANGELES-AL - d	.358	54	193	39	69	14	0	13	43	0	5	4	32	23	2	0	3	.449	.632
2009	YANKEES - e	.292	156	609	103	178	43	3	#39	*122	0	5	12	81	114	2	0	4	.383	.565
2010	YANKEES	.256	158	601	*113	154	36	0	33	108	0	5	13	93	122	0	1	3	.365	.481
Minor League Totals		.313	88	326	63	102	21	5	19	69	0	1	8	48	61	5	2	21	.413	.583
AL Totals		.284	1061	4035	681	1147	266	15	238	772	0	29	71	524	814	15	4	40	.374	.535
NL Totals		.295	157	589	101	174	36	1	37	134	0	3	7	92	116	0	0	6	.395	.548
Major League Totals		.286	1218	4624	782	1321	302	16	275	906	0	32	78	616	930	15	4	46	.377	.536
NYY Total		.274	314	1210	216	332	79	3	72	230	0	10	25	174	236	2	1	7	.374	.523

*Denotes league leader   #Tied for league lead
Selected by Boston in the ninth round of the 1998 First-Year Player Draft but did not sign.
Selected by Texas in the first round (fifth pick overall) of the 2001 First-Year Player Draft.

a – Placed on the 15-day disabled list from April 13-29, 2004 with a strained left oblique.
b – Placed on the 15-day disabled list from June 9 – July 13, 2007 with a strained left quadriceps.
c – Traded to the Atlanta Braves along with LHP Ron Mahay from the Texas Rangers in exchange for C Jarrod Saltalamacchia, INF Elvis Andrus, RHP Neftali Perez and LHPs Matt Harrison and Beau Jones on July 31, 2007.
d – Traded to the Los Angeles Angels from the Atlanta Braves in exchange for INF Casey Kotchman and RHP Steve Marek on July 29, 2008.
e – Signed as a free agent by the Yankees to an eight-year contract on January 6, 2009.

MARK TEIXEIRA

	2010					CAREER				
	AVG	AB	H	HR	RBI	AVG	AB	H	HR	RBI
Overall	.256	601	154	33	108	.286	4624	1321	275	906
Minnesota	.400	25	10	1	4	.374	222	83	16	46
Tampa Bay	.162	68	11	2	6	.264	295	78	16	53
Texas	.167	24	4	1	3	.263	95	25	5	23
Atlanta	-	-	-	-	-	.188	32	6	2	4
Cincinnati	-	-	-	-	-	.260	50	13	6	16
Philadelphia	.100	10	1	1	1	.250	112	28	10	23
San Francisco	-	-	-	-	-	.297	431	128	25	67
March	-	-	-	-	-	.100	10	1	0	0
April	.136	81	11	2	9	.237	637	151	24	83
May	.280	118	33	6	25	.293	809	237	45	167
June	.250	100	25	5	14	.273	721	197	45	142
July	.344	96	33	8	26	.291	762	222	49	145
August	.289	97	28	9	21	.308	853	263	58	183
September	.232	95	22	3	12	.296	790	234	53	178
October	.143	14	2	0	1	.381	42	16	1	8
Home	.288	292	84	19	64	.305	2302	701	155	517
Road	.227	309	70	14	44	.267	2322	620	120	389
vs. Left	.278	180	50	10	39	.305	1379	420	71	274
vs. Right	.247	421	104	23	69	.278	3245	901	204	632

Teixeira's Career by Ballpark

Park	AVG	AB	H	HR	RBI	Park	AVG	AB	H	HR	RBI
AT&T Park	.000	11	0	0	1	Target Field	.308	13	4	0	0
Citizens Bank Park	.250	56	14	6	17	Tropicana Field	.257	144	37	5	20
Great American Ball Park	.275	40	11	6	15	Turner Field	.293	317	93	21	70
Rangers Ballpark	.301	1363	410	87	305	Yankee Stadium	.300	600	180	43	135

Teixeira's Division Series Record

Year	Club vs. Opp.	AVG	G	AB	R	H	2B	3B	HR	RBI	SH	SF	HP	BB	SO	SB	CS	E	OBP	SLG
2008	LAA vs. BOS	.467	4	15	4	7	0	0	0	1	0	1	0	4	3	0	0	0	.550	.467
2009	NYY vs. MIN	.167	3	12	3	2	0	0	1	1	0	0	0	1	1	0	0	0	.231	.417
Division Series Totals		**.333**	**7**	**27**	**7**	**9**	**0**	**0**	**1**	**2**	**0**	**1**	**0**	**5**	**4**	**0**	**0**	**0**	**.424**	**.444**

Teixeira's League Championship Series Record

Year	Club vs. Opp.	AVG	G	AB	R	H	2B	3B	HR	RBI	SH	SF	HP	BB	SO	SB	CS	E	OBP	SLG
2009	NYY vs. LAA	.222	6	27	2	6	1	0	0	4	0	1	0	3	8	0	0	0	.290	.259
LCS Totals		**.222**	**6**	**27**	**2**	**6**	**1**	**0**	**0**	**4**	**0**	**1**	**0**	**3**	**8**	**0**	**0**	**0**	**.290**	**.259**

Teixeira's World Series Record

Year	Club vs. Opp.	AVG	G	AB	R	H	2B	3B	HR	RBI	SH	SF	HP	BB	SO	SB	CS	E	OBP	SLG
2009	NYY vs. PHI	.136	6	22	5	3	1	0	1	3	0	0	3	2	8	0	0	0	.296	.318
World Series Totals		**.136**	**6**	**22**	**5**	**3**	**1**	**0**	**1**	**3**	**0**	**0**	**3**	**2**	**8**	**0**	**0**	**0**	**.296**	**.318**
POSTSEASON TOTALS		**.237**	**19**	**76**	**14**	**18**	**2**	**0**	**2**	**9**	**0**	**2**	**3**	**10**	**20**	**0**	**0**	**0**	**.341**	**.342**

Teixeira's All-Star Game Record

Year	Club, Site	AVG	G	AB	R	H	2B	3B	HR	RBI	SH	SF	HP	BB	SO	SB	CS	E	OBP	SLG
2005	TEX, Detroit	.333	1	3	1	1	0	0	1	2	0	0	0	0	0	0	0	0	.333	1.333
2009	NYY, St. Louis	.000	1	3	0	0	0	0	0	0	0	0	0	0	0	0	0	0	.000	.000
All-Star Game Totals		**.167**	**2**	**6**	**1**	**1**	**0**	**0**	**1**	**2**	**0**	**0**	**0**	**0**	**0**	**0**	**0**	**0**	**.167**	**.667**

Teixeira's World Baseball Classic Record

Year	Country, Site	AVG	G	AB	R	H	2B	3B	HR	RBI	SH	SF	HP	BB	SO	SB	CS	E	OBP	SLG
2006	USA, USA	0	4	15	0	0	0	0	0	0	0	0	0	0	4	1	0	0	.000	.000

Teixeira's Career Fielding Record

Position	PCT	G	PO	A	E	TC
First Base	.996	1154	9949	663	38	10650
Third Base	.811	15	10	20	7	37
Outfield	.974	32	37	0	1	38

Teixeira's Career Home Run Chart

MULTI-HOMER GAMES: 29. **TWO-HOMER GAMES:** 26, last on 9/24/10 vs. Boston. **THREE-HOMER GAMES:** 3, last on 5/8/10 at Boston. **GRAND SLAMS:** 5, last on 6/20/10 vs. New York-NL (Johan Santana). **PINCH-HIT HR:** None. **INSIDE-THE-PARK HR:** None. **WALK-OFF HR:** None. **LEADOFF HR:** None.

Marcus Thames

38

Outfield/Designated Hitter

6-2 • 220 • B/T: Right/Right

Opening Day Age: 33

Birthdate
March 6, 1977

Birthplace
Louisville, Miss.

Resides
Starkville, Miss.

M.L. Service
6 years, 108 days

Status

▸ Signed a minor league contract with the Yankees on February 8, 2010...was signed to a Major League contract and selected to the Yankees' 25-man roster on April 3, 2010.

Postseason Notes

▸ Made his only postseason appearance in 2006 with the Detroit Tigers, batting .238 (5-for-21) with 3R, 2 doubles and 1RBI in eight games.

Career Notes

▸ Since 2006, has averaged 1HR every 14.93AB, marking the fourth-best ratio in the American League over the stretch (min. 1,200AB).

▸ In his career, has appeared in 276 games (235 starts) in LF, 75 games (53 starts) in RF, 44 games (34 starts) at 1B and one game at 3B.

2010

▸ Hit .288 (61-for-212) with 22R, 7 doubles, 12HR and 33RBI in 82 games (16 starts in LF and six in RF) with the Yankees in 2010...made his fifth career Opening Day roster and first with the Yankees...hit .300 (39-for-130) with 5 doubles, 5HR and 14RBI off left-handed pitching and .268 (22-for-82) with 2 doubles, 7HR and 19RBI off right-handers.

▸ Batted .308 (33-for-107) on the road, hitting 8HR...eight of his 12HR overall came with runners on base.

▸ Reached base in each of his first 12 starts of the season vs. left-handed starters.

▸ Hit his first home run of the season in 4/22 loss at Oakland, marking his second career homer as a Yankee and first since 6/10/02 vs. Arizona off Randy Johnson in his first Major League plate appearance – a span of 7 years, 316 days...the *Elias Sports Bureau* notes it was the longest stretch between homers as a Yankee since Jack Quinn homered on 9/11/1911 and 5/15/1920 (8 years, 247 days).

▸ Hit "walk-off" home run on 5/17 vs. Boston's Jonathan Papelbon, marking his second career "walk-off" home run (also 6/19/09 w/ Detroit vs. Milwaukee off Chris Narveson) and third career "walk-off" hit (also RBI single on 5/21/05 w/ Detroit vs. Arizona)...snapped a 53AB homerless stretch vs. right-handed pitching (last on 8/12/09 w/ Detroit at Boston off Josh Beckett)...also tallied 4RBI in the game, his most since 6/19/09 w/ Detroit vs. Milwaukee (also 4RBI).

▸ Walked a career-high three times in 5/18 loss vs. Boston.

▸ Missed two games from 5/20-21 with a sprained right ankle...was scratched from the lineup with a stiff neck prior to 6/5 loss at Toronto.

▸ Was placed on the 15-day disabled list with a strained right hamstring from 6/13-7/3 (missed 18 team games)...hit .200 (3-for-15) with 1RBI in four game rehab assignment with Triple-A Scranton/Wilkes Barre (2GS-LF/1GS-RF/1GS-DH).

2010 Highs and Streaks	
Hits	3 - 4 times
	Last: at TEX, 9/10/10
Runs	2 - 4 times
	Last: at CWS, 8/28/10
2B	1 - 7 times
	Last: at TEX, 9/10/10
3B	N/A
HR	2 - at CWS, 8/28/10
RBI	4 - vs. BOS, 5/17/10
BB	3 - vs. BOS, 5/18/10
SO	3 - 3 times
	Last: at TEX, 9/10/10
SB	N/A
Hit Streak	6g - 8/2-12/10

Career Highs and Streaks	
Hits	4 - vs. CLE, 7/12/09
Runs	3 - 4 times
	Last: vs. CLE, 7/12/09
2B	2 - 2 times
	Last: at OAK, 9/2/07
3B	1 - 3 times
	Last: at TOR, 4/9/09
HR	2 - 9 times
	Last: at CWS, 8/28/10
RBI	5 - 3 times
	Last: vs. BOS, 7/6/07
BB	3 - vs. BOS, 5/18/10
SO	4 - 4 times
	Last: at CLE, 7/30/08
SB	1 - 3 times
	Last: vs. CLE, 7/4/07
Hit Streak	11g - 6/8-18/06

MARCUS THAMES

- In his first game back from the D.L., hit 10th-inning game-winning pinch-hit "walk-off" single on 7/4 vs. Toronto…marked the Yankees' first "walk-off" hit by a pinch hitter since 6/5/08 vs. Toronto, when Jason Giambi hit a two-run HR off B.J. Ryan.
- Hit .344 (21-for-61) in 19 games in the month August, marking the sixth-highest average by an American Leaguer in the month…his 14RBI in August were his most for any calendar month since driving in 16 runs in June 2008 w/ Detroit.
- Hit solo-HR and had game-winning RBI single in the ninth and was 3-for-5 with 2R and 2RBI in 8/11 win at Texas.
- Homered in five consecutive starts from 8/24-30 (6HR total)…became the first Yankee to homer in five straight starts since Alex Rodriguez from 9/4-9/07…had 4HR in a three-game span from 8/28-30 and 7HR in a 10-game stretch from 8/24-9/4.
- Collected his ninth career multi-HR game—and first since 6/19/09 w/ Detroit vs. Milwaukee—in 8/29 win at Chicago-AL, hitting a two-run HR and solo HR and going 2-for-5.
- Was 3-for-6 with 1R, 1 double and 1RBI in 9/10 loss at Texas, matching his season high in hits (fourth time).
- Hit safely in four of his final five starts of the season.
- Hit .135 (7-for-52) with 4R, 1 double, 2HR and 2RBI in 19 spring training games with the Yankees.

Thames' Career Hitting Record

Year	Team	AVG	G	AB	R	H	2B	3B	HR	RBI	SH	SF	HP	BB	SO	SB	CS	E	OBP	SLG
1997	GCL Yankees	.344	57	195	51	67	17	4	7	36	1	4	3	16	26	6	4	2	.394	.579
	Greensboro	.313	4	16	2	5	1	0	0	2	0	0	0	0	3	1	0	0	.313	.375
1998	Tampa	.284	122	457	62	130	18	3	11	59	1	5	8	24	78	13	6	9	.328	.409
1999	Norwich	.225	51	182	25	41	6	2	4	26	1	2	3	22	40	0	1	7	.316	.346
	Tampa	.244	69	266	47	65	12	4	11	38	1	2	3	33	58	3	0	3	.332	.444
2000	Norwich	.241	131	474	72	114	30	2	15	79	0	8	4	50	89	1	5	9	.313	.407
2001	Norwich	.321	139	520	114	167	43	4	31	97	0	3	7	73	101	10	4	8	.410	.598
2002	YANKEES	.231	7	13	2	3	1	0	1	2	0	0	0	0	4	0	0	0	.231	.538
	Columbus	.207	107	386	51	80	21	3	13	45	0	2	7	43	71	5	4	5	.297	.378
2003	Columbus	.278	52	194	26	54	15	2	2	28	0	5	1	17	48	3	4	5	.332	.407
	Oklahoma - b	.258	18	66	9	17	4	0	2	7	0	0	0	8	12	1	0	0	.338	.409
	TEXAS - a	.205	30	73	12	15	2	0	1	4	0	1	2	8	18	0	1	0	.298	.274
2004	Toledo	.329	64	234	57	77	21	1	24	59	1	4	2	33	40	4	1	2	.410	.735
	DETROIT	.255	61	165	24	42	12	0	10	33	0	1	2	16	42	0	1	0	.326	.509
2005	Toledo	.340	73	265	53	90	18	3	22	56	0	5	3	41	59	4	1	2	.427	.679
	DETROIT	.196	38	107	11	21	2	0	7	16	0	1	1	9	38	0	0	1	.263	.411
2006	DETROIT	.256	110	348	61	89	20	2	26	60	0	1	4	37	92	1	1	2	.333	.549
2007	Toledo	.375	2	8	2	3	0	0	1	2	0	0	0	0	1	0	0	0	.375	.750
	DETROIT - c	.242	86	269	37	65	15	0	18	54	0	1	1	13	72	2	1	2	.278	.498
2008	DETROIT	.241	103	316	50	76	12	0	25	56	0	2	0	24	95	0	3	5	.292	.516
2009	Toledo	.245	12	49	6	12	0	0	2	6	0	0	0	5	14	0	0	0	.315	.367
	DETROIT - d	.252	87	258	33	65	11	1	13	36	0	6	1	29	72	0	2	0	.323	.453
2010	YANKEES - e, f	.288	82	212	22	61	7	0	12	33	0	3	3	19	61	0	0	3	.350	.491
	Scranton/WB	.200	4	15	0	3	0	0	0	1	0	0	0	0	1	0	0	0	.200	.200
Minor League Totals		**.278**	**905**	**3327**	**577**	**925**	**206**	**28**	**145**	**541**	**5**	**40**	**41**	**365**	**641**	**51**	**30**	**51**	**.353**	**.488**
Major League Totals		**.248**	**604**	**1761**	**252**	**437**	**82**	**3**	**113**	**294**	**0**	**16**	**14**	**155**	**494**	**3**	**9**	**15**	**.311**	**.491**

Thames' Division Series Record

Year	Club vs. Opp.	AVG	G	AB	R	H	2B	3B	HR	RBI	SH	SF	HP	BB	SO	SB	CS	E	OBP	SLG
2006	DET vs. NYY	.333	4	15	2	5	2	0	0	1	0	0	0	1	5	0	0	0	.375	.467
Division Series Totals		**.333**	**4**	**15**	**2**	**5**	**2**	**0**	**0**	**1**	**0**	**0**	**0**	**1**	**5**	**0**	**0**	**0**	**.375**	**.467**

Thames' League Championship Series Record

Year	Club vs. Opp.	AVG	G	AB	R	H	2B	3B	HR	RBI	SH	SF	HP	BB	SO	SB	CS	E	OBP	SLG
2006	DET vs. OAK	.000	2	5	1	0	0	0	0	0	0	0	0	0	1	0	0	0	.000	.000
LCS Totals		**.000**	**2**	**5**	**1**	**0**	**0**	**0**	**0**	**0**	**0**	**0**	**0**	**0**	**1**	**0**	**0**	**0**	**.000**	**.000**

Thames' World Series Record

Year	Club vs. Opp.	AVG	G	AB	R	H	2B	3B	HR	RBI	SH	SF	HP	BB	SO	SB	CS	E	OBP	SLG
2006	DET vs. STL	.000	2	1	0	0	0	0	0	0	0	0	0	0	0	0	0	0	.000	.000
World Series Totals		**.000**	**2**	**1**	**0**	**0**	**0**	**0**	**0**	**0**	**0**	**0**	**0**	**0**	**0**	**0**	**0**	**0**	**.000**	**.000**
POSTSEASON TOTALS		**.238**	**8**	**21**	**3**	**5**	**2**	**0**	**0**	**1**	**0**	**0**	**1**	**1**	**6**	**0**	**0**	**0**	**.273**	**.333**

Thames' Career Home Run Chart

MULTI-HOMER GAMES: 9. **TWO-HOMER GAMES:** 9, last on 8/28/10 at Chicago-AL. **GRAND SLAMS:** 6, last on 9/14/08 at Chicago-AL (Octavio Dotel). **PINCH-HIT HR:** 4, last on 6/8/09 at Chicago-AL (Matt Thorton). **INSIDE-THE-PARK HR:** None. **WALK-OFF HR:** 2, last on 5/17/10 vs. Boston (Jonathan Papelbon). **LEADOFF HR:** None.

Javier Vazquez

31

Right-handed Pitcher
6-2 • 210 • B/T: Right/Right
Opening Day Age: 33

Birthdate
July 25, 1976

Birthplace
Ponce, P.R.

Resides
Ponce, P.R.

M.L. Service
12 years, 141 days

Career Highlights
A.L. All-Star Team
▸ 2004

Status
▸ Acquired by the Yankees along with LHP Boone Logan in exchange for OF Melky Cabrera, RHP Arodys Vizcaino and LHP Mike Dunn on December 22, 2009…is in the fifth year of a five-year contract extending through 2010.

Postseason Notes
▸ Has made four career postseason appearances (two starts), going 1-1 with a 10.34 ERA (15.2IP, 18ER)…made his first career postseason start in 2004 ALDS Game 4 at Minnesota on 10/9/04…earned his only career playoff win with the Yankees in a 19-8 ALCS Game 3 victory on 10/16/04 at Boston, pitching 4.1 IP of relief (7H, 4ER, 2BB, 4K, 1HR).

Career Notes
▸ Has won at least 10 games in 11 consecutive seasons (2000-10), marking the longest such streak among active Major League pitchers…only Andy Pettitte (15) and Jamie Moyer (15) have more 10-win seasons among active pitchers.

▸ Has never appeared on the disabled list in his entire career…the only Major League pitchers with longer service time never to have gone on the disabled list are Derek Lowe and Livan Hernandez.

▸ Is one of three active Major Leaguers to have defeated all 30 teams, joining San Francisco's Barry Zito, Philadelphia's Jamie Moyer and the Dodgers' Vincente Padilla (credit: *Elias*)…has started in 44 different stadiums, second most among active pitchers (Jamie Moyer-49).

▸ Owns 10 seasons of at least 200.0IP…has missed 200.0IP just twice over the last 11 years (2000-10), in each of his two seasons with the Yankees (2010-157.1IP; 2004-198.0IP).

▸ Struck out at least one batter in 349 consecutive games from 5/16/00-9/10/10, tying Dwight Gooden for the third longest streak since 1900, behind Nolan Ryan (382) and Randy Johnson (351)…also struck out at least one batter in 345 consecutive starts over that same stretch, marking the fifth-longest streak since 1900, trailing only Tom Seaver (411), Nolan Ryan (382), Curt Schilling (378), David Cone (347) and Dwight Gooden (347).

▸ Has recorded 10-or-more-K in a game 40 times, the third-highest total among pitchers currently on a 40-man roster behind Johan Santana (49) and Kerry Wood (41).

▸ Has not committed an error over his last 105G/100GS since 8/16/07 and has made just two miscues over the last five seasons (2006-10).

2010 Highs and Streaks	
Low hit CG	N/A
IP (start)	7.0 - 8 times
	Last: at CLE, 7/26/10
IP (relief)	4.2 - vs. OAK, 8/30/10
Hits	10 - at TOR, 9/29/10
Runs	8 - at TB, 4/9/10
BB	4 - 5 times
	Last: vs. TOR, 9/4/10
SO	9 - at TOR, 6/6/10
HR	3 - 3 times
	Last: at TOR, 9/29/10
Winning Streak	3g - 2 times
	Last: 7/5-26/10
Losing Streak	2g - 4 times
	Last: 8/6-16/10

Career Highs and Streaks	
Low hit CG	1 - at LAD, 9/14/99
IP (start)	9.0 - 23 times
	Last: at WAS, 9/25/09
IP (relief)	4.2 - vs. OAK, 8/30/10
Hits	12 - 3 times
	Last: at PIT, 9/6/05
Runs	9 - 2 times
	Last: vs. HOU, 6/25/06
BB	6 - 2 times
	Last: vs. NYY, 8/10/06
SO	14 - at CHC, 4/9/03
HR	3 - 17 times
	Last: at TOR, 9/29/10
Winning Streak	6g - 8/12-9/7/01
Losing Streak	7g - 8/4-9/5/02

▸ Went 14-10 with a 4.91 ERA and was named to the AL All-Star team in 2004 in his other season with the Yankees...following the season, was traded to the Diamondbacks in exchange for LHP Randy Johnson.

2010

▸ Went 10-10 with a 5.32 ERA (157.1IP, 93ER), 65BB and 121K in 31 games (26 starts) with the Yankees in 2010...marked his lowest IP and strikeout totals since 1999 (154.2IP, 113K) and his most walks since his 1998 rookie season (68BB)...opponents batted .257 (155-for-602, 32HR); LH .275 (83-for-302, 19HR) and RH .240 (72-for-300, 13HR)...the Yankees went 13-13 in his starts.

▸ Made 26 starts in 2010, going 8-10 with a 5.56 ERA (144.0IP, 89ER)...was 2-0 with a 2.70 ERA (13.1IP, 4ER) in five relief appearances, including wins on 5/17 vs. Boston and 8/30 vs. Oakland.

Vazquez's 2010 Pitching Lines

Date/Opp	Score	W/L	IP	H	R	ER	HR	BB	K	NP/K	ERA	Left game
4/9 at TB	3-9	L	5.2	8	**8**	8	2	3	5	98-62	12.71	Trailing 7-2
4/14 vs. LAA	3-5	L	5.1	6	4	4	0	2	4	100-60	9.82	Trailing 3-1
4/20 at OAK	7-3	W	5.1	6	3	3	2	3	6	107-72	8.27	Leading 6-3
4/25 at LAA	4-8	L	3.2	5	5	5	1	3	3	78-47	9.00	Trailing 3-5
5/1 vs. CWS	6-7	ND	3.0	7	5	5	**3**	**4**	2	83-46	9.78	Trailing5-1
5/12 at DET (G1)*	0-2	L	**7.0**	5	2	2	0	2	7	97-66	8.10	Trailing 2-0
*5/17 vs. BOS**	*11-9*	*W*	*0.1*	*0*	*0*	*0*	*0*	*0*	*1*	*---*	*8.01*	*---*
5/21 at NYM*	2-1	W	6.0	1	0	0	0	2	6	70-46	6.69	Leading 2-0
5/27 at MIN	2-8	L	5.2	8	5	5	1	3	2	112-64	6.86	Trailing 1-2
6/1 vs. BAL	3-1	W	**7.0**	4	1	1	1	1	7	103-63	6.06	Leading 3-1
6/6 at TOR*	4-3	W	**7.0**	1	2	2	1	**4**	**9**	106-65	5.63	Leading 4-2
6/12 vs. HOU	9-3	W	**7.0**	6	3	3	2	0	6	95-58	5.43	Leading 9-3
6/18 vs. NYM*	0-4	L	**7.0**	3	1	1	0	3	4	109-67	5.01	Trailing 1-0
6/23 at ARI	6-5 (10)	ND	5.0	6	4	4	0	2	1	85-51	5.16	Tied 4-4
6/30 vs. SEA*	0-7	L	6.0	6	3	3	2	2	8	113-71	5.11	Trailing 3-0
7/5 at OAK	3-1	W	**7.0**	3	1	1	0	2	2	110-72	4.81	Leading 3-1
7/10 at SEA	1-4	ND	**7.0**	3	0	0	0	2	7	**117**-77	4.45	Leading 1-0
7/21 vs. LAA	10-6	W	5.0	9	5	5	2	0	1	80-59	4.68	Leading 6-5
7/26 at CLE	3-2	W	**7.0**	5	2	2	1	3	5	102-64	4.54	Leading 3-2
7/31 at TB	5-4	ND	6.1	8	4	4	1	1	3	102-66	4.61	Trailing 4-3
8/6 vs. BOS	3-6	L	5.1	6	6	3	2	**4**	5	109-66	4.63	Trailing 6-3
8/11 at TEX*	7-6	ND	4.1	8	6	6	1	2	1	82-49	4.90	Trailing 6-1
8/16 vs. DET	1-3	L	4.0	5	2	2	1	4	6	106-64	4.89	Trailing 2-0
8/21 vs. SEA*	9-5	ND	3.0	8	4	4	**3**	1	2	65-40	5.05	Tied 4-4
8/25 at TOR	*3-6*	*ND*	*4.1*	*2*	*1*	*1*	*1*	*1*	*2*	*55-36*	*4.96*	*Trailing 6-3*
8/30 vs. OAK	*11-5*	*W*	*4.2*	*2*	*1*	*1*	*0*	*1*	*6*	*70-47*	*4.86*	*Leading 4-2*
9/4 vs. TOR	7-5	ND	4.2	4	5	5	2	**4**	6	88-50	5.01	Leading 5-3
9/10 at TEX	5-6 (13)	ND	5.0	6	4	4	0	2	4	88-59	5.09	Leading 5-3
9/21 vs. TB	*8-3*	*ND*	*1.0*	*3*	*0*	*0*	*0*	*0*	*0*	*21-14*	*5.05*	*Leading 7-3*
9/23 vs. TB	*3-10*	*ND*	*3.0*	*1*	*2*	*2*	*0*	*2*	*3*	*60-33*	*5.07*	*Trailing10-3*
9/29 at TOR	4-8	L	4.2	**10**	7	7	3	2	0	89-55	5.32	Trailing 7-0
Totals		10-10	157.1	155	96	93	32	65	121		5.32	

*start came after a Yankees loss – **Bold**-season high – *italics*= relief appearance

▸ Received the worst run support of any Yankees starter in 2010, averaging 4.65R/9.0IP during his starts.

▸ Was the starter in three of the eight games the Yankees were shut out in 2010 (5/12-G1 at Detroit, 6/18 vs. Mets and 6/30 vs. Seattle) allowing six combined runs over 20.0IP in those starts.

▸ Was 2-1 with a 2.88 ERA (25.0IP, 8ER) in four Interleague starts.

▸ Allowed just 4SB (7/31 at TB by Carl Crawford; 4/14 vs. LAA by Brandon Wood; and 4/9 vs. TB by B.J. Upton)...had a 16-start stretch from 4/20-7/26 without allowing a stolen base, marking the longest such stretch by a Yankee since Vazquez went 23 straight starts without allowing a steal from 4/8-8/6/04 (credit: *Elias Sports Bureau*).

▸ Allowed 32 homers, tying for the fourth-most ever allowed by a Yankees pitcher in a single season...also allowed 33 homers as a Yankee during the 2004 season, which ranks third on the list...surrendered home runs in eight straight starts from 7/21-9/4, marking the longest such stretch by a Yankees starter since Andy Pettitte had a nine-game streak over his last eight starts of 1999 and his first start in 2000...marks the longest such streak by a Yankees right-hander since Hideki Irabu had an eight-game streak in 1997.

▸ Yankees fielders did not make an error through his first 114.2IP, according to the *Elias Sports Bureau*, and he allowed just three unearned runs all season (all on 8/6 vs. Boston).

▸ Went 1-3 with a 9.78 ERA (23.0IP, 25ER) over his first five starts of the season from 4/9-5/1.

▸ Made his first start on 4/9 at Tampa Bay, recording the loss in a 9-3 Rays victory (5.2IP, 8H, 8R, 8ER, 3BB, 5K, 2HR)...marked his most runs and earned runs allowed since 6/25/06 vs. Houston (w/ Chicago-AL), when he surrendered a career-high-tying 9R/9ER.

▸ Also took the loss in his second start on 4/14 vs. Los Angeles-AL, (5.1IP, 6H, 4ER, 2BB, 4K), marking the first time in his career he lost the first two starts of a season and the third time he started a season 0-2 (also 1998 and 2005).

▸ Surpassed 2,500.0 career IP in his start on 4/14 vs. Los Angeles-AL, becoming the 189th pitcher all-time to reach the plateau and one of just five active players – including teammate Andy Pettitte – to reach the mark.

▸ Earned his first win of the season on 4/20 at Oakland…allowed 3ER (all on home runs) in 5.1IP (6H, 3BB, 6K, 2HR).

▸ Tied his career high with 3HR (15th time) on 5/1 vs. Chicago-AL, allowing 5ER on 7H in 3.0IP (4BB, 2K)…marked his shortest non-injury outing since 8/14/05 (w/ Arizona) at Atlanta (2.0IP, 9ER).

▸ Made his third career relief appearance and recorded the win in 5/17 victory vs. Boston, striking out his only batter faced (Kevin Youkilis) to end the top of the ninth…Yankees scored 4R in the bottom of the ninth, including a "walk-off" HR off Papelbon…was his first career relief win after making 391 career starts…no Major League pitcher had made as many starts before his first relief win since 8/16/02, when Kevin Brown earned his first career relief win w/ Los Angeles-NL vs. Montreal after 408 career starts.

▸ Limited the Mets to just 1H over 6.0 scoreless innings (2BB, 6K) on 5/21 at Citi Field, recording the win in the 2-1 Yankees victory…held the Mets hitless over his first 4.1IP…was forced to exit after bruising his right index finger while hitting a sacrifice bunt in the top of the seventh inning.

▸ Went 3-2 with a 3.23 ERA (39.0IP, 14ER) and a .187 opponent's batting average in six June starts…prior to the stretch was 2-5 with a 6.91ERA and a .289 opponent's batting average from the start of the season through May.

MAJOR LEAGUE PITCHERS LAST 10 YEARS (since 2001)	
Most Strikeouts	
1. JAVIER VAZQUEZ	1,926
2. Johan Santana	1,813
3. CC SABATHIA	1,787
4. Roy Oswalt	1,666
5. Roy Halladay	1,575
Most IP	
1. Mark Buehrle	2,220.0
2. Livan Hernandez	2,173.0
3. CC SABATHIA	2127.0
4. Barry Zito	2,105.2
5. JAVIER VAZQUEZ	2,102.2
Most Starts	
1. Barry Zito	339
2. Livan Hernandez	332
3. Mark Buehrle	331
4. CC SABATHIA	322
5. JAVIER VAZQUEZ	320

▸ Held an opponent to 1H for the second time on 6/6 at Toronto, recording the win in a 4-3 Yankees victory…held the Jays to just 1H (a Vernon Wells two-run HR) over 7.0IP, striking out a season-high nine batters (also 4BB)…carried a no-hitter through two outs in the sixth inning.

▸ Went undefeated in July, going 3-0 with 2ND in five starts (3.34 ERA in 32.1IP, 28H, 12ER).

▸ Made his 400th career start on 7/5 at Oakland, becoming the 120th pitcher in Major League history to reach the plateau and sixth active player…became the seventh pitcher to reach the plateau as a Yankee, joining Catfish Hunter, Whitey Ford, Mike Mussina, Herb Pennock, Andy Pettitte and Red Ruffing.

▸ Carried a no-hitter until a two-out, sixth-inning hit (single by Ichiro Suzuki) on 7/10 at Seattle, tossing 7.0 scoreless IP in a no-decision (3H, 2BB, 7K, 1WP)…threw a season-high 117 pitches.

▸ Defeated the Angels on 7/21 at Yankee Stadium, completing the feat of winning against all 30 current franchises.

▸ Recorded the loss on 8/6 vs. Boston, marking his first defeat since 6/30 vs. Seattle…Francisco Cervelli's second-inning fielding error led to three unearned runs, the only unearned runs that Vazquez allowed in 2010…his 6R allowed in 5.1IP marked his most since his first start of the season on 4/9 at Tampa Bay (8R).

▸ Made back-to-back relief appearances on 8/25 at Toronto (4.1IP, 2H, 1ER, 1BB, 2K, 1HR) and 8/30 vs. Oakland (4.2IP, 4H, 5ER, 4BB, 6K, 2HR).

▸ Earned his 10th win of the season on 8/30 vs. Oakland in relief, reaching the total for the 11th consecutive season…tossed a relief-outing career-high 4.2IP (2H, 1ER, 1BB, 6K, 1WP).

▸ Recorded no-decisions in back-to-back starts on 9/4 vs. Toronto (4.2IP, 5ER) and 9/10 at Texas, (5.0IP, 4ER).

▸ Did not pitch for 10 days before tossing 1.0 inning of scoreless relief in 9/21 win vs. Tampa Bay, allowing 3H without striking out a batter…was the first time he did not strike out a batter in a game since 5/10/00 w/Montreal vs. Philadelphia, snapping a streak of 349 consecutive appearance with at least 1K.

▸ Hit three consecutive batters (Jennings, Aybar and Shoppach) in the seventh inning of 9/23 relief appearance vs. Tampa Bay (3.0IP, 1H, 2ER, 2BB, 3K, 3HBP), tying a Major League record (eighth time)…became the first Yankee in franchise history to hit three consecutive batters and the first pitcher in the Majors since the Dodgers' Jeff Weaver (8/21/04 vs. Atlanta)…joined Harry Harper (8/25/21 at Cleveland) and Tom Morgan (6/30/54 at Boston) as the only Yankees to hit three batters in a single inning—credit: *Elias Sports Bureau* record book…allowed two runs in the seventh without allowing a hit.

▸ Started and allowed a season-high 10H and a season-high-tying 3HR on 9/29 at Toronto in his final 2010 start or appearance…recorded the loss in an 8-4 defeat (4.2IP, 7ER, 2BB, 0K, 3HR, 1WP) without recording a strikeout, snapping a 345-start stretch with at least 1K.

JAVIER VAZQUEZ

Vazquez' Career Pitching Record

Year	Team	W	L	ERA	G	GS	CG	SHO	SV	IP	H	R	ER	HR	HB	BB	SO	WP	BK
1994	GCL Expos	5	2	2.53	15	11	1	1	0	67.2	37	25	19	0	3	15	56	9	2
1995	Albany	6	6	5.08	21	21	1	0	0	102.2	109	67	58	8	9	47	87	2	2
1996	Delmarva	14	3	2.68	27	27	1	0	0	164.1	138	64	49	12	7	57	173	12	2
1997	West Palm Beach	6	3	2.16	19	19	1	0	0	112.2	98	40	27	8	6	28	100	2	2
	Harrisburg	4	0	1.07	6	6	1	0	0	42.0	15	5	5	2	2	12	47	2	0
1998	MONTREAL	5	15	6.06	33	32	0	0	0	172.1	196	121	116	31	11	68	139	2	0
1999	WASHINGTON	9	8	5.00	26	26	3	1	0	154.2	154	98	86	20	4	52	113	2	0
	Ottawa	4	2	4.85	7	7	0	0	0	42.2	45	24	23	7	2	16	46	0	0
2000	WASHINGTON	11	9	4.05	33	33	2	1	0	217.2	247	104	98	24	5	61	196	3	0
2001	WASHINGTON	16	11	3.42	32	32	5	3	0	223.2	197	92	85	24	4	44	208	3	1
2002	WASHINGTON	10	13	3.91	34	34	2	0	0	230.1	243	111	100	28	4	49	179	3	0
2003	WASHINGTON	13	12	3.24	34	34	4	1	0	230.2	198	93	83	28	4	57	241	11	1
2004	YANKEES - a	14	10	4.91	32	32	0	0	0	198.0	195	114	108	33	11	60	150	12	2
2005	ARIZONA - b	11	15	4.42	33	33	3	1	0	215.2	223	112	106	35	5	46	192	7	0
2006	CHICAGO - AL - c	11	12	4.84	33	32	1	0	0	202.2	206	116	109	23	15	56	184	7	0
2007	CHICAGO - AL	15	8	3.74	32	32	2	0	0	216.2	197	95	90	29	7	50	213	5	0
2008	CHICAGO - AL	12	16	4.67	33	33	1	0	0	208.1	214	113	108	25	6	61	200	2	0
2009	ATLANTA - d, e	15	10	2.87	32	32	3	0	0	219.1	181	75	70	20	4	44	238	6	0
2010	YANKEES	10	10	5.32	31	26	0	0	0	157.1	155	96	93	32	7	65	121	8	0
Minor League Totals		**39**	**16**	**3.06**	**95**	**91**	**5**	**1**	**0**	**532.0**	**442**	**225**	**181**	**37**	**29**	**175**	**509**	**27**	**8**
AL Totals		**62**	**56**	**4.65**	**161**	**155**	**4**	**0**	**0**	**983.0**	**967**	**534**	**508**	**142**	**46**	**292**	**868**	**34**	**2**
NL Totals		**90**	**93**	**4.02**	**257**	**256**	**22**	**7**	**0**	**1664.1**	**1639**	**806**	**744**	**210**	**40**	**421**	**1506**	**37**	**2**
Major League Totals		**152**	**149**	**4.26**	**418**	**411**	**26**	**7**	**0**	**2647.1**	**2606**	**1340**	**1252**	**352**	**86**	**713**	**2374**	**71**	**4**
NYY Total		**24**	**20**	**5.09**	**63**	**58**	**0**	**0**	**0**	**355.1**	**350**	**210**	**201**	**65**	**18**	**125**	**271**	**20**	**2**

Selected by the Montreal Expos in the fifth round of the 1994 First-Year Player Draft.

a – Acquired by the Yankees from Montreal in exchange for LHP Randy Choate, INF Nick Johnson and OF Juan Rivera on December 16, 2003.

b – Acquired by Arizona from the Yankees along with LHP Brad Halsey, C Dioner Navarro and cash considerations in exchange for LHP Randy Johnson on January 11, 2005.

c – Acquired by Chicago-AL from Arizona along with cash considerations in exchange for RHPs Orlando Hernandez and Luis Vizcaino and OF Chris Young on December 20, 2005.

d – Acquired by Atlanta from Chicago-AL along with LHP Boone Logan in exchange for INFs Jonny Gilmore and Brent Lillibridge, C Tyler Flowers and LHP Santos Rodriguez on December 4, 2008.

e – Acquired by the Yankees from Atlanta along with LHP Boone Logan in exchange for OF Melky Cabrera, RHP Arodys Vizcaino and LHP Mike Dunn on December 22, 2009.

Vazquez' Division Series Record

Year	Club vs. Opp.	W	L	ERA	G	GS	CG	SHO	SV	IP	H	R	ER	HR	HP	BB	SO	WP	BK
2004	NYY vs. MIN	0	0	9.00	1	1	0	0	0	5.0	7	5	5	1	2	2	6	0	0
2008	CWS vs. TB	0	1	12.46	1	1	0	0	0	4.1	8	6	6	2	0	1	6	0	0
Division Series Totals		**0**	**1**	**10.61**	**2**	**2**	**0**	**0**	**0**	**9.1**	**15**	**11**	**11**	**3**	**2**	**3**	**12**	**0**	**0**

Vazquez' Championship Series Record

Year	Club vs. Opp.	W	L	ERA	G	GS	CG	SHO	SV	IP	H	R	ER	HR	HP	BB	SO	WP	BK
2004	NYY vs. BOS	1	0	9.95	2	0	0	0	0	6.1	9	7	7	3	0	7	6	0	0
LCS Totals		**1**	**0**	**9.95**	**2**	**0**	**0**	**0**	**0**	**6.1**	**9**	**7**	**7**	**3**	**0**	**7**	**6**	**0**	**0**
POSTSEASON TOTALS		**1**	**1**	**10.34**	**4**	**2**	**0**	**0**	**0**	**15.2**	**24**	**18**	**18**	**6**	**2**	**10**	**18**	**0**	**0**

Vazquez' All-Star Game Record

Year	Club, Site	W	L	ERA	G	GS	CG	SHO	SV	IP	H	R	ER	HR	HP	BB	SO	WP	BK
2004	NYY, Houston	0	0	0.00	1	0	0	0	0	1.0	0	0	0	0	0	0	2	0	0

Vazquez' World Baseball Classic Record

Year	Country, Site	W	L	ERA	G	GS	CG	SHO	SV	IP	H	R	ER	HR	HP	BB	SO	WP	BK
2006	Puerto Rico	1	0	2.25	2	2	0	0	0	8.0	6	2	2	1	1	2	7	0	0
2009	Puerto Rico	2	0	0.96	2	2	0	0	0	9.1	8	1	1	0	0	1	5	0	0
WBC Totals		**3**	**0**	**1.56**	**4**	**4**	**0**	**0**	**0**	**17.1**	**14**	**3**	**3**	**1**	**1**	**3**	**12**	**0**	**0**

Vazquez' Regular Season Batting Record

Year	Team	AVG	G	AB	R	H	2B	3B	HR	RBI	SH	SF	HP	BB	SO	SB	CS
2010	NYY	.000	31	1	0	0	0	0	0	0	2	0	0	2	0	0	0
Major League Totals		**.206**	**418**	**504**	**38**	**104**	**13**	**2**	**1**	**27**	**96**	**2**	**1**	**22**	**85**	**0**	**1**

Vazquez' Career Fielding Record

Position	PCT	G	PO	A	E	TC	DP
Pitcher	.979	418	155	398	12	565	42

Kerry Wood

39 Right-handed Pitcher

6-5 4 210 4B/T: Right/Right

Opening Day Age: 32

Birthdate
June 16, 1977

Birthplace
Irving, Tex.

Resides
Chicago, Ill.

M.L. Service
12 years, 169 days

Career Highlights
N.L. All-Star Team
▸ 2003, 2008

N.L. Rookie of the Year
▸ 1998

Status
▸ Was acquired by the Yankees from the Cleveland Indians along with cash considerations on July 31, 2010 in exchange for a player to be named later or cash…signed a two-year contract with Cleveland on December 13, 2008…contract extends through the 2010 season with a club option for 2011.

Postseason Notes
▸ Is 2-2 with a 3.68 ERA in eight career postseason appearances (five starts)…both wins came in the 2003 NLDS w/ Chicago-NL vs. Atlanta, allowing 7H and 3ER in 15.1IP over two starts…last appeared in the playoffs in the 2008 NLDS with Chicago-NL vs. Los Angeles-NL, making one relief outing.

Career Notes
▸ Since 1950, ranks second among all Major Leaguers with 10.35 strikeouts per nine innings (1,519K, 1,320.1IP), trailing only Randy Johnson (10.61)—min. 1,000.0IP.
▸ Reached the 1,500-strikeout plateau in 8/18/10 win vs. Detroit after pitching only 1,303.0IP in the Majors, the fastest any pitcher has ever reached the mark…according to the *Elias Sports Bureau*, surpassed the previous record holder Pedro Martinez who had thrown 1,337.0IP at the time of his 1,500th strikeout.

2010
▸ Combined to go 3-4 with eight saves (in 12 opportunities) and a 3.13 ERA in 47 relief appearances with the Yankees and Indians in 2010…opponents batted .210 (35-for-167, 4HR); LH .211 (16-for-76, 1HR), RH .209 (19-for-91, 3HR)…appeared in consecutive games seven times and three straight games once.
▸ Was 2-0 with a 0.69 ERA in 24 relief appearances with the Yankees in 2010, striking out 31 batters in 26.0IP…retired 18-of-24 first batters faced (75.0%)…prevented seven-of-eight inherited runners from scoring…the Yankees were 12-12 in his appearances…22 of his 24 outings with the Yankees were scoreless.
▸ His 0.69 ERA was the lowest single-season ERA in franchise history (min. 25.0IP), surpassing Goose Gossage's 0.77 ERA in 1981—credit: Stats LLC.
▸ Held opponents scoreless in 31 of his 35 appearances from 6/13 through the end of the season, striking out 41 batters in 35.2IP over the stretch (22H, 5ER, 22BB).
▸ From 8/1 through the end of the season, the Yankees bullpen pitched to a 2.79 ERA and held opponents to a .218 batting average…prior to Wood's acquisition, Yankees relievers had a 3.95 ERA with a .238 opponents' BA.
▸ Made his Yankees debut in 8/1 loss at Tampa Bay, allowing 1H and 2BB in 1.0IP (3K)…allowed 1ER in his next outing in 8/3 loss vs. Toronto on an Aaron Hill solo HR (0.2IP, 1H).
▸ Did not allow a run in a career-high 21 straight appearances from 8/6-9/26…surpassed his previous career high of 11 games from 5/20-6/17/09…tossed

2010 Highs and Streaks		
Low hit CG	N/A	
IP (start)	N/A	
IP (relief)	2.0 - at TEX, 8/11/10	
Hits	4 - vs. KC, 5/19/10	
Runs	5 - vs. KC, 5/19/10	
BB	3 - at BOS, 10/2/10(G1)	
SO	3 - 2 times	
	Last: at TB, 8/1/10	
HR	1 - 4 times	
	Last: vs. TOR, 8/3/10	
Winning Streak	2g - 8/11-9/3/10	
Losing Streak	2g - 6/23-7/11/10	

Career Highs and Streaks		
Low hit CG	1 - 2 times	
	Last: vs. MIL, 5/25/01	
IP (start)	9.0 - 9 times	
	Last: vs. NYM, 9/17/03	
IP (relief)	2.0 - 10 times	
	Last: at TEX, 8/11/10	
Hits	11 - vs. FLA, 9/10/04	
Runs	8 - 3 times	
	Last: vs. HOU, 8/27/04	
BB	8 - vs. STL, 9/22/00	
SO	20 - vs. HOU, 5/6/98	
HR	4 - vs. HOU, 8/27/04	
Single Season Winning Streak		
	6g - 5/19-6/17/01	
Winning Streak	6g - 2 times	
	Last: 7/23/01-4/15/02	
Losing Streak	3g - 2 times	
	Last: 7/5-9/7/08	

23.1 straight scoreless innings over the stretch, the longest single-season streak of his career, surpassing his 21.0 scoreless-inning stretch in his rookie season with the Cubs in 1998…marked the fifth-longest single-season consecutive scoreless appearance streak by a Yankee since 1920, behind Mariano Rivera (28 straight in 1999 and 22 straight in 2005), Boone Logan (25 straight in 2010) and Steve Farr (23 straight in 1991).

MOST CONSECUTIVE SCORELESS APPEARANCES, YANKEES, SINCE 1920	
Player	Number of seasons
MARIANO RIVERA.................	28 (7/22-10/2/99, 30.2IP)
BOONE LOGAN	25 (7/21-9/13/10, 15.1IP)
Steve Farr........................	23 (5/29-8/2/91, 26.0IP)
MARIANO RIVERA.................	22 (5/9-7/4/05, 23.0IP)
KERRY WOOD.................	**.21 (8/6-9/26/10, 23.1IP)**
MARIANO RIVERA.................	21 (6/16-8/9/09, 21.1IP)
Mike Myers	21 (5/3-7/3/06, 9.2IP)
Baseball-reference.com	

▸ Tossed 2.0 scoreless innings on 8/11 at Texas to record his first win as a Yankee (2H, 1BB, 2K)…was his longest outing since 9/18/08 w/ Chicago-NL vs. Milwaukee (also 2.0IP).

▸ His strikeout of Ramon Santiago in the seventh inning of 8/18 win vs. Detroit was the 1,500th of his career.

▸ Allowed just his second run as a Yankee in 10/2 Game 1 win at Boston, snapping his career-high 21-appearance scoreless streak.

▸ Opened the year with Cleveland, going 1-4 with eight saves and a 6.30 ERA (20.0IP, 14ER) in 23 relief appearances prior to being traded.

▸ Began the season on the 15-day disabled list with a strained right lat, suffered in spring training…made two rehab appearances with Triple-A Akron (1.2IP, 4H, 6ER, 2BB, 2K, 1WP)…was returned from rehab and reinstated from the D.L. on 5/7.

▸ Allowed 12 runs combined in his first 12 appearances of the season, pitching to a 9.58 ERA (10.1IP, 11ER, 7BB, 8K) through 6/10.

▸ Held opponents scoreless in nine of his next 11 appearances – his final outings with the Indians – from 6/13-7/11, striking out 10 batters in 9.2IP over the stretch (8H, 3ER, 4BB, 4-for-5 in save chances).

▸ Converted his final three save chances with the Indians on three consecutive days from 6/27-29.

▸ Returned to the 15-day disabled list on 7/17 (retroactive to 7/12) with a blister on his right index finger…made one rehab appearance with Akron, tossing 1.0 scoreless inning…was returned from rehab and reinstated on 7/31, hours before being traded to the Yankees.

Wood's Career Pitching Record

Year	Team	W	L	ERA	G	GS	CG	SHO	SV	IP	H	R	ER	HR	HB	BB	SO	WP	BK
1995	GCL Cubs	0	0	0.00	1	1	0	0	0	3.0	0	0	0	0	0	1	2	0	0
	Williamsport	0	0	10.38	2	2	0	0	0	4.1	5	8	5	0	0	5	5	1	0
1996	Daytona	10	2	2.91	22	22	0	0	0	114.1	72	51	37	6	14	70	136	10	7
1997	Orlando	6	7	4.50	19	19	0	0	0	94.0	58	49	47	2	10	79	106	10	4
	Iowa	4	2	4.68	10	10	0	0	0	57.2	35	35	30	2	6	52	80	8	2
1998	Iowa	1	0	0.00	1	1	0	0	0	5.0	1	0	0	0	0	2	11	0	0
	CHICAGO-NL	13	6	3.40	26	26	1	1	0	166.2	117	69	63	14	11	85	233	6	3
1999						Injured - Did Not Pitch - a													
2000	Daytona	2	0	1.50	2	2	0	0	0	12.0	3	2	2	0	0	5	17	0	1
	Iowa	0	0	2.57	1	1	0	0	0	7.0	4	2	2	1	0	4	7	1	0
	CHICAGO-NL - b, c	8	7	4.80	23	23	1	0	0	137.0	112	77	73	17	9	87	132	5	1
2001	CHICAGO-NL - d	12	6	3.36	28	28	1	1	0	174.1	127	70	65	16	10	92	217	9	0
2002	CHICAGO-NL	12	11	3.66	33	33	4	1	0	213.2	169	92	87	22	16	97	217	8	1
2003	CHICAGO-NL	14	11	3.20	32	32	4	2	0	211.0	152	77	75	24	21	100	266	10	0
2004	CHICAGO-NL - e	8	9	3.72	22	22	0	0	0	140.1	127	62	58	16	11	51	144	7	0
	Iowa	1	0	0.00	1	1	0	0	0	5.0	2	0	0	0	0	1	4	0	0
2005	CHICAGO-NL - f, g, h	3	4	4.23	21	10	0	0	0	66.0	52	32	31	14	2	26	77	0	0
	Iowa	0	0	2.84	3	3	0	0	0	12.2	11	4	4	1	1	6	18	0	0
	Peoria	0	0	0.00	2	0	0	0	0	2.1	1	0	0	0	0	0	5	0	0
2006	Peoria	0	0	0.00	1	1	0	0	0	5.0	1	0	0	0	1	1	12	0	0
	Iowa	0	1	1.80	1	1	0	0	0	5.0	5	1	1	0	0	2	3	0	0
	CHICAGO-NL - i, j	1	2	4.12	4	4	0	0	0	19.2	19	13	9	5	1	8	13	1	0
2007	AZL Cubs	0	1	2.25	4	4	0	0	0	4.0	4	2	1	0	0	1	5	1	0
	Peoria	1	0	0.00	3	1	0	0	0	3.0	1	0	0	0	0	1	3	1	0
	Tennessee	0	0	0.00	1	0	0	0	0	1.2	1	0	0	0	0	1	1	0	0
	CHICAGO-NL - k	1	1	3.33	22	0	0	0	0	24.1	18	9	9	0	0	13	24	1	0
2008	CHICAGO-NL - l, m	5	5	3.26	65	0	0	0	34	66.1	54	24	24	3	7	18	84	1	0
2009	CLEVELAND	3	3	4.25	58	0	0	0	20	55.0	48	26	26	7	3	28	63	5	0
2010	CLEVELAND - n, o	1	4	6.30	23	0	0	0	8	20.0	21	15	14	3	2	11	18	2	1
	Akron	0	1	20.25	3	1	0	0	0	2.2	4	6	6	0	0	3	2	1	0
	YANKEES - p	2	0	0.69	24	0	0	0	0	26.0	14	2	2	1	1	18	31	3	0
Minor League Totals		25	14	3.59	77	70	0	0	0	338.2	207	160	135	12	32	234	417	33	14
AL Totals		6	7	3.74	105	0	0	0	28	101.0	83	43	42	11	6	57	112	10	1
NL Totals		77	61	3.65	276	178	11	5	34	1219.1	947	525	494	131	88	577	1407	48	5
Major League Totals		83	68	3.65	381	178	11	5	62	1320.1	1030	568	536	142	142	634	1519	58	6

Selected by Chicago-NL in the first round (fourth pick overall) of the 1995 First-Year Player Draft.

KERRY WOOD

a – Placed on the 60-day disabled list from March 31, 1999 through the end of the season after having right elbow surgery.
b – Placed on the 15-day disabled list from March 25-May 2, 2000 while rehabbing from right elbow surgery.
c – Placed on the 15-day disabled list from July 30-August 22, 2000 with a left oblique strain.
d – Placed on the 15-day disabled list from August 4-September 7, 2001 with right shoulder tendinitis.
e – Placed on the 15-day disabled list from May 12-July 11, 2004 with a lower right triceps strain.
f – Placed on the 15-day disabled list from May 1-June 29, 2005 with a right shoulder supraspinatus muscle strain.
g – Placed on the 15-day disabled list from July 21-August 5, 2005 with right shoulder inflammation.
h – Placed on the 15-day disabled list on August 30, 2005 after having right shoulder surgery…was transferred to the 60-day disabled list from September 12, 2005 through the end of the season.
i – Placed on the 15-day disabled list from March 27-May 18, 2006 while rehabbing from right shoulder surgery.
j – Placed on the 15-day disabled list on June 7, 2006 with right shoulder stiffness…was transferred to the 60-day disabled list from August 27, 2006 through the end of the season.
k – Placed on the 15-day disabled list on March 29, 2007 with right shoulder tendinitis…was transferred to the 60-day disabled list on May 15-August 3, 2007.
l – Placed on the 15-day disabled list from July 14-August 5, 2008 with a blister on his right index finger.
m – Signed by Cleveland as a free agent on December 16, 2008.
n – Placed on the 15-day disabled list from March 26-May 7, 2010 with a strained right latissimus muscle.
o – Placed on the 15-day disabled list from July 12-31, 2010 with a blister on his right index finger.
p – Acquired by the Yankees from Cleveland on July 31, 2010 in exchange for a player to be named later or cash considerations.

Wood's Division Series Record

Year	Club vs. Opp.	W	L	ERA	G	GS	CG	SHO	SV	IP	H	R	ER	HR	HP	BB	SO	WP	BK
1998	CHC vs. ATL	0	1	1.80	1	1	0	0	0	5.0	3	1	1	0	0	4	5	0	0
2003	CHC vs. ATL	2	0	1.76	2	2	0	0	0	15.1	7	3	3	1	0	7	18	1	0
2007	CHC vs. ARI	0	0	3.00	2	0	0	0	0	3.0	3	1	1	1	0	0	2	0	0
2008	CHC vs. LAD	0	0	0.00	1	0	0	0	0	1.0	2	1	0	0	0	0	0	0	0
Division Series Totals		**2**	**1**	**1.85**	**6**	**3**	**0**	**0**	**0**	**24.1**	**15**	**6**	**5**	**2**	**0**	**11**	**25**	**1**	**0**

Wood's League Championship Series Record

Year	Club vs. Opp.	W	L	ERA	G	GS	CG	SHO	SV	IP	H	R	ER	HR	HP	BB	SO	WP	BK
2003	CHC vs. FLA	0	1	7.30	2	2	0	0	0	12.1	14	10	10	1	0	7	13	0	0
LCS Totals		**0**	**1**	**7.30**	**2**	**2**	**0**	**0**	**0**	**12.1**	**14**	**10**	**10**	**1**	**0**	**7**	**13**	**0**	**0**
POSTSEASON TOTALS		**2**	**2**	**3.68**	**8**	**5**	**0**	**0**	**0**	**36.2**	**29**	**16**	**15**	**3**	**0**	**18**	**38**	**1**	**0**

Wood's All-Star Game Record

Year	Club, Site	W	L	ERA	G	GS	CG	SHO	SV	IP	H	R	ER	HR	HP	BB	SO	WP	BK
2003	CHC, Chicago (AL)	0	0	0.00	1	0	0	0	0	1.0	1	0	0	0	0	0	2	0	0
2008	CHC, New York (AL)							Selected - Did Not Attend											
All-Star Game Totals		**0**	**0**	**0.00**	**1**	**0**	**0**	**0**	**0**	**1.0**	**1**	**0**	**0**	**0**	**0**	**0**	**2**	**0**	**0**

	2010										Career									
	W	L	SV	ERA	G	GS	IP	H	HR	ER	SO	W	L	SV	ERA	G	GS	IP	H	HR	ER	SO
Overall	3	4	8	3.13	47	0	46.0	35	4	16	49	83	68	62	3.65	381	178	1320.1	1030	142	536	1519
Minnesota	-	-	-	-	-	-	-	-	-	-	-	1	1	4	2.93	8	2	15.1	10	0	5	18
Tampa Bay	0	1	0	1.35	7	0	6.2	4	0	1	8	0	1	1	1.00	10	0	9.0	5	0	1	10
Texas	1	0	0	0.00	3	0	4.0	3	0	0	2	1	0	0	1.80	4	0	5.0	5	0	1	5
Atlanta	-	-	-	-	-	-	-	-	-	-	-	4	3	0	2.91	13	8	58.2	51	6	19	70
Cincinnati	0	0	2	3.00	3	0	3.0	2	1	1	6	13	5	6	2.97	38	21	151.2	108	16	50	191
Philadelphia	0	1	0	13.50	2	0	1.1	1	1	2	0	4	2	1	4.03	10	6	44.2	44	4	20	49
San Francisco	-	-	-	-	-	-	-	-	-	-	-	4	3	2	4.79	14	10	62.0	55	8	33	67
Home	2	2	3	4.01	25	0	24.2	23	3	11	28	41	33	33	3.38	191	84	653.1	493	63	245	776
Road	1	2	5	2.11	22	0	21.1	12	1	5	21	42	35	29	3.93	190	94	667.0	537	79	291	743

Wood's Career By Ballpark

Park	W	L	SV	ERA	G	GS	IP	ER	Park	W	L	SV	ERA	G	GS	IP	ER
AT&T Park	2	2	0	2.77	4	4	26.0	8	Target Field	1	0	0	0.00	1	1	5.0	0
Citizens Bank Park	2	3	0	5.04	6	5	30.1	17	Tropicana Field	6	2	0	2.09	11	11	81.2	19
Great American BP	-	-	-	-	-	-	-	-	Turner Field	1	7	0	5.08	11	11	56.2	32
Rangers Ballpark	2	1	0	4.00	6	6	36.0	16	Yankee Stadium	10	10	0	3.98	30	30	185.1	82

Wood's Career Fielding Record

Position	PCT	G	PO	A	E	TC	DP
Pitcher	.959	381	71	116	8	195	11

Wood's Regular Season Batting Record

Year	Team	AVG	G	AB	R	H	2B	3B	HR	RBI	SH	SF	HP	BB	SO	SB	CS
2010	NYY						Did Not Bat										
Major League Totals		**.171**	**381**	**345**	**23**	**59**	**6**	**0**	**7**	**32**	**46**	**1**	**0**	**11**	**113**	**0**	**0**

Wear the Gear of Champions

Get yours today at the Official Online Shop
of the 27-time World Series® Champion
New York Yankees™

Additional Yankees in 2010

RHP ALFREDO ACEVES   #91

▸ Was 3-0 with one save and a 3.00 ERA in 10 relief appearances with the Yankees in 2010…opponents batted .208 (10-for-48, 1HR); LH .235 (4-for-17), RH .194 (6-for-31, 1HR)…retired nine-of-10 first batters faced (90.0%)…prevented five-of-six inherited runners from scoring (83.3%).

▸ Half of his outings were more than 1.0 inning…held opponents scoreless in seven of his appearances and did not surrender an earned run over his final seven games (8.0IP).

▸ Made his first career Opening Day roster…tossed 2.0 scoreless innings of relief on 4/6 at Boston to earn the win in the Yankees' first victory of 2010.

▸ Also picked up the win on 4/30 vs. Chicago-AL and 5/8 at Boston…became just the second pitcher since 1900 to record at least three wins in a season while pitching 12.0 innings or fewer (also the Mets' Don Florence in 1995)—credit: *Elias Sports Bureau.*

▸ Has won 13 straight regular season decisions, the longest current streak in the Majors.

▸ Earned a save in 5/5 win vs. Baltimore, retiring his only batter faced…was the second save of his career (also 7/5/09 vs. Toronto).

▸ Earned the win on 5/8 at Boston despite leaving the game with two outs in the sixth inning with a stiff lower back (1.0IP, 2H, 1K)…was placed on the 15-day disabled list on 5/12 with a strained lower back, missing the remainder of the season (131 games).

▸ Attempted a rehab assignment with Triple-A Scranton/Wilkes-Barre and Double-A Trenton, working to a 6.17 ERA (11.2IP, 8ER) with no decisions in seven combined appearances (five starts) from 8/10-30 before being shut down for the season.

Aceves' 2010 Pitching Record

Year	Club	W	L	ERA	G	GS	CG	SHO	SV	IP	H	R	ER	HR	HB	BB	SO	WP	BK
2010	YANKEES	3	1	3.00	10	0	0	0	1	12.0	10	5	4	1	1	4	2	0	0
	Scranton/WB	0	0	7.36	3	2	0	0	0	3.2	4	4	3	0	1	5	4	0	0
	Trenton	0	0	5.63	4	3	0	0	0	8.0	10	5	5	1	0	1	7	0	0

RHP JONATHAN ALBALADEJO   #63

▸ Posted a 3.97 ERA without recording a decision in 10 appearances over two stints with the Yankees in 2010 (7/20-24; 9/1-10/3)…opponents batted .231 (9-for-39, 1HR); LH .222 (4-for-18, 0HR), RH .238 (5-for-21, 1HR)…seven of his 10 appearances were scoreless…retired 4-of-10 first batters faced (40.0%)…stranded 7-of-10 inherited runners (70.0%).

▸ Was recalled from Triple-A Scranton/Wilkes-Barre on 7/20 when Andy Pettitte was placed on the disabled list…made two appearances (2.2IP, 2H, 1ER, 1BB, 3K) before being optioned back to Scranton/WB when Sergio Mitre was activated from the disabled list.

▸ Returned to the Yankees as a September callup on 9/1…in eight relief outings during the month, allowed 7H and 4ER in 8.2IP (4.15 ERA).

▸ Began the season with Scranton/WB, going 4-2 with 43 saves and a 1.42 ERA in 57 appearances (63.1IP, 38H, 10ER, 18BB, 82K, 3HR)…Scranton/WB was 53-4 in games he appeared in this season, with wins in 43 of his final 44 appearances…struck out at least one batter in 49 of his 57 appearances…was named to the International League postseason All-Star team…led the IL in games finished (54) and ranked fourth in games…among IL relievers, ranked first in opponents batting average (.170) and strikeouts/9.0IP (11.65).

▸ His 43 saves this season set a Scranton/WB club record and an International League all-time single season record (surpassing Matt Whiteside's 38 saves for the Richmond Braves in 2004)…finished three saves shy of tying the overall Minor League single-season record of 46 set by Jamie Cochran of the SAL's Savannah Sand Gnats in 1993.

▸ Was named the International League "Pitcher of the Week" for the period from 7/15-18, earning the honor for the second consecutive week…converted each of his two save opportunities in the four-day span, striking out two batters in 2.0IP…became the first pitcher to earn IL "Pitcher of the Week" in two straight weeks since Cole Hamels in 2006.

▸ Allowed just 1ER in 33.1IP over a 29-appearance stretch from 5/20-8/6…struck out 47 batters during the span, while holding opponents to 15H and 8BB.

Albaladejo's 2010 Pitching Record

Year	Club	W	L	ERA	G	GS	CG	SHO	SV	IP	H	R	ER	HR	HB	BB	SO	WP	BK
2010	Scranton/WB	4	2	1.42	57	0	0	0	43	63.1	38	10	10	3	2	18	82	6	1
	YANKEES	0	0	3.97	10	0	0	0	0	11.1	9	5	5	1	2	8	8	0	0

RHP ANDREW BRACKMAN   #66

▸ Was recalled from Double-A Trenton on 9/23…did not appear in a game.
▸ Combined at Single-A Tampa and Double-A Trenton to go 10-11 with a 3.90 ERA in 27 appearances (26 starts), allowing 144H and 61ER in 140.2IP (76R, 39BB, 126K, 8HR).
▸ Began the season with Tampa, going 5-4 with a 5.10 ERA (60.0IP, 34ER) in 12 starts…was transferred to Trenton on 6/25, where he went 5-7 with a 3.01 ERA in 15 games (14 starts).
▸ Made one postseason start for Trenton, allowing just 1H in 5.0 scoreless innings to earn the win in Game 1 of the Eastern League Championship Series on 9/14 at Altoona (1IBB, 2HBP, 4K).

Brackman's 2010 Pitching Record

Year	Club	W	L	ERA	G	GS	CG	SHO	SV	IP	H	R	ER	HR	HB	BB	SO	WP	BK
2010	Tampa	5	4	5.10	12	12	0	0	0	60.0	67	38	34	5	5	9	56	6	0
	Trenton	5	7	3.01	15	14	0	0	0	80.2	77	38	27	3	7	30	70	6	0

OF COLIN CURTIS   #27/#22

▸ Hit .186 (11-for-59) with 7R, 3 doubles, 1HR and 8RBI in 31 games (nine starts in RF, two in LF, one at DH) over two stints with the Yankees in 2010 (6/21-7/31 and 9/6-10/3).
▸ Was signed to a Major League contract and selected to the Yankees' 25-man roster from Triple-A Scranton/Wilkes-Barre on 6/21…made his Major League debut that night at Arizona, pinch-hitting for Burnett in the fifth and going 0-for-1 in the Yankees' loss.
▸ Collected his first Major League hit and RBI with a pinch hit two-run double off Chad Qualls in the eighth inning of 6/22 win at Arizona.
▸ Drove in the game-tying run with his ninth-inning groundout in 6/27 win at Los Angeles-NL to complete the Yankees' four-run rally in the ninth and send the game to extra innings.
▸ Made his first Major League start—in LF—in 6/30 loss vs. Seattle, going 1-for-3 with 1 double.
▸ Hit three-run HR—the first of his Major League career—and was 1-for-1 in 7/21 win vs. Los Angeles-AL…entered the game as a pinch-hitter with an 0-2 count after Gardner was ejected…remained in the game in LF…became the first Yankee to hit his first career home run as a pinch-hitter since Andy Phillips on 9/26/04 at Boston…was the Yankees' first pinch-hit homer of 2010.
▸ Scored a career-high 3R, going 2-for-4 in 7/29 win at Cleveland.
▸ Was optioned to Scranton/WB on 7/31 when the Yankees acquired OF Austin Kearns from the Cleveland Indians…returned to the Yankees as a September callup on 9/6.
▸ Played in nine games from 9/6 through the end of the season, making three starts in RF and going 0-for-16 overall with 1BB…finished the season hitless in his final 19AB.
▸ Batted .289 (69-for-239) with 28R, 24 doubles, 5HR and 27RBI in 66 games with Scranton/Wilkes-Barre…appeared at all three OF positions…hit .293 (22-for-75) off LH pitching in 2010 and .287 (47-for-164) against righties with Scranton/WB.
▸ Went 4-for-5 with 3RBI and tied a franchise single-game record with 3 doubles in Scranton/WB's 6-3 victory vs. Lehigh Valley on 4/23.
▸ Compiled a 14-game hitting streak from 8/18-9/1, batting .354 (17-for-48) over the stretch…hit safely in 18 of his final 21 games of the season, carrying a .450 (27-for-60) average from 8/14 through the end of the Triple-A regular season.
▸ Attended spring training with the Yankees as a non-roster invitee in each of the last three years (2008-10)…this spring, went 6-for-12 (.500) with 2HR and 8RBI in 12 games.

Curtis' 2010 Batting Record

Year	Club	AVG	G	AB	R	H	2B	3B	HR	RBI	SH	SF	HB	BB	SO	SB	CS	E	OBP	SLG
2010	Scranton/WB	.289	66	239	28	69	24	0	5	27	1	2	6	21	38	1	2	0	.452	.358
	YANKEES	.186	31	59	7	11	3	0	1	8	0	0	1	4	15	0	0	0	.250	.288

OF GREG GOLSON   #27/#26

▸ Hit .261 (6-for-23) with 3R, 2 doubles and 2RBI in 24 games (four starts in RF, one in CF and one in LF) over three stints with the Yankees in 2010 (also 5/4-7, 5/12-18, 9/1-10/3).
▸ Was recalled from Triple-A Scranton/Wilkes-Barre on 5/4…made his Yankees debut in that night's win vs. Baltimore, entering the game defensively in the eighth in CF (did not bat)…did not appear in another game before being optioned back to Scranton/WB on 5/7.
▸ Recalled for a second time on 5/12 when Alfredo Aceves was placed on the 15-day disabled list…appeared in five games, making one start in RF in 5/13 loss at Detroit.
▸ Collected his first Major League hit in 5/12 Game 2 win at Detroit, entering game in the seventh in CF and singling off Phil Coke in the ninth.

- Joined the Yankees a third time as a September callup on 9/1…played in 18 games over the final month of the season, batting .222 (4-for-18) with 3R, 2 doubles and 2RBI.
- Recorded his first career extra-base hit with a third-inning double in 9/5 loss vs. Toronto.
- Entered 9/14 win at Tampa Bay defensively in the ninth in RF…threw out Carl Crawford at third base on a fly ball out to complete a double play and end the game…according to the *Elias Sports Bureau*, marked the Yankees first extra-inning win to end on an outfield assist since 8/16/03 when Karim Garcia started a 9-4-5-2-5 putout of Baltimore's Jack Cust in the 12th inning to preserve a 5-4 win.
- Collected his first career multi-hit game in 9/23 loss vs. Tampa Bay, going 2-for-4 with 1R and 1 double.
- Began the season with Triple-A Scranton/Wilkes-Barre, batting .263 (109-for-415) with 51R, 23 doubles, 5 triples, 10HR and 40RBI in 116 games…hit safely in each of his last nine games with Scranton/WB, batting .382 (13-for-34) with 7R, 5 doubles, 1 triple, 1HR and 2RBI over the stretch.
- Hit an inside-the-park home run in the third inning of 4/30 win vs. Louisville off the Bats' Matt Maloney.
- Collected a season-high four hits with 1R and 1RBI in 7/4 win at Rochester…had six extra-base hits over a four-game span from 8/3-8, going 8-for-17 with 5R, 2 doubles, 1 triple, 3HR, and 7RBI.

Golson's 2010 Batting Record

Year	Club	AVG	G	AB	R	H	2B	3B	HR	RBI	SH	SF	HB	BB	SO	SB	CS	E	OBP	SLG
2010	Scranton/WB	.263	116	415	51	109	23	5	10	40	6	2	6	25	99	17	4	5	.313	.414
	YANKEES	.261	24	23	3	6	2	0	0	2	0	0	0	0	3	0	2	0	.261	.348

OF CHAD HUFFMAN #22

- Appeared in nine games (two starts in LF, two in RF) with the Yankees in 2010, batting .167 (3-for-18) with 2RBI.
- Was recalled from Triple-A Scranton/Wilkes-Barre prior to 6/13 win vs. Houston…made his Major League debut that day, starting in RF and going 1-for-4 with 1BB…singled in his first career plate appearance (off Brian Moehler), becoming the second Yankee to accomplish the feat over the last four seasons (also Ramiro Pena on 4/9/09 at Baltimore)…became the first Yankee to record a hit when his first career plate appearance came at home since Marcus Thames on 6/10/02 vs. Arizona.
- Collected his first Major League RBI with a two-run single in the ninth in 6/27 win at Los Angeles-NL, entering the game in LF in the fourth inning for an injured Brett Gardner and going 2-for-3.
- Scored his first Major League run and was 0-for-3 with 1HBP in 7/3 win vs. Toronto.
- Was optioned to Triple-A Scranton/Wilkes-Barre on 7/4 when OF Marcus Thames was returned from rehab and reinstated from the 15-day disabled list.
- Began the season with Triple-A Scranton/Wilkes-Bare, batting .274 (101-for-368) with 48R, 20 doubles, 10HR and 45RBI in 104 games…ranked second on the team with 40BB…starting games in LF, RF, 1B and DH…carried a .341 average (14-for-41) with runners in scoring position and two outs.
- Acquired by the Yankees off waivers from the San Diego Padres on 4/7/10…was designated for assignment on 9/15 when LHP Royce Ring was added to the Major League roster.

Huffman's 2010 Batting Record

Year	Club	AVG	G	AB	R	H	2B	3B	HR	RBI	SH	SF	HB	BB	SO	SB	CS	E	OBP	SLG
2010	Scranton/WB	.274	104	368	48	101	20	0	10	45	1	1	5	40	81	0	2	3	.353	.410
	YANKEES	.167	9	18	1	3	0	0	0	2	0	0	1	2	5	0	0	0	.286	.167

DH/1B NICK JOHNSON #26/#36

- Batted .167 (12-for-72) with 12R, 4 doubles, 2HR and 8RBI in 24 games with the Yankees in 2010 (19 starts at DH, two at 1B)…made his seventh career Opening Day roster.
- Recorded his first RBI of the season in 4/6 win at Boston, drawing a bases-loaded walk in the eighth inning to score the game-winning run of the Yankees first victory of the season.
- Hit his first home run of the season and was 2-for-3 with 3R, 1 double and 2BB in 4/13 win vs. Los Angeles-AL…was his first home run as a Yankee since 9/23/03 at Chicago-AL…according to the *Elias Sports Bureau*, became the first player to go six-or-more full seasons between Yankees homers since Ruben Sierra (homered for the Yankees in 1996, then next in 2003)…joined Eric Hinske as the only players to homer in their first at-bat as a Yankee at the current Yankee Stadium.
- Snapped an 0-for-21 stretch with a fourth-inning single in 4/23 loss at Los Angeles-AL…fell 1AB shy of his longest career single-season hitless stretch (22AB from 9/16-10/2/09).
- Missed two games with a stiff lower back (4/24-25).
- Reached base five times in five plate appearances in 5/5 win vs. Baltimore (3-for-3 with 1R, 1 double and 2BB), marking the first time he reached base five times in a nine-inning game since 4/20/06 w/ Washington at Philadelphia (also five times).

- Left 5/7 win at Boston after his fourth-inning at-bat with a sore right wrist…was examined by Hand Specialist, Dr. Melvin Rosenwasser and Yankees Team Physician Dr. Christopher Ahmad at NewYork-Presbyterian Hospital and placed on the 15-day disabled list on 5/8 with an inflamed tendon in his right wrist.
- Underwent surgery at NewYork-Presbyterian Hospital to remove the inflamed tissue on 5/18…the surgery was performed by Dr. Rosenwasser…was transferred to the 60-day D.L. on 5/20, missing the remainder of the season (135 games).
- Signed by the Yankees as a free agent on 12/23/09…contract extends through the 2010 season.

Johnson's 2010 Batting Record

Year	Club	AVG	G	AB	R	H	2B	3B	HR	RBI	SH	SF	HB	BB	SO	SB	CS	E	OBP	SLG
2010	YANKEES	.167	24	72	12	12	4	0	2	8	0	0	2	24	23	0	1	0	.388	.306

LHP DAMASO MARTE   #43

- Was 0-0 with a 4.08 ERA in 30 relief appearances with the Yankees in 2010…opponents batted .161 (10-for-62, 2HR); LH .146 (6-for-41, 1HR), RH .190 (4-for-21, 1HR)…retired 23-of-30 first batters faced (76.7%)…prevented 16-of-22 inherited runners from scoring (72.7%)…appeared in consecutive games six times.
- Tossed less than 1.0 inning in 22 of his outings…held opponents scoreless in his first seven appearances and 21 of his first 23 games through 6/13…included was nine straight scoreless outings from 5/15-6/13 (4.1IP).
- Made his ninth career Opening Day roster in 2010, second with the Yankees.
- Tossed 1.2IP in 5/17 win at Boston, marking his longest outing since throwing 2.0 innings of relief on 6/20 vs. Toronto.
- Threw 29 pitches in 6/17 loss vs. Philadelphia, allowing 1ER in 0.2IP (2BB)…marked his most pitches since 8/10/08 at Los Angeles-AL (also 29 pitches).
- Retired 23 of his final 25 left-handed batters faced from 5/15-7/7 (1H, 1BB).
- Held opponents hitless in 17 straight at-bats from 5/17-6/30 prior to Chone Figgins' single in 6/30 loss vs. Seattle, marking his longest such streak as a Yankee…also allowed a Russell Branyan home run in the game, snapping an 0-for-19 stretch by left-handed batters (dating back to a double by Minnesota's Justin Morneau on 5/14 at Yankee Stadium)—credit: Elias.
- Was placed on the 15-day disabled list prior to 7/17 game with left shoulder inflammation (retroactive to 7/8)…was transferred to the 60-day disabled list on 9/1, missing the remainder of the season (78 games).
- Went 0-1 with a 9.00 ERA in four spring training relief outings with the Yankees (3.0IP, 6H, 4R, 3ER, 1BB, 2K).

Marte's 2010 Pitching Record

Year	Club	W	L	ERA	G	GS	CG	SHO	SV	IP	H	R	ER	HR	HB	BB	SO	WP	BK
2010	YANKEES	0	0	4.08	30	0	0	0	0	17.2	10	8	8	2	1	11	12	2	1

RHP MARK MELANCON   #39

- Made two relief appearances over two stints with the Yankees in 2010 (5/2-4 and 5/18-20), allowing 5R (4ER) in 4.0IP.
- Was recalled from Triple-A Scranton/Wilkes-Barre on 5/2 when OF Curtis Granderson was placed on the 15-day disabled list…made his season debut that night vs. Chicago-AL, allowing 2H and 2ER in 2.0IP (3R, 1K, 1HR)…was optioned back to Scranton/WB on 5/4.
- Was recalled for a second time on 5/18, making one appearance in 5/19 loss vs. Tampa Bay (2.0IP, 5H, 2ER, 2K) before being optioned back to Scranton/WB on 5/20.
- Began the season with Triple-A Scranton/Wilkes-Barre, making 40 relief appearances and going 6-1 with six saves and a 3.67 ERA (56.1IP, 23ER).
- Was part of a deadline deal on 7/31 and was traded to Houston along with minor league INF Jimmy Paredes in exchange for DH/1B Lance Berkman and cash.
- Made six spring training relief appearances with the Yankees, posting a 2.45 ERA with one save (7.1IP, 6H, 2ER, 1BB)…led all Yankees relievers with 10K.

Melancon's 2010 Pitching Record

Year	Club	W	L	ERA	G	GS	CG	SHO	SV	IP	H	R	ER	HR	HB	BB	SO	WP	BK
2010	Scranton/WB	6	1	3.67	40	0	0	0	6	56.1	63	24	23	5	3	31	58	7	0
	YANKEES	0	0	9.00	2	0	0	0	0	4.0	7	5	4	1	0	0	3	0	0

INF JUAN MIRANDA #53

- Hit .219 (14-for-64) with 7R, 2 doubles, 1 triple, 3HR and 10RBI in 33 games (10 starts at DH, four at 1B) over three stints with the Yankees in 2010 (5/13-6/2, 7/16-31, 9/12-10/3).
- Was recalled from Triple-A Scranton/Wilkes-Barre on 5/13 and made his season debut that day at Detroit, starting at 1B and going 0-for-3 with 1BB.
- Hit his first career triple in 5/20 loss vs. Tampa Bay and went 2-for-3 with a career-high 3R, 1HR, 2RBI and 1BB.
- Was optioned to Scranton/WB on 6/2 when Jorge Posada was reinstated from the 15-day disabled list.
- Was recalled for a second stint from 7/16, batting .267 (4-for-15) with 1HR before being optioned to Scranton/WB on 7/31 when Lance Berkman was acquired from the Houston Astros.
- Rejoined the Yankees a third time on 9/12…appeared in five games following his recall, going 0-for-3 with 1BB and 1RBI.
- Was credited with the game-winning RBI, drawing a 10th-inning "walk-off" walk on 9/26 vs. Boston…was his second career "walk-off" plate appearance (also 9/29/09 vs. Kansas City – off Kyle Farnsworth)…entered the game in the top of the 10th as a defensive replacement at 1B…became the first Yankee to record a "walk-off" walk since Jorge Posada on 9/5/04 vs. Baltimore (off Jorge Julio) and the first Yankee to do so in an extra-inning game since Paul O'Neill in the 10th inning of 5/9/00 win vs. Tampa Bay (off Jim Morris).
- Began the season with Triple-A Scranton/Wilkes-Barre, batting .285 (84-for-295) with 52R, 15 doubles, 15HR and 43RBI in 80 games…ranked fourth on the team and fifth among all Yankees minor leaguers in home runs…reached base safely (via hit, walk or HBP) in 68 of his 80G with an official AB.
- Reached base safely (via hit, walk or hit by pitch) in 26 of his 27 games with an official at-at-bat prior to his first recall on 5/13.
- Scored a season-high 4R in 7/4 win at Rochester…collected a season-high-tying 4H the next day at Rochester and matched the mark on 8/18 at Columbus.
- Fashioned a season-high 11-game hitting streak from 8/7-19, batting .429 (18-for-42) with 13R, 2 doubles, 1 triple, 3HR, 9RBI and 5BB over the stretch.
- In four postseason games for Scranton/WB, hit .143 (2-for-14) with 1R, 1 double, 2RBI and 1BB.
- Appeared in 17 spring training games for the Yankees in 2010, batting .256 (10-for-39) with 3R, 4 doubles, 2HR and 6RBI.

Miranda's 2010 Batting Record

Year	Club	AVG	G	AB	R	H	2B	3B	HR	RBI	SH	SF	HB	BB	SO	SB	CS	E	OBP	SLG
2010	Scranton/WB	.285	80	295	52	84	15	1	15	43	0	3	9	33	71	1	0	4	.495	.371
	YANKEES	.219	33	64	7	14	2	1	3	10	0	0	0	7	12	0	0	0	.296	.422

C CHAD MOELLER #17/#18

- Hit .214 (3-for-14) with 2R and 3 doubles in nine games (four starts at C) over two stints with the Yankees in 2010 (5/20-6/21, 9/1-10/3).
- Was signed to a Major League contract and selected to the Yankees' 25-man roster from Triple-A Scranton/Wilkes-Barre on 5/20 when Jorge Posada went on the disabled list.
- Made his first appearance of the season in 5/28 win vs. Cleveland, starting at C and going 1-for-4 with 1 double…had not played in previous seven games since joining the Yankees…made four starts before being designated for assignment on 6/21…cleared waivers and was outrighted to Scranton/WB on 6/24.
- Was signed to a Major League contract and selected to the Yankees active roster from Scranton/WB again on 9/1…appeared in five games in September, all as a defensive replacement at C, going 1-for-3 with 1 double.
- Was signed by the Yankees as a minor league free agent on 4/6 and reported to Triple-A Scranton/Wilkes-Barre…in 28 games with Scranton/WB in 2010, batted .230 (20-for-87) with 8R, 6 doubles, 1HR and 9RBI.
- Attended spring training with Baltimore as a non-roster invitee, batting .300 (6-for-20) with 4R, 1 double, 2HR and 3RBI in nine games before his release on 4/1.

Moeller's 2010 Batting Record

Year	Club	AVG	G	AB	R	H	2B	3B	HR	RBI	SH	SF	HB	BB	SO	SB	CS	E	OBP	SLG
2010	Scranton/WB	.230	28	87	8	20	6	0	1	9	0	0	3	6	15	0	0	1	.333	.302
	YANKEES	.214	9	14	2	3	3	0	0	0	0	0	0	1	4	0	0	0	.267	.429

RHP IVAN NOVA #41

- Was 1-2 with a 4.50 ERA in 10 games (seven starts) with the Yankees in 2010…opponents batted .268 (44-for-164, 4HR); LH .276 (27-for-98, 3HR), RH .258 (17-for-98, 7HR).
- Went 0-1 with a 1.69 ERA (5.1IP, 1ER) in his three relief outings…posted a 1-1 record with a 4.91 ERA in his seven starts.
- Opposing batters hit .230 (17-for-74) with two extra-base hits their first time through the order, .262 (17-for-65) with eight extra-base hits their second pass and .400 (10-for-25) with two extra-base hits the third time through.
- Was recalled from Triple-A Scranton/Wilkes-Barre on 5/10…made his Major League debut in 5/13 loss at Detroit, tossing 2.0 scoreless innings (2H, 1K) of relief…made one additional relief appearance (5/16 vs. Minnesota) before being optioned back to Scranton/WB on 5/17 when Chan Ho Park was reinstated from the 15-day disabled list.

- Was recalled a second time on 8/22, joining the starting rotation…completed 6.0 innings just once and exited before 5.0IP three times…was removed with a lead in four of his seven starts.
- Made his first Major League start against Toronto at the Rogers Centre on 8/23, recording a no-decision, (5.1IP, 6H, 2ER, 1BB, 3K, 1HR)…pitched out of a bases-loaded, no-out jam in the first inning…his only runs allowed came on a two-run HR by Jose Bautista in the third.
- Recorded his first Major League win in his second start on 8/29 at Chicago-AL, allowing 1ER in 5.2IP (5H, 1BB, 7K)…became the first Yankees rookie starter to earn a win since Alfredo Aceves on 9/9/08 (credit: Elias) as the Yankees became the last Major League team in 2010 to have a rookie earn a win.
- Made his first career Yankee Stadium start on 9/3 vs. Toronto…allowed 3ER in 4.2IP, receiving a no-decision (6H, 1HR, 2BB, 0K)…was removed despite needing one more out to qualify for the win.
- Suffered his first loss on 9/25 vs. Boston (4.2IP, 4H, 4ER, 3BB, 2K, 1HP)…according to the *Elias Sports Bureau*, became one of two Yankees since 1980 to go undefeated in his first six career starts, joining Joba Chamberlain (first 7GS in 2008).
- Made his final appearance on 10/2 at Boston in Game 2 of a doubleheader, suffering the loss after allowing the game-winning run in the bottom of the 10th at 1:22 a.m. (4H, 3BB, 1K).
- Went 12-3 with a 2.86 ERA in 23 starts at Triple-A Scranton/WB (145.0IP, 135H, 50R, 46ER, 48BB, 115K, 10HR, .250 opp. BA)…ranked second in the International League in ERA, trailing only *Baseball America* "Player of the Year" Jeremy Hellickson…tied for first in winning percentage and ranked third in wins.
- Tossed at least 7.0 innings in seven starts, recording a season-high-tying 8.0IP twice.
- Won 10 of his final 11 decisions with SWB, going 10-1 with a 2.19 ERA (94.2IP, 23ER) over 14 starts from 6/5-8/18.
- Did not record a decision in three spring training relief appearances with the Yankees, allowing 1ER in 4.0IP (2.25 ERA, 4H, 2BB, 3K, 1HR).

Nova's 2010 Pitching Record

Year	Club	W	L	ERA	G	GS	CG	SHO	SV	IP	H	R	ER	HR	HB	BB	SO	WP	BK
2010	Scranton/WB	12	3	2.86	23	23	0	0	0	145.0	135	50	46	10	2	48	115	4	1
	YANKEES	1	2	4.50	10	7	0	0	0	42.0	44	22	21	4	1	17	26	2	0

INF EDUARDO NUNEZ   #12

- Hit .280 (14-for-50) with 12R, 1 double, 1HR and 7RBI in 30 games (10 starts at 3B and three at SS) with the Yankees in 2010…stole five bases without being caught…struck out just twice in 53 plate appearances.
- Was recalled from Triple-A Scranton/WB on 8/19 when Lance Berkman went on the 15-day disabled list…made his Major League debut in that night's win vs. Detroit, entering the game defensively in the seventh at SS and going 0-for-1.
- Made his first Major League start (at 3B) in 8/21 win vs. Seattle, going 1-for-3 with 1R and 1RBI…collected his first Major League hit—a go-ahead RBI-single off Jason Vargas in the seventh inning.
- Made 11 starts from 8/21-9/4 (nine at 3B and two at SS) while Alex Rodriguez was on the disabled list…hit .293 (12-for-41) over the stretch, committing just one error in 27 chances.
- Collected his first multi-hit game in 8/25 loss at Toronto, going 2-for-4 with 1RBI.
- Hit two-run HR—the first of his Major League career—and was 3-for-4 with 2R, 4RBI, 1BB and 1SB in 8/29 win at Chicago-AL…marked the most RBI in a game by a Yankees rookie since Brett Gardner on 9/26/08 at Boston (also 4RBI)…became the first Yankee to drive in at least four runs in a game within his first 10 Major League games since Shelley Duncan on 7/22/07 vs. Tampa Bay (4RBI) and just the fifth to do so in the last 44 years (since 1967), joining Andy Phillips (4RBI on 4/24/05 vs. Texas), Hideki Matsui (4RBI on 4/8/03 vs. Minnesota) and Brian Dayett (4RBI on 9/18/83 Game 2 at Cleveland)…according to Elias, became just the fifth Yankee in franchise history to hit his first Major League home run and steal his first base in the same game, joining Willie Randolph (1976), Roy White (1966), Gil McDougald (1951) and Wally Pipp (1915).
- Broke up Cliff Lee's no-hit bid on 9/12 at Rangers Ballpark with a sixth-inning single and was 1-for-3 in the Yankees loss.
- Pinch-ran in the ninth inning of 9/26 win vs. Boston…stole second base and then scored the game-tying run…the Yankees won the game on Juan Miranda's "walk-off" walk in the 10th inning.
- Made just one more start—in 10/2 Game 2 loss at Boston—going 0-for-3 with 1R.
- Began the season with Triple-A Scranton/Wilkes-Barre, batting .289 (134-for-464) with 55R, 25 doubles, 3 triples, 4HR and 50RBI in 118 games…recorded the third-highest average among all Yankees farmhands in 2010…at the time of his recall, was leading the International League in hits…recorded 35 multi-hit games, including 10 three-hit games and two four-hit contests…was named to the International League postseason All-Star team as the league's top shortstop.
- Was named to the International League midseason All-Star team, starting at SS and going 0-for-2 in the IL's 2-1 victory.
- Led Scranton/WB batters in hits, doubles and stolen bases (23).
- Hit .377 (29-for-77) in 20 games in April, hitting safely in all but four contests that month.
- Appeared in 17 official spring training games with the Yankees in 2010, batting .231 (6-for-17) with 5R, 3 doubles and 4RBI.

Nunez's 2010 Batting Record

Year	Club	AVG	G	AB	R	H	2B	3B	HR	RBI	SH	SF	HB	BB	SO	SB	CS	E	OBP	SLG
2010	Scranton/WB	.289	118	464	55	134	25	3	4	50	3	2	5	32	60	23	5	14	.340	.381
	YANKEES	.280	30	50	12	14	1	0	1	7	0	0	0	3	2	5	0	1	.321	.360

RHP CHAN HO PARK #61

- Was 2-1 with a 5.60 ERA in 27 relief appearances with the Yankees in 2010…opponents batted .280 (40-for-143, 7HR); LH .328 (22-for-67 4HR), RH .237 (18-for-76, 3HR)…retired 19-of-27 first batters faced (70.4%)…allowed five-of-seven inherited runners to score (71.4%)…12 of his appearances were more than 1.0 inning, including nine outings of at least 2.0IP…allowed runs in 14 of his 27 outings (51.9%).
- Appeared on an Opening Day roster with his fifth different team in 2010 (also Los Angeles-NL, Texas, San Diego and Philadelphia).
- Suffered the loss (and blown save) in his first appearance as a Yankee in 4/4 Opening Day game at Boston, allowing 3H and 3R (2ER) in 0.2IP (1K, 1HR)…was his first home run allowed as a reliever since 8/27/08 at Washington (Ryan Zimmerman).
- Earned his first win as a Yankee on 4/7 at Boston, tossing 3.0 scoreless innings (1H, 1K).
- Was placed on the D.L. from 4/16 (retroactive to 4/14)-5/16 with a right hamstring strain, missing 30 team games…was the first Yankees player to be placed on the D.L. in 2010…made one rehab appearance with Triple-A Scranton/Wilkes-Barre on 5/14 vs. Charlotte, starting and tossing 1.0 scoreless inning (1H, 2K, 1WP)…also appeared in an extended spring training game in Tampa on 5/12, allowing 1H with 3K…tossed 45 pitches in a side-session in Tampa on 5/10.
- Was returned from rehab and reinstated from the 15-day disabled list on 5/17, and appeared in that night's win vs. Boston…allowed 3ER in 1.0IP for his second blown save…Yankees scored four in the ninth for the "walk-off" victory.
- Held opponents scoreless over five consecutive outings from 6/5-17, allowing just 3H in 5.2IP with 7K…earned his second win of the season on 7/18 vs. Tampa Bay (1.1IP, 2K).
- Made his final appearance with the Yankees in 7/29 win at Cleveland, allowing 2H and 2ER in 2.0IP (3R, 3BB, 2K, 2WP).
- Was designated for assignment on 7/31 when the Yankees acquired RHP Kerry Wood from the Cleveland Indians…was claimed off waivers by the Pittsburgh Pirates on 8/4.
- Was signed by the Yankees as a free agent to a one-year contract on 2/28/10…did not allow a run over six spring training relief appearances with the Yankees (7.0IP, 4H, 0BB, 8K)…became the first Korean-born player ever to appear in a game for the Yankees.

Park's 2010 Pitching Record

Year	Club	W	L	ERA	G	GS	CG	SHO	SV	IP	H	R	ER	HR	HB	BB	SO	WP	BK
2010	YANKEES	2	1	5.60	27	0	0	0	0	35.1	40	25	22	7	1	12	29	2	0

LHP ROYCE RING #61

- Made five relief appearances with the Yankees in 2010, allowing 3H and 4ER in 2.1IP (15.43 ERA)…allowed runs in three of his five outings…nine of his 12 batters faced were left-handed hitters (3-for-8, 1BB).
- Was signed to a Major League contract and selected to the Yankees' active roster from Triple-A Scranton/Wilkes-Barre on 9/15…made his Yankees debut in 9/22 loss vs. Tampa Bay, allowing 1ER in 1.2IP (1BB, 2K).
- Began the season with Triple-A Scranton/Wilkes-Barre, going 2-1 with two saves and a 1.93 ERA in 52 relief appearances (42.0IP, 12ER)…led the staff in appearances, holding opponents without an earned run in 45 of the 52 outings…tossed less than 1.0 inning 26 times…opponents batted .222 (35-for-158, 2HR); LH .202 (18-for-89, 2HR), RH .246 (17-for-69).
- Held opponents scoreless in his first 10 relief appearances (8.2IP).
- Made one postseason relief appearance for Scranton/WB, walking one batter in 0.1IP.
- In nine official spring training relief appearances with the Yankees in 2010, allowed 2ER in 8.0IP (2.25 ERA).

Ring's 2010 Pitching Record

Year	Club	W	L	ERA	G	GS	CG	SHO	SV	IP	H	R	ER	HR	HB	BB	SO	WP	BK
2010	Scranton/WB	2	1	1.93	52	0	0	0	2	42.0	35	12	9	2	5	11	39	2	0
	YANKEES	0	0	15.43	5	0	0	0	0	2.1	3	4	4	0	0	2	2	0	0

INF KEVIN RUSSO #27/#26/#60

- Hit .184 (9-for-49) with 5R, 2 doubles and 4RBI in 31 games (10 starts in LF, three at 3B) over three stints with the Yankees in 2010 (5/8-13, 5/20-7/16, 9/12-10/3)…also appeared defensively at 2B in two games.
- Was recalled from Triple-A Scranton/Wilkes-Barre on 5/8 and made his Major League debut that day at Boston, entering the game in the eighth at 2B and going 0-for-1…was 0-for-2 in four games before being optioned back to Scranton/WB on 5/13 when Juan Miranda was recalled.
- Was recalled from Scranton/WB for a second time on 5/20 when C Jorge Posada went on the disabled list.
- Made his first Major League start in 5/21 win at the Mets, driving in both Yankees runs in the 2-1 win…recorded his first Major League hit—a third-inning single off Hisanori Takahashi—and going 2-for-3 with 2RBI before being removed defensively in the seventh…recorded his first career RBI with a game-winning two-run double in the seventh.

- According to the *Elias Sports Bureau*, became the first Major Leaguer to drive in all of his team's runs in a victory in his first Major League start since Montreal's Shane Andrews in a 2-1 win at Pittsburgh on 4/27/95…Elias also notes that no Yankee had accomplished that feat in the Expansion Era (since 1961) and Archie Moore was the last Yankee to drive in all of his club's runs in his first Major League start (in a 2-1 Yankees loss on 10/4/64 vs. Cleveland).
- Was optioned to Scranton/WB on 7/16 when Juan Miranda was recalled.
- Returned to the Yankees a third time as a September recall on 9/12…appeared in two games following his recall, going 0-for-1.
- Began the season with Triple-A Scranton/Wilkes-Barre, batting .259 (86-for-332) with 41R, 16 doubles, 1HR and 24RBI in 81 games…saw time at 2B, 3B, SS, LF, CF, RF and DH…combined for a .966 fielding percentage (9E, 256TC).
- Hit safely in a season-high 12 straight games from 4/28-5/16, batting .380 (19-for-50) with 9R, 3 doubles, 1 triple, 1HR and 9RBI…had three 3H games during the stretch (4/29 vs. Louisville, 5/2 at Norfolk and 5/6 at Durham).
- In four postseason games for Scranton/WB, hit .143 (2-for-14) with 2R, 1 triple, 1RBI, 3BB and 1SB.
- Appeared in 19 spring training games for the Yankees in 2010, batting .265 (9-for-34) with 3 doubles and 3RBI.

Russo's 2010 Batting Record

Year	Club	AVG	G	AB	R	H	2B	3B	HR	RBI	SH	SF	HB	BB	SO	SB	CS	E	OBP	SLG
2010	Scranton/WB	.259	81	332	41	86	16	2	1	24	1	0	9	28	65	9	4	9	.333	.328
	YANKEES	.184	31	49	5	9	2	0	0	4	1	0	1	3	9	1	0	1	.245	.224

RHP ROMULO SANCHEZ   #47/#64

- Allowed 1H in 4.1IP in two scoreless relief appearances over two stints with the Yankees in 2010 (5/7-10 and 9/17-10/3).
- Was recalled from Triple-A Scranton/Wilkes-Barre on 5/7…made one relief appearance in 5/9 loss at Boston, allowing just 1H in 3.2 scoreless IP (1BB, 3K)…was optioned back to Scranton/WB on 5/10.
- Returned to the Yankees as a September callup on 9/17…made his second—and final—appearance in 9/25 loss vs. Boston, tossing 0.2 scoreless innings (2BB, 2K).
- Began the season with Scranton/WB, going 10-8 with a 3.97 ERA in 31 games (14 starts), holding opponents to a .232 batting average (88-for-380).
- Worked exclusively as a reliever from 7/5 through the end of the season, allowing just 5ER in 25.0IP (1.80 ERA)…overall as a reliever, went 7-1 with a 1.69 ERA, striking out 37 batters in 32.0IP…posted a 3-7 record with a 4.98 ERA as a starter.
- Did not record a decision in three spring training relief appearances with the Yankees, allowing 1ER in 4.0IP (2.25 ERA, 4H, 2BB, 3K, 1HR).

Sanchez' 2010 Pitching Record

Year	Club	W	L	ERA	G	GS	CG	SHO	SV	IP	H	R	ER	HR	HB	BB	SO	WP	BK
2010	Scranton/WB	10	8	3.97	31	14	0	0	0	104.1	88	50	46	8	1	59	96	6	1
	YANKEES	0	0	0.00	2	0	0	0	0	4.1	1	0	0	0	0	3	5	0	0

OF RANDY WINN   #22

- Hit .213 (13-for-61) with 7R, 1 triple, 1HR and 8RBI in 29 games (14 starts in LF, two in RF) with the Yankees in 2010…made his 11th career Opening Day roster, 10th straight (since 2001).
- Recorded his first hit as a Yankee in 4/27 loss at Baltimore—a third-inning single off Kevin Millwood.
- Hit game-winning three-run HR and was 1-for-3 on 5/3 vs. Baltimore…snapped a 491AB homerless stretch, dating back to 4/25/09 w/ San Francisco at Arizona (off Max Scherzer).
- Made his final appearance with the Yankees in 5/22 loss at the Mets, going 1-for-2 with 1BB…was designated for assignment on 5/28 when OF Curtis Granderson was returned from rehab and reinstated from the 15-day disabled list…was released on 6/4 and signed by St. Louis on 6/5.

Winn's 2010 Batting Record

Year	Club	AVG	G	AB	R	H	2B	3B	HR	RBI	SH	SF	HB	BB	SO	SB	CS	E	OBP	SLG
2010	YANKEES	.213	29	61	7	13	0	1	1	8	1	1	0	8	15	1	0	0	.300	.295

2010 Transactions

Jan. 7	Signed **RHP Sergio Mitre** to a one-year contract, avoiding arbitration.
Jan. 18	Signed **RHP Chad Gaudin** and **LHP Boone Logan** to one-year contracts, avoiding arbitration.
Jan. 26	Acquired **OF Greg Golson** from the Texas Rangers in exchange for minor league **INF Mitch Hilligoss**.
Feb. 8	Signed **OF Randy Winn** to a one-year contract.
	Invited 20 non-roster players to spring training: **LHP Wilkins Arias, LPH Jeremy Bleich, OF Colin Curtis, RHP Grant Duff, OF Reid Gorecki, C Kyle Higashioka, RHP Jason Hirsh, LHP Kei Igawa, RHP Zach McAllister, C Jesus Montero, C P.J. Pilittere, LHP Royce Ring, C Mike Rivera, C Austin Romine, RHP Amaury Sanit, RHP Zack Segovia, OF Marcus Thames, RHP Kevin Whelan and OF David Winfree.**
Feb. 16	Invited **RHP's D.J. Mitchell** and **Justin Pope** and **INF's Brandon Laird** and **Jorge Vazquez** to spring training.
Feb. 19	Invited **C Jose Gil** to spring training.
Feb. 28	Signed **RHP Chan Ho Park** to a one-year contract; designated **RHP Edwar Ramirez** for assignment.
Mar. 9	Traded **RHP Edwar Ramirez** to the Texas Rangers for cash considerations.
Mar. 13	Optioned **LHP Wilkin De La Rosa** to Triple-A Scranton/Wilkes-Barre, optioned **RHP Christian Garcia** to Double-A Trenton, optioned **RHP Andrew Brackman** to Single-A Tampa and reassigned **LHP Wilkins Arias, LHP Jeremy Bleich, RHP Grant Duff, C Jose Gil, C Kyle Higashioka, LHP Kei Igawa, RHP D.J. Mitchell** and **RHP Kevin Whelan** to minor league camp.
Mar. 14	Reassigned **RHP Zach McAllister** to minor league camp.
Mar. 15	Optioned **RHP Ivan Nova** to Triple-A Scranton/Wilkes-Barre and optioned **RHP Hector Noesi** to Single-A Tampa.
Mar. 19	Optioned **RHP Romulo Sanchez** to Triple-A Scranton/Wilkes-Barre; reassigned **RHP Jason Hirsh** and **RHP Ryan Pope** to minor league camp.
Mar. 20	Reassigned **RHP Dustin Moseley** to minor league camp.
Mar. 21	Reassigned **OF Colin Curtis, OF Reid Gorecki, C Jesus Montero, C Austin Romine** to minor league camp.
Mar. 22	**OF Jamie Hoffmann** was returned to the Los Angeles Dodgers after the Yankees selected him in the 2009 Rule 5 Draft; optioned **INF Reegie Corona** and **INF Eduardo Nunez** to Triple-A Scranton/Wilkes-Barre; reassigned **INF Brandon Laird** and **INF Jorge Vazquez** to minor league camp.
Mar. 24	Optioned **RHP Jonathan Albaladejo, OF Greg Golson, RHP Mark Melancon, 1B Juan Miranda,** and **INF Kevin Russo** to Triple-A Scranton/Wilkes-Barre.
Mar. 25	Released **RHP Chad Gaudin**.
Mar. 26	Reassigned **RHP Amaury Sanit** to minor league camp.
Mar. 30	Reassigned **OFs Jon Weber** and **David Winfree** to minor league camp.
Apr. 1	Reassigned **RHP Zack Segovia** to minor league camp.
Apr. 2	Reassigned **LHP Royce Ring** to minor league camp.
Apr. 3	Signed **OF Marcus Thames** to a Major League contract and selected him to the 25-man roster; optioned **LHP Boone Logan** to Triple-A Scranton/Wilkes-Barre; reassigned **C P.J. Piliterre** to minor league camp; and gave **C Mike Rivera** his outright release.
Apr. 7	Acquired **OF Chad Huffman** off waivers from San Diego and added him to the 40-man roster.
Apr. 16	Placed **RHP Chan Ho Park** on the 15-day disabled list with a right hamstring strain; recalled **LHP Boone Logan** from Triple-A Scranton/Wilkes-Barre.
May 2	Placed **CF Curtis Granderson** on the 15-day disabled list with a Grade 2 left groin strain…recalled **RHP Mark Melancon** from Triple-A Scanton/Wilkes-Barre.
May 5	Recalled **OF Greg Golson** from Triple-A Scranton/Wilkes-Barre; optioned **RHP Mark Melancon** to Scranton/WB.
May 7	Recalled **RHP Romulo Sanchez** from Triple-A Scranton/Wilkes-Barre; optioned **OF Greg Golson** to Scranton/WB.
May 8	Placed **DH/1B Nick Johnson** on the 15-day disabled list with an inflamed right wrist tendon…recalled **INF Kevin Russo** from Triple-A Scranton/Wilkes-Barre.
May 10	Recalled **RHP Ivan Nova** from Triple-A Scranton/Wilkes-Barre; optioned **RHP Romulo Sanchez** to Scranton/WB.
May 12	Placed **RHP Alfredo Aceves** on the 15-day disabled list with a strained lower back…recalled **OF Greg Golson** from Triple-A Scranton/Wilkes-Barre.
May 13	Recalled **INF Juan Miranda** from Triple-A Scranton/Wilkes-Barre; optioned **INF Kevin Russo** to Scranton/WB.
May 14	Claimed **RHP Shane Lindsay** off waivers from the Colorado Rockies and assigned him to Single-A Tampa; released **RHP Christian Garcia**.
May 17	Returned from rehab and reinstated **RHP Chan Ho Park** from the 15-day disabled list…optioned **RHP Ivan Nova** to Triple-A Scranton/Wilkes-Barre.
May 18	Recalled **RHP Mark Melancon** from Triple-A Scranton/Wilkes-Barre; optioned **OF Greg Golson** to Scranton/WB.
May 20	Placed **C Jorge Posada** on the 15-day diabled list with a fractured right foot; signed **C Chad Moeller** to a Major League contract and selected him to the 25-man roster; recalled **INF Kevin Russo** from Triple-A Scranton/Wilkes-Barre; transferred **DH Nick Johnson** from the 15-day disabled list to the 60-day disabled list.; optioned **RHP Mark Melancon** to Triple-A Scranton/WB.
May 26	Signed **RHP Chad Gaudin** to a Major League contract and selected him to the 25-man roster; optioned **LHP**

2010 Transactions

	Boone Logan to Triple-A Scranton/Wilkes-Barre; designated **RHP Shane Lindsay** for assignment.
May 28	Returned from rehab and reinstated **OF Curtis Granderson** from the 15-day disabled list; designated **OF Randy Winn** for assignment.
June 1	**RHP Shane Lindsay** was claimed off waivers by the Cleveland Indians.
June 2	Reinstated **C Jorge Posada** from the 15-day disabled list; optioned **INF Juan Miranda** to Triple-A Scranton/Wilkes-Barre.
June 4	Released **OF Randy Winn**.
June 13	Placed **OF Marcus Thames** on the 15-day diabled list with strained right hamstring…recalled **OF Chad Huffman** from Triple-A Scranton/Wilkes-Barre.
June 15	Placed **RHP Sergio Mitre** on the 15-day diabled list with strained left oblique; recalled **LHP Boone Logan** from Triple-A Scranton/Wilkes-Barre.
June 21	Designated **C Chad Moeller** for assignment; signed **OF Colin Curtis** to a Major League contract and selected him to the 25-man roster.
June 26	**C Chad Moeller** cleared waivers and was outrighted to Triple-A Scranton/WB.
July 2	Signed **RHP Dustin Moseley** to a Major League contract and selected him to the 25-man roster from Triple-A Scranton/Wilkes-Barre; optioned **LHP Boone Logan** to Triple-A Scranton/Wilkes-Barre.
July 4	Returned from rehab and reinstated **OF Marcus Thames** from the 15-day disabled list; optioned **OF Chad Huffman** to Triple-A Scranton/Wilkes-Barre.
July 16	Recalled **1B Juan Miranda** from Triple-A Scranton/Wilkes-Barre; optioned **INF Kevin Russo** to Scranton/WB; returned **RHP Sergio Mitre** from rehab.
July 17	Placed **LHP Damaso Marte** on the 15-day disabled list with left shoulder inflammation; recalled **LHP Boone Logan** from Triple-A Scranton/Wilkes-Barre.
July 20	Placed **LHP Andy Pettitte** on the 15-day disabled list with a Grade 1 left groin strain; recalled **RHP Jonathan Albaladejo** from Triple-A Scranton/Wilkes-Barre.
July 24	Returned from rehab and reinstated **RHP Sergio Mitre** from the 15-day disabled list; optioned **RHP Jonathan Albaladejo** to Triple-A Scranton/Wilkes-Barre.
July 30	Acquired **OF Austin Kearns** from the Cleveland Indians for a player to be named later (RHP Zach McAllister).
July 31	Acquired **1B/DH Lance Berkman** and cash from the Houston Astros in exchange for RHP Mark Melancon and minor league INF Jimmy Paredes; acquired **RHP Kerry Wood** and cash from the Cleveland Indians for a player to be named later or cash considerations; optioned **OF Colin Curtis** and **1B/DH Juan Miranda** to Triple-A Scranton/Wilkes-Barre; designated **RHP Chan Ho Park** for assignment.
Aug. 4	**RHP Chan Ho Park** was claimed off waivers by the Pittsburgh Pirates.
Aug 19	Placed **1B/DH Lance Berkman** on the 15-day disabled list with a right ankle sprain (retroactive to 8/16); recalled **INF Eduardo Nunez** from Triple-A Scranton/Wilkes-Barre.
Aug. 21	Placed **3B Alex Rodriguez** on the 15-day disabled list with a strained left calf.
Aug. 22	Recalled **RHP Ivan Nova** from Triple-A Scranton/Wilkes-Barre.
Sept. 1	Recalled **RHP Jonathan Albaladejo** and **OF Greg Golson** from Triple-A Scranton/Wilkes-Barre; signed **C Chad Moeller** to a Major League contract and added him to the 40-man roster; returned **DH/1B Lance Berkman** from rehab and reinstated from the 15-day D.L.; transferred **LHP Damaso Marte** to the 60-day D.L.
Sept. 5	Reinstated **3B Alex Rodriguez** from the 15-day disabled list.
Sept. 6	Recalled **OF Colin Curtis** from Triple-A Scranton/Wilkes-Barre.
Sept. 9	Claimed **LHP Steve Garrison** off waivers from the San Diego Padres; designated **LHP Wilkin De La Rosa** for assignment.
Sept. 12	Recalled **1B Juan Miranda** and **INF Kevin Russo** from Triple-A Scranton/Wilkes-Barre; outrighted **LHP Wilkin De La Rosa** to Double-A Trenton.
Sept. 15	Signed **LHP Royce Ring** to a Major League contract and added him to the active roster; designated **OF Chad Huffman** for assignment.
Sept. 17	Recalled **RHP Romulo Sanchez** from Triple-A Scranton/Wilkes-Barre; **OF Chad Huffman** was claimed off waivers by Cleveland.
Sept. 19	Returned from rehab and reinstated **LHP Andy Pettitte** from the 15-day D.L.
Sept. 24	Recalled **RHP Andrew Brackman** from Double-A Trenton.

2010 Day-by-Day

Gm	Date	Opponent	W/L	Score	Winning Pitcher	Losing Pitcher	Save	Rec.	Pos.	GA/GB	Att.
1	4/4	at Boston	L	7-9	Okajima (1-0)	Park (0-1)	Papelbon (1)	0-1	5th	-1.0	*37,440
	4/5	OFF DAY							T4th	-1.0	
2	4/6	at Boston	W	6-4	Aceves (1-0)	Okajima (1-1)	Rivera (1)	1-1	T2nd	-0.5	*38,000
3	4/7	at Boston	W	3-1 (10)	Park (1-1)	Papelbon (0-1)	Rivera (2)	2-1	2nd	-0.5	*38,238
	4/8	OFF DAY							T1st	---	
4	4/9	at Tampa Bay	L	3-9	Price (1-0)	Vazquez (0-1)	-	2-2	3rd	-1.0	33,221
5	4/10	at Tampa Bay	W	10-0	Sabathia (1-0)	Davis (0-1)	-	3-2	T2nd	-1.0	29,892
6	4/11	at Tampa Bay	W	7-3	Burnett (1-0)	Choate (0-1)	-	4-2	2nd	-1.0	31,253
	4/12	OFF DAY							2nd	-0.5	
7	4/13	Los Angeles-AL	W	7-5	Pettitte (1-0)	Santana (0-2)	Rivera (3)	5-2	2nd	-0.5	*49,293 (1)
8	4/14	Los Angeles-AL	L	3-5	Pineiro (1-1)	Vazquez (0-2)	Rodney (1)	5-3	3rd	-0.5	42,372
9	4/15	Los Angeles-AL	W	6-2	Hughes (1-0)	Kazmir (0-1)	Rivera (4)	6-3	T2nd	-0.5	44,722
10	4/16	Texas	W	5-1 (6)	**Sabathia** (2-0)	**Wilson** (0-1)	-	7-3	T1st	---	42,145
11	4/17	Texas	W	7-3	Burnett (2-0)	Feldman (1-1)	-	8-3	T1st	---	44,963
12	4/18	Texas	W	5-2	Pettitte (2-0)	Harden (0-1)	Rivera (5)	9-3	T1st	---	44,121
	4/19	OFF DAY							2nd	-0.5	
13	4/20	at Oakland	W	7-3	Vazquez (1-2)	Gonzalez (1-1)	-	10-3	1st	+0.5	19,849
14	4/21	at Oakland	W	3-1	Hughes (2-0)	Sheets (1-1)	Rivera (6)	11-3	1st	+0.5	30,211
15	4/22	at Oakland	L	2-4	Braden (3-0)	**Sabathia** (2-1)	Bailey (2)	11-4	2nd	-0.5	21,986
16	4/23	at Los Angeles-AL	L	4-6	Rodney (1-1)	Chamberlain (0-1)	Fuentes (2)	11-5	2nd	-0.5	44,002
17	4/24	at Los Angeles-AL	W	7-1	Pettitte (3-0)	Pineiro (2-2)	-	12-5	2nd	-0.5	43,390
18	4/25	at Los Angeles-AL	L	4-8	Kazmir (2-1)	Vazquez (1-3)	-	12-6	2nd	-1.5	42,284
	4/26	OFF DAY							2nd	-1.5	
19	4/27	at Baltimore	L	4-5	Castillo (1-0)	Robertson (0-1)	Simon (1)	12-7	2nd	-2.5	20,536
20	4/28	at Baltimore	W	8-3	Sabathia (3-1)	Guthrie (0-3)	-	13-7	2nd	-2.5	17,248
21	4/29	at Baltimore	W	4-0	Burnett (3-0)	Matusz (2-1)	-	14-7	2nd	-2.5	26,439
22	4/30	Chicago-AL	W	6-4	Aceves (2-0)	Thornton (2-2)	Rivera (7)	15-7	2nd	-1.5	44,783
23	5/1	Chicago-AL	L	6-7	Linebrink (1-0)	Robertson (0-2)	Jenks (5)	15-8	2nd	-1.5	45,465
24	5/2	Chicago-AL	W	12-3	Hughes (3-0)	Buehrle (2-4)	-	16-8	2nd	-1.5	45,303
25	5/3	Baltimore	W	4-1	Sabathia (4-1)	Guthrie (0-4)	Chamberlain (1)	17-8	2nd	-1.0	41,571
26	5/4	Baltimore	W	4-1	Burnett (4-0)	Matusz (2-2)	Chamberlain (2)	18-8	2nd	-1.0	43,260
27	5/5	Baltimore	W	7-5	Pettitte (4-0)	Hernandez (0-4)	Aceves (1)	19-8	2nd	-1.0	43,425
	5/6	OFF DAY							2nd	-1.5	
28	5/7	at Boston	W	10-3	Hughes (4-0)	Beckett (1-1)	-	20-8	2nd	-1.5	*37,898
29	5/8	at Boston	W	14-3	Aceves (3-0)	Buchholz (3-3)	-	21-8	2nd	-0.5	*37,138
30	5/9	at Boston	L	3-9	Lester (3-2)	Burnett (4-1)	-	21-9	2nd	-0.5	*37,618
31	5/10	at Detroit	L	4-5	Bonine (3-0)	Mitre (0-1)	Valverde (9)	21-10	2nd	-0.5	34,365
	5/11	at Detroit	Ppd., rain						2nd	-1.0	
32	5/12	at Detroit	L	0-2	Porcello (3-3)	Vazquez (1-4)	Valverde (10)	21-11	2nd	-1.5	27,376
33	5/12	at Detroit	W	8-0	Hughes (5-0)	Bonderman (1-2)	-	22-11	2nd	-1.5	28,514
34	5/13	at Detroit	L	0-6	Verlander (4-2)	Sabathia (4-2)	-	22-12	2nd	-2.0	31,130
35	5/14	Minnesota	W	8-4	Chamberlain (1-1)	Baker (4-3)	-	23-12	2nd	-1.0	45,195
36	5/15	Minnesota	W	7-1	Pettitte (5-0)	Liriano (4-2)	-	24-12	2nd	-1.0	46,347
37	5/16	Minnesota	L	3-6	Blackburn (4-1)	Chamberlain (1-2)	Rauch (10)	24-13	2nd	-2.0	46,628
38	5/17	Boston	W	11-9	Vazquez (2-4)	Papelbon (1-3)	-	25-13	2nd	-2.0	48,271
39	5/18	Boston	L	6-7	Bard (1-1)	Rivera (0-1)	Papelbon (10)	25-14	2nd	-3.0	47,734
40	5/19	Tampa Bay	L	6-10	Davis (4-3)	Burnett (4-2)	Benoit (1)	25-15	2nd	-4.0	43,283
41	5/20	Tampa Bay	L	6-8	Shields (5-1)	Pettitte (5-1)	Soriano (11)	25-16	2nd	-5.0	45,483
42	5/21	at New York-NL	W	2-1	Vazquez (3-4)	Dessens (0-1)	Rivera (8)	26-16	2nd	-4.0	*41,382
43	5/22	at New York-NL	L	3-5	Pelfrey (6-1)	Hughes (5-1)	Rodriguez (7)	26-17	2nd	-5.0	*41,343
44	5/23	at New York-NL	L	4-6	Santana (4-2)	Sabathia (4-3)	Rodriguez (8)	26-18	2nd	-6.0	*41,422
	5/24	OFF DAY							2nd	-5.5	
45	5/25	at Minnesota	W	1-0	Burnett (5-2)	Duensing (2-1)	Rivera (9)	27-18	2nd	-4.5	*38,962
46	5/26	at Minnesota	W	3-2	Pettitte (6-1)	Rauch (1-1)	Rivera (10)	28-18	2nd	-3.5	*39.353
47	5/27	at Minnesota	L	2-8	Blackburn (6-1)	Vazquez (3-5)	-	28-19	2nd	-4.5	*39,087
48	5/28	Cleveland	W	8-2	Hughes (6-1)	Carmona (4-3)	-	29-19	2nd	-3.5	44,634
49	5/29	Cleveland	L	11-13	Perez, R. (1-0)	Chamberlain (1-3)	Wood (2)	29-20	2nd	-4.5	46,599
50	5/30	Cleveland	W	7-3	Burnett (6-2)	Sipp (0-1)	-	30-20	2nd	-3.5	45,706
51	5/31	Cleveland	W	11-2	Pettitte (7-1)	Talbot (6-4)	-	31-20	2nd	-2.5	44,976
52	6/1	Baltimore	W	3-1	Vazquez (4-5)	Matusz (2-6)	Rivera (11)	32-20	2nd	-2.5	43,059
53	6/2	Baltimore	W	9-1	Hughes (7-1)	Bergesen (3-4)	-	33-20	2nd	-2.5	44,465
54	6/3	Baltimore	W	6-3	Sabathia (5-3)	Millwood (0-6)	Rivera (12)	34-20	2nd	-2.0	44,927

2010 Day-by-Day

Gm	Date	Opponent	W/L	Score	Winning Pitcher	Losing Pitcher	Save	Rec.	Pos.	GA/GB	Att.
55	6/4	at Toronto	L	1-6	Cecil (6-2)	Burnett (6-3)	-	34-21	2nd	-2.0	30,089
56	6/5	at Toronto	L	2-3 (14)	Janssen (4-0)	Gaudin (0-3)	-	34-22	2nd	-2.0	37,165
57	6/6	at Toronto	W	4-3	Vazquez (5-5)	Downs (1-5)	Rivera (13)	35-22	2nd	-2.0	33,622
	6/7		OFF DAY						2nd	-2.0	
58	6/8	at Baltimore	W	12-7	Hughes (8-1)	Millwood (0-7)	-	36-22	2nd	-2.0	23,171
59	6/9	at Baltimore	W	4-2	Sabathia (6-3)	Tillman (0-2)	Rivera (14)	37-22	2nd	-2.0	16,451
60	6/10	at Baltimore	L	3-4	Arrieta (1-0)	Burnett (6-4)	Hernandez (1)	37-23	2nd	-2.0	27,064
61	6/11	Houston	W	4-3	Pettitte (8-1)	Myers (4-4)	Rivera (15)	38-23	2nd	-1.0	46,883
62	6/12	Houston	W	9-3	Vazquez (6-5)	Rodriguez (3-9)	-	39-23	2nd	-1.0	46,159
63	6/13	Houston	W	9-5	Hughes (9-1)	Moehler (0-3)	-	40-23	T1st	---	46,832
	6/14		OFF DAY						T1st	---	
64	6/15	Philadelphia	W	8-3	Sabathia (7-3)	Halladay (8-5)	-	41-23	T1st	---	47,135
65	6/16	Philadelphia	L	3-6	Moyer (7-6)	Burnett (6-5)	-	41-24	T1st	---	47,414
66	6/17	Philadelphia	L	1-7	Kendrick (4-2)	Pettitte (8-2)	-	41-25	T1st	---	47,204
67	6/18	New York-NL	L	0-4	Takahashi (6-2)	Vazquez (6-6)	Rodriguez (16)	41-26	T1st	---	*49,220 (2)
68	6/19	New York-NL	W	5-3	Hughes (10-1)	Pelfrey (9-2)	Rivera (16)	42-26	T1st	---	*49,073 (3)
69	6/20	New York-NL	W	4-0	Sabathia (8-3)	Santana (5-4)	-	43-26	1st	+1.0	*49,240 (4)
70	6/21	at Arizona	L	4-10	Lopez (3-6)	Burnett (6-6)	-	43-27	1st	+0.5	47,229
71	6/22	at Arizona	W	9-3	Pettitte (9-2)	Haren (7-6)	-	44-27	1st	+1.5	45,776
72	6/23	at Arizona	W	6-5 (10)	Rivera (1-1)	Rosa (0-2)	-	45-27	1st	+2.5	46,325
	6/24		OFF DAY						1st	+2.0	
73	6/25	at Los Angeles-NL	W	2-1	Sabathia (9-3)	Padilla (1-2)	Rivera (17)	46-27	1st	+3.0	*56,000
74	6/26	at Los Angeles-NL	L	4-9	Kuroda (7-5)	Burnett (6-7)	-	46-28	1st	+2.0	*56,000
75	6/27	at Los Angeles-NL	W	8-6 (10)	Rivera (2-1)	Troncoso (1-2)	-	47-28	1st	+2.0	*56,000
	6/28		OFF DAY						1st	+2.0	
76	6/29	Seattle	L	4-7	Lee (7-3)	Hughes (10-2)	-	47-29	1st	+1.0	45,780
77	6/30	Seattle	L	0-7	Hernandez (6-5)	Vazquez (6-7)	-	47-30	1st	+1.0	46,309
78	7/1	Seattle	W	4-2	Sabathia (10-3)	Aardsma (0-5)	Rivera (18)	48-30	1st	+1.5	45,591
79	7/2	Toronto	L	1-6 (11)	Frasor (3-1)	Robertson (0-3)	-	48-31	1st	+0.5	45,792
80	7/3	Toronto	W	11-3	Pettitte (10-2)	Romero (6-5)	-	49-31	1st	+0.5	46,364
81	7/4	Toronto	W	7-6 (10)	Robertson (1-3)	Purcey (0-1)	-	50-31	1st	+1.5	46,810
82	7/5	at Oakland	W	3-1	Vazquez (7-7)	Sheets (3-8)	Rivera (19)	51-31	1st	+2.0	27,405
83	7/6	at Oakland	W	6-1	Sabathia (11-3)	Cahill (8-3)	-	52-31	1st	+2.0	20,473
84	7/7	at Oakland	W	6-2	Burnett (7-7)	Gonzalez (7-6)	-	53-31	1st	+2.0	31,518
85	7/8	at Seattle	W	3-1	Pettitte (11-2)	Aardsma (0-6)	Rivera (20)	54-31	1st	+2.0	37,432
86	7/9	at Seattle	W	6-1	Hughes (11-2)	Pauley (0-1)	-	55-31	1st	+3.0	39,645
87	7/10	at Seattle	L	1-4	Hernandez (7-5)	Chamberlain (1-4)	-	55-32	1st	+2.0	42,558
88	7/11	at Seattle	W	8-2	Sabathia (12-3)	Rowland-Smith (1-9)	-	56-32	1st	+2.0	42,069
	7/12 – 7/15				(81st All-Star Game on 7/13 at Angel Stadium of Anaheim)						
89	7/16	Tampa Bay	W	5-4	Rivera (3-1)	Choate (2-3)	-	57-32	1st	+3.0	47,524
90	7/17	Tampa Bay	L	5-10	Niemann (8-2)	Burnett (7-8)	-	57-33	1st	+2.0	*48,957 (5)
91	7/18	Tampa Bay	W	9-5	Park (2-1)	Price (12-5)	-	58-33	1st	+3.0	46,969
	7/19		OFF DAY						1st	+2.5	
92	7/20	Los Angeles-AL	L	2-10	O'Sullivan (1-0)	Hughes (11-3)	-	58-34	1st	+2.5	47,775
93	7/21	Los Angeles-AL	W	10-6	Vazquez (8-7)	Pineiro (10-7)	-	59-34	1st	+2.5	47,521
94	7/22	Kansas City	W	10-4	Sabathia (13-3)	Chen (5-4)	-	60-34	1st	+3.0	47,484
95	7/23	Kansas City	W	7-1	Burnett (8-8)	Bannister (7-9)	-	61-34	1st	+4.0	46,801
96	7/24	Kansas City	L	5-6	Davies (9-6)	Mitre (0-2)	Soria (27)	61-35	1st	+3.0	*48,138 (6)
97	7/25	Kansas City	W	12-6	Hughes (12-3)	O'Sullivan (1-1)	-	62-35	1st	+3.0	47,890
98	7/26	at Cleveland	W	3-2	Vazquez (9-7)	Westbrook (6-7)	Rivera (21)	63-35	1st	+3.0	27,224
99	7/27	at Cleveland	L	1-4	Tomlin (1-0)	Sabathia (13-4)	Perez (10)	63-36	1st	+2.0	27,416
100	7/28	at Cleveland	W	8-0	Burnett (9-8)	Carmona (10-8)	-	64-36	1st	+2.0	22,965
101	7/29	at Cleveland	W	11-4	Moseley (1-0)	Herrmann (0-1)	-	65-36	1st	+2.0	34,455
102	7/30	at Tampa Bay	L	2-3	Hughes (12-4)	Davis (9-9)	Soriano (29)	65-37	1st	+1.0	*36,973
103	7/31	at Tampa Bay	W	5-4	Robertson (2-3)	Soriano (2-1)	Rivera (22)	66-37	1st	+2.0	*36,973
104	8/1	at Tampa Bay	L	0-3	Shields (10-9)	Sabathia (13-5)	Soriano (30)	66-38	1st	+1.0	*36,973
105	8/2	Toronto	L	6-8	Morrow (8-6)	Burnett (9-9)	Gregg (24)	66-39	T1st	---	47,034
106	8/3	Toronto	L	2-8	Romero (10-6)	Moseley (1-1)	-	66-40	2nd	-1.0	46,480
107	8/4	Toronto	W	5-1	Hughes (13-4)	Marcum (10-5)	-	67-40	T1st	---	47,659
	8/5		OFF DAY						1st	+0.5	

2010 Day-by-Day

Gm	Date	Opponent	W/L	Score	Winning Pitcher	Losing Pitcher	Save	Rec.	Pos.	GA/GB	Att.
108	8/6	Boston	L	3-6	Buchholz (12-5)	Vazquez (9-8)	Papelbon (27)	67-41	1st	+0.5	*49,555 (7)
109	8/7	Boston	W	5-2	Sabathia (14-5)	Lackey (10-7)	Rivera (23)	68-41	1st	+1.5	*49,716 (8)
110	8/8	Boston	W	7-2	Moseley (2-1)	Beckett (3-2)	-	69-41	1st	+2.5	*49,096 (9)
111	8/9	Boston	L	1-2	Lester (12-7)	Hughes (13-5)	Papelbon (28)	69-42	1st	+1.5	*49,476 (10)
112	8/10	at Texas	L	3-4 (10)	Feliz (3-2)	Rivera (3-2)	-	69-43	1st	+0.5	46,121
113	8/11	at Texas	W	7-6	Wood (2-4)	Feliz (3-3)	Rivera (24)	70-43	1st	+1.5	*48,676
114	8/12	at Kansas City	W	4-3	Sabathia (15-5)	Chen (7-6)	Robertson (1)	71-43	1st	+2.0	23,337
115	8/13	at Kansas City	L	3-4	Davies (6-7)	Moseley (2-2)	Soria (32)	71-44	1st	+2.0	30,680
116	8/14	at Kansas City	W	8-3	Hughes (14-5)	O'Sullivan (1-4)	-	72-44	1st	+2.0	34,206
117	8/15	at Kansas City	L	0-1	Bullington (1-2)	**Burnett** (9-10)	Soria (33)	72-45	1st	+1.0	26,012
118	8/16	Detroit	L	1-3	Scherzer (8-9)	Vazquez (9-9)	Valverde (23)	72-46	T1st	---	46,098
119	8/17	Detroit	W	6-2	Sabathia (16-5)	Verlander (13-8)	-	73-46	T1st	---	46,906
120	8/18	Detroit	W	9-5	Moseley (3-2)	Bonderman (6-9)	-	74-46	1st	---	46,479
121	8/19	Detroit	W	11-5	Hughes (15-5)	Porcello (5-11)	Mitre (1)	75-46	1st	+1.0	*48,143 (11)
122	8/20	Seattle	L	0-6	Hernandez (10-9)	Burnett (9-11)	-	75-47	1st	+1.0	46,493
123	8/21	Seattle	W	9-5	Logan (1-0)	Vargas (9-6)	Rivera (25)	76-47	1st	+1.0	*48,158 (12)
124	8/22	Seattle	W	10-0	Sabathia (17-5)	French (2-4)	-	77-47	1st	+1.0	46,778
125	8/23	at Toronto	L	2-3	Downs (5-5)	Robertson (2-4)	Gregg (28)	77-48	T1st	---	29,198
126	8/24	at Toronto	W	11-5	Moseley (4-2)	Rzepczynski (1-2)	-	78-48	T1st	---	30,567
127	8/25	at Toronto	L	3-6	Cecil (11-6)	Hughes (15-6)	Gregg (29)	78-49	T1st	---	31,449
	8/26		OFF DAY						T1st	---	
128	8/27	at Chicago-AL	L	4-9	Garcia (11-5)	Burnett (9-12)	-	78-50	T1st	---	*38,596
129	8/28	at Chicago-AL	W	12-9	Sabathia (18-5)	Danks (12-9)	Rivera (26)	79-50	1st	---	*38,811
130	8/29	at Chicago-AL	W	2-1	Nova (1-0)	Floyd (9-11)	Rivera (27)	80-50	1st	---	*39,433
131	8/30	Oakland	W	11-5	Vazquez (10-9)	Cahill (14-6)	-	81-50	T1st	---	46,356
132	8/31	Oakland	W	9-3	Hughes (16-6)	Mazzaro (6-7)	-	82-50	1st	+1.0	44,575
133	9/1	Oakland	W	4-3	Burnett (10-12)	Anderson (3-6)	Rivera (28)	83-50	1st	+1.0	45,222
134	9/2	Oakland	W	5-0	Sabathia (19-5)	Braden (9-10)	-	84-50	1st	+1.5	44,644
135	9/3	Toronto	W	7-3	Wood (3-4)	Morrow (10-7)	-	85-50	1st	+1.5	44,739
136	9/4	Toronto	W	7-5	Chamberlain (2-4)	Frasor (3-4)	Rivera (29)	86-50	1st	+2.5	47,478
137	9/5	Toronto	L	3-7	Cecil (12-7)	Hughes (16-7)	-	86-51	1st	+2.5	47,737
138	9/6	Baltimore	L	3-4	Matusz (8-12)	Burnett (10-13)	Uehara (7)	86-52	1st	+2.5	46,103
139	9/7	Baltimore	L	2-6	Arrieta (5-6)	Sabathia (19-6)	-	86-53	1st	+1.5	46,432
140	9/8	Baltimore	W	3-2	Chamberlain (3-4)	Uehara (1-1)	-	87-53	1st	+2.5	44,163
	9/9		OFF DAY						1st	+2.5	
141	9/10	at Texas	L	5-6 (13)	Feldman (7-10)	Gaudin (0-4)	-	87-54	1st	+1.5	46,179
142	9/11	at Texas	L	6-7	Ogando (4-1)	Rivera (3-3)	-	87-55	1st	+0.5	*49,210
143	9/12	at Texas	L	1-4	Lee (11-8)	Moseley (4-3)	Feliz (36)	87-56	1st	+0.5	42,007
144	9/13	at Tampa Bay	L	0-1 (11)	Balfour (2-1)	Mitre (0-3)	-	87-57	2nd	-0.5	26,907
145	9/14	at Tampa Bay	W	8-7 (10)	Robertson (3-4)	Wheeler (2-3)	Rivera (30)	88-57	1st	+0.5	28,713
146	9/15	at Tampa Bay	L	3-4	Qualls (1-0)	Hughes (16-8)	Soriano (43)	88-58	2nd	-0.5	29,733
	9/16		OFF DAY						2nd	-0.5	
147	9/17	at Baltimore	W	4-3	Robertson (4-4)	Uehara (1-2)	Rivera (31)	89-58	1st	+0.5	32,874
148	9/18	at Baltimore	W	11-3	Sabathia (20-6)	Guthrie (10-14)	-	90-58	1st	+0.5	*48,775
149	9/19	at Baltimore	L	3-4 (11)	Gonzalez (1-3)	Robertson (4-5)	-	90-59	1st	+0.5	39,537
150	9/20	Tampa Bay	W	8-6	Gaudin (1-4)	Garza (14-9)	Rivera (32)	91-59	1st	+1.5	47,437
151	9/21	Tampa Bay	W	8-3	Hughes (17-8)	Shields (13-13)	Chamberlain (3)	92-59	1st	+2.5	46,609
152	9/22	Tampa Bay	L	2-7	Hellickson (4-0)	Burnett (10-14)	-	92-60	1st	+1.5	46,986
153	9/23	Tampa Bay	L	3-10	Price (18-6)	Sabathia (20-7)	-	92-61	1st	+0.5	47,646
154	9/24	Boston	L	8-10	Beckett (6-5)	Hughes (11-3)	Papelbon (37)	92-62	2nd	-0.5	*49,457 (13)
155	9/25	Boston	L	3-7	Lester (19-8)	Nova (1-1)	-	92-63	2nd	-1.5	*49,588 (14)
156	9/26	Boston	W	4-3 (10)	Logan (2-0)	Okajima (4-4)	-	93-63	2nd	-0.5	*49,199 (15)
157	9/27	at Toronto	L	5-7	Rzepczynski (3-4)	Burnett (10-15)	-	93-64	2nd	-0.5	16,004
158	9/28	at Toronto	W	6-1	Sabathia (21-7)	Drabek (0-3)	-	94-64	2nd	-0.5	18,193
159	9/29	at Toronto	L	4-8	Cecil (15-7)	Vazquez (10-10)	-	94-65	2nd	-0.5	33,143
	9/30		OFF DAY						T1st	---	
	10/1	at Boston	Ppd., rain						1st	+0.5	
160	10/2	at Boston	W	6-5 (10)	Hughes (18-8)	Papelbon (5-7)	Rivera (33)	95-65	1st	+1.0	*37,467
161	10/2	at Boston	L	6-7 (10)	Manuel (1-0)	Nova (1-2)	-	95-66	T1st	---	*37,589
162	10/3	at Boston	L	4-8	Lackey (14-11)	Moseley (4-4)	-	95-67	2nd	-1.0	*37,453

BOLD (Complete Game)   *Denotes Sellout (#Home Sellouts)

2010 Major League Standings

AMERICAN LEAGUE

	WON	LOST	PCT.	GB
*TAMPA BAY	96	66	.593	--
#NEW YORK	95	67	.586	1.0
BOSTON	89	73	.549	7.0
TORONTO	85	77	.525	11.0
BALTIMORE	66	96	.407	30.0

AL CENTRAL	WON	LOST	PCT.	GB
*MINNESOTA	94	68	.580	--
CHICAGO	88	74	.543	6.0
DETROIT	81	81	.500	13.0
CLEVELAND	69	93	.426	25.0
KANSAS CITY	67	95	.414	27.0

AL WEST	WON	LOST	PCT.	GB
*TEXAS	90	72	.556	--
OAKLAND	81	81	.500	9.0
LOS ANGELES	80	82	.494	10.0
SEATTLE	61	101	.377	29.0

* - DIVISION WINNER
# - WILD CARD WINNER

NATIONAL LEAGUE

NL EAST	WON	LOST	PCT.	GB
*PHILADELPHIA	97	65	.599	--
#ATLANTA	91	71	.562	6.0
FLORIDA	80	82	.494	17.0
NEW YORK	79	83	.488	18.0
WASHINGTON	69	93	.426	28.0

NL CENTRAL	WON	LOST	PCT.	GB
*CINCINNATI	91	71	.562	--
ST. LOUIS	86	76	.531	5.0
MILWAUKEE	77	85	.475	14.0
HOUSTON	76	86	.469	15.0
CHICAGO	75	87	.463	16.0
PITTSBURGH	57	105	.352	34.0

NL WEST	WON	LOST	PCT.	GB
*SAN FRANCISCO	92	70	.568	--
SAN DIEGO	90	72	.556	2.0
COLORADO	83	79	.512	9.0
LOS ANGELES	80	82	.494	12.0
ARIZONA	65	97	.401	27.0

2010 Yankees Club Statistics

	HOME W	HOME L	ROAD W	ROAD L	TOTALS W	TOTALS L
VS. BALTIMORE	7	2	6	3	13	5
VS. BOSTON	4	5	5	4	9	9
VS. TAMPA BAY	4	5	4	5	8	10
VS. TORONTO	5	4	3	6	8	10
TOTALS VS. EAST	20	16	18	18	38	34

	HOME W	HOME L	ROAD W	ROAD L	TOTALS W	TOTALS L
VS. CLEVELAND	3	1	3	1	6	2
VS. CHICAGO	2	1	2	1	4	2
VS. DETROIT	3	1	1	3	4	4
VS. KANSAS CITY	3	1	2	2	5	3
VS. MINNESOTA	2	1	2	1	4	2
TOTALS VS. CENTRAL	13	5	10	8	23	13

	HOME W	HOME L	ROAD W	ROAD L	TOTALS W	TOTALS L
VS. LOS ANGELES	3	2	1	2	4	4
VS. OAKLAND	4	0	5	1	9	1
VS. SEATTLE	3	3	3	1	6	4
VS. TEXAS	3	0	1	4	4	4
TOTALS VS. WEST	13	5	10	8	23	13

TOTALS VS. AL	46	26	38	34	84	60

	HOME W	HOME L	ROAD W	ROAD L	TOTALS W	TOTALS L
VS. ARIZONA	0	0	2	1	2	1
VS. HOUSTON	3	0	0	0	3	0
VS. LOS ANGELES	0	0	2	1	2	1
VS. NEW YORK	2	1	1	2	3	3
VS. PHILADELPHIA	1	2	0	0	1	2
TOTALS VS. NL	6	3	5	4	11	7

OVERALL TOTALS	52	29	43	38	95	67

	HOME W	HOME L	ROAD W	ROAD L	TOTALS W	TOTALS L
SHUTOUTS	3	3	5	5	8	8
SHO – INDIVIDUAL	0	1	0	0	0	1
EXTRA INNINGS	2	1	5	6	7	7
ONE-RUN DECISIONS	6	4	14	15	20	19
TWO-RUN DECISIONS	9	6	7	7	16	13
VS. LH STARTERS	17	12	14	15	31	27
VS. RH STARTERS	35	17	29	23	64	40
GRASS FIELDS	52	29	36	27	88	56
ARTIFICIAL FIELDS	0	0	7	11	7	11
DAY GAMES	28	11	8	11	36	22
NIGHT GAMES	24	18	35	27	59	45

	NYY	OPP
DOUBLE PLAYS	161	143
TRIPLE PLAYS	1	0
LEFT ON BASE	1228	1082
GRAND SLAM HR	10	3
HOME RUNS – HOME	115	108
HOME RUNS – ROAD	86	71

	WON	LOST	
DOUBLEHEADERS (HOME)	WON 0	LOST 0	SPLIT 0
DOUBLEHEADERS (ROAD)	WON 0	LOST 0	SPLIT 2

	WON	LOST
STARTERS	72	50
RELIEVERS	23	17
STREAKS	8	4

ATTENDANCE

HOME	3,765,807	(81 DATES)	46,491 AVG
ROAD	2,830,138	(81 DATES)	34,940 AVG

2010 Final Yankees Statistics

PLAYER	AVG	G	AB	R	H	TB	2B	3B	HR	RBI	SH	SF	HP	BB	IBB	SO	SB	CS	DP	E	SLG	OBP
Berkman	.255	37	106	9	27	37	7	0	1	9	0	0	0	17	3	15	0	0	6	1	.349	.358
Burnett	.000	33	1	0	0	0	0	0	0	0	2	0	0	0	0	1	0	0	0	4	.000	.000
Cano	.319	160	626	103	200	334	41	3	29	109	0	5	8	57	14	77	3	2	19	3	.534	.381
Cervelli	.271	93	266	27	72	89	11	3	0	38	8	4	6	33	1	42	1	1	7	13	.335	.359
Curtis	.186	31	59	7	11	17	3	0	1	8	0	0	1	4	0	15	0	0	0	0	.288	.250
Gardner	.277	150	477	97	132	181	20	7	5	47	5	3	5	79	1	101	47	9	6	1	.379	.383
Golson	.261	24	23	3	6	8	2	0	0	2	0	0	0	0	0	3	0	2	0	0	.348	.261
Granderson	.247	136	466	76	115	218	17	7	24	67	4	3	2	53	1	116	12	2	3	2	.468	.324
Huffman	.167	9	18	1	3	3	0	0	0	2	0	0	1	2	0	5	0	0	1	0	.167	.286
Hughes	.000	31	1	0	0	0	0	0	0	0	1	0	0	0	0	0	0	0	0	0	.000	.000
Jeter	.270	157	663	111	179	245	30	3	10	67	1	3	9	63	4	106	18	5	22	6	.370	.340
Johnson	.167	24	72	12	12	22	4	0	2	8	0	0	2	24	0	23	0	1	2	0	.306	.388
Kearns	.235	36	102	13	24	33	3	0	2	7	0	0	5	12	0	38	0	0	4	0	.324	.345
Miranda	.219	33	64	7	14	27	2	1	3	10	0	0	0	7	0	12	0	0	1	0	.422	.296
Moeller	.214	9	14	2	3	6	3	0	0	0	0	0	0	1	0	4	0	0	0	0	.429	.267
Nunez	.280	30	50	12	14	18	1	0	1	7	0	0	0	3	0	2	5	0	4	1	.360	.321
Pena	.227	85	154	18	35	38	1	1	0	18	4	2	1	6	0	27	7	1	4	5	.247	.258
Pettitte	.250	21	4	0	1	1	0	0	0	0	3	0	0	0	0	3	0	0	0	3	.250	.250
Posada	.248	120	383	49	95	174	23	1	18	57	0	2	7	59	3	99	3	1	6	8	.454	.357
Rivera	.000	61	1	0	0	0	0	0	0	0	0	0	0	0	0	0	0	0	0	0	.000	.000
Rodriguez	.270	137	522	74	141	264	29	2	30	125	0	11	3	59	1	98	4	3	7	7	.506	.341
Russo	.184	31	49	5	9	11	2	0	0	4	1	0	1	3	0	9	1	0	0	1	.224	.245
Sabathia	.200	34	5	0	1	1	0	0	0	0	0	0	0	0	0	3	0	0	0	1	.200	.200
Swisher	.288	150	566	91	163	289	33	3	29	89	3	2	6	58	0	139	1	2	13	4	.511	.359
Teixeira	.256	158	601	113	154	289	36	0	33	108	0	5	13	93	6	122	0	1	15	3	.481	.365
Thames	.288	82	212	22	61	104	7	0	12	33	0	3	3	19	0	61	0	0	3	3	.491	.350
Vazquez	.000	31	1	0	0	0	0	0	0	0	2	0	0	2	0	0	0	0	0	0	.000	.667
Winn	.213	29	61	7	13	18	0	1	1	8	1	1	0	8	0	15	1	0	1	0	.295	.300
YANKEES	**.267**	**162**	**5567**	**859**	**1485**	**2427**	**275**	**32**	**201**	**823**	**33**	**44**	**73**	**662**	**36**	**1136**	**103**	**30**	**124**	**69**	**.436**	**.350**
OPPONENTS	**.249**	**162**	**5411**	**693**	**1349**	**2160**	**246**	**14**	**179**	**662**	**36**	**52**	**62**	**540**	**37**	**1154**	**132**	**23**	**137**	**96**	**.399**	**.322**

PITCHER	W	L	ERA	G	GS	CG	GF	SHO	SV	IP	H	R	ER	HR	HB	BB	IBB	SO	WP	BK	AVG
Aceves	3	0	3.00	10	0	0	2	0	1	12.0	10	5	4	1	1	4	1	2	0	0	.208
Albaladejo	0	0	3.97	10	0	0	5	0	0	11.1	9	5	5	1	2	8	1	8	0	0	.231
Burnett	10	15	5.26	33	33	1	0	0	0	186.2	204	118	109	25	19	78	2	145	16	0	.285
Chamberlain	3	4	4.40	73	0	0	18	0	3	71.2	71	37	35	6	1	22	2	77	5	1	.253
Gaudin	1	2	4.50	30	0	0	17	0	0	48.0	46	27	24	11	5	20	0	33	3	0	.254
Hughes	18	8	4.19	31	29	0	0	0	0	176.1	162	83	82	25	0	58	1	146	9	1	.244
Logan	2	0	2.93	51	0	0	8	0	0	40.0	34	13	13	3	1	20	3	38	1	0	.231
Marte	2	0	4.08	30	0	0	3	0	0	17.2	10	8	8	2	1	11	1	12	2	1	.161
Melancon	0	0	9.00	2	0	0	2	0	0	4.0	7	5	4	1	0	0	0	3	0	0	.389
Mitre	0	3	3.33	27	3	0	13	0	1	54.0	43	23	20	7	2	16	0	29	1	0	.223
Moseley	4	4	4.96	16	9	0	2	0	0	65.1	66	36	36	13	2	27	0	33	0	0	.269
Nova	1	2	4.50	10	7	0	3	0	0	42.0	44	22	21	4	1	17	2	26	2	0	.268
Park	2	1	5.60	27	0	0	15	0	0	35.1	40	25	22	7	1	12	0	29	2	0	.280
Pettitte	11	3	3.28	21	21	0	0	0	0	129.0	123	52	47	13	3	41	3	101	2	0	.257
Ring	0	0	15.43	5	0	0	0	0	0	2.1	3	4	4	0	0	2	0	2	0	0	.300
Rivera	3	3	1.80	61	0	0	55	0	33	60.0	39	14	12	2	5	11	3	45	0	0	.183
Robertson	4	5	3.82	64	0	0	10	0	1	61.1	59	26	26	5	3	33	6	71	7	2	.258
Sabathia	21	7	3.18	34	34	2	0	0	0	237.2	209	92	84	20	7	74	6	197	8	1	.239
Sanchez	0	0	0.00	2	0	0	1	0	0	4.1	1	0	0	0	0	3	0	5	0	0	.071
Vazquez	10	10	5.32	31	26	0	4	0	0	157.1	155	96	93	32	7	65	4	121	8	0	.257
Wood	2	0	0.69	24	0	0	1	0	0	26.0	14	2	2	1	1	18	2	31	3	0	.161
YANKEES	**95**	**67**	**4.06**	**162**	**162**	**3**	**159**	**8**	**39**	**1442.1**	**1349**	**693**	**651**	**179**	**62**	**540**	**37**	**1154**	**69**	**6**	**.249**
OPPONENTS	**67**	**95**	**5.10**	**162**	**162**	**5**	**157**	**8**	**34**	**1430.2**	**1485**	**859**	**811**	**201**	**73**	**662**	**36**	**1136**	**73**	**4**	**.267**

2010 Yankees Fielding Statistics

PITCHERS	PCT	G	GS	PO	A	E	TC	DP	TP
Aceves	1.000	10	0	0	2	0	2	0	0
Albaladejo	1.000	10	0	0	2	0	2	0	0
Burnett	.862	33	33	9	16	4	29	1	0
Chamberlain	1.000	73	0	2	6	0	8	1	0
Gaudin	.750	30	0	1	2	1	4	0	0
Hughes	1.000	31	29	7	13	0	20	1	0
Logan	1.000	51	0	1	3	0	4	0	0
Marte	.500	30	0	0	1	1	2	0	0
Melancon	.000	2	0	0	0	0	0	0	0
Mitre	1.000	27	3	5	7	0	12	0	0
Moseley	1.000	16	9	7	10	0	17	1	0
Nova	.909	10	7	5	5	1	11	0	0
Park	1.000	27	0	3	3	0	6	0	0
Pettitte	.857	21	21	3	15	3	21	1	0
Ring	.000	5	0	0	0	0	0	0	0
Rivera	1.000	61	0	2	16	0	18	0	0
Robertson	1.000	64	0	0	5	0	5	0	0
Sabathia	.971	34	34	4	30	1	35	3	0
Sanchez	.000	2	0	0	0	0	0	0	0
Vazquez	1.000	31	26	14	23	0	37	2	0
Wood	1.000	24	0	3	3	0	6	0	0

FIRST BASE	PCT	G	GS	PO	A	E	TC	DP	TP
Berkman	.982	8	7	54	2	1	57	8	0
Huffman	.000	1	0	0	0	0	0	0	0
Johnson	1.000	2	2	18	0	0	18	1	1
Miranda	1.000	13	4	53	5	0	58	5	0
Posada	.000	1	0	0	0	0	0	0	0
Swisher	1.000	6	1	19	2	0	21	2	0
Teixeira	.998	149	148	1227	80	3	1310	137	0

SECOND BASE	PCT	G	GS	PO	A	E	TC	DP	TP
Cano	.996	158	157	341	432	3	776	114	1
Nunez	.000	1	0	0	0	0	0	0	0
Pena	.967	8	5	12	17	1	30	6	0
Russo	1.000	2	0	2	1	0	3	0	0

THIRD BASE	PCT	G	GS	PO	A	E	TC	DP	TP
Cervelli	1.000	2	0	1	0	0	1	0	0
Nunez	.944	15	10	3	14	1	18	1	0
Pena	.966	48	27	17	67	3	87	5	0
Rodriguez	.976	124	122	61	224	7	292	25	1
Russo	1.000	16	3	4	6	0	10	1	0
Thames	.000	1	0	0	0	1	1	0	0

SHORTSTOP	PCT	G	GS	PO	A	E	TC	DP	TP
Jeter	.989	151	150	182	365	6	553	94	0
Nunez	1.000	11	3	7	16	0	23	4	0
Pena	.979	23	9	22	24	1	47	7	0

OUTFIELDERS	PCT	G	GS	PO	A	E	TC	DP	TP
Curtis	1.000	23	11	22	0	0	22	0	0
Gardner	.997	146	134	287	12	1	300	2	0
Golson	1.000	23	6	25	1	0	26	1	0
Granderson	.994	134	123	316	5	2	323	2	0
Huffman	1.000	7	4	14	0	0	14	0	0
Kearns	1.000	34	28	55	1	0	56	1	0
Pena	1.000	2	0	1	0	0	1	0	0
Russo	.933	11	10	14	0	1	15	0	0
Swisher	.986	134	131	265	10	4	279	1	0
Thames	.947	32	23	34	2	2	38	1	0
Winn	1.000	27	16	31	1	0	32	0	0

CATCHERS	PCT	G	GS	PO	A	E	TC	DP	TP	PB
Cervelli	.980	90	80	579	45	13	637	2	0	2
Moeller	1.000	9	4	33	6	0	39	0	0	2
Posada	.986	83	78	562	22	8	592	2	0	8

2010 Yankees Starting Pitchers

STARTERS	W	L	PCT	ERA	G	GS	CG	IP	H	TBF	R	ER	HR	SH	SF	HB	BB	IBB	SO	WP	BK	AVG
Burnett	10	15	.400	5.26	33	33	1	186.2	204	829	118	109	25	7	10	19	78	2	145	16	0	.285
Hughes	17	8	.680	4.23	29	29	0	174.1	162	724	83	82	25	2	5	0	58	1	143	9	1	.246
Mitre	0	2	.000	5.93	3	3	0	13.2	16	62	12	9	3	1	1	1	4	0	8	0	0	.291
Moseley	4	4	.500	5.29	9	9	0	51.0	52	218	30	30	10	0	3	2	22	0	26	0	0	.272
Nova	1	1	.500	4.91	7	7	0	36.2	36	159	21	20	4	0	1	1	14	2	24	2	0	.254
Pettitte	11	3	.786	3.28	21	21	0	129.0	123	536	52	47	13	8	5	3	41	3	101	2	0	.257
Sabathia	21	7	.750	3.18	34	34	2	237.2	209	970	92	84	20	5	8	7	74	6	197	8	1	.239
Vazquez	8	10	.444	5.56	26	26	0	144.0	147	628	92	89	31	2	6	4	61	4	109	7	0	.265
TOTALS	72	50	.590	4.35	162	162	3	973.0	949	4126	500	470	131	25	39	37	352	18	753	44	2	.258

2010 Yankees Relievers

RELIEVERS	W	L	PCT	ERA	APP	GF	SV	IP	H	TBF	R	ER	HR	SH	SF	HB	BB	IBB	SO	WP	BK	AVG
Aceves	3	0	1.000	3.00	10	2	1	12.0	10	53	5	4	1	0	0	1	4	1	2	0	0	.208
Albaladejo	0	0	.000	3.97	10	5	0	11.1	9	50	5	5	1	0	1	2	8	1	8	0	0	.231
Chamberlain	3	4	.429	4.40	73	18	3	71.2	71	305	37	35	6	0	1	1	22	2	77	5	1	.253
Gaudin	1	2	.333	4.50	30	17	0	48.0	46	209	27	24	11	2	1	5	20	0	33	3	0	.254
Hughes	1	0	1.000	0.00	2	0	0	2.0	0	6	0	0	0	0	0	0	0	0	3	0	0	.000
Logan	2	0	1.000	2.93	51	8	0	40.0	34	169	13	13	3	0	1	1	20	3	38	1	0	.231
Marte	0	0	.000	4.08	30	3	0	17.2	10	76	8	8	2	0	2	1	11	1	12	2	1	.161
Melancon	0	0	.000	9.00	2	2	0	4.0	7	19	5	4	1	0	1	0	0	0	3	0	0	.389
Mitre	0	1	.000	2.45	24	13	1	40.1	27	151	11	11	4	0	0	1	12	0	21	1	0	.196
Moseley	0	0	.000	3.77	7	2	0	14.1	14	60	6	6	3	0	1	0	5	0	7	0	0	.259
Nova	0	1	.000	1.69	3	3	0	5.1	8	26	1	1	0	1	0	0	3	0	2	0	0	.364
Park	2	1	.667	5.60	27	15	0	35.1	40	157	25	22	7	1	0	1	12	0	29	2	0	.280
Ring	0	0	.000	15.43	5	0	0	2.1	3	12	4	4	0	0	0	0	2	0	2	0	0	.300
Rivera	3	3	.500	1.80	61	55	33	60.0	39	230	14	12	2	0	1	5	11	3	45	0	0	.183
Robertson	4	5	.444	3.82	64	10	1	61.1	59	273	26	26	5	5	3	3	33	6	71	7	2	.258
Sanchez	0	0	.000	0.00	2	1	0	4.1	1	17	0	0	0	0	0	0	3	0	5	0	0	.071
Vazquez	2	0	1.000	2.70	5	2	0	13.1	8	55	4	4	1	0	1	3	4	0	12	1	0	.170
Wood	2	0	1.000	0.69	24	1	0	26.0	14	108	2	2	1	2	0	1	18	2	31	3	0	.161
TOTALS	23	17	.575	3.47	430	159	39	469.1	400	1976	193	181	48	11	13	25	188	19	401	25	4	.230

Yankees Pinch Hitters

BATTER	AVG	APP	AB	R	H	TB	2B	3B	HR	RBI	SH	SF	HP	BB	IBB	SO	SB	CS	GDP	SLG	OBP
Berkman	.286	9	7	0	2	3	1	0	0	0	0	0	0	2	0	2	0	0	0	.429	.444
Cano	.000	1	1	0	0	0	0	0	0	0	0	0	0	0	0	0	0	0	0	.000	.000
Cervelli	.000	4	4	0	0	0	0	0	0	0	0	0	0	0	0	2	0	0	0	.000	.000
Curtis	.364	12	11	1	4	8	1	0	1	7	0	0	1	0	3	0	0	0	0	.727	.417
Gardner	.000	3	3	1	0	0	0	0	0	0	0	0	0	0	0	0	0	0	0	.000	.000
Granderson	.000	8	7	1	0	0	0	0	0	0	0	0	0	1	0	4	0	0	0	.000	.125
Huffman	.000	2	2	0	0	0	0	0	0	0	0	0	0	0	0	0	0	0	0	.000	.000
Jeter	.500	2	2	0	1	1	0	0	0	0	0	0	0	0	0	0	0	0	0	.500	.500
Johnson	.000	3	1	0	0	0	0	0	0	0	0	0	0	2	0	0	0	0	0	.000	.667
Kearns	.000	6	5	0	0	0	0	0	0	0	0	0	1	0	0	4	0	0	0	.000	.167
Miranda	.222	11	9	1	2	2	0	0	0	0	0	0	0	2	0	4	0	0	1	.222	.364
Pena	.250	5	4	0	1	1	0	0	0	1	1	0	0	0	0	1	0	0	0	.250	.250
Posada	.077	14	13	1	1	4	0	0	1	1	0	0	0	1	0	5	0	0	1	.308	.143
Rodriguez	.000	3	2	0	0	0	0	0	0	0	0	0	0	1	0	1	0	0	0	.000	.333
Swisher	.000	7	6	0	0	0	0	0	0	0	0	0	0	0	0	1	0	0	0	.000	.000
Teixeira	.000	1	0	0	0	0	0	0	0	0	0	0	1	1	0	0	0	0	0	.000	1.000
Thames	.211	24	19	0	4	4	0	0	0	1	0	0	0	3	0	6	0	0	0	.211	.318
Winn	.000	1	1	0	0	0	0	0	0	0	0	0	0	0	0	1	0	0	0	.000	.000
TOTALS	.155		97	5	15	23	2	0	2	12	1	0	1	14	1	34	0	0	2	.237	.268

2010 Yankees Highs & Lows

CLUB

MOST RUNS, GAME -
14	NEW YORK AT BOSTON	5/08/10
12	NEW YORK VS KANSAS CITY	7/25/10
12	NEW YORK VS CHICAGO	5/02/10
12	NEW YORK AT CHICAGO	8/28/10
12	NEW YORK AT BALTIMORE	6/08/10

MOST RUNS, GAME, BOTH CLUBS -
24	CLEVELAND (13) AT NEW YORK (11)	5/29/10
21	NEW YORK (12) AT CHICAGO (9)	8/28/10

MOST RUNS, INNING -
11	NEW YORK VS TORONTO	7/03/10 (INNING 3)
9	NEW YORK VS DETROIT	8/19/10 (INNING 6)

MOST HITS, GAME -
18	NEW YORK VS CLEVELAND	5/31/10
17	NEW YORK AT TORONTO	8/24/10
17	NEW YORK AT BOSTON	5/08/10

MOST HITS, GAME, BOTH CLUBS -
30	LOS ANGELES (15) AT NEW YORK (15)	7/21/10
30	NEW YORK (14) AT CHICAGO (16)	8/28/10
30	NEW YORK (15) AT BALTIMORE (15)	6/08/10
28	KANSAS CITY (14) AT NEW YORK (14)	7/22/10

MOST TOTAL BASES, GAME -
33	NEW YORK AT TORONTO	8/24/10
31	NEW YORK AT KANSAS CITY	8/14/10

MOST DOUBLES, GAME -
5	NEW YORK AT SEATTLE	7/11/10
5	NEW YORK VS TAMPA BAY	9/21/10
5	NEW YORK VS KANSAS CITY	7/22/10
5	NEW YORK VS MINNESOTA	5/14/10
4	15 GAMES/CLUBS TIED	
4	NEW YORK AT TAMPA BAY	9/14/10 (10 INN.)
4	NEW YORK AT BOSTON	10/02/10 -G1 (10 INN.)

MOST TRIPLES, GAME -
2	NEW YORK AT OAKLAND	4/21/10
2	NEW YORK VS LOS ANGELES	4/15/10
1	27 GAMES/CLUBS TIED	
1	NEW YORK AT BOSTON	10/02/10 - G1 (10 INN.)

MOST HOME RUNS, GAME -
6	NEW YORK VS BOSTON	9/24/10
5	NEW YORK AT TORONTO	8/24/10
5	NEW YORK AT KANSAS CITY	8/14/10

MOST HOME RUNS, GAME, BOTH CLUBS -
8	BOSTON (2) AT NEW YORK (6)	9/24/10
7	BOSTON (5) AT NEW YORK (2)	5/17/10
7	NEW YORK (4) AT CHICAGO (3)	8/28/10

MOST EXTRA BASE HITS, GAME -
8	NEW YORK VS DETROIT	8/18/10
8	NEW YORK VS MINNESOTA	5/14/10
8	NEW YORK VS LOS ANGELES	4/15/10
7	NEW YORK VS KANSAS CITY	7/22/10
7	NEW YORK VS LOS ANGELES	7/21/10
7	NEW YORK VS CHICAGO	5/02/10
7	NEW YORK AT KANSAS CITY	8/14/10
7	NEW YORK AT CHICAGO	8/28/10
7	NEW YORK AT TAMPA BAY	9/14/10 (10 INN.)

MOST WALKS, GAME -
12	NEW YORK AT CLEVELAND	7/29/10
10	NEW YORK AT OAKLAND	4/20/10
10	NEW YORK VS HOUSTON	6/13/10
10	NEW YORK AT BOSTON	5/08/10
13	NEW YORK AT ARIZONA	6/23/10 (10 INN.)
10	NEW YORK AT BOSTON	10/02/10 (10 INN.)

MOST WALKS, GAME, BOTH CLUBS -
17	NEW YORK (12) AT CLEVELAND (5)	7/29/10
16	NEW YORK (9) AT TEXAS (7)	9/11/10
19	NEW YORK (13) AT ARIZONA (6)	6/23/10 (10 INN.)
16	NEW YORK (10) AT BOSTON (6)	10/02/10 - G2 (10 INN.)

MOST STRIKEOUTS, GAME -
17	NEW YORK AT TEXAS	8/11/10
15	NEW YORK AT TORONTO	8/23/10
15	NEW YORK AT TEXAS	9/10/10 (13 INN.)

MOST STRIKEOUTS, GAME, BOTH CLUBS -
22	NEW YORK (15) AT TORONTO (7)	8/23/10
21	NEW YORK (11) AT TORONTO (10)	6/06/10
21	NEW YORK (17) AT TEXAS (4)	8/11/10
21	NEW YORK (10) AT OAKLAND (11)	4/20/10
21	TORONTO (9) AT NEW YORK (12)	8/02/10
32	NEW YORK (14) AT BOSTON (18)	10/02/10 - G2 (10 INN.)
30	NEW YORK (14) AT TORONTO (16)	6/05/10 (14 INN.)
22	TORONTO (10) AT NEW YORK (12)	7/04/10 (10 INN.)

MOST STOLEN BASES, GAME -
4	NEW YORK VS TEXAS	4/18/10
3	NEW YORK VS OAKLAND	8/31/10
3	NEW YORK VS DETROIT	8/17/10
3	NEW YORK VS BOSTON	8/07/10
3	NEW YORK VS KANSAS CITY	7/25/10
3	NEW YORK AT KANSAS CITY	8/14/10
4	NEW YORK AT BOSTON	10/02/10 - G1 (10 INN.)
4	NEW YORK AT BOSTON	10/02/10 - G2 (10 INN.)

MOST STOLEN BASES, GAME, BOTH CLUBS -
7	BOSTON (6) AT NEW YORK (1)	8/09/10
6	TAMPA BAY (6) AT NEW YORK	5/19/10
6	NEW YORK (2) AT KANSAS CITY (4)	8/13/10
6	BOSTON (5) AT NEW YORK (1)	9/26/10 (10 INN.)

MOST DOUBLE PLAYS, GAME -
4	NEW YORK VS BALTIMORE	5/05/10
3	NEW YORK AT TAMPA BAY	4/11/10
3	NEW YORK AT OAKLAND	4/20/10
3	NEW YORK VS KANSAS CITY	7/23/10
3	NEW YORK AT MINNESOTA	5/26/10
3	NEW YORK AT KANSAS CITY	8/15/10
3	NEW YORK AT CLEVELAND	7/27/10

MOST DOUBLE PLAYS, GAME, BOTH CLUBS -
4	10 GAMES/CLUBS TIED	
6	NEW YORK (1) AT ARIZONA (5)	6/23/10 (10 INN.)
4	NEW YORK (2) AT TORONTO (2)	6/05/10 (14 INN.)
4	NEW YORK (1) AT BALTIMORE (3)	9/19/10 (11 INN.)

MOST ERRORS, GAME -
3	NEW YORK AT KANSAS CITY	8/15/10
3	NEW YORK AT BOSTON	4/06/10
2	NEW YORK VS KANSAS CITY	7/25/10
2	NEW YORK VS TAMPA BAY	7/16/10
2	NEW YORK VS SEATTLE	6/29/10
2	NEW YORK VS BOSTON	5/18/10
2	NEW YORK AT CLEVELAND	7/27/10
2	NEW YORK AT BALTIMORE	4/27/10
4	NEW YORK AT BOSTON	10/02/10 - G2 (10 INN.)
2	NEW YORK AT LOS ANGELES	6/27/10 (10 INN.)

MOST ERRORS, GAME, BOTH CLUBS -
4	SEATTLE (3) AT NEW YORK (1)	8/22/10
4	KANSAS CITY (2) AT NEW YORK (2)	7/25/10
4	BOSTON (2) AT NEW YORK (2)	5/18/10
4	NEW YORK (3) AT BOSTON (1)	4/06/10
4	NEW YORK (2) AT BALTIMORE (2)	4/27/10
3	10 GAMES/CLUBS TIED	
6	NEW YORK (4) AT BOSTON (2)	10/02/10 - G2 (10 INN.)
5	NEW YORK AT TEXAS (3)	8/10/10 (10 INN.)

MOST LEFT ON BASE, GAME -
14	NEW YORK AT TEXAS	9/11/10
14	NEW YORK AT CLEVELAND	7/29/10
13	NEW YORK AT NEW YORK	5/22/10
18	NEW YORK AT TEXAS	9/10/10 (13 INN.)
15	NEW YORK AT BOSTON	10/02/10 - G2 (10 INN.)

MOST LEFT ON BASE, GAME, BOTH CLUBS -
27	NEW YORK (14) AT TEXAS (13)	9/11/10
21	NEW YORK (13) AT NEW YORK (8)	5/22/10
21	DETROIT (12) AT NEW YORK (9)	8/16/10
21	KANSAS CITY (14) AT NEW YORK (7)	7/22/10
21	NEW YORK (11) AT BALTIMORE (10)	6/09/10
26	NEW YORK (18) AT TEXAS (8)	9/10/10 (13 INN.)
26	NEW YORK (15) AT BOSTON (11)	10/02/10 - G2 (10 INN.)
24	NEW YORK (12) AT BOSTON (12)	10/02/10 - G1 (10 INN.)
22	NEW YORK (9) AT TORONTO (13)	6/05/10 (14 INN.)
21	TORONTO (13) AT NEW YORK (8)	7/02/10 (11 INN.)

2010 Yankees Highs & Lows

MOST INN., GAME -
14.0	TORONTO VS NEW YORK	6/05/10
13.0	TEXAS VS NEW YORK	9/10/10

LONGEST TIME, GAME -
4:22	NEW YORK VS CLEVELAND	5/29/10
4:16	TEXAS VS NEW YORK	9/11/10
5:12	TEXAS VS NEW YORK	9/10/10 (13 INN.)
4:18	BOSTON VS NEW YORK	10/02/10 - G1 (10 INN.)

SHORTEST TIME, GAME -
1:58	NEW YORK VS TEXAS	4/16/10 (6 INN.)
2:07	OAKLAND VS NEW YORK	4/22/10
2:07	KANSAS CITY VS NEW YORK	8/15/10

HIGHEST ATTENDANCE, GAME -
49,716	NEW YORK VS BOSTON	8/07/10
49,558	NEW YORK VS BOSTON	9/25/10

LONGEST WINNING STREAK -
8	NEW YORK	8/28/10 THRU 9/04/10
7	NEW YORK	7/03/10 THRU 7/09/10

LONGEST LOSING STREAK -
4	NEW YORK	9/10/10 THRU 9/13/10
4	NEW YORK	9/22/10 THRU 9/25/10

INDIVIDUAL BATTING

LONGEST HITTING STREAK -
17	Cano	NEW YORK	5/17/10 THRU 6/03/10
14	Jeter	NEW YORK	9/10/10 THRU 9/25/10

MOST RUNS, GAME -
3	Rodriguez	NEW YORK AT LOS ANGELES	6/27/10 9 INN.
3	Jeter	NEW YORK AT ARIZONA	6/23/10 9 INN.
3	27 PLAYERS TIED		

MOST HITS, GAME -
4	12 PLAYERS TIED

MOST TOTAL BASES, GAME -
13	Rodriguez	NEW YORK AT KANSAS CITY	8/14/10
13	Teixeira	NEW YORK AT BOSTON	5/08/10
10	Cano	NEW YORK AT BALTIMORE	4/29/10

MOST DOUBLES, GAME -
2	18 PLAYERS TIED		
2	Cano	NEW YORK AT BOSTON	10/02/10 - G1 (10 INN.)
2	Granderson	NEW YORK AT TAMPA BAY	9/14/10 (10 INN.)
2	Teixeira	NEW YORK VS TORONTO	7/04/10 (10 INN.)

MOST TRIPLES, GAME -
2	Granderson	NEW YORK VS LOS ANGELES 4/15/10	
1	29 PLAYERS TIED		
1	Granderson	NEW YORK AT BOSTON	10/02/10 - G1 (10 INN.)

MOST HOME RUNS, GAME -
3	Rodriguez	NEW YORK AT KANSAS CITY	8/14/10
3	Teixeira	NEW YORK AT BOSTON	5/08/10
2	15 PLAYERS TIED		

MOST EXTRA BASES, GAME -
3	Rodriguez	NEW YORK AT KANSAS CITY	8/14/10
3	Cano	NEW YORK AT TAMPA BAY	7/31/10
3	Rodriguez	NEW YORK AT KANSAS CITY	7/22/10
3	Teixeira	NEW YORK AT BOSTON	5/08/10
3	Cano	NEW YORK AT BALTIMORE	4/29/10
2	52 PLAYERS TIED		
3	Cano	NEW YORK AT BOSTON	10/02/10 - G1 (10 INN.)
2	5 PLAYERS TIED		

MOST RUNS BATTED IN, GAME -
6	Cano	NEW YORK VS SEATTLE	8/22/10
6	Rodriguez	NEW YORK VS CLEVELAND	5/31/10
5	Granderson	NEW YORK VS TAMPA BAY	9/20/10
5	Rodriguez	NEW YORK AT KANSAS CITY	8/14/10
5	Rodriguez	NEW YORK AT OAKLAND	7/06/10
5	Swisher	NEW YORK AT BALTIMORE	6/08/10
5	Cervelli	NEW YORK AT BOSTON	5/08/10
5	Teixeira	NEW YORK AT BOSTON	5/08/10

MOST STOLEN BASES, GAME -
2	Gardner	NEW YORK VS OAKLAND	8/31/10
2	Gardner	NEW YORK VS TEXAS	4/18/10
1	80 PLAYERS TIED		
3	Gardner	NEW YORK AT BOSTON	10/02/10 - G2 (10 INN.)
2	Gardner	NEW YORK AT BOSTON	10/02/10 - G1 (10 INN.)

INDIVIDUAL PITCHING

MOST STRIKEOUTS GAME (STARTER) -
10	Sabathia	NEW YORK AT OAKLAND	7/06/10
10	Hughes	NEW YORK AT OAKLAND	4/21/10
9	6 PLAYERS TIED		
10	Pettitte	NEW YORK AT TORONTO	6/05/10 (14 INN.)
9	Sabathia	NEW YORK AT TAMPA BAY	9/13/10 (11 INN.)

MOST STRIKEOUTS GAME (RELIEVER) -
6	Vazquez	NEW YORK VS OAKLAND	8/30/10
5	Gaudin	NEW YORK VS TAMPA BAY	7/17/10

MOST INN., GAME (STARTER) -
8.2	Sabathia	NEW YORK AT KANSAS CITY	8/12/10
8.1	Sabathia	NEW YORK AT TORONTO	9/28/10

MOST INN., GAME (RELIEVER) -
4.2	Vazquez	NEW YORK VS OAKLAND	8/30/10
4.2	Mitre	NEW YORK AT CHICAGO	8/27/10
4.2	Moseley	NEW YORK VS KANSAS CITY	7/24/10
4.1	Vazquez	NEW YORK AT TORONTO	8/25/10

MOST HOME RUNS ALLOWED, GAME -
3	Vazquez	NEW YORK AT TORONTO	9/29/10
3	Hughes	NEW YORK VS TORONTO	9/05/10
3	Vazquez	NEW YORK VS SEATTLE	8/21/10
3	Moseley	NEW YORK VS DETROIT	8/18/10
3	Burnett	NEW YORK AT ARIZONA	6/21/10
3	Burnett	NEW YORK AT TORONTO	6/04/10
3	Pettitte	NEW YORK VS TAMPA BAY	5/20/10
3	Vazquez	NEW YORK VS CHICAGO	5/01/10
2	30 PLAYERS TIED		
3	Hughes	NEW YORK VS TORONTO	7/04/10 (10 INN.)
2	Pettitte	NEW YORK AT TORONTO	6/05/10 (14 INN.)

LONGEST WINNING STREAK -
9	Sabathia	NEW YORK	6/03/10 THRU 7/22/10
6	Sabathia	NEW YORK	8/07/10 THRU 9/02/10

LONGEST LOSING STREAK -
5	Burnett	NEW YORK	6/04/10 THRU 6/26/10
4	Burnett	NEW YORK	8/02/10 THRU 8/27/10

MOST CONSECUTIVE SCORELESS INN. -
23.1	Wood	NEW YORK	8/03/10 THRU 10/02/10
18.1	Robertson	NEW YORK	7/02/10 THRU 8/23/10

YANKEES BY THE NUMBERS, 2010

Pre-All-Star Break	56-32
Post-All-Star Break	39-24
vs. LH starters	31-27
vs. RH starters	64-40
Yankees Score First	55-20
Opponents Score First	40-47
Yankees Score 4 Runs or More	83-25
Yankees Score 3 Runs or Fewer	12-42
Yankees Outhit Opp.:	69-9
Opp. Outhits Yankees:	15-44
Hit Totals Are Even:	11-13
One-Run Games:	20-19
Leading After 6:	74-9
Trailing After 6:	12-51
Tied After 6:	9-7
Leading After 7:	80-7
Trailing After 7:	9-56
Tied After 7:	5-4
Leading After 8:	81-2
Trailing After 8:	6-58
Tied After 8:	6-8
Extra-Inning Games:	7-7
On Grass:	88-56
On Turf:	7-11
Day	36-22
Night	59-45
Series Record:	30-16-6
Series Record, home:	16-6-4
Series Record, road:	14-10-2
Series Openers:	27-25
Series Finales	30-22
vs. AL East	38-34
vs. AL Central	23-13
vs. AL West	23-13
vs. NL	11-7

Yankees vs. Right

BATTER	AVG	G	AB	R	H	2B	3B	HR	RBI	SH	SF	HP	BB	SO	SB	CS	DP	SLG	OBP
Berkman	.284	36	88	8	25	6	0	1	8	0	0	0	15	12	0	0	5	.386	.388
TOTAL	.267	120	322	41	86	19	1	13	53	0	0	0	67	70	3	2	13	.453	.393
Cano	.337	144	412	63	139	33	2	16	66	0	1	4	40	46	3	2	10	.544	.400
Cervelli	.246	81	179	19	44	8	1	0	28	6	4	5	15	29	1	1	4	.302	.315
Curtis	.180	30	50	6	9	2	0	1	8	0	0	1	3	11	0	0	0	.280	.241
Gardner	.287	137	338	73	97	16	5	3	30	3	1	2	54	67	38	8	3	.391	.387
Golson	.000	19	6	0	0	0	0	0	1	0	0	0	0	1	0	1	0	.000	.000
Granderson	.253	124	308	66	78	12	6	20	55	1	3	2	40	75	10	2	1	.526	.340
Huffman	.286	6	7	0	2	0	0	0	2	0	0	0	2	2	0	0	0	.286	.444
Jeter	.246	147	451	66	111	18	1	4	43	1	2	8	38	78	14	4	17	.317	.315
Johnson	.157	23	51	7	8	1	0	2	4	0	0	0	21	17	0	0	2	.294	.403
Kearns	.218	28	55	6	12	2	0	0	5	0	0	3	5	22	0	0	2	.255	.317
TOTAL	.270	106	256	35	69	14	0	6	37	0	2	8	27	78	3	1	9	.395	.355
Miranda	.224	31	58	7	13	1	1	3	9	0	0	0	5	11	0	0	1	.431	.286
Moeller	.111	7	9	1	1	1	0	0	0	0	0	0	1	3	0	0	0	.222	.200
Nunez	.292	27	24	6	7	0	0	0	3	0	0	0	3	2	4	0	3	.292	.370
Pena	.244	80	123	16	30	1	1	0	15	2	1	1	5	21	6	0	3	.268	.277
Posada	.243	107	247	37	60	15	1	10	32	0	2	4	45	61	3	0	4	.433	.366
Rodriguez	.290	127	379	56	110	17	1	24	90	0	5	2	37	73	3	1	4	.530	.352
Russo	.136	25	22	3	3	1	0	0	3	0	0	1	3	4	1	0	0	.182	.269
Swisher	.285	142	386	64	110	20	3	25	73	3	2	1	26	110	0	0	9	.547	.330
Teixeira	.247	144	421	77	104	21	0	23	69	0	4	9	55	89	0	0	9	.461	.344
Thames	.268	47	82	9	22	2	0	7	19	0	2	1	10	27	0	0	2	.549	.347
Winn	.260	28	50	6	13	0	1	1	8	1	1	0	8	11	1	0	1	.360	.356
TOTALS	**.266**		**3755**	**596**	**999**	**177**	**23**	**140**	**571**	**21**	**28**	**44**	**432**	**777**	**84**	**19**	**80**	**.437**	**.346**

PITCHER	AVG	AB	H	HR	HB	BB	SO
Aceves	.194	31	6	1	0	2	1
Albaladejo	.238	21	5	1	2	4	4
Burnett	.285	330	94	14	9	30	72
Chamberlain	.258	155	40	3	1	9	38
Gaudin	.241	83	20	3	4	10	15
Hughes	.253	320	81	8	0	19	69
Logan	.279	68	19	3	0	10	8
Marte	.190	21	4	1	1	8	1
Melancon	.455	11	5	1	0	0	3
Mitre	.218	87	19	4	2	11	12
Moseley	.256	117	30	5	1	13	19
Nova	.269	67	18	1	0	7	8
Park	.237	76	18	3	1	8	20
Pettitte	.283	350	99	11	3	34	62
Ring	.000	2	0	0	0	1	0
Rivera	.155	110	17	0	4	5	31
Robertson	.250	132	33	3	2	15	37
Sabathia	.232	673	156	16	4	60	135
Sanchez	.000	7	0	0	0	1	1
Vazquez	.240	300	72	13	4	21	62
Wood	.140	50	7	1	0	2	15
TOTALS	**.247**	**3011**	**743**	**92**	**38**	**270**	**613**

Yankees vs. Left

BATTER	AVG	G	AB	R	H	2B	3B	HR	RBI	SH	SF	HP	BB	SO	SB	CS	DP	SLG	OBP
Berkman	.111	13	18	1	2	1	0	0	1	0	0	0	2	3	0	0	1	.167	.200
TOTAL	.171	49	82	7	14	4	0	1	5	0	0	0	10	15	0	0	5	.256	.261
Cano	.285	101	214	40	61	8	1	13	43	0	4	4	17	31	0	0	9	.514	.343
Cervelli	.322	49	87	8	28	3	2	0	10	2	0	1	18	13	0	0	3	.402	.443
Curtis	.222	9	9	1	2	1	0	0	0	0	0	0	1	4	0	0	0	.333	.300
Gardner	.252	88	139	24	35	4	2	2	17	2	2	3	25	34	9	1	3	.353	.373
Golson	.353	8	17	3	6	2	0	0	1	0	0	0	0	2	0	1	0	.471	.353
Granderson	.234	84	158	10	37	5	1	4	12	3	0	0	13	41	2	0	2	.354	.292
Huffman	.091	5	11	1	1	0	0	0	0	0	0	1	0	3	0	0	1	.091	.167
Jeter	.321	89	212	45	68	12	2	6	24	0	1	1	25	28	4	1	5	.481	.393
Johnson	.190	10	21	5	4	3	0	0	4	0	0	2	3	6	0	1	0	.333	.346
Kearns	.255	21	47	7	12	1	0	2	2	0	0	2	7	16	0	0	2	.404	.375
TOTAL	.252	66	147	20	37	7	1	4	12	0	0	2	19	38	1	0	7	.395	.345
Miranda	.167	7	6	0	1	1	0	0	1	0	0	0	2	1	0	0	0	.333	.375
Moeller	.400	3	5	1	2	2	0	0	0	0	0	0	0	1	0	0	0	.800	.400
Nunez	.269	10	26	6	7	1	0	1	4	0	0	0	0	0	1	0	1	.423	.269
Pena	.161	25	31	2	5	0	0	0	3	2	1	0	1	6	1	1	1	.161	.182
Posada	.257	64	136	12	35	8	0	8	25	0	0	3	14	38	0	1	2	.493	.340
Rodriguez	.217	68	143	18	31	12	1	6	35	0	6	1	22	25	1	2	3	.441	.314
Russo	.222	12	27	2	6	1	0	0	1	1	0	0	0	5	0	0	0	.259	.222
Swisher	.294	88	180	27	53	13	0	4	16	0	0	5	32	29	1	2	4	.433	.415
Teixeira	.278	94	180	36	50	15	0	10	39	0	1	4	38	33	0	1	6	.528	.413
Thames	.300	58	130	13	39	5	0	5	14	0	1	2	9	34	0	0	1	.454	.352
Winn	.000	9	11	1	0	0	0	0	0	0	0	0	0	4	0	0	0	.000	.000
TOTALS	**.268**		**1812**	**263**	**486**	**98**	**9**	**61**	**252**	**12**	**16**	**29**	**230**	**359**	**19**	**11**	**44**	**.433**	**.357**

PITCHER	AVG	AB	H	HR	HB	BB	SO
Aceves	.235	17	4	0	1	2	1
Albaladejo	.222	18	4	0	0	4	4
Burnett	.286	385	110	11	10	48	73
Chamberlain	.246	126	31	3	0	13	39
Gaudin	.265	98	26	8	1	10	18
Hughes	.235	345	81	17	0	39	77
Logan	.190	79	15	0	1	10	30
Marte	.146	41	6	1	0	3	11
Melancon	.286	7	2	0	0	0	0
Mitre	.226	106	24	3	0	5	17
Moseley	.281	128	36	8	1	14	14
Nova	.268	97	26	3	1	10	18
Park	.328	67	22	4	0	4	9
Pettitte	.186	129	24	2	0	7	39
Ring	.375	8	3	0	0	1	2
Rivera	.214	103	22	2	1	6	14
Robertson	.268	97	26	2	1	18	34
Sabathia	.261	203	53	4	3	14	62
Sanchez	.143	7	1	0	0	2	4
Vazquez	.275	302	83	19	3	44	59
Wood	.189	37	7	0	1	16	16
TOTALS	**.253**	**2400**	**606**	**87**	**24**	**270**	**541**

Yankees at Home

BATTER	AVG	G	AB	R	H	2B	3B	HR	RBI	SH	SF	HP	BB	SO	SB	CS	GDP	E
Berkman	.286	20	56	7	16	5	0	1	5	0	0	0	6	9	0	0	0	0
TOTAL	.286	65	220	30	63	15	0	10	36	0	0	0	32	43	2	1	3	1
Cano	.298	80	309	52	92	19	1	16	67	0	2	2	29	38	1	0	7	0
Cervelli	.262	44	122	14	32	6	3	0	14	6	3	4	11	21	1	0	5	6
Curtis	.333	10	15	3	5	1	0	1	3	0	0	0	1	5	0	0	0	0
Gardner	.274	75	237	60	65	11	2	5	29	2	3	2	42	41	20	5	3	0
Golson	.500	10	8	2	4	2	0	0	0	0	0	0	0	2	0	2	0	0
Granderson	.262	69	233	42	61	10	3	14	32	1	0	1	25	54	6	1	1	2
Huffman	.077	5	13	1	1	0	0	0	0	0	0	0	1	5	0	0	1	0
Jeter	.295	78	322	62	95	17	2	7	38	1	1	3	33	54	10	2	10	4
Johnson	.233	11	30	6	7	3	0	2	6	0	0	1	11	9	0	1	2	0
Kearns	.270	16	37	5	10	2	0	1	6	0	0	3	4	13	0	0	1	0
TOTAL	.251	58	179	23	45	6	1	5	24	0	2	4	23	48	0	0	9	3
Miranda	.267	20	45	6	12	2	1	3	8	0	0	0	6	10	0	0	0	0
Moeller	.143	6	7	0	1	1	0	0	0	0	0	0	0	3	0	0	0	0
Nunez	.250	16	24	7	6	1	0	0	1	0	0	0	0	3	0	0	2	0
Pena	.242	48	95	10	23	0	1	0	16	2	2	1	4	15	3	1	3	4
Posada	.288	60	198	32	57	15	1	11	33	0	0	5	25	56	2	0	2	6
Rodriguez	.294	63	228	32	67	14	0	15	62	0	4	3	26	45	2	0	2	3
Russo	.136	12	22	3	3	0	0	0	0	0	0	0	1	4	1	0	0	0
Swisher	.287	75	279	49	80	12	1	15	47	0	0	2	28	61	1	0	6	3
Teixeira	.288	81	292	67	84	22	0	19	64	0	2	9	53	61	0	0	6	3
Thames	.267	38	105	9	28	3	0	4	15	0	2	2	11	29	0	0	2	1
Winn	.182	12	33	4	6	0	1	1	7	1	1	0	1	9	1	0	1	0
TOTALS	**.279**	**81**	**2710**	**473**	**755**	**146**	**16**	**115**	**453**	**13**	**20**	**39**	**318**	**544**	**51**	**12**	**54**	**35**

PITCHER	ERA	W	L	G	GS	CG	SHO	SV	IP	AB	H	R	ER	HR	HB	BB	SO	WP	AVG
Aceves	6.75	1	0	6	0	0	0	1	5.1	22	6	4	4	1	1	3	0	0	.273
Albaladejo	5.63	0	0	7	0	0	0	0	8.0	29	7	5	5	1	2	6	6	0	.241
Burnett	4.59	5	7	14	14	0	0	0	80.1	304	85	45	41	10	8	33	67	7	.280
Chamberlain	5.30	3	2	37	0	0	0	3	35.2	146	41	22	21	2	1	13	35	1	.281
Gaudin	4.09	1	0	17	0	0	0	0	33.0	122	28	15	15	8	4	10	20	1	.230
TOTAL	4.62	1	1	22	0	0	0	0	39.0	146	35	20	20	9	4	11	27	1	.240
Hughes	4.66	11	4	18	18	0	0	0	106.1	400	99	56	55	20	0	39	83	6	.248
Logan	2.74	2	0	26	0	0	0	0	23.0	88	21	7	7	2	1	10	21	0	.239
Marte	3.86	0	0	16	0	0	0	0	9.1	34	8	4	4	1	0	4	9	0	.235
Melancon	9.00	0	0	2	0	0	0	0	4.0	18	7	5	4	1	0	0	3	0	.389
Mitre	4.76	0	1	12	2	0	0	1	28.1	109	31	17	15	5	1	9	10	0	.284
Moseley	5.24	2	1	9	4	0	0	0	34.1	131	37	20	20	9	1	13	18	0	.282
Nova	4.50	0	1	5	4	0	0	0	22.0	83	21	12	11	2	1	9	12	2	.253
Park	4.74	1	0	16	0	0	0	0	19.0	75	19	11	10	5	1	5	15	0	.253
Pettitte	3.89	7	3	12	12	0	0	0	69.1	262	68	34	30	10	1	23	44	2	.260
Ring	5.40	0	0	2	0	0	0	0	1.2	6	1	1	1	0	0	1	2	0	.167
Rivera	2.20	1	1	31	0	0	0	14	28.2	103	18	9	7	1	3	2	25	0	.175
Robertson	4.60	1	2	29	0	0	0	0	29.1	106	23	15	15	3	2	17	34	3	.217
Sabathia	3.00	11	2	16	16	1	0	0	111.0	409	90	41	37	8	4	34	97	5	.220
Sanchez	0.00	0	0	1	0	0	0	0	0.2	6	0	0	0	0	0	2	2	0	.000
Vazquez	5.29	5	5	15	11	0	0	0	66.1	263	70	42	39	18	5	28	61	4	.266
Wood	0.63	1	0	13	0	0	0	0	14.1	50	8	1	1	1	1	8	17	0	.160
TOTAL	4.01	2	2	25	0	0	0	3	24.2	94	23	11	11	3	3	13	28	2	.245
TOTALS	**4.22**	**52**	**29**	**81**	**81**	**1**	**3**	**19**	**730.0**	**2762**	**688**	**366**	**342**	**108**	**37**	**269**	**581**	**31**	**.249**

Yankees on the Road

BATTER	AVG	G	AB	R	H	2B	3B	HR	RBI	SH	SF	HP	BB	SO	SB	CS	GDP	E
Berkman	.220	17	50	2	11	2	0	0	4	0	0	0	11	6	0	0	6	1
TOTAL	.201	57	184	18	37	8	1	4	22	0	0	0	45	42	1	1	15	1
Cano	.341	80	317	51	108	22	2	13	42	0	3	6	28	39	2	2	12	3
Cervelli	.278	49	144	13	40	5	0	0	24	2	1	2	22	21	0	1	2	7
Curtis	.136	21	44	4	6	2	0	0	5	0	0	1	3	10	0	0	0	0
Gardner	.279	75	240	37	67	9	5	0	18	3	0	3	37	60	27	4	3	1
Golson	.133	14	15	1	2	0	0	0	2	0	0	0	0	1	0	0	0	0
Granderson	.232	67	233	34	54	7	4	10	35	3	3	1	28	62	6	1	2	0
Huffman	.400	4	5	0	2	0	0	0	2	0	0	0	1	0	0	0	0	0
Jeter	.246	79	341	49	84	13	1	3	29	0	2	6	30	52	8	3	12	2
Johnson	.119	13	42	6	5	1	0	0	2	0	0	1	13	14	0	0	0	0
Kearns	.215	20	65	8	14	1	0	1	1	0	0	2	8	25	0	0	3	0
TOTAL	.272	62	224	32	61	15	0	5	25	0	0	6	23	68	4	1	7	1
Miranda	.105	13	19	1	2	0	0	0	2	0	0	0	1	2	0	0	1	0
Moeller	.286	3	7	2	2	2	0	0	0	0	0	0	1	1	0	0	0	0
Nunez	.308	14	26	5	8	0	0	1	6	0	0	0	3	2	2	0	2	1
Pena	.203	37	59	8	12	1	0	0	2	2	0	0	2	12	4	0	1	1
Posada	.205	60	185	17	38	8	0	7	24	0	2	2	34	43	1	1	4	2
Rodriguez	.252	74	294	42	74	15	2	15	63	0	7	0	33	53	2	3	5	4
Russo	.222	19	27	2	6	2	0	0	4	1	0	1	2	5	0	0	0	1
Swisher	.289	75	287	42	83	21	2	14	42	3	2	4	30	78	0	2	7	1
Teixeira	.227	77	309	46	70	14	0	14	44	0	3	4	40	61	0	1	9	0
Thames	.308	44	107	13	33	4	0	8	18	0	1	1	8	32	0	0	1	2
Winn	.250	17	28	3	7	0	0	0	1	0	0	0	7	6	0	0	0	0
TOTALS	.256	81	2857	386	730	129	16	86	370	20	24	34	344	592	52	18	70	34

PITCHER	ERA	W	L	G	GS	CG	SHO	SV	IP	AB	H	R	ER	HR	HB	BB	SO	WP	AVG
Aceves	0.00	2	0	4	0	0	0	0	6.2	26	4	1	0	0	0	1	2	0	.154
Albaladejo	0.00	0	0	3	0	0	0	0	3.1	10	2	0	0	0	0	2	2	0	.200
Burnett	5.76	5	8	19	19	1	0	0	106.1	411	119	73	68	15	11	45	78	9	.290
Chamberlain	3.50	2	0	36	0	0	0	0	36.0	135	30	15	14	4	0	9	42	4	.222
Gaudin	5.40	0	2	13	0	0	0	0	15.0	59	18	12	9	3	1	10	13	2	.305
TOTAL	7.18	0	3	20	0	0	0	0	26.1	110	38	25	21	7	4	14	26	2	.345
Hughes	3.47	7	4	13	11	0	0	0	70.0	265	63	27	27	5	0	19	63	3	.238
Logan	3.18	0	0	25	0	0	0	0	17.0	59	13	6	6	1	0	10	17	1	.220
Marte	4.32	0	0	14	0	0	0	0	8.1	28	2	4	4	1	1	7	3	2	.071
Mitre	1.75	0	2	15	1	0	0	0	25.2	84	12	6	5	2	1	7	19	1	.143
Moseley	4.65	2	3	7	5	0	0	0	31.0	114	29	16	16	4	1	14	15	0	.254
Nova	4.50	1	1	5	3	0	0	0	20.0	81	23	10	10	2	0	8	14	0	.284
Park	6.61	1	0	11	0	0	0	0	16.1	68	21	14	12	2	0	7	14	2	.309
Pettitte	2.56	4	0	9	9	0	0	0	59.2	217	55	18	17	3	2	18	57	0	.253
Ring	40.50	0	0	3	0	0	0	0	0.2	4	2	3	3	0	0	1	0	0	.500
Rivera	1.44	2	2	30	0	0	0	19	31.1	110	21	5	5	1	2	9	20	0	.191
Robertson	3.09	3	3	35	0	0	0	1	32.0	123	36	11	11	2	1	16	37	4	.293
Sabathia	3.34	10	5	18	18	1	0	0	126.2	467	119	51	47	12	3	40	100	3	.255
Sanchez	0.00	0	0	1	0	0	0	0	3.2	12	1	0	0	0	0	1	3	0	.083
Vazquez	5.34	5	5	16	15	0	0	0	91.0	339	85	54	54	14	2	37	60	4	.251
Wood	0.77	1	0	11	0	0	0	0	11.2	37	6	1	1	0	0	10	14	3	.162
TOTAL	2.11	1	2	22	0	0	0	5	21.1	73	12	6	5	1	0	16	21	3	.164
TOTALS	3.90	43	38	81	81	2	5	20	712.1	2649	661	327	309	71	25	271	573	38	.250

Yankees with Runners in Scoring Position

PLAYER	OUTS	AVG	AB	H	2B	3B	HR	TOT RBI	SP RBI	MISP	MOB	BB	IBB	SO	SH	SF	GIDP
Berkman	<2	.333	15	5	2	0	0	4	4	25	33	6	2	1	0	0	2
Berkman	2	.250	12	3	2	0	0	4	3	18	25	2	1	2	0	0	0
Berkman		.296	27	8	4	0	0	8	7	43	58	8	3	3	0	0	2
Cano	<2	.410	83	34	8	1	4	51	43	121	172	8	3	8	0	5	7
Cano	2	.239	88	21	4	2	1	26	21	121	180	18	11	11	0	0	0
Cano		.322	171	55	12	3	5	77	64	242	352	26	14	19	0	5	7
Cervelli	<2	.243	37	9	1	1	0	13	13	65	94	8	0	7	5	4	3
Cervelli	2	.381	42	16	1	0	0	24	23	62	89	4	1	6	0	0	0
Cervelli		.316	79	25	2	1	0	37	36	127	183	12	1	13	5	4	3
Curtis	<2	.143	14	2	0	0	1	6	4	16	21	0	0	5	0	0	0
Curtis	2	.286	7	2	1	0	0	2	2	11	17	1	0	2	0	0	0
Curtis		.190	21	4	1	0	1	8	6	27	38	1	0	7	0	0	0
Gardner	<2	.269	67	18	4	1	0	24	23	108	153	16	1	11	2	3	2
Gardner	2	.194	62	12	0	0	1	15	13	92	130	14	0	25	0	0	0
Gardner		.233	129	30	4	1	1	39	36	200	283	30	1	36	2	3	2
Golson	<2	.500	2	1	0	0	0	2	2	3	5	0	0	0	0	0	0
Golson	2	.000	3	0	0	0	0	0	0	4	6	0	0	1	0	0	0
Golson		.200	5	1	0	0	0	2	2	7	11	0	0	1	0	0	0
Granderson	<2	.215	65	14	2	1	3	21	15	96	134	12	2	17	2	3	1
Granderson	2	.245	49	12	2	2	2	18	14	70	99	8	1	11	0	0	0
Granderson		.228	114	26	4	3	5	39	29	166	233	20	3	28	2	3	1
Jeter	<2	.290	93	27	6	3	2	35	31	139	188	13	3	20	1	3	8
Jeter	2	.257	74	19	5	0	2	24	21	101	137	7	1	11	0	0	0
Jeter		.275	167	46	11	3	4	59	52	240	325	20	4	31	1	3	8
Kearns	<2	.176	17	3	1	0	0	3	3	23	39	1	0	8	0	0	2
Kearns	2	.077	13	1	1	0	0	2	2	22	33	2	0	5	0	0	0
Kearns		.133	30	4	2	0	0	5	5	45	72	3	0	13	0	0	2
Miranda	<2	.444	9	4	1	0	0	5	5	16	25	3	0	1	0	0	0
Miranda	2	.133	15	2	0	0	1	1	1	20	25	0	0	4	0	0	0
Miranda		.250	24	6	1	0	1	6	6	36	50	3	0	5	0	0	0
Nunez	<2	.333	6	2	0	0	0	2	2	10	16	1	0	0	0	0	1
Nunez	2	.600	5	3	0	0	0	3	3	9	14	1	0	0	0	0	0
Nunez		.455	11	5	0	0	0	5	5	19	30	2	0	0	0	0	1
Pena	<2	.136	22	3	0	0	0	6	6	34	47	1	0	3	2	2	1
Pena	2	.296	27	8	0	0	0	11	11	36	53	1	0	4	0	0	0
Pena		.224	49	11	0	0	0	17	17	70	100	2	0	7	2	2	1
Posada	<2	.213	61	13	3	0	3	22	18	84	114	9	1	18	0	2	3
Posada	2	.192	52	10	3	0	2	17	12	72	107	8	2	19	0	0	0
Posada		.204	113	23	6	0	5	39	30	156	221	17	3	37	0	2	3
Rodriguez	<2	.269	78	21	9	0	5	58	47	131	188	11	0	16	0	11	3
Rodriguez	2	.297	74	22	3	0	2	31	26	102	142	11	1	10	0	0	0
Rodriguez		.283	152	43	12	0	7	89	73	233	330	22	1	26	0	11	3
Russo	<2	.167	6	1	1	0	0	3	3	10	16	1	0	2	1	0	0
Russo	2	.000	8	0	0	0	0	0	0	10	16	0	0	1	0	0	0
Russo		.071	14	1	1	0	0	3	3	20	32	1	0	3	1	0	0
Swisher	<2	.282	71	20	3	0	1	25	22	104	144	12	0	24	3	2	7
Swisher	2	.293	58	17	4	2	2	26	21	84	114	8	0	14	0	0	0
Swisher		.287	129	37	7	3	3	51	43	188	258	20	0	38	3	2	7
Teixeira	<2	.269	93	25	7	0	6	45	36	160	214	26	6	10	0	5	7
Teixeira	2	.279	61	17	2	0	4	28	21	92	128	15	0	17	0	0	0
Teixeira		.273	154	42	9	0	10	73	57	252	342	41	6	27	0	5	7
Thames	<2	.286	28	8	1	0	3	15	11	42	57	3	0	8	0	3	1
Thames	2	.143	28	4	0	0	0	3	3	35	53	2	0	9	0	0	0
Thames		.214	56	12	1	0	3	18	14	77	110	5	0	17	0	3	1
YANKEES	**<2**	**.274**	**788**	**216**	**51**	**8**	**28**	**349**	**297**	**1223**	**1714**	**133**	**18**	**164**	**20**	**44**	**50**
YANKEES	**2**	**.242**	**712**	**172**	**28**	**7**	**17**	**242**	**201**	**1014**	**1446**	**111**	**18**	**161**	**0**	**0**	**0**
YANKEES		**.259**	**1500**	**388**	**79**	**15**	**45**	**591**	**498**	**2237**	**3160**	**244**	**36**	**325**	**20**	**44**	**50**

Yankees with Bases Loaded

PLAYER	OUTS	AVG	AB	H	2B	3B	HR	TOT RBI	SP RBI	MISP	MOB	BB	IBB	SO	SH	SF	GIDP
Berkman	<2	.000	2	0	0	0	0	0	0	4	6	0	0	0	0	0	2
Berkman	2	.000	2	0	0	0	0	1	1	6	9	1	0	0	0	0	0
Berkman		.000	4	0	0	0	0	1	1	10	15	1	0	0	0	0	2
Cano	<2	.667	12	8	2	0	2	21	16	30	45	0	0	1	0	3	2
Cano	2	.500	6	3	1	0	0	5	5	12	18	0	0	0	0	0	0
Cano		.611	18	11	3	0	2	26	21	42	63	0	0	1	0	3	2
Cervelli	<2	.000	3	0	0	0	0	3	3	12	18	1	0	1	0	1	1
Cervelli	2	.750	8	6	0	0	0	14	14	20	30	2	0	0	0	0	0
Cervelli		.545	11	6	0	0	0	17	17	32	48	3	0	1	0	1	1
Curtis	<2	.000	0	0	0	0	0	0	0	0	0	0	0	0	0	0	0
Curtis	2	.000	1	0	0	0	0	0	0	2	3	0	0	0	0	0	0
Curtis		.000	1	0	0	0	0	0	0	2	3	0	0	0	0	0	0
Gardner	<2	.286	7	2	0	0	0	8	8	20	30	1	0	1	0	2	0
Gardner	2	.333	6	2	0	0	1	7	5	16	24	2	0	3	0	0	0
Gardner		.308	13	4	0	0	1	15	13	36	54	3	0	4	0	2	0
Golson	<2	.000	1	0	0	0	0	1	1	2	3	0	0	0	0	0	0
Golson	2	.000	1	0	0	0	0	0	0	2	3	0	0	0	0	0	0
Golson		.000	2	0	0	0	0	1	1	4	6	0	0	0	0	0	0
Granderson	<2	.200	5	1	0	0	0	2	2	10	15	0	0	3	0	0	0
Granderson	2	.333	6	2	0	0	1	6	4	12	18	0	0	1	0	0	0
Granderson		.273	11	3	0	0	1	8	6	22	33	0	0	4	0	0	0
Jeter	<2	.000	11	0	0	0	0	4	4	26	39	1	0	5	0	0	2
Jeter	2	.111	9	1	0	0	0	2	2	20	30	1	0	2	0	0	0
Jeter		.050	20	1	0	0	0	6	6	46	69	2	0	7	0	0	2
Kearns	<2	.333	3	1	1	0	0	2	2	6	9	0	0	2	0	0	0
Kearns	2	.250	4	1	1	0	0	2	2	8	12	0	0	1	0	0	0
Kearns		.286	7	2	2	0	0	4	4	14	21	0	0	3	0	0	0
Miranda	<2	.500	2	1	0	0	0	3	3	8	12	2	0	1	0	0	0
Miranda	2	.500	2	1	0	0	0	1	1	4	6	0	0	0	0	0	0
Miranda		.500	4	2	0	0	0	4	4	12	18	2	0	1	0	0	0
Nunez	<2	.000	2	0	0	0	0	1	1	4	6	0	0	0	0	0	0
Nunez	2	.500	2	1	0	0	0	2	2	4	6	0	0	0	0	0	0
Nunez		.250	4	1	0	0	0	3	3	8	12	0	0	0	0	0	0
Pena	<2	.000	3	0	0	0	0	1	1	8	12	0	0	2	0	1	0
Pena	2	.750	4	3	0	0	0	6	6	8	12	0	0	0	0	0	0
Pena		.429	7	3	0	0	0	7	7	16	24	0	0	2	0	1	0
Posada	<2	.143	7	1	0	0	1	7	5	16	24	0	0	3	0	1	1
Posada	2	.429	7	3	0	0	1	7	5	14	21	0	0	0	0	0	0
Posada		.286	14	4	0	0	2	14	10	30	45	0	0	3	0	1	1
Rodriguez	<2	.556	9	5	1	0	2	22	17	32	48	2	0	2	0	4	0
Rodriguez	2	.364	11	4	1	0	1	12	9	24	36	1	0	4	0	0	0
Rodriguez		.450	20	9	2	0	3	34	26	56	84	3	0	6	0	4	0
Russo	<2	.000	0	0	0	0	0	1	1	2	3	1	0	0	0	0	0
Russo	2	.000	1	0	0	0	0	0	0	2	3	0	0	0	0	0	0
Russo		.000	1	0	0	0	0	1	1	4	6	1	0	0	0	0	0
Swisher	<2	.333	6	2	0	0	0	6	6	16	24	2	0	1	0	0	2
Swisher	2	.300	10	3	1	0	0	8	7	22	33	1	0	4	0	0	0
Swisher		.313	16	5	1	0	0	14	13	38	57	3	0	5	0	0	2
Teixeira	<2	.500	8	4	1	0	1	14	12	22	33	0	0	1	0	2	1
Teixeira	2	.571	7	4	0	0	0	8	8	16	24	1	0	0	0	0	0
Teixeira		.533	15	8	1	0	1	22	20	38	57	1	0	1	0	2	1
Thames	<2	.400	5	2	0	0	0	2	2	10	15	0	0	1	0	0	1
Thames	2	.000	4	0	0	0	0	0	0	8	12	0	0	3	0	0	0
Thames		.222	9	2	0	0	0	2	2	18	27	0	0	4	0	0	1
YANKEES	<2	.330	91	30	6	0	6	104	90	238	357	10	0	24	0	14	13
YANKEES	2	.358	95	34	4	0	4	83	73	212	318	11	0	19	0	0	0
YANKEES		.344	186	64	10	0	10	187	163	450	675	21	0	43	0	14	13

Yankees Pitchers as Batters (career)

PITCHER	AVG	AB	R	H	HR	RBI	In 2010	Last Hit
Burnett	.131	267	12	35	3	9	0-for-1	6/20/09 at FLA
In postseason	*.000*	*1*	*0*	*0*	*0*	*0*		---
Chamberlain	.000	5	0	0	0	0	---	---
Gaudin	.031	32	1	1	0	0	---	5/31/09 at COL(w/SD)
Hughes	.000	1	0	0	0	0	0-for-1	---
Logan	---	-	-	-	-	-	-	-
Mitre	.141	78	5	11	0	2	---	7/14/07 vs. WAS (w/ FLA)
Moseley	---	-	-	-	-	-	-	-
Pettitte	.137	190	6	26	1	13	1-for-4	6/22/10 at ARZ
In postseason	*.158*	*19*	*2*	*3*	*0*	*1*		*10/31/09 at PHI (G3)*
Rivera	.000	3	0	0	0	1	0-for-1	---
In postseason	*.000*	*3*	*0*	*0*	*0*	*0*		---
Robertson	---	-	-	-	-	-	-	-
Sabathia	.258	97	7	25	3	14	1-for-5	5/23/10 at NYM
In postseason	*.000*	*5*	*0*	*0*	*0*	*0*		---
Vazquez	.206	504	38	104	1	27	0-for-1	9/8/09 at HOU
In postseason	---	-	-	-	-	-		-
Wood	.171	345	23	59	7	32	---	5/29/06 vs. CIN
In postseason	*.273*	*11*	*2*	*3*	*1*	*5*		*10/15/03 vs. FLA (G7)*

HOME RUNS BY YANKEE PITCHERS

No Yankee pitcher has ever homered in a postseason game…the first home run hit by a Yankee pitcher was by Clark Griffith on July 14, 1903…the last was hit by Lindy McDaniel on September 28, 1972 off Mickey Lolich at Detroit.

Yankees Lineups

2010 STARTS BY POSITION

PLAYER	C	1B	2B	3B	SS	LF	CF	RF	DH
Berkman	--	7	--	--	--	--	--	--	21
Cano	--	--	157	--	--	--	--	--	2
Cervelli	80	--	--	--	--	--	--	--	--
Curtis	--	--	--	--	--	2	--	9	1
Gardner	--	--	--	--	--	96	38	--	--
Golson	--	--	--	--	--	1	1	4	--
Granderson	--	--	--	--	--	--	123	--	--
Huffman	--	--	--	--	--	2	--	2	--
Jeter	--	--	--	--	150	--	--	--	5
Johnson	--	2	--	--	--	--	--	--	19
Kearns	--	--	--	--	--	20	--	8	1
Miranda	--	4	--	--	--	--	--	--	10
Moeller	4	--	--	--	--	--	--	--	--
Nunez	--	--	--	10	3	--	--	--	--
Pena	--	--	5	27	9	--	--	--	--
Posada	78	--	--	--	--	--	--	--	28
Rodriguez	--	--	--	122	--	--	--	--	12
Russo	--	--	--	3	--	10	--	--	--
Swisher	--	1	--	--	--	--	--	131	11
Teixeira	--	148	--	--	--	--	--	--	9
Thames	--	--	--	--	--	17	--	6	34
Winn	--	--	--	--	--	14	--	2	--

2010 STARTS BY BATTING ORDER

PLAYER	1	2	3	4	5	6	7	8	9
Berkman	--	2	2	--	--	13	10	1	--
Cano	--	1	--	26	132	--	--	--	--
Cervelli	--	--	--	--	--	4	13	42	21
Curtis	--	--	--	--	--	--	1	5	6
Gardner	25	17	--	--	--	--	8	28	56
Golson	--	--	--	--	--	--	--	1	5
Granderson	--	21	--	--	--	4	63	32	3
Huffman	--	--	--	--	--	--	--	4	--
Jeter	137	18	--	--	--	--	--	--	--
Johnson	--	21	--	--	--	--	--	--	--
Kearns	--	--	--	--	1	1	20	7	--
Miranda	--	--	--	--	--	2	7	5	--
Moeller	--	--	--	--	--	--	--	--	4
Nunez	--	--	--	--	--	--	1	5	7
Pena	--	--	--	--	--	--	--	7	34
Posada	--	--	--	--	5	93	8	--	--
Rodriguez	--	--	--	134	--	--	--	--	--
Russo	--	--	--	--	--	--	--	5	8
Swisher	--	82	1	1	13	30	6	10	--
Teixeira	--	--	157	--	--	--	--	--	--
Thames	--	--	2	1	11	15	24	4	--
Winn	--	--	--	--	--	--	1	6	9

2010 Season Summary

APRIL 2010 YANKEES 15-7 • HOME 6-1 • ROAD 9-6 (thru games of 4/30)			
Tampa Bay	17	6	.739	--
NEW YORK	15	7	.682	-1.5
Toronto	12	12	.500	-5.5
Boston	11	12	.478	-6.0
Baltimore	5	18	.217	-12.0

Sunday, April 4
at Boston, Lost, 7-9   **0-1, 5th, -0.5**
The Yankees lost their season opener at Fenway Park, 9-7...fell to 62-45-1 all time on Opening Day and 28-31 in road openers...marked the Yankees' second consecutive Opening Day road defeat (lost 10-5 at Baltimore in on 4/6/09)...**LHP CC Sabathia** allowed 5ER in 5.1IP in recording a no-decision (6H, 2BB, 4K)...**C Jorge Posada** (3-for-4) and **CF Curtis Granderson** (1-for-4) hit back-to-back solo HRs in the second inning to open the scoring, becoming the first pair of Yankees teammates to hit back-to-back homers on Opening Day since Dave Winfield and Steve Kemp on 4/5/83 at Seattle, according to the *Elias Sports Bureau*...Granderson's HR came in his first plate appearance as a Yankee, making him the first Yankee to accomplish the feat on an Opening Day since Jim Wynn on 4/7/77 vs. Milwaukee...**LF Brett Gardner** (2-for-4) stole home as part of a fourth-inning double steal with **SS Derek Jeter** (2-for-5)...was the Yankees' first steal of home since 7/31/04 vs. Baltimore (fourth inning) when Alex Rodriguez accomplished the feat as part of a double steal with Hideki Matsui...was the Majors' first steal of home on Opening Day since Oakland's Mike Bordick on 4/6/92 vs. Kansas City...**Granderson, PR-DH Randy Winn** (0-for-0) and **RHP Chan Ho Park** each made their Yankees debuts.

Monday, April 5
Off Day   **0-1, T4th, -1.0**

Tuesday, April 6
at Boston, Won, 6-4   **1-1, T2nd, -0.5**
The Yankees recorded their first win of the season, defeating Boston, 6-4, at Fenway Park...**RHP A.J. Burnett** started and recorded a no-decision, allowing 4R/3ER in 5.0IP (7H, 1BB, 5K, 1HP, 1HR)...**2B Robinson Cano** (2-for-3) drove in a pair of runs with a fifth-inning sacrifice fly and a ninth-inning solo homer...**DH Nick Johnson** (0-for-2) put the Yankees ahead in the eighth, drawing a bases-loaded walk...**RHP Alfredo Aceves** earned the win, tossing a scoreless sixth and seventh inning (2.0IP)...**RHP Joba Chamberlain** struck out his only two batters faced in the eighth...**RHP Mariano Rivera** earned his first save of the season with a scoreless ninth (1.0IP, 1H, 1K).

Wednesday, April 7
at Boston, Won, 3-1 (10)   **2-1, 2nd, -0.5**
The Yankees won their second straight game at Boston, scoring two runs in the 10th inning for a 3-1 win...**LHP Andy Pettitte** started and allowed just 1ER in 6.0IP, in recording a no-decision (6H, 3BB, 4K)...became just the sixth pitcher to start at least one game in 13 different seasons with the Yankees (also W. Ford-16; Ruffing-15; Guidry-13; Gomez-13; Shawkey-13)...**RHP Chan Ho Park** came on in relief and tossed 3.0 scoreless innings to earn the win (1H, 1K)...**CF Curtis Granderson**

broke a 1-1 tie in the top of the 10th with a solo HR off Jonathan Papelbon, his second career go-ahead HR in the ninth inning or later (also 9/26/05 w/ Detroit vs. White Sox off Cliff Politte)...**RHP Mariano Rivera** tossed a perfect 10th to record the save for the second consecutive night (1.0IP).

Thursday, April 8
Off Day   **2-1, T1st, --**

Friday, April 9
at Tampa Bay, Lost, 3-9   **2-2, 3rd, -1.0**
The Yankees lost the series opener at Tampa Bay, 9-3...**RHP Javier Vazquez** made his first regular season start as a Yankee since 9/30/04 vs. Minnesota...picked up the loss, allowing 8R/8ER in 5.2IP in his worst outing since surrendering 9R/9ER on 6/25/06 w/ White Sox vs. Houston...snapped a nine-start road undefeated streak dating back to 7/7/09...**DH Nick Johnson** (2-for-5) broke an 0-for-10 stretch, getting his first hit of the season with a fourth-inning single.

Saturday, April 10
at Tampa Bay, Won, 10-0   **3-2, T2nd, -1.0**
The Yankees shut out the Rays, 10-0, at Tropicana Field...was the second-most lopsided shut out win in the history of the series (13-0 Yankees win, 5/16/02 at original Yankee Stadium)...**LHP CC Sabathia** started and carried a no-hitter through two out in the eighth inning until Kelly Shoppach singled to left field (7.2IP, 1H, 2BB, 5K, 111/69)...was removed by manager Joe Girardi immediately following the single...was the furthest he had gone in a game without allowing a hit (previous best was on 4/7/02 w/ Cleveland at Detroit, 7.0 no-hit IP)...was the deepest a Yankee had taken a no-hitter since Mike Mussina took a perfect game 8.2IP on 9/2/01 at Boston (Carl Everett single)...**1B Mark Teixeira** (3-for-4) had a double and 1RBI and snapped a career-worst 0-for-17 start to his season...**3B Alex Rodriguez** (2-for-4) recorded his 1,000th hit as a Yankee with a second-inning single...**2B Robinson Cano** (2-for-5) opened the scoring with a two-run homer in the second inning and had 3RBI on the day...Teixeira, Rodriguez and Cano each made noteworthy defensive plays to preserve the no-hitter while intact.

Sunday, April 11
at Tampa Bay, Won, 7-3   **4-2, 2nd, -1.0**
The Yankees won the series finale at Tampa Bay, 7-3...**RHP A.J. Burnett** started and allowed 2ER (both in the first inning) in 7.0IP, earning his first win of the year (6H, 3BB, 1K)...**CF Curtis Granderson** (2-for-4) had an RBI double...**3B Alex Rodriguez** (2-for-4) had 2 doubles and 2RBI...**C Jorge Posada** (1-for-3) hit his second HR of the season—a two-run, go-ahead homer in the sixth...**RHP Mariano Rivera** tossed a scoreless ninth in a non-save situation (1.0IP, 1H, 1BB, 1K).

Monday, April 12
Off Day   **4-2, 2nd, -0.5**

Tuesday, April 13
vs. Los Angeles-AL, Lost 5-7   **5-2, 2nd, -1.0**
The Yankees won their home opener, 7-5, vs. the Angels...won their home opener for the 12th time in the last 13 years...**LHP Andy Pettitte** started and recorded a win, tossing 6.0 shutout innings (5H, 3BB, 6K) in the first scoreless outing by a Yankees starter on a home Opening Day since he turned the trick on 4/5/02 vs.

Tampa Bay…**DH Nick Johnson** (2-for-3) hit a solo HR in his first at-bat…according to the *Elias Sports Bureau*, marked the Yankees' *first run or hit in the first inning* in 2010…**SS Derek Jeter** (2-for-5) hit a solo HR in the third inning…**C Jorge Posada** (3-for-4) hit his 345th career double in the seventh inning, passing Mickey Mantle (344) for sole possession of seventh place on the Yankees' all-time list…reached base safely in four of five plate appearances…**RHP Mariano Rivera** retired both of his batters faced in the ninth for his third save of the season (0.2IP, 1K)…marks his fifth career save in a Yankees home opener…the attendance of 49,293 was the largest regular season attendance in Yankee Stadium history (2009-10) to that point.

Wednesday, April 14
vs. Los Angeles-AL, Lost 3-5   5-3, 3rd, -0.5
The Yankees had their three-game winning streak snapped, losing, 5-3, to the Los Angeles Angels at Yankee Stadium…no home runs were hit by either team…**RHP Javier Vazquez** started and allowed 4ER in 5.1IP (6H, 2BB, 4K, 1WP)…with his 5.1IP, reached the 2,500IP plateau…this was the first season in his career he took the loss in his first two starts of the year (also 4/9 at Tampa Bay)…**RF Nick Swisher** (1-for-4) had an RBI triple in the fifth inning, marking his first triple since 4/11/09 at Kansas City off Horacio Ramirez.

Thursday, April 15
vs. Los Angeles-AL, Won, 6-2   6-3, T2nd, -0.5
The Yankees defeated the Angels , 6-2, taking the rubber match of the series on Jackie Robinson Day…all players, coaches and umpires wore No. 42…Jackie Robinson's grandson Jesse Sims threw out the first pitch…**RHP Phil Hughes** allowed 2ER in 5.0IP in his first start of the season, earning the win (3H, 5BB, 6K, 1BK, 1HR)…**2B Robinson Cano** (2-for-4) had 3RBI, recording his fifth-career two-homer game and first since 4/25/09 at Boston…was his first time hitting 2HR in a game *off left-handed pitching*…**CF Curtis Granderson** (2-for-4) tripled twice in the same game for the fifth time in his career and first since 8/18/08 at Texas (w/ Detroit)…the triples came in consecutive ABs, marking a first by a Yankee since Clay Bellinger on 8/26/00 at Oakland…**SS Derek Jeter** (2-for-5) hit a solo homer, marking his second HR in three games…**RHP Mariano Rivera** (0.1IP) recorded his fourth save in four chances.

Friday, April 16
vs. Texas, Won 5-1   7-3, T1st, --
The Yankees defeated the Rangers, 5-1, in a rain-shortened six-inning game…neither team hit a home run, marking the second such game at Yankee Stadium in 2010 (also 4/14 vs. Los Angeles-AL)…four of the Yankees' five runs were scored without the ball leaving the infield (PB, FC, E, INF hit)…**LHP CC Sabathia** improved to 2-0, limiting the Rangers to 1ER in 6.0IP (3H, 0BB, 9K, 1HP) while recording his 29th career complete game…struck out six straight batters beginning with Nelson Cruz to end the first inning through Julio Borbon in the third inning…according to the *Elias Sports Bureau*, marked the most consecutive strikeouts in his career and most by a Yankees pitcher since David Cone on 8/8/99 (also six straight)…retired 17 of his final 19 batters faced…**2B Robinson Cano** (1-for-3) and **SS Derek Jeter** (2-for-3) each hit safely, extending their hitting streaks to 10 games to start the season, and becoming the first Yankees tandem to accomplish the feat.

Saturday, April 17
vs. Texas, Won 7-3   8-3, T1st, --
The Yankees defeated the Rangers, 7-3…clinched their fourth series win in a row to start the season for just the third time in franchise history (also 1922 and 1926)…**Manager Joe Girardi** recorded his 200th regular season win as Yankees skipper…**RHP A.J. Burnett** started and earned the win, tossing 7.0 scoreless IP (6H, 2BB, 7K, 1WP)…**SS Alex Rodriguez** (2-for-4) hit his 584th career home run in the third inning off Scott Feldman, breaking a tie with Mark McGwire (583) for sole possession of eighth place on Baseball's all-time list…**SS Derek Jeter** (3-for-4) hit a two-run homer in the third inning and extended his hitting streak to a career-best 11 games *from the start of the season*…**LF Brett Gardner** (3-for-4) had three infield hits, which the *Elias Sports Bureau* notes was the most by a Yankee since Don Mattingly also had three on 8/19/92 vs. Oakland…**C Jorge Posada** (2-for-4) recorded his 1,500th career hit.

Sunday, April 18
vs. Texas, Won 5-2   9-3, 2nd, -0.5
The Yankees defeated Texas, 5-2, to complete their first series sweep of the season…did not commit an error for the 10th straight game, marking the longest such streak in April in franchise history (credit: *Elias*)…**LHP Andy Pettitte** started and earned the win, allowing just 2ER in 8.0IP (4H, 3BB, 4K)…**1B Mark Teixeira** (1-for-4) snapped a 40AB homerless stretch from the start of the season (the second-longest of his career) with a solo home run to lead off the third inning…**SS Ramiro Pena** (1-for-4) put the Yankees ahead for good with a two-run bases-loaded single in the third in his first start of the season as **SS Derek Jeter** missed the game due to a head cold…**3B Alex Rodriguez** (1-for-1) reached base in all four of his plate appearances (single, 3BB)…**RHP Mariano Rivera** recorded his fifth save in five chances (1.0IP, 2K)…the Yankees dedicated the game to the memory of longtime employee Harvey Winston, a 22-year member of the Yankees organization who passed away unexpectedly in January.

Monday, April 19
Off Day   9-3, 2nd, -0.5

Tuesday, April 20
at Oakland, Won 7-3   10-3, 1st, +0.5
The Yankees defeated Oakland, 7-3, at Oakland Alameda Coliseum to win the opening game of their three-game series…had just 5H but drew 10BB…was the first time the Yankees scored seven-or-more runs on five-or-fewer hits since 7/25/06 at Texas (7R, 4H)…**RHP Javier Vazquez** won his first game of the season, allowing 3ER in 5.1IP (6H, 3BB, 6K, 2HR)…**3B Alex Rodriguez** (1-for-2) reached base four times with 3BB and a three-run fifth-inning HR…**SS Derek Jeter** (0-for-5) was held hitless for the first time in 2010, snapping his 11-game hitting streak to start the season…**LHP Boone Logan** made his first appearance *as a Yankee* (1.1IP, 2H, 1BB, 1K)…**RHP Mariano Rivera** recorded his sixth save in six chances in 2010 (1.0IP, 1K).

Wednesday, April 21
at Oakland, Won 3-1   11-3, 1st, +0.5
The Yankees defeated Oakland, 3-1, at Oakland-Alameda Coliseum to win the second game of their three-game series…marked their fifth straight series win to start the season, tying the 1926 Yankees' all-time franchise record…according to the *Elias Sports Bureau*, the Yankees joined the 1904 Red Sox and 1922 Giants as the only defending World Series champions to begin the season with five straight series wins…held the A's to

just three hits…**RHP Phil Hughes** struck out a career-high 10 batters and took a no-hitter through 7.0IP before allowing a leadoff infield single in the eighth to Eric Chavez on a hard-hit ball which deflected off the heel of Hughes' glove…allowed just 1ER on 1H and 2BB in 7.1IP…**3B Alex Rodriguez** (2-for-4) and **2B Robinson Cano** (2-for-4) tripled in consecutive at-bats in the fourth, marking the first such instance for the Yankees since Melky Cabrera and Johnny Damon on 8/25/07 at Detroit…**RHP Mariano Rivera** recorded his sixth save in six chances (1.0IP, 1H, 1HP).

Thursday, April 22
at Oakland, Lost 2-4   11-4, 2nd, -0.5
The Yankees lost, 4-2, to the A's at Oakland-Alameda Coliseum…held to 3H on Wednesday…turned a triple play in the sixth inning (5-4-3; Rodriguez to Cano to Johnson; hit by Suzuki), snapping a 6,632-game stretch without a triple play since 6/3/68 vs. Minnesota (1-5-3; Womack to Cox to Mantle; hit by Roseboro)…**LHP CC Sabathia** took a complete game loss, allowing 3ER in 8.0IP (4H, 4R, 6BB, 5K, 1WP, 1HR)…tied his career high in walks (third time), marking his most since 9/11/04 w/ Cleveland at Oakland…set a career high with 4BB *to left-handed-hitters*…tossed a complete game for his second consecutive start on 4/16 (6.0IP-rain shortened loss vs. Texas), marking a first by a Yankee since David Wells in 1998…**1B Mark Teixeira** (1-for-4) hit a solo homer in the sixth…**LF Marcus Thames** (1-for-2) hit a solo homer in the fifth, snapping an 83AB homerless stretch dating back to last season…the Yankees and A's played the game in 2:07, the club's shortest game since a 2 hour, 4 minute, 2-0 win on 6/18/96 vs. Minnesota.

Friday, April 23
at Los Angeles, Lost 4-6   11-5, 2nd, -0.5
The Yankees lost, 6-4, to the Angels at Angel Stadium…the defeat – after the game was tied, 4-4, after seven innings – snapped the Yankees' Modern Era-record 17-game winning streak in games tied at the end of the seventh…**RHP A.J. Burnett** started and did not record a decision, allowing 4ER in 6.1IP (9H, 2BB, 3K, 2HP)…**RF Nick Swisher** (1-for-3) hit a solo home run in the fourth…**LF Brett Gardner** (1-for-3) doubled in the third…his prior 19 hits dating to 9/16/09 were all singles…**RHP Joba Chamberlain** allowed a game-winning two-run home run to Kendry Morales in the eighth inning (1.0IP, 3H, 2ER, 1HR).

Saturday, April 24
at Los Angeles, Won 7-1   12-5, 2nd, -0.5
The Yankees defeated the Angels, 7-1, at Angel Stadium…**LHP Andy Pettitte** started and allowed just 1ER in 8.0IP (6H, 0BB, 8K)…improved to 3-0 with a 1.29 ERA (28.0IP, 4ER, 22K) in 2010…marked his lowest ERA, runs allowed and most K through four starts in his career…**LF Brett Gardner** (3-for-5) tripled in the fifth, stole a base and scored two runs…**2B Robinson Cano** (4-for-5) matched his career high in hits (16th time) and scored three runs for the first time since scoring 4R on 4/9/09 at Baltimore…**RF Nick Swisher** (2-for-4) recorded 2RBI and drove in a least one run for the third time in four games…**C Francisco Cervelli** (1-for-3) doubled and drove in two runs.

Sunday, April 25
at Los Angeles, Lost 4-8   12-6, 2nd, -1.5
The Yankees lost 8-4 at the Angels, marking their first series loss of the season…Yankees batters tallied just 3H and Yankees 1-4 hitters went 0-for-13…were outscored, 8-1, after taking a 3-0 lead after two innings…**RHP**

Javier Vazquez started and fell to 1-3 on the season, allowing 5ER in 3.2IP (5H, 3BB, 3K, 1HP, 1HR)…**DH Jorge Posada** opened the scoring with a two-run homer in the second inning…**2B Robinson Cano** (1-for-3) hit a solo homer in the sixth and scored two runs.

Monday, April 26
Off Day (White House Visit)   12-6, 2nd, -1.5

Tuesday, April 27
at Baltimore, Lost 4-5   12-7, 2nd, -2.5
The Yankees lost, 5-4, despite outhitting the Orioles 9H to 7H…was the Yankees' first one-run game of the year…**RHP Phil Hughes** started allowed just 1ER on 2H in 5.2IP but did not figure in the decision (4BB, 2K)…held his opponent under 3H for the third straight start to begin the year…**2B Robinson Cano** (3-for-4) extended his hitting streak to six games…**RF Nick Swisher** (3-for-4) scored two runs…**C Jorge Posada** (1-for-3) hit a solo homer in the fourth inning, marking the Yankees' only extra-base hit.

Wednesday, April 28
at Baltimore, Won 8-3   13-7, 2nd, -2.5
The Yankees won, 8-3, recording 15H…led 5-0 after two innings…**LHP CC Sabathia** started and improved to 3-1 in 2010, allowing 3ER in 7.2IP (11H, 2BB, 5K, 1HR)…allowed a seventh-inning HR to Nick Markakis, snapping a 54.0-inning streak from the start of his career having never allowed a HR at Camden Yards…**SS Derek Jeter** (2-for-4) doubled to lead off the game, marking the 442nd double of his career and tying Don Mattingly for third place on the club's all-time list…also had 2RBI…**C Jorge Posada** (0-for-0) left the game in the bottom of the second after getting hit by a pitch (right knee) by Orioles starter Jeremy Guthrie.

Thursday, April 29
at Baltimore, Won 4-0   14-7, 2nd, -2.5
The Yankees won, 4-0, in the series finale at Baltimore…Yankees pitchers allowed just 3H in their second shutout of 2010…**RHP A.J. Burnett** limited the O's to 3H in 8.0 scoreless IP (1BB, 4K, 1WP)…was his longest scoreless start with three-or-fewer hits allowed since 8/9/05 w/ Florida vs. Arizona (9.0IP, 3H)…**2B Robinson Cano** (3-for-4) hit solo HRs in the fourth and eighth innings, doubled and scored three runs…was his second 2HR game of the season (also on 4/15 vs. Los Angeles-AL)…**DH Marcus Thames** (3-for-4) reached base four times in four plate appearances with 2 singles, 1 double and 1BB…also had 1RBI.

Friday, April 30
vs. Chicago-AL, Won 6-4   15-7, 2nd, -1.5
The Yankees won, 6-4, vs. Chicago-AL…were down 3-0 after the bottom of the first and overcame a three-or-more run deficit for the first time in 2010…**LHP Andy Pettitte** started and did not record a decision, allowing 4ER on 7H in 6.0IP (2BB, 3K, 1HR)…**SS Derek Jeter** (3-for-4) hit a two-run home run in the fifth and a game-winning two-run triple in the seventh to break a 4-4 tie…his 4RBI were his most in a game since 9/10/06 at Baltimore (also 4RBI)…finished 1 double shy of a cycle…surpassed Ken Griffey, Jr. (2,776) for the most hits among active players…**2B Robinson Cano** (1-for-4) drove in one run on a first-inning single and extended his hitting streak to nine games…**RHP Mariano Rivera** tossed a scoreless ninth (1.0IP, 2K) to record his seventh save in seven chances this season…his 2K gave him 1,015 for his career, tying and surpassing Roger Clemens for 10th place on the Yankees' all-time list.

YANKEES 16-13 • HOME 10-6 • ROAD 6-7
(thru games of 5/31)

Tampa Bay	34	18	.654	--
NEW YORK	**31**	**20**	**.608**	**-2.5**
Toronto	31	22	.585	-3.5
Boston	29	23	.558	-5.0
Baltimore	15	36	.294	-18.5

Saturday, May 1
vs. Chicago-AL, Lost 6-7   **15-8, 2nd, -1.5**
The Yankees lost, 7-6, vs. Chicago-AL...came back from a 5-1 deficit after the top of the third, scoring one run in the fifth and four runs in the sixth before surrendering two runs in the seventh...**RHP Javier Vazquez** started and did not record a decision, allowing 5ER on 7H in 3.0IP (4BB, 2K, 3HR)...**RF Nick Swisher** (2-for-5) put the Yankees ahead with a two-run sixth-inning homer.... snapped a 22AB home hitless stretch...**1B Mark Teixeira** (2-for-4) reached base three times (2 singles, 1BB) and drove in a run, for his second multi-hit game of the season (also 4/10 at Tampa Bay, 3-for-4)...**LF/ CF Brett Gardner** (2-for-4) singled home a run, stole one base and scored two runs...**RHP Sergio Mitre** tossed 3.0 hitless innings of relief (2BB, 1K)...**CF Curtis Granderson** (1-for-3) left the game in the bottom of the sixth inning with left groin strain.

Sunday, May 2
vs. Chicago-AL, Won 12-3   **16-8, 2nd, -1.5**
The Yankees won, 12-3, and scored five runs in the seventh inning...**RHP Phil Hughes** improved to 3-0 in his first four starts of the season, tossing 7.0 scoreless innings (4H, 1BB, 6K, 1WP)...**CF Brett Gardner** (2-for-4) drove in a run on a second-inning single and hit a fourth-inning solo HR...was his first career HR off a left-handed pitcher and snapped 167AB homerless stretch against all pitchers...**2B Robinson Cano** (2-for-4) reached base safely three times with 1 double, 1BB and a fifth-inning three-run HR...**1B Mark Teixeira** (4-for-5) tied his career high in hits (18th time)...was his second consecutive multi-hit game...**RF Nick Swisher** (3-for-4) reached base in four of five PAs (1BB, 2 singles, 1HR) and hit a two-run sixth-inning homer -- his second consecutive game with a home run...**3B Francisco Cervelli** (0-for-1) entered the game defensively in the eighth, marking his first career game at a position other than catcher.

Monday, May 3
vs. Baltimore, Won 4-1   **17-8, 2nd, -1.0**
The Yankees won, 4-1, defeating Baltimore for the 12th time in the two clubs' last 14 games at Yankee Stadium...the Yankees scored all of their runs in the fourth inning...**LHP CC Sabathia** started and recorded victory, allowing 1ER in 8.0IP (6H, 2BB, 2K, 1WP, 1HR)...**LF Randy Winn** (1-for-3) snapped a 491AB homerless streak with a three-run, fourth-inning homer that put the Yankees ahead...was his first homer since 4/25/09 w/ San Francisco at Arizona off Max Scherzer...**C Jorge Posada** (0-for-2) was replaced defensively in the top of the sixth inning, leaving the game with tightness in his right calf...was diagnosed with a mild calf strain after undergoing a postgame MRI at New York-Presbyterian Hospital...**RHP Joba Chamberlain** tossed a scoreless ninth inning (1.0IP, 1BB, 1K), recording his second career save.

Tuesday, May 4
vs. Baltimore, Won 4-1   **18-8, 2nd, -1.0**
The Yankees won, 4-1, winning by the same score for the second straight night...Yankees 7-9 hitters went 4-for-8, with 1 triple and 1SF, scoring all 4R and recording 2RBI...**RHP A.J. Burnett** did not allow an earned run in 7.1IP (5H, 1R, 2BB, 8K)...improved to 4-0 for the first time in his career...**DH Derek Jeter** (1-for-5) recorded his 443rd career double to lead off the game, surpassing Don Mattingly for sole possession of third place in franchise history...**C Francisco Cervelli** (3-for-3) tied his career high with 3H and 2R...hit his first career triple and had a bunt single in the sixth...**CF Greg Golson** (0-for-0) made his Yankees debut, entering the game defensively in the eighth (did not bat)...**RHP Joba Chamberlain** tossed a scoreless ninth inning (1.0IP, 1H, 2K), recording his third career save and his second in as many nights.

Wednesday, May 5
vs. Baltimore, Won 7-5   **19-8, 2nd, -1.5**
The Yankees won, 7-5, completing a series sweep of Baltimore...the Yankees scored in each of the first four innings...Yankees fielders turned four inning-ending double plays...**LHP Andy Pettitte** started and allowed 1ER in 5.0IP (6H, 2BB, 2K), remaining undefeated in his last 9GS against the Orioles, (7-0, 3.02 ERA)...**SS Derek Jeter** (1-for-5) played in his 2,164th career game, tying Lou Gehrig for second place on the Yankees' all-time list behind Mickey Mantle (2,401)...**DH Nick Johnson** (3-for-3) reached base five times in 5PA with 1 single, 1 double, 1HR and 2BB...marked the first time he reached base five times in a nine-inning game since 4/20/06 w/ Washington at Philadelphia (also five times)...**RHP Alfredo Aceves** retired his only batter faced, recording his first save of 2010 and second of his career.

Thursday, May 6
Off Day   **19-8, 2nd, -1.5**

Friday, May 7
at Boston, Won 10-3   **20-8, 2nd, -1.5**
The Yankees defeated the Red Sox, 10-3, marking their third straight win at Fenway Park...scored six runs in the sixth inning...seven different Yankees drove in at least one run in the game...**RHP Phil Hughes** started and allowed 2ER in 7.0IP (7H, 1BB, 7K), improving to 4-0 with a 1.69 ERA in 2010...**SS Derek Jeter** (0-for-4) played in his 2,165th career game, surpassing Lou Gehrig (2,164) for second place on the Yankees' all-time list behind Mickey Mantle (2,401G)...**RF Nick Swisher** (1-for-5) put the Yankees ahead, 3-0, with a three-run, fourth-inning home run...**DH Nick Johnson** (0-for-2) left the game in the top of the fifth with soreness in his right wrist...**2B Robinson Cano** (0-for-2) left the game in the top of the sixth after getting hit by a pitch by Josh Beckett.

Saturday, May 8
at Boston, Won 14-3   **21-8, 2nd, -0.5**
The Yankees defeated the Red Sox, 14-3, setting a season high in margin of victory (11)...also tallied 17H, 3HR and 10 batter walks...scored in six different innings, including eight runs in the final three frames...the Yankees bullpen tossed 4.1 scoreless IP (4H, 2BB, 5K)...**LHP CC Sabathia** started and allowed 3ER in 4.2IP (2BB, 4K, 1WP, 2HR) before a being removed after a 1:14 rain delay...**1B Mark Teixeira** (4-for-6) hit a career-high-tying three home runs (third time), marking the first 3HR game by a Yankee since Alex Rodriguez on 4/26/05 vs. Los Angeles-AL...became the second Yankee with 3HR in a game vs. Boston – also Lou Gehrig on 6/23/27 at Fenway Park...also homered from both sides of the

plate, marking the first time a Yankee accomplished the feat in 2010…**C Francisco Cervelli** (3-for-4) had a career-high 5RBI on three run-scoring singles, marking the most RBI by a Yankee in Fenway Park since Yogi Berra had 6RBI on 5/29/54…**3B Alex Rodriguez** (2-for-2) reached base five times (2 singles and 3BB)…**2B Kevin Russo** (0-for-1) made his Major League debut as a defensive replacement in the eighth inning…**RHP Alfredo Aceves** improved to 3-0 this season tossing 1.0 scoreless IP (2H, 1K) before leaving the game with a stiff lower back.

Sunday, May 9
at Boston, Lost 3-9   **21-9, 2ⁿᵈ, -0.5**
The Yankees lost to the Red Sox, 9-3, snapping their four-game Fenway Park winning streak…**RHP A.J. Burnett** started and allowed a career-high-tying 9R in 4.1IP (9H, 8ER, 3BB, 4K, 1WP, 1HR)…**RF Nick Swisher** (2-for-4) led off the fourth inning with a solo HR…**3B Alex Rodriguez** (1-for-3) also hit a solo homer in the fourth, his 586th career home run, tying Frank Robinson for seventh place on Baseball's all-time list…also snapped a 61AB homerless stretch…**CF Brett Gardner** (1-for-4) extended his hitting streak to a career-high-tying 11 games…**RHP Romulo Sanchez** made his Yankees debut, tossing 3.2 scoreless IP (1H, 1BB, 3K)…**Manager Joe Girardi** was ejected from the game in the fourth inning by Home Plate Umpire Tim McClelland.

Monday, May 10
at Detroit, Lost 4-5   **21-10, 2ⁿᵈ, -0.5**
The Yankees dropped their second consecutive game, falling, 5-4, at Detroit…**RHP Sergio Mitre** made his first start of the season and recorded the loss, allowing 4R/3ER in 4.1IP (5H, 2BB, 4K, 1HR)…**1B Mark Teixeira** (1-for-5) had the Yankees' only extra-base hit of the game, a two-run homer in the third inning…**CF Brett Gardner** (0-for-3) had his career-high-tying 11 game-hitting streak snapped…**RHP Joba Chamberlain** struck out the side in the eighth inning (1.0IP, 3K).

Tuesday, May 11
at Detroit, Rain Out   **21-10, 2ⁿᵈ, -1.0**

Wednesday, May 12
at Detroit (DH), Lost 0-2; Won 8-0 22-11, 2ⁿᵈ, -1.5
The Yankees split their first doubleheader of the season, dropping Game 1, 2-0, and winning Game 2, 8-0…marked the Yankees' *first doubleheader with both games ending in shutouts* since 9/24/76 at Detroit's Tiger Stadium (3-0; 8-0)…in Game 1, the Yankees were shut out for the first time this season and held to just 4H…marked their first three-game losing streak in 2010…**RHP Javier Vazquez** allowed just 2ER and 5H in 7.0IP (2BB, 7K) in his first start since 5/1 vs. Chicago-AL…**C Jorge Posada** (1-for-3) had 1 double, marking the game's only extra-base hit…in Game 2, Yankees pitchers posted their third shutout of the season in an 8-0 win…Yankees batters were 6-for-12 with RISP…scored six runs in the ninth, sending 11 batters to the plate…marked the most runs the club scored in a ninth inning since 9/2/09 (7R)…**RHP Phil Hughes** allowed just 5H in 7.0 scoreless IP (1BB, 8K), improving to 5-0 with a 1.38 ERA this season…**CF Brett Gardner** (3-for-5) scored two runs and recorded his third three-hit game of the year…**CF/RF Greg Golson** (1-for-2) recorded his first Major League hit, a ninth-inning single off Phil Coke…**RHP Mariano Rivera** made his first appearance since 4/30 vs. Chicago-AL, tossing 1.0 perfect inning (1K).

Thursday, May 13
at Detroit, Lost 0-6   **22-12, 2ⁿᵈ, -2.0**
The Yankees were shut out at Detroit, 6-0, just one day after getting blanked, 2-0, in Game 1 of a doubleheader on 5/12 at Comerica Park…marked just the second time since 1998 that the Yankees had been shut out twice in a single series (also 5/12-13/99 vs. Anaheim)…Yankees batters were 0-for-8 with RISP…had just 4H in the game…**LHP CC Sabathia** started and recorded the loss, allowing 6ER in 6.0IP (9H, 0BB, 4K)…**C Jorge Posada** (2-for-4) doubled in the sixth and was the only Yankee to record a multi-hit game or an extra-base hit…**RHP Ivan Nova** made his Major League debut, tossing 2.0 scoreless IP in relief (2H, 1K).

Friday, May 14
vs. Minnesota, Won 8-4   **23-12, 2ⁿᵈ, -1.0**
The Yankees won their series opener vs. Minnesota, 8-4…was their eighth straight regular season win against the Twins and 11th straight including the 2009 ALDS (3-0) dating to the start of the 2009 season…had eight extra-base hits…**RHP A.J. Burnett** started but did not record a decision, allowing 3R/2ER in 6.2IP (7H, 4BB, 4K, 1HR)…**3B Alex Rodriguez** (2-for-3) hit a game-winning grand slam off Matt Guerrier in the seventh to put the Yankees in the lead…was his 587th career home run, breaking a tie with Frank Robinson (586) for sole possession of seventh place on Baseball's all-time home run list…was his 19th career grand slam, tying Eddie Murray for third place on Baseball's all-time list…**RHP Joba Chamberlain** struck out the side in a perfect eighth inning (1.0IP, 3K)…was credited with the win despite not being the pitcher of record when the Yankees took the lead…**RF Nick Swisher** (0-for-1) left the game after the third inning with a sore left biceps.

Saturday, May 15
vs. Minnesota, Won 7-1   **24-12, 2ⁿᵈ, -1.0**
The Yankees defeated Minnesota, 7-1…was their ninth straight regular season win against the Twins and 12th straight including the 2009 ALDS (3-0) dating to the start of the 2009 season…**LHP Andy Pettitte** started and earned the win, tossing 6.1 scoreless IP (2H, 3BB, 2K)…his 1.79 ERA and nine runs allowed were the lowest of his career *through seven starts of a season*…was the second time in his career he won his first five decisions (also 5-0 start in 1997)…**1B Mark Teixeira** (2-for-4) hit a two-run homer in the seventh inning…**C Jorge Posada** (3-for-4) also hit a two-run seventh-inning homer, marking the club's third multi-homer inning of 2010…was his first three-hit game since 4/13 vs. Los Angeles-AL (also went 3-for-4)…**SS Derek Jeter** (2-for-5) scored the Yankees' first run of the game and drove in their second run…his two hits equaled his hit total from his previous six games combined (5/9-14), in which he went 2-for-25…**CF Brett Gardner** (0-for-4) had his 16-game streak of reaching base safely (since 4/28) snapped.

Sunday, May 16
vs. Minnesota, Lost 6-3   **24-13, 2ⁿᵈ, -2.0**
The Yankees lost to Minnesota, 6-3, after allowing five runs in the eighth inning…snapped the Yankees' nine-game regular season winning streak against Minnesota and their 10-game *home regular season* winning streak vs. the Twins…**RHP Sergio Mitre** made his second start of the season, allowing 1ER in 5.0IP (4H, 1BB, 3K, 1HR)…left with a 3-1 lead…**LF Randy Winn** (2-for-4) drove in two runs with a two-run triple in the second inning…**RHP David Robertson** tossed 2.0 hitless IP (2BB, 2K, 1BK)…**SS/RF Ramiro Pena** (2-for-4) made his first career appearance in the outfield, moving to RF in the ninth inning…**RHP Joba Chamberlain** was charged with 3ER, snapping a streak of eight scoreless

relief appearances since 4/28...**RHP Mariano Rivera** allowed his first runs of the season and blew his first save of 2010 (0.1IP, 1H, 2ER, 1BB, 1K)...also had his streak of 51 successfully converted saves at home snapped (tied with Eric Gagne, 2002-04, for the longest such streak all time)...entered the game with two outs and bases loaded in the eighth and walked in a run (BB to Jim Thome) for just the fourth time in his career...then allowed just his fourth career grand slam to Jason Kubel.

Monday, May 17
vs. Boston, Won 11-9   25-13, 2nd, -2.0
The Yankees recorded their first "walk-off" win of the season, scoring four runs in the ninth to win, 11-9, vs. Boston...scored five runs in the first inning before falling behind, 9-7, going into the bottom of the ninth...was their 12th comeback win of the season and first when trailing after eight innings (had been 0-12)...Yankees pitchers allowed a season-high five home runs...according to the Elias Sports Bureau, was just the second time in franchise history that the Yankees won a game in which an opponent hit at least five homers (also allowed 5HR in 9-8 win on 7/21/02 vs. Boston)...**RF Marcus Thames** (2-for-4) hit his second career "walk-off" home run (third career "walk-off" hit)...also had a first-inning sacrifice fly and a run-scoring fifth-inning double...**DH/3B Alex Rodriguez** (2-for-5) hit a game-tying two-run home run in the ninth off Jonathan Papelbon...also singled in two runs in the first inning...**RHP Phil Hughes** started and did not record a decision, despite leaving with a 6-5 lead (5.0IP, 6H, 5ER, 1BB, 3K, 2HR, 1WP)...**CF Brett Gardner** (2-for-4) scored a career-high-tying three runs...**RHP Javier Vazquez** recorded the win in his third career relief appearance, striking out his only batter faced (Youkilis) to end the top of the ninth.

Tuesday, May 18
vs. Boston, Lost 7-6   25-14, 2nd, -3.0
The Yankees lost to Boston, 7-6, despite having leads of 5-0 after five innings and 5-1 after seven innings...marked their largest blown lead in a loss since 4/25/09 at Boston (led 6-0, lost 16-11) and their largest blown lead in a loss at home since 5/4/07 vs. Seattle (led 5-0, lost 15-11)...snapped an eight-game home winning streak vs. Boston...**LHP CC Sabathia** started and allowed just 1ER in 7.0IP (4H, 3BB, 5K, 1HR)...exited with a 5-1 lead...allowed just one runner past second base (Youkilis solo HR)...**DH Juan Miranda** (2-for-5) hit his first home run of the season, and second of his career (also 10/2/09 at Tampa Bay)...**2B Robinson Cano** (2-for-5) had 2 doubles and 3RBI...**RHP Mariano Rivera** was charged with two unearned runs in the ninth, recording his first loss of the season (1.0IP, 2H).

Wednesday, May 19
vs. Tampa Bay, Lost 6-10   25-15, 2nd, -4.0
The Yankees lost, 10-6, to the Tampa Bay Rays at Yankee Stadium...lost consecutive home games for the first time this season...allowed 6SB, their most in a game since permitting 6SB on 8/10/92 at Detroit...the Yankees scored four runs in the bottom of the ninth...**RHP A.J. Burnett** started and recorded the loss, allowing 6ER in 6.2IP (9H, 4BB, 4K, 1HP, 1HR)...**3B Alex Rodriguez** (2-for-4) hit a solo HR in the sixth inning, the 589th of his career...**2B Robinson Cano** (4-for-5) tied his career high in hits (17th time)...was his second four-hit game of 2010 (also 4/24 at Los Angeles-AL)...**RF Marcus Thames** (1-for-2) left the game in the bottom of the sixth with a sprained left ankle.

Thursday, May 20
vs. Tampa Bay, Lost 6-8   25-16, 2nd, -5.0
The Yankees lost, 8-6, to the Tampa Bay Rays at Yankee Stadium, marking their first series loss at home in 2010 and first sweep at home since last May, also against Tampa Bay...**LHP Andy Pettitte** started and allowed a season-high-tying 7R/6ER in 5.0IP, while dropping to 5-1 on the season (9H, 2BB, 3K, 3HR)...allowed his most home runs in a game since surrendering a career-high 4HR on 5/7/09 vs. Tampa Bay...had allowed just 1HR in 45.1IP this season entering the game...**DH Juan Miranda** (2-for-3) hit his second home run of the season (and second in three games) in the second inning...recorded his first career triple in his next at-bat in the fourth...scored a career-high three runs...**SS Derek Jeter** (3-for-5) drove in a pair of runs with a ninth-inning double.

Friday, May 21
at New York Mets, Won 2-1   26-16, 2nd, -4.0
The Yankees defeated the Mets, 2-1, in the first Subway Series game of the season...Yankees pitchers allowed just four hits...was the Yankees' first one-run win of the season...**RHP Javier Vazquez** allowed just 1H in 6.0 scoreless IP (2BB, 6K)...marked his fewest hits allowed in a start since 4/7/07 w/ Chicago-AL vs. Minnesota (1H in 6.2IP)...left the game with a bruised right index finger suffered while bunting in the seventh (X-rays were negative)...**LF Kevin Russo** (2-for-3) made his first Major League start and recorded his first Major League hit (third-inning single off Hisanori Takahashi)...drove in the Yankees' only runs of the game with a two-run seventh-inning double, becoming the first Yankee in the Expansion Era (since 1961) to drive in all his team's runs in a win in his first career start (credit: Elias)...**RHP Joba Chamberlain** struck out three batters in 1.2IP...**RHP Mariano Rivera** recorded his eighth save of the season, despite allowing 1ER in the ninth (1.0IP, 2H)...marked his 932nd career appearance, surpassing Gene Garber (931) for sole possession of 19th place on Baseball's all-time list behind 18th place Rollie Fingers (944).

Saturday, May 22
at New York Mets, Lost 3-5   26-17, 2nd, -5.0
The Yankees lost, 5-3, at Citi Field...marked their first-ever loss at the Mets' new stadium after winning their first four games there...**RHP Phil Hughes** recorded his first loss of the season, allowing 4ER in 5.2IP (8H, 3BB, 7K)...Yankees 4-7 batters (Rodriguez, Cano, Swisher, Cervelli) combined to go 9-for-19 with 3R and 1RBI...**RF Nick Swisher** (3-for-4) reached base four times (also 1HBP), doubled and scored 1R...**3B Alex Rodriguez** (2-for-5) collected two hits in a game for the 12th time in May.

Sunday, May 23
at New York Mets, Lost 4-6   26-18, 2nd, -6.0
The Yankees lost for the second straight game at Citi Field, falling 6-4...were down 4-0 after two innings and 6-0 after five...scored three runs in the ninth...**LHP CC Sabathia** allowed 6R in 5.0IP (10H, 5ER, 2BB, 6K, 2HR)...was his first Interleague loss since 6/15/07 w/ Cleveland vs. Atlanta...went 1-for-2 at the plate, recording the first hit by a Yankees pitcher this season (single off Johan Santana)...**SS Derek Jeter** (3-for-5) had the Yankees' only extra-base hit of the game, a ninth-inning run-scoring double...**RHP Sergio Mitre** (2.0IP, 1K, 1HP) and **LHP Boone Logan** (1.0IP, 1H) tossed 3.0 combined scoreless innings of relief.

Monday, May 24
Off Day   26-18, 2nd, -5.5

Tuesday, May 25 (Suspended game)
at Minnesota, Won 1-0   27-18, 2nd, -4.5
The Yankees' first-ever game at Target Field was a 1-0 win in a game that was suspended after five innings (and a 1 hour, 23 minute rain delay) with a score of 0-0 and resumed the next day…was the Yankees' first 1-0 victory over Minnesota since 5/22/82 at the original Yankee Stadium…**RHP A.J. Burnett** earned the win, despite not pitching on the day the game was won…tossed five scoreless innings, allowing just three hits (2BB, 5K)…was the pitcher of record when **SS Derek Jeter** (2-for-4) won the game on a sixth-inning solo HR off Brian Duensing…marked the Yankees' first 1-0 win on a solo HR since 4/27/08 at Cleveland (Melky Cabrera solo HR)…**CF Brett Gardner** (1-for-1) snapped a 16AB hitless stretch with his first-inning single…**RHP Mariano Rivera** tossed a scoreless ninth (1.0IP, 1BB) to earn his ninth save in 10 save opportunities this season.

Wednesday, May 26
at Minnesota, Won 3-2   28-18, 2nd, -3.5
The Yankees defeated Minnesota, 3-2, in the scheduled matchup…game followed the resumption of the previous night's suspended contest…**LHP Andy Pettitte** allowed just 2ER in 8.0IP in improving to 6-1 on the season…**SS Derek Jeter** (1-for-5) doubled and extended his *hitting streak vs. Minnesota* to 10 games…**RF Nick Swisher** (2-for-5) hit a solo-HR in the ninth inning to provide the margin of victory…**RHP Mariano Rivera** recorded his second save of the day, tossing a perfect ninth inning (1.0IP) to earn his 10th save in 11 opportunities in 2010…recorded two saves in one day for the first time since 5/3/07 at Texas.

Thursday, May 27
at Minnesota, Lost 2-8   28-18, 2nd, -4.5
The Yankees dropped the final game of their three-game series at Minnesota, 8-2…was just their second loss in their last 16 overall games against Minnesota, including their three-game 2009 ALDS sweep…**RHP Javier Vazquez** started and took the loss, allowing 5ER in 5.2IP (8H, 3BB, 2K, 1HR)…**2B Robinson Cano** (2-for-4) doubled and drove in both of the Yankees' runs…**RHP Chad Gaudin** made his 2010 Yankees debut, allowing 1ER in relief (1.2IP, 2H, 1BB, 3K, 1HR).

Friday, May 28
vs. Cleveland, Won 8-2   29-18, 2nd, -3.5
The Yankees defeated Cleveland, 8-2, to begin their seven-game homestand…**RHP Phil Hughes** started and allowed 2ER in 7.0IP (5H, 1BB, 8K, 1HR), improving to 6-1 with a 2.70 ERA on the season…struck out his first five batters faced…**RF Nick Swisher** (2-for-4) opened the scoring with a two-run second-inning homer…**2B Robinson Cano** (3-for-4) hit his third career grand slam in the seventh inning…snapped a 96AB homerless stretch…made his first career start batting in the fourth spot in the lineup…extended his hitting streak to 11 games… **C Chad Moeller** (1-for-4) played in his first game this season, starting at catcher…**CF Curtis Granderson** (1-for-3) played for the first time after missing 24 games with a Grade 2 left groin strain, starting in CF…was returned from rehab and reinstated from the 15-day disabled list prior to the game.

Saturday, May 29
vs. Cleveland, Lost 11-13   29-20, 2nd, -4.5
The Yankees lost to Cleveland, 13-11, marking their largest blown lead (led 10-4 after 5 innings) since 4/25/09 at Boston (led 6-0 going into the bottom of

the fourth, lost 16-11)…had not lost a home game in which they held a lead of six-or-more runs since 5/22/92 vs. Milwaukee (led 9-3 after six innings, lost 10-9 in 14 innings), snapping a streak of 291 such *home* victories…according to the *Elias Sports Bureau*, was the second-longest such streak in AL history behind the Philadelphia Athletics' 314-game streak from 1908 to 1934…**LHP CC Sabathia** started and allowed 5ER in 6.0IP (7H, 2BB, 5K, 1WP)…did not allow a home run, snapping a career-long streak of seven-straight games allowing at least 1HR (credit: *Elias*)…was his fifth straight start without a win, his longest such stretch *as a Yankee*…**2B Robinson Cano** (3-for-4) had 3RBI and extended his hitting streak to 12 games…**3B Alex Rodriguez** (2-for-4) had 3RBI, snapping a streak of seven games without an RBI…was his longest RBI drought since a nine-game stretch from 5/9-18/07…**1B Mark Teixeira** (0-for-3) drove in a run in the fourth inning on a bases-loaded hit-by-pitch, snapping a 10-game streak without an RBI…**RHP Joba Chamberlain** took the loss, allowing 4ER in 0.1IP (4H, 1BB, 1K).

Sunday, May 30
vs. Cleveland, Won 7-3   30-20, 2nd, -3.5
The Yankees overcame a 3-0 deficit going into the bottom of the seventh to win, 7-3…scored five runs in the seventh (all with 2 outs) and two in the eighth…**RHP A.J. Burnett** improved to 6-2 on the season, limiting the Indians to 3R/1ER in 8.0IP (5H, 0BB, 8K, 2HP)…was the fourth time in his career tossing at least 8.0 innings without allowing a walk (previously done on 6/27/06 w/ Toronto vs. Washington)…**SS Derek Jeter** (2-for-5) collected 2RBI on his seventh-inning single, giving him 1,099 career RBI, tying Don Mattingly for ninth place on the franchise's all-time list…was his seventh consecutive multi-hit game vs. Cleveland, becoming the first Yankee ever to accomplish the feat, according to the *Elias Sports Bureau*…**1B Mark Teixeira** (2-for-4) put the Yankees ahead with his seventh-inning three-run home run…was the 250th homer of his career…**Manager Joe Girardi** earned his 300th career managerial win.

Monday, May 31
vs. Cleveland, Won 11-2   31-20, 2nd, -2.5
The Yankees won 11-2 vs. Cleveland, improving to 21-17 all time on Memorial Day…Yankees batters had a season-high 18H and six Yankees had multi-hit games…were 6-for-11 with RISP…scored six runs on seven hits in the seventh inning…**LHP Andy Pettitte** improved to 7-1, allowing just 1ER in 7.0IP (4H, 0BB, 5K, 1HR)…retired his final 14 batters faced…**3B Alex Rodriguez** (3-for-4) drove in a season-high 6RBI…hit his 20th career grand slam in the seventh, surpassing Eddie Murray (19) for the third-most in Baseball history…**2B Robinson Cano** (2-for-5) followed Rodriguez's slam with a solo home run, marking the Yankees second set of back-to-back HRs this season…**LF Brett Gardner** (3-for-4) was caught stealing twice in the same game for the first time in his career, becoming the first Yankee with 2CS in the same game since Bobby Abreu on 9/23/07 vs. Toronto.

JUNE 2010			
YANKEES 16-10 • HOME 9-5 • ROAD 7-5			
(thru games of 6/30)			
NEW YORK	**47**	**30**	**.610**	**--**
Boston	47	32	.595	-1.0
Tampa Bay	45	32	.584	-2.0
Toronto	40	39	.506	-8.0
Baltimore	24	53	.312	-23.0

Tuesday, June 1
vs. Baltimore, Won 7-3   32-20, 2nd, -2.5
The Yankees opened their series vs. Baltimore with a 3-1 win...game was tied 1-1 after six innings...the Yankees won on a two-run Miguel Tejada throwing error in the seventh inning on a ground-ball hit by **3B Alex Rodriguez** (1-for-4)...**RHP Javier Vazquez** allowed just 1ER in 7.0IP (4H, 1IBB, 7K, 1HR, 1HP)...**CF Curtis Granderson** (1-for-4) hit his third home run of the season and first since 4/7 at Fenway Park...was his first homer off a lefthander since 4/22/09 w/Detroit at Los Angeles-AL (off Joe Saunders)...**RHP Mariano Rivera** (1.0IP, 1H) converted his 11th save in 12 chances this season...marked his first save *at home* since 4/30 vs. Chicago-AL...**1B Mark Teixeira** (0-for-1) left the game in the top of the fourth inning with a bruised left foot, suffered on foul ball in his first-inning AB...underwent X-rays, the results of which were negative.

Wednesday, June 2
vs. Baltimore, Won 7-3   33-20, 2nd, -2.5
The Yankees won their fourth straight, a 9-1 victory vs. Baltimore...led 4-0 after two innings and 6-0 after three innings...**RHP Phil Hughes** allowed just 1ER in 7.0IP (6H,1BB, 7K), improving to 7-1 with a 2.54 ERA...**2B Robinson Cano** (3-for-4) hit his 12th home run of the season and matched a season high with 3R (fourth time)...also extended hitting streak to 16 games...**RF Nick Swisher** (3-for-5) had a game-high 3RBI.

Thursday, June 3
vs. Baltimore, Win 6-3   34-20, 2nd, -2.0
The Yankees completed the series sweep of Baltimore with a 6-3 win...was their second straight sweep of the O's and their eighth straight win against the Orioles dating to their second meeting of the season on 4/28...**LHP CC Sabathia** earned the win in his 300th career start, allowing 3ER on just 3H in 7.0IP (1BB, 7K, 2HR)...retired the first 21 batters faced (1HR, 1E)...snapped his five-start winless stretch, his longest such streak as a Yankee...**2B Robinson Cano** (1-for-3) extended his hitting streak to 17 games with a run-scoring first-inning double, marking the longest hitting streak by a Yankee this season...**3B Alex Rodriguez** (2-for-5) hit a two-run HR in the third...**LF Brett Gardner** (2-for-4) hit his third homer of the season, a solo HR in the sixth...**RHP Mariano Rivera** tossed a scoreless ninth for his 12th save of the season in 13 chances.

Friday, June 4
at Toronto, Lost 1-6   34-21, 2nd, -2.0
The Yankees lost at Toronto, 6-1, snapping their five-game winning streak...**RHP A.J. Burnett** took the loss, dropping to 6-3 on the season...allowed 6ER in 6IP (6H, 4BB, 2K, 1WP, 3HR) while surrendering runs in the second, fourth, fifth and sixth innings...matched a career high with the 3HR allowed (seventh time)...**2B Robinson Cano** (0-for-4) saw his 17-game hitting streak come to an end...**3B Alex Rodriguez** (1-for-4) and **C Chad Moeller** (1-for-3) each doubled, marking the Yankees' only extra-base hits of the game.

Saturday, June 5
at Toronto, Lost 2-3 (14 inn.)   34-22, 2nd, -2.0
The Yankees fell, 3-2, in 14 innings at Rogers Centre...was the Yankees' longest game of the season (in innings)...Yankees pitchers combined to strike out 16, fanning their most batters since 7/19/08 vs. Oakland (18K in a 12-inning contest)...**LHP Andy Pettitte** did not record a decision in the start, allowing 2ER on 5H in 7.2IP and striking out a season-high 10 batters...marked his 13th career double-digit strikeout game...**SS Derek Jeter**

(2-for-6) hit a two-run home run in the fifth, accounting for the Yankees' only runs...**CF/LF Brett Gardner** (2-for-4) reached base four times in the game (also 2BB) and stole a base...**1B Mark Teixeira** (0-for-6) became just the sixth Yankee all time to strike out five times in a game, first since Melky Cabrera on 7/7/07 vs. Los Angeles-AL.

Sunday, June 6
at Toronto, Won 4-3   35-22, 2nd, -2.0
The Yankees won, 4-3, in the final game of a three-game set at Rogers Centre...trailed, 2-0, entering the eighth and scored four runs in the inning, marking their first win this season when trailing after seven...**RHP Javier Vazquez** started and earned the win, limiting the Blue Jays to 1H in 7.0IP (2ER, 4BB, 9K, 1HR)...carried a no-hitter through 5.2IP before walking Adam Lind and allowing a two-run HR to Vernon Wells...marked just the second time in his career he tossed at least 7.0 innings and allowed no more than 1H (also 9/14/99 w/ Montreal at Los Angeles-NL)...**2B Robinson Cano** (3-for-4) doubled and drove in the game-winning run with a two-run, eighth-inning single...**RHP Mariano Rivera** tossed a perfect five-pitch ninth for his 13th save in 14 chances this season...**Manager Joe Girardi** was ejected by Home Plate Umpire Bruce Dreckman in the top of the eighth inning for arguing balls and strikes.

Monday, June 7
Off Day   35-22, 2nd, -2.0

Tuesday, June 8
at Baltimore, Won 12-7   36-22, 2nd, -2.0
The Yankees won, 12-7, at Baltimore, marking their ninth consecutive win over the Orioles in 2010...both clubs had 15 hits, tying the most combined hits (30) in a Yankees game this season (also 7/21 vs. Los Angeles-AL and 8/25 at Chicago-AL)...had a 6-0 lead after three innings and scored six runs in the seventh...**RHP Phil Hughes** notched his eighth win of the season, allowing 3ER in 6.0IP (9H, 0BB, 4K)...**RF Nick Swisher** (3-for-6) hit a two-run first-inning homer and bases-loaded seventh-inning double...matched his career high with 5RBI (fourth time)...**CF Curtis Granderson** (2-for-5) hit his second career grand slam in the third inning off Kevin Millwood (also 4/4/07 w/ Detroit vs. Toronto, off Shaun Marcum)...also stole his first base since returning from the D.L., marking his first stolen base attempt and steal since 4/13 vs. the Angels...**1B Mark Teixeira** (3-for-4) reached base safely five times (2 singles, 1HR, 2BB).

Wednesday, June 9
at Baltimore, Won 4-2   37-22, 2nd, -2.0
The Yankees came back from a 2-0 deficit after three innings to win, 4-2 at Baltimore...**LHP CC Sabathia** allowed just 2ER in 7.0IP, earning his fourth victory over the O's this season (9H, 3BB, 8K)...**2B Robinson Cano** (3-for-4) had an RBI single in the sixth in his career-high third consecutive three-hit game...**RHP Mariano Rivera** recorded his 14th save of the season in 15 save opportunities, tossing a perfect ninth (1.0IP, 1K).

Thursday, June 10
at Baltimore, Lost 3-4   37-23, 2nd, -2.0
The Yankees lost 4-3 at Baltimore, snapping their 10-game winning streak against the O's...Yankees batters had just 4H...**RHP A.J. Burnett** allowed 4ER in 6.2IP (8H, 1BB, 5K, 2HP, 1HR)...**1B Mark Teixeira** (1-for-3) had 1RBI and a sixth-inning leadoff double, which was the Yankees' final hit of the game...**3B Alex Rodriguez** (did not bat) was removed for a pinch-hitter in the second inning with right groin stiffness.

Friday, June 11
vs. Houston, Won 4-3   **38-23, 2nd, -1.0**
The Yankees defeated Houston, 4-3, at Yankee Stadium in their shortest nine-inning home game of the season (2:19)…Yankees pitchers allowed just 4H…neither club homered for the fourth time at Yankee Stadium in 2010…**LHP Andy Pettitte** won his 200th career game as a Yankee, allowing just 3R/2ER in 7.1IP (4H, 1BB, 4K)…was also his 237th career game, passing Whitey Ford (236) and tying Hall-of-Famer and former Yankee Waite Hoyt for 57th place on Baseball's all-time list…also surpassed 3,000 career IP in the game….**RF Nick Swisher** (0-for-2) drove in the game's first run with a first-inning bases loaded walk…**C Francisco Cervelli** (1-for-3) had 2RBI with a two-out bases loaded single in the first…**RHP Mariano Rivera** recorded his 15th save in 16 chances with a perfect ninth (1.0IP, 2K).

Saturday, June 12
vs. Houston, Won 9-3   **39-23, 2nd, -1.0**
The Yankees defeated Houston, 9-3…**RHP Javier Vazquez** won his third straight start and improved to 6-5 on the season, allowing just 3ER in 7.0IP (6H, 6K, 2HR)….**SS Derek Jeter** (2-for-4) led off the game with his 24th career lead-off home run, tying Rickey Henderson for the all-time franchise mark…also hit a three-run homer in the sixth inning, marking his ninth career multi-homer game and first since 8/26/06 at Los Angeles-AL…his 4RBI tied a season high (also 4/30 vs. Chicago-AL)…**C Jorge Posada** (2-for-3) hit his eighth career grand slam in the third inning, first since 7/26/04 at Toronto (off Sean Douglass)…was Posada's 250th career home run, tying Graig Nettles for seventh place on the Yankees' all-time list…**RHP David Robertson** (1.0IP, 2H, 1K) and **RHP Chad Gaudin** (1.0IP, 1H, 1K) tossed a scoreless eighth and ninth inning, respectively…**LF Marcus Thames** (0-for-1) left the game with a strained right hamstring…had an MRI at NewYork Presbyterian Hospital which came back negative.

Sunday, June 13
vs. Houston, Won 9-5   **40-23, T1st, --**
The Yankees completed a three-game sweep of Houston, defeating the Astros, 9-5…scored all of their runs in a three-inning stretch, tallying 3R in the fourth, 4R in the fifth and 2R in the sixth…Yankees batters recorded 10BB…**RHP Phil Hughes** recorded his ninth win of the season (5.2IP, 7H, 5ER, 2BB, 6K, 1HR)…**C Jorge Posada** (1-for-3) hit his ninth career grand slam – and second in as many days – in the fifth…became the first Yankee to hit a grand slam in consecutive games since Bill Dickey in 1937 on 8/3 (G2) and 8/4 vs. Chicago-AL and only the third Yankee ever to accomplish the feat (also Babe Ruth who did so in 1927 and 1929 – credit: Elias Sports Bureau)…was his 251st career HR, breaking a tie with Graig Nettles for sole possession of seventh place on the franchise's all-time list…his 8RBI over his last two games were his most in consecutive contests since 9/10-11/03 (9RBI)…was his first start at catcher since returning from the disabled list on 6/2…**2B Robinson Cano** (1-for-3) hit his 100th career home run (solo in fourth)…**3B Ramiro Pena** (1-for-3) drove in the go-ahead run with his fourth-inning, two-run single, marking his first RBI since 5/19 vs.Tampa Bay…**RF Chad Huffman** (1-for-4) started and made his Major League debut…had an infield single in his first career plate appearance off Brian Moehler.

Monday, June 14
Off Day   **40-23, T1, --**

Tuesday, June 15
vs. Philadelphia, Won 8-3   **41-23, T1st, --**
The Yankees defeated Philadelphia, 8-3 in the series opener…had a 5-0 lead after three innings…hit 3HR, all off Roy Halladay…**LHP CC Sabathia** allowed 3ER in 7.0IP (5H, 3BB/1IBB, 7K, 1WP, 1HP), improving to 7-3 with a 4.00 ERA this season…in the third inning, **CF Curtis Granderson** (2-for-5) hit a solo HR and **RF Nick Swisher** (2-for-5) hit a two-run HR…**1B Mark Teixeira** (1-for-4) hit a solo HR in the fifth…**C Francisco Cervelli** drove in two runs with a bases-loaded single in the seventh…**RHP David Robertson** (1.0IP, 1BB, 1K) and **RHP Chan Ho Park** (1.0IP, 1K) tossed 2.0 innings of scoreless relief

Wednesday, June 16
vs. Philadelphia, Lost 3-6   **41-24, T1st, --**
The Yankees had their four-game winning streak snapped, losing, 6-3 vs. Philadelphia…had just four baserunners through the first eight innings of the game…Phillies starter Jamie Moyer (47 yrs. 210 days) recorded the win, becoming the oldest pitcher to ever record a win against the Yankees…**RHP A.J. Burnett** lost his third straight start, dropping to 6-5 with a 4.33 ERA this season…allowed 6ER in 3.1IP (6H, 4BB, 3K, 1HP, 1WP, 2HR), marking his shortest outing in over a year (6/9/09 at Boston – 2.2IP)…**2B Robinson Cano** (2-for-4) was the only Yankee to have a multi-hit game, hitting a solo HR in the second inning and a single in the ninth…**C Jorge Posada** (1-for-4) hit a solo HR in the fifth, marking his third HR in his last four games…Yankees relievers **LHP Boone Logan** (2.2IP, 1BB, 3K) and **RHP Chad Gaudin** (3.0IP, 3K) tossed 5.2 combined innings of scoreless relief.

Thursday, June 17
vs. Philadelphia, Lost 1-7   **41-25, T1st, --**
The Yankees lost, 7-1, vs. Philadelphia, dropping just their second series at home this season…lost consecutive games at home for the first time since a three-game losing streak from 5/18-20…Yankees batters totaled just four hits…Yankees 1-4 batters (Jeter, Granderson, Teixeira and Rodriguez) went a combined 1-for-15 with 1BB…**LHP Andy Pettitte** lost for just the second time, allowing 3R/2ER in 7.0IP (6H, 3BB/1IBB, 7K, 1HR)…retired the Phillies' first nine batters…surpassed Ron Guidry (1,778K) for sole possession of second place on the Yankees' all-time strikeout list and surpassed Bob Shawkey (2,493.0IP) for sole possession of fifth place on the Yankees' all-time IP list…**2B Robinson Cano** (2-for-4) drove in the Yankees' only run on a sixth-inning single, extending his hitting streak to 10 games…**LHP Damaso Marte** threw 29 pitches, his most since 8/10/08 at Los Angeles-AL (also 29 pitches).

Friday, June 18
vs. the Mets, Lost 0-4   **41-26, T1st, --**
The Yankees lost, 4-0, to the Mets at Yankee Stadium, dropping their third consecutive home game for just the second time this season(also 5/18-20)…also lost a home series opener for just the second time this season (also 5/19 vs. Tampa Bay)…were shut out for the third time this season…were held scoreless for just the second time in the current Yankee Stadium (also 6/18/09 vs. Washington, 3-0)…Yankees batters were 2-for-17 with runners on base and 0-for-9 with runners in scoring position…**RHP Javier Vazquez** allowed just 1ER in 7.0IP (3H, 3BB, 4K, 1WP)…the loss snapped his personal three-game winning streak…did not allow a hit to his final 18 hitters faced (3BB)…**2B Robinson Cano** (0-for-3) had his 10-game hitting streak come to an end.

Saturday, June 19
vs. the Mets, Won 5-3 42-26, T1st, --
The Yankees snapped their three-game losing streak, defeating the Mets, 5-3…according to the *Elias Sports Bureau*, the pitching matchup (the Yankees' Phil Hughes at 9-1 vs. the Mets' Mike Pelfrey at 9-1) was *just the second time in Major League history* in which both starters came into the game with *at least nine wins for the season and a winning pct. of .900 or higher*…the only other such game was on 6/22/1900 when Brooklyn's Joe McGinnity faced Philadelphia-NL's Bill Bernhard at Baker Bowl, with both pitchers entering the game with 12-1 records…**RHP Phil Hughes** allowed 3ER in 7.0IP (5H, 3BB, 4K, 1WP, 2HR), improving to 10-1…**1B Mark Teixeira** (1-for-4) and **CF Curtis Granderson** (1-for-3) each hit two-run HRs…**LF Brett Gardner** (2-for-4) replaced Derek Jeter in the lead-off spot and scored 2R…Jeter was scratched from the starting lineup with a bruised right heel…**RHP Mariano Rivera** recorded his 16th save in 17 opportunities with a perfect ninth (1.0IP, 1K).

Sunday, June 20
vs. the Mets, Won 4-0 43-26, 1st, +1.0
The Yankees recorded their fifth shutout win of the season (and first at home), defeating the Mets, 4-0…**LHP CC Sabathia** won his fourth straight start, tossing 8.0 scoreless IP (4H, 2BB, 6K)…marked his second scoreless start of the season (also 4/10 at Tampa Bay – 7.2IP)…**1B Mark Teixeira** (1-for-3) hit his fifth career grand slam in the third inning, to account for all the scoring…according to *Elias*, the win marked the first time a Major League game finished 4-0 on a grand slam since 6/20/04 (San Francisco's Edgardo Alfonso GS vs. Boston)…was just the third time in franchise history the Yankees had won in such a fashion (also on a Cliff Johnson GS in 1977 and a Bernie Williams GS in 1993)…**RHP Mariano Rivera** tossed a scoreless ninth in a non-save situation (1.0IP).

Monday, June 21
at Arizona, Lost 4-10 43-27, 1st, +0.5
The Yankees fell in their series opener at Arizona, 10-4…**RHP A.J. Burnett** started and allowed 7ER in 4.0IP (9H, 2BB, 4K, 3HR), including five runs (on 3HR) in the first inning…**LF Brett Gardner** (4-for-4) set a season high in hits…also scored 2R and had 1SB…**RF Nick Swisher** (2-for-4) had 2RBI, with a third-inning RBI triple and a ninth-inning sacrifice fly…**PH Colin Curtis** (0-for-1) made his Major League debut after being called up earlier in the day, pinch-hitting for Burnett in the fifth and flying out to center field…**RHP Chad Gaudin** tossed 2.0 scoreless IP in relief of Burnett (1H, 1BB, 1K).

Tuesday, June 22
at Arizona, Won 9-3 44-27, 1st, +1.5
The Yankees defeated Arizona, 9-3, at Chase Field…Yankees batters were 5-for-8 with RISP…scored a six runs in the eighth inning…**LHP Andy Pettitte** allowed just 2ER in 7.0IP (7H, 2BB, 7K), improving to 9-2 with a 2.48 ERA…reached 2,501.0 career IP as a Yankee, passing Lefty Gomez (2,497.0IP) for sole possession of fourth place on the Yankees' all-time IP list…trails only Whitey Ford (3,171.0IP), Red Ruffing (3,168.0IP) and Mel Stottlemyre (2,662.0IP)…was his sixth straight outing of at least 7.0IP, marking his longest such streak since a 10-start streak of at least 7.0IP from 7/15-8/31/05 w/ Houston…**3B Alex Rodriguez** (2-for-5) drove in the Yankees' first three runs of the game with a two-run HR in the first and a third-inning RBI single…**PH Colin Curtis** (1-for-1) recorded his first Major League hit and RBI with his eighth-inning, two-run double off Chad Qualls.

Wednesday, June 23
at Arizona, Won 6-5 (10 inn.) 45-27, 1st, +2.5
The Yankees defeated Arizona, 6-5 in 10 innings…marked their second win of the season when trailing after eight innings (also 5/17 vs. Boston)…Yankees batters walked a season-high 13 times…**RHP Javier Vazquez** started and allowed 4ER in 5.0IP (6H, 2BB, 1K) and did not record a decision…as a batter, drew a career-high 2BB…**CF Curtis Granderson** (3-for-5) hit a game-winning solo HR in the 10th inning…was his third career extra-inning HR and second of 2010 (also 4/7 win at Boston)…**3B Alex Rodriguez** (0-for-1) tied the game in the ninth with a sacrifice fly…also had 3BB…**SS Derek Jeter** (0-for-4, 3R) scored at least three runs without recording a hit for the second time in his career (also 9/12/06 vs. Tampa Bay)…**RHP Mariano Rivera** pitched 2.0 scoreless innings, earning his first win of the season (2.0IP, 2H, 1BB, 2K)…pitched out of bases loaded, no out situation in the bottom of the 10th without allowing the any runs…with his 2K, collected his 1,029th career K, surpassing Al Downing (1,028) for sole possession of ninth place on the Yankees' all-time list…also had his fourth career plate appearance, grounding out to first in the 10th…was his 944th career plate appearance, tying Rollie Fingers for 18th place on Baseball's all-time list…had his streak of retiring 24 consecutive hitters snapped (Stephen Drew leadoff single in 10th).

Thursday, June 24
Off Day 45-27, 1st, +2.0

Friday, June 25
at Los Angeles-NL, Won 2-1 46-27, 1st, +3.0
The Yankees defeated the Dodgers, 2-1, in the clubs' first meeting since 6/20/04…**LHP CC Sabathia** started and allowed just 1ER in 8.0IP (4H, 3BB, 7K), improving to 9-3 on the season and winning his fifth straight start…**3B Alex Rodriguez** (2-for-4) scored both of the Yankees' runs and had two of the Yankees' three extra-base hits, including a second-inning double and a sixth-inning solo HR…marked his 593rd career HR and the 31st different ballpark in which he has homered…**SS Derek Jeter** (2-for-5) had the Yankees' other multi-hit game and extra-base hit (third-inning double)…**RHP Mariano Rivera** struck out the side in the ninth to record his 17th save in 18 opportunities this season (1.0IP, 3K).

Saturday, June 26
at Los Angeles-NL, Lost 4-9 46-28, 1st, +2.0
The Yankees had their three-game winning streak snapped, falling 9-4 at Dodger Stadium…**1B Mark Teixeira** (1-for-5) put the Yankees on the board first with a first-inning three-run home run…**LF/CF Brett Gardner** (2-for-3) collected his fourth multi-hit game in seven contests…**SS Derek Jeter** (1-for-4) scored 2R and had 1SB on his 36th birthday…**RHP A.J. Burnett** lost his fifth straight start, his longest skid since dropping five in-a-row from 8/24-9/14/05 w/ Florida…allowed 6H and 6ER in 3.0IP with 6BB, 5K and 1WP, marking his most walks this season…Yankees pitchers combined to walk a season-high 10 batters.

Sunday, June 27
at Los Angeles-NL, Won 6-2 47-28, 1st, +2.0
The Yankees came back from a 6-2 deficit after eight innings, scoring four in the ninth and two in the 10th to win, 8-6 at Dodger Stadium…overcame a four-run deficit in the ninth inning or later for the first time since 4/19/2007 vs. Cleveland and the first time *on the road* since 5/20/06 at the Mets, according to the *Elias Sports*

Bureau…also trailed 5-0 after five innings, tying the largest deficit the club overcame this season (also 8/11 vs. Texas)…**LHP Andy Pettitte** allowed 5R/4ER in 5.0IP (6H, 3BB/1IBB, 5K, 1HR), snapping a six-start streak of lasting at least 7.0IP…committed a career-high tying 2E, both in the third inning…**3B Alex Rodriguez** (2-for-5) hit a two-run HR in the sixth (#594 of his career)…tied his season high with 3R (third time)…**SS Derek Jeter** (3-for-4) reached base four times (3 singles, 1IBB)…**LF Chad Huffman** (2-for-3) had his first career multi-hit game, including his first career RBI with a two-run, ninth-inning single…entered the game as a defensive replacement in the fourth…**2B Robinson Cano** (2-for-5) doubled in a run in the ninth and won the game with a two-run 10th-inning HR off LHP George Sherrill…**RHP Mariano Rivera** tossed 2.0 scoreless innings to earn his second win of the season (1H, 3K).

Monday, June 28
Off Day   47-28, 1st, +2.0

Tuesday, June 29
vs. Seattle, Lost 4-7   47-29, 1st, +1.0
The Yankees dropped their series opener vs. Seattle, 7-4…**RHP Phil Hughes** allowed a career-high 10H and a season high 7R (5.2IP, 6ER, 2BB/1IBB, 3K, 1HR)…was his first loss at home since 5/4/09 vs. Boston, snapping a 10-game winning streak at Yankee Stadium…**RF Nick Swisher** (2-for-4) hit two solo HRs (first and sixth innings) off LHP Cliff Lee, marking his 15th career multi-HR game…**1B Mark Teixeira** (1-for-4) extended his hitting streak to 10 games…**CF Curtis Granderson** (2-for-4) had two hits off Lee, marking his first game with more than one hit off LHP since 9/16/09 w/ Detroit vs. Kansas City…**RHP Chan Ho Park** did not allow any runs in 2.0 perfect IP (1K), snapping a streak of allowing at least two runs in three consecutive appearances (6/18-26).

Wednesday, June 30
vs. Seattle, Lost 0-7   47-30, 1st, +1.0
The Yankees dropped their second straight game to the M's, falling, 7-0, at Yankee Stadium…was the fourth time this season the Yankees were shut out and the second time at home (also 6/18 vs. the Mets)…Seattle's Felix Hernandez became the first pitcher (Yankees or opponent) to toss a complete game shutout in the current Yankee Stadium…the Yankees were on the losing end of *back-to-back complete game wins* for the first time since 4/21-22/00, when Toronto's Chris Carpenter and Kelvim Escobar turned the trick at the Rogers Centre…had not happened in consecutive *home* games since 5/15-16/91 at the original Yankee Stadium, when the Angels' Mark Langston and Jim Abbott accomplished the feat…Yankees batters had a season-low-tying 2H, marking its fewest *in a home game* since 8/31/07 vs. Tampa Bay (2H in 9-1 loss)…**RHP Javier Vazquez** allowed 3ER in 6.0IP (6H, 2BB, 8K, 1HP, 2HR)…**1B Mark Teixeira** (1-for-3) extended his hitting streak to 11 games with a fourth-inning double…**LF Colin Curtis** (1-for-3) had the Yankees' other hit, a fifth-inning double

JULY 2010
YANKEES 19-7 • HOME 9-4 • ROAD 10-3
(thru games of 7/31)

NEW YORK	66	37	.641	--
Tampa Bay	64	39	.621	-2.0
Boston	59	45	.567	-7.5
Toronto	54	50	.519	-12.5
Baltimore	32	72	.308	-34.5

Thursday, July 1
vs. Seattle, Won 4-2   48-30, 1st, +1.5
The Yankees defeated Seattle, 4-2, snapping their two-game losing streak…**LHP CC Sabathia** won his sixth straight start, allowing just 2R/1ER in 8.0IP (5H, 2BB, 4K)…surpassed 2,000.0 career IP…**2B Robinson Cano** (1-for-3) hit a solo HR in the fourth…**DH Alex Rodriguez** (2-for-4) hit a game-winning two-run HR in the eighth, breaking a 2-2 tie…was his 595th career homer and 250th as a Yankee, tying Graig Nettles for eighth on the Yankees' all-time list…**1B Mark Teixeira** (2-for-4) extended his hitting streak to 12 games with a fourth-inning single…**RHP Mariano Rivera** recorded his 18th save in 19 chances.

Friday, July 2
vs. Toronto, Lost 1-6 (11 inn.)   48-31, 1st, +0.5
The Yankees lost, 6-1, in 11 innings in their first extra-inning home game of 2010…Yankees batters had just five hits (all singles)…were 0-for-8 with RISP…Jays pitchers retired the final 13 Yankees faced…the Yankees had a 1-0 lead after seven innings before allowing the tying run in the eighth…**RHP A.J. Burnett** tossed 6.2 scoreless IP but received a no-decision (4H, 3BB, 6K, 1HP, 2WP), snapping a stretch of recording the loss in five consecutive starts…**3B Alex Rodriguez** (0-for-4) drove in the Yankees' only run with a first-inning sacrifice fly…**1B Mark Teixeira** (0-for-3) had his hitting streak snapped at 12 games…**C Francisco Cervelli** (2-for-4) was the only Yankee to record a multi-hit game.

Saturday, July 3
vs. Toronto, Won 11-3   49-31, 1st, +0.5
The Yankees defeated Toronto, 11-3, at Yankee Stadium…Yankees batters scored 11 runs in the third inning, marking their highest single-inning output since 6/21/05 vs. Tampa Bay (13R in the eighth)…the half-inning lasted 37 minutes…sent 15 men to the plate…tied a season high with 7H in the inning (also 5/31 vs. Cleveland – 7th)…had three bases loaded AB in the inning, resulting in 9RBI (Teixeira double-2RBI; Gardner grand slam-4RBI; Rodriguez double-3RBI)…**LHP Andy Pettitte** improved to 10-2, allowing 3ER in 6.0IP (5H, 1BB, 4K, 2HR)…marked his 391st start as a Yankee, tying Red Ruffing for second-most in club history behind Whitey Ford (438)…was his 400th career appearance as a Yankee…retired 17 of his final 19 batters faced…**LF Brett Gardner** (2-for-3) hit his first career grand slam…tied his career high with 4RBI (also 9/26/08 at Boston)…**3B Alex Rodriguez** (1-for-4) had 4RBI on a ground out and a three-run double, both in the third inning…**SS Derek Jeter** (0-for-1) had 3BB (in his first three plate appearances), tying his career high now done 21 times…**RHP Dustin Moseley** made his Yankees debut, tossing 2.0 perfect IP (2K).

Sunday, July 4
vs. Toronto, Won 7-6   50-31, 1st, +2.0
The Yankees recorded their second "walk-off" win of the season with a pinch-hit RBI single by **OF Marcus Thames** (who came off the D.L. that morning) in the 10th inning…the Yankees' 14H in the game were their most in nearly a month (since 15H on 6/8 at Baltimore)…**RHP Phil Hughes** did not draw a decision, allowing 5ER in 6.0IP (6H, 2BB, 5K, 1WP)…also matched his career high with 3HR (also 3HR on 8/26/07 at Detroit)…**LF Brett Gardner** (2-for-4) hit his second career inside-the-park HR…**1B Mark Teixeira** (3-for-4) had two doubles and drove in two runs…**RHP Mariano Rivera** (1.0IP, 3H, 1ER, 1K) suffered his second blown save of the season, snapping a stretch of 16 consecutive scoreless outings dating back to 5/25.

Monday, July 5
at Oakland, Won 6-1   **51-31, 1ˢᵗ, +2.0**

The Yankees won their third straight game, with a 3-1 victory at Oakland…**RHP Javier Vazquez** earned his seventh win of the season, limiting the A's to 1ER on 3H in 7.0IP (2BB, 2K)…retired his final nine batters faced and 14 of the last 17…**RHP Joba Chamberlain** tossed a scoreless eighth (1.0IP, 2K) and RHP Mariano Rivera (1.0IP) tossed a perfect ninth to record his 19th save of the season…**DH Nick Swisher** (2-for-4), **CF Curtis Granderson** (1-for-3) and **C Francisco Cervelli** (1-for-4) had consecutive two-out hits in the second to plate two runs…**1B Mark Teixeira** (1-for-5) hit his 14th home run of the season, a solo HR in the sixth inning.

Tuesday, July 6
at Oakland, Won 6-1   **52-31, 1ˢᵗ, +2.0**

The Yankees won their fourth straight game, defeating the Athletics, 6-1, at Oakland-Alameda County Coliseum…**3B Alex Rodriguez** (2-for-3) recorded his first multi-HR game of the year, including his 21st career grand slam…drove in five of the Yankees' six runs in the game…**LHP CC Sabathia** earned his team-high 11th win of the season, limiting the A's to 1ER in 7.0IP with a season-high 10K (7H, 3BB, 1WP).

Wednesday, July 7
at Oakland, Won 6-2   **53-31, 1ˢᵗ, +2.0**

The Yankees won their fifth straight game, defeating the Athletics, 6-2, to complete the series sweep at Oakland Coliseum…**RHP A.J. Burnett** (7.0IP, 5H, 2ER, 2BB, 3K) earned his first win since 5/30 vs. Cleveland, snapping a personal five-game losing streak…the Yankees scored five runs in the fourth inning – all with two outs – including a three-run HR by **1B Mark Teixeira** (1-for-4) who homered for the second time in his last three games…**RF Nick Swisher** (3-for-4) finished a triple shy of the cycle and scored twice.

Thursday, July 8
at Seattle, Won 3-1   **54-31, 1ˢᵗ, +2.0**

The Yankees extended their winning streak to six games (matching their season high) with a 3-1 win at Seattle…**LHP Andy Pettitte** improved to 11-2, holding the M's to 5H and 1ER in 8.0IP with 4BB and 9K…**RHP Mariano Rivera** (1.0IP, 1K) recorded his 20th save of the season, reaching the plateau for the 14th consecutive season, extending his Major League record…**RF Nick Swisher** (4-for-4) reached base five times (also 1BB) and tied his career high in hits (also 9/8/06 w/ Oakland at Tampa Bay)…was his 11th game with at least three hits this season, surpassing his previous career high (10 games with at least 3H in 2007)…**3B Alex Rodriguez** (1-for-4) hit a two-out, two-run single in the ninth to put the Yankees ahead…**CF Curtis Granderson** (3-for-4) matched his season high in hits (third time).

Friday, July 9
at Seattle, Won 6-1   **55-31, 1ˢᵗ, +3.0**

The Yankees ran their winning streak to seven games with a 6-1 victory at Seattle…**RHP Phil Hughes** became the team's third 11-game winner, holding the Mariners to 1ER on 6H in 7.0IP with 5K and no walks…**1B Mark Teixeira** (2-for-4) recorded his second multi-homer game of the season (solo HRs in the first and the ninth innings) and matched his season high with 3R…homered from both sides of the plate in a game for the second time this season and 10th time in his career (fifth as a Yankee)…**2B Robinson Cano** (1-for-5) hit a two-run triple.

Saturday, July 10
at Seattle, Lost 4-1   **55-32, 1ˢᵗ, +2.0**

The Yankees had their seven-game winning streak snapped with a 4-1 loss at Seattle…allowed all four runs in the eighth inning on a Jose Lopez grand slam off **RHP Joba Chamberlain**…scored just 1R despite collecting 10H…also snapped a six-game road winning streak…**RHP Javier Vazquez** tossed 7.0 scoreless innings, limiting the Mariners to 3H and 2BB with 7K…carried a no-hitter through 5.2 innings, allowing just one baserunner (Branyan walk in first)…**DH Nick Swisher** (1-for-4) plated the Yankees' only run with a third-inning solo home run.

Sunday, July 11
at Seattle, Won 8-2   **56-32, 1ˢᵗ, +2.0**

The Yankees headed into the All-Star break with an 8-2 win at Seattle…**LHP CC Sabathia** won his eighth consecutive start, limiting the Mariners to 1ER in 7.0IP (6H, 1BB, 1K)…was his 12th win of the season, tied for tops in the AL prior to the All-Star break…retired 16 of his first 18 batters faced and 11 straight from the 2nd inning through the fifth…**1B Mark Teixeira** (4-for-5) matched his season high in hits (third time) with 2R, 2 doubles and 1RBI…**DH Marcus Thames** (2-for-5) hit a two-run home run in the fifth inning.

Monday, July 12 – Thursday, July 15
All-Star break   **56-32, 1ˢᵗ, +2.0**

Friday, July 16
vs. Tampa Bay, Won 5-4   **57-32, 1ˢᵗ, +3.0**

The Yankees recorded their third "walk-off" win of the season, with a 5-4 victory vs. Tampa Bay…honored the passings of both George M. Steinbrenner III and Bob Sheppard prior to the game…**RF Nick Swisher** (3-for-5) – an Ohio State alum – drove in **CF Curtis Granderson** (1-for-4) with a ninth-inning single for the game-winning run…Swisher also homered in the eighth to tie the game at 4-4…**2B Robinson Cano** (1-for-4) and **C Jorge Posada** (1-for-3) hit back-to-back HRs in the sixth…**LHP CC Sabathia** (7.0IP, 8H, 4R, 3ER, 4BB, 6K) did not draw a decision…**RHP David Robertson** struck out all three batters he faced in a scoreless inning of relief…**RHP Mariano Rivera** (1.0IP, 1H, 1K) earned his third win of the season…also picked off B.J. Upton in the ninth, marking his fifth career pickoff and first since 5/21/03 at Boston (Damian Jackson).

Saturday, July 17
vs. Tampa Bay, Lost 5-10   **57-33, 1ˢᵗ, +2.0**

The Yankees fell to the Rays, 10-5, on Old-Timers' Day at Yankee Stadium…**RHP A.J. Burnett** lost for the sixth time in his last eight starts, exiting after 2.0IP with lacerations on his right hand (4H, 4ER, 0BB, 1K, 1HR, 1WP, 2HP)…marked his shortest outing as a Yankee…**1B Mark Teixeira** (1-for-4) hit his team-leading 18th home run and fifth HR in his last nine games…**DH Jorge Posada** (2-for-5) homered for the second straight game…**LF Brett Gardner** (1-for-3) had a two-run bases-loaded single in the second inning to get the Yankees on the board.

Sunday, July 18
vs. Tampa Bay, Won 9-4   **58-33, 1ˢᵗ, +3.0**

The Yankees won the series finale vs. Tampa Bay, 9-5…seven different Yankees scored at least 1R and six different players had at least 1RBI…were 6-for-16 with runners in scoring position, including a 4-for-8 mark with RISP and two outs…scored six of their nine runs with two outs…trailed 3-0 after the top of the first…**LHP Andy Pettitte** exited the game in the third inning with a strained left groin (2.1IP, 6H, 3ER, 3BB, 3K, 1HR, 1HP)…was taken to New York-Presbyterian Hospital to undergo an MRI which revealed a Grade 1 strain…the Yankees bullpen (**Robertson, Park, Logan, Chamberlain** and **Rivera**) combined to allow just 2ER in 6.2IP (6H, 0BB, 8K)…**3B Alex Rodriguez** (2-for-4) hit the 598th HR of his career in the seventh inning…**2B Robinson Cano** (2-for-3) collected his team-leading 35th multi-hit game.

Monday, July 19
Off Day   58-33, 1st, +2.5

Tuesday, July 20
vs. Los Angeles-AL, Lost 2-10   58-34, 1st, +2.5
The Yankees fell to the Angels, 10-2…allowed double-digits in runs for the fifth time this season and second time in their last three games (10-5 loss on Saturday vs. Tampa Bay)…**RHP Phil Hughes** recorded his third loss of the season, allowing a season-high-tying 6ER in 5.0IP (9H, 3BB, 2K, 2HR)…**C Jorge Posada** (0-for-2) had 1RBI, recording an RBI in his fifth straight game to tie a career high (fourth time, first since 5/29-6/3/07)…also caught Abreu stealing second base twice, marking the first time he caught the same runner twice in the same game since 7/29/04 vs. Baltimore (Jerry Hairston, Jr.)…**Manager Joe Girardi** was ejected from the game in the sixth inning for arguing a call that when Mark Teixeira was called out at first base.

Wednesday, July 21
vs. Los Angeles-AL, Win 10-6   59-34, 1st, +2.5
The Yankees salvaged a series split with the Angels with a 10-6 victory…**RHP Javier Vazquez** (5.0IP, 9H, 5ER, 0BB, 1K, 2HR) won his 150th career game…**SS Derek Jeter** (3-for-5) tied his season high with 3R (fourth time)…**PH/LF Colin Curtis** (1-for-1) hit his first career homer, a three-run HR, after entering the game in the seventh inning and continuing Brett Gardner's plate appearance with an 0-2 count…**Gardner** (0-for-3) was ejected from the game by Home Plate Umpire Paul Emmel…**2B Robinson Cano** (1-for-3) hit his 18th homer of the season, tying Mark Teixeira for the team lead.

Thursday, July 22
vs. Kansas City, Won 10-4   60-34, 1st, +3.0
The Yankees won their second straight, defeating the Royals, 10-4, and improved to 4-2 since the All-Star break…**LHP CC Sabathia** became the AL's first 13-game winner (6.1IP, 11H, 4R, 3ER, 4BB, 9K, 1WP, 1BK), winning his 7th straight decision at home…**3B Alex Rodriguez** (3-for-5) hit his 599th career homer in the seventh off Robinson Tejeda…also had two doubles and 4RBI…**SS Derek Jeter** (2-for-5) hit his second career inside-the-park HR…**1B Mark Teixeira** (3-for-5) reached base in his 38th straight game, extending his career high…**LF Brett Gardner** (0-for-3) recorded two outfield assists in the same game for the first time in his career, becoming the Yankees' first left fielder with two assists in the same game since Melky Cabrera had two assists on 5/16/06 vs. Texas

Friday, July 23
vs. Kansas City, Won 7-1   61-34, 1st, +4.0
The Yankees won their third straight game, defeating the Royals, 7-1…the game was interrupted with two out in the bottom of the fifth inning with a 1 hour and 25 minute rain delay…the Yankees scored four runs in the first inning, including a bases-clearing double by **2B Robinson Cano** (2-for-4)…**RHP A.J. Burnett** tossed 5.0 scoreless innings (4H, 1BB, 3K) in the rain-shortened outing, winning at home for the first time since 5/30 vs. Cleveland…**DH Jorge Posada** (2-for-3) doubled in Cano in the first inning for his 1,000th career RBI.

Saturday, July 24
vs. Kansas City, Lost 4-7   61-35, 1st, +3.0
The Yankees had their three-game winning streak snapped with a 7-4 loss vs. Kansas City…**1B Mark Teixeira** (2-for-5) homered twice for his 28th career multi-homer game and third this season…**C Jorge Posada** (1-for-3) also homered, collecting his 1,000 career RBI, and extending his career-long streak to eight consecutive games with at least one RBI…**RHP Sergio Mitre** (4.1IP, 7H, 7R, 5ER, 1BB, 1K, 1HR, 1HP) made the start for the injured Andy Pettitte and recorded the loss…**RHP Dustin Moseley** tossed 4.2 scoreless innings of relief.

Sunday, July 25
vs. Kansas City, Won 12-6   62-35, 1st, +3.0
The Yankees finished off the homestand with a 12-6 win v. Kansas City…scored four runs in the third and five runs in the eighth…game was interrupted by a 2 hour, 32 minute rain delay…**CF Curtis Granderson** (2-for-4) collected his fifth career multi-homer game, with a pair of solo HRs…**RHP Phil Hughes** (5.1IP, 6H, 3ER, 0BB, 3K, 2HR) earned his 12th win of the season in the rain-shortened outing…**2B Robinson Cano** (2-for-5) recorded his 1,000th career hit…**SS Derek Jeter** (3-for-4) hit his season high in hits (eighth time).

Monday, July 26
at Cleveland, Won 3-2   63-35, 1st, +3.0
The Yankees started their seven-game road trip with a 3-2 comeback win at Cleveland…**CF Curtis Granderson** (2-for-3) hit a two-run HR in the eighth-inning to put the Yankees in the lead…**RF Nick Swisher** (1-for-3) scored his 500th career run, homering to tie the game at 1-1 in the fourth inning…**RHP Javier Vazquez** limited the Indians to 2ER on 5H in 7.0IP (3BB, 5K, 1HR) for his third straight win…**RHP Mariano Rivera** recorded his 21st save of the season with a scoreless ninth inning (1.0IP, 1H).

Tuesday, July 27
at Cleveland, Lost 1-4   63-36, 1st, +2.0
The Yankees lost for just the fourth time since the All-Star break, falling 4-1 at Cleveland…the Yankees managed just one baserunner (Jeter single) through the first six innings…**LHP CC Sabathia** (7.0IP, 9H, 4R, 2ER, 3BB, 5K) lost for the first time since 5/23, snapping his nine-game winning streak…**SS Derek Jeter** (2-for-4) collected two of the Yankees' five hits in the game…**2B Robinson Cano** (1-for-3) doubled and scored the Yankees' lone run in the eighth…**1B Mark Teixeira** (0-for-4) failed to reach base for the first time since 6/5, snapping his career-long stretch of 42 consecutive games reaching base safely.

Wednesday, July 28
at Cleveland, Won 8-0   64-36, 1st, +2.0
The Yankees shut out the Indians, 8-0…scored in each of the first four innings…collected 13 hits, marking their most hits in a road game since 6/8 at Baltimore (15H)…**RHP A.J. Burnett** tossed 6.1 scoreless innings (7H, 3BB, 7K) for his second straight win and third victory in his last four starts…**2B Robinson Cano** (2-for-5) doubled, homered, scored two runs and drove in one run…**CF Curtis Granderson** (2-for-4) had an RBI triple and scored twice…**LF/CF Brett Gardner** (2-for-4) doubled, scored two runs and had 2RBI.

Thursday, July 29
at Cleveland, Won 11-4   **65-36, 1st, +2.0**
The Yankees closed out their series at Cleveland with an 11-4 win…scored seven runs in the seventh inning – all with two outs – sending 12 men to the plate in the frame…according to *Elias*, it marked just the second time in the last 32 seasons that the Yankees scored seven runs in an inning, all after there were two outs and no runners on base (also 4/23/00 at Toronto)…11 of the 12 position players that appeared in the game reached base…the Yankees had 21AB with runners in scoring position (7H)…drew 12BB, their most in a nine-inning game since 8/19/06 at Boston (13BB)…**RHP Dustin Moseley** made his first start as a Yankee, limiting the Indians to 4H and 1ER in 6.0IP (2BB, 4K) for the win…**2B Robinson Cano** (1-for-5) homered in his second straight game for his 20th HR of the season (five shy of his total from last year)…**RF/LF Colin Curtis** (2-for-4) recorded his second multi-hit game and scored a career-high 3R…**Marcus Thames** (0-for-2) made his first career appearance at 3B in the ninth inning…**LF Brett Gardner** (1-for-1) scored twice and matched his career high with 3BB (also 5/29/10 vs. Cleveland).

Friday, July 30
at Tampa Bay, Lost 2-3   **65-37, 1st, +1.0**
The Yankees suffered a 3-2 loss at Tampa Bay…had three hits in the first inning, then went 1-for-24 with 3BB over the remainder of the game…**RF Nick Swisher** (1-for-4) hit his 19th homer of the season, accounting for all the Yankees runs with the two-run HR in the first…**2B Robinson Cano** (2-for-4) had the team's only multi-hit game…**RHP Phil Hughes** (6.0IP, 4H, 3ER, 2BB, 6K, 1HR) took his fourth loss of the season, just his second on the road (also 5/22 at the Mets), allowing all three runs on a Matt Joyce home run in the sixth…marked his first road homer allowed in 2010…**RHP Joba Chamberlain** tossed 2.0 scoreless innings of relief, marking his longest relief outing since 9/10/08 at Los Angeles-AL.

Saturday, July 31
at Tampa Bay, Won 6-5   **66-37, 1st, +2.0**
The Yankees returned to the win column with a 5-4 come-from-behind victory at Tampa Bay…four of the five runs scored on three home runs, tying their team season high (10th time)…had six hits in the game – all for extra bases…**2B Robinson Cano** (3-for-4) had two doubles and a ninth-inning solo home run – his team-high-tying 21st – that gave the Yankees the win…**RF Nick Swisher** (1-for-4) hit a solo HR in the seventh to tie the game at 4-4…**1B Mark Teixeira** (1-for-4) tied the game 3-3 in the top of the sixth with a two-run homer, his 21st…**RHP Javier Vazquez** did not draw a decision in the start, allowing 4ER on 8H in 6.1IP…**RHP Mariano Rivera** collected his 22nd save of the season with a scoreless ninth.

Sunday, August 1
at Tampa Bay, Lost 0-3   **66-38, 1st, +1.0**
The Yankees fell to Tampa Bay, 3-0, in the series finale…suffered their fifth shutout of the season (third on the road)…marked the fifth time the Yankees were held scoreless by the Rays, first since 9/23/06 at Tropicana Field…Yankees batters struck out 11 times…**RF Nick Swisher** (2-for-4) had two of the Yankees' five hits in the game…**LHP CC Sabathia** lost his second straight start, allowing 8H and 3ER in 6.2IP (3BB, 3K)…was his first loss in August since 2007…did not allow a home run, extending his homerless streak to 80.2IP…**LF Austin Kearns** (0-for-2) and **RHP Kerry Wood** (1.0IP, 1H, 2BB, 3K) each made their Yankees debut.

Monday, August 2
vs. Toronto, Lost 6-8   **66-39, T1st, --**
The Yankees lost to Toronto, 8-6, in the opening game of their series at Yankee Stadium…allowed 7R on 7H (6 doubles, 1HR) in the fifth, tying their single-inning season high (also on 5/29 vs. Cleveland–7th inn.)…<u>matched the most doubles surrendered in a single inning in AL history</u> (also on 6/9/34 Boston vs. Washington – 8th inn.; and 7/31/02 by the Yankees at Texas – 2nd inning)…**RHP A.J. Burnett** started and allowed 8ER in 4.2IP (8H, 2BB, 4K, 1WP, 2HR)…had his two-game scoreless streak snapped…**RF/CF Nick Swisher** (2-for-5) recorded his 16th career multi-HR game and second in 2010 (also 6/29 vs. Seattle)…hit a two-run HR in the first and a solo shot in the ninth…**1B Mark Teixeira** (1-for-5) hit a two-run HR in the fifth and is tied with Swisher for the team lead with 22HR…**DH Lance Berkman** (1-for-3) batted seventh in the starting lineup for the first time since 7/4/00 vs. Arizona (his second season in the Majors)…drove in his first run as a Yankee with a sixth-inning single…**RHP David Robertson** tossed a scoreless seventh (1BB, 2K) marking his 11th straight scoreless outing.

Tuesday, August 3
vs. Toronto, Lost 2-8   **66-60, 2nd, -1.0**
The Yankees dropped their third straight game, falling, 8-2, vs. Toronto…collected just 2H in the game, matching their season low (also 6/30 vs. Seattle)…**1B Mark Teixeira** (1-for-4) accounted for both Yankees runs with a first-inning two-run homer, his team-leading 23rd…following Teixeira's homer, 26 of the final 27 Yankees batters were retired (Thames infield single in the fifth)…**RHP Dustin Moseley** suffered his first loss of the season in his second start, allowing 5ER in a career-high 7.1IP (9H, 1BB, 2K, 1HP, 2HR).

Wednesday, August 4
vs. Toronto, Won 5-1   **67-40, T1st, --**
The Yankees snapped their three-game losing streak with a 5-1 win vs. Toronto…**3B Alex Rodriguez** hit his 600th career home run in the first inning off RHP Shaun Marcum…**RHP Phil Hughes** (5.1IP, 4H, 1ER, 2BB, 5K) improved to 13-4 this season, tying CC Sabathia for the most wins on the staff in 2010…improved to 8-0 in his last 10 starts immediately following a Yankees loss (since May 2009)…**SS Derek Jeter** (4-for-4) collected a season-high 4H and hit two doubles in the same game for the first time since 6/25/08 at Pittsburgh…had at least 4H, 2 doubles and 3R in the same game for just the second time (also 7/17/98 at Toronto).

AUGUST 2010
YANKEES 16-13 • HOME 10-6 • ROAD 6-7
(thru games of 8/31)

NEW YORK	82	50	.621	--
Tampa Bay	61	51	.614	-1.0
Boston	74	58	.561	-8.0
Toronto	69	63	.523	-13.0
Baltimore	49	83	.371	-33.0

Thursday, August 5
Off Day   **67-40, 1ˢᵗ, +0.5**

Friday, August 6
vs. Boston, Lost 3-6   **67-41, 1ˢᵗ, +0.5**
The Yankees dropped the series opener to Boston, 6-3, at Yankee Stadium…allowed three unearned runs in the second inning after a Francisco Cervelli error…**1B Mark Teixeira** (1-for-4) hit a two-run homer in the first-inning, his team-leading 24ᵗʰ HR this season and fourth in his last six games…**RHP Javier Vazquez** (5.1IP, 6H, 6R, 3ER, 4BB, 5K, 2HR) lost for the first time since 6/30, allowing his most runs since his first start of the season (4/9 at Tampa Bay – 8R)…Cervelli's error was the first by the Yankees this season with Vazquez on the mound…**2B Robinson Cano** (3-for-4) collected his team-leading multi-hit game and 12ᵗʰ three-hit game of 2010…**SS Derek Jeter** (1-for-3) tied Babe Ruth (2,873) on Baseball's all-time hits list.

Saturday, August 7
vs. Boston, Won 5-2   **68-41, 1ˢᵗ, +1.5**
The Yankees returned to the win column with a 5-2 victory vs. Boston…came back from a 2-0 deficit to score five unanswered runs…**LHP CC Sabathia** (8.0IP, 6H, 2ER, 1BB, 4K, 1HR) snapped his two-game losing streak and won for the 10ᵗʰ time in his last 13 starts…**CF Curtis Granderson** (2-for-4) collected his team-leading sixth triple of 2010…**3B Alex Rodriguez** was scratched from the original lineup with a lower left leg contusion…underwent X-rays, the results of which were negative…**3B Ramiro Pena** (1-for-3) was inserted in the lineup, driving in two runs.

Sunday, August 8
vs. Boston, Won 7-2   **69-41, 1ˢᵗ, +2.5**
The Yankees won their second straight, defeating Boston, 7-2…recorded a season-high 12H against the Red Sox for the fourth time this season…**RHP Dustin Moseley** (6.1IP, 6H, 2ER, 2BB, 5K, 1HR) made the start and recorded the win after **RHP A.J. Burnett** was scratched with back spasms…**1B Mark Teixeira** (2-for-5) hit a solo HR in the fifth, his team-leading 25ᵗʰ of the season…**DH Lance Berkman** (3-for-4) doubled twice and recorded his first multi-hit game with the Yankees…**SS Derek Jeter** (2-for-5) surpassed Babe Ruth (2,873) on the all-time hits list and drove in three runs, his most RBI since 6/12 vs. Houston (4RBI).

Monday, August 9
vs. Boston, Lost 1-2   **69-42, 1ˢᵗ, +1.5**
The Yankees dropped the series finale, 2-1, vs. Boston…Yankees batters were held hitless over the first 4.1IP…were 0-for-9 with runners in scoring position and 2-for-17 with runners on base…allowed 6SB in the game, marking the second time that happened this season (also 6SB on 5/19 vs. Tampa Bay)…**RHP Phil Hughes** allowed 6H and 2ER in 6.0IP (1BB, 3K), losing for the fourth time in his last eight starts…retired 14 of his final 15 batters faced…**1B Mark Teixeira** (1-for-5) homered in his second straight game, hitting his team-leading 26ᵗʰ home run of the season…**LF Austin Kearns** (1-for-2) collected the Yankees' first hit of the game with a fifth-inning single…was his first hit as a Yankee.

Tuesday, August 10
at Texas, Lost 3-4 (10 inn.)   **69-43, 1ˢᵗ, +0.5**
The Yankees lost their second straight game, falling in 10 innings at Texas, 4-3…was their second "walk-off" loss this season (also 6/5 at Toronto)…the Yankees starting lineup was without **Mark Teixeira** (birth of his son) and **Robinson Cano** (cold-like symptoms)…failed

to win a game in which their opponent made three or more errors and they made none for the first time since 6/27/08 vs. the Mets…**RHP A.J. Burnett** started and held the Rangers to 3ER in 7.0IP (6H, 2BB, 4K, 1HR) in the no-decision…**RHP Mariano Rivera** surrendered the game-winning RBI single…**3B Alex Rodriguez** (1-for-4) tied the game at 3-3 with an eighth-inning solo HR, the 601ˢᵗ of his career…**RF Nick Swisher** (2-for-5) and **C Francisco Cervelli** (1-for-4) each had RBI hits.

Wednesday, August 11
at Texas, Won 7-6   **70-43, 1ˢᵗ, +1.0**
The Yankees overcame a five-run deficit for the 7-6 win at Texas…trailed 6-1 after the fifth and 6-5 entering the ninth…struck out 17 times, matching their franchise record (also 9/30/01 vs. Baltimore, a 15-inning, 1-1 tie; and 9/10/99 vs. Boston, a 3-1 loss in 9.0 innings)…according to *Elias*, the win marked the first time in franchise history the Yankees won a game in which they fanned at least 17 times…**DH Marcus Thames** (3-for-5) drove in the go-ahead run with a ninth-inning RBI single…also hit a solo HR in the eighth…**SS Derek Jeter** (3-for-5) tripled, scored 1R and drove in a run…also surpassed Mel Ott (2,876) for sole possession of 38ᵗʰ place on Baseball's all-time list…**RHP Javier Vazquez** started and did not record a decision, allowing 6ER on 8H in 4.1IP (2BB, 1K, 1HR)…the Yankees bullpen (**RHP Sergio Mitre**, **RHP Kerry Wood** and **RHP Mariano Rivera**) combined to toss 4.2 scoreless innings.

Thursday, August 12
at Kansas City, Won 4-3   **71-43, 1ˢᵗ, +2.0**
The Yankees won their second straight, defeating the Royals, 4-3…**LHP CC Sabathia** came within one out of a complete game, limiting Kansas City to 3ER in a season-high 8.2IP (10H, 2BB, 3K) for his 15ᵗʰ win of the season…**RF Nick Swisher** (3-for-4) reached base four times (also 1BB)…**LF/RF Austin Kearns** (2-for-4) hit his first home run as a Yankee, a solo HR in the fourth inning…**SS Derek Jeter** (2-for-5) recorded his second straight multi-hit game and fifth in his last 10 contests…**RHP David Robertson** (2H, 1K) recorded the final out for his second career save.

Friday, August 13
at Kansas City, Lost 3-4   **71-44, 1ˢᵗ, +2.0**
The Yankees fell to the Royals, 4-3, at Kauffman Stadium…the game was interrupted by two rain delays (31 minutes and 2 hour, 10 minutes)…**RHP Dustin Moseley** stated and took the loss, allowing all 4ER on 8H in 4.1IP (3BB, 1K)…allowed go-ahead solo HR just prior to second rain delay and did not return to the game…Yankees relievers combined to toss 3.2 hitless, scoreless IP (1BB, 5K)…Yankees scored all 3R in the third inning, capped by a **DH Lance Berkman** (1-for-3) game-tying RBI double…**3B Alex Rodriguez** (2-for-5) and **SS Derek Jeter** (2-for-5) both had multi-hit games.

Saturday, August 14
at Kansas City, Won 8-3   **72-44, 1ˢᵗ, +2.0**
The Yankees returned to the win column with an 8-3 victory at Kansas City…the Yankees hit 5HR, including three by **3B Alex Rodriguez** (4-for-5) who set a season high in hits, tied a season high with 3R and drove in five runs (one shy of his season high)…**C Jorge Posada** (1-for-3) and **CF Curtis Granderson** (1-for-5) also went deep, hitting back-to-back HRs in the sixth…**RHP Phil Hughes** (6.0IP, 9H, 3ER, 1BB, 1HR) earned his 14ᵗʰ win of the season…**Yankees relievers** (Chamberlain, Logan, Robertson and Mitre) combined to allow just 1H in 4.0 scoreless IP (2K).

Sunday, August 15
at Kansas City, Lost 0-1   **72-45, 1st, +1.0**
The Yankees wrapped up their six-game road trip, suffering a 1-0 shutout at Kansas City...were held to 2H in the contest, matching their season low (third time, also 8/3 at Toronto and 6/30 vs. Seattle)...were shut out for the sixth time this season, fourth time on the road...marked the first time the Royals blanked the Yankees since 4/9/08 at Kauffman Stadium (4-0) and their first 1-0 loss against Kansas City since 6/11/72...**RHP A.J. Burnett** took a complete-game loss (8.0IP, 4H, 1ER, 3BB, 6K), retiring 18 of his final 22 batters faced (2H, 2BB)...**2B Robinson Cano** (1-for-3) and **LF Brett Gardner** (1-for-3) recorded both Yankees hits.

Monday, August 16
vs. Detroit, Lost 1-3   **72-46, T1st, --**
The Yankees lost their second straight game, falling to the Tigers, 3-1...were 0-for-7 with RISP, stranding a runner in scoring position in each of the last four innings...**RHP Javier Vazquez** started and lost his second straight decision (4.0IP, 5H, 2ER, 4BB, 6K, 1HR)...**LF Brett Gardner** (0-for-2) drove in the Yankees' only run with a bases-loaded walk in the ninth, snapping a 17.0-inning scoreless stretch for the Yankees...**CF Curtis Granderson** (3-for-3) reached base four times (also 1BB) in his first game against his former club...**3B Alex Rodriguez** (0-for-2) left the game in the fifth with tightness in his left calf and RF Nick Swisher (0-for-2) was removed for a pinch-hitter in the sixth with tightness in his right forearm...both players are listed as day-to-day.

Tuesday, August 17
vs. Detroit, Won 6-2   **73-46, T1st, --**
The Yankees snapped their two-game losing streak, defeating the Tigers, 6-2...**LHP CC Sabathia** earned his AL-leading 16th win of the season, allowing 5H and 2ER in 7.0IP (3BB, 9K, 2HR, 1WP)...was his 15th straight start of tossing at least 6.0 innings and allowing no more than 3ER...**C Jorge Posada** (1-for-2) collected his 1,558th career hit with a fifth-inning single, tying Thurman Munson for 17th place on the Yankees' all-time hits list...**2B Robinson Cano** (1-for-4) and **CF Curtis Granderson** (1-for-3) each hit solo home runs...**RHP Mariano Rivera** tossed a scoreless ninth inning (1.0IP, 1H).

Wednesday, August 18
vs. Detroit, Won 9-5   **74-46, T1st, --**
The Yankees won their second straight with a 9-5 victory vs. Detroit...marked the Yankees' most runs since an 11-4 win at Cleveland on 7/29...eight of the Yankees' 9H went for extra bases (4 doubles, 1 triple, 3HR)...the Yankees homered three times, including back-to-back HRs by **1B Mark Teixeira** (3-for-4) and **2B Robinson Cano** (1-for-3) in the first inning...**RHP Dustin Moseley** started and recorded the win (5.0IP, 5H, 4ER, 2BB, 2K, 3HR)...allowed 3H over his final 4.0IP, all home runs...**RHP David Robertson** (1.0IP) entered the game with the bases loaded and no outs in the eighth inning and retired each of his three batters faced, for his 18th consecutive scoreless appearance.

Thursday, August 19
vs. Detroit, Won 11-5   **75-46, 1st, +1.0**
The Yankees recorded their third straight win with an 11-5 victory vs. Detroit...scored nine runs in the sixth inning, marking their second-biggest inning this season behind an 11-run third inning on 7/3 vs. Toronto...**RHP Phil Hughes** improved to 15-5, limiting the Tigers to 2ER on 4H in 6.0IP with no walks and 6K

(1HR)...allowed both runs on a Cabrera first-inning home run...retired his last 11 batters faced...**2B Robinson Cano** (3-for-5) homered for the third straight game for the first time in his career and matched his season high with 3R (sixth time)...**RHP Sergio Mitre** (3.0IP, 6H, 3ER, 1BB, 3K, 1HR) earned his first Major League save.

Friday, August 20
vs. Seattle, Lost 0-6   **75-47, 1st, +1.0**
The Yankees were shut out for the seventh time this season, losing 6-0 vs. Seattle...was the third time this season they were blanked at home...**SS Derek Jeter** (1-for-4) recorded the Yankees' first hit of the game in the fourth inning, doubling for the team's only extra-base hit of the contest...**RHP A.J. Burnett** suffered his 11th loss of the season, allowing 12H and 6ER in 7.0IP (3BB, 4K, 2HR)...matched his career high for hits allowed (fifth time)...tossed a season-high 122 pitches...**DH Alex Rodriguez** (0-for-1) left after 1AB with tightness in his left calf...faced RHP Felix Hernandez who held the Yankees to 1ER in 26.0IP (0.35 ERA) this season, going 3-0.

Saturday, August 21
vs. Seattle, Won 9-5   **76-47, 1st, +1.0**
The Yankees came back from a 2-0 first-inning deficit to win 9-5 vs. the Mariners...eight different Yankees recorded at least 1H and scored at least 1R, and six different Yankees drove in at least one run...**RHP Javier Vazquez** exited after 3.0IP (8H, 4ER, 1BB, 2K, 3HR)...matched his shortest start this season (5/1 vs. Chicago-AL)...tied his career high in home runs allowed...the Yankees bullpen allowed just 1ER in 6.0IP (4H, 1ER, 0BB, 6K), including 3.0 scoreless innings from **RHP Chad Gaudin**...**3B Eduardo Nunez** (1-for-3) made his first Major League hit and RBI, recording his first Major League hit and RBI with a go-ahead seventh-inning run-scoring single...**LF Austin Kearns** (1-for-3) extended his hitting streak to 10 games.

Sunday, August 22
vs. Seattle, Won 10-0   **77-47, 1st, +1.0**
The Yankees shut out the Mariners, 10-0, in the series finale at Yankee Stadium...nine different Yankees had a hit and nine different Yankees scored a run...**LHP CC Sabathia** tossed 6.0 shutout innings (3H, 0BB, 8K, 1HP) and recorded his AL-leading 17th win of the season...ran his winning streak at Yankee Stadium to 15 games...**2B Robinson Cano** (2-for-5) hit his fourth career grand slam and collected a career-high 6RBI...**C Jorge Posada** (1-for-5) homered for the second straight day...**LF/RF Austin Kearns** (1-for-4) extended his hitting streak to a season-high 11 games with a solo HR in the fourth.

Monday, August 23
at Toronto, Lost 2-3   **77-48, T1st, --**
The Yankees started their road trip with a 3-2 loss at Toronto...three of the Yankees' six hits were doubles and four of the hits came with two outs...**RHP Ivan Nova** made his first Major League start, limiting the Blue Jays to 2ER on 6H in 5.1IP (1BB, 3K, 1HR) in the no-decision...**RHP David Robertson** took the loss, allowing a go-ahead solo HR in the eighth to snap a streak of 19 consecutive scoreless appearances...**2B Robinson Cano** (1-for-2) and **DH Jorge Posada** (1-for-4) each had RBI doubles...**3B Ramiro Pena** (2-for-3) collected his first multi-hit game since 7/7 at Oakland and fourth such contest of the year.

Tuesday, August 24
at Toronto, Won 11-5   **78-48, T1st, --**
The Yankees recorded an 11-5 win at Toronto…collected 17H, matching their most in a road game this season (also 5/8 at Boston)…hit 5HR, including a three-homer third inning that featured back-to-back HRs from **DH Marcus Thames** (3-for-4) and **C Jorge Posada** (4-for-5), who tied his career high in hits (17th time)…**1B Mark Teixeira** (4-for-5) also tied their career high in hits (21st time, eighth as a Yankee)…**RHP Dustin Moseley** earned the win, limiting the Blue Jays to 2ER on 5H in 6.0IP (4BB, 4K).

Wednesday, August 25
at Toronto, Lost 3-6   **78-49, T1st, --**
The Yankees dropped the series finale, losing 6-3 at Toronto…**RHP Phil Hughes** had his shortest outing of the season, allowing 5ER on 6H in 3.2IP (5BB, 6K, 1HR, 1WP)…**RHP Javier Vazquez** tossed 4.1IP in relief, limiting the Jays to 1ER in 4.1IP (2H, 1BB, 2K, 1HR)…**DH Marcus Thames** (2-for-4) doubled and hit a two-run home run…**3B Eduardo Nunez** (2-for-4) collected his first career multi-hit game, including a two-out RBI single in the ninth…**LF Brett Gardner** (2-for-3) had the Yankees only other multi-hit game.

Thursday, August 26
Off day   **78-49, T1st, --**

Friday, August 27
at Chicago-AL, Lost 4-9   **78-50, T1st, --**
The Yankees fell in the series opener at Chicago-AL, 4-9…**RHP A.J. Burnett** lost his fourth straight decision, allowing a career-high-tying 9R in 3.1IP (8H, 8ER, 3BB, 3K, 1WP)…marked the fourth time this season the hurler failed to complete 4.0IP…**RHP Sergio Mitre** tossed 4.2 scoreless innings of relief, matching the longest relief outing by a Yankee this season (Moseley-7/24 vs. Kansas City)…**RF Nick Swisher** (2-for-4) doubled and hit a two-run HR in the ninth, accounting for the Yankees' only extra-base hits in the contest…**LF Brett Gardner** (2-for-3) collected the Yankees' only other multi-hit game, also scoring 1R and driving one in.

Saturday, August 28
at Chicago-AL, Won 12-9   **79-50, T1st, --**
The Yankees snapped their two-game losing streak with a 12-9 win at U.S. Cellular Field…scored double-digits in runs for the fourth time in their last nine games…**LHP CC Sabathia** (7.0IP, 9H, 5ER, 1BB, 9K) became the Majors' first 18-game winner…won his fifth consecutive start…**DH Marcus Thames** (2-for-5) recorded his ninth career multi-homer game with a two-run HR and a solo HR…**3B/SS Eduardo Nunez** (3-for-4) hit his first Major League homer, drove in a career-high four runs and stole his first base…became the first Yankee to drive in at least four runs within his first 10 Major League games since Shelley Duncan in 2007 and just the fifth such Yankee in the last 44 years (since 1967)…**RF/1B Nick Swisher** (2-for-5) also homered for the Yankees, driving in three runs in the game.

Sunday, August 29
at Chicago-AL, Won 2-1   **80-50, T1st, --**
The Yankees won their second straight, with a 2-1 win at Chicago-AL in the series finale…won for just the fourth time this season when scoring two runs or less…**RHP Ivan Nova** earned his first Major League win, limiting the White Sox to 1ER on 5H in 5.2IP with 1BB and 7K…became the first rookie starter to earn a win for the Yankees since Alfredo Aceves on 9/9/08 (credit: *Elias*)…**DH Marcus Thames** (1-for-3) put the Yankees on

the board with a solo HR in the second, his fifth homer in his last four starts…**C Francisco Cervelli** (4-for-4) set a career high in hits and caught a runner stealing second in the eighth.

Monday, August 30
vs. Oakland, Won 11-5   **81-50, T1st, --**
The Yankees began their 10-game homestand with an 11-5 win vs. Oakland…overcame a 3-0 first-inning deficit for their sixth comeback of three-or-more runs…scored double digits in runs for the fifth time in their last 11 games…**1B Mark Teixeira** (3-for-3) and **2B Robinson Cano** (3-for-4) hit back-to-back homers in the third inning and combined to score 6R in the game…was Cano's 26th homer of the season, setting a single-season career high…**DH Marcus Thames** (1-for-4) homered for the sixth time in his last five starts…**RHP Dustin Moseley** started and did not record a decision (4.1IP, 5H, 4ER, 4BB, 4K, 1HR)…**RHP Javier Vazquez** earned the win in relief (4.2IP, 2H, 1ER, 1BB, 6K), his 10th of the year, extending his streak to 11 consecutive seasons with at least 10 wins – the longest active streak in the Majors.

Tuesday, August 31
vs. Oakland, Won 9-3   **82-50, 1st, +1.0**
The Yankees won their fourth straight game with a 9-3 win vs. Oakland…took over first place (+1.0G) with Tampa Bay's loss…hit at least 3HR for the fourth time in their last seven games…**1B Mark Teixeira** (2-for-3) hit his 30th home run of the season and second in as many days…**RF Nick Swisher** (1-for-4) hit his 25th homer of the season, making him the third Yankee to reach the plateau in 2010…**C Jorge Posada** (2-for-3) collected his 10th career triple (first since 4/26/08 at Cleveland) and recorded his 1,014th career RBI, surpassing Bob Meusel (1,013) for sole possession of 11th place on the franchise's all-time list…**RHP Phil Hughes** won his 16th game of the season, holding the A's to 2ER on 4H in 5.0IP (5BB, 1K, 1WP).

SEPTEMBER/OCTOBER 2010
YANKEES 13-17 • HOME 8-7 • ROAD 5-10
(thru games of 10/3)

Tampa Bay	96	66	.593	---
NEW YORK	**95**	**67**	**.586**	**-1.0**
Boston	89	73	.549	-7.0
Toronto	85	77	.525	-11.0
Baltimore	66	96	.407	-30.0

Wednesday, September 1
vs. Oakland, Won 4-3   **83-50, 1st, +1.0**
The Yankees won their fifth straight game with a 4-3 win vs. Oakland…scored all four runs over the first two innings, including three in the second…**RHP A.J. Burnett** earned his first win since 7/28 at Cleveland, holding the A's to 3ER in 6.0IP (6H, 2BB, 8K, 1HR)…matched his season high in strikeouts (third time, also 5/4 vs. BAL and 5/30 vs. CLE)…became the fifth Yankee to reach 10 wins this season…the Yankees bullpen combined for 3.0 scoreless innings…**1B Mark Teixeira** (3-for-4) reached base at least three times in a game for the third consecutive contest…**PH Lance Berkman** (1-for-1) doubled on the first pitch he saw as a pinch-hitter in the eighth after being returned from rehab and reinstated from the 15-day D.L. (right ankle sprain) prior to the game.

Thursday, September 2
vs. Oakland, Won 5-0   **84-50, 1st, +1.5**
The Yankees shut out the A's, 5-0, in the series finale to complete the four-game sweep...**LHP CC Sabathia** tossed 8.0 shutout innings, holding Oakland to just 1H with 3BB, 5K and 1HP, winning his Major League-leading 19th game and matching his career high...was the fourth time he was the starting and winning pitcher in a Yankees shutout in 2010...was his 16th straight win at home...**CF Curtis Granderson** (2-for-3) recorded his sixth career multi-homer game and second this season (also 7/25 vs. Kansas City)...entered the game in the second inning after **RF Nick Swisher** (0-for-1) left the game after the first inning with stiffness in his left knee...**C Jorge Posada** (2-for-3) hit his 17th HR of the season and fourth in his last 11 games.

Friday, September 3
vs. Toronto, Won 7-3   **85-50, 1st, +1.5**
The Yankees won their seventh straight game, defeating Toronto, 7-3...**LF Brett Gardner** (1-for-3) walked twice and scored a career-high-tying three runs (fourth time, second this season)...also tripled, his fifth of the season...**RHP Ivan Nova** started and did not draw a decision leaving after 4.2IP (6H, 3ER, 2BB, 1HR)...**Yankees relievers** combined for 4.1 hitless and scoreless innings (Logan, Robertson, Wood, Rivera)...**CF Curtis Granderson** (2-for-3) recorded his third straight multi-hit game and drove in three runs.

Saturday, September 4
vs. Toronto, Won 7-5   **86-50, 1st, +2.5**
The Yankees won their season-high eighth straight game, defeating the Blue Jays, 7-5...**DH Marcus Thames** (1-for-4) hit a go-ahead two-run home run in the seventh...**2B Robinson Cano** (2-for-4) drove in a pair of runs with a bases-loaded single...**C Francisco Cervelli** (2-for-4) had two doubles and scored twice...**RHP Javier Vazquez** (4.2IP, 4H, 5ER, 4BB, 6K, 2HR) started but did not earn a decision...**the Yankees bullpen** (Moseley, Logan, Chamberlain, Wood, Rivera) combined to toss 4.1 scoreless innings.

Sunday, September 5
vs. Toronto, Lost 3-7   **86-51, 1st, +2.5**
The Yankees had their eight-game winning streak snapped with a 7-3 loss vs. Toronto...**RHP Phil Hughes** took the loss, allowing 6ER in 6.0IP (7H, 1BB, 5K, 3HR)...matched his season high in earned runs allowed (third time) and matched his career high in homers allowed...two of the HRs came on 0-2 pitches...**3B Alex Rodriguez** (2-for-5) was activated from the D.L. prior to the game and also drove in a run...**LF Brett Gardner** (2-for-3) drew a walk in his 10th consecutive game with an AB...**2B Ramiro Pena** (2-for-3) extended his career high hitting streak to seven games.

Monday, September 6
vs. Baltimore, Lost 3-4   **86-52, 1st, +2.5**
The Yankees dropped their second straight, falling, 4-3, vs. Baltimore...was the Yankees' last game of five consecutive day games (went 3-2)...fell to 33-27 on Labor Day in the Expansion Era...**RHP A.J. Burnett** lost for the fifth time in his last seven starts, allowing 4ER on 7H in 7.0IP (4BB, 5K, 1WP)...**SS Derek Jeter** (1-for-4) recorded his 150th hit of the season with his first-inning double, extending his streak to 15 consecutive seasons reaching the plateau...**3B Alex Rodriguez** (1-for-2) hit his 605th career home run in the fourth and reached 100RBI for a record 14th season.

Tuesday, September 7
vs. Baltimore, Lost 2-6   **86-53, 1st, +1.5**
The Yankees lost their third straight, losing 6-2 vs. Baltimore...**LHP CC Sabathia** lost in his bid to record his 20th win of the season, allowing 5ER on 9H in 6.1IP (6R, 1BB, 5K, 1HR)...lost at Yankee Stadium for the first time since 7/2/09 vs. Seattle, snapping his 21-start undefeated stretch which remains tied with Whitey Ford (8/8/64-8/18/65) for the longest undefeated streak of starts at *any* stadium by a Yankee...**DH Lance Berkman** (3-for-4) tied his season high in hits (eighth time)...reached base to lead off the second, fifth and seventh innings, scoring just once (in the fifth).

Wednesday, September 8
vs. Baltimore, Won 3-2   **87-53, 1st, +2.5**
The Yankees won their series finale vs. Baltimore, 3-2, with a ninth-inning "walk-off" home run by **RF Nick Swisher** off Orioles closer Koji Uehara...Swisher (2-for-4) collected his second game-ending hit of the season and third career "walk-off" homer...**RHP Ivan Nova** limited the O's to 2ER – both coming on a Matt Wieters HR – in 6.0IP (6H, 2IBB, 6K, 2WP, 1HR)...retired 12 of his first 14 batters faced...**Yankees relievers** (Robertson, Logan and Chamberlain) combined for 3.0 hitless and scoreless innings (6K).

Thursday, September 9
Off day   **87-53, 1st, +2.5**

Friday, September 10
at Texas, Lost 5-6 (13 inn.)   **87-54, 1st, +1.5**
The Yankees suffered their third "walk-off" loss of the season, falling 6-5 in the 13th inning at Texas...both teams combined to use 19 pitchers in the game, setting an AL record...**RHP Chad Gaudin** (the Yankees' eighth pitcher of the night) suffered the loss, allowing the game-winning solo HR...**RHP Javier Vazquez** started and did not record a decision (5.0IP, 6H, 4ER, 2BB, 1K)...the Yankees scored four of their runs in the third inning...**3B Alex Rodriguez** (3-for-6) and **DH Marcus Thames** (3-for-6) led the Yankees offense with 3H apiece.

Saturday, September 11
at Texas, Lost 6-7   **87-55, 1st, +0.5**
The Yankees suffered their second straight "walk-off" loss, falling 7-6 at Texas...the game lasted 4 hours and 16 minutes with an additional 59 minute rain delay...**RHP Mariano Rivera** blew his third save of the season, allowing two runs in the bottom of the ninth, including a bases loaded HBP to force in the winning run, the first such occurrence in his career...was the first HBP to force in the game-ending run by a Yankees pitcher since Jim Kaat plunked Detroit's Steve Kemp with the bases loaded on 5/23/79 in a 4-3 loss at Tiger Stadium...**RHP A.J. Burnett** was forced out of the game by the rain after 4.0IP (4H, 2ER, 3BB, 6K, 1WP)...**3B Alex Rodriguez** (1-for-4) had a bases-clearing double in the eighth.

Sunday, September 12
at Texas, Lost 1-4   **87-56, 1st, +0.5**
The Yankees suffered the series sweep, dropping the finale 4-1...were held to just 2H, matching their season low (fourth time)...**SS Derek Jeter** (1-for-2) walked twice and doubled home **3B Eduardo Nunez** (1-for-3) for the Yankees' lone run of the game...**CF Curtis Granderson** (0-for-3) walked in the sixth, accounting for the Yankees' only other baserunner in the contest...**RHP Dustin Moseley** allowed 4ER in 6.2IP in the starting effort (5H, 2BB, 1K), holding the Rangers scoreless over his first five frames.

Monday, September 13
at Tampa Bay, Lost 0-1 (11 inn.)   **87-57, 2nd, -0.5**
The Yankees suffered a 1-0 "walk-off" loss in the 11th inning...marked the eighth time the Yankees were shut out this season, fifth time on the road and the sixth time ever vs. Tampa Bay (second this season – also 8/1 at Tropicana Field)...marked the Yankees' second 1-0, extra-inning loss in the last 20 years (also 5/18/04 at the Angels, 11 inn.)...**LHP CC Sabathia** tossed 8.0 scoreless innings, limiting the Rays to 2H with 2BB and 9K...was denied his 20th win of the season for the second straight start...opposed David Price (17-6), marking the first game since 9/11/85 in which each starting pitcher had at least 17 wins and went at least eight scoreless innings...according the *Elias*, in that game John Tudor (17-8) threw a 10.0-inning shutout at the Mets against Dwight Gooden who entered the game 20-4...all four Yankees (Jeter, Cano, Kearns, Granderson) hits were singles...no Yankees reached third base.

Tuesday, September 14
at Tampa Bay, Won 8-7 (10 inn.)   **88-57, 1st, +0.5**
The Yankees won, 8-7, in 10 innings at Tampa Bay, snapping their season-high-tying four-game losing streak...was the Yankees' 13th win in their last at-bat this season and second straight...**PH/C Jorga Posada** (1-for-1) hit a go-ahead pinch-hit HR, the fifth of his career, in the top of the 10th for the game-winning run...the Yankees led 6-0 at one point...**2B Robinson Cano** (3-for-4) collected his team-high 16th 3H game this season, also hitting a two-run HR...**3B Alex Rodriguez** (2-for-6) hit his 606th career homer...**RHP Ivan Nova** (4.2IP, 6H, 6ER, 3BB, 2K, 1HR) did not record a decision in his fifth start...Yankees relievers (**Logan**, **Chamberlain**, **Wood**, **Robertson** and **Rivera**) combined to allow just 1ER in 5.1IP (2H, 1BB, 7K, 1HR)...**RF Greg Golson** (0-for-0) who entered defensively in the 10th inning, threw out Carl Crawford at third base to end the game.

Wednesday, September 15
at Tampa Bay, Lost 3-4   **88-58, 2nd, -0.5**
The Yankees fell in the series finale at Tampa Bay, losing 4-3...all three games in the series were decided by one run...**CF Curtis Granderson** (1-for-5) hit a go-ahead two-run homer in the seventh...**2B Robinson Cano** (3-for-4) recorded his second straight 3H game–and team-high 17th the season...drove in the Yankees' first run with a bases-loaded single in the first...**RHP Phil Hughes** lost his second straight decision, allowing 4ER on 6H in 6.2IP with no walks and 5K...all four runs were surrendered on two, two-run homers by Dan Johnson.

Thursday, September 16
Off Day   **88-58, 2nd, -0.5**

Friday, September 17
at Baltimore, Won 4-3   **89-58, 1st, +0.5**
The Yankees came away with a 4-3 win at Baltimore after **3B Alex Rodriguez** (2-for-5) hit a two-strike, two-out, three-run homer in the top of the ninth off closer Koji Uehara to bring the Yankees back from a 3-1 deficit...was his second homer of the game after a solo HR in the second inning off Kevin Millwood, driving in all four Yankees runs in the game...**RHP A.J. Burnett** did not record a decision after holding the Orioles to 3ER in 7.0IP (6H, 1BB, 5K, 2HR, 2HP)...**2B Robinson Cano** (2-for-5) collected his third straight multi-hit game.

Saturday, September 18
at Baltimore, Won 11-3   **90-58, 1st, +0.5**
The Yankees won their second straight game, defeating Baltimore 11-3...**LHP CC Sabathia** earned his career-high 20th win, becoming the first pitcher to reach the mark in 2010 and the first Yankees lefty to reach the plateau since Andy Pettitte in 2003...limited the Orioles to 3ER in 7.0IP (7H, 1BB, 4K, 1HR)...**2B Robinson Cano** (2-for-4) collected his fourth straight multi-hit game...also connected for his 28th HR of the season...**SS Derek Jeter** (2-for-3) reached base four times (also 2BB) and score a pair of runs...**LF Brett Gardner** (3-for-5) fell a homer shy of the cycle, also scoring 2R.

Sunday, September 19
at Baltimore, Lost 3-4 (10 inn.)   **90-59, 1st, +0.5**
The Yankees completed their nine-game road trip with a 4-3 loss in 11 innings at Baltimore...**LHP Andy Pettitte** made his first start since 7/18, limiting the Orioles to 1ER on 3H in 6.0IP with 1BB and 2K in the no-decision...exited with a 3-1 lead...**RHP Mariano Rivera** (1.0IP, 2H, 1ER, 1K) suffered his fourth blown save of the season, allowing a game-tying homer in the ninth...all eight of the Yankees' hits were singles...also drew 9BB...**2B Robinson Cano** (2-for-4) collected his fifth consecutive multi-hit game, hitting safely in his 12th straight game vs. Baltimore and 13th consecutive game at Camden Yards.

Monday, September 20
vs. Tampa Bay, Won 8-6   **91-59, 1st, +1.5**
The Yankees began their final homestand with an 8-6 win vs. Tampa Bay...**CF Curtis Granderson** (2-for-3) collected his seventh career multi-homer game (third this season) and tied his career high with 5RBI (third time, first since 4/4/07 vs. Toronto)...**C Francisco Cervelli** (3-for-4) tied his career high with 3H and became the first Yankees catcher with 3H and 3R in a game since Jose Molina on 8/2/08 vs. the Angels...**RHP Ivan Nova** (5.2IP, 3H, 3ER, 2BB, 4K) started but did not record a decision, retiring 15 of his first 17 batters faced...**RHP Mariano Rivera** (1.0IP, 2H, 1ER) improved to 57-for-58 in career save chances against Tampa Bay.
• Prior to the game, the Yankees held a ceremony to dedicate and unveil a monument in honor of George M. Steinbrenner III, in Yankee Stadium's Monument Park...Frank Sinatra Jr., sang the national anthem...Mr. Steinbrenner's granddaughter, Haley Swindal, sang "God Bless America" during the seventh-inning stretch.

Tuesday, September 21
vs. Tampa Bay, Won 8-3   **92-59, 1st, +2.5**
The Yankees won their second straight game, defeating the Rays 8-3...the Yankees scored five runs in the first inning, batting around in the 20-minute bottom of the frame...the scoring began with **RF Nick Swisher** (2-for-5) hitting a solo homer...the Yankees went 5-for-10 with RISP...**RHP Phil Hughes** had his 17th win, holding the Rays to 4H and 3ER in 6.1IP (5BB, 6K, 1HR, 1WP) to become the first Yankee to win at least 17 games in a season at age 24 or younger since Andy Pettitte (21 wins in 1996)...**RHP Joba Chamberlain** (1.2IP, 1H, 1K) recorded his third save of the season.

Wednesday, September 22
vs. Tampa Bay, Lost 2-7   **92-60, 1st, +1.5**
The Yankees fell to the Rays, 7-2, at Yankee Stadium in a game that was interrupted by a 2 hour, 11 minute minute rain delay...**RHP A.J. Burnett** suffered the loss, allowing 1ER in just 3.0IP (2H, 2BB, 2K)...was the second time in his last three starts he had a

rain-shortened outing (also 9/11 at Texas)...Yankees relievers combined to allow 6ER in 6.0IP, their most allowed since 7/17...**DH Lance Berkman** (2-for-4) hit his first home run as a Yankee in the fifth inning, the team's first hit of the game...**SS Derek Jeter** (2-for-4) extended his hitting streak to 11 games and scored a run in the sixth inning – the 1,678th of his career, surpassing Mickey Mantle (1,677) for sole possession of third place in franchise history.

Thursday, September 23
vs. Tampa Bay, Lost 3-10   92-61, 1st, +0.5
The Yankees fell in the series finale vs. Tampa Bay, 10-3...surrendered seven runs in the sixth inning, matching their season high (third time)...**LHP CC Sabathia** allowed 7ER in 5.1IP (10H, 3BB, 6K), losing his second straight home start...marked his most earned runs allowed as a Yankee...**DH/LF Marcus Thames** (1-for-4) put the Yankees on the board first with a two-run home run...**LF/CF Greg Golson** (2-for-4) collected his first career multi-hit game...**SS Derek Jeter** extended his hitting streak to 12 games.

Friday, September 24
vs. Boston, Lost 8-10   92-62, 2nd, -0.5
The Yankees lost their third straight, falling to Boston, 10-8 at Yankee Stadium...hit a season-high 6HR in the losing effort, marking the third such occurrence in club history...**3B Alex Rodriguez** (2-for-4) and **1B Mark Teixeira** (2-for-4) each homered twice in the game...with 2HR, **Rodriguez** tied and surpassed Sammy Sosa (609) for sixth on the all-time list...**CF Curtis Granderson** (3-for-4) and **RF Nick Swisher** (1-for-5) also went deep...**SS Derek Jeter** (1-for-4) extended his hitting streak to 13 games...**LHP Andy Pettitte** allowed 7R (6ER) on 10H in 3.1IP in the losing effort (0BB, 1K, 1HR)...marked a season-high in hits allowed and tied a season high in runs and earned runs surrendered.

Saturday, September 25
vs. Boston, Lost 3-7   92-63, 2nd, -1.5
The Yankees lost their fourth straight game, falling 7-3 vs. Boston...was their season-high fourth straight home defeat...were held hitless by Jon Lester until **C Francisco Cervelli** (1-for-2) had a one out single in the sixth...**CF Curtis Granderson** (1-for-3) put the Yankees on the board in the eighth with his second homer in as many games...**3B Alex Rodriguez** (1-for-3) homered in the ninth, the 611th of his career...**SS Derek Jeter** (1-for-4) extended his season-high hitting streak to 14 games...**RHP Ivan Nova** (4.2IP, 4H, 4ER, 3BB, 2K, 1HP) suffered his first career loss.

Sunday, September 26
vs. Boston, Won 4-3 (10 inn.)   93-63, 2nd, -0.5
The Yankees recorded their fifth "walk-off" win of the season in the 10th inning with a bases-loaded walk of **1B Juan Miranda** to force in the winning run...**3B Alex Rodriguez** (1-for-3) put the Yankees ahead in the seventh with a two-run home run, the 612th of his career...**2B Robinson Cano** (2-for-4) collected his team-leading 57th multi-hit game and sent the game into extra innings with a bases loaded single in the ninth off Jonathan Papelbon...**RHP Phil Hughes** started and limited the Red Sox to 1ER in 6.0IP in the no-decision (3H, 4BB, 4K)...**RHP Mariano Rivera** (1.1IP, 2H, 2ER) suffered his third blown save of September and fifth of the season, allowing 2ER in the ninth in which the Red Sox stole four bases, including third base twice...was his third straight outing allowing at least one run.

Monday, September 27
at Toronto, Lost 5-7   93-64, 2nd, -0.5
The Yankees lost in their first attempt to clinch a playoff spot, falling, 7-5, at Toronto...trailed 7-0 after three innings...**RHP A.J. Burnett** suffered his 15th loss of the season, allowing 7ER in 2.1IP (7H, 1BB, 1K, 2HR)...became the Yankees'first 15-game loser since Melido Perez went 13-16 in 1992...**CF Curtis Granderson** (1-for-4) homered for the third time in his last four games...**1B Mark Teixeira** (2-for-5) hit a three-run homer in the seventh.

Tuesday, September 28
at Toronto, Won 6-1   94-64, 2nd, -0.5
The Yankees clinched a postseason berth with a 6-1 win at Toronto...all six runs scored on plays that did not involve a hit (3SF, one fielder's choice, one RBI groundout and 1BB with the bases loaded)...**LHP CC Sabathia** earned win No. 21 of the season, limiting the Jays to 3H and 1ER in 8.1IP (2BB, 8K, 1HR)...**SS Derek Jeter** (2-for-4) scored three runs, tying a season high (sixth time), and drove in a run...**LF Brett Gardner** (2-for-4) recorded the Yankees' other multi-hit effort...**2B Robinson Cano** (0-for-3) collected his 500th career RBI with an eighth-inning sacrifice fly.

Wednesday, September 29
at Toronto, Lost 4-8   94-65, 2nd, -0.5
The Yankees fell in their final game against Toronto in 2010, 8-4...**3B Alex Rodriguez** (1-for-5) hit his 30th home run of the season to put the Yankees on the board in the sixth...**C Francisco Cervelli** (3-for-3) recorded his second three-hit game in his last five contests...**RHP Javier Vazquez** (4.2IP, 10H, 7ER, 2BB, 0K, 3HR) suffered the loss in a spot start.

Thursday, September 30
Off Day   94-65, T1st, --

Friday, October 1
at Boston, Rain out   94-65, 1st, +0.5

Saturday, October 2
at Boston   95-66, T1st, --
The Yankees and Red Sox split a doubleheader at Fenway Park that included a combined 8 hours, 18 minutes of baseball, 775 pitches, 23 different pitchers, 50 runners left on base, 49K and 31BB...**LF Brett Gardner** played all 20 innings, becoming the first player in franchise history to steal five bases in a single day (credit: *Elias*).
   The Yankees won Game 1, 6-5, in 10 innings...Yankees pitchers combined to strike out 18, tying their third-highest single-game total...**LHP Andy Pettitte** (4.0IP, 9H, 3ER, 2BB, 8K) started and did not earn a decision...**RHP Phil Hughes** (1.0IP, 2K) earned his18th win in relief...**LF Brett Gardner** (0-for-3) scored the winning run on an infield hit by **SS Derek Jeter** (2-for-5)...**2B Robinson Cano** (3-for-5) had 2 doubles and 1HR.
   The Yankees fell in Game 2, 7-6, in 10 innings...committed a season-high 4E, including three in the fourth, leading to two unearned runs...**RHP Ivan Nova** (2.1IP, 4H, 1ER, 3BB, 1K) allowed the game-winning run...**RHP A.J. Burnett** started and allowed 2ER in 6.0IP (6H, 4R, 2BB, 5K)...**C Francisco Cervelli** (2-for-3) had two, two-out RBI...**LF Brett Gardner** (1-for-5) matched a single-game career high with 3SB (also 5/26/09 at Texas).

Sunday, October 3   95-67, 2nd, -1.0
at Boston,
The Yankees fell in the regular season finale, 8-4, at Fenway Park...**DH Robinson Cano** (1-for-4) had an RBI single in his final AB, reaching 200H for the season...**RF Nick Swisher** (1-for-3) hit his 29th HR of the season...**RHP Dustin Moseley** started and suffered the loss, allowing 4ER on two, two-run home runs in 5.0IP (5H, 2BB, 3K).

Yankees vs. Minnesota

IN THE POSTSEASON: Overall: 9-2
at home: 4-2   **(at original Yankee Stadium:** 2-2; **at current Yankee Stadium:** 2-0)
at Minnesota (all games played at the Metrodome): 5-0

The Yankees and Twins have played each other three times in postseason play, meeting in the 2003, 2004 and 2009 American League Division Series…swept Minnesota in last year's ALDS, en route to their 27th World Championship…the Yankees have lost just two of 11 all-time postseason games vs. the Twins and have won the last six postseason games against Minnesota…never lost a postseason game in the Metrodome, winning the final game in the building, 4-1, to complete their 2009 ALDS sweep.

IN 2010: 4-2
at Yankee Stadium: 2-1   **at Target Field:** 2-1

The Yankees were 4-2 against the Twins in 2010, playing all six games over a 14-day span from 5/14-27…won the season series for the fourth straight year (2007-10) and recorded their ninth straight non-losing season series (2002-10) against Minnesota…their loss on 5/16 at Yankee Stadium snapped a streak of 12 consecutive home wins vs. Minnesota, including the postseason…have won 11 of their last 13 regular season games against Minnesota and 14 of their last 16 overall games including the 2009 ALDS…the Yankees are 25-8 against the Twins in both regular season and postseason contests since 2007 and 54-18 since the start of the 2002 season.

NYY vs. MINNESOTA in 2010				
Date	**H/A**	**W/L**	**Score**	**Record**
5/14	at NYY	W	8-4	1-0
5/15	at NYY	W	7-1	2-0
5/16	at NYY	L	3-6	2-1
5/25	at MIN	W	1-0	3-1
5/26	at MIN	W	3-2	4-1
5/27	at MIN	L	2-8	4-2
Total in 2010			**24-21**	**4-2**

The Yankees won two out of three vs. the Twins at home from 5/14-16, winning their ninth consecutive home season series vs. the Twins (2002-10)…took two of three games in their first-ever visit to Target Field from 5/25-27 and have won 11 of their last 17 regular season games in Minnesota and 28 of their last 44 overall games in Minnesota (regular and postseason) since 2000.

BATTER	2010								Career							
	AVG	**G**	**AB**	**R**	**H**	**HR**	**RBI**	**BB**	**SO**	**AVG**	**G**	**AB**	**R**	**H**	**HR**	**RBI**	**BB**	**SO**
Berkman	---	-	-	-	-	-	-	-	-	.293	12	41	7	12	5	13	2	6
Cano	.348	6	23	0	8	0	3	0	2	.321	42	165	25	53	5	22	6	17
Cervelli	.188	5	16	2	3	0	1	2	4	.320	9	25	3	8	0	4	2	5
Gardner	.240	6	25	3	6	1	2	1	6	.288	14	52	9	15	2	9	2	12
Golson	1.000	3	1	0	1	0	0	0	0	1.000	3	1	0	1	0	0	0	0
Granderson	---	-	-	-	-	-	-	-	-	.294	82	309	47	91	16	37	32	69
Jeter	.321	6	28	3	9	1	2	0	4	.322	110	451	73	145	11	52	45	78
Kearns	.286	7	21	0	6	0	2	2	8	.273	10	33	0	9	0	2	4	10
Miranda	.077	5	13	1	1	0	0	0	2	.077	5	13	1	1	0	0	0	2
Nunez	---	-	-	-	-	-	-	-	-	---	-	-	-	-	-	-	-	-
Pena	.500	1	4	1	2	0	0	0	0	.273	5	11	3	3	0	0	0	1
Posada	.714	2	7	3	5	1	2	1	2	.299	69	241	33	72	8	31	28	62
Rodriguez	.273	6	22	2	6	1	5	2	5	.328	128	488	102	160	45	115	61	82
Swisher	.235	6	17	2	4	1	1	1	6	.254	57	181	27	46	10	28	27	44
Teixeira	.400	6	25	4	10	1	4	1	3	.374	54	222	39	83	16	46	15	36
Thames	.300	4	10	2	3	0	1	1	4	.257	67	202	26	52	15	27	12	62
TOTALS	**.297**	**6**	**209**	**24**	**62**	**6**	**24**	**9**	**41**							

PITCHER	2010											Career									
	W-L	**ERA**	**G**	**GS**	**SV**	**IP**	**H**	**R**	**ER**	**BB**	**SO**	**W-L**	**ERA**	**G**	**GS**	**SV**	**IP**	**H**	**R**	**ER**	**BB**	**SO**
Burnett	1-0	1.54	2	2	0	11.2	10	3	2	6	9	3-1	3.22	8	8	0	50.1	44	20	18	25	50
Chamberlain	1-1	9.00	3	0	0	3.0	3	3	3	2	5	1-1	5.00	4	1	0	9.0	6	5	5	6	11
Gaudin	0-0	5.40	1	0	0	1.2	2	1	1	1	3	2-1	4.19	6	3	0	19.1	23	9	9	13	11
Hughes	-	---	-	-	-	-	-	-	-	-	-	0-0	3.68	3	1	0	7.1	7	3	3	4	4
Logan	0-0	4.50	1	0	0	2.0	4	1	1	0	1	0-0	9.64	17	0	0	14.0	25	16	15	7	10
Mitre	0-0	1.80	1	1	0	5.0	4	1	1	1	3	0-0	1.80	1	1	0	5.0	4	1	1	1	3
Moseley	-	---	-	-	-	-	-	-	-	-	-	0-0	5.68	4	1	0	6.1	9	4	4	2	5
Nova	0-0	0.00	1	0	0	1.0	2	0	0	0	0	0-0	0.00	1	0	0	1.0	2	0	0	0	0
Pettitte	2-0	1.26	2	2	0	14.1	10	2	2	3	6	11-5	3.46	21	21	0	145.2	148	63	56	45	110
Ring	-	---	-	-	-	-	-	-	-	-	-	-	---	-	-	-	-	-	-	-	-	-
Rivera	0-0	5.40	4	0	2	3.1	1	2	2	2	1	4-3	1.42	47	1	28	63.1	41	11	10	13	60
Robertson	0-0	0.00	3	0	0	4.0	3	0	0	4	2	1-0	0.00	7	0	0	8.1	4	0	0	7	6
Sabathia	-	---	-	-	-	-	-	-	-	-	-	13-8	3.05	28	28	0	191.2	173	74	65	62	143
Vazquez	0-1	7.94	1	1	0	5.2	8	5	5	3	2	6-7	5.26	17	17	0	106.0	117	63	62	24	83
Wood	-	---	-	-	-	-	-	-	-	-	-	1-1	2.93	8	2	4	15.1	10	9	5	10	18
TOTALS	**4-2**	**3.40**	**6**	**6**	**2**	**53.0**	**51**	**21**	**20**	**24**	**33**											

Yankees vs. Tampa Bay

IN THE POSTSEASON:
The Yankees and Rays have never met in the postseason.

IN 2010: 8-10
at Yankee Stadium: 4-5 **at Tropicana Field:** 4-5
The Yankees lost the season series vs. Tampa Bay, 8-10, marking just their second season series loss in the 13-year history of the Tampa Bay franchise (also 2005, 8-11)...the Yankees' .641 (141-79) winning percentage against the Rays is the highest of any AL club vs. Tampa Bay all time...went 4-5 this season at Tampa Bay, losing the road season series for just the second time (also 2-4 in 2000)...marked their most losses at Tropicana Field since 2005 (5-5)...went 4-5 at home vs. the Rays, losing the home season series for just the second time (also 3-6 in 2005).

NYY vs. TAMPA BAY in 2010				
Date	H/A	W/L	Score	Record
4/9	at TB	L	3-9	0-1
4/10	at TB	W	10-0	1-1
4/11	at TB	W	7-3	2-1
5/19	at NYY	L	6-10	2-2
5/20	at NYY	L	6-8	2-3
7/16	at NYY	W	5-4	3-3
7/17	at NYY	L	5-10	3-4
7/18	at NYY	W	9-5	4-4
7/30	at TB	L	2-3	4-5
7/31	at TB	W	5-4	5-5
8/1	at TB	L	0-3	5-6
9/13	at TB	L	0-1 (11)	5-7
9/14	at TB	W	8-7 (10)	6-7
9/15	at TB	L	3-4	6-8
9/20	at NYY	W	8-6	7-8
9/21	at NYY	W	8-3	8-8
9/22	at NYY	L	2-7	8-9
9/23	at NYY	L	3-10	8-10
Total in 2010			**90-97**	**8-10**

				2010									Career					
BATTER	AVG	G	AB	R	H	HR	RBI	BB	SO	AVG	G	AB	R	H	HR	RBI	BB	SO
Berkman	.290	10	31	3	9	2	4	6	4	.235	16	51	8	12	3	10	8	10
Cano	.378	18	74	11	28	4	14	3	11	.323	99	375	57	121	15	63	18	52
Cervelli	.250	8	24	3	6	0	5	6	4	.194	15	31	3	6	0	5	6	5
Gardner	.195	16	41	7	8	0	4	8	7	.169	34	83	16	14	0	6	10	23
Golson	.333	4	6	1	2	0	0	0	0	.333	4	6	1	2	0	0	0	0
Granderson	.228	16	57	9	13	3	11	7	18	.256	47	172	28	44	6	24	21	48
Jeter	.301	18	83	13	25	0	6	2	11	.311	209	855	166	266	19	115	73	130
Kearns	.244	11	45	3	11	0	3	1	16	.267	17	60	6	16	2	6	4	19
Nunez	.000	1	1	0	0	0	0	0	0	.000	1	1	0	0	0	0	0	0
Pena	.250	5	4	1	1	0	2	0	0	.286	15	21	3	6	0	3	3	1
Posada	.250	12	36	5	9	4	8	8	12	.261	176	587	76	153	22	107	97	129
Rodriguez	.250	18	68	13	17	3	11	8	16	.277	173	676	127	187	44	133	75	147
Swisher	.364	15	55	9	20	5	11	6	16	.306	66	235	47	72	18	42	40	63
Teixeira	.162	18	68	9	11	2	6	11	15	.264	79	295	49	78	16	53	37	63
Thames	.200	6	15	1	3	1	2	2	3	.281	34	96	8	27	5	13	6	32
TOTALS	**.256**	**18**	**620**	**90**	**159**	**24**	**87**	**71**	**139**									

				2010									Career					
PITCHER	W-L	ERA	G	GS	SV	IP	H	R	ER	BB	SO	W-L	ERA	G	GS	SV	IP	H	R	ER	BB	SO
Burnett	1-3	6.27	4	4	0	18.2	21	13	13	9	8	12-7	3.15	25	25	0	168.1	128	63	59	57	164
Chamberlain	0-0	2.89	7	0	1	9.1	8	3	3	1	12	1-0	2.02	18	3	1	35.2	23	8	8	8	32
Gaudin	1-0	5.40	8	0	0	10.0	11	6	6	6	12	2-2	4.06	14	3	0	31.0	32	15	14	16	36
Hughes	1-2	4.74	3	3	0	19.0	14	10	10	7	17	3-3	4.50	10	5	0	34.0	30	18	17	14	28
Logan	0-0	10.38	6	0	0	4.1	6	5	5	2	5	0-0	7.36	12	0	0	11.0	13	10	9	5	10
Mitre	0-1	7.71	2	0	0	2.1	3	2	2	0	1	1-1	3.86	3	1	0	9.1	8	5	4	0	4
Moseley	0-0	10.38	2	0	0	4.1	10	5	5	3	2	0-0	16.20	3	0	0	5.0	12	9	9	5	2
Nova	0-0	6.97	2	2	0	10.1	9	9	8	5	6	0-0	6.97	2	2	0	10.1	9	9	8	5	6
Pettitte	0-1	11.05	2	2	0	7.1	15	10	9	5	6	16-6	4.11	31	30	0	177.1	203	92	81	59	144
Ring	0-0	5.40	1	0	0	1.2	0	1	1	1	2	0-0	5.40	1	0	0	1.2	0	1	1	1	2
Rivera	1-0	1.69	6	0	3	5.1	6	1	1	1	3	3-5	1.63	89	0	57	94.0	68	18	17	23	103
Robertson	2-0	1.04	7	0	0	8.2	4	1	1	0	13	2-0	2.19	11	0	1	12.1	8	3	3	0	15
Sabathia	1-2	3.38	5	5	0	34.2	29	14	13	14	29	8-5	3.24	20	20	0	139.0	121	60	50	45	126
Vazquez	0-1	7.88	4	2	0	16.0	20	14	14	6	11	5-5	4.97	16	14	0	92.1	99	51	51	29	79
Wood	0-1	1.35	7	0	0	6.2	4	1	1	6	8	0-1	1.00	10	0	1	9.0	5	1	1	7	10
TOTALS	**8-10**	**5.29**	**18**	**18**	**4**	**160.0**	**163**	**97**	**94**	**66**	**139**											

Yankees vs. Texas

IN THE POSTSEASON: Overall: 9-1
at original Yankee Stadium: 5-1 **at Rangers Ballpark:** 4-0

The Yankees and Rangers have met three times in postseason play with the Yankees defeating Texas in the ALDS in 1996 (3-1), '98 (3-0) and '99 (3-0)…the Yankees have won nine straight postseason games against the Rangers, including shutout victories in four of the last six meetings…according to the *Elias Sports Bureau*, is their longest postseason winning streak against any opponent in franchise history and the longest current winning streak between any teams…all three Yankees wins in 1996 were come-from-behind…in 1998, the Yankees outscored the Rangers, 9-1, in the series, throwing shutouts in Game 1 and Game 3…in 1999, the Yankees again shutout the Rangers in Game 1 and Game 3, outscoring Texas, 14-1 overall.

IN 2010: 4-4
at Yankee Stadium: 3-0 **at Rangers Ballpark:** 1-4

The Yankees and Rangers split the 2010 season series, marking the Yankees' sixth non-losing season series in the last seven seasons…swept a three-game series vs. Texas from 4/16-18, in the Rangers' only trip to the Bronx in 2010…have won 18 of their last 29 regular season home games vs. Texas…have outscored the Rangers 77-45 over their last 10 home games…made two trips to Rangers Ballpark, splitting a two-game set from 8/10-11 and getting swept in a three-game series from 9/10-12…four of the five games between the teams in Texas were decided by one run, including two extra-inning games and three "walk-off" wins by the Rangers…the Yankees own the best winning percentage by any AL club in the history of Rangers Ballpark (44-32, .579).

NYY vs. TEXAS in 2010				
Date	H/A	W/L	Score	Record
4/16	at NYY	W	5-1 (6)	1-0
4/17	at NYY	W	7-3	2-0
4/18	at NYY	W	5-2	3-0
8/10	at TEX	L	3-4 (10)	3-1
8/11	at TEX	W	7-6	4-1
9/10	at TEX	L	5-6 (13)	4-2
9/11	at TEX	L	6-7	4-3
9/12	at TEX	L	1-4	4-4
Total in 2010			**39-33**	**4-4**

	2010								Career								
BATTER	AVG	G	AB	R	H	HR	RBI	BB	SO	AVG	G	AB	R	H	HR	RBI	BB	SO
Berkman	.226	11	31	3	7	1	4	9	7	.283	64	230	34	65	11	39	36	49
Cano	.233	8	30	3	7	0	1	2	4	.309	44	181	28	56	4	26	8	18
Cervelli	.556	4	9	2	5	0	4	6	1	.412	6	17	3	7	0	5	6	2
Gardner	.333	7	21	5	7	0	2	3	6	.326	16	46	10	15	0	4	6	11
Golson	.000	3	3	0	0	0	0	0	0	.000	3	3	0	0	0	0	0	0
Granderson	.200	8	20	2	4	0	1	5	7	.236	42	148	27	35	7	25	28	34
Jeter	.385	6	26	4	10	1	5	3	4	.318	130	532	97	169	22	84	62	101
Kearns	.231	9	26	3	6	0	0	3	10	.250	12	36	5	9	0	1	6	13
Nunez	.500	3	4	1	2	0	0	0	0	.500	3	4	1	2	0	0	0	0
Pena	.100	4	10	0	1	0	2	0	1	.158	8	19	1	3	0	2	1	3
Posada	.250	6	16	4	4	1	1	1	5	.308	94	302	60	93	18	71	58	71
Rodriguez	.360	7	25	5	9	2	8	7	8	.316	109	412	87	130	18	76	63	92
Swisher	.103	7	29	3	3	0	1	2	12	.246	79	289	58	71	16	49	47	83
Teixeira	.167	6	24	4	4	1	3	3	6	.263	27	95	22	25	5	23	14	18
Thames	.435	6	23	3	10	1	3	0	10	.330	31	88	15	29	5	13	8	23
TOTALS	**.301**	**18**	**662**	**101**	**199**	**31**	**99**	**79**	**126**									

	2010									Career									
PITCHER	W-L	ERA	G	GS	SV	IP	H	R	ER	BB	SO	W-L	ERA	G	GS	SV	IP	H	R	ER	BB	SO
Burnett	1-0	2.50	3	3	0	18.0	16	5	5	7	17	4-3	3.66	12	11	0	71.1	62	29	29	25	78
Chamberlain	0-0	4.50	2	0	0	2.0	1	1	1	1	2	0-1	8.68	6	4	0	18.2	27	18	18	14	23
Gaudin	0-1	14.73	3	0	0	3.2	8	6	6	0	1	4-7	5.89	24	8	0	65.2	77	44	43	32	53
Hughes	0-0	0.00	1	0	0	1.0	0	0	0	0	1	2-0	0.00	3	2	0	15.1	3	0	0	4	13
Logan	0-0	0.00	3	0	0	0.2	0	0	0	2	2	0-2	14.29	10	0	0	5.2	15	11	9	4	5
Mitre	0-0	0.00	1	0	0	1.2	0	0	0	0	1	0-0	0.00	1	0	0	1.2	0	0	0	0	1
Moseley	0-1	5.40	1	1	0	6.2	5	4	4	2	1	0-2	5.46	10	5	0	31.1	39	19	19	12	16
Nova	-	---	-	-	-	-	-	-	-	-	-	0-0	---	-	-	-	-	-	-	-	-	-
Pettitte	1-0	2.25	1	1	0	8.0	4	2	2	3	4	11-9	5.24	23	23	0	146.0	178	93	85	51	105
Ring	-	---	-	-	-	-	-	-	-	-	-	0-0	0.00	2	0	0	1.1	0	0	0	0	1
Rivera	0-2	5.79	5	0	2	4.2	7	3	3	3	4	5-4	2.49	64	1	34	79.2	82	24	22	22	56
Robertson	0-0	2.25	3	0	0	4.0	3	1	1	3	2	1-0	3.00	10	0	0	12.0	5	4	4	9	14
Sabathia	1-0	1.50	1	1	0	6.0	3	1	1	0	9	8-3	4.29	14	14	0	86.0	89	44	41	33	77
Vazquez	0-0	9.64	2	2	0	9.1	14	10	10	4	2	2-2	6.64	7	7	0	40.2	49	30	30	11	36
Wood	1-0	0.00	3	0	0	4.0	3	0	0	1	2	1-0	1.80	4	0	0	5.0	5	1	1	2	5
TOTALS	**4-4**	**4.20**	**8**	**8**	**2**	**70.2**	**64**	**33**	**33**	**28**	**51**											

Yankees vs. Atlanta

IN THE POSTSEASON: Overall: 15-9
at original Yankee Stadium: 7-5
at Milwaukee: 3-4　　　**at Atlanta:** 5-0

The Yankees have played the Braves four times in the World Series, twice while the club was in Milwaukee (1957 and '58) and twice in their current location in Atlanta (1996 and '99)…lost the '57 Series but have won their last three postseason series.

The 1957 World Series went the distance with the Yankees falling in Game 7 on a 5-0 shutout…in a rematch the next year, the Yankees lost the first two games, but came back and emerged victorious in the deciding Game 7…the two teams would not meet again until 1996, when the Yankees again came back after being down 2-games-to-0 to win the final four games of the Series, and win their first championship since 1978…the 1999 Fall Classic saw a four-game sweep by the Yankees, extending the franchise's World Series winning streak to 12 games.

IN 2010:

Did not meet…the Yankees hold a 12-10 advantage in regular season Interleague play, traveling to Atlanta in 1998, 2000 and 2009 and hosting the Braves in the Bronx in 1997, 1998, 1999, 2001 and 2006.

| | | | 2010 | | | | | | | | | Career | | | | | |
BATTER	AVG	G	AB	R	H	HR	RBI	BB	SO	AVG	G	AB	R	H	HR	RBI	BB	SO
Berkman	.000	1	5	0	0	0	1	2	1	.292	58	195	33	57	12	45	33	33
Cano	---	-	-	-	-	-	-	-	-	.143	2	7	0	1	0	0	1	1
Cervelli	---	-	-	-	-	-	-	-	-	.333	1	3	1	1	1	1	1	0
Gardner	---	-	-	-	-	-	-	-	-	.250	3	12	1	3	0	0	2	2
Golson	---	-	-	-	-	-	-	-	-	---	2	0	1	0	0	0	0	0
Granderson	---	-	-	-	-	-	-	-	-	.091	3	11	1	1	0	0	0	6
Jeter	---	-	-	-	-	-	-	-	-	.344	22	96	20	33	2	7	11	14
Kearns	---	-	-	-	-	-	-	-	-	.219	71	242	31	53	4	35	34	61
Nunez	---	-	-	-	-	-	-	-	-	---	-	-	-	-	-	-	-	-
Pena	---	-	-	-	-	-	-	-	-	---	-	-	-	-	-	-	-	-
Posada	---	-	-	-	-	-	-	-	-	.213	15	47	6	10	1	4	7	13
Rodriguez	---	-	-	-	-	-	-	-	-	.300	12	50	8	15	2	9	6	7
Swisher	---	-	-	-	-	-	-	-	-	.160	6	25	3	4	1	2	3	5
Teixeira	---	-	-	-	-	-	-	-	-	.188	9	32	7	6	2	4	10	10
Thames	---	-	-	-	-	-	-	-	-	.000	2	3	0	0	0	0	0	0

| | | | 2010 | | | | | | | | | Career | | | | | |
PITCHER	W-L	ERA	G	GS	SV	IP	H	R	ER	BB	SO	W-L	ERA	G	GS	SV	IP	H	R	ER	BB	SO
Burnett	-	---	-	-	-	-	-	-	-	-	-	5-9	3.74	18	17	0	98.2	90	50	41	48	88
Chamberlain	-	---	-	-	-	-	-	-	-	-	-	1-0	2.84	1	1	0	6.1	7	3	2	0	5
Gaudin	-	---	-	-	-	-	-	-	-	-	-	0-1	8.53	3	1	0	6.1	10	6	6	3	5
Hughes	-	---	-	-	-	-	-	-	-	-	-	0-0	0.00	1	0	0	2.0	0	0	0	0	2
Logan	-	---	-	-	-	-	-	-	-	-	-	-	---	-	-	-	-	-	-	-	-	-
Mitre	-	---	-	-	-	-	-	-	-	-	-	0-1	4.58	5	3	0	19.2	22	10	10	5	9
Moseley	-	---	-	-	-	-	-	-	-	-	-	-	---	-	-	-	-	-	-	-	-	-
Nova	-	---	-	-	-	-	-	-	-	-	-	-	---	-	-	-	-	-	-	-	-	-
Pettitte	-	---	-	-	-	-	-	-	-	-	-	5-1	3.39	10	10	0	58.1	60	26	22	18	45
Ring	-	---	-	-	-	-	-	-	-	-	-	0-0	0.00	3	0	0	4.2	0	0	0	0	1
Rivera	-	---	-	-	-	-	-	-	-	-	-	0-1	3.27	10	0	8	11.0	7	4	4	3	14
Robertson	-	---	-	-	-	-	-	-	-	-	-	0-0	10.80	2	0	0	1.2	4	2	2	0	3
Sabathia	-	---	-	-	-	-	-	-	-	-	-	1-1	3.24	2	2	0	16.2	18	7	6	2	16
Vazquez	-	---	-	-	-	-	-	-	-	-	-	7-10	3.80	20	20	0	132.2	134	68	56	38	113
Wood	-	---	-	-	-	-	-	-	-	-	-	4-3	2.91	13	8	0	58.2	51	19	19	25	70

Yankees vs. Cincinnati

IN THE POSTSEASON: Overall: 8-5
at original Yankee Stadium: 3-3
at Cincinnati: 5-2   **(at Crosley Field:** 5-0; **at Riverfront Stadium:** 0-2)

The Yankees and Reds have met in three World Series, squaring off in the 1939, 1961 and 1976 Fall Classic…the Yankees swept the '39 Series, won the '61 Series 4-games-to-1 and were swept in the '76 Series.

The Yankees completed the 1939 sweep as the pitching staff combined for a 1.22 ERA, holding Cincinnati to just four extra-base hits and no home runs…the 1961 World Series victory was highlighted by Whitey Ford's 14.0 scoreless innings in his two wins (Games 1 and 4), as well as the Yankees outscoring the Red 20-5 over the final two games…the 1976 World Series was the first to take place in the remodeled original Yankee Stadium and the team's first under George M. Steinbrenner's ownership.

IN 2010:

Did not meet…have met twice during the regular season in Interleague play (2003 and 2008), with the Reds holding a 4-2 advantage.

BATTER	2010									Career							
	AVG	G	AB	R	H	HR	RBI	BB	SO	AVG	G	AB	R	H	HR	RBI	BB	SO
Berkman	.167	9	30	2	5	1	4	8	7	.318	152	525	121	167	49	137	114	86
Cano	----	-	-	-	-	-	-	-	-	.222	3	9	0	2	0	2	0	0
Cervelli	----	-	-	-	-	-	-	-	-	---	-	-	-	-	-	-	-	-
Gardner	----	-	-	-	-	-	-	-	-	---	-	-	-	-	-	-	-	-
Golson	----	-	-	-	-	-	-	-	-	---	-	-	-	-	-	-	-	-
Granderson	----	-	-	-	-	-	-	-	-	.182	3	11	1	2	1	1	0	3
Jeter	----	-	-	-	-	-	-	-	-	.269	6	26	2	7	0	0	2	6
Kearns	.286	6	21	0	6	0	1	2	4	.310	23	84	9	26	2	10	5	20
Nunez	----	-	-	-	-	-	-	-	-	---	-	-	-	-	-	-	-	-
Pena	----	-	-	-	-	-	-	-	-	---	-	-	-	-	-	-	-	-
Posada	----	-	-	-	-	-	-	-	-	.188	5	16	2	3	0	2	5	6
Rodriguez	----	-	-	-	-	-	-	-	-	.182	6	22	4	4	0	0	2	7
Swisher	----	-	-	-	-	-	-	-	-	.444	3	9	0	4	0	2	3	1
Teixeira	----	-	-	-	-	-	-	-	-	.260	13	50	9	13	6	16	12	12
Thames	----	-	-	-	-	-	-	-	-	.500	2	6	2	3	1	1	1	2

PITCHER	2010											Career								
	W-L	ERA	G	GS	SV	IP	H	R	ER	BB	SO	W-L	ERA	G	GS	SV	IP	H	R	ER	BB	SO
Burnett	-	---	-	-	-	-	-	-	-	-	-	2-3	5.75	7	7	0	40.2	44	27	26	20	47
Chamberlain	-	---	-	-	-	-	-	-	-	-	-	-	---	-	-	-	-	-	-	-	-	-
Gaudin	-	---	-	-	-	-	-	-	-	-	-	0-1	5.19	2	1	0	8.2	9	5	5	2	4
Hughes	-	---	-	-	-	-	-	-	-	-	-	-	---	-	-	-	-	-	-	-	-	-
Logan	-	---	-	-	-	-	-	-	-	-	-	-	---	-	-	-	-	-	-	-	-	-
Mitre	-	---	-	-	-	-	-	-	-	-	-	0-1	6.14	8	3	0	22.0	30	16	15	9	16
Moseley	-	---	-	-	-	-	-	-	-	-	-	0-1	27.00	1	0	0	0.1	2	1	1	0	0
Pettitte	-	---	-	-	-	-	-	-	-	-	-	4-3	3.64	10	10	0	59.1	72	30	24	23	55
Ring	-	---	-	-	-	-	-	-	-	-	-	1-1	0.00	4	0	0	2.1	3	1	0	0	1
Rivera	-	---	-	-	-	-	-	-	-	-	-	0-0	0.00	2	0	1	2.1	3	0	0	1	3
Robertson	-	---	-	-	-	-	-	-	-	-	-	-	---	-	-	-	-	-	-	-	-	-
Sabathia	-	---	-	-	-	-	-	-	-	-	-	4-1	2.33	11	11	0	73.1	62	25	19	20	75
Vazquez	-	---	-	-	-	-	-	-	-	-	-	4-3	5.05	11	11	0	73.0	79	43	41	14	65
Wood	0-0	3.00	3	0	2	3.0	2	1	1	0	6	13-5	2.97	38	21	6	151.2	108	56	50	59	191

Yankees vs. San Diego

IN THE POSTSEASON: Overall: 4-0
at original Yankee Stadium: 2-0   **at Qualcomm Stadium:** 2-0

The Yankees and Padres have met once in the postseason, facing off in the 1998 World Series…the Yankees swept the series 4-games-to-0, outscoring San Diego, 26-13…came back from three-run deficits to win in Games 1 and 3…was the seventh time the Yankees swept an opponent in the World Series.

IN 2010:

Did not meet…the Yankees and Padres have met three times in Interleague play, with the Yankees holding a 7-2 advantage…swept the Padres in their last meeting from 6/17-19/08 at the original Yankee Stadium.

BATTER	2010 AVG	G	AB	R	H	HR	RBI	BB	SO	Career AVG	G	AB	R	H	HR	RBI	BB	SO
Berkman	.160	7	25	2	4	1	2	4	8	.301	68	239	51	72	19	49	43	49
Cano	---	-	-	-	-	-	-	-	-	.300	3	10	3	3	0	0	0	1
Cervelli	---	-	-	-	-	-	-	-	-	---	-	-	-	-	-	-	-	-
Gardner	---	-	-	-	-	-	-	-	-	---	-	-	-	-	-	-	-	-
Golson	---	-	-	-	-	-	-	-	-	---	-	-	-	-	-	-	-	-
Granderson	---	-	-	-	-	-	-	-	-	.545	3	11	3	6	1	1	0	1
Jeter	---	-	-	-	-	-	-	-	-	.324	9	37	4	12	0	4	4	8
Kearns	---	-	-	-	-	-	-	-	-	.274	26	84	10	23	0	12	12	15
Nunez	---	-	-	-	-	-	-	-	-	---	-	-	-	-	-	-	-	-
Pena	---	-	-	-	-	-	-	-	-	---	-	-	-	-	-	-	-	-
Posada	---	-	-	-	-	-	-	-	-	.172	8	29	1	5	0	2	5	3
Rodriguez	---	-	-	-	-	-	-	-	-	.302	26	106	17	32	6	16	10	16
Swisher	---	-	-	-	-	-	-	-	-	.067	3	15	0	1	0	0	0	8
Teixeira	---	-	-	-	-	-	-	-	-	.171	9	35	6	6	0	4	4	4
Thames	---	-	-	-	-	-	-	-	-	.400	4	10	1	4	1	2	0	2

PITCHER	2010 W-L	ERA	G	GS	SV	IP	H	R	ER	BB	SO	Career W-L	ERA	G	GS	SV	IP	H	R	ER	BB	SO
Burnett	-	---	-	-	-	-	-	-	-	-	-	1-4	4.54	5	5	0	33.2	25	19	17	27	30
Chamberlain	-	---	-	-	-	-	-	-	-	-	-	0-0	1.59	1	1	0	5.2	4	1	1	3	9
Gaudin	-	---	-	-	-	-	-	-	-	-	-	1-0	1.17	4	1	0	7.2	10	1	1	3	4
Hughes	-	---	-	-	-	-	-	-	-	-	-	-	---	-	-	-	-	-	-	-	-	-
Logan	-	---	-	-	-	-	-	-	-	-	-	0-0	9.00	2	0	0	2.0	4	3	2	1	2
Mitre	-	---	-	-	-	-	-	-	-	-	-	1-3	5.34	5	5	0	28.2	26	19	17	11	12
Moseley	-	---	-	-	-	-	-	-	-	-	-	-	---	-	-	-	-	-	-	-	-	-
Pettitte	-	---	-	-	-	-	-	-	-	-	-	4-1	2.10	5	5	0	30.0	23	7	7	7	36
Ring	-	---	-	-	-	-	-	-	-	-	-	0-0	0.00	3	0	0	1.0	1	0	0	1	1
Rivera	-	---	-	-	-	-	-	-	-	-	-	0-0	0.00	4	0	3	4.0	1	0	0	1	9
Robertson	-	---	-	-	-	-	-	-	-	-	-	-	---	-	-	-	-	-	-	-	-	-
Sabathia	-	---	-	-	-	-	-	-	-	-	-	3-0	2.12	4	4	0	29.2	30	7	7	4	31
Vazquez	-	---	-	-	-	-	-	-	-	-	-	5-4	3.00	17	17	0	120.0	98	44	40	27	104
Wood	-	---	-	-	-	-	-	-	-	-	-	2-3	3.82	9	5	3	35.1	31	16	15	18	43

Yankees vs. San Francisco

IN THE POSTSEASON: Overall: 23-19-1 (4-3 vs. San Francisco)
at home: 10-9-1   **(at the Polo Grounds:** 1-4-1; **at original Yankee Stadium:** 9-5)
on the road: 13-10   **(at the Polo Grounds:** 11-8; **at Candlestick Park:** 2-2)

The Yankees and Giants have met seven times in the World Series with the Giants winning their first two meetings in 1921 and 1922 and Yankees winning each of the last five in 1923, '36, '37, '51 and '62…the 43 World Series games between the teams are the second-most for any two opponents behind the 66 Fall Classic games between the Yankees and Dodgers (credit: *Elias*).

In 1921, Babe Ruth's first season in pinstripes, the Yankees played their crosstown rivals in the franchise's first World Series appearance, losing 5-games-to-3 in Baseball's last nine-game Fall Classic format…the Yankees were held without a win in the 1922 World Series, one of only three such instances in their history…Game 2 of the Series featured the only tie in the history of World Series play…the Yankees' win in 1923 marked the franchise's first of 27 World Championships…led by rookie Joe DiMaggio, the Yankees' 1936 World Series win vs. the Giants marked their first of four consecutive titles from '36-39…their 18-4 win in Game 2 still marks the most runs ever scored by a team in a World Series game…the Yankees' 1951 Series win over the Giants featured rookies Willie Mays and Mickey Mantle…the 1962 World Series, in which the Yankees faced the San Francisco Giants, went seven games with the Yankees emerging victorious after a 1-0 shutout in Game 7 by Series MVP Ralph Terry.

IN 2010:

The Yankees and Giants did not play each other in 2010…the two teams have met twice in Interleague play, splitting the all-time series, 3-3…the Yankees took two out of three games in 2002 at the original Yankee Stadium and lost two out of three at AT&T Park in 2007.

BATTER	2010									Career								
	AVG	G	AB	R	H	HR	RBI	BB	SO	AVG	G	AB	R	H	HR	RBI	BB	SO
Berkman	.318	6	22	1	7	0	3	3	2	.250	63	216	30	54	11	35	37	44
Cano	---	-	-	-	-	-	-	-	-	.286	3	14	1	4	0	1	0	2
Cervelli	---	-	-	-	-	-	-	-	-	---	-	-	-	-	-	-	-	-
Gardner	---	-	-	-	-	-	-	-	-		-	-	-	-	-	-	-	-
Golson	---	-	-	-	-	-	-	-	-	---	-	-	-	-	-	-	-	-
Granderson	---	-	-	-	-	-	-	-	-	.231	3	13	2	3	0	2	1	2
Jeter	---	-	-	-	-	-	-	-	-	.261	6	23	3	6	0	2	2	5
Kearns	---	-	-	-	-	-	-	-	-	.226	34	115	17	26	4	16	22	26
Nunez	---	-	-	-	-	-	-	-	-	---	-	-	-	-	-	-	-	-
Pena	---	-	-	-	-	-	-	-	-		-	-	-	-	-	-	-	-
Posada	---	-	-	-	-	-	-	-	-	.238	6	21	1	5	0	2	4	8
Rodriguez	---	-	-	-	-	-	-	-	-	.478	17	69	17	33	6	24	9	10
Swisher	---	-	-	-	-	-	-	-	-	.231	18	65	11	15	3	14	13	19
Teixeira	---	-	-	-	-	-	-	-	-	.143	6	21	2	3	1	4	3	7
Thames	---	-	-	-	-	-	-	-	-	.273	3	11	3	3	3	4	1	4

PITCHER	2010											Career										
	W-L	ERA	G	GS	SV	IP	H	R	ER	BB	SO	W-L	ERA	G	GS	SV	IP	H	R	ER	BB	SO
Burnett	-	---	-	-	-	-	-	-	-	-	-	5-2	1.84	7	7	0	49.0	33	12	10	18	37
Chamberlain	-	---	-	-	-	-	-	-	-	-	-	-	---	-	-	-	-	-	-	-	-	-
Gaudin	-	---	-	-	-	-	-	-	-	-	-	2-0	2.76	11	3	0	29.1	27	10	9	16	15
Hughes	-	---	-	-	-	-	-	-	-	-	-	-	---	-	-	-	-	-	-	-	-	-
Logan	-	---	-	-	-	-	-	-	-	-	-	0-0	0.00	2	0	0	0.2	1	1	0	0	2
Mitre	-	---	-	-	-	-	-	-	-	-	-	1-0	7.30	3	2	0	12.1	18	10	10	6	2
Moseley	-	---	-	-	-	-	-	-	-	-	-	-	---	-	-	-	-	-	-	-	-	-
Pettitte	-	---	-	-	-	-	-	-	-	-	-	0-3	5.40	3	3	0	18.1	23	13	11	6	17
Ring	-	---	-	-	-	-	-	-	-	-	-	0-0	0.00	1	0	0	0.2	0	0	0	2	0
Rivera	-	---	-	-	-	-	-	-	-	-	-	0-1	0.00	3	0	2	3.2	2	1	0	1	4
Robertson	-	---	-	-	-	-	-	-	-	-	-	-	---	-	-	-	-	-	-	-	-	-
Sabathia	-	---	-	-	-	-	-	-	-	-	-	2-0	1.59	2	2	0	17.0	9	3	3	2	16
Vazquez	-	---	-	-	-	-	-	-	-	-	-	5-7	3.65	15	15	0	93.2	97	40	38	34	57
Wood	-	---	-	-	-	-	-	-	-	-	-	4-3	4.79	14	10	2	62.0	55	34	33	39	67

Yankees vs. Philadelphia

IN THE POSTSEASON: Overall: 8-2
at home: 4-1   **(at original Yankee Stadium:** 2-0; **at current Yankee Stadium:** 2-1)
at Philadelphia: 4-1   **(at Shibe Park:** 2-0; **at Citizens Bank Park:** 2-1)

The Yankees and Phillies have met twice in postseason play, facing off in the 1950 World Series and the 2009 World Series…the Yankees swept the '50 series, 4-0, winning their 13th championship, and won last year's Fall Classic, 4-2, for their 27th title…in the 1950 Series, Yankees pitchers allowed just five runs (three earned) all series, tallying a 0.73 combined ERA in 37.0IP…each of the first three games were decided by one run, including a 1-0 victory behind Vic Raschi in Game 1 and a 2-1, 10-inning win behind Allie Reynolds in Game 2.

IN 2010: 1-2
at Yankee Stadium: 1-2   **at Citizens Bank Park:** 0-0

The Yankees and Phillies met in a three-game series at Yankee Stadium from 6/15-17 with the Phillies taking two out of three games…the Yankees won the series opener, hitting three home runs and scoring six runs against Roy Halladay…marked the second straight season the two teams squared off in Interleague play, with the Yankees also dropping two of three games at Yankee Stadium from 5/22-24/09.

NYY vs. PHILADELPHIA in 2010				
Date	H/A	W/L	Score	Record
6/15	at NYY	W	8-3	1-0
6/16	at NYY	L	3-6	1-1
6/17	at NYY	L	1-7	1-2
Total in 2010	-		**12-16**	**1-2**

	2010									Career								
BATTER	AVG	G	AB	R	H	HR	RBI	BB	SO	AVG	G	AB	R	H	HR	RBI	BB	SO
Berkman	---	-	-	-	-	-	-	-	-	.292	64	219	34	64	10	46	44	44
Cano	.385	3	13	2	5	1	2	0	1	.303	9	33	5	10	1	2	1	3
Cervelli	.333	2	6	0	2	0	2	0	1	.273	4	11	1	3	0	2	0	1
Gardner	.222	3	9	0	2	0	2	1	0	.286	5	14	0	4	0	2	1	0
Golson	---	-	-	-	-	-	-	-	-	---	-	-	-	-	-	-	-	-
Granderson	.167	3	12	1	2	1	1	0	3	.320	6	25	7	8	2	2	0	4
Jeter	.000	3	11	0	0	0	0	2	3	.296	24	98	17	29	5	14	13	20
Kearns	.000	2	8	0	0	0	0	1	2	.270	63	215	35	58	5	23	34	43
Nunez	---	-	-	-	-	-	-	-	-	---	-	-	-	-	-	-	-	-
Pena	.000	2	6	0	0	0	0	0	2	.000	4	9	1	0	0	0	0	4
Posada	.333	2	6	3	2	1	1	1	3	.264	15	53	7	14	4	11	9	18
Rodriguez	.286	2	7	0	2	0	1	1	0	.250	8	28	3	7	2	5	6	6
Swisher	.167	3	12	2	2	1	1	2	1	.074	8	27	2	2	1	3	2	8
Teixeira	.100	3	10	4	1	1	1	2	2	.250	29	112	21	28	10	23	13	30
Thames	---	-	-	-	-	-	-	-	-	.000	3	5	0	0	0	0	0	3
TOTALS	**.200**	**3**	**95**	**12**	**19**	**5**	**12**	**8**	**18**									

	2010										Career									
PITCHER	W-L	ERA	G	GS	SV	IP	H	R	ER	BB	SO	W-L	ERA	G	GS	SV	IP	H	R	ER	BB	SO
Burnett	0-1	16.20	1	1	0	3.1	6	6	6	4	3	5-9	5.13	18	17	0	100.0	104	60	57	50	90
Chamberlain	0-0	---	1	0	0	0.0	2	3	3	1	0	0-0	---	1	0	0	0.0	2	3	3	1	0
Gaudin	0-0	0.00	1	0	0	3.0	0	0	0	0	3	0-0	0.00	3	0	0	5.1	3	0	0	1	5
Hughes	-	---	-	-	-	-	-	-	-	-	-	-	-	-	-	-	-	-	-	-	-	-
Logan	0-0	0.00	1	0	0	2.2	0	0	0	1	3	0-0	0.00	5	0	0	4.2	2	0	0	2	6
Mitre	-	---	-	-	-	-	-	-	-	-	-	0-3	5.75	4	4	0	20.1	24	17	13	8	16
Moseley	-	---	-	-	-	-	-	-	-	-	-	-	-	-	-	-	-	-	-	-	-	-
Nova	-	---	-	-	-	-	-	-	-	-	-	-	-	-	-	-	-	-	-	-	-	-
Pettitte	0-1	2.57	1	1	0	7.0	6	3	2	3	7	2-3	3.51	8	8	0	48.2	51	23	19	15	35
Ring	-	---	-	-	-	-	-	-	-	-	-	0-1	6.61	21	0	0	16.1	19	12	12	11	14
Rivera	-	---	-	-	-	-	-	-	-	-	-	1-0	1.69	9	0	5	10.2	6	2	2	0	11
Robertson	0-0	0.00	2	0	0	2.0	0	0	0	1	2	0-0	0.00	2	0	0	2.0	0	0	0	1	2
Sabathia	1-0	3.86	1	1	0	7.0	5	3	3	3	7	2-1	4.23	4	4	0	27.2	27	13	13	7	19
Vazquez	-	---	-	-	-	-	-	-	-	-	-	12-8	4.27	28	28	0	185.1	183	95	88	50	156
Wood	0-1	13.50	2	0	0	1.1	1	2	2	1	0	4-2	4.03	10	6	1	44.2	44	20	20	16	49
TOTALS	**5.00**	**1-2**	**3**	**3**	**0**	**27.0**	**21**	**16**	**15**	**15**	**26**											

Organizational Summary

AAA	Scranton/Wilkes-Barre Yankees	International League	87-56 (.608)
AA	Trenton Thunder	Eastern League	83-59 (.585)
A	Tampa Yankees	Florida State League	78-57 (.578)
A	Charleston RiverDogs	South Atlantic League	65-74 (.468)
Short-A	Staten Island Yankees	New York-Penn League	34-40 (.459)
R	GCL Yankees	Gulf Coast League	24-32 (.429)

WINNING BASEBALL: Yankees affiliates combined for a 443-389 (.532) record in 2010, finishing the regular season with the third-best winning percentage among American League organizations…in fact, Yankees farm clubs have combined for a winning record in each of the last 21 seasons (1990-2010).

CHAMPS AGAIN: The **Single-A Tampa Yankees** (78-57) won their second consecutive Florida State League championship in 2010 and fifth in franchise history, marking the first time that a FSL team has won back-to-back league titles since the Lakeland Flying Tigers from 1975-76…the **Triple-A Scranton/Wilkes-Barre Yankees** (83-56) won their fifth straight International League North Division title and fourth consecutive as an affiliate of the New York Yankees, extending their record for most consecutive division championships in league history…the **Double-A Trenton Thunder** went 83-59, winning the Eastern League's North Division title for the third time in the last four years.

CREAM OF THE CROP: INF Brandon Laird (EL) and **OF Melky Mesa** (FSL) were each named Player of the Year in their respective leagues…marked the second straight year that the Yankees had two players awarded with the honor after Shelley Duncan (IL) and Austin Romine (FSL) accomplished the feat in 2009…Laird was also named to the *Sporting News* 2010 All-Minor League team…**C Jesus Montero** made the IL's midseason and postseason All-Star squad…entered the 2010 season tabbed by *Baseball America* as the Yankees' top prospect and the fifth-best prospect in all of Baseball (top catcher).

2010 DRAFT SUMMARY: With their first-round pick (32nd selection) in the 2010 First-Year Player Draft, the Yankees selected **INF Cito Culver** out of Irondequoit High School (N.Y.)…was ranked as the third best prospect from the state of New York…was also a three-time all county selection as well as an Under Armour All-American…the Yankees drafted a total of 21 pitchers, four catchers, five infielders and 13 outfielders…the Yankees signed 25 of their draft picks, including each of the top eight and 18 of the top 24.

DSL YANKEES: The Dominican Summer League Yankees 1 completed the 2010 season with a 44-27 record, finishing second in the Boca Chica South Division…the Dominican Summer League Yankees 2 finished 28-44, ranking eighth in the Boca Chica North Division…**RHPs Cristofer Cabrera** and **Deivi Mojica** and **OF Yeicok Calderon**, of the DSL Yankees 1, and **INF Rafael Polo**, of the DSL Yankees 2, were each selected to the DSL All-Star team…Cabrera went 3-1 with a 0.51 ERA in eight starts, allowing just 2ER in 35.0IP…in 13G/2GS, Mojica was 8-2 with a 2.00 ERA, limiting opposing batters to a .193 (36-for-187) batting average…Calderon hit .339 (83-for-245), leading the DSL in extra-base hits (30), slugging percentage (.551) and total bases (135), ranking second in HRs and hits, third in on-base percentage (.439) and fifth in batting average…Polo batted .323 (80-for-248) with 17 doubles, nine triples and 30RBI in 63G…ranked second in extra-base hits (27) and triples, third in total bases (118), fifth in hits and slugging percentage (.476) and ninth in average.

The Tampa Yankees captured their second straight Florida State League Championship in 2010.

ORGANIZATIONAL LEADERS

Batting Average

Robert Lyerly	CHA	.312
Jesus Montero	SWB	.289
Eduardo Nunez	SWB	.289
Justin Christian	SWB	.289
Marcos Vechionacci	TRE	.283

HR

Brandon Laird	SWB	.25
Jesus Montero	SWB	.21
Melky Mesa	TAM	.19
Jorge Vazquez	SWB	.18
Juan Miranda	SWB	.15

RBI

Brandon Laird	SWB	102
Daniel Brewer	TRE	84
Bradley Suttle	TAM	.80
Jesus Montero	SWB	.75
Melky Mesa	TAM	.74

SB

Raymond Kruml	TAM	.42
Jimmy Paredes	CHA	.36
Melky Mesa	TAM	.31
Jose Pirela	TAM	.30
Daniel Brewer	TRE	.29

ERA

Michael O'Brien	STA	2.08
Graham Stoneburner	TAM	2.41
David Phelps	SWB	2.50
Adam Warren	TRE	2.59
Ivan Nova	SWB	2.86

Wins

Hector Noesi	SWB	.14
D.J. Mitchell	SWB	.13
Ivan Nova	SWB	.12
Lance Pendleton	SWB	.12
2 others tied		.11

Strikeouts

Hector Noesi	SWB	153
David Phelps	SWB	141
Graham Stoneburner	TAM	137
Lance Pendleton	SWB	133
2 others tied		126

Saves

Jonathan Albaladejo	SWB	.43
Jonathan Ortiz	TAM	.21
Ryan Pope	TRE	.17
Chase Whitley	TAM	.15
Ryan Flannery	TAM	.14

2010 Scranton/Wilkes-Barre Yankees (AAA)

2010 INTERNATIONAL LEAGUE FINAL STANDINGS

NORTH DIVISION	W	L	PCT	GB
Scranton/WB Yankees	87	56	.608	-
Syracuse Chiefs	76	67	.531	11.0
Buffalo Bisons	76	68	.528	11.5
Pawtucket Red Sox	66	78	.458	21.5
Lehigh Valley IronPigs	58	86	.403	29.5
Rochester Red Wings	49	95	.340	38.5
SOUTH DIVISION	W	L	PCT	GB
Durham Bulls	88	55	.615	-
Gwinnett Braves	72	71	.503	16.0
Charlotte Knights	67	77	.465	21.5
Norfolk Tides	67	77	.465	21.5
WEST DIVISION	W	L	PCT	GB
Louisville Bats	79	64	.552	-
Columbus Clippers	79	65	.549	0.5
Indianapolis Indians	71	73	.493	8.5
Toledo Mud Hens	70	73	.490	9.0

2010 SCRANTON/WILKES-BARRE YANKEES HIGHLIGHTS

The Scranton/Wilkes-Barre Yankees went 87-56 in 2010, finishing with the second-best record in the International League…won the IL's North Division title for a league-record fifth consecutive year as a franchise, and fourth consecutive year as an affiliate of the New York Yankees…dropped a best-of-five first-round series to the Columbus Clippers, three-games-to-one, and did not advance to the Governor's Cup Championship Series for the first time in three years…was the ninth time in the last 13 seasons that Scranton/WB has reached the playoffs…were a league-best 60-10 (.857) when scoring first this season and 34-14 (.708) in one-run games.

BATTING NOTES: The Yankees batted .267, ranking fifth in the International League…were led by **C Jesus Montero** who ended the regular season batting .289 (131-for-453) with 34 doubles, three triples, 21HR and 75RBI in 123 games with the Yankees…led the team in home runs and RBI and ranked third in the IL in extra-base hits (58), tied for third in doubles and ranked fifth in both slugging percentage (.517) and total bases (234)…was named to the league's postseason All-Star team alongside teammate **INF Eduardo Nunez**…in 118 games with Scranton/WB, Nunez hit .289 (134-for-464) with 25 doubles, 4HR, 53RBI and 23SB, prior to being promoted to the Major League team on 8/19…hit .316 (42-for-133) with seven doubles and 43RBI with runners in scoring position.

PITCHING NOTES: The Scranton/WB Yankees ranked third in the International League with a combined 3.78 team ERA…were led by **RHP Ivan Nova** who went 12-3 with a 2.86 ERA with Scranton/WB, allowing 3ER or less in 18 of his 23 starts (145.0IP, 46ER)…finished the year ranked second in the league in ERA and tied for third in wins, despite his promotion to the Major League team on 8/22…**RHP Jonathan Albaladejo** established an IL record with 43 saves in 45 save opportunities, earning a spot on the league's postseason All-Star team…fell just three saves shy of tying the overall Minor League record of 46 set by Jamie Cochran of the SAL's Savannah Sand Gnats in 1993…allowed just 10ER and recorded 82K in 63.1IP in relief, ranking first in the league in games finished (54) and fourth in appearances (57)…the SWB Yankees pitching staff earned a league-high four IL Pitcher of the Week Awards (Albaladejo 7/5-7/11 and 7/15-7/18, **RHP Tim Redding** 7/26-8/1, and **RHP Jason Hirsh** 8/2-8/8).

SCRANTON/WB ALL-STARS
Midseason: RHP Jonathan Albaladejo, C Jesus Montero, INF Eduardo Nunez
Postseason: RHP Jonathan Albaladejo, C Jesus Montero, INF Eduardo Nunez

2010 Scranton/Wilkes-Barre Yankees (AAA)

BATTERS	AVG	G	AB	R	H	2B	3B	HR	RBI	BB	SO	SB	CS	OBP	SLG	E
Bruntlett, Eric	.265	70	253	35	67	14	0	9	38	16	59	4	0	.316	.427	7
Christian, Justin	.242	16	66	9	16	0	0	0	4	8	9	2	0	.324	.242	0
#Corona, Reegie	.238	105	387	46	92	20	5	5	31	36	58	14	1	.306	.354	6
*Curtis, Colin	.289	66	239	28	69	24	0	5	27	21	38	1	2	.358	.452	0
*Cusick, Matthew	.265	29	83	11	22	6	0	0	9	10	7	0	0	.337	.337	5
Golson, Greg	.263	116	415	51	109	23	5	10	40	25	99	17	4	.313	.414	5
Gonzalez, Edwar	.154	4	13	1	2	0	0	0	0	1	5	0	0	.214	.154	0
Gorecki, Reid	.253	78	281	45	71	18	5	3	30	32	67	12	3	.332	.384	5
*Granderson, Curtis	.250	5	16	0	4	0	0	0	2	2	2	0	0	.333	.250	0
Hammock, Robby	.180	22	61	6	11	2	0	0	4	11	13	0	1	.306	.213	1
Huffman, Chad	.274	104	368	48	101	20	0	10	45	40	81	0	2	.353	.410	3
Laird, Brandon	.246	31	122	13	30	6	0	2	12	4	27	0	0	.268	.344	2
*Miranda, Juan	.285	80	295	52	84	15	1	15	43	33	71	1	0	.371	.495	4
Moeller, Chad	.230	28	87	8	20	6	0	1	9	6	15	0	0	.302	.333	1
Montero, Jesus	.289	123	453	66	131	34	3	21	75	46	91	0	0	.353	.517	6
Natale, Jeff	.182	14	22	3	4	1	0	0	6	3	1	0	0	.286	.227	1
Nunez, Eduardo	.289	118	464	55	134	25	3	4	50	32	60	23	5	.340	.381	14
Pilittere, P.J.	.357	22	56	6	20	4	0	1	5	5	13	0	1	.419	.482	1
Rivera, Rene	.250	19	68	3	17	3	0	2	11	1	17	0	0	.257	.382	0
Russo, Kevin	.259	81	332	41	86	16	2	1	24	28	65	9	4	.333	.328	9
*Snyder, Justin	.333	2	6	0	2	0	0	0	1	0	0	0	0	.333	.333	0
Thames, Marcus	.200	4	15	0	3	0	0	0	1	0	1	0	0	.200	.200	0
*Tracy, Chad	.324	18	68	14	22	5	0	6	18	4	6	0	0	.356	.662	2
Vazquez, Jorge	.270	76	293	47	79	21	0	18	62	17	95	0	0	.313	.526	6
*Weber, Jon	.258	47	163	18	42	7	2	0	11	18	25	0	2	.333	.325	2
Winfree, David	.264	52	201	24	53	16	0	5	33	9	32	0	0	.301	.418	3
Team Total	**.267**	**143**	**4827**	**630**	**1291**	**286**	**26**	**118**	**591**	**408**	**957**	**83**	**25**	**.330**	**.411**	**93**

PITCHERS	W-L	ERA	G	GS	CG	SHO	SV	IP	H	R	ER	HR	HB	BB	SO	WP
Aceves, Alfredo	0-0	7.36	3	2	0	0	0	3.2	4	4	3	0	2	5	4	0
Albaladejo, Jonathan	4-2	1.42	57	0	0	0	43	63.1	38	10	10	3	2	18	82	6
Duff, Grant	0-0	6.00	4	0	0	0	0	6.0	8	4	4	0	0	2	6	0
Hirsh, Jason	9-7	3.90	26	19	0	0	0	122.1	102	55	53	17	8	39	95	1
*Igawa, Kei	3-4	4.32	22	10	0	0	0	77.0	81	37	37	9	0	23	68	2
Kontos, George	0-1	10.12	2	0	0	0	0	2.2	5	3	3	1	0	1	2	0
*Logan, Boone	0-1	2.11	14	0	0	0	0	21.1	18	5	5	1	2	4	23	1
McAllister, Zach	8-10	5.09	24	24	1	0	0	132.2	165	82	75	20	6	38	88	7
Melancon, Mark	6-1	3.67	40	0	0	0	6	56.1	63	24	23	5	3	31	58	7
Mitchell, D.J.	2-0	3.57	3	3	0	0	0	17.2	19	7	7	0	0	7	16	2
Mitre, Sergio	0-1	7.04	2	2	0	0	0	7.2	9	6	6	1	1	2	7	1
Moseley, Dustin	4-4	4.21	12	12	0	0	0	72.2	83	40	34	6	4	18	55	4
Noesi, Hector	1-1	4.82	3	3	1	0	0	18.2	23	10	10	1	1	4	14	1
Norton, Tim	0-0	0.00	1	0	0	0	0	1.0	1	0	0	0	0	1	0	0
Nova, Ivan	12-3	2.86	23	23	0	0	0	145.0	135	50	46	10	2	48	115	4
Park, Chan Ho	0-0	0.00	1	1	0	0	0	1.0	1	0	0	0	0	0	2	1
Pendleton, Lance	2-1	4.24	6	5	0	0	0	34.0	29	17	16	6	0	12	22	1
Phelps, David	4-2	3.07	12	11	0	0	0	70.1	76	31	24	4	1	13	57	1
Redding, Tim	7-4	2.46	13	12	1	0	0	84.0	68	24	23	2	2	17	62	2
*Ring, Royce	2-1	1.93	52	0	0	0	2	42.0	35	12	9	2	5	11	39	2
Sanchez, Romulo	10-8	3.97	31	14	0	0	0	104.1	88	50	46	8	1	59	96	6
Sanit, Amaury	3-2	7.75	21	1	0	0	0	33.2	47	29	29	7	0	15	22	5
Schmidt, Josh	1-0	7.20	2	0	0	0	0	5.0	6	4	4	0	1	2	3	0
Segovia, Zack	3-2	4.19	44	0	0	0	4	62.1	68	32	29	6	2	14	51	5
Van Benschoten, John	2-0	2.31	6	1	0	0	1	11.2	13	3	3	1	0	6	8	1
Whelan, Kevin	2-1	6.30	17	0	0	0	1	20.0	19	15	14	2	1	10	22	3
Wordekemper, Eric	2-0	3.13	24	0	0	0	1	31.2	31	11	11	2	0	9	29	2
Team Total	**87-56**	**3.78**	**143**	**143**	**3**	**7**	**58**	**1248.0**	**1235**	**565**	**524**	**114**	**44**	**409**	**1046**	**65**

KEY: *- Lefthanded hitter/pitcher, # - switch hitter

2010 Trenton Thunder (AA)

2010 EASTERN LEAGUE FINAL STANDINGS

EASTERN DIVISION	W	L	PCT	GB
Trenton Thunder	83	59	.585	-
New Hampshire Fisher Cats	79	62	.560	3.5
Portland Sea Dogs	70	71	.496	12.5
Reading Phillies	69	72	.489	13.5
Binghamton Mets	66	76	.465	17.0
New Britain Rock Cats	44	98	.310	39.0
WESTERN DIVISION	W	L	PCT	GB
Altoona Curve	82	60	.577	-
Harrisburg Senators	77	65	.542	5.0
Bowie Baysox	75	67	.528	7.0
Akron Aeros	71	71	.500	11.0
Richmond Flying Squirrels	68	73	.482	13.5
Erie SeaWolves	66	76	.465	16.0

2010 TRENTON THUNDER HIGHLIGHTS

The Trenton Thunder completed the 2010 season with a 83-59 record, winning the Eastern League's North Division…marked **Manager Tony Franklin's** third division title in four years at the helm…swept the New Hampshire Fisher Cats, three-games-to-none, in a best-of-five first round playoff matchup, but fell to the Altoona Curve, three-games-to-one, in the EL Championship series.

BATTING NOTES: The Thunder offense batted .259, ranking seventh in the Eastern League…**INF Brandon Laird** was awarded both the FSL Player and Rookie of the Year and was named to the *Sporting News* 2010 All-Minor League team…appeared in 107 games with the Thunder this season and batted .291 (119-for-409) with 22 doubles, two triples, 23 home runs, 90RBI, and 73 runs scored prior to his promotion to Triple-A Scranton/WB on 8/2…led all Yankees minor league hitters with 102RBI…became the second player in Trenton history to hit for the cycle when he completed the feat with a "walk-off" home run in the Thunder's 7-6 victory over the Erie SeaWolves on 5/26…was the only member of the team to be named to the league's postseason All-Star roster…in his first season at the Double-A level, **C Austin Romine** hit .268 (122-for-455) with 31 doubles, 10HR and 69RBI in 115 games with Trenton and was named an EL midseason All-Star…batted .319 (37-for-116) with 11 doubles, 4HR and 11RBI off left-handed pitching this season…**OF Daniel Brewer** led all Thunder batters with 34 doubles and 29SB, hitting .270 (137-for-508) with 10HR and 84RBI in 136 games…among all EL postseason batters, ranked second in batting average (.400), stolen bases (2) and hits (10), third in on-base percentage (.483) and fourth in slugging percentage (.560).

PITCHING NOTES: The Thunder pitching staff ranked third in the EL with a 3.66 overall team ERA…were led by **RHP Lance Pendleton** who went 10-4 with a 3.43 ERA in 23G/22GS…prior to his promotion to Triple-A Scranton/WB on 8/10, led the team in wins, allowing 3ER or less in 18 of his starts, 2ER or less in 16 of his outings and 1ER or less in nine of his appearances…**RHPs Josh Schmidt** and **D.J. Mitchell** were each named to the league's midseason All-Star team…Schmidt went 3-3 with a 2.67 ERA in 47 appearances out of the bullpen, recording 71K in 60.2IP…in 23G/22GS, Mitchell was 11-4 with a 4.06 ERA, holding batters to a .183 (26-for-142) batting average with runners in scoring position…**RHP Ryan Pope** led all Thunder relievers, converting 17-of-20 save opportunities…tied for third in the league in saves, ranked third in fewest walks per 9.0IP ratio (1.88) and ranked fifth in fewest base runners per 9.0IP ratio (10.52).

TRENTON ALL-STARS
Midseason: RHP Josh Schmidt, RHP D.J. Mitchell, C Austin Romine
Postseason: INF Brandon Laird

2010 Trenton Thunder (AA)

BATTERS	AVG	G	AB	R	H	2B	3B	HR	RBI	BB	SO	SB	CS	OBP	SLG	E
Adams, David	.309	39	152	31	47	15	3	3	32	18	31	5	2	.393	.507	0
Baker, Ryan J.	.000	3	3	0	0	0	0	0	0	0	1	0	0	.000	.000	0
#Berkman, Lance	.250	2	8	1	2	0	0	0	0	1	3	0	0	.333	.250	0
Brewer, Daniel	.270	136	508	83	137	34	3	10	53	117	29	10	.346	.407	2
Christian, Justin	.297	87	343	65	102	21	6	9	51	40	47	20	5	.374	.472	1
*Cusick, Matthew	.234	59	201	17	47	7	3	3	26	22	31	3	1	.310	.343	1
Gil, Jose	.236	31	106	19	25	6	1	5	25	9	23	0	0	.305	.453	3
Gonzalez, Edwar	.235	74	243	37	57	8	4	6	35	28	59	4	2	.333	.374	1
Gorecki, Reid	.257	29	105	10	27	7	0	2	15	13	20	8	3	.347	.381	0
*Grote, Taylor	.000	1	1	0	0	0	0	0	0	1	1	0	0	.500	.000	0
*Joseph, Corban	.216	31	111	11	24	6	4	0	13	15	33	1	0	.305	.342	7
*Krum, Austin	.229	120	459	77	105	17	1	5	44	64	86	16	7	.328	.303	3
Laird, Brandon	.291	107	409	73	119	22	2	23	90	38	84	2	2	.355	.523	20
*Mahoney, Kevin	.267	6	15	2	4	1	0	0	1	5	6	0	0	.476	.333	2
Nunez, Luis	.241	131	449	60	108	24	5	8	44	25	70	7	10	.284	.370	14
Rivera, Rene	.319	25	94	13	30	10	0	5	17	7	17	0	0	.369	.585	1
Romine, Austin	.268	115	455	61	122	31	0	10	69	37	94	2	0	.324	.402	5
*Rye, Jack	.212	15	52	5	11	3	1	1	7	6	9	1	0	.293	.365	2
*Smith, Kevin	.168	41	131	9	22	6	0	0	5	17	49	0	0	.273	.214	3
*Snyder, Justin	.245	90	261	56	64	13	2	3	27	49	44	2	1	.365	.345	12
*Sublett, Damon	.214	35	112	14	24	4	1	2	14	22	37	1	1	.343	.321	2
Vazquez, Jorge	.390	10	41	4	16	4	0	0	6	1	8	0	0	.405	.488	1
#Vechionacci, Marcos	.283	114	406	56	115	17	3	11	55	40	111	6	2	.350	.421	8
Team Total	**.259**	**142**	**4665**	**704**	**1208**	**256**	**39**	**106**	**660**	**511**	**981**	**107**	**46**	**.337**	**.399**	**97**

PITCHERS	W-L	ERA	G	GS	CG	SHO	SV	IP	H	R	ER	HR	HB	BB	SO	WP
Aceves, Alfredo	0-0	5.63	4	3	0	0	0	8.0	10	5	5	1	0	1	7	0
Arbiso, Cory	5-5	4.38	32	11	0	0	0	84.1	100	46	41	9	1	22	49	6
*Arias, Wilkins	4-3	3.65	57	0	0	0	0	61.2	61	27	25	5	2	30	70	6
*Banuelos, Manuel	0-1	3.52	3	3	0	0	0	15.1	15	8	6	2	0	8	17	1
Betances, Dellin	0-0	3.77	3	3	0	0	0	14.1	10	7	6	3	1	3	20	3
*Bleich, Jeremy	3-2	4.79	8	8	0	0	0	41.1	35	22	22	2	3	28	26	3
Brackman, Andrew	5-7	3.01	15	14	0	0	0	80.2	77	38	27	3	7	30	70	6
Bush, Paul	0-2	15.00	3	0	0	0	0	3.0	3	5	5	1	1	4	4	0
Castillo, Noel	3-2	6.27	17	0	0	0	0	18.2	12	15	13	4	1	16	20	3
Cox, J.B.	3-0	4.28	26	0	0	0	2	33.2	34	18	16	1	2	12	23	3
*De La Rosa, Wilkin	2-4	5.33	36	8	0	0	0	72.2	82	51	43	7	3	41	56	3
Duff, Grant	1-4	2.84	28	0	0	0	8	31.2	30	16	10	4	0	16	38	3
Garcia, Christian	1-0	0.00	1	0	0	0	0	5.2	2	0	0	0	1	1	3	0
Kontos, George	0-2	3.38	17	0	0	0	0	32.0	30	13	12	2	0	11	28	0
Mitchell, D.J.	11-4	4.06	23	22	0	0	0	133.0	128	69	60	11	6	57	96	12
Noesi, Hector	8-4	3.10	17	16	2	1	0	98.2	90	37	34	7	2	18	86	5
Norton, Tim	1-0	0.90	6	0	0	0	1	10.0	4	1	1	0	0	3	15	0
Olbrychowski, Adam	0-0	2.08	2	0	0	0	0	4.1	4	1	1	0	0	1	4	1
Pendleton, Lance	10-4	3.43	23	22	0	0	0	120.2	95	50	46	9	4	45	111	4
Phelps, David	6-0	2.04	14	14	0	0	0	88.1	63	21	20	2	2	23	84	2
Pope, Ryan	4-6	4.20	46	7	0	0	17	94.1	88	48	44	10	7	31	85	7
Schmidt, Josh	3-3	2.67	47	0	0	0	2	60.2	41	18	18	3	4	28	71	0
Snyder, Justin	0-0	0.00	1	0	0	0	0	1.0	1	0	0	0	0	1	0	0
Van Benschoten, John	2-0	0.00	3	0	0	0	0	6.0	4	1	0	0	1	4	4	0
Venditte, Pat	1-1	9.00	2	0	0	0	0	2.0	4	2	2	0	0	1	4	0
Warren, Adam	4-2	3.15	10	10	0	0	0	54.1	49	26	19	2	3	16	59	4
Whelan, Kevin	3-3	5.83	24	0	0	0	3	29.1	20	19	19	1	1	21	40	5
Wordekemper, Eric	3-0	2.88	23	0	0	0	8	34.1	26	12	11	5	1	8	35	5
Team Total	**83-59**	**3.66**	**142**	**142**	**2**	**12**	**41**	**1240.0**	**1118**	**576**	**504**	**94**	**53**	**480**	**1125**	**82**

KEY: *- Lefthanded hitter/pitcher, # - switch hitter

2010 Tampa Yankees (A)

2010 FLORIDA STATE LEAGUE FINAL STANDINGS

FIRST HALF

North Division	W	L	PCT	GB
Dunedin Blue Jays	41	29	.625	-
Tampa Yankees	36	32	.529	4.0
Clearwater Threshers	37	33	.529	4.0
Lakeland Flying Tigers	37	33	.529	4.0
Daytona Cubs	34	36	.486	7.0
Brevard County Manatees	27	42	.391	13.5

South Division	W	L	PCT	GB
Charlotte Stone Crabs	43	26	.623	-
Bradenton Marauders	39	31	.557	4.5
Palm Beach Cardinals	39	31	.557	4.5
St. Lucie Mets	33	35	.485	9.5
Fort Myers Miracle	28	42	.400	15.5
Jupiter Hammerheads	22	46	.324	20.5

SECOND HALF

North Division	W	L	PCT	GB
Tampa Yankees	42	25	.627	-
Daytona Cubs	41	28	.594	2.0
Brevard County Manatees	37	33	.529	6.5
Lakeland Flying Tigers	34	34	.500	8.5
Dunedin Blue Jays	31	38	.449	12.0
Clearwater Threshers	30	39	.435	13.0

South Division	W	L	PCT	GB
Bradenton Marauders	37	31	.544	-
Fort Myers Miracle	36	32	.529	1.0
Charlotte Stone Crabs	37	33	.529	1.0
Palm Beach Cardinals	36	34	.514	2.0
St. Lucie Mets	29	41	.414	9.0
Jupiter Hammerheads	24	46	.343	14.0

2010 TAMPA YANKEES HIGHLIGHTS

In his first season as Tampa's manager, **Torre Tyson** led the Yankees to their second consecutive Florida State League championship and fifth in franchise history…marked the first back-to-back league titles in the FSL since the Lakeland Flying Tigers accomplished the feat from 1975-76…Tampa finished with a 78-57 overall record, winning the North Division's second half title and earning a playoff berth in successive years after previously not qualifying for the postseason in each of their prior four seasons…recorded a league-high 19 shutout victories in 2010…four different Yankees players were selected as either a FSL Pitcher or Player of the Week.

BATTING NOTES: The Tampa Yankees offense ranked third in the Florida State League in both batting average (.263) and home runs (72)…**OF Melky Mesa** was named the FSL "Player of the Year"…batted .260 (116-for-446) with 19HR and 74RBI in 121G with Tampa…led the team in home runs and RBI and ranked second in the league in slugging percentage (.475), tied for second in home runs, ranked third in extra-base hits (49) and triples (9) and fifth in runs scored (81)…joined **INF Bradley Suttle** on the postseason All-Star team…Suttle hit .272 (140-for-514) with 33 doubles, 10HR and 80RBI in 133G and led all FSL third basemen with a .951 fielding percentage…ranked second in the league in RBI, fourth in hits and fifth in doubles…led all FSL batters during the postseason with 3HR and 9RBI in six games.

PITCHING NOTES: The Tampa Yankees pitching staff tied for second in the FSL with a 3.30 ERA during the regular season…combined to go 5-1 with a 1.00 ERA in six postseason games, striking out 53 batters and allowing just 6ER in 54.0IP…**RHPs Hector Noesi** (4/8-18) and **Dellin Betances** (6/21-27) were each awarded "Pitcher of the Week" honors in 2010…Noesi went 5-2 with a 2.72 ERA in eight starts with Tampa before being promoted to Double-A Trenton on 5/16…in 14GS with the Yankees, Betances went 8-1 with a 1.77 ERA, recording 88K and allowing just 14ER in 71.0IP prior to his promotion to Trenton on 8/23…allowed 2ER or less in 13 of his 14 starts with Tampa and 1ER or less in nine of those outings…**RHP Jonathan Ortiz** converted 21 of his 27 save opportunities, going 7-1 with a 2.47 ERA in 46 appearances out of the bullpen…ranked fourth in the league in saves and fifth in games finished (41).

TAMPA ALL-STARS
Midseason: C Mitch Abeita, OF Jack Rye, INF Corban Joseph, RHP Adam Warren, RHP Hector Noesi
Postseason: OF Melky Mesa, INF Bradley Suttle, Manager Torre Tyson

2010 Tampa Yankees (A)

BATTERS	AVG	G	AB	R	H	2B	3B	HR	RBI	BB	SO	SB	CS	OBP	SLG	E
Abeita, Mitch	.273	77	256	33	70	15	1	1	26	42	60	0	0	.375	.352	6
#Almonte, Abraham	.263	15	57	9	15	3	1	0	3	6	16	5	3	.333	.351	1
#Almonte, Zoilo	.261	63	238	26	62	10	3	3	26	23	65	8	1	.322	.366	4
Baker, Ryan J.	.086	15	35	6	3	0	0	0	2	7	15	0	0	.250	.086	0
#Feliz, Anderson	.280	10	25	6	7	1	0	1	4	3	9	2	0	.357	.440	1
*Flores, Ramon	.250	8	28	0	7	0	0	0	2	0	5	0	0	.250	.250	0
Gil, Jose	.255	40	141	17	36	4	0	5	19	11	31	4	0	.316	.390	1
#Ibarra, Walter	.301	72	246	28	74	12	1	1	14	15	46	15	7	.348	.370	10
*Joseph, Corban	.302	98	381	52	115	27	3	6	52	43	74	5	8	.378	.436	13
*Kruml, Raymond	.271	66	291	44	79	14	2	1	21	21	63	30	6	.325	.344	3
#Leslie, Myron	.262	80	260	40	68	14	1	6	39	30	53	8	0	.339	.392	8
*Lockwood, Trent	.257	86	292	37	75	17	0	4	37	35	67	2	0	.334	.356	8
*Mahoney, Kevin	.400	3	5	0	2	2	0	0	1	1	2	0	0	.500	.800	0
Maruszak, Addison	.284	68	243	32	69	16	0	1	34	11	40	3	2	.312	.362	10
*Medchill, Neil	.178	51	180	17	32	5	1	3	21	18	70	3	2	.260	.267	0
Mesa, Melky	.260	121	446	81	116	21	9	19	74	44	129	31	9	.338	.475	4
*Pena, Henry	.000	1	3	0	0	0	0	0	0	0	2	0	0	.000	.000	0
Pirela, Jose	.252	130	497	68	125	15	13	5	61	57	87	30	7	.329	.364	30
*Rye, Jack	.274	92	332	49	91	22	3	6	45	34	41	7	1	.342	.413	3
*Santana, Francisco	.135	23	74	3	10	4	1	0	8	1	23	1	0	.145	.216	0
#Suttle, Bradley	.272	133	514	61	140	33	4	10	80	53	136	12	2	.340	.411	15
Team Total	**.263**	**135**	**4544**	**609**	**1196**	**235**	**43**	**72**	**569**	**455**	**1034**	**166**	**48**	**.333**	**.381**	**125**

PITCHERS	W-L	ERA	G	GS	CG	SHO	SV	IP	H	R	ER	HR	HB	BB	SO	WP
*Banuelos, Manuel	0-3	2.23	10	10	0	0	0	44.1	38	16	11	1	1	14	62	2
Bartleski, Philip	3-3	4.54	37	0	0	0	3	69.1	82	41	35	8	3	17	57	4
Betances, Dellin	8-1	1.77	14	14	0	0	0	71.0	43	18	14	1	3	19	88	3
Black, Sean	1-0	1.59	2	2	0	0	0	11.1	9	2	2	0	2	1	12	0
Braboy, Brandon	0-0	3.57	11	2	0	0	1	22.2	31	11	9	0	1	4	17	4
Brackman, Andrew	5-4	5.10	12	12	0	0	0	60.0	67	38	34	5	5	9	56	6
Castillo, Noel	2-2	2.28	16	0	0	0	0	27.2	18	8	7	2	3	13	36	5
Claiborne, Preston	0-1	3.68	5	0	0	0	0	7.1	7	3	3	1	1	4	6	1
Cox, J.B.	0-1	8.59	5	0	0	0	0	7.1	14	11	7	1	1	2	4	1
Flannery, Ryan	1-0	2.25	2	0	0	0	0	4.0	2	1	1	0	0	0	6	0
Forer, Nathan	0-0	9.39	6	0	0	0	0	7.2	16	8	8	0	0	4	5	0
*Hall, Shaeffer	9-5	3.91	15	14	0	0	0	69.0	81	38	30	7	0	10	57	1
Heredia, Jairo	0-6	6.93	6	6	0	0	0	24.2	37	28	19	2	4	11	14	1
Heyer, Craig	8-4	3.52	26	12	1	0	0	92.0	92	42	36	1	5	6	66	3
Kapala, Daniel	1-6	4.53	12	11	0	0	0	57.2	61	33	29	2	7	30	26	6
Kontos, George	0-1	2.61	5	2	0	0	0	10.1	7	3	3	0	0	3	8	0
*Lare, Trenton	1-2	4.00	42	1	0	0	0	74.1	95	46	33	6	1	19	73	4
Leslie, Myron	0-0	9.00	1	0	0	0	0	1.0	3	1	1	0	0	0	0	0
*Marcano, Juan	1-0	0.00	3	0	0	0	0	5.0	1	0	0	0	0	3	8	0
Marshall, Brett	0-0	4.50	1	1	0	0	0	4.0	5	3	2	0	0	0	6	0
Marte, Ronny	1-0	2.93	9	0	0	0	0	15.1	16	9	5	0	0	8	11	2
Mitre, Sergio	0-0	0.00	1	0	0	0	0	1.0	0	0	0	0	0	0	1	0
Noesi, Hector	5-2	2.72	8	8	0	0	0	43.0	35	14	13	3	2	6	53	5
Norton, Tim	0-0	1.69	12	0	0	0	2	21.1	16	7	4	2	0	3	32	2
Olbrychowski, Adam	3-2	4.02	30	1	0	0	1	62.2	59	33	28	1	3	27	52	6
Ortiz, Jonathan	7-1	2.47	46	0	0	0	21	54.2	41	17	15	4	0	11	62	1
*Romanski, Josh	0-1	4.50	3	3	0	0	0	12.0	15	6	6	2	0	4	12	1
Rulon, Brad	1-0	2.50	11	0	0	0	0	18.0	18	8	5	1	0	6	16	3
Sanit, Amaury	0-0	1.80	3	0	0	0	0	5.0	0	1	1	0	0	2	6	0
Stoneburner, Graham	8-5	2.53	19	19	1	0	0	103.0	80	35	29	4	8	24	93	4
Van Benschoten, John	2-1	4.50	12	2	0	0	0	26.0	30	14	13	4	1	8	24	0
Venditte, Pat	4-1	1.73	41	0	0	0	6	72.2	49	17	14	2	2	14	85	0
Warren, Adam	7-5	2.22	15	15	1	0	0	81.0	72	23	20	2	6	17	67	0
Whitley, Chase	0-0	3.00	2	0	0	0	0	3.0	1	1	1	1	1	0	6	0
Team Total	**78-57**	**3.30**	**135**	**135**	**3**	**19**	**34**	**1189.1**	**1141**	**536**	**436**	**63**	**60**	**299**	**1127**	**65**

KEY: *- Lefthanded hitter/pitcher, # - switch hitter

2010 Charleston RiverDogs (A)

2010 SOUTH ATLANTIC LEAGUE FINAL STANDINGS

FIRST HALF

NORTHERN DIVISION	W	L	PCT	GB
Lakewood BlueClaws	42	28	.600	-
Hickory Crawdads	40	30	.571	2.0
Hagerstown Suns	36	34	.514	6.0
Delmarva Shorebirds	32	38	.457	10.0
Greensboro Grasshoppers	32	38	.457	10.0
Kannapolis Intimidators	31	38	.449	10.5
West Virginia Power	31	39	.443	11.0

SOUTHERN DIVISION	W	L	PCT	GB
Savannah Sand Gnats	42	28	.600	-
Augusta GreenJackets	41	29	.586	1.0
Greenville Drive	36	34	.514	6.0
Lexington Legends	35	35	.500	7.0
Charleston RiverDogs	31	38	.449	10.5
Rome Braves	30	39	.435	11.5
Asheville Tourists	29	40	.420	12.5

SECOND HALF

NORTHERN DIVISION	W	L	PCT	GB
Lakewood BlueClaws	42	27	.609	-
Hickory Crawdads	35	34	.507	7.0
West Virginia Power	34	35	.493	8.0
Greensboro Grasshoppers	34	36	.486	8.5
Kannapolis Intimidators	34	36	.486	8.5
Hagerstown Suns	29	41	.414	13.5
Delmarva Shorebirds	27	43	.386	15.5

SOUTHERN DIVISION	W	L	PCT	GB
Greenville Drive	41	28	.594	-
Asheville Tourists	40	30	.571	1.5
Augusta GreenJackets	38	30	.559	2.5
Lexington Legends	36	33	.522	5.0
Charleston RiverDogs	34	36	.486	7.5
Savannah Sand Gnats	33	36	.478	8.0
Rome Braves	29	41	.414	12.5

2010 CHARLESTON RIVERDOGS HIGHLIGHTS

The Charleston RiverDogs finished the 2010 regular season with a 65-74 overall record…went 34-36 during the second half of the season and finished the year with a 35-35 home record, marking the 12th time in the team's 14-year history that the team has finished with a .500 or better record at home…three different Charleston players earned Player of the Week honors in 2010 (**RHP Graham Stoneburner** 4/19-4/25, **INF Luke Murton** 5/24-5/30 and **RHP Michael Solbach** 8/16-8/22)….the RiverDogs drew 269,023 fans at home this season, marking the third-highest total in club history.

BATTING NOTES: Charleston combined for a .258 overall team batting average in 2010…were led by **INF Robert Lyerly**, who hit .312 (157-for-503) with 36 doubles, 7HR and 71RBI in 131 games…finished third in the South Atlantic League in both batting average and hits and was the lone RiverDogs player to be named to the SAL postseason All-Star team…**OF Zoilo Almonte** and **INF Luke Murton** were each named to the league's midseason All-Star team…Almonte batted .278 (63-for-227) with 13 doubles, 10HR and 35RBI with Charleston prior to his promotion to Single-A Tampa on 6/24…in 106 games with the RiverDogs, Murton batted .282 (112-for-397) with 32 doubles, 12HR and 55RBI…was named the SAL's Player of the Week for the week of 5/24-5/30 and ended the season reaching base safely in 15 of his last 16 games played…**OF Slade Heathcott**, the Yankees first overall pick in the 2009 First Year Player Draft out of Texas HS, batted .258 (77-for-298) with 16 doubles, 15SB and 30RBI in his first full professional season…hit .321(36-for-112) with 29RBI and 18BB with runners on base.

PITCHING NOTES: Charleston's pitching staff ranked third in the league in overall team ERA (3.43)…**LHP Josh Romanski** led the team in wins, going 8-4 with a 3.16 ERA in 15GS prior to his promotion to Single-A Tampa on 8/24…**RHP Ryan Flannery** was the only RiverDogs pitcher to have been named to either the midseason or post-season All-Star teams when he was awarded the honor midseason…was promoted to Tampa on 9/1, after going 7-6 with 14 saves and a 2.26 ERA in 45 appearances out of the bullpen with Charleston, recording 70K and walking just 14 batters in 79.2IP…**RHP Graham Stoneburner** made seven starts with the RiverDogs, going 1-3 with a 2.08 ERA…retired 20 consecutive batters in Charleston's 12-inning, 4-3 loss to the Rome Braves on 4/24 and recorded 11K, including seven in-a-row, in the team's 2-0 victory over the Lakewood BlueClaws on 5/5…the 11K marked the first time that a Charleston hurler fanned 10 or more batters since Dellin Betances recorded 12K on 8/16/08.

CHARLESTON ALL-STARS
Midseason: RHP Ryan Flannery, OF Zoilo Almonte, INF Luke Murton
Postseason: INF Robert Lyerly

2010 Charleston RiverDogs (A)

BATTERS	AVG	G	AB	R	H	2B	3B	HR	RBI	BB	SO	SB	CS	OBP	SLG	E
#Almonte, Zoilo	.278	58	227	33	63	13	2	10	35	21	65	7	6	.341	.485	3
#Arcia, Francisco	.314	17	51	2	16	4	0	0	3	7	8	1	0	.397	.392	2
Castro, Kelvin	.224	123	437	55	98	20	5	2	39	30	96	15	11	.274	.307	37
*Flores, Ramon	.250	14	48	3	12	3	0	0	2	3	15	1	0	.294	.313	0
*Grote, Taylor	.278	28	90	11	25	7	0	2	9	16	30	1	2	.383	.422	0
*Heathcott, Slade	.258	76	298	48	77	16	3	2	30	42	101	15	10	.359	.352	7
Higashioka, Kyle	.225	90	320	35	72	18	0	6	24	31	64	0	2	.303	.338	6
*Kruml, Raymond	.261	51	184	21	48	9	1	0	11	7	35	12	2	.297	.321	0
#Landoni, Emerson	.280	84	261	39	73	13	1	3	32	21	44	13	8	.330	.372	17
*Lassiter, Garrison	.102	27	88	2	9	1	0	0	4	14	36	1	1	.223	.114	5
Liccien, Jhorge	.200	2	5	0	1	0	0	0	0	1	2	0	0	.333	.200	0
*Lyerly, Robert	.312	131	503	72	157	36	0	7	71	34	129	9	7	.352	.425	33
*Mack, Deangelo	.252	116	424	52	107	20	5	12	56	46	99	5	7	.333	.408	8
*Mahoney, Kevin	.298	26	84	15	25	8	0	2	7	13	25	1	1	.404	.464	1
*Medchill, Neil	.215	65	237	29	51	10	1	9	32	23	84	5	4	.295	.380	2
*Milo, Justin	.231	16	52	8	12	0	0	0	4	11	15	3	1	.359	.231	1
Murphy, JR	.255	87	330	46	84	15	2	7	54	36	64	4	5	.327	.376	11
Murton, Luke	.282	106	397	48	112	32	2	12	55	39	71	2	0	.361	.463	4
#Paredes, Jimmy	.282	99	404	59	114	24	6	5	48	18	82	36	10	.312	.408	36
Rabago, Hector	.160	40	119	7	19	3	0	3	16	9	29	0	0	.239	.261	13
*Santana, Francisco	.257	34	101	16	26	5	2	2	15	5	22	2	1	.292	.406	1
Toussen, Jose	.000	2	3	1	0	0	0	0	0	0	0	0	0	.000	.000	0
Team Total	**.258**	**139**	**4663**	**602**	**1201**	**257**	**30**	**84**	**547**	**427**	**1116**	**133**	**78**	**.324**	**.380**	**203**

PITCHERS	W-L	ERA	G	GS	CG	SHO	SV	IP	H	R	ER	HR	HB	BB	SO	WP
Acosta, Ryan	5-4	3.50	42	0	0	0	1	61.2	61	31	24	0	3	23	46	8
Barreda, Manuel	1-0	0.00	6	0	0	0	0	7.1	8	0	0	0	1	5	7	0
Black, Sean	7-8	3.88	23	22	1	1	0	116.0	118	75	50	6	10	40	92	9
Flannery, Ryan	7-6	2.26	45	0	0	0	14	79.2	61	25	20	2	4	14	70	4
Gil, Francisco	1-3	1.25	28	0	0	0	9	36.0	32	10	5	0	2	12	27	3
Gipson, Mike	0-2	7.88	3	2	0	0	0	8.0	11	7	7	1	2	3	6	0
Greene, Shane	0-2	4.58	4	4	0	0	0	19.2	14	10	10	1	5	8	22	1
*Hall, Shaeffer	2-2	1.85	10	10	0	0	0	68.0	52	19	14	1	2	11	46	0
Heredia, Jairo	4-2	3.45	20	9	0	0	0	70.1	74	34	27	4	2	19	65	2
Marquez, Dickson	0-5	10.62	15	0	0	0	1	20.1	30	25	24	1	2	12	10	1
Marshall, Brett	4-2	2.50	13	13	1	1	0	72.0	52	26	20	2	1	22	56	5
Marte, Ronny	2-3	3.13	35	2	0	0	4	54.2	67	30	19	4	3	15	36	10
Martinez, Richard	1-0	3.60	1	1	0	0	0	5.0	5	2	2	0	0	2	4	0
Perez, Kelvin	5-5	3.18	30	13	0	0	0	104.2	93	53	37	6	5	36	80	14
*Quintana, Jose	0-1	4.70	5	3	0	0	0	15.1	11	10	8	1	1	10	12	0
Ramirez, Jose A.	6-5	3.60	22	21	0	0	0	115.0	106	56	46	3	9	42	105	20
Rodriguez, Wilton	0-1	7.71	1	1	0	0	0	4.2	4	4	4	0	0	4	3	0
*Romanski, Josh	8-4	3.16	15	15	0	0	0	88.1	84	39	31	8	4	17	73	4
*Rondon, Francisco	1-2	7.71	10	0	0	0	1	11.2	12	10	10	3	1	7	16	2
Shive, Andrew	1-1	3.38	6	0	0	0	0	8.0	4	7	3	0	1	8	4	3
Solbach, Michael	4-6	3.90	30	15	0	0	0	99.1	109	47	43	4	5	23	95	11
Stoneburner, Graham	1-3	2.08	7	7	0	0	0	39.0	27	11	9	2	1	10	44	1
Tatis, Gabriel	2-3	4.14	37	0	0	0	0	58.2	56	38	27	2	11	18	49	12
Watkins, Benjamin	3-4	3.88	35	1	0	0	0	58.0	59	28	25	3	3	16	34	4
Team Total	**65-74**	**3.43**	**139**	**139**	**2**	**12**	**30**	**1221.1**	**1150**	**597**	**465**	**54**	**78**	**377**	**1002**	**114**

KEY: *- Lefthanded hitter/pitcher, # - switch hitter

2010 Staten Island Yankees (Short-Season A)

2010 NEW YORK-PENN LEAGUE FINAL STANDINGS

MCNAMARA DIVISION	W	L	PCT	GB
Brooklyn Cyclones	51	24	.680	-
Hudson Valley Renegades	39	36	.520	12.0
Aberdeen IronBirds	34	40	.459	16.5
Staten Island Yankees	**34**	**40**	**.459**	**16.5**

PINCKNEY DIVISION	W	L	PCT	GB
Batavia Muckdogs	45	29	.608	-
Jamestown Jammers	43	32	.573	2.5
Williamsport Crosscutters	43	33	.566	3.0
Auburn Doubledays	35	40	.467	10.5
State College Spikes	33	42	.440	12.5
Mahoning Valley Scrappers	30	46	.395	16.0

STEDLER DIVISION	W	L	PCT	GB
Tri-City ValleyCats	38	36	.514	-
Connecticut Tigers	38	37	.507	0.5
Vermont Lake Monsters	36	38	.486	2.0
Lowell Spinners	24	50	.324	14.0

2010 STATEN ISLAND YANKEES HIGHLIGHTS

The Staten Island Yankees went 34-40 in 2010, tying for third in the New York-Penn League's McNamara Division…missed the playoffs for the first time in the last six years, after winning the league championship last season…Richmond County Bank Ballpark played host to the 2010 NYPL All-Star game, marking the first time in the team's 12-year history that the team's home field served as host for the Mid-Summer Classic…six different members of the Yankees were named to the American League All-Star squad for the second consecutive year, including **Manager Josh Paul**.

BATTING NOTES: INF Jose Mojica and **OF Eduardo Sosa** were each named NYPL midseason All-Stars…in 53 games with Staten Island, Mojica hit .241 (45-for-187) with 10 doubles…enjoyed his best month of the season in June, when he hit .347 (17-for-49) with six doubles and 6RBI…Sosa batted .256 (46-for-180) with 13 doubles, three triples, 2HR and 15SB in 47 games with Staten Island…fashioned a season-high 10-game hitting streak from 6/30-7/10, batting .426 (20-for-47) with five doubles and 6SB over the stretch.

PITCHING NOTES: Staten Island pitchers combined for a 3.86 overall team ERA…were led by **RHP Michael O'Brien** who went 6-2 with a 2.08 ERA in 11GS with the Yankees, allowing just 14ER in 60.2IP…ranked third in the league in ERA and allowed 2ER or less in nine of his 11 starts…was joined by **RHPs Preston Claiborne** and **Chase Whitley** on the American League All-Star team…in 19 outings out of the bullpen, Claiborne went 1-2 with a 2.28 ERA, recording 30K in 23.2IP prior to his promotion to Single-A Tampa on 8/23…Whitley was 4-2 with a 1.31 ERA and 15 saves in 34.1IP in relief…led all Staten Island relievers with 44K and tied for second in the NYPL in saves…**RHP Zachary Varce**, the Yankees' 11th round pick in the 2010 First-Year Player Draft, recorded a league-best 74K in 71.1IP.

STATEN ISLAND ALL-STARS:
Midseason: RHP Michael O'Brien, RHP Preston Claiborne, RHP Chase Whitley, INF Jose Mojica, OF Eduardo Sosa

2010 Staten Island Yankees (Short-Season A)

BATTERS	AVG	G	AB	R	H	2B	3B	HR	RBI	BB	SO	SB	CS	OBP	SLG	E
#Arcia, Francisco	.224	25	98	13	22	4	0	2	14	5	13	1	0	.267	.327	5
Brown, Isaiah	.218	24	78	7	17	5	1	1	5	10	26	4	1	.307	.346	3
Brown, Shane	.234	60	209	30	49	7	0	2	25	37	28	2	4	.375	.297	6
#Culver, Cito	.186	15	43	2	8	1	0	0	0	8	10	1	1	.340	.209	6
De Leon, Kelvin	.236	69	259	33	61	12	1	6	37	17	80	5	1	.288	.359	6
*Duran, Kelvin	.172	18	58	4	10	3	0	0	4	2	31	2	2	.213	.224	1
Farnham, Jeffrey	.227	36	110	15	25	5	0	0	11	13	19	4	1	.331	.273	5
*Ferraro, Michael	.204	43	152	14	31	10	0	1	13	5	47	1	1	.252	.289	4
*Lassiter, Garrison	.285	39	123	10	35	3	1	0	10	19	29	1	3	.389	.325	3
*Mahoney, Kevin	.276	38	134	18	37	5	2	6	22	18	35	4	1	.384	.478	4
McCoy, Nick	.237	20	59	5	14	4	0	0	7	9	16	1	0	.366	.305	2
Mojica, Jose	.241	53	187	16	45	10	0	0	12	11	20	2	1	.284	.294	19
*Parache, Luis	.235	45	149	17	35	9	1	3	20	10	20	4	2	.284	.369	9
*Roller, Kyle	.272	67	246	36	67	11	3	5	31	31	65	3	2	.367	.402	5
Sanchez, Gary	.278	16	54	8	15	2	0	2	7	3	16	1	1	.333	.426	1
Segedin, Rob	.243	20	70	13	17	6	1	1	7	7	7	0	1	.321	.400	3
*Sosa, Eduardo	.256	47	180	31	46	13	3	2	15	24	48	15	6	.353	.394	4
*Stevenson, Casey	.217	52	198	18	43	8	0	6	23	10	35	0	2	.266	.348	5
Urena, Carlos	.182	6	22	0	4	2	0	0	3	0	5	0	0	.182	.273	1
Team Total	**.239**	**74**	**2429**	**290**	**581**	**120**	**13**	**37**	**266**	**239**	**550**	**51**	**30**	**.320**	**.345**	**101**

PITCHERS	W-L	ERA	G	GS	CG	SHO	SV	IP	H	R	ER	HR	HB	BB	SO	WP
Barreda, Manuel	0-0	4.76	7	0	0	0	0	17.0	14	9	9	0	3	11	18	1
*Brooks, Gavin	0-0	0.00	1	0	0	0	0	0.1	1	0	0	0	0	0	0	0
Burawa, Daniel	0-0	7.71	6	0	0	0	0	7.0	8	7	6	0	0	7	10	1
Claiborne, Preston	1-2	2.28	19	0	0	0	2	23.2	20	9	6	0	0	8	30	2
Cotton, Bryant	1-1	6.20	14	0	0	0	0	20.1	24	15	14	1	0	6	23	1
*Elam, Sam	0-1	8.68	4	2	0	0	0	9.1	9	13	9	2	3	15	9	4
Farnham, Jeffrey	0-0	0.00	1	0	0	0	0	2.0	1	0	0	0	0	4	2	0
Forer, Nathan	0-0	1.99	16	0	0	0	0	22.2	19	7	5	2	1	7	14	0
Gipson, Mike	3-1	4.42	12	6	0	0	0	38.2	37	21	19	4	2	11	50	6
Greene, Shane	2-6	4.59	10	10	0	0	0	49.0	57	28	25	1	7	21	44	3
Hobbs, Dustin	0-2	9.00	2	2	0	0	0	9.0	11	10	9	0	1	7	5	1
*Jernstad, Matthew	2-2	3.32	14	3	0	0	0	43.1	38	18	16	3	3	11	44	1
Kahnle, Thomas	0-0	0.56	11	0	0	0	3	16.0	3	1	1	0	3	5	25	2
*Lewis, Fred	1-0	2.45	5	0	0	0	0	3.2	3	2	1	0	0	5	3	0
Mahoney, Kevin	0-1	13.50	1	0	0	0	0	2.0	6	4	3	1	0	2	1	1
Martinez, Richard	4-1	1.69	16	2	0	0	0	32.0	22	9	6	1	0	16	34	4
Mitchell, Bryan	0-1	6.75	1	1	0	0	0	4.0	7	4	3	0	2	1	3	1
O'Brien, Michael	6-2	2.08	11	11	0	0	0	60.2	49	19	14	1	1	18	38	5
Oliver, William	0-0	5.06	4	0	0	0	0	5.1	6	4	3	0	0	4	7	3
Recchia, Michael	0-1	4.93	22	0	0	0	1	34.2	30	22	19	1	1	12	30	5
Rodriguez, Wilton	1-3	4.39	6	4	0	0	0	26.2	38	22	13	0	1	7	17	2
Shive, Andrew	0-1	5.17	10	0	0	0	0	15.2	17	10	9	0	2	12	10	2
*Sneed, Kramer	1-3	4.09	8	7	0	0	0	33.0	35	20	15	3	2	7	42	2
*Turley, Nik	4-4	4.38	12	12	1	0	0	61.2	57	36	30	0	2	29	47	4
Varce, Zachary	4-6	4.54	15	14	0	0	0	71.1	75	42	36	4	1	17	74	5
Whitley, Chase	4-2	1.31	28	0	0	0	15	34.1	18	8	5	0	1	15	44	2
Team Total	**34-40**	**3.86**	**74**	**74**	**1**	**6**	**21**	**643.1**	**605**	**340**	**276**	**24**	**36**	**258**	**624**	**58**

KEY: *- Lefthanded hitter/pitcher, # - switch hitter

2010 Gulf Coast Yankees (Rookie)

2010 GULF COAST LEAGUE FINAL STANDINGS

NORTH DIVISION	W	L	PCT	GB
GCL Phillies	32	24	.571	-
GCL Blue Jays	31	28	.525	2.5
GCL Tigers	30	28	.517	3.0
GCL Pirates	29	30	.492	4.5
GCL Braves	27	31	.466	6.0
GCL Yankees	**24**	**32**	**.429**	**8.0**

EAST DIVISION	W	L	PCT	GB
GCL Marlins	37	19	.661	-
GCL Mets	31	25	.554	6.0
GCL Cardinals	28	28	.500	9.0
GCL Nationals	24	32	.429	13.0
GCL Astros	20	36	.357	17.0

SOUTH DIVISION	W	L	PCT	GB
GCL Rays	34	26	.567	-
GCL Red Sox	31	28	.525	2.5
GCL Twins	29	31	.483	5.0
GCL Orioles	25	34	.424	8.5

2010 GULF COAST YANKEES HIGHLIGHTS

The GCL Yankees ended the 2010 season with a record of 24-32, finishing last in the GCL's North Division…missed the playoffs for the first time in the last three years…won a season-high four consecutive games on two separate occasions, from 7/27-30 and from 8/3-5…owned a 21-1 record when leading after seven innings and a 19-1 record when leading after eight.

BATTING NOTES: The GCL Yankees ranked third in the league with a .258 overall team batting average…were led by **OF Ramon Flores** who finished second in the GCL with a .329 batting average…ranked first among all GCL hitters in on-base percentage (.436), second in slugging percentage (.481) and third in walks (28)…prior to his promotion to Short-Season Single-A Staten Island on 8/19, **C Gary Sanchez** hit .353 (42-for-119) with 6HR and 36RBI in 31G with the Yankees…began the season by hitting safely in each of his first 10G, batting .459 (17-for-37) with three doubles, 3HR and 12RBI over the stretch…hit .394 (13-for-33) with 3HR and 18RBI off GCL left-handed pitching.

PITCHING NOTES: The Yankees' pitching staff finished the season with a 4.03 combined ERA…**RHP Dustin Hobbs**, the organization's 21st round pick in the 2010 First-Year Player Draft out of Yavapai College, led all Yankees starters in wins, going 3-1 with a 2.30 ERA (7ER)…allowed 1ER or less in six of his seven starts and recorded 33K in 27.1IP…**RHP Conor Mullee**, the Yankees' 24th round pick in the 2010 draft out of St. Peter's College (N.J.), went 2-1 with a 1.64 ERA in 14 appearances out of the bullpen, allowing just 4ER in 22.0IP…did not allow an earned run in 10 of his 14 relief appearances and held right-handed batters to a .228 (13-for-57) average…in 15G prior to his promotion to Single-A Charleston on 8/18, **LHP Jose Quintana** went 3-1 with a 2.31 ERA, recording 32K in 23.1IP in relief.

2010 Gulf Coast Yankees (Rookie)

BATTERS	AVG	G	AB	R	H	2B	3B	HR	RBI	BB	SO	SB	CS	OBP	SLG	E
Alcantara, Jorge	.229	10	35	2	8	3	0	0	2	0	10	0	1	.229	.314	4
Aron, Nathan	.240	9	25	5	6	1	0	0	2	5	8	0	0	.394	.280	0
Austin, Tyler	.000	2	2	0	0	0	0	0	0	0	1	0	0	.500	.000	0
#Culver, Cito	.269	41	160	21	43	7	1	2	18	13	41	6	3	.320	.363	13
*Duran, Kelvin	.221	35	136	18	30	5	0	2	10	17	35	10	4	.303	.301	2
#Feliz, Anderson	.273	47	198	33	54	9	6	4	27	15	44	11	7	.324	.439	12
*Flores, Ramon	.329	43	158	33	52	10	4	2	22	28	22	4	1	.436	.481	9
*Gamel, Benjamin	.280	7	25	3	7	1	0	0	0	3	8	1	2	.357	.320	1
*Golsan, Judd	.188	35	101	9	19	4	0	0	9	8	35	9	3	.261	.228	2
Gumbs, Angelo	.192	7	26	1	5	1	0	0	0	1	3	3	0	.222	.231	3
Hammock, Robby	.500	4	12	4	6	2	0	2	4	1	1	1	0	.538	1.167	0
Kuo, Fu-Lin	.243	42	136	21	33	4	0	4	23	15	34	0	0	.329	.360	16
Liccien, Jhorge	.215	27	79	9	17	5	1	1	14	7	22	0	1	.279	.342	7
Maruszak, Addison	.375	2	8	1	3	1	0	0	2	0	0	0	0	.375	.500	0
Moronta, Eladio	.107	9	28	1	3	0	0	0	3	2	10	1	1	.188	.107	1
Nunez, Reymond	.222	27	108	10	24	4	1	3	20	5	30	1	0	.263	.361	6
*Pena, Henry	.302	26	86	12	26	7	0	3	7	14	25	3	0	.406	.512	1
Perkins, Kyle	.083	13	24	1	2	0	0	0	1	6	9	0	0	.258	.083	2
Rosario, Jose	.245	36	110	22	27	4	1	2	7	8	22	6	0	.320	.355	14
Sanchez, Gary	.353	31	119	25	42	11	0	6	36	11	28	1	1	.419	.597	7
Segedin, Rob	.250	2	8	3	2	0	0	1	3	0	1	0	0	.333	.625	1
*Sublett, Damon	.158	5	19	3	3	0	0	1	3	3	3	0	1	.273	.316	0
Taveras, Damian	.252	31	107	14	27	5	0	2	14	10	30	2	0	.336	.355	7
Toussen, Jose	.277	45	148	24	41	4	0	1	15	11	20	9	1	.333	.324	9
*Williams, Mason	.222	5	18	0	4	0	0	0	0	1	4	1	2	.263	.222	0
Team Total	**.258**	**56**	**1876**	**275**	**484**	**88**	**15**	**36**	**242**	**184**	**446**	**69**	**28**	**.332**	**.378**	**132**

PITCHERS	W-L	ERA	G	GS	CG	SHO	SV	IP	H	R	ER	HR	HB	BB	SO	WP
Arias, Justo	2-2	5.40	14	0	0	0	0	26.2	37	19	16	2	2	4	27	1
*Banuelos, Manuel	0-0	1.80	2	0	0	0	0	5.0	1	1	1	0	0	3	6	1
Checo, Mariel	0-1	5.92	10	2	0	0	0	24.1	26	21	16	4	1	11	24	7
*DeLuca, Evan	1-3	9.35	9	6	0	0	0	26.0	37	36	27	4	7	24	30	4
*Iam, Sam	0-0	4.26	10	0	0	0	0	12.2	8	9	6	0	4	15	15	3
Garce, Harold	2-0	2.79	12	0	0	0	1	19.1	13	7	6	0	1	13	9	2
Garcia, Charlyn	0-0	10.29	7	0	0	0	0	7.0	15	8	8	0	2	1	4	1
Gerritse, Brett	2-2	3.82	9	2	0	0	1	35.1	39	20	15	3	2	12	27	2
Hobbs, Dustin	3-1	2.30	7	7	0	0	0	27.1	23	10	7	0	2	7	33	1
Isabel, George	0-0	18.00	2	0	0	0	0	2.0	5	4	4	1	0	1	3	3
*Johnson, Trevor	0-2	9.00	7	0	0	0	0	7.0	9	9	7	1	0	5	2	3
*Lewis, Fred	0-1	2.25	9	0	0	0	0	12.0	9	4	3	0	0	11	15	0
*Marcano, Juan	1-1	1.05	6	3	0	0	1	25.2	15	3	3	0	0	2	21	0
Marshall, Brett	0-0	2.25	2	1	0	0	0	8.0	6	5	2	0	1	4	8	0
Marte, Joel	0-2	3.43	18	0	0	0	2	21.0	25	13	8	0	3	7	25	2
Mitchell, Bryan	2-1	3.67	10	9	0	0	0	41.2	28	24	17	2	3	22	36	5
Mitre, Sergio	0-1	1.80	2	2	0	0	0	5.0	2	1	1	0	0	0	8	0
Mullee, Conor	2-1	1.64	14	0	0	0	0	22.0	19	9	4	0	1	6	20	1
Nuding, Zachary	0-1	4.50	1	1	0	0	0	2.0	4	2	1	0	0	1	2	0
Oliver, William	2-0	4.38	8	0	0	0	1	12.1	12	9	6	2	2	4	10	0
*Quintana, Jose	3-1	2.31	15	0	0	0	1	23.1	14	11	6	0	3	8	32	1
Reyes, Yobanny	0-1	21.21	2	0	0	0	0	4.2	11	11	11	0	1	3	4	2
Richardson, Matthew	1-4	5.00	11	9	0	0	0	45.0	38	36	25	1	5	29	36	5
Rodriguez, Wilton	0-3	4.05	6	4	0	0	0	20.0	16	13	9	2	0	9	21	2
*Rutckyj, Evan	0-0	0.00	1	0	0	0	0	1.0	0	0	0	0	0	0	0	0
Sanit, Amaury	0-0	2.70	3	3	0	0	0	6.2	4	2	2	0	1	0	10	0
*Sneed, Kramer	0-0	2.70	4	0	0	0	0	6.2	3	3	2	0	0	3	9	0
*Tapia, Erick	2-1	1.15	9	0	0	0	0	15.2	7	3	2	1	1	5	14	0
Triplet, David	0-0	0.00	2	0	0	0	0	2.0	0	0	0	0	0	0	2	0
*Turley, Nik	0-2	0.84	3	2	0	0	0	10.2	11	7	1	0	0	2	9	0
Van Benschoten, John	1-1	1.29	4	3	0	0	0	7.0	5	1	1	1	0	2	8	0
Team Total	**24-32**	**4.03**	**56**	**56**	**0**	**1**	**8**	**485.0**	**442**	**301**	**217**	**24**	**42**	**214**	**470**	**46**

KEY: *- Lefthanded hitter/pitcher, # - switch hitter

Yankees Championship Clubs

40 American League Pennant Winners, 27 World Championship Teams

Year	Won	Lost	Pct.	GA	Manager	World Series Opponent	Record W	L
1921	98	55	.641	4.5	Miller Huggins	Giants	3	5
1922	94	60	.610	1.0	Miller Huggins	Giants**	0	4
1923*	98	54	.645	16.0	Miller Huggins	Giants	4	2
1926	91	63	.591	3.0	Miller Huggins	Cardinals	3	4
1927*	110	44	.714	19.0	Miller Huggins	Pirates	4	0
1928*	101	53	.656	2.5	Miller Huggins	Cardinals	4	0
1932*	107	47	.695	13.0	Joe McCarthy	Cubs	4	0
1936*	102	51	.667	19.5	Joe McCarthy	Giants	4	2
1937*	102	52	.662	13.0	Joe McCarthy	Giants	4	1
1938*	99	53	.651	9.5	Joe McCarthy	Cubs	4	0
1939*	106	45	.702	17.0	Joe McCarthy	Reds	4	0
1941*	101	53	.656	17.0	Joe McCarthy	Dodgers	4	1
1942	103	51	.689	9.0	Joe McCarthy	Cardinals	1	4
1943*	98	56	.636	13.5	Joe McCarthy	Cardinals	4	1
1947*	97	57	.630	12.0	Bucky Harris	Dodgers	4	3
1949*	97	57	.630	1.0	Casey Stengel	Dodgers	4	1
1950*	98	56	.636	3.0	Casey Stengel	Phillies	4	0
1951*	98	56	.636	5.0	Casey Stengel	Giants	4	2
1952*	95	59	.617	2.0	Casey Stengel	Dodgers	4	3
1953*	99	52	.656	8.5	Casey Stengel	Dodgers	4	2
1955	96	58	.623	3.0	Casey Stengel	Dodgers	3	4
1956*	97	57	.630	9.0	Casey Stengel	Dodgers	4	3
1957	98	56	.636	8.0	Casey Stengel	Braves	3	4
1958*	92	62	.597	10.0	Casey Stengel	Braves	4	3
1960	97	57	.630	8.0	Casey Stengel	Pirates	3	4
1961*	109	53	.673	8.0	Ralph Houk	Reds	4	1
1962*	96	66	.593	5.0	Ralph Houk	Giants	4	3
1963	104	57	.646	10.5	Ralph Houk	Dodgers	0	4
1964	99	63	.611	1.0	Yogi Berra	Cardinals	3	4
1976	97	62	.610	10.5	Billy Martin	Reds	0	4
1977*	100	62	.617	2.5	Billy Martin	Dodgers	4	2
1978*	100	63	.613	1.0	Martin-Lemon	Dodgers	4	2
1981†	34	22	.607	2.0	Gene Michael			
	25	26	.490	-5.0	Michael-Lemon	Dodgers	2	4
1996*	92	70	.568	4.0	Joe Torre	Braves	4	2
1998*	114	48	.704	22.0	Joe Torre	Padres	4	0
1999*	98	64	.605	4.0	Joe Torre	Braves	4	0
2000*	87	74	.540	2.5	Joe Torre	Mets	4	1
2001	95	65	.594	13.5	Joe Torre	Diamondbacks	3	4
2003	101	61	.623	6.0	Joe Torre	Marlins	2	4
2009*	103	59	.636	8.0	Joe Girardi	Phillies	4	2

Yankees World Series Totals   ****Tie game in 1922**   **134   90**

* World Champions   † 1st-Half Winner

60th Anniversary of the 1950 World Champion Yankees

The 2010 season marks the 60th anniversary of the Yankees' 1950 World Championship season. Led by Manager Casey Stengel and AL MVP Phil Rizzuto, who batted .324 with 125 runs scored, the Yankees went 98-56 in capturing the pennant by 3.0 games. In the World Series, the Yankees swept four games from the Philadelphia Phillies to win the 13th championship in team history. Yankees pitchers allowed just five runs (three earned) all Series, tallying a 0.73 combined ERA in 37.0IP. Each of the first three games were decided by one run, including a 1-0 victory behind Vic Raschi in Game 1, and a 2-1, 10-inning win behind Allie Reynolds in Game 2. Whitey Ford earned the first of his record 10 career World Series wins in the Game 4 clincher as Reynolds came out of the bullpen to strike out the final batter of the game with two runners on base. The victory marked the second of five consecutive Fall Classics won by the Yankees from 1949 through 1953.

Front Row: Whitey Ford, Phil Rizzuto, Billy Martin, Ed Lopat, Jim Turner, Frank Crosetti, Casey Stengel, Bill Dickey, Jackie Jensen, Billy Johnson, Gene Woodling, Charley Silvera, John Mize. **Second Row:** Gus Mauch, Bob Porterfield, Wally Hood, Dave Madison, Jerry Coleman, Bobby Brown, Tommy Henrich, Hank Bauer, Joe Collins, Lou Burdette, Joe Ostrowski, Ernie Nevel, Johnny Hopp. **Back Row:** Tommy Byrne, Cliff Mapes, Hank Workman, Fred Sanford, Tom Ferrick, Yogi Berra, Joe Page, Ralph Houk, Joe DiMaggio, Allie Reynolds, Vic Raschi. **Seated on Ground (Batboys):** Bert Padell, Joseph Carrieri.

All-Time New York Yankees Managers

MANAGER	YEARS	WON	LOST	PCT	A. L. PENNANTS	WORLD CHAMPIONSHIPS
Joe McCarthy	1931-46	1460	867	.627	8	7
Casey Stengel	1949-60	1149	696	.623	10	7
Joe Torre	1996-2007	1173	767	.605	6	4
Miller Huggins	1918-29	1067	719	.597	6	3
Ralph Houk	1961-63, 1966-73	944	806	.539	3	2
Billy Martin	1975-78, 1979, 1983, 1985, 1988	556	385	.591	2	1
Clark Griffith	1903-08	419	370	.531	0	0
Buck Showalter	1992-95	313	268	.539	0	0
Lou Piniella	1986-87, 1988	224	193	.537	0	0
Bill Donovan	1915-17	220	239	.479	0	0
JOE GIRARDI	**2008-10**	**287**	**199**	**.591**	**1**	**1**
Yogi Berra	1964, 1984-85	192	148	.565	1	0
Bucky Harris	1947-48	191	117	.620	1	1
George Stallings	1909-10	153	138	.526	0	0
Bill Virdon	1974-75	142	124	.534	0	0
Stump Merrill	1990-91	120	155	.436	0	0
Frank Chance	1913-14	117	168	.411	0	0
Dick Howser	1980	103	60	.632	0	0
Bob Lemon	1978-79, 1981-82	99	73	.576	2	1
Gene Michael	1981, 1982	92	76	.548	0	0
Bob Shawkey	1930	86	68	.558	0	0
Hal Chase	1910-11	85	78	.521	0	0
Johnny Keane	1965-66	81	101	.445	0	0
Bill Dickey	1946	57	48	.543	0	0
Dallas Green	1989	56	65	.463	0	0
Harry Wolverton	1912	50	102	.329	0	0
Bucky Dent	1989-90	36	53	.404	0	0
Clyde King	1982	29	33	.468	0	0
Norm Elberfeld	1908	27	71	.276	0	0
Roger Peckinpaugh	1914	10	10	.500	0	0
Johnny Neun	1946	8	6	.571	0	0
Art Fletcher	1929	6	5	.545	0	0
Totals	**1903-2010**	**9552**	**7208**	**.570**	**40**	**27**

Yankees in ALDS/ALCS Play

Year	Series	Opponent	NYY Manager	W	L
1976*	LCS	Kansas City	Billy Martin	3	2
1977*	LCS	Kansas City	Billy Martin	3	2
1978*	LCS	Kansas City	Bob Lemon	3	1
1980	LCS	Kansas City	Dick Howser	0	3
1981*	DIV	Milwaukee - a	Bob Lemon	3	2
	LCS	Oakland	Bob Lemon	3	0
1995	DIV	Seattle	Buck Showalter	2	3
1996*	DIV	Texas	Joe Torre	3	1
	LCS	Baltimore	Joe Torre	4	1
1997	DIV	Cleveland	Joe Torre	2	3
1998*	DIV	Texas	Joe Torre	3	0
	LCS	Cleveland	Joe Torre	4	2
1999*	DIV	Texas	Joe Torre	3	0
	LCS	Boston	Joe Torre	4	1
2000*	DIV	Oakland	Joe Torre	3	2
	LCS	Seattle	Joe Torre	4	2
2001*	DIV	Oakland	Joe Torre	3	2
	LCS	Seattle	Joe Torre	4	1
2002	DIV	Anaheim	Joe Torre	1	3
2003*	DIV	Minnesota	Joe Torre	3	1
	LCS	Boston	Joe Torre	4	3
2004	DIV	Minnesota	Joe Torre	3	1
	LCS	Boston	Joe Torre	3	4
2005	DIV	Los Angeles	Joe Torre	2	3
2006	DIV	Detroit	Joe Torre	1	3
2007	DIV	Cleveland	Joe Torre	1	3
2009*	DIV	Minnesota	Joe Girardi	3	0
	LCS	Los Angeles	Joe Girardi	4	2
	American League Division Series Totals			**36**	**27**
	American League Championship Series Totals			**43**	**24**
	American League Postseason Totals			**79**	**51**

a - Eastern Division Series, NY finished first in first half of season (prior to player strike) and finished sixth in second half of season.

* American League Champions

Year-by-Year Results

Year	AL/WS	Position	GA/GB	Won	Lost	Pct.	Manager	Attendance	Stadium
1903		Fourth	-17.0	72	62	.537	Clark Griffith	211,808	Hilltop Park
1904		Second	-1.5	92	59	.609	Clark Griffith	438,919	Hilltop Park
1905		Sixth	-21.5	71	78	.477	Clark Griffith	309,100	Hilltop Park
1906		Second	-3.0	90	61	.596	Clark Griffith	434,700	Hilltop Park
1907		Fifth	-21.0	70	78	.473	Clark Griffith	350,020	Hilltop Park
1908		Eighth	-39.5	51	103	.331	Griffith-Kid Elberfeld	305,500	Hilltop Park
1909		Fifth	-23.5	74	77	.490	George Stallings	501,000	Hilltop Park
1910		Second	-14.5	88	63	.583	Stallings-Hal Chase	355,857	Hilltop Park
1911		Sixth	-25.5	76	76	.500	Hal Chase	302,444	Hilltop Park
1912		Eighth	-55.0	50	102	.329	Harry Wolverton	242,194	Hilltop Park
1913		Seventh	-38.0	57	94	.377	Frank Chance	357,551	Polo Grounds
1914		Sixth	-30.0	70	84	.455	Chance-Roger Peckinpaugh	359,477	Polo Grounds
1915		Fifth	-32.5	69	83	.454	Bill Donovan	256,035	Polo Grounds
1916		Fourth	-11.0	80	74	.519	Bill Donovan	469,211	Polo Grounds
1917		Sixth	-28.5	71	82	.464	Bill Donovan	330,294	Polo Grounds
1918		Fourth	-13.5	60	63	.488	Miller Huggins	282,047	Polo Grounds
1919		Third	-7.5	80	59	.576	Miller Huggins	619,164	Polo Grounds
1920		Third	-3.0	95	59	.617	Miller Huggins	1,289,422	Polo Grounds
1921	AL	First	+4.5	98	55	.641	Miller Huggins	1,230,696	Polo Grounds
1922	AL	First	+1.0	94	60	.610	Miller Huggins	1,026,134	Polo Grounds
1923	WS	First	+16.0	98	54	.645	Miller Huggins	1,007,066	Orig. Yankee Stadium
1924		Second	-2.0	89	63	.586	Miller Huggins	1,053,533	Orig. Yankee Stadium
1925		Seventh	-28.5	69	85	.448	Miller Huggins	697,267	Orig. Yankee Stadium
1926	AL	First	+3.0	91	63	.591	Miller Huggins	1,027,095	Orig. Yankee Stadium
1927	WS	First	+19.0	110	44	.714	Miller Huggins	1,164,015	Orig. Yankee Stadium
1928	WS	First	+2.5	101	53	.656	Miller Huggins	1,072,132	Orig. Yankee Stadium
1929		Second	-18.0	88	66	.571	Huggins-Art Fletcher	960,148	Orig. Yankee Stadium
1930		Third	-16.0	86	68	.558	Bob Shawkey	1,169,230	Orig. Yankee Stadium
1931		Second	-13.5	94	59	.614	Joe McCarthy	912,437	Orig. Yankee Stadium
1932	WS	First	+13.0	107	47	.695	Joe McCarthy	962,320	Orig. Yankee Stadium
1933		Second	-7.0	91	59	.607	Joe McCarthy	728,014	Orig. Yankee Stadium
1934		Second	-7.0	94	60	.610	Joe McCarthy	854,682	Orig. Yankee Stadium
1935		Second	-3.0	89	60	.597	Joe McCarthy	657,508	Orig. Yankee Stadium
1936	WS	First	+19.5	102	51	.667	Joe McCarthy	976,913	Orig. Yankee Stadium
1937	WS	First	+13.0	102	52	.662	Joe McCarthy	998,148	Orig. Yankee Stadium
1938	WS	First	+9.5	99	53	.651	Joe McCarthy	970,916	Orig. Yankee Stadium
1939	WS	First	+17.0	106	45	.702	Joe McCarthy	859,785	Orig. Yankee Stadium
1940		Third	-2.0	88	66	.571	Joe McCarthy	988,975	Orig. Yankee Stadium
1941	WS	First	+17.0	101	53	.656	Joe McCarthy	964,722	Orig. Yankee Stadium
1942	AL	First	+9.0	103	51	.669	Joe McCarthy	988,251	Orig. Yankee Stadium
1943	WS	First	+13.5	98	56	.636	Joe McCarthy	645,006	Orig. Yankee Stadium
1944		Third	-6.0	83	71	.539	Joe McCarthy	789,995	Orig. Yankee Stadium
1945		Fourth	-6.5	81	71	.533	Joe McCarthy	881,846	Orig. Yankee Stadium
1946		Third	-17.0	87	67	.565	McCarthy-Bill Dickey-Johnny Neun	2,265,512	Orig. Yankee Stadium
1947	WS	First	+12.0	97	57	.630	Bucky Harris	2,178,937	Orig. Yankee Stadium
1948		Third	-2.5	94	60	.610	Bucky Harris	2,373,901	Orig. Yankee Stadium
1949	WS	First	+1.0	97	57	.630	Casey Stengel	2,281,676	Orig. Yankee Stadium
1950	WS	First	+3.0	98	56	.636	Casey Stengel	2,081,380	Orig. Yankee Stadium
1951	WS	First	+5.0	98	56	.636	Casey Stengel	1,950,107	Orig. Yankee Stadium
1952	WS	First	+2.0	95	59	.617	Casey Stengel	1,629,665	Orig. Yankee Stadium
1953	WS	First	+8.5	99	52	.656	Casey Stengel	1,537,811	Orig. Yankee Stadium
1954		Second	-8.0	103	51	.669	Casey Stengel	1,475,171	Orig. Yankee Stadium
1955	AL	First	+3.0	96	58	.623	Casey Stengel	1,490,138	Orig. Yankee Stadium
1956	WS	First	+9.0	97	57	.680	Casey Stengel	1,491,138	Orig. Yankee Stadium
1957	AL	First	+8.0	98	56	.636	Casey Stengel	1,497,134	Orig. Yankee Stadium
1958	WS	First	+10.0	92	62	.597	Casey Stengel	1,428,438	Orig. Yankee Stadium
1959		Third	-15.0	79	75	.513	Casey Stengel	1,552,030	Orig. Yankee Stadium
1960	AL	First	+8.0	97	57	.630	Casey Stengel	1,627,349	Orig. Yankee Stadium
1961	WS	First	+8.0	109	53	.673	Ralph Houk	1,747,725	Orig. Yankee Stadium
1962	WS	First	+5.0	96	66	.593	Ralph Houk	1,493,574	Orig. Yankee Stadium
1963	AL	First	+10.5	104	57	.646	Ralph Houk	1,308,920	Orig. Yankee Stadium

Year-by-Year Results

Year		Position	GA/GB	Won	Lost	Pct.	Manager	Attendance	
1964	AL	First	+1.0	99	63	.611	Yogi Berra	1,305,638	Orig. Yankee Stadium
1965		Sixth	-25.0	77	85	.475	Johnny Keane	1,213,552	Orig. Yankee Stadium
1966		Tenth	-26.5	70	89	.440	Keane-Houk	1,124,648	Orig. Yankee Stadium
1967		Ninth	-20.0	72	90	.444	Ralph Houk	1,259,514	Orig. Yankee Stadium
1968		Fifth	-20.0	83	79	.512	Ralph Houk	1,185,666	Orig. Yankee Stadium
1969		Fifth	-28.5	80	81	.497	Ralph Houk	1,067,996	Orig. Yankee Stadium
1970		Second	-15.0	93	69	.574	Ralph Houk	1,136,879	Orig. Yankee Stadium
1971		Fourth	-21.0	82	80	.506	Ralph Houk	1,070,771	Orig. Yankee Stadium
1972		Fourth	-6.5	79	76	.510	Ralph Houk	966,328	Orig. Yankee Stadium
1973		Fourth	-17.0	80	82	.494	Ralph Houk	1,262,103	Orig. Yankee Stadium
1974		Second	-2.0	89	73	.549	Bill Virdon	1,273,075	Shea Stadium
1975		Third	-12.0	83	77	.519	Virdon-Billy Martin	1,288,048	Shea Stadium
1976	AL	First	+10.5	97	62	.610	Billy Martin	2,012,434	Orig. Yankee Stadium (R)
1977	WS	First	+2.5	100	62	.617	Billy Martin	2,103,092	Orig. Yankee Stadium (R)
1978	WS	First	+1.0	100	63	.613	Martin-Bob Lemon	2,335,871	Orig. Yankee Stadium (R)
1979		Fourth	-13.5	89	71	.556	Lemon-Martin	2,537,765	Orig. Yankee Stadium (R)
1980		First	+3.0	103	59	.636	Dick Howser	2,627,417	Orig. Yankee Stadium (R)
1981	AL	First	+2.0	34	22	.607	Gene Michael		
		Sixth	-5.0	25	26	.490	Michael-Lemon	1,614,353	Orig. Yankee Stadium (R)
1982		Fifth	-16.0	79	83	.488	Lemon-Michael-Clyde King	2,041,219	Orig. Yankee Stadium (R)
1983		Third	-7.0	91	71	.562	Billy Martin	2,257,976	Orig. Yankee Stadium (R)
1984		Third	-17.0	87	75	.537	Yogi Berra	1,821,815	Orig. Yankee Stadium (R)
1985		Second	-2.0	97	64	.602	Berra-Martin	2,214,587	Orig. Yankee Stadium (R)
1986		Second	-5.5	90	72	.556	Lou Piniella	2,268,030	Orig. Yankee Stadium (R)
1987		Fourth	-9.0	89	73	.549	Lou Piniella	2,427,672	Orig. Yankee Stadium (R)
1988		Fifth	-3.5	85	76	.528	Martin-Piniella	2,633,701	Orig. Yankee Stadium (R)
1989		Fifth	-14.5	74	87	.460	Dallas Green-Bucky Dent	2,170,485	Orig. Yankee Stadium (R)
1990		Seventh	-21.0	67	95	.414	Dent-Stump Merrill	2,006,436	Orig. Yankee Stadium (R)
1991		Fifth	-21.0	71	91	.438	Stump Merrill	1,863,733	Orig. Yankee Stadium (R)
1992		Fourth	-20.0	76	86	.469	Buck Showalter	1,748,773	Orig. Yankee Stadium (R)
1993		Second	-7.0	88	74	.543	Buck Showalter	2,416,965	Orig. Yankee Stadium (R)
1994		First	+6.5	70	43	.619	Buck Showalter	1,675,556	Orig. Yankee Stadium (R)
1995		Second	-7.0	79	65	.549	Buck Showalter	1,705,263	Orig. Yankee Stadium (R)
1996	WS	First	+4.0	92	70	.568	Joe Torre	2,250,877	Orig. Yankee Stadium (R)
1997		Second	-2.0	96	66	593	Joe Torre	2,580,445	Orig. Yankee Stadium (R)
1998	WS	First	+22.0	114	48	.704	Joe Torre	2,919,046	Orig. Yankee Stadium (R)
1999	WS	First	+4.0	98	64	.605	Joe Torre	3,292,736	Orig. Yankee Stadium (R)
2000	WS	First	+2.5	87	74	.540	Joe Torre	3,227,657	Orig. Yankee Stadium (R)
2001	AL	First	+13.5	95	65	.594	Joe Torre	3,264,777	Orig. Yankee Stadium (R)
2002		First	+10.5	103	58	.640	Joe Torre	3,461,644	Orig. Yankee Stadium (R)
2003	AL	First	+6.0	101	61	.623	Joe Torre	3,465,585	Orig. Yankee Stadium (R)
2004		First	+3.0	101	61	.623	Joe Torre	3,775,292	Orig. Yankee Stadium (R)
2005		First*	0.0	95	67	.586	Joe Torre	4,090,692	Orig. Yankee Stadium (R)
2006		First	+10.0	97	65	.599	Joe Torre	4,243,780	Orig. Yankee Stadium (R)
2007		Second	-2.0	94	68	.580	Joe Torre	4,271,083	Orig. Yankee Stadium (R)
2008		Third	-8.0	89	73	.549	Joe Girardi	4,298,543	Orig. Yankee Stadium (R)
2009	WS	First	+8.0	103	59	.636	Joe Girardi	3,719,358	Yankee Stadium
2010		Second	-1.0	95	67	.586	Joe Girardi	3,765,803	Yankee Stadium
Totals	**27WS/40AL**			**9,552**	**7,208**	**.570**		(R) Remodeled Orig. Yankee Stadium	

* Won head-to-head tie-breaker

Notable Postseason Home Runs

GRAND SLAMS

DIVISION SERIES . . . . .Paul O'Neill, October 4, 1997 at Cleveland (Game 3)

LEAGUE CHAMPIONSHIP SERIES . . . . .Ricky Ledee, October 17, 1999 at Boston (Game 4)

WORLD SERIES. . . . . .Tony Lazzeri, October 2, 1936 at New York Giants (Game 2)
Gil McDougald, October 9, 1951 at New York Giants (Game 5)
Mickey Mantle, October 4, 1953 at Brooklyn (Game 5)
Yogi Berra, October 5, 1956 at Brooklyn (Game 2)
Bill Skowron, October 10, 1956 at Brooklyn (Game 7)
Bobby Richardson, October 8, 1960 vs. Pittsburgh (Game 3)
Joe Pepitone, October 14, 1964 at St. Louis (Game 6)
Tino Martinez, October 17, 1998 vs. San Diego (Game 1)

PINCH-HIT HOME RUNS

DIVISION SERIES . . . . .David Justice, October 15, 2001 vs. Oakland (Game 5)

LEAGUE CHAMPIONSHIP SERIES . . . . .Ricky Ledee, October 17, 1999 at Boston (Game 4)
Ruben Sierra, October 13, 2003 at Boston (Game 4)

WORLD SERIES. . . . . .Yogi Berra, October 2, 1947 at Boston (Game 3)
Johnny Mize, October 3, 1952 vs. Brooklyn (Game 3)
Bob Cerv, October 2, 1955 at Brooklyn (Game 5)
Elston Howard, October 5, 1960 at Pittsburgh (Game 1)
John Blanchard, October 7, 1961 at Cincinnati (Game 3)
Jim Leyritz, October 27, 1999 vs. Atlanta (Game 4)
Jason Giambi, October 23, 2003 at Florida (Game 5)
Hideki Matsui, October 31, 2009 at Philadelphia (Game 3)

INSIDE-THE-PARK HOME RUNS

DIVISION SERIES . . . . .Never accomplished by a Yankees player.

LEAGUE CHAMPIONSHIP SERIES . . . . .Graig Nettles, October 9, 1980 at Kansas City (Game 2)

WORLD SERIES. . . . . .Never accomplished by a Yankees player.

LEADOFF HOME RUNS

DIVISION SERIES . . . . .Derek Jeter, October 6, 2004 vs. Minnesota (Game 2)
Johnny Damon, October 4, 2007 at Cleveland (Game 1)

LEAGUE CHAMPIONSHIP SERIES . . . . .Derek Jeter, October 19, 2009 at Los Angeles-AL (Game 3)

WORLD SERIES. . . . . .Phil Rizzuto, October 5, 1942 vs. St. Louis (Game 5)
Gene Woodling, October 4, 1953 at Brooklyn (Game 5)
Derek Jeter, October 25, 2000 at New York Mets (Game 4)
Derek Jeter is the only player ever to hit a leadoff homer in each of the three postseason rounds.

WALK-OFF HOME RUNS

DIVISION SERIES . . . . .Jim Leyritz, October 4, 1995 vs. Seattle (Game 2), 15th inning
Mark Teixeira, October 9, 2009 vs. Minnesota (Game 2), 11th inning

LEAGUE CHAMPIONSHIP SERIES . . . . .Chris Chambliss, October 14, 1976 vs. Kansas City (Game 5)*
Bernie Williams, October 9, 1996 vs. Baltimore (Game 1), 11th inning
Bernie Williams, October 13, 1999 vs. Boston (Game 1), 10th inning
Alfonso Soriano, October 21, 2001 vs. Seattle (Game 4)
Aaron Boone, October 16, 2003 vs. Boston (Game 7), 11th inning*

WORLD SERIES. . . . . .Tommy Henrich, October 5, 1949 vs. Brooklyn (Game 1)
Mickey Mantle, October 10, 1964 vs. St. Louis (Game 3)
Chad Curtis, October 26, 1999 vs. Atlanta (Game 3), 10th inning
Derek Jeter, October 31, 2001 vs. Arizona (Game 4), 10th inning

*clinched series

GRAND SLAMS ALLOWED

DIVISION SERIES . . . . .Edgar Martinez, October 7, 1995 (Game 4) at Seattle off John Wetteland

LEAGUE CHAMPIONSHIP SERIES . . . . .Jim Thome, October 13, 1998 (Game 6) vs. Cleveland off David Cone
Johnny Damon, October 20, 2004 (Game 7) vs. Boston off Javier Vazquez

WORLD SERIES. . . . . .Chuck Hiller, October 8, 1962 (Game 4) vs. San Francisco off Marshall Bridges
Ken Boyer, October 11, 1964 (Game 4) vs. St. Louis off Al Downing

WALK-OFF HOME RUNS ALLOWED (14 walk-off losses total in postseason play)

DIVISION SERIES . . . . .Never allowed.

LEAGUE CHAMPIONSHIP SERIES . . . . .David Ortiz, October 17, 2004 (Game 4) at Boston (12th inning) off Paul Quantrill

WORLD SERIES. . . . . .Eddie Mathews, October 6, 1957 (Game 4) at Milwaukee (10th inning) off Bob Grim
Bill Mazeroski, October 13, 1960 (Game 7) at Pittsburgh off Ralph Terry*
Alex Gonzalez, October 22, 2003 (Game 4) at Florida (12th inning) off Jeff Weaver

*clinched series

YANKEES TO HOMER IN FIRST CAREER WORLD SERIES AT-BAT
(According to *Elias Sports Bureau* Record Book)

Chick Fewster . . . . . . 10/11/21 in Game 6 loss vs. the New York Giants off Jesse Barnes (second inning, 1 on)*
George Selkirk . . . . . 9/30/36 in Game 1 loss at the New York Giants off Carl Hubbell (third inning, solo)
Elston Howard . . . . . 9/28/55 in Game 1 win vs. Brooklyn off Don Newcombe (second inning, 1 on)
Roger Maris. . . . . 10/5/60 in Game 1 loss at Pittsburgh off Vern Law (first inning, solo)
Jim Mason . . . . 10/19/76 in Game 3 loss vs. Cincinnati off Pat Zachry (seventh inning, solo) –
pinch-hit HR was his only career World Series plate appearance.
Bob Watson. . . . . 10/20/81 in Game 1 win vs. Los Angeles (NL) off Jerry Reuss (first inning, 2 on)

*All but Fewster homered in their first plate appearance.

IN A PINCH: There have been 24 pinch-hit home runs all time in World Series play, eight of which have been hit by a Yankee…the first pinch-hit home run during a World Series game was hit by Yogi Berra on 10/2/47 in a Game 3 loss at Brooklyn…Berra's solo homer came in the seventh inning off Ralph Branca and was his first career postseason hit.

Chris Chambliss hits a walk-off home run off Kansas City reliever Mark Littell to win Game 5 and clinch the 1976 League Championship Series, catapulting the Yankees to their first World Series appearance since 1964.

Yankees Postseason Reference Sheet

YANKEES ALL-TIME POSTSEASON LEADERS

GAMES PLAYED
1. DEREK JETER 138
2. Bernie Williams 121
3. JORGE POSADA. 111
4. MARIANO RIVERA 88
5. Tino Martinez 81

RUNS
1. DEREK JETER 99
2. Bernie Williams 83
3. JORGE POSADA 46
4. Mickey Mantle 42
5. Yogi Berra 41

HITS
1. DEREK JETER 175
2. Bernie Williams 128
3. JORGE POSADA 89
4. Paul O'Neill 76
5. Yogi Berra 71

HOME RUNS
1. Bernie Williams 22
2. DEREK JETER 20
3. Mickey Mantle 18
4. Babe Ruth 15
5. Yogi Berra, Reggie Jackson 12

RBI
1. Bernie Williams 80
2. DEREK JETER 55
3. Mickey Mantle 40
T4. Yogi Berra, Hideki Matsui, JORGE POSADA . . 39

BATTING AVERAGE (min. 75PA)
1. Lou Gehrig .361
2. Thurman Munson. 357
3. Babe Ruth .347
4. Billy Martin 333
5. Reggie Jackson 328

WINS
1. ANDY PETTITTE 17
2. Whitey Ford 10
3. Orlando Hernandez 9
4. MARIANO RIVERA 8
5. Four tied 7

SAVES (official stat since 1969)
1. MARIANO RIVERA 39
2. Goose Gossage 7
   John Wetteland 7
4. Ken Clay, Sparky Lyle . . . . . .
   and Ramiro Mendoza 1

GAMES
1. MARIANO RIVERA 88
2. Jeff Nelson 44
3. ANDY PETTITTE 36
4. Mike Stanton 31
5. Whitey Ford 22

GAMES STARTED
1. ANDY PETTITTE 36
2. Whitey Ford 22
3. Roger Clemens 18
4. Mike Mussina 15
5. Orlando Hernandez . . 14

INNINGS PITCHED
1. ANDY PETTITTE 223.2
2. Whitey Ford 146.0
3. MARIANO RIVERA 133.1
4. Roger Clemens 102.1
5. Orlando Hernandez 102.0

STRIKEOUTS
1. ANDY PETTITTE 148
2. MARIANO RIVERA 107
3. Orlando Hernandez 101
4. Roger Clemens 99
5. Whitey Ford .94

ERA (min. 40.0IP)
1. MARIANO RIVERA 0.74
2. Waite Hoyt 1.62
3. Herb Pennock 2.06
4. Vic Raschi 2.24
5. Ed Lopat 2.60

Yankees All-Time Postseason Highs

TEAM BATTING
Runs, game, Yankees – 19 – 2004 ALCS Game 3 at BOS
Runs, game, Opponent – 15 – 2001 WS Game 6 at ARI
Runs, inn., Yankees – 7 – 7x, last 2000 ALCS Game 2 vs. SEA – 8th inn.
Runs, inn., Opp. – 8 – 3x, last 2002 ALDS Game 4 at ANA – 5th inn.
Hits, game, Yankees – 20 – 2004 ALCS Game 3 at BOS
Hits, game, Opponent – 22 – 2001 WS Game 6 at ARI
Extra-base hits, game, Yankees – 13 – 2004 ALCS Game 3 at BOS
Extra-base hits, game, Opponent – 10 – 1999 ALCS Game 3 at BOS
Home runs, game, Yankees – 5 – 1928 WS Game 4 at STL
Home runs, game, Opponent – 4 – 6x, last 2007 ALDS at CLE
Singles, game, Yankees – 16 – 1978 WS Game 5 vs. LAD
Singles, game, Opponent – 16 – 2001 WS Game 6 at ARI
Doubles, game, Yankees – 8 – 2004 ALCS Game 3 at BOS
Doubles, game, Opp. – 6 – 4x, last 2001 WS Game 6 at ARI
Triples, game, Yankees – 3 – 2x, last 1960 WS Game 6 at PIT
Triples, game, Opponents – 2 – 8x, last 2005 ALDS Game 3 vs. LAA
Left on base, game, Yankees – 18 – 2004 ALCS Game 5 at BOS
Left on base, game, Opponent – 17 – 2009 ALDS Game 2 vs. MIN
Stolen bases, game, Yankees – 4 – 1998 ALCS Game 4 at CLE
Stolen bases, game, Opp. – 3 – 4x, last 1995 ALDS Game 3 at SEA

TEAM FIELDING
Double plays turned, game, Yankees – 4 – 1951 WS at NYG
Double plays turned, game, Opp. – 5 – 2004 ALDS Game 1 vs. MIN
Errors, game, Yankees – 5 – 1976 ALCS Game 2 at Kansas City
Errors, game, Opponent – 4 – 8x, last 1999 ALCS Game 4 at BOS

TEAM PITCHING
Strikeouts, game, Yankees – 15 – 2000 ALCS Game 4 at SEA
Strikeouts, game, Opponent – 16 – 2x, last 2004 ALCS Game 5 at BOS
Walks, game, Yankees – 11 – 1956 WS Game 2 at BRO
Walks, game, Opponent – 11 – 2x, last 2001 ALCS Game 4 vs. SEA

INDIVIDUAL BATTING
At-bats, game – 7 – 5x, last by four players, 2004 ALCS Game 5 at BOS
Runs, game – 5 – 2x, Alex Rodriguez and Hideki Matsui
   2004 ALCS Game 3 at BOS
Hits, game – 5 – 2x, Derek Jeter, 2006 ALDS Game 1 vs. DET;
   Hideki Matsui, 2004 ALCS Game 3 at BOS
Doubles, game – 2 – Done by many, last by Alex Rodriguez,
   2009 WS Game 5 at PHI
Triples, game – 2 – Bobby Richardson, 1960 WS Game 6 at PIT
HR, game – 3 – 3x, Reggie Jackson, 1977 WS Game 6 vs. LAD;
   Babe Ruth, 1926 WS Game 4 at STL;
   Babe Ruth, 1928 WS Game 4 at STL
Grand slams – 1 – 10x, last Ricky Ledee, 1999 ALCS Game 4 at BOS
RBI, game – 6 – 3x, Hideki Matsui, 2009 WS Game 6 vs. PHI;
   Bernie Williams, 1999 ALDS Game 1 vs. TEX;
   Bobby Richardson, 1960 WS Game 3 vs. PIT
Walks, game – 4 – 2x, Bernie Williams, 1995 ALDS Game 5 at SEA;
   Babe Ruth, 1926 WS Game 7 vs. STL
Strikeouts, game – 5 – George Pipgras, 1932 WS Game 3 at CHC

INDIVIDUAL PITCHING
Strikeouts, game – 15 – Roger Clemens, 2000 ALCS Game 4 at SEA
Walks, game – 10 – Bill Bevens – 1947 WS Game 4 at BRO
ER allowed, game – 8 – 3x, C. Wang, 2007 ALDS Game 1 vs. CLE;
   Jay Witasick, 2001 WS Game 6 at ARI;
   David Wells, 2002 ALDS Game 4 at ANA
Hits allowed, game – 14 – Waite Hoyt, 1926 WS Game 4 at STL

TEAM MISCELLANEOUS
Longest game, innings – 15 – 1995 ALDS Game 2 vs. SEA
Margin of victory – 13 runs – 16-3 win in 1960 WS Game 2 at PIT
Margin of defeat – 13 runs – 15-2 loss in 2001 WS Game 6 at ARI
Largest crowd, home – 74,065 – 1947 WS Game 6 vs. BRO
Largest crowd, road – 65,975 – 2003 WS Game 5 at FLA

Yankees Postseason Results

1921 WORLD SERIES

Marked the Yankees' first ever World Series appearance in Baseball's last nine-game Fall Classic…Waite Hoyt went 2-1 despite not allowing an earned run in 27.0IP (18H, 11BB) over three starts…is tied with Christy Mathewson (1905) for the most IP without allowing an ER in a single World Series…lost, 1-0, in the Game 8 clincher, tossing a complete game and allowing an unearned run in the first inning…Carl Mays went 1-2 with a 1.73 ERA (26.0IP, 5ER) in his three starts, setting a still-standing record for most innings pitched in a single postseason without allowing a walk…Babe Ruth hit the first of his 15 career World Series home runs in a losing effort in Game 4.

New York Yankees (AL) 3
New York Giants (NL) 5

GAME 1 at Polo Grounds, Manhattan, N.Y., Oct. 5
NYY	1 0 0	0 1 1	0 0 0	- 3	7	0
NYG	0 0 0	0 0 0	0 0 0	- 0	5	0
W - Mays   L - Douglas   A - 30,202

GAME 2 at Polo Grounds, Manhattan, N.Y., Oct. 6
NYG	0 0 0	0 0 0	0 0 0	- 0	2	3
NYY	0 0 0	1 0 0	0 2 X	- 3	3	0
W - Hoyt   L - Nehf   A - 34,939

GAME 3 at Polo Grounds, Manhattan, N.Y., Oct. 7
NYY	0 0 4	0 0 0	0 1 0	- 5	8	0
NYG	0 0 4	0 0 0	8 1 X	- 13	20	0
W - Barnes   L - Quinn   A - 36,509

GAME 4 at Polo Grounds, Manhattan, N.Y., Oct. 9
NYG	0 0 0	0 0 0	0 3 1	- 4	9	1
NYY	0 0 0	0 1 0	0 0 1	- 2	7	1
W - Douglas   L - Mays   A - 36,372

GAME 5 at Polo Grounds, Manhattan, N.Y., Oct. 10
NYY	0 0 1	2 0 0	0 0 0	- 3	6	1
NYG	1 0 0	0 0 0	0 0 0	- 1	10	1
W - Hoyt   L - Nehf   A - 35,758

GAME 6 at Polo Grounds, Manhattan, N.Y., Oct. 11
NYG	0 3 0	4 0 1	0 0 0	- 8	13	0
NYY	3 2 0	0 0 0	0 0 0	- 5	7	2
W - Barnes   L - Shawkey   A - 34,283

GAME 7 at Polo Grounds, Manhattan, N.Y., Oct. 12
NYY	0 1 0	0 0 0	0 0 0	- 1	8	1
NYG	0 0 0	1 0 0	1 0 X	- 2	6	0
W - Douglas   L - Mays   A - 36,503

GAME 8 at Polo Grounds, Manhattan, N.Y., Oct. 13
NYG	1 0 0	0 0 0	0 0 0	- 1	6	0
NYY	0 0 0	0 0 0	0 0 0	- 0	4	1
W - Nehf   L - Hoyt   A - 25,410

Babe Ruth hit the first of his 15 career World Series home runs in Game 4 of the 1921 World Series.

1922 WORLD SERIES

The Yankees went 0-4-1 against the Giants, marking just one of three times in 40 World Series appearances that the Yankees have been held without a win (were swept in 1963 vs. Los Angeles and 1976 vs. Cincinnati)…hit just .203 as a team…Game 2 marked the Yankees' only tie in 225 overall World Series games (134-90-1).

New York Yankees (AL) 0
New York Giants (NL) 4

GAME 1 at Polo Grounds, Manhattan, N.Y., Oct. 4
NYY	0 0 0	0 0 1	1 0 0	- 2	7	0
NYG	0 0 0	0 0 0	0 3 X	- 3	11	3
W - Ryan   L - Bush   A - 36,514

GAME 2 at Polo Grounds, Manhattan, N.Y., Oct. 5
NYG	3 0 0	0 0 0	0 0 0 0	- 3	8	1
NYY	1 0 0	1 0 0	0 1 0 0	- 3	8	0
(Called after 10 innings because of darkness)   A - 37,020

GAME 3 at Polo Grounds, Manhattan, N.Y., Oct. 6
NYY	0 0 0	0 0 0	0 0 0	- 0	4	1
NYG	0 0 2	0 0 0	1 0 X	- 3	12	1
W - Scott   L - Hoyt   A - 37,620

GAME 4 at Polo Grounds, Manhattan, N.Y., Oct. 7
NYG	0 0 0	0 4 0	0 0 0	- 4	9	1
NYY	2 0 0	0 0 0	1 0 0	- 3	8	0
W - McQuillan L - Mays   A - 36,242

GAME 5 at Polo Grounds, Manhattan, N.Y., Oct. 8
NYY	1 0 0	0 1 0	1 0 0	- 3	5	0
NYG	0 2 0	0 0 0	0 3 X	- 5	10	0
W - Nehf   L - Bush   A - 38,551

1923 WORLD SERIES

Won the first World Series in franchise history in the inaugural season of the original Yankee Stadium…their Game 2 win snapped a nine-game World Series winless streak dating to 1921 (0-8-1)…scored five runs in the eighth inning of the Game 6 clincher to win, 6-4…Babe Ruth and Bob Meusel led the Yankees in HR (3) and RBI (8), respectively.

New York Giants (NL) 2
New York Yankees (AL) 4

GAME 1 at Yankee Stadium, Bronx, N.Y., Oct. 10
NYG	0 0 4	0 0 0	0 0 1	- 5	8	0
NYY	1 2 0	0 0 0	1 0 0	- 4	12	1
W - Ryan   L - Bush   A - 55,307

GAME 2 at Polo Grounds, Manhattan, N.Y., Oct. 11
NYY	0 1 0	2 1 0	0 0 0	- 4	10	0
NYG	0 1 0	0 0 1	0 0 0	- 2	9	2
W - Pennock   L - McQuillan   A - 40,402

GAME 3 at Yankee Stadium, Bronx, N.Y., Oct. 12
NYG	0 0 0	0 0 0	1 0 0	- 1	4	0
NYY	0 0 0	0 0 0	0 0 0	- 0	6	1
W - Nehf   L - Jones   A - 62,430

GAME 4 at Polo Grounds, Manhattan, N.Y., Oct. 13
NYY	0 6 1	1 0 0	0 0 0	- 8	13	1
NYG	0 0 0	0 0 0	0 3 1	- 4	13	1
W - Shawkey   L - Scott   A - 46,302

GAME 5 at Yankee Stadium, Bronx, N.Y., Oct. 14
NYG	0 1 0	0 0 0	0 0 0	- 1	3	2
NYY	3 4 0	1 0 0	0 0 X	- 8	14	0
W - Bush   L - Bentley   A - 62,817

GAME 6 at Polo Grounds, Manhattan, N.Y., Oct. 15
NYY	1 0 0	0 0 0	0 5 0	- 6	5	0
NYG	1 0 0	1 1 1	0 0 0	- 4	10	1
W - Pennock   L - Nehf   A - 34,172

1926 WORLD SERIES

The Series is most remembered for Game 7, which featured Pete Alexander's bases-loaded, seventh-inning strikeout of Tony Lazzeri, and Babe Ruth making the final out of the series attempting to steal second base with the Yankees down, 3-2, in the ninth…Ruth became the first player to hit 3HR in a single World Series game (Game 4 at St. Louis) and the first to hit 4HR over an entire World Series.

St. Louis Cardinals (NL)   4
New York Yankees (AL)   3

GAME 1 at Yankee Stadium, Bronx, N.Y., Oct. 2

STL	1 0 0	0 0 0	0 0 0	- 1	3	1
NYY	1 0 0	0 0 1	0 0 X	- 2	6	0

W - Pennock   L - Sherdel   A - 61,658

GAME 2 at Yankee Stadium, Bronx, N.Y., Oct. 3

STL	0 0 2	0 0 0	3 0 1	- 6	12	1
NYY	0 2 0	0 0 0	0 0 0	- 2	4	0

W - Alexander   L - Shocker   A - 63,600

GAME 3 at Sportsman's Park, St. Louis, Oct. 5

NYY	0 0 0	0 0 0	0 0 0	- 0	5	1
STL	0 0 0	3 1 0	0 0 X	- 4	8	0

W - Haines   L - Ruether   A - 37,708

GAME 4 at Sportsman's Park, St. Louis, Oct. 6

NYY	1 0 1	1 4 2	1 0 0	- 10	14	1
STL	1 0 0	3 0 0	0 0 1	- 5	14	0

W - Hoyt   L - Reinhart   A - 38,825

GAME 5 at Sportsman's Park, St. Louis, Oct. 7

NYY	0 0 0	0 0 1	0 0 1 1	- 3	9	1
STL	0 0 0	1 0 0	1 0 0 0	- 2	7	1

W - Pennock   L - Sherdel   A - 39,552

GAME 6 at Yankee Stadium, St. Louis, Oct. 9

STL	3 0 0	0 1 0	5 0 1	- 10	13	2
NYY	0 0 0	1 0 0	1 0 0	- 2	8	1

W - Alexander   L - Shawkey   A - 48,615

GAME 7 at Yankee Stadium, St. Louis, Oct. 10

STL	0 0 0	3 0 0	0 0 0	- 3	8	0
NYY	0 0 1	0 0 1	0 0 0	- 2	8	3

W - Haines   L - Hoyt   A - 38,093

1927 WORLD SERIES

The Murderers' Row Yankees became the first AL team to sweep a World Series…Babe Ruth had a Series-high 7RBI and his 2HR were the only homers of the Series…Herb Pennock was perfect through his first 22 batters of Game 3 before a Pie Traynor single…Yankees completed the sweep on a ninth-inning wild pitch from Pirates pitcher Johnny Miljus in Game 4…marked the first of eight consecutive winning World Series appearances for the franchise (1927-28, 32, '36-39, '41).

New York Yankees (AL)   4
Pittsburgh Pirates (NL)   0

GAME 1 at Forbes Field, Pittsburgh, Oct. 5

NYY	1 0 3	0 1 0	0 0 0	- 5	6	1
PIT	1 0 1	0 1 0	0 1 0	- 4	9	2

W - Hoyt   L - Kremer   A - 41,467

GAME 2 at Forbes Field, Pittsburgh, Oct. 6

NYY	0 0 3	0 0 0	0 3 0	- 6	11	0
PIT	1 0 0	0 0 0	0 1 0	- 2	7	2

W - Pipgras   L - Aldridge   A - 41,634

GAME 3 at Yankee Stadium, Bronx, N.Y., Oct. 7

PIT	0 0 0	0 0 0	0 1 0	- 1	3	1
NYY	2 0 0	0 0 0	6 0 X	- 8	9	0

W - Pennock   L - Meadows   A - 60,695

GAME 4 at Yankee Stadium, Bronx, N.Y., Oct. 8

PIT	1 0 0	0 0 0	2 0 0	- 3	10	1
NYY	1 0 0	0 2 0	0 0 1	- 4	12	2

W - Moore   L - Miljus   A - 57,909

1928 WORLD SERIES

The Yankees' win marked their first back-to-back titles…was the sixth and last Series for manager Miller Huggins, who died during the 1929 season…used only three pitchers in the entire Series as each earned complete-game wins (Waite Hoyt in Games 1 and 4; George Pipgras in Game 2 and Tom Zachary in Game 3)…Lou Gehrig led the Yankees with 4HR and 9RBI…Babe Ruth tied his own record with 3HR in Game 4 at St. Louis.

St. Louis Cardinals (NL)   0
New York Yankees (AL)   4

GAME 1 at Yankee Stadium, Bronx, N.Y., Oct. 4

STL	0 0 0	0 0 0	1 0 0	- 1	3	1
NYY	1 0 0	2 0 0	0 1 X	- 4	7	0

W - Hoyt   L - Sherdel   A - 61,425

GAME 2 at Yankee Stadium, Bronx, N.Y., Oct. 5

STL	0 3 0	0 0 0	0 0 0	- 3	4	1
NYY	3 1 4	0 0 0	1 0 X	- 9	8	2

W - Pipgras   L - Alexander   A - 60,714

GAME 3 at Sportsman's Park, St. Louis, Oct. 7

NYY	0 1 0	2 0 3	1 0 0	- 7	7	2
STL	2 0 0	0 1 0	0 0 0	- 3	9	3

W - Zachary   L - Haines   A - 39,602

GAME 4 at Sportsman's Park, St. Louis, Oct. 9

NYY	0 0 0	1 0 0	4 2 0	- 7	15	2
STL	0 0 1	1 0 0	0 0 1	- 3	11	0

W - Hoyt   L - Sherdel   A - 37,331

1932 WORLD SERIES

The Yankees swept the Cubs to run their World Series winning streak to 12 games…was the first of Manager Joe McCarthy's eight Series appearances and seven titles with the club…Babe Ruth hit his "called shot" off Cubs pitcher Charlie Root in the fifth inning of Game 3…he and Gehrig each hit 2HR in the game…the Yankees outscored the Cubs 37-19 in the Series…Gehrig batted .529 (9-for-17) with 9R, 3HR and 8RBI…was Ruth's last World Series with the Yankees.

Chicago Cubs (NL)   0
New York Yankees (AL)   4

GAME 1 at Yankee Stadium, Bronx, N.Y., Sept. 28

CHC	2 0 0	0 0 0	2 2 0	- 6	10	1
NYY	0 0 0	3 0 5	3 1 X	- 12	8	2

W - Ruffing   L - Bush   A - 41,459

GAME 2 at Yankee Stadium, Bronx, N.Y., Sept. 29

CHC	1 0 1	0 0 0	0 0 0	- 2	9	0
NYY	2 0 2	0 1 0	0 0 X	- 5	10	1

W - Gomez   L - Warneke   A - 50,709

GAME 3 at Wrigley Field, Chicago, Oct. 1

NYY	3 0 1	0 2 0	0 0 1	- 7	8	1
CHC	1 0 2	1 0 0	0 0 1	- 5	9	4

W - Pipgras   L - Root   A - 49,986

GAME 4 at Wrigley Field, Chicago, Oct. 2

NYY	1 0 2	0 0 2	4 0 4	- 13	19	4
CHC	4 0 0	0 0 1	0 0 1	- 6	9	1

W - Moore   L - May   A - 49,844

1936 WORLD SERIES

The Yankees' victory was the first of four consecutive titles…had their 12-game World Series winning streak snapped with a Game 1 loss…the Yankees' 18-4 Game 2 win still marks the most runs scored by one team in a World Series game…Bill Dickey and Tony Lazzeri (grand slam) each had 5RBI in the game…rookie Joe DiMaggio batted .346 (9-for-26) with 3RBI in the Series.

New York Yankees (AL)   4
New York Giants (NL)   2

GAME 1 at Polo Grounds, Manhattan, N.Y., Sept. 30

NYY	0 0 1	0 0 0	0 0 0	-	1	7	2
NYG	0 0 0	0 1 1	0 4 X	-	6	9	1

W - Hubbell   L - Ruffing   A - 39,419

GAME 2 at Polo Grounds, Manhattan, N.Y., Oct. 2

NYY	2 0 7	0 0 1	2 0 6	-	18	17	0
NYG	0 1 0	3 0 0	0 0 0	-	4	6	1

W - Gomez   L - Schumacher   A - 43,543

GAME 3 at Yankee Stadium, Bronx, N.Y., Oct. 3

NYG	0 0 0	0 1 0	0 0 0	-	1	11	0
NYY	0 1 0	0 0 0	0 1 X	-	2	4	0

W - Hadley   L - Fitzsimmons   A - 64,842

GAME 4 at Yankee Stadium, Bronx, N.Y., Oct. 4

NYG	0 0 0	1 0 0	0 1 0	-	2	7	1
NYY	0 1 3	0 0 0	0 1 X	-	5	10	1

W - Pearson   L - Hubbell   A - 66,669

GAME 5 at Yankee Stadium, Bronx, N.Y., Oct. 5

NYG	3 0 0	0 0 1	0 0 0	1	-	5	8	3
NYY	0 1 1	0 0 0	2 0 0	0	-	4	10	1

W - Schumacher   L - Malone   A - 50,024

GAME 6 at Polo Grounds, Manhattan, N.Y., Oct. 6

NYY	0 2 1	2 0 0	0 1 7	-	13	17	2
NYG	2 0 0	0 0 0	1 1 0	-	5	9	1

W - Gomez   L - Fitzsimmons   A - 38,427

1937 WORLD SERIES

The Yankees defeated the Giants for the second year in a row…Yankees pitchers posted a 2.45 ERA (44.0, 12ER) in the Series…Lefty Gomez recorded complete-game wins in Game 1 and in the Game 5 clincher…George Selkirk led the Yankees with 5R and 6RBI.

New York Giants (NL)   1
New York Yankees (AL)   4

GAME 1 at Yankee Stadium, Bronx, N.Y., Oct. 6

NYG	0 0 0	0 1 0	0 0 0	-	1	6	2
NYY	0 0 0	0 0 7	0 1 X	-	8	7	0

W - Gomez   L - Hubbell   A - 60,573

GAME 2 at Yankee Stadium, Bronx, N.Y., Oct. 7

NYG	1 0 0	0 0 0	0 0 0	-	1	7	0
NYY	0 0 0	0 2 4	2 0 X	-	8	12	0

W - Ruffing   L - Melton   A - 57,675

GAME 3 at Polo Grounds, Manhattan, N.Y., Oct. 8

NYY	0 1 2	1 1 0	0 0 0	-	5	9	0
NYG	0 0 0	0 0 0	1 0 0	-	1	5	4

W - Pearson   L - Schumacher   A - 37,385

GAME 4 at Polo Grounds, Manhattan, N.Y., Oct. 9

NYY	1 0 1	0 0 0	0 0 1	-	3	6	0
NYG	0 6 0	0 0 0	1 0 X	-	7	12	3

W - Hubbell   L - Hadley   A - 44,293

GAME 5 at Polo Grounds, Manhattan, N.Y., Oct. 10

NYY	0 1 1	0 2 0	0 0 0	-	4	8	0
NYG	0 0 2	0 0 0	0 0 0	-	2	10	0

W - Gomez   L - Melton   A - 38,216

1938 WORLD SERIES

The Yankees ran their all-time World Series mark vs. the Cubs to 8-0…became the first team to win three consecutive Series…middle infielders Joe Gordon and Frank Crosetti each drove in a team-high 6R in the series…used just four pitchers, who sported a 1.75 combined ERA (36.0IP, 7ER)…Red Ruffing recorded complete-game wins in Game 1 and 4, compiling a 1.50 ERA in the Series (18.0IP, 3ER).

New York Yankees (AL)   4
Chicago Cubs (NL)   0

GAME 1 at Wrigley Field, Chicago, Oct. 5

NYY	0 2 0	0 0 0	1 0 0	-	3	12	1
CHC	0 0 1	0 0 0	0 0 0	-	1	9	1

W - Ruffing   L - Lee   A - 43,642

GAME 2 at Wrigley Field, Chicago, Oct. 6

NYY	0 2 0	0 0 0	0 2 2	-	6	7	2
CHC	1 0 2	0 0 0	0 0 0	-	3	11	0

W - Gomez   L - Dean   A - 42,108

GAME 3 at Yankee Stadium, Bronx, N.Y., Oct. 8

CHC	0 0 0	0 1 0	0 1 0	-	2	5	1
NYY	0 0 0	0 2 2	0 1 X	-	5	7	2

W - Pearson   L - Bryant   A - 55,236

GAME 4 at Yankee Stadium, Bronx, N.Y., Oct. 9

CHC	0 0 0	1 0 0	0 2 0	-	3	8	1
NYY	0 3 0	0 0 1	0 4 X	-	8	11	1

W - Ruffing   L - Lee   A - 59,847

1939 WORLD SERIES

The Yankees won the last of four consecutive World Series with their second straight sweep…were led by Charlie Keller, who batted .438 (7-for-16) with 8R, 3HR and 6RBI…the Yankees hit just .206 (27-for-131) as a team…Yankees pitching compiled a 1.22 ERA, holding the Reds to just four extra-base hits (0HR) in the Series…Game 4 was won in the 10th inning on Joe DiMaggio's single with Charlie Keller on first and Frank Crosetti on third…after the Cincinnati RF misplayed the ball, Keller successfully scored from first, crashing into Reds catcher Ernie Lombardi and dazing him long enough for DiMaggio to score as in a play since known as "Lombardi's Snooze."

Cincinnati Reds (NL)   0
New York Yankees (AL)   4

GAME 1 at Yankee Stadium, Bronx, N.Y., Oct. 4

CIN	0 0 0	1 0 0	0 0 0	-	1	4	0
NYY	0 0 0	0 1 0	0 0 1	-	2	6	0

W - Ruffing   L - Derringer   A - 58,541

GAME 2 at Yankee Stadium, Bronx, N.Y., Oct 5

CIN	0 0 0	0 0 0	0 0 0	-	0	2	0
NYY	0 0 3	1 0 0	0 0 X	-	4	9	0

W - Pearson   L - Walters   A - 59,791

GAME 3 at Crosley Field, Cincinnati, Oct. 7

NYY	2 0 2	0 3 0	0 0 0	-	7	5	1
CIN	1 2 0	0 0 0	0 0 0	-	3	10	0

W - Hadley   L - Thompson   A - 32,723

GAME 4 at Crosley Field, Cincinnati, Oct. 8

NYY	0 0 0	0 0 0	2 0 2	3	-	7	7	1
CIN	0 0 0	0 0 0	3 1 0	0	-	4	11	4

W - Murphy   L - Walters   A - 32,794

1941 WORLD SERIES

Marked the first World Series meeting between the Yankees and Dodgers…Game 4 featured the famous passed ball by Dodgers catcher Mickey Owen, which would have been the final out of the game and evened the Series at 2-2…the Yankees went on to score 4R with two out in the ninth to win, 7-4, at Ebbets Field…in the Game 5 clincher, Tiny Bonham tossed a complete game (1ER, 5H) and Tommy Henrich hit a solo homer…Joe Gordon (.500, 1HR, 5RBI) and Charlie Keller (.389, 5RBI) paced Yankees hitters…capped a run of 32 wins in 36 World Series games dating to 1927.

Brooklyn Dodgers (NL)   **1**
New York Yankees (AL)   **4**

GAME 1 at Yankee Stadium, Bronx, N.Y., Oct. 1
BRO	000	010	100	-	2	6	0
NYY	010	101	00X	-	3	6	1

W - Ruffing   L - Davis   A - 68,540

GAME 2 at Yankee Stadium, Bronx, N.Y., Oct. 2
BRO	000	021	000	-	3	6	2
NYY	011	000	000	-	2	9	1

W - Wyatt   L - Chandler   A - 66,248

GAME 3 at Ebbets Field, Brooklyn, N.Y., Oct. 4
NYY	000	000	020	-	2	8	0
BRO	000	000	010	-	1	4	0

W - Russo   L - Casey   A - 33,100

GAME 4 at Ebbets Field, Brooklyn, N.Y., Oct. 5
NYY	100	200	004	-	7	12	0
BRO	000	220	000	-	4	9	1

W - Murphy   L - Casey   A - 33,813

GAME 5 at Ebbets Field, Brooklyn, N.Y., Oct. 6
NYY	020	010	000	-	3	6	0
BRO	001	000	000	-	1	4	1

W - Bonham   L - Wyatt   A - 34,072

1942 WORLD SERIES

The Yankees won Game 1 behind Red Ruffing but lost the next four games…marked the Yankees' first losing World Series since falling in seven games to the Cardinals in 1926…Joe DiMaggio went 7-for-21 (.333) and Phil Rizzuto went 8-for-21 (.381), while Charlie Keller led the Yankees with 2HR and 5RBI.

New York Yankees (AL)   **1**
St. Louis Cardinals (NL)   **4**

GAME 1 at Sportsman's Park, St. Louis, Sept. 30
NYY	000	110	032	-	7	11	0
STL	000	000	004	-	4	7	4

W - Ruffing   L - M.Cooper   A - 34,769

GAME 2 at Sportsman's Park, St. Louis, Oct. 1
NYY	000	000	030	-	3	10	2
STL	200	000	11X	-	4	6	0

W - Beazley   L - Bonham   A - 34,255

GAME 3 at Yankee Stadium, Bronx, N.Y., Oct. 3
STL	001	000	001	-	2	5	1
NYY	000	000	000	-	0	6	1

W - White   L - Chandler   A - 69,123

GAME 4 at Yankee Stadium, Bronx, N.Y., Oct. 4
STL	000	600	201	-	9	12	1
NYY	100	005	000	-	6	10	1

W - Lanier   L - Donald   A - 69,902

GAME 5 at Yankee Stadium, Bronx, N.Y., Oct. 5
STL	000	101	002	-	4	9	4
NYY	100	100	000	-	2	7	1

W - Beazley   L - Ruffing   A - 69,052

1943 WORLD SERIES

The Yankees reversed the prior year's result, winning in five games…Spud Chandler was dominant, allowing just 1ER over 18.0IP for complete-game wins in Games 1 and 5…Bill Dickey's two-run homer in the Game 5 clincher marked the only runs of the game…Yankees Joe DiMaggio, Tommy Henrich, Phil Rizzuto, George Selkirk, Red Ruffing and Buddy Hassett were all serving in the military and did not appear in the Series…marked the seventh and final World Series title in eight appearances under manager Joe McCarthy.

St. Louis Cardinals (NL)   **1**
New York Yankees (AL)   **4**

GAME 1 at Yankee Stadium, Bronx, N.Y., Oct. 5
STL	010	010	000	-	2	7	2
NYY	000	202	00X	-	4	8	2

W - Chandler   L - Lanier   A - 68,676

GAME 2 at Yankee Stadium, Bronx, N.Y., Oct. 6
STL	001	300	000	-	4	7	2
NYY	000	100	002	-	3	6	0

W - M.Cooper   L - Bonham   A - 68,578

GAME 3 at Yankee Stadium, Bronx, N.Y., Oct. 7
STL	000	200	000	-	2	6	4
NYY	000	001	05X	-	6	8	0

W - Borowy   L - Brazle   A - 69,990

GAME 4 at Sportsman's Park, St.Louis, Oct. 10
NYY	000	100	010	-	2	6	2
STL	000	000	100	-	1	7	1

W - Russo   L - Brecheen   A - 36,196

GAME 5 at Sportsman's Park, St.Louis, Oct. 11
NYY	000	002	000	-	2	7	1
STL	000	000	000	-	0	10	1

W - Chandler   L - M.Cooper   A - 33,872

1947 WORLD SERIES

The Yankees were piloted by Bucky Harris in his only World Series managing the team…in Game 4, Yankees pitcher Bill Bevens lost both his no-hit bid and the game with two outs in the bottom of the ninth as pinch-hitter Cookie Lavagetto doubled home two runs for a 3-2 Brooklyn win…Spec Shea recorded two wins and Johnny Lindell batted .500 (9-for-18) with 7RBI.

Brooklyn Dodgers (NL)   **3**
New York Yankees (AL)   **4**

GAME 1 at Yankee Stadium, Bronx, N.Y., Sept. 30
BRO	100	001	100	-	3	6	0
NYY	000	050	00X	-	5	4	0

W - Shea   L - Branca   A - 73,365

GAME 2 at Yankee Stadium, Bronx, N.Y., Oct. 1
BRO	001	100	001	-	3	9	2
NYY	101	124	0X	-	10	15	1

W - Reynolds   L - Lombardi   A - 69,865

GAME 3 at Ebbets Field, Brooklyn, N.Y., Oct. 2
NYY	002	221	100	-	8	13	0
BRO	061	200	00X	-	9	13	1

W - Casey   L - Newsom   A - 33,098

GAME 4 at Ebbets Field, Brooklyn, N.Y., Oct. 3
NYY	100	100	000	-	2	8	1
BRO	000	010	002	-	3	1	3

W - Casey   L - Bevens   A - 33,443

GAME 5 at Ebbets Field, Brooklyn, N.Y., Oct. 4
NYY	000	110	000	-	2	5	0
BRO	000	001	000	-	1	4	1

W - Shea   L - Barney   A - 34,379

GAME 6 at Yankee Stadium, Bronx, N.Y., Oct. 5

BRO	2 0 2	0 0 4	0 0 0	-	8	12	1
NYY	0 0 4	1 0 0	0 0 1	-	6	15	2

W - Branca   L - Page   A - 74,065

GAME 7 at Yankee Stadium, Bronx, N.Y., Oct. 6

BRO	0 2 0	0 0 0	0 0 0	-	2	7	0
NYY	0 1 0	2 0 1	1 0 X	-	5	7	0

W - Page   L - Gregg   A - 71,548

1949 WORLD SERIES

Marked the first of five straight World Series championships...was the first of 10 World Series appearances in a 12-year stretch under manager Casey Stengel (won seven)...Allie Reynolds allowed just 2H, winning Game 1, 1-0, over Don Newcombe on Tommy Henrich's leadoff homer in the bottom of the ninth...also pitched 3.1 scoreless innings to close out Game 4...Commissioner Happy Chandler ordered lights turned on during Game 5, marking the first time a World Series game was finished under electric light.

Brooklyn Dodgers (NL)   1
New York Yankees (AL)   4

GAME 1 at Yankee Stadium, Bronx, N.Y., Oct. 5

BRO	0 0 0	0 0 0	0 0 0	-	0	2	0
NYY	0 0 0	0 0 0	0 0 1	-	1	5	1

W - Reynolds   L - Newcombe A - 66,224

GAME 2 at Yankee Stadium, Bronx, N.Y., Oct. 6

BRO	0 1 0	0 0 0	0 0 0	-	1	7	2
NYY	0 0 0	0 0 0	0 0 0	-	0	6	1

W - Roe   L - Raschi   A - 70,053

GAME 3 at Ebbets Field, Brooklyn, N.Y., Oct. 7

NYY	0 0 1	0 0 0	0 0 3	-	4	5	0
BRO	0 0 0	1 0 0	0 0 2	-	3	5	0

W - Page   L - Branca   A - 32,788

GAME 4 at Ebbets Field, Brooklyn, N.Y., Oct. 8

NYY	0 0 0	3 3 0	0 0 0	-	6	10	0
BRO	0 0 0	0 0 4	0 0 0	-	4	9	1

W - Lopat   L - Newcombe A - 33,934

GAME 5 at Ebbets Field, Brooklyn, N.Y., Oct. 9

NYY	2 0 3	1 1 3	0 0 0	-	10	11	1
BRO	0 0 1	0 0 1	4 0 0	-	6	11	2

W - Raschi   L - Barney   A - 33,711

Manager Casey Stengel led the Yankees to a record five-consecutive World Series titles from 1949-53.

1950 WORLD SERIES

Yankees pitchers allowed just 5R (3ER) all Series, tallying a 0.73 combined ERA in 37.0IP...each of the first three games were decided by one run, including a 1-0 victory behind Vic Raschi in Game 1 and a 2-1, 10-inning win behind Allie Reynolds in Game 2...Whitey Ford earned the first of his record 10 career World Series wins in the Game 4 clincher as Reynolds came out of the bullpen to strike out the final batter of the game with two runners on base.

New York Yankees (AL)   4
Philadelphia Phillies (NL)   0

GAME 1 at Shibe Park, Philadelphia, Oct. 4

NYY	0 0 0	1 0 0	0 0 0	-	1	5	0
PHI	0 0 0	0 0 0	0 0 0	-	0	2	1

W - Raschi   L - Konstanty A - 30,746

GAME 2 at Shibe Park, Philadelphia, Oct. 5

NYY	0 1 0	0 0 0	0 0 0 1	-	2	10	0
PHI	0 1 0	0 0 0	0 0 0 0	-	1	7	0

W - Reynolds   L - Roberts   A - 32,660

GAME 3 at Yankee Stadium, Bronx, N.Y., Oct. 6

PHI	0 0 0	0 0 1	1 0 0	-	2	10	2
NYY	0 0 1	0 0 0	0 1 1	-	3	7	0

W - Ferrick   L - Meyer   A - 64,505

GAME 4 at Yankee Stadium, Bronx, N.Y., Oct. 7

PHI	0 0 0	0 0 0	0 0 2	-	2	7	1
NYY	2 0 0	0 0 3	0 0 X	-	5	8	2

W - Ford   L - Miller   A - 68,098

1951 WORLD SERIES

The Yankees defeated the Giants in Joe DiMaggio's final World Series...Willie Mays and Mickey Mantle made their Series debuts, both in their rookie seasons...in Game 2, Mantle seriously injured his right knee after getting his cleat caught in a drainpipe, ending his Series...Ed Lopat allowed just 1ER in 18.0IP, notching wins in Games 2 and 5.

New York Giants (NL)   2
New York Yankees (AL)   4

GAME 1 at Yankee Stadium, Bronx, N.Y., Oct. 4

NYG	2 0 0	0 0 3	0 0 0	-	5	10	1
NYY	0 1 0	0 0 0	0 0 0	-	1	7	1

W - Koslo   L - Reynolds   A - 65,673

GAME 2 at Yankee Stadium, Bronx, N.Y., Oct. 5

NYG	0 0 0	0 0 0	1 0 0	-	1	5	1
NYY	1 1 0	0 0 0	0 1 X	-	3	6	0

W - Lopat   L - Jansen   A - 66,018

GAME 3 at the Polo Grounds, Manhattan, N.Y., Oct. 6

NYY	0 0 0	0 0 0	0 1 1	-	2	5	2
NYG	0 1 0	0 5 0	0 0 X	-	6	7	2

W - Hearn   L - Reynolds   A - 52,035

GAME 4 at the Polo Grounds, Manhattan, N.Y., Oct. 8

NYY	0 1 0	1 2 0	2 0 0	-	6	12	0
NYG	1 0 0	0 0 0	0 0 1	-	2	8	2

W - Reynolds   L - Maglie   A - 49,010

GAME 5 at the Polo Grounds, Manhattan, N.Y., Oct. 9

NYY	0 0 5	2 0 2	4 0 0	-	13	12	1
NYG	1 0 0	0 0 0	0 0 0	-	1	5	3

W - Lopat   L - Jansen   A - 47,530

GAME 6 at Yankee Stadium, Bronx, N.Y., Oct. 10

NYG	0 0 0	0 1 0	0 0 2	-	3	11	1
NYY	1 0 0	0 0 3	0 0 X	-	4	7	0

W - Raschi   L - Koslo   A - 61,711

1952 WORLD SERIES

Led by Mickey Mantle (.345, 5R, 2HR), Johnny Mize (.400, 3HR, 6RBI) and Gene Woodling (.348), the Yankees won in seven games…Allie Reynolds and Vic Raschi each recorded a pair of victories…the Yankees slugged 10HR in the Series…in Game 7, second baseman Billy Martin made a running catch on a two-out, seventh-inning, based-loaded pop-up from Jackie Robinson to preserve the Yankees' lead.

New York Yankees (AL)   4
Brooklyn Dodgers (NL)   3

GAME 1 at Ebbets Field, Brooklyn, N.Y., Oct. 1

NYY	0 1 0	0 0 0	0 1 0	- 2	6 2
BRO	0 1 0	0 0 2	0 1 X	- 4	6 0

W - Black   L - Reynolds   A - 34,861

GAME 2 at Ebbets Field, Brooklyn, N.Y., Oct. 2

NYY	0 0 0	1 1 5	0 0 0	- 7	10 0
BRO	0 0 1	0 0 0	0 0 0	- 1	3 1

W - Raschi   L - Erskine   A - 33,792

GAME 3 at Yankee Stadium, Bronx, N.Y., Oct. 3

BRO	0 0 1	0 1 0	0 1 2	- 5	11 0
NYY	0 1 0	0 0 0	0 1 1	- 3	6 2

W - Roe   L - Lopat   A - 66,698

GAME 4 at Yankee Stadium, Bronx, N.Y., Oct. 4

BRO	0 0 0	0 0 0	0 0 0	- 0	4 1
NYY	0 0 0	1 0 0	0 1 X	- 2	4 1

W - Reynolds   L - Black   A - 71,787

GAME 5 at Yankee Stadium, Bronx, N.Y., Oct. 5

BRO	0 1 0	0 3 0	1 0 0	0 1 - 6	10 0
NYY	0 0 0	0 5 0	0 0 0	0 0 - 5	5 1

W - Erskine   L - Sain   A - 70,536

GAME 6 at Ebbets Field, Brooklyn, N.Y., Oct. 6

NYY	0 0 0	0 0 0	2 1 0	- 3	9 0
BRO	0 0 0	0 0 1	0 1 0	- 2	8 1

W - Raschi   L - Loes   A - 30,037

GAME 7 at Ebbets Field, Brooklyn, N.Y., Oct. 7

NYY	0 0 0	1 1 1	1 0 0	- 4	10 4
BRO	0 0 0	1 1 0	0 0 0	- 2	8 1

W - Reynolds   L - Black   A - 33,195

Billy Martin makes a game-saving catch on a two-out, seventh-inning, based-loaded pop-up from Jackie Robinson to preserve the win in Game 7 of the 1952 World Series.

1953 WORLD SERIES

The Yankees won their all-time record fifth consecutive title…Billy Martin batted .500 (12-for-24) with 2HR and 8RBI…still shares the all-time mark for hits in a six-game World Series…Mickey Mantle won Game 2 with a two-run homer in the eighth inning…added a grand slam in the Game 5 win…Martin drove in the winning run in the Game 6 clincher with a single in the bottom of the ninth.

Brooklyn Dodgers (NL)   2
New York Yankees (AL)   4

GAME 1 at Yankee Stadium, Bronx, N.Y., Sept. 30

BRO	0 0 0	0 1 3	1 0 0	- 5	12 2
NYY	4 0 0	0 1 0	1 3 X	- 9	12 0

W - Sain   L - Labine   A - 69,374

GAME 2 at Yankee Stadium, NY Oct. 1

BRO	0 0 0	2 0 0	0 0 0	- 2	9 1
NYY	1 0 0	0 0 0	1 2 X	- 4	5 0

W - Lopat   L - Roe   A - 66,786

GAME 3 at Ebbets Field, Brooklyn, N.Y., Oct. 2

NYY	0 0 0	0 1 0	0 1 0	- 2	6 0
BRO	0 0 0	0 1 1	0 1 X	- 3	9 0

W - Erskine   L - Raschi   A - 35,270

GAME 4 at Ebbets Field, Brooklyn, N.Y., Oct. 3

NYY	0 0 0	0 2 0	0 0 1	- 3	9 0
BRO	3 0 0	1 0 2	1 0 X	- 7	12 0

W - Loes   L - Ford   A - 36,775

GAME 5 at Ebbets Field, Brooklyn, N.Y., Oct. 4

NYY	1 0 5	0 0 0	3 1 1	- 11	11 1
BRO	0 1 0	0 1 0	0 4 1	- 7	14 1

W - McDonald   L - Podres   A - 36,775

GAME 6 at Yankee Stadium, Bronx, N.Y., Oct. 5

BRO	0 0 0	0 0 1	0 0 2	- 3	8 3
NYY	2 1 0	0 0 0	0 0 1	- 4	13 0

W - Reynolds   L - Labine   A - 62,370

1955 WORLD SERIES

Marked the Yankees' first Series loss to the Dodgers after five successive wins (1941, '47, '49, '52, '53)…is the only time the Dodgers triumphed over the Yankees before relocating to Los Angeles in 1958…Brooklyn's Johnny Podres tossed an eight-hit, 2-0, shutout in the Game 7 clincher at Yankee Stadium…with two on and no out in the sixth, Yogi Berra's slicing line drive was famously caught by Brooklyn's Sandy Amoros, who then threw the ball back to the infield to double off Gil McDougald, preventing a potential rally.

New York Yankees (AL)   3
Brooklyn Dodgers (NL)   4

GAME 1 at Yankee Stadium, Bronx, N.Y., Sept. 28

BRO	0 2 1	0 0 0	0 2 0	- 5	10 0
NYY	0 2 1	1 0 2	0 0 X	- 6	9 1

W - Ford   L - Newcombe   A - 63,869

GAME 2 at Yankee Stadium, Bronx, N.Y., Sept.29

BRO	0 0 0	1 1 0	0 0 0	- 2	5 2
NYY	0 0 0	4 0 0	0 0 X	- 4	8 0

W - Byrne   L - Loes   A - 64,707

GAME 3 at Ebbets Field, Brooklyn, N.Y., Sept. 30

NYY	0 2 0	0 0 0	1 0 0	- 3	7 0
BRO	2 2 0	2 0 0	2 0 X	- 8	11 1

W - Podres   L - Turley   A - 34,209

GAME 4 at Ebbets Field, Brooklyn, N.Y., Oct. 1

NYY	1 1 0	1 0 2	0 0 0	- 5	9 0
BRO	0 0 1	3 3 0	1 0 X	- 8	14 0

W - Labine   L - Larsen   A - 36,242

GAME 5 at Ebbets Field, Brooklyn, N.Y., Oct. 2

NYY	0 0 0	1 0 0	1 1 0	- 3	6 0
BRO	0 2 1	0 1 0	0 1 X	- 5	9 2

W - Craig   L - Grim   A - 36,796

GAME 6 at Yankee Stadium, Bronx, N.Y., Oct. 3

BRO	0 0 0	1 0 0	0 0 0	- 1	4 1
NYY	5 0 0	0 0 0	0 0 X	- 5	8 0

W - Ford   L - Spooner   A - 64,022

GAME 7 at Yankee Stadium, Bronx, N.Y., Oct. 4

BRO	0 0 0	1 0 1	0 0 0	- 2	5 0
NYY	0 0 0	0 0 0	0 0 0	- 0	8 1

W - Podres   L - Byrne   A - 62,465

1956 WORLD SERIES

Lost the first two games in Brooklyn, then came back to win in seven...was highlighted by Don Larsen's Game 5 perfect game caught by Yogi Berra, the only no-hitter in postseason history...Larsen didn't know he was pitching until he got to the park that day...had lasted only 1.2 innings in his Game 2 start, (4R, 0ER, 1H, 4BB)...Berra led the Yankees with a .360 (9-for-25) batting average, 3HR and a then-record 10 RBI...the Yankees hit 12HR, the second-highest total in Series history (San Francisco 14HR in 2002).

New York Yankees (AL)   4
Brooklyn Dodgers (NL)   3

GAME 1 at Ebbets Field, Brooklyn, N.Y., Oct. 3

NYY	2 0 0	1 0 0	0 0 0	-	3	9	1
BRO	0 2 3	1 0 0	0 0 X	-	6	9	0

W - Maglie   L - Ford   A - 34,479

GAME 2 at Ebbets Field, Brooklyn, N.Y., Oct. 5

NYY	1 5 0	1 0 0	0 0 1	-	8	12	2
BRO	0 6 1	2 2 0	0 2 X	-	13	12	0

W - Bessent   L - Morgan   A - 36,217

GAME 3 at Yankee Stadium, Bronx, N.Y., Oct. 6

BRO	0 1 0	0 0 1	1 0 0	-	3	8	1
NYY	0 1 0	0 0 3	0 1 X	-	5	8	1

W - Ford   L - Craig   A - 73,977

GAME 4 at Yankee Stadium, Bronx, N.Y., Oct. 7

BRO	0 0 0	1 0 0	0 0 1	-	2	6	0
NYY	1 0 0	2 0 1	2 0 X	-	6	7	2

W - Sturdivant   L - Erskine   A - 69,705

GAME 5 at Yankee Stadium, Bronx, N.Y., Oct. 8

BRO	0 0 0	0 0 0	0 0 0	-	0	0	0
NYY	0 0 0	1 0 1	0 0 X	-	2	5	0

W - Larsen   L - Maglie   A - 64,519

GAME 6 at Ebbets Field, Brooklyn, N.Y., Oct. 9

NYY	0 0 0	0 0 0	0 0 0	0	-	0	7	0
BRO	0 0 0	0 0 0	0 0 1	-	1	4	0

W - Labine   L - Turley   A - 33,224

GAME 7 at Ebbets Field, Brooklyn, N.Y., Oct. 10

NYY	2 0 2	1 0 0	4 0 0	-	9	10	0
BRO	0 0 0	0 0 0	0 0 0	-	0	3	1

W - Kucks   L - Newcombe   A - 33,782

1957 WORLD SERIES

The Yankees dropped their second seven-game World Series in three years in their first-ever meeting against Milwaukee...the Braves' Lew Burdette won Games 2, 5 and 7, the latter two on seven-hit shutouts...second baseman Jerry Coleman batted .364 (8-for-22) with 2 doubles and 2RBI in a losing effort.

Milwaukee Braves (NL)   4
New York Yankees (AL)   3

GAME 1 at Yankee Stadium, Bronx, N.Y., Oct. 2

MIL	0 0 0	0 0 0	1 0 0	-	1	5	0
NYY	0 0 0	0 1 2	0 0 X	-	3	9	1

W - Ford   L - Spahn   A - 69,476

GAME 2 at Yankee Stadium, Bronx, N.Y., Oct. 3

MIL	0 1 1	2 0 0	0 0 0	-	4	8	0
NYY	1 0 0	0 0 0	0 0 0	-	2	7	2

W - Burdette   L - Shantz   A - 65,202

GAME 3 at County Stadium, Milwaukee, Oct. 5

NYY	3 0 2	2 0 0	5 0 0	-	12	9	0
MIL	0 1 0	0 2 0	0 0 0	-	3	8	1

W - Larsen   L - Buhl   A - 45,804

GAME 4 at County Stadium, Milwaukee, Oct. 6

NYY	1 0 0	0 0 0	0 0 3	1	-	5	11	0
MIL	0 0 0	4 0 0	0 0 0	3	-	7	7	0

W - Spahn   L - Grim   A - 45,804

GAME 5 at County Stadium, Milwaukee, Oct. 7

NYY	0 0 0	0 0 0	0 0 0	-	0	7	0
MIL	0 0 0	0 0 1	0 0 X	-	1	6	0

W - Burdette   L - Ford   A - 45,811

GAME 6 at Yankee Stadium, Bronx, N.Y., Oct. 9

MIL	0 0 0	0 1 0	1 0 0	-	2	4	0
NYY	0 0 2	0 0 0	1 0 X	-	3	7	0

W - Turley   L - Johnson   A - 61,408

GAME 7 at Yankee Stadium, Bronx, N.Y., Oct. 10

MIL	0 0 4	0 0 0	0 1 0	-	5	9	1
NYY	0 0 0	0 0 0	0 0 0	-	0	7	3

W - Burdette   L - Larsen   A - 61,207

1958 WORLD SERIES

The Yankees came back from two-games-to-none and three-games-to-one deficits to win in seven...after getting bombed for 4ER in just 0.1IP in his Game 2 start, Yankees pitcher Bob Turley tossed a five-hit shutout in Game 5, came on with two on and a one-run lead in the 10th innning to get the final out in Game 6, and earned the victory in Game 7 with 6.2 innings (1ER) in relief of Don Larsen...winning the title gave the Yankees a World Series championship over each of the eight modern NL teams (since 1900)...Hank Bauer batted .323 (10-for-31) with 4HR, making him just one of four Yankees in franchise history to hit four-or-more homers in a single Series (also Ruth 4HR in 1926; Gehrig 4HR in 1928; and Reggie Jackson 5HR in 1977)...was held hitless in Game 4, snapping an all-time Major League-best 17-game World Series hitting streak.

New York Yankees (AL)   4
Milwaukee Braves (NL)   3

GAME 1 at County Stadium, Milwaukee, Oct. 1

NYY	0 0 0	1 2 0	0 0 0	0	-	3	8	1
MIL	0 0 0	2 0 0	0 1 0	1	-	4	10	0

W - Spahn   L - Duren   A - 46,367

GAME 2 at County Stadium, Milwaukee, Oct. 2

NYY	1 0 0	1 0 0	0 0 3	-	5	7	0
MIL	7 1 0	0 0 0	2 3 X	-	13	15	1

W - Burdette   L - Turley   A - 46,367

GAME 3 at Yankee Stadium, Bronx, N.Y., Oct. 4

MIL	0 0 0	0 0 0	0 0 0	-	0	6	0
NYY	0 0 0	0 2 0	2 0 X	-	4	4	0

W - Larsen   L - Rush   A - 71,599

GAME 4 at Yankee Stadium, Bronx, N.Y., Oct. 5

MIL	0 0 0	0 0 1	1 1 0	-	3	9	0
NYY	0 0 0	0 0 0	0 0 0	-	0	2	1

W - Spahn   L - Ford   A - 71,563

GAME 5 at Yankee Stadium, Bronx, N.Y., Oct. 6

MIL	0 0 0	0 0 0	0 0 0	-	0	5	0
NYY	0 0 1	0 0 6	0 0 X	-	7	10	0

W - Turley   L - Burdette   A - 65,279

GAME 6 at County Stadium, Milwaukee, Oct. 8

NYY	1 0 0	0 0 1	0 0 0	2	-	4	10	1
MIL	1 1 0	0 0 0	0 0 0	1	-	3	10	4

W - Duren   L - Spahn   A - 46,367

GAME 7 at County Stadium, Milwaukee, Oct. 9

NYY	0 2 0	0 0 0	0 4 0	-	6	8	0
MIL	1 0 0	0 0 1	0 0 0	-	2	5	2

W - Turley   L - Burdette   A - 46,367

1960 WORLD SERIES

Despite outscoring Pittsburgh 55-27 and setting still-standing World Series marks for runs scored and team batting average (.338), the Yankees lost the decisive Game 7, 10-9, on Bill Maseroski's ninth-inning "walk-off" homer off Ralph Terry...marked Casey Stengel's final game as Yankees manager...Bobby Richardson batted .367 (11-for-30) and recorded a still-standing record 12RBI, becoming the only player in Baseball history to win the World Series MVP Award on a losing team...Whitey Ford tossed complete game shutouts in Games 3 and 6, allowing just 11H and 2BB in 18.0 Series IP.

New York Yankees (AL)   3
Pittsburgh Pirates (NL)   4

GAME 1 at Forbes Field, Pittsburgh, Oct. 5

NYY	1 0 0	1 0 0	0 0 2	-	4	13	2
PIT	3 0 0	2 0 1	0 0 X	-	6	8	0
W - Law	L - Ditmar	A - 36,676					

GAME 2 at Forbes Field, Pittsburgh, Oct. 6

NYY	0 0 2	1 2 7	3 0 1	-	16	19	1
PIT	0 0 0	1 0 0	0 0 2	-	3	13	1
W - Turley	L - Friend	A - 37,308					

GAME 3 at Yankee Stadium, Bronx, N.Y., Oct. 8

PIT	0 0 0	0 0 0	0 0 0	-	0	4	0
NYY	6 0 0	4 0 0	0 0 X	-	10	16	1
W - Ford	L - Mizell	A - 70,001					

GAME 4 at Yankee Stadium, Bronx, N.Y., Oct. 9

PIT	0 0 0	0 3 0	0 0 0	-	3	7	0
NYY	0 0 0	1 0 0	1 0 0	-	2	8	0
W - Law	L - Terry	A - 67,812					

GAME 5 at Yankee Stadium, Bronx, N.Y., Oct. 10

PIT	0 3 1	0 0 0	0 0 1	-	5	10	2
NYY	0 1 1	0 0 0	0 0 0	-	2	5	2
W - Haddix	L - Ditmar	A - 62,753					

GAME 6 at Forbes Field, Pittsburgh, Oct. 12

NYY	0 1 5	0 0 2	2 2 0	-	12	17	1
PIT	0 0 0	0 0 0	0 0 0	-	0	7	1
W - Ford	L - Friend	A - 38,580					

GAME 7 at Forbes Field, Pittsburgh, Oct. 13

NYY	0 0 0	0 1 4	0 2 2	-	9	13	1
PIT	2 2 0	0 0 0	0 5 1	-	10	11	0
W - Haddix	L - Terry	A - 36,683					

Bobby Richardson [crossing home plate] drove in an all-time record 12 runs in the 1960 Fall Classic, becoming the only player to win World Series MVP honors on a losing team.

1961 WORLD SERIES

With the Series tied 1-1, the Yankees won Game 3 on a game-tying solo homer by Johnny Blanchard in the eighth and Roger Maris' game-winning solo shot in the ninth...outscored Cincinnati 20-5 in the final two games...Manager Ralph Houk became the third Yankees skipper to win the World Series with the Yankees in his first season with the club...Hector Lopez led the Yankees with 7RBI in just 9AB...Whitey Ford pitched 14.0 scoreless innings, notching wins in Games 1 and 4.

Cincinnati Reds (NL)   1
New York Yankees (AL)   4

GAME 1 at Yankee Stadium, Bronx, N.Y., Oct. 4

CIN	0 0 0	0 0 0	0 0 0	-	0	2	0
NYY	0 0 0	1 0 1	0 0 X	-	2	6	0
W - Ford	L - O'Toole	A - 62,397					

GAME 2 at Yankee Stadium, Bronx, N.Y., Oct. 5

CIN	0 0 0	2 1 1	0 2 0	-	6	9	0
NYY	0 0 0	2 0 0	0 0 0	-	2	4	3
W - Jay	L - Terry	A - 63,083					

GAME 3 at Crosley Field, Cincinnati, Oct. 7

NYY	0 0 0	0 0 0	1 1 1	-	3	6	1
CIN	0 0 1	0 0 0	1 0 0	-	2	8	0
W - Arroyo	L - Purkey	A - 32,589					

GAME 4 at Crosley Field, Cincinnati, Oct. 8

NYY	0 0 0	1 1 2	3 0 0	-	7	11	0
CIN	0 0 0	0 0 0	0 0 0	-	0	5	1
W - Ford	L - O'Toole	A - 32,589					

GAME 5 at Crosley Field, Cincinnati, Oct. 9

NYY	5 1 0	5 0 2	0 0 0	-	13	15	1
CIN	0 0 3	0 2 0	0 0 0	-	5	11	3
W - Daley	L - Jay	A - 32,589					

1962 WORLD SERIES

The Yankees clinched a tight seven-game Series on a 1-0, four-hit, Game 7 shutout from Ralph Terry...scored their only run when Tony Kubek grounded into a fifth-inning double play...Terry allowed just 17H and 5ER in 25.0 Series IP, taking home the MVP Award...the teams combined for just 41 total runs in a Series that stretched over 13 days due to rainouts.

New York Yankees (AL)   4
San Francisco Giants (NL)   3

GAME 1 at Candlestick Park, San Francisco, Oct. 4

NYY	2 0 0	0 0 0	1 2 1	-	6	11	0
SF	0 1 1	0 0 0	0 0 0	-	2	10	0
W - Ford	L - O'Dell	A - 43,852					

GAME 2 at Candlestick Park, San Francisco, Oct. 5

NYY	0 0 0	0 0 0	0 0 0	-	0	3	1
SF	1 0 0	0 0 0	1 0 X	-	2	6	0
W - Sanford	L - Terry	A - 43,910					

GAME 3 at Yankee Stadium, Bronx, N.Y., Oct. 7

SF	0 0 0	0 0 0	0 0 2	-	2	4	3
NYY	0 0 0	0 0 0	3 0 X	-	3	5	1
W - Stafford	L - Pierce	A - 71,434					

GAME 4 at Yankee Stadium, Bronx, N.Y., Oct. 8

SF	0 2 0	0 0 0	4 0 1	-	7	9	1
NYY	0 0 0	0 0 2	0 0 1	-	3	9	1
W - Larsen	L - Coates	A - 66,607					

GAME 5 at Yankee Stadium, Bronx, N.Y., Oct. 10

SF	0 0 1	0 1 0	0 0 1	-	3	8	2
NYY	0 0 0	1 0 1	0 3 X	-	5	6	0
W - Terry	L - Sanford	A - 63,165					

GAME 6 at Candlestick Park, San Francisco, Oct. 15

NYY	000	010	010	-	2	3	2
SF	000	320	00X	-	5	10	1

W - Pierce   L - Ford   A - 43,948

GAME 7 at Candlestick Park, San Francisco, Oct. 16

NYY	000	010	000	-	1	7	0
SF	000	000	000	-	0	4	1

W - Terry   L - Sanford   A - 43,948

1963 WORLD SERIES

The Yankees were swept despite allowing just 12 overall runs, marking just one of two four-game Series exits in franchise history (also 1976 vs. Cincinnati)...scored just four runs and batted .171 over the four games, marking the third and four-lowest all-time totals, respectively, by any team in a World Series.

Los Angeles Dodgers (NL)   4
New York Yankees (AL)   0

GAME 1 at Yankee Stadium, Bronx, N.Y., Oct. 2

LAD	041	000	000	-	5	9	0
NYY	000	000	020	-	2	6	0

W - Koufax   L - Ford   A - 69,000

GAME 2 at Yankee Stadium, Bronx, N.Y., Oct. 3

LAD	200	100	010	-	4	10	1
NYY	000	000	001	-	1	7	0

W - Podres   L - Downing   A - 66,455

GAME 3 at Dodger Stadium, Los Angeles, Oct. 5

NYY	000	000	000	-	0	3	0
LAD	100	000	00x	-	1	4	1

W - Drysdale   L - Bouton   A - 55,912

GAME 4 at Dodger Stadium, Los Angeles, Oct. 6

NYY	000	000	100	-	1	6	1
LAD	000	010	10X	-	2	2	1

W - Koufax   L - Ford   A - 55,912

1964 WORLD SERIES

The Yankees' seven-game loss marked Mickey Mantle's final World Series...batted .333 (8-for-24) with 3HR, giving him a record 18 World Series HR for his career...Jim Bouton won both of his starts, allowing just 3ER in 17.1IP...Bobby Richardson batted .406 (13-for-32), setting an all-time record for hits in a Series (since tied by Lou Brock in 1968 and Marty Barrett in 1986).

New York Yankees (AL)   3
St. Louis Cardinals (NL)   4

GAME 1 at Busch Stadium, St. Louis, Oct. 7

NYY	030	010	010	-	5	12	2
STL	110	004	03X	-	9	12	0

W - Sadecki   L - Ford   A - 30,805

GAME 2 at Busch Stadium, St. Louis, Oct. 8

NYY	000	101	204	-	8	12	0
STL	001	000	011	-	3	7	0

W - Stottlemyre   L - Gibson   A - 30,805

GAME 3 at Yankee Stadium, Bronx, N.Y., Oct. 10

STL	000	010	000	-	1	6	0
NYY	010	000	001	-	2	5	2

W - Bouton   L - Schultz   A - 67,101

GAME 4 at Yankee Stadium, Bronx, N.Y., Oct. 11

STL	000	004	000	-	4	6	1
NYY	300	000	000	-	3	6	1

W - Craig   L - Downing   A - 66,312

GAME 5 at Yankee Stadium, Bronx, N.Y., Oct. 12

STL	000	020	000	3	-	5	10	1
NYY	000	000	002	0	-	2	6	2

W - Gibson   L - Mikkelsen   A - 65,633

GAME 6 at Busch Stadium, St. Louis, Oct. 14

NYY	000	012	050	-	8	10	0
STL	100	000	011	-	3	10	1

W - Bouton   L - Simmons   A - 30,805

GAME 7 at Busch Stadium, St. Louis, Oct. 15

NYY	000	003	002	-	5	9	2
STL	000	330	10X	-	7	10	1

W - Gibson   L - Stottlemyre   A - 30,346

1976 CHAMPIONSHIP SERIES

Chris Chambliss batted .524 (11-for-21) with 2HR and 8RBI, including the Series-winning "walk-off" home run off the Royals' Mark Littell in Game 5.

Kansas City Royals (AL)   2
New York Yankees (AL)   3

GAME 1 at Royals Stadium, Kansas City, Mo., Oct. 9

NYY	200	000	002	-	4	12	0
KC	000	000	010	-	1	5	2

W - Hunter   L - Gura   S - (none)   A - 41,077

GAME 2 at Royals Stadium, Kansas City, Mo., Oct. 10

NYY	012	000	000	-	3	12	5
KC	200	002	03X	-	7	9	0

W - Splittorff   L - Figueroa   S - (none)   A - 41,091

GAME 3 at Yankee Stadium, Bronx, N.Y., Oct. 12

KC	300	000	000	-	3	6	0
NYY	000	203	00X	-	5	9	0

W - Ellis   L - Hassler   S - Lyle   A - 56,808

GAME 4 at Yankee Stadium, Bronx, N.Y., Oct. 13

KC	030	201	010	-	7	9	1
NYY	020	000	101	-	4	11	0

W - Bird   L - Hunter   S - Mingori   A - 56,355

GAME 5 at Yankee Stadium, Bronx, N.Y., Oct. 14

KC	210	000	030	-	6	11	1
NYY	202	002	001	-	7	11	1

W - Tidrow   L - Littell   S - (none)   A - 56,821

1976 WORLD SERIES

Marked the Yankees' first World Series appearance after an 11-year drought...was the first Series appearance under the majority ownership of George M. Steinbrenner...also was the club's first Series following the 1974-75 remodeling of the original Yankee Stadium...was the second and last time the Yankees have been swept in a Series...Thurman Munson led the Yankees, batting .529 (9-for-17) with 2R and 2RBI.

New York Yankees (AL)   0
Cincinnati Reds (NL)   4

GAME 1 at Riverfront Stadium, Cincinnati, Oct. 16

NYY	010	000	000	-	1	5	1
CIN	101	001	20X	-	5	10	1

W - Gullett   L - Alexander   S - (none)   A - 54,826

GAME 2 at Riverfront Stadium, Cincinnati, Oct. 17

NYY	000	100	200	-	3	9	1
CIN	000	000	001	-	4	10	0

W - Billingham   L - Hunter   S - (none)   A - 54,816

GAME 3 at Yankee Stadium, Bronx, N.Y., Oct. 19

CIN	030	100	020	-	6	13	2
NYY	000	100	100	-	2	8	0

W - Zachary   L - Ellis   S - McEnaney   A - 56,667

GAME 4 at Yankee Stadium, Bronx, N.Y., Oct. 21

CIN	000	300	004	-	7	9	2
NYY	100	010	000	-	2	8	0

W - Nolan   L - Figueroa   S - McEnaney   A - 56,700

1977 CHAMPIONSHIP SERIES

Sparky Lyle appeared in four of the five games and recorded wins in relief in Game 4 (5.1IP, 2H, 0R, 0BB, 1K) and Game 5 (1.1IP, 1H, 0R, 1K)...Yankees scored 1R in the eighth and 3R in the ninth to win the Game 5 clincher, 5-3.

New York Yankees (AL)   **3**
Kansas City Royals (AL)   **2**

GAME 1 at Yankee Stadium, Bronx, N.Y., Oct. 5

KC	2 2 2	0 0 0	0 1 0	-	7	9	0
NYY	0 0 2	0 0 0	0 0 0	-	2	9	0

W - Splittorff   L - Gullett   S - (none)   A - 54,930

GAME 2 at Yankee Stadium, Bronx, N.Y., Oct. 6

KC	0 0 1	0 0 1	0 0 0	-	2	3	1
NYY	0 0 0	0 2 3	0 1 X	-	6	10	1

W - Guidry   L - Hassler   S - (none)   A - 56,230

GAME 3 at Royals Stadium, Kansas City, Mo., Oct. 7

NYY	0 0 0	0 1 0	0 0 1	-	2	4	1
KC	0 1 1	0 1 2	1 0 X	-	6	12	1

W - Leonard   L - Torrez   S - (none)   A - 41,285

GAME 4 at Royals Stadium, Kansas City, Mo., Oct. 8

NYY	1 2 1	1 0 0	0 0 1	-	6	13	0
KC	0 0 2	2 0 0	0 0 0	-	4	8	2

W - Lyle   L - Gura   S - (none)   A - 41,135

GAME 5 at Royals Stadium, Kansas City, Mo., Oct. 9

NYY	0 0 1	0 0 0	0 1 3	-	5	10	0
KC	2 0 1	0 0 0	0 0 0	-	3	10	1

W - Lyle   L - Leonard   S - (none)   A - 41,133

1977 WORLD SERIES

The Yankees snapped a 14-season championship drought, defeating the Dodgers in six games...in the Game 6 clincher, Reggie Jackson joined Babe Ruth (twice) as the only players to hit 3HR in a single World Series game...batted .450 (9-for-20) with 10R (tied for most all-time), 5HR (tied for most all-time) and 8RBI, taking home the Series MVP...Mike Torrez won both of his starts, tossing complete-game wins in Games 3 and 6.

Los Angeles Dodgers (NL)   **2**
New York Yankees (AL)   **4**

GAME 1 at Yankee Stadium, Bronx, N.Y., Oct. 11

LAD	2 0 0	0 0 0	0 0 1 0 0 0	-	3	6	0
NYY	1 0 0	0 0 1	0 1 0 0 0 1	-	4	11	0

W - Lyle   L - Rhoden   S - (none)   A - 56,668

GAME 2 at Yankee Stadium, Bronx, N.Y., Oct. 12

LAD	2 1 2	0 0 0	0 0 1	-	6	9	0
NYY	0 0 0	1 0 0	0 0 0	-	1	5	0

W - Hooton   L - Hunter   S - (none)   A - 56,691

GAME 3 at Dodger Stadium, Los Angeles, Oct. 14

NYY	3 0 0	1 1 0	0 0 0	-	5	10	0
LAD	0 0 3	0 0 0	0 0 0	-	3	7	1

W - Torrez   L - John   S - (none)   A - 55,992

GAME 4 at Dodger Stadium, Los Angeles, Oct. 15

NYY	0 3 0	0 0 1	0 0 0	-	4	7	0
LAD	0 0 2	0 0 0	0 0 0	-	2	4	0

W - Guidry   L - Rau   S - (none)   A - 55,995

GAME 5 at Dodger Stadium, Los Angeles, Oct. 16

NYY	0 0 0	0 0 0	2 2 0	-	4	9	2
LAD	1 0 0	4 3 2	0 0 X	-	10	13	0

W - Sutton   L - Gullett   S - (none)   A - 55,955

GAME 6 at Yankee Stadium, Bronx, N.Y., Oct. 18

LAD	2 0 1	0 0 0	0 0 1	-	4	9	0
NYY	0 2 0	3 2 0	0 1 X	-	8	8	1

W - Torrez   L - Hooton   S - (none)   A - 56,407

1978 CHAMPIONSHIP SERIES

Reggie Jackson led the Yankees in batting .462 (6-for-13), HR (2) and RBI (6)...Ron Guidry (8.0IP, 1ER) and Goose Gossage (1.0IP, 0ER) pitched the Yankees to a Game 4 win.

Kansas City Royals (AL)   **1**
New York Yankees (AL)   **3**

GAME 1 at Royals Stadium, Kansas City, Mo., Oct. 3

NYY	0 1 1	0 2 0	0 3 0	-	7	16	0
KC	0 0 0	0 0 1	0 0 0	-	1	2	2

W - Beattie   L - Leonard   S - Clay   A - 41,143

GAME 2 at Royals Stadium, Kansas City, Mo., Oct. 4

NYY	0 0 0	0 0 0	2 2 0	-	4	12	1
KC	1 4 0	0 0 0	3 2 X	-	10	16	1

W - Gura   L - Figueroa   S - (none)   A - 41,158

GAME 3 at Yankee Stadium, Bronx, N.Y., Oct. 6

KC	1 0 1	0 1 0	0 2 0	-	5	10	1
NYY	0 1 0	2 0 1	0 2 X	-	6	10	0

W - Gossage   L - Bird   S - (none)   A - 55,535

GAME 4 at Yankee Stadium, Bronx, N.Y., Oct. 7

KC	1 0 0	0 0 0	0 0 0	-	1	7	0
NYY	0 1 0	0 0 1	0 0 X	-	2	4	0

W - Guidry   L - Leonard   S - Gossage   A - 56,356

1978 WORLD SERIES

The Yankees defeated the Dodgers for the second consecutive year, 4-games-to-2...Series cemented Graig Nettles' reputation for defensive excellence...Bucky Dent won the MVP, batting .417 (10-for-24) with 7RBI...second baseman Brian Doyle, filling in for the injured Willie Randolph, batted .438 (7-for-16) with 4R...Catfish Hunter allowed just 2ER in 7.0IP in recording the win in the Game 6 clincher at Los Angeles.

New York Yankees (AL)   **4**
Los Angeles Dodgers (NL)   **2**

GAME 1 at Dodger Stadium, Los Angeles, Oct. 10

NYY	0 0 0	0 0 0	3 2 0	-	5	9	1
LAD	0 3 0	3 1 0	3 1 X	-	11	15	2

W - John   L - Figueroa   S - (none)   A - 55,997

GAME 2 at Dodger Stadium, Los Angeles, Oct. 11

NYY	0 0 2	0 0 0	1 0 0	-	3	11	0
LAD	0 0 0	1 0 3	0 0 X	-	4	7	0

W - Hooton   L - Hunter   S - Welch   A - 55,982

GAME 3 at Yankee Stadium, Bronx, N.Y., Oct. 13

LAD	0 0 1	0 0 0	0 0 0	-	1	8	0
NYY	1 1 0	0 0 0	3 0 X	-	5	10	1

W - Guidry   L - Sutton   S - (none)   A - 56,447

GAME 4 at Yankee Stadium, Bronx, N.Y., Oct. 14

LAD	0 0 0	0 3 0	0 0 0	-	3	6	1
NYY	0 0 0	0 0 2	0 1 0 1	-	4	9	0

W - Gossage   L - Welch   S - (none)   A - 56,445

GAME 5 at Yankee Stadium, Bronx, N.Y., Oct. 15

LAD	1 0 1	0 0 0	0 0 0	-	2	9	3
NYY	0 0 4	3 0 0	4 1 X	-	12	18	0

W - Beattie   L - Hooton   S - (none)   A - 56,448

GAME 6 at Dodger Stadium, Los Angeles, Oct. 17

NYY	0 3 0	0 0 2	2 0 0	-	7	11	0
LAD	1 0 1	0 0 0	0 0 0	-	2	7	1

W - Hunter   L - Sutton   S - (none)   A - 55,985

1980 CHAMPIONSHIP SERIES

The Yankees' scored just two runs in each game, marking the only time in franchise history the Yankees have been swept in the ALCS or ALDS.

Kansas City Royals (AL)   **3**
New York Yankees (AL)   **0**

GAME 1 at Royals Stadium, Kansas City, Mo., Oct. 8

NYY	0 2 0	0 0 0	0 0 0	- 2 10 1
KC	0 2 2	0 0 0	1 2 X	- 7 10 0

W - Gura   L - Guidry   S - (none)   A - 42,598

GAME 2 at Royals Stadium, Kansas City, Mo., Oct. 9

NYY	0 0 0	0 2 0	0 0 0	- 2 8 0
KC	0 0 3	0 0 0	0 0 X	- 3 6 0

W - Leonard   L - May   S - Quisenberry   A - 42,633

GAME 3 at Yankee Stadium, Bronx, N.Y., Oct. 10

KC	0 0 0	0 1 0	3 0 0	- 4 12 1
NYY	0 0 0	0 0 2	0 0 0	- 2 8 0

W - Quisenberry   L - Gossage   S - (none)   A - 56,588

1981 DIVISION SERIES

The Yankees almost squandered a two-games-to-none lead but defeated Milwaukee behind two wins from Dave Righetti (one as a starter, one as a reliever)...Oscar Gamble went 6-for-10 with 2HR and 4RBI.

Milwaukee Brewers (AL)   **2**
New York Yankees (AL)   **3**

GAME 1 at County Stadium, Milwaukee, Oct. 7

NYY	0 0 0	4 0 0	0 0 1	- 5 13 1
MIL	0 1 1	0 1 0	0 0 0	- 3 8 3

W - Davis   L - Haas   S - Gossage   A - 35,064

GAME 2 at County Stadium, Milwaukee, Oct. 8

NYY	0 0 0	1 0 0	0 0 2	- 3 7 0
MIL	0 0 0	0 0 0	0 0 0	- 0 7 0

W - Righetti   L - Caldwell   S - Gossage   A - 26,395

GAME 3 at Yankee Stadium, Bronx, N.Y., Oct. 9

MIL	0 0 0	0 0 0	3 2 0	- 5 9 0
NYY	0 0 0	1 0 0	0 0 0	- 3 8 2

W - Fingers   L - John   S - (none)   A - 54,171

GAME 4 at Yankee Stadium, Bronx, N.Y., Oct. 10

MIL	0 0 0	2 0 0	0 0 0	- 2 4 2
NYY	0 0 0	0 0 1	0 0 0	- 1 5 0

W - Vuckovich   L - Reuschel   S - Fingers   A - 52,077

GAME 5 at Yankee Stadium, Bronx, N.Y., Oct. 11

MIL	0 1 1	0 0 0	1 0 0	- 3 8 0
NYY	0 0 0	4 0 0	1 2 X	- 7 13 0

W - Righetti   L - Haas   S - Gossage   A - 47,505

1981 CHAMPIONSHIP SERIES

The Yankees outscored Oakland 20-4 in their only ALCS sweep in franchise history...Graig Nettles drove in three runs in each game, batting .500 (6-for-12) with 1HR.

New York Yankees (AL)   **3**
Oakland Athletics (AL)   **0**

GAME 1 at Yankee Stadium, Bronx, N.Y., Oct. 13

OAK	0 0 0	0 1 0	0 0 0	- 1 6 1
NYY	3 0 0	0 0 0	0 0 X	- 3 7 1

W - John   L - Norris   S - Gossage   A - 55,740

GAME 2 at Yankee Stadium, Bronx, N.Y., Oct. 14

OAK	0 0 1	2 0 0	0 0 0	- 3 11 1
NYY	1 0 0	7 0 1	4 0 X	- 13 19 0

W - Frazier   L - McCatty   S - (none)   A - 48,497

GAME 3 at Oakland-Alameda County Coliseum, Oak, Oct. 15

NYY	0 0 0	0 0 1	0 0 3	- 4 10 0
OAK	0 0 0	0 0 0	0 0 0	- 0 5 2

W - Righetti   L - Keough   S - (none)   A - 47,302

1981 WORLD SERIES

After winning the first two games of the Series, the Yankees dropped the next four, falling to 8-3 in their World Series appearances vs. the Dodgers...pitcher George Frazier became the first pitcher to lose three games in a best-of-seven World Series...future GM Bob Watson led the club with 7RBI.

Los Angeles Dodgers (NL)   **4**
New York Yankees (AL)   **2**

GAME 1 at Yankee Stadium, Bronx, N.Y., Oct. 20

LAD	0 0 0	0 1 0	0 2 0	- 3 5 0
NYY	3 0 1	1 0 0	0 0 X	- 5 6 0

W - Guidry   L - Reuss   S - Gossage   A - 56,470

GAME 2 at Yankee Stadium, Bronx, N.Y., Oct. 21

LAD	0 0 0	0 0 0	0 0 0	- 0 4 2
NYY	0 0 0	1 0 0	2 0 X	- 3 6 1

W - John   L - Hooton   S - Gossage   A - 56,505

GAME 3 at Dodger Stadium, Los Angeles, Oct. 23

NYY	0 2 2	0 0 0	0 0 0	- 4 9 0
LAD	3 0 0	0 2 0	0 0 X	- 5 11 1

W - Valenzuela   L - Frazier   S - (none)   A - 56,236

GAME 4 at Dodger Stadium, Los Angeles, Oct. 24

NYY	2 1 1	0 0 2	0 1 0	- 7 13 1
LAD	0 0 2	0 1 3	2 0 X	- 8 14 2

W - Howe   L - Frazier   S - (none)   A - 56,242

GAME 5 at Dodger Stadium, Los Angeles, Oct. 25

NYY	0 1 0	0 0 0	0 0 0	- 1 5 0
LAD	0 0 0	0 0 0	2 0 X	- 2 4 3

W - Reuss   L - Guidry   S - (none)   A - 56,115

GAME 6 at Yankee Stadium, Bronx, N.Y., Oct. 28

LAD	0 0 0	1 3 4	0 1 0	- 9 13 1
NYY	0 0 1	0 0 1	0 0 0	- 2 7 2

W - Hooton   L - Frazier   S - Howe   A - 56,513

1995 DIVISION SERIES

The Yankees snapped a 13-year playoff drought...Don Mattingly batted .417 (10-for-24) with 1HR and 6RBI in his only career postseason series...won the first two games at home before dropping three straight in Seattle...won Game 2, 7-5, on Jim Leyritz's 15th-inning "walk-off" homer in the longest postseason game in franchise history...after throwing 135 pitches in a Game 1 win, David Cone threw 147 pitches in a Game 5 no-decision.

New York Yankees (AL)   **2**
Seattle Mariners (AL)   **3**

GAME 1 at Yankee Stadium, Bronx, N.Y., Oct. 3

SEA	0 0 0	1 0 1	2 0 2	- 6 9 0
NYY	0 0 2	0 0 2	4 1 X	- 9 13 0

W - Cone   L - Nelson   S - (none)   A - 57,178

GAME 2 at Yankee Stadium, Bronx, N.Y., Oct. 4

SEA	0 0 1	0 0 1	2 0 0	0 0 0 - 5 16 2
NYY	0 0 0	0 1 2	1 0 0	0 0 2 - 7 11 0

W - Rivera   L - Belcher   S - (none)   A - 57,126

GAME 3 at Kingdome, Seattle, Oct. 6

NYY	0 0 0	1 0 0	1 2 0	- 4 6 2
SEA	0 0 0	0 2 4	1 0 X	- 7 7 0

W - Johnson   L - McDowell   S - Charlton   A - 57,944

GAME 4 at Kingdome, Seattle, Oct. 7

NYY	3 0 2	0 0 0	0 1 2	- 8 14 1
SEA	0 0 4	0 1 1	0 5 X	- 11 16 0

W - Charlton   L - Wetteland   S - Risley   A - 57,180

GAME 5 at Kingdome, Seattle, Oct. 8

NYY	0 0 0	2 0 2	0 0 0	0 1 - 5 6 0
SEA	0 0 1	1 0 0	0 2 0	0 2 - 6 15 0

W - Johnson   L - McDowell   S - (none)   A - 57,411

1996 DIVISION SERIES

The Yankees bullpen recorded wins in Games 2, 3 and 4, allowing just 1ER in 19.2IP over the series.

Texas Rangers (AL)	1
New York Yankees (AL)	3

GAME 1 at Yankee Stadium, Bronx, N.Y., Oct. 1

TEX	0 0 0	5 0 1	0 0 0	-	6	8	0
NYY	1 0 0	1 0 0	0 0 0	-	2	10	0

W - Burkett L - Cone S - (none) A - 57,205

GAME 2 at Yankee Stadium, Bronx, N.Y., Oct. 2

TEX	0 1 3	0 0 0	0 0 0	0 0 0 -	4	8	1
NYY	0 1 0	1 0 0	1 1 0	0 0 1 -	5	8	0

W - Boehringer L - Stanton S - (none) A - 57,156

GAME 3 at The Ballpark in Arlington, Texas, Oct. 4

NYY	1 0 0	0 0 0	0 0 2	-	3	7	1
TEX	0 0 0	1 1 0	0 0 0	-	2	6	1

W - Nelson L - Oliver S - Wetteland A - 50,860

GAME 4 at The Ballpark in Arlington, Texas, Oct. 5

NYY	0 0 0	3 1 0	1 0 1	-	6	12	1
TEX	0 2 2	0 0 0	0 0 0	-	4	9	0

W - Weathers L - Pavlik S - Wetteland A - 50,066

1996 CHAMPIONSHIP SERIES

Down, 4-3, going into the bottom of the eighth inning of Game 1, the Yankees tied the score on Derek Jeter's disputed home run to right field...Bernie Williams (9-for-19) batted .474 with 6R, 2HR and 6RBI, earning ALCS MVP honors.

Baltimore Orioles (AL)	1
New York Yankees (AL)	4

GAME 1 at Yankee Stadium, Bronx, N.Y., Oct. 9

BAL	0 1 1	1 0 1	0 0 0 0 0	-	4	11	1
NYY	1 1 0	0 0 0	1 1 0 1	-	5	11	0

W - Rivera L - Myers S - (none) A - 56,495

GAME 2 at Yankee Stadium, Bronx, N.Y., Oct. 10

BAL	0 0 2	0 0 0	2 1 0	-	5	10	0
NYY	2 0 0	0 0 0	1 0 0	-	3	11	1

W - Wells L - Nelson S - Benitez A - 56,432

GAME 3 at Camden Yards, Baltimore, Oct. 11

NYY	0 0 0	1 0 0	0 4 0	-	5	8	0
BAL	2 0 0	0 0 0	0 0 0	-	2	3	2

W - Key L - Mussina S - Wetteland A - 48,635

GAME 4 at Camden Yards, Baltimore, Oct. 12

NYY	2 1 0	2 0 0	0 3 0	-	8	9	0
BAL	1 0 1	2 0 0	0 0 0	-	4	11	0

W - Weathers L - Coppinger S - (none) A - 48,974

GAME 5 at Camden Yards, Baltimore, Oct. 13

NYY	0 0 6	0 0 0	0 0 0	-	6	11	0
BAL	0 0 0	0 0 1	0 1 2	-	4	4	1

W - Pettitte L - Erickson S - (none) A - 48,718

Third baseman Charlie Hayes catches the final out of the 1996 World Series.

1996 WORLD SERIES

The Yankees snapped a 17-year World Championship drought, coming back from a two-games-to-none deficit...Manager Joe Torre won in his first year at the helm...club came back from a 6-0 deficit in Game 4, with Jim Leyritz knotting the score at 6-6 with a three-run, eighth inning homer...Andy Pettitte outdueled John Smoltz, 1-0, in Game 5...Jimmy Key defeated Greg Maddux in the Game 6 clincher...John Wetteland saved each of the Yankees' victories, earning MVP honors.

Atlanta Braves (NL)	2
New York Yankees (AL)	4

GAME 1 at Yankee Stadium, Bronx, N.Y., Oct. 20

ATL	0 2 6	0 1 3	0 0 0	-	12	13	0
NYY	0 0 0	0 1 0	0 0 0	-	1	4	1

W - Smoltz L - Pettitte S - (none) A - 56,365

GAME 2 at Yankee Stadium, Bronx, N.Y., Oct. 21

ATL	1 0 1	0 1 1	0 0 0	-	4	10	0
NYY	0 0 0	0 0 0	0 0 0	-	0	7	1

W - Maddux L - Key S - (none) A - 56,340

GAME 3 at Fulton County Stadium, Atlanta, Oct. 22

NYY	1 0 0	1 0 0	0 3 0	-	5	8	1
ATL	0 0 0	0 0 1	0 1 0	-	2	6	1

W - Cone L - Glavine S - Wetteland A - 51,843

GAME 4 at Fulton County Stadium, Atlanta, Oct. 23

NYY	0 0 0	0 0 3	0 3 0 2	-	8	12	0
ATL	0 4 1	0 1 0	0 0 0 0	-	6	9	2

W - Lloyd L - Avery S - Wetteland A - 51,881

GAME 5 at Fulton County Stadium, Atlanta, Oct. 24

NYY	0 0 0	1 0 0	0 0 0	-	1	4	1
ATL	0 0 0	0 0 0	0 0 0	-	0	5	1

W - Pettitte L - Smoltz S - Wetteland A - 51,881

GAME 6 at Yankee Stadium, Bronx, N.Y., Oct. 26

ATL	0 0 0	1 0 0	0 0 1	-	2	8	0
NYY	0 0 3	0 0 0	0 0 X	-	3	8	1

W - Key L - Maddux S - Wetteland A - 56,375

1997 DIVISION SERIES

The Yankees' Game 1 win featured the first-ever back-to-back-to-back postseason homers (Tim Raines, Derek Jeter and Paul O'Neill)...O'Neill finished the series with a .421 batting average (8-for-19), 2HR and 7RBI, including a grand slam in Game 3...Mariano Rivera suffered a blown save in Game 4, on Sandy Alomar, Jr.'s eighth-inning solo home run...would not allow another run in his next 23 postseason appearances, spanning 33.1IP.

New York Yankees (AL)	2
Cleveland Indians (AL)	3

GAME 1 at Yankee Stadium, Bronx, N.Y., Sept. 30

CLE	5 0 0	1 0 0	0 0 0	-	6	10	0
NYY	0 1 0	1 1 5	0 0 X	-	8	11	0

W - Mendoza L - Plunk S - Rivera A - 57,398

GAME 2 at Yankee Stadium, Bronx, N.Y., Oct. 2

CLE	0 0 0	5 2 0	0 0 0	-	7	11	1
NYY	3 0 0	0 0 0	0 1 1	-	5	7	2

W - Wright L - Pettitte S - (none) A - 57,360

GAME 3 at Jacobs Field, Cleveland, Oct. 4

NYY	1 0 1	4 0 0	0 0 0	-	6	4	1
CLE	0 1 0	0 0 0	0 0 0	-	1	5	1

W - Wells L - Nagy S - (none) A - 45,274

GAME 4 at Jacobs Field, Cleveland, Oct. 5

NYY	2 0 0	0 0 0	0 0 0	-	2	9	1
CLE	0 1 0	0 0 0	0 1 1	-	3	9	0

W - Jackson L - Mendoza S - (none) A - 45,231

GAME 5 at Jacobs Field, Cleveland, Oct. 6

NYY	0 0 0	0 2 1	0 0 0	-	3	12	0
CLE	0 0 3	1 0 0	0 0 X	-	4	7	2

W - Wright L - Pettitte S - Mesa A - 45,203

1998 DIVISION SERIES

The Yankees outscored Texas, 9-1, in the series, behind wins from David Wells, Andy Pettitte and David Cone… outfielder Shane Spencer recorded 4RBI in the series, including a three-run homer in Game 3.

New York Yankees (AL)	**3**
Texas Rangers (AL)	**0**

GAME 1 at Yankee Stadium, Bronx, N.Y., Sept. 29

TEX	000 000 000	-	0	5	0
NYY	020 000 00X	-	2	6	0

W - Wells   L - Stottlemyre   S - Rivera   A - 57,362

GAME 2 at Yankee Stadium, Bronx, N.Y., Sept. 30

TEX	000 010 000	-	1	5	0
NYY	010 200 00X	-	3	8	0

W - Pettitte   L - Helling   S - Rivera   A - 57,360

GAME 3 at The Ballpark in Arlington, Texas, Oct. 2

NYY	000 004 000	-	4	9	1
TEX	000 000 000	-	0	3	1

W - Cone   L - Sele   S - (none)   A - 49,950

1998 CHAMPIONSHIP SERIES

The Yankees won the final three games of the series, taking the series in six…their Game 4 win featured 7.0 scoreless IP from starter Orlando Hernandez…David Wells earned series MVP honors with wins in Games 1 and 5.

Cleveland Indians (AL)	**2**
New York Yankees (AL)	**4**

GAME 1 at Yankee Stadium, Bronx, N.Y., Oct. 6

CLE	000 000 002	-	2	5	0
NYY	500 001 10X	-	7	11	0

W - Wells   L - Wright   S - (none)   A - 57,138

GAME 2 at Yankee Stadium, Bronx, N.Y., Oct. 7

CLE	000 100 000 003	-	4	8	1
NYY	000 000 100 000	-	1	7	1

W - Burba   L - Nelson   S - Jackson   A - 57,128

GAME 3 at Jacobs Field, Cleveland, Oct. 9

NYY	100 000 000	-	1	4	0
CLE	020 040 00X	-	6	12	0

W - Colon   L - Pettitte   S - (none)   A - 44,904

GAME 4 at Jacobs Field, Cleveland, Oct. 10

NYY	100 200 001	-	4	4	0
CLE	000 000 000	-	0	4	3

W - Hernandez   L - Gooden   S - (none)   A - 44,981

GAME 5 at Jacobs Field, Cleveland, Oct. 11

NYY	310 100 000	-	5	6	0
CLE	200 001 000	-	3	8	0

W - Wells   L - Ogea   S - Rivera   A - 44,966

GAME 6 at Yankee Stadium, Bronx, N.Y., Oct.13

CLE	000 050 000	-	5	8	3
NYY	213 003 00X	-	9	11	1

W - Cone   L - Nagy   S - (none)   A - 57,142

Orlando Hernandez recorded the first of nine career post-season wins with the Yankees in Game 4 of the 1998 ALCS vs. Cleveland.

1998 WORLD SERIES

The Yankees swept the Padres to finish with a 125-50 overall record (including the postseason), setting the all-time mark for most wins in a season…trailing, 5-2, in Game 1 at Yankee Stadium, Chuck Knoblauch's three-run HR tied the game and Tino Martinez's grand slam put the Yankees ahead in the seventh…also came back from a 3-0 deficit after six innings in Game 3 with Series MVP Scott Brosius hitting a leadoff HR in the seventh and a three-run HR in the eighth…Mariano Rivera notched three saves, marking his highest total in a single World Series.

San Diego Padres (NL)	**0**
New York Yankees (AL)	**4**

GAME 1 at Yankee Stadium, Bronx, N.Y., Oct. 17

SD	002 030 010	-	6	8	1
NYY	020 000 70X	-	9	9	1

W - Wells   L - Wall   S - Rivera   A - 56,712

GAME 2 at Yankee Stadium, Bronx, N.Y., Oct. 18

SD	000 010 020	-	3	10	1
NYY	331 020 00X	-	9	16	0

W - Hernandez   L - Ashby   S - (none)   A - 56,692

GAME 3 at Qualcomm Stadium, San Diego, Oct. 20

NYY	000 000 230	-	5	9	1
SD	000 003 010	-	4	7	1

W - Mendoza   L - Hoffman   S - Rivera   A - 64,667

GAME 4 at Qualcomm Stadium, San Diego, Oct. 21

NYY	000 001 020	-	3	9	0
SD	000 000 000	-	0	7	0

W - Pettitte   L - Brown   S - Rivera   A - 65,427

Mariano Rivera [L] celebrates with Joe Girardi after the final out of the 1998 World Series.

1999 DIVISION SERIES

The Yankees defeated the Rangers in the ALDS for the third time in three attempts over a four-year stretch…outscored them 14-1 in the series…in Game 1, Orlando Hernandez limited Texas to 2H over 8.0 scoreless IP and Bernie Williams drove in six runs, which ties Bobby Richardson (1960 WS, Game 3) and Hideki Matsui (2009 WS, Game 6) for the most in a single postseason game franchise history.

Texas Rangers (AL)	**0**
New York Yankees (AL)	**3**

GAME 1 at Yankee Stadium, Bronx, N.Y., Oct. 5

TEX	000 000 000	-	0	2	1
NYY	010 024 01X	-	8	10	0

W - O. Hernandez   L - Sele   S - (none)   A - 57,099

GAME 2 at Yankee Stadium, Bronx, N.Y., Oct. 7

TEX	000 100 000	-	1	7	0
NYY	000 010 11X	-	3	7	2

W - Pettitte   L - Helling   S - Rivera   A - 57,485

GAME 3 at The Ballpark in Arlington, Texas, Oct. 9

NYY	300 000 000	-	3	6	0
TEX	000 000 000	-	0	5	1

W - Clemens   L - Loaiza   S - (none)   A - 50,269

1999 CHAMPIONSHIP SERIES

The Yankees won their first-ever postseason meeting vs. Boston…Bernie Williams won Game 1 with a 10th-inning walk-off home run…the club had a 12-game postseason winning streak snapped in a Game 3 loss…Derek Jeter led the Yankees with a .350 (7-for-20) batting average.

Boston Red Sox (AL)   **1**
New York Yankees (AL)   **4**

GAME 1 at Yankee Stadium, Bronx, N.Y., Oct. 13

												R	H	E
BOS	2	1	0	0	0	0	0	0	0	-	3	8	3
NYY	0	2	0	0	0	0	1	0	1	-	4	10	1

W - Rivera   L - Beck   S - (none)   A - 57,181

GAME 2 at Yankee Stadium, Bronx, N.Y., Oct. 14

										R	H	E
BOS	0	0	0	0	2	0	0	0	-	2	10	0
NYY	0	0	0	1	0	0	2	0 X	-	3	7	0

W - Cone   L - R. Martinez   S - Rivera   A - 57,180

GAME 3 at Fenway Park, Boston, Oct. 16

										R	H	E
NYY	0	0	0	0	0	0	0	1	0	-	1	3	3
BOS	2	2	2	0	2	1	4	0 X	-	13	21	1

W - P. Martinez   L - Clemens   S - (none)   A - 33,190

GAME 4 at Fenway Park, Boston, Oct. 17

										R	H	E
NYY	0	1	0	2	0	0	0	0	6	-	9	11	0
BOS	0	1	1	0	0	0	0	0	0	-	2	10	4

W - Pettitte   L - Saberhagen   S - Rivera   A - 33,586

GAME 5 at Fenway Park, Boston, Oct. 18

										R	H	E
NYY	2	0	0	0	0	0	2	0	2	-	6	11	1
BOS	0	0	0	0	0	0	0	1	0	-	1	5	2

W - Hernandez   L - Mercker   S - Mendoza   A - 33,589

1999 WORLD SERIES

The Yankees recorded their second straight World Series sweep… Orlando Hernandez allowed just 1R on 1H in 7.0IP (10K) in Game 1…David Cone followed with 7.0 scoreless innings on 1H in Game 2…Chad Curtis hit a 10th-inning walk-off homer in Game 3…the Game 4 win extended the Yankees' World Series winning streak to 12 games.

Atlanta Braves (NL)   **0**
New York Yankees (AL)   **4**

GAME 1 at Turner Field, Atlanta, Oct. 23

										R	H	E
NYY	0	0	0	0	0	0	0	4	0	-	4	6	0
ATL	0	0	0	1	0	0	0	0	0	-	1	2	2

W - Hernandez   L - Maddux   S - Rivera   A - 51,342

GAME 2 at Turner Field, Atlanta, Oct. 24

										R	H	E
NYY	3	0	2	1	1	0	0	0	0	-	7	14	1
ATL	0	0	0	0	0	0	0	0	2	-	2	5	1

W - Cone   L - Millwood   S - (none)   A - 51,226

GAME 3 at Yankee Stadium, Bronx, N.Y., Oct. 26

											R	H	E
ATL	1	0	3	1	0	0	0	0	0	-	5	14	1
NYY	1	0	0	0	1	0	1	2	0 1	-	6	9	0

W - Rivera   L - Remlinger   S - (none)   A - 56,794

GAME 4 at Yankee Stadium, Bronx, N.Y., Oct. 27

										R	H	E
ATL	0	0	0	0	0	0	0	1	0	-	1	5	0
NYY	0	0	3	0	0	0	0	1 X	-	4	8	0

W - Clemens   L - Smoltz   S - Rivera   A - 56,752

2000 DIVISION SERIES

Dropped Game 1 of a postseason series for the first time since the 1996 World Series, snapping a winning streak of seven such games…also lost Game 4 at Yankee Stadium, snapping their home postseason winning streak at 10 games…Andy Pettitte and Mariano Rivera shut out the A's, 4-0, in Game 2…the Yankees scored 6R in the first inning of the deciding Game 5 in Oakland to provide the margin of victory in a 7-5 win.

New York Yankees (AL)   **3**
Oakland Athletics (AL)   **2**

Game 1 at Network Associates Coliseum, Oak., Oct. 3

										R	H	E
NYY	0	2	0	0	0	1	0	0	0	-	3	7	0
OAK	0	0	0	3	1	0	1	X	-	5	10	2

W - Heredia   L - Clemens   S - Isringhausen   A - 47,360

Game 2 at Network Associates Coliseum, Oak., Oct. 4

										R	H	E
NYY	0	0	0	0	0	3	0	0	1	-	4	8	1
OAK	0	0	0	0	0	0	0	0	0	-	0	6	1

W - Pettitte   L - Appier   S - Rivera   A - 47,860

Game 3 at Yankee Stadium, Bronx, N.Y., Oct. 6

										R	H	E
OAK	0	1	0	0	1	0	0	0	0	-	2	4	2
NYY	0	2	0	1	0	0	0	1 X	-	4	6	1

W - Hernandez   L - Hudson   S - Rivera   A - 56,606

Game 4 at Yankee Stadium, Bronx, N.Y., Oct. 7

										R	H	E
OAK	3	0	0	0	0	3	0	1	4	-	11	11	0
NYY	0	0	0	0	0	1	0	0	0	-	1	8	0

W - Zito   L - Clemens   S - (none)   A - 56,915

Game 5 at Network Associates Coliseum, Oak., Oct. 8

										R	H	E
NYY	6	0	0	1	0	0	0	0	0	-	7	12	0
OAK	0	2	1	2	0	0	0	0	0	-	5	13	0

W - Stanton   L - Heredia   S - Rivera   A - 41,170

2000 CHAMPIONSHIP SERIES

The Yankees scored 19 of their 31 total runs in the series in the seventh-inning-or-later, including three come-from-behind victories…MVP David Justice hit 2HR and had a series-best 8RBI…Bernie Williams hit .435 (10-for-23)…Roger Clemens struck out 15 batters while tossing a 1H, 2BB complete-game shutout in Game 4 at Seattle.

Seattle Mariners (AL)   **2**
New York Yankees (AL)   **4**

Game 1 at Yankee Stadium, Bronx, N.Y., Oct. 10

										R	H	E
SEA	0	0	0	0	1	1	0	0	0	-	2	5	0
NYY	0	0	0	0	0	0	0	0	0	-	0	6	1

W - Garcia   L - Neagle   S - Sasaki   A - 54,481

Game 2 at Yankee Stadium, Bronx, N.Y., Oct. 11

										R	H	E
SEA	0	0	1	0	0	0	0	0	0	-	1	7	2
NYY	0	0	0	0	0	0	7	X	-	7	14	0

W - Hernandez   L - Rhodes   S - (none)   A - 55,317

Game 3 at Safeco Field, Seattle, Oct. 13

										R	H	E
NYY	0	2	1	0	0	1	0	0	4	-	8	13	0
SEA	1	0	0	0	1	0	0	0	0	-	2	10	1

W - Pettitte   L - Sele   S - Rivera   A - 47,827

Game 4 at Safeco Field, Seattle, Oct. 14

										R	H	E
NYY	0	0	0	0	3	0	0	2	0	-	5	5	0
SEA	0	0	0	0	0	0	0	0	0	-	0	1	0

W - Clemens   L - Abbott   S - (none)   A - 47,803

Game 5 at Safeco Field, Seattle, Oct. 15

										R	H	E
NYY	0	0	0	2	0	0	0	0	0	-	2	8	0
SEA	1	0	0	0	5	0	0	0 X	-	6	8	0

W - Garcia   L - Neagle   S - (none)   A - 47,802

Game 6 at Yankee Stadium, Bronx, N.Y., Oct. 17

										R	H	E
SEA	2	0	0	2	0	0	0	3	0	-	7	10	0
NYY	0	0	0	3	0	0	6	0 X	-	9	11	0

W - Hernandez L - Paniagua S - (none) A - 56,598

2000 WORLD SERIES

Marked the first "Subway Series" since the Yankees-Dodgers matchup in 1956...the Yankees were victorious in Games 1 and 5 in their last at-bat, winning on a 12th-inning single from Jose Vizcaino and a ninth-inning Luis Sojo single, respectively...Derek Jeter was named Series MVP, batting .409 (9-for-22) with 6R and 2 solo HR, including one on the first pitch of Game 4.

New York Mets (NL)	1
New York Yankees (AL)	4

Game 1 at Yankee Stadium, Bronx, N.Y., Oct. 21

													R	H	E
NYM	0 0 0	0 0 0	3 0 0	0 0 0	-	3	10	0
NYY	0 0 0	0 0 2	0 0 1	0 0 1	-	4	12	0

W - Stanton   L - Wendell   S - (none)   A - 55,913

Game 2 at Yankee Stadium, Bronx, N.Y., Oct. 22

				R	H	E
NYM	0 0 0	0 0 0	0 0 5	-	5	7	3
NYY	2 1 0	0 1 0	1 1 X	-	6	12	1

W - Clemens   L - Hampton   S - (none)   A - 56,059

Game 3 at Shea Stadium, Bronx, N.Y., Oct. 24

				R	H	E
NYY	0 0 1	1 0 0	0 0 0	-	2	8	0
NYM	0 1 0	0 0 1	0 2 X	-	4	9	0

W - J. Franco   L - Hernandez   S - Benitez   A - 55,299

Game 4 at Shea Stadium, Bronx, N.Y., Oct. 25

				R	H	E
NYY	1 1 1	0 0 0	0 0 0	-	3	8	0
NYM	0 0 2	0 0 0	0 0 0	-	2	6	1

W - Nelson   L - B. Jones   S - Rivera   A - 55,290

Game 5 at Shea Stadium, Bronx, N.Y., Oct. 26

				R	H	E
NYY	0 1 0	0 0 1	0 0 2	-	4	7	1
NYM	0 2 0	0 0 0	0 0 0	-	2	8	1

W - Stanton   L - Leiter   S - Rivera   A - 55,292

2001 DIVISION SERIES

The postseason began less than a month after the attacks of 9/11...after losing Games 1 and 2, the Yankees won three straight...were held to just two hits in Game 3 at Oakland but won, 1-0, behind Mike Mussina (7.0IP), Mariano Rivera (2.0IP) and Jorge Posada's fifth-inning solo home run...the game also featured Derek Jeter's famous "Flip Play," which nailed Jeremy Giambi at the plate in the seventh.

New York Yankees (AL)	3
Oakland Athletics (AL)	2

Game 1 at Yankee Stadium, Bronx, N.Y., Oct. 10

				R	H	E
OAK	1 0 0	1 0 0	1 2 0	-	5	10	1
NYY	0 0 0	0 1 0	0 2 0	-	3	10	1

W - Mulder   L - Clemens   S - Isringhausen   A - 56,697

Game 2 at Yankee Stadium, Bronx, N.Y., Oct. 11

				R	H	E
OAK	0 0 0	1 0 0	0 0 1	-	2	9	0
NYY	0 0 0	0 0 0	0 0 0	-	0	7	1

W - Hudson   L - Pettitte   S - Isringhausen   A - 56,684

Game 3 at Network Associates Coliseum, Oak., Oct. 13

				R	H	E
NYY	0 0 0	0 1 0	0 0 0	-	1	2	0
OAK	0 0 0	0 0 0	0 0 0	-	0	6	1

W - Mussina   L - Zito   S - Rivera   A - 55,861

Game 4 at Network Associates Coliseum, Oak., Oct. 14

				R	H	E
NYY	0 2 2	3 0 0	0 0 2	-	9	11	1
OAK	0 0 2	0 0 0	0 0 0	-	2	11	1

W - Hernandez   L - Lidle   S - (none)   A - 43,681

Game 5 at Yankee Stadium, Bronx, N.Y., Oct. 15

				R	H	E
OAK	1 1 0	0 1 0	0 0 0	-	3	7	3
NYY	0 2 1	1 0 1	0 0 X	-	5	10	1

W - Stanton   L - Mulder   S - Rivera   A - 56,642

Derek Jeter [R] makes his famous "Flip Play" relay throw to Jorge Posada in Game 3 of the 2001 ALDS at Oakland.

2001 CHAMPIONSHIP SERIES

The Yankees defeated a Seattle club that won an AL-record 116 games during the regular season...Andy Pettitte was named Series MVP, going 2-0 with a 2.51 ERA...Game 4 ended on Alfonso Soriano's two-run walk-off homer in the ninth...Bernie Williams homered in three consecutive games (Games 3-5).

New York Yankees (AL)	4
Seattle Mariners (AL)	1

Game 1 at Safeco Field, Seattle, Oct. 17

				R	H	E
NYY	0 1 0	2 0 0	0 0 1	-	4	9	0
SEA	0 0 0	0 1 0	0 0 1	-	2	4	0

W - Pettitte   L - Sele   S - Rivera   A - 47,644

Game 2 at Safeco Field, Seattle, Oct. 18

				R	H	E
NYY	0 3 0	0 0 0	0 0 0	-	3	9	1
SEA	0 0 0	2 0 0	0 0 0	-	2	6	0

W - Mussina   L - Garcia   S - Rivera   A - 47,791

Game 3 at Yankee Stadium, Bronx, N.Y., Oct. 20

				R	H	E
SEA	0 0 0	0 2 7	2 1 2	-	14	15	0
NYY	2 0 0	0 0 0	0 1 0	-	3	7	2

W - Moyer   L - Hernandez   S - (none)   A - 56,517

Game 4 at Yankee Stadium, Bronx, N.Y., Oct. 21

				R	H	E
SEA	0 0 0	0 0 0	0 1 0	-	1	2	0
NYY	0 0 0	0 0 0	0 1 2	-	3	4	0

W - Rivera   L - Sasaki   S - (none)   A - 56,375

Game 5 at Yankee Stadium, Bronx, N.Y., Oct. 22

				R	H	E
SEA	0 0 0	0 0 0	3 0 0	-	3	9	1
NYY	0 0 4	1 0 4	0 3 X	-	12	13	1

W - Pettitte   L - Sele   S - (none)   A - 56,370

2001 WORLD SERIES

All games were won by the home team in one of the most thrilling World Series of all time...President George W. Bush threw out the ceremonial first pitch prior Game 3 at Yankee Stadium...the Yankees came back from two-run deficits with two outs in the ninth vs. Arizona's Byung-Hyun Kim in both Games 4 and 5...Tino Martinez tied Game 4 with a two-run home run and Derek Jeter earned the nickname, "Mr. November," with a solo HR to win it in the 10th...Scott Brosius hit a two-run homer to tie Game 5 before Alfonso Soriano won the game with an RBI-single in the 12th...despite taking a 2-1 lead on a Soriano solo homer in the eighth inning of Game 7, the Yankees lost the Series after allowing two runs in the ninth.

New York Yankees (AL)	3
Arizona Diamondbacks (NL)	4

Game 1 at Bank One Ballpark, Phoenix, Ariz., Oct. 27
```
NYY   1 0 0   0 0 0   0 0 0    -  1   3  2
ARI   1 0 4   4 0 0   0 0 X    -  9  10  0
```
W-Schilling   L-Mussina   S-(none)   A-49,646

Game 2 at Bank One Ballpark, Phoenix, Ariz., Oct. 28
```
NYY   0 0 0   0 0 0   0 0 0    -  0   3  0
ARI   0 1 0   0 0 3   0 X      -  4   5  0
```
W-Johnson   L-Pettitte   S-(none)   A-49,646

Game 3 at Yankee Stadium, Bronx, N.Y., Oct. 30
```
ARI   0 0 0   1 0 0   0 0 0    -  1   3  3
NYY   0 1 0   0 0 1   0 0 X    -  2   7  1
```
W-Clemens   L-Anderson   S-Rivera   A-55,820

Game 4 at Yankee Stadium, Bronx, N.Y., Oct. 31
```
ARI   0 0 0   1 0 0   0 2 0  0   -  3   6  0
NYY   0 0 1   0 0 0   0 0 2  1   -  4   7  0
```
W-Rivera   L-Kim   S-(none)   A-55,863

Game 5 at Yankee Stadium, Bronx, N.Y., Nov. 1
```
ARI   0 0 0   0 2 0   0 0 0  0 0 0   -  2   8  0
NYY   0 0 0   0 0 0   0 0 2  0 0 1   -  3   9  1
```
W-Hitchcock   L-Lopez   S-(none)   A-56,018

Game 6 at Bank One Ballpark, Phoenix, Ariz., Nov. 3
```
NYY   0 0 0   0 0 2   0 0 0    -   2   7  1
ARI   1 3 8   3 0 0   0 0 X    -  15  22  0
```
W-Johnson   L-Pettitte   S-(none)   A-49,707

Game 7 at Bank One Ballpark, Phoenix, Ariz., Nov. 4
```
NYY   0 0 0   0 0 0   1 1 0    -  2   6  3
ARI   0 0 0   0 0 1   0 0 2    -  3  11  0
```
W-Johnson   L-Rivera   S-(none)   A-49,589

Tino Martinez sets the stage for an improbable Yankees comeback with a game-tying, two-out, two-run, ninth-inning home run in Game 4 of the 2001 World Series.

Derek Jeter becomes "Mr. November" with his game-winning home run in Game 4 of the 2001 World Series vs. Arizona.

Scott Brosius ties Game 5 of the 2001 World Series with his two-out, ninth-inning HR off Arizona's Byung-Hyun Kim.

2002 DIVISION SERIES
The Yankees had their Division Series winning streak snapped at four, losing their first DS since 1997 vs. Cleveland...Derek Jeter batted .500 (8-for-16) with 2HR and 3RBI.

Anaheim Angels (AL) 3
New York Yankees (AL) 1

Game 1 at Yankee Stadium, Bronx, N.Y., Oct. 1
```
ANA   0 0 1   0 2 1   0 1 0    -  5  12  0
NYY   1 0 0   2 1 0   0 4 X    -  8   8  1
```
W-Karsay   L-Weber   S-Rivera   A-56,710

Game 2 at Yankee Stadium, Bronx, N.Y., Oct. 2
```
ANA   1 2 1   0 0 0   0 3 1    -  8  17  1
NYY   0 0 1   2 0 2   0 0 1    -  6  12  1
```
W-Rodriguez   L-Hernandez   S-Percival   A-56,695

Game 3 at Edison International Field, Anaheim, Oct. 4
```
NYY   3 0 3   0 0 0   0 0 0    -  6   6  0
ANA   0 1 2   1 0 1   1 3 X    -  9  12  0
```
W-Rodriguez   L-Stanton   S-Percival   A-45,072

Game 4 at Edison International Field, Anaheim, Oct. 5
```
NYY   0 1 0   0 1 1   1 0 1    -  5  12  2
ANA   0 0 1   0 8 0   0 0 X    -  9  15  1
```
W-Washburn   L-Wells   S-(none)   A-45,067

2003 DIVISION SERIES
The Yankees held Minnesota to just six runs in four games, including one run in each of Games 2, 3 and 4...Derek Jeter batted .429 (6-for-14) with 1HR.

Minnesota Twins (AL) 1
New York Yankees (AL) 3

GAME 1 at Yankee Stadium, Bronx, N.Y., Sept. 30
```
MIN   0 0 1   0 0 2   0 0 0    -  3   8  0
NYY   0 0 0   0 0 0   0 0 1    -  1   9  1
```
W-Hawkins   L-Mussina   S-Guardado   A-56,292

GAME 2 at Yankee Stadium, Bronx, N.Y., Oct. 2
```
MIN   0 0 0   0 1 0   0 0 0    -  1   4  1
NYY   1 0 0   0 0 0   3 0 X    -  4   8  1
```
W-Pettitte   L-Radke   S-Rivera   A-56,479

GAME 3 at Metrodome, Minneapolis, Oct. 4
```
NYY   0 2 1   0 0 0   0 0 0    -  3   8  1
MIN   0 0 1   0 0 0   0 0 0    -  1   5  0
```
W-Clemens   L-Lohse   S-Rivera   A-55,915

GAME 4 at Metrodome, Minneapolis, Oct. 5
```
NYY   0 0 0   6 0 0   0 1 1    -  8  13  0
MIN   0 0 0   1 0 0   0 0 0    -  1   9  1
```
W-Wells   L-Santana   S-(none)   A-55,875

2003 CHAMPIONSHIP SERIES

Defined by the final game, the Series was won on Aaron Boone's first pitch leadoff home run off Tim Wakefield in the bottom of the 11th inning of Game 7…in the contest, the Yankees came back from a 5-2 deficit heading into the bottom of the eighth…Mike Mussina made his first-ever relief appearance, getting a strikeout and double play with two on and no outs in the fourth to keep the Yankees in the game…tossed 3.0 scoreless IP on two days' rest…Jason Giambi hit solo homers in the fifth and seventh…the Yankees scored three runs in the eighth off Pedro Martinez to tie the game, 5-5…Mariano Rivera tossed 3.0 scoreless innings, pitching the ninth, 10th and 11th, to earn the win.

| Boston Red Sox (AL) | 3 |
| New York Yankees (AL) | 4 |

GAME 1 at Yankee Stadium, Bronx, N.Y., Oct. 8

BOS	0 0 0	2 2 0	1 0 0	-	5	13	0
NYY	0 0 0	0 0 0	2 0 0	-	2	3	0

W - Wakefield L - Mussina S - Williamson A - 56,281

GAME 2 at Yankee Stadium, Bronx, N.Y., Oct. 9

BOS	0 1 0	0 0 1	0 0 0	-	2	10	1
NYY	0 2 1	0 1 0	2 0 X	-	6	8	0

W - Pettitte L - Lowe S - (none) A - 56,295

GAME 3 at Fenway Park, Boston, Oct. 11

NYY	0 1 1	2 0 0	0 0 0	-	4	7	0
BOS	2 0 0	0 0 0	1 0 0	-	3	6	0

W - Clemens L - Martinez S - Rivera A - 34,209

GAME 4 at Fenway Park, Boston, Oct. 13

NYY	0 0 0	0 1 0	0 0 1	-	2	6	1
BOS	0 0 0	1 1 0	1 0 X	-	3	6	0

W - Wakefield L - Mussina S - Williamson A - 34,599

GAME 5 at Fenway Park, Boston, Oct. 14

NYY	0 3 0	0 0 0	0 1 0	-	4	7	1
BOS	0 0 0	1 0 0	0 1 0	-	2	6	1

W - Wells L - Lowe S - Rivera A - 34,619

GAME 6 at Yankee Stadium, Bronx, N.Y., Oct. 15

BOS	0 0 4	0 0 0	3 0 2	-	9	16	1
NYY	1 0 0	4 1 0	0 0 0	-	6	12	2

W - Embree L - Contreras S - Williamson A - 56,277

GAME 7 at Yankee Stadium, Bronx, N.Y., Oct. 16

BOS	0 3 0	1 0 0	0 1 0	0 0	-	5	11	0
NYY	0 0 0	0 1 0	1 3 0	0 1	-	6	11	1

W - Rivera L - Wakefield S - (none) A - 56,279

Aaron Boone wins Game 7 of the 2003 ALCS with his 11th inning home run off Boston's Tim Wakefield.

2003 WORLD SERIES

The Yankees outscored Florida, 21-17, in defeat…Andy Pettitte allowed just 3R (1ER) in 15.2IP over two starts, including a win in Game 2 and a loss in the decisive Game 6…Bernie Williams batted .400 (10-for-25) with 5R, 2HR and 5RBI.

| Florida Marlins (NL) | 4 |
| New York Yankees (AL) | 2 |

GAME 1 at Yankee Stadium, Bronx, N.Y., Oct. 18

FLA	1 0 0	0 2 0	0 0 0	-	3	7	1
NYY	0 0 1	0 0 1	0 0 0	-	2	9	0

W - Penny L - Wells S - Urbina A - 55,769

GAME 2 at Yankee Stadium, Bronx, N.Y., Oct. 19

FLA	0 0 0	0 0 0	0 0 1	-	1	6	0
NYY	3 1 0	0 0 0	0 0 X	-	6	10	2

W - Pettitte L - Redman S - (none) A - 55,750

GAME 3 at Pro Player Stadium, Miami, Oct. 21

NYY	0 0 0	1 0 0	0 1 4	-	6	6	1
FLA	1 0 0	0 0 0	0 0 0	-	1	8	0

W - Mussina L - Beckett S - Rivera A - 65,731

GAME 4 at Pro Player Stadium, Miami, Oct. 22

NYY	0 1 0	0 0 0	0 0 2 0 0 0	-	3	12	0
FLA	3 0 0	0 0 0	0 0 0 0 0 1	-	4	10	0

W - Looper L - Weaver S - (none) A - 65,934

GAME 5 at Pro Player Stadium, Miami, Oct. 23

NYY	1 0 0	0 0 0	1 0 2	-	4	12	1
FLA	0 3 0	1 2 0	0 0 X	-	6	9	1

W - Penny L - Contreras S - Urbina A - 65,975

GAME 6 at Yankee Stadium, Bronx, N.Y., Oct. 25

FLA	0 0 0	0 1 1	0 0 0	-	2	7	0
NYY	0 0 0	0 0 0	0 0 0	-	0	5	1

W - Beckett L - Pettitte S - (none) A - 55,773

2004 DIVISION SERIES

The Yankees defeated Minnesota in the ALDS for the second straight season…won Game 2 scoring twice in the 12th inning and Game 4 with one run in the 11th…Alex Rodriguez batted .421 (8-for-19) with 1HR and 3RBI.

| Minnesota Twins (AL) | 1 |
| New York Yankees (AL) | 3 |

GAME 1 at Yankee Stadium, Bronx, N.Y., Oct. 5

MIN	0 0 1	0 0 1	0 0 0	-	2	7	0
NYY	0 0 0	0 0 0	0 0 0	-	0	9	0

W - Santana L - Mussina S - Nathan A - 55,749

GAME 2 at Yankee Stadium, Bronx, N.Y., Oct. 6

MIN	1 2 0	0 0 0	0 2 0	0 0 1	-	6	12	0
NYY	1 0 2	0 1 0	1 0 0	0 0 2	-	7	9	0

W - Quantrill L - Nathan S - (none) A - 56,354

GAME 3 at Metrodome, Minneapolis, Oct. 8

NYY	0 3 0	0 0 4	1 0 0	-	8	14	1
MIN	1 0 0	0 0 0	0 0 3	-	4	12	1

W - Brown L - Silva S - (none) A - 54,803

GAME 4 at Metrodome, Minneapolis, Oct. 9

NYY	0 0 1	0 0 0	0 4 0	0 1	-	6	11	0
MIN	1 0 0	1 3 0	0 0 0	0 0	-	5	12	1

W - Rivera L - Lohse S - (none) A - 52,498

2004 CHAMPIONSHIP SERIES

The Yankees lost their first-ever postseason series after being up 3-games-to-0…scored 19 runs in their Game 3 win, marking the most ever by one team in an ALCS game…Hideki Matsui batted .412 (14-for-34) with 6 doubles, 1 triple, 2HR and 10RBI in the series, establishing the all-time mark for extra-base hits in a postseason series and ALCS marks for hits, total bases and doubles.

Boston Red Sox (AL)	4
New York Yankees (AL)	3

GAME 1 at Yankee Stadium, Bronx, N.Y., Oct. 12

BOS	0 0 0	0 0 0	5 2 0	-	7	10	0
NYY	2 0 4	0 0 2	0 2 X	-	10	14	0

W - Mussina   L - Schilling   S - Rivera   A - 56,135

GAME 2 at Yankee Stadium, Bronx, N.Y., Oct. 13

BOS	0 0 0	0 0 0	0 1 0	-	1	5	0
NYY	1 0 0	0 0 2	0 0 X	-	3	7	0

W - Lieber   L - Martinez   S - Rivera   A - 56,136

GAME 3 at Fenway Park, Boston, Oct. 16

NYY	3 0 3	5 2 0	4 0 2	-	19	22	1
BOS	0 4 2	0 0 0	2 0 0	-	8	15	0

W - Vazquez   L - Mendoza   S - (none)   A - 35,126

GAME 4 at Fenway Park, Boston, Oct. 17

NYY	0 0 2	0 0 2	0 0 0	0 0 0	-	4	12	1
BOS	0 0 0	0 0 0	3 0 0	1 0 0 2	-	6	8	0

W - Leskanic   L - Quantrill   S - (none)   A - 35,826

GAME 5 at Fenway Park, Boston, Oct. 18

NYY	0 1 0	0 0 3	0 0 0	0 0 0 0 0	-	4	12	1
BOS	2 0 0	0 0 0	0 2 0	0 0 0 0 1	-	5	13	1

W - Wakefield   L - Loaiza   S - (none)   A - 35,120

GAME 6 at Yankee Stadium, Bronx, N.Y., Oct. 19

BOS	0 0 0	4 0 0	0 0 0	-	4	11	0
NYY	0 0 0	0 0 0	1 1 0	-	2	6	0

W - Schilling   L - Lieber   S - Foulke   A - 56,128

GAME 7 at Yankee Stadium, Bronx, N.Y., Oct. 20

BOS	2 4 0	2 0 0	0 1 1	-	10	13	0
NYY	0 0 1	0 0 0	2 0 0	-	3	5	1

W - Lowe   L - Brown   S - (none)   A - 56,129

2005 DIVISION SERIES

Mariano Rivera saved both of the Yankees' victories… Derek Jeter tied for the team lead in both RBI (5) and runs scored (4).

New York Yankees (AL)	2
Los Angeles Angels of Anaheim (AL)	3

GAME 1 at Angel Stadium, Anaheim, Oct. 4

NYY	3 1 0	0 0 0	0 0 0	-	4	9	0
LAA	0 0 0	0 0 0	1 0 1	-	2	7	0

W - Mussina   L - Colon   S - Rivera   A - 45,142

GAME 2 at Angel Stadium, Anaheim, Oct. 5

NYY	0 1 0	0 1 0	0 0 1	-	3	6	3
LAA	0 0 0	0 1 1	2 1 X	-	5	7	0

W - Escobar   L - Wang   S - Rodriguez   A - 45,150

GAME 3 at Yankee Stadium, Bronx, N.Y., Oct. 7

LAA	3 0 2	0 0 2	2 2 0	-	11	19	1
NYY	0 0 0	4 2 0	1 0 0	-	7	12	2

W - Shields   L - Small   S - (none)   A - 56,277

GAME 4 at Yankee Stadium, Bronx, N.Y., Oct. 9

LAA	0 0 0	0 0 2	0 0 0	-	2	4	0
NYY	0 0 0	0 0 1	2 0 X	-	3	4	1

W - Leiter   L - Shields   S - Rivera   A - 56,226

GAME 5 at Angel Stadium, Anaheim, Oct. 10

NYY	0 2 0	0 0 0	1 0 0	-	3	11	0
LAA	0 3 2	0 0 0	0 0 X	-	5	9	0

W - Santana   L - Mussina   S - Rodriguez   A - 45,133

2006 DIVISION SERIES

Chien-Ming Wang recorded his first career postseason win in Game 1…Derek Jeter (8-for-16) and Jorge Posada (7-for-14) combined for 15 of the team's 33 overall hits.

Detroit Tigers (AL)	3
New York Yankees (AL)	1

GAME 1 at Yankee Stadium, Bronx, N.Y., Oct. 3

DET	0 0 0	0 3 0	1 0 0	-	4	12	1
NYY	0 0 5	0 0 2	0 1 X	-	8	14	0

W - Wang   L - Robertson   S - (none)   A - 56,291

GAME 2 at Yankee Stadium, Bronx, N.Y., Oct. 5

DET	0 1 0	0 1 1	1 0 0	-	4	8	0
NYY	0 0 0	3 0 0	0 0 0	-	3	8	1

W - Walker   L - Mussina   S - Jones   A - 56,252

GAME 3 at Comerica Park, Detroit, Oct. 6

NYY	0 0 0	0 0 0	0 0 0	-	0	5	0
DET	0 3 0	0 0 2	1 0 X	-	6	10	0

W - Rogers   L - Johnson   S - (none)   A - 43,440

GAME 4 at Comerica Park, Detroit, Oct. 7

NYY	0 0 0	0 0 0	1 0 2	-	3	6	2
DET	0 3 1	0 3 1	0 0 X	-	8	13	0

W - Bonderman   L - Wright   S - (none)   A - 43,126

2007 DIVISION SERIES

The Yankees were outhit, .315 to .228, in the series…the Yankees' 2-1, 11-inning loss in Game 2 featured the unusual postseason debut of Joba Chamberlain, who allowed the go-ahead run in the eighth on 2BB, 2WP and 1HP while "midges" descended on the pitcher's mound.

New York Yankees (AL)	1
Cleveland Indians (AL)	3

GAME 1 at Jacobs Field, Cleveland, Oct. 4

NYY	1 0 0	1 1 0	0 0 0	-	3	5	0
CLE	3 0 1	0 5 2	0 1 X	-	12	14	0

W – Sabathia   L – Wang   S – (none)   A – 44,608

GAME 2 at Jacobs Field, Cleveland, Oct. 5

NYY	0 0 1	0 0 0	0 0 0	0 0	-	1	3	0
CLE	0 0 0	0 0 0	0 1 0	0 1	-	2	9	1

W – Perez   L – Vizcaino   S – (none)   A – 44,732

GAME 3 at Yankee Stadium, Bronx, N.Y., Oct. 7

CLE	1 1 1	0 0 0	0 1 0	-	4	9	1
NYY	0 0 1	0 4 3	0 0 x	-	8	11	1

W – Hughes   L – Westbrook   S – (none)   A – 56,358

GAME 4 at Yankee Stadium, Bronx, N.Y., Oct. 8

CLE	2 2 0	2 0 0	0 0 0	-	6	13	0
NYY	0 1 0	0 0 1	1 0 1	-	4	12	0

W – Byrd   L – Wang   S – Borowski   A – 56,315

2009 DIVISION SERIES

The Yankees recorded their third all time ALDS sweep (also 1998-99 vs. Texas) and fourth "best-of-five" series sweep (also 1981 ALCS vs. Oakland)…came back from deficits in all three games…out-homered the Twins, 6-0…Yankees starters allowed just 3ER and three extra-base hits in 19.0IP with a 1.42 ERA…Alex Rodriguez batted a team-high .455 (5-for-11) with 2HR and 6RBI.

Minnesota Twins (AL)	0
New York Yankees (AL)	3

GAME 1 at Yankee Stadium, Bronx, N.Y., Oct. 7

MIN	0 0 2	0 0 0	0 0 0	-	2	10	1
NYY	0 0 2	1 3 0	1 0 x	-	7	9	0

W – Sabathia   L – Duensing   S – (none)   A – 44,464

GAME 2 at Yankee Stadium, Bronx, N.Y., Oct. 9

MIN	0 0 0	0 0 1	0 2 0	0 0	-	3	12	1
NYY	0 0 0	0 0 1	0 0 2	0 1	-	4	7	0

W – Robertson   L – Mijares   S – (none)   A – 50,006

GAME 3 at Metrodome, Minneapolis, Oct. 11

NYY	0 0 0	0 0 0	2 0 2	-	4	7	0
MIN	0 0 0	0 0 1	0 0 0	-	1	7	0

W – Pettitte   L – Pavano   S – Rivera   A – 54,735

2009 CHAMPIONSHIP SERIES

The Yankees won their 40th AL pennant...hit 8HR and drew 38BB over the six games, while holding the Majors' second-highest scoring team to an average of 3.2R/G...won Game 2 in 13 innings on a throwing error by Maicer Izturis... CC Sabathia earned ALCS MVP honors, going 2-0 with a 1.13 ERA (16.0IP, 2ER) in two starts...Alex Rodriguez batted a team-high .429 (9-for-21) with 6R, 3HR, 6RBI and 8BB.

Los Angeles Angels (AL) 2
New York Yankees (AL)   4

GAME 1 at Yankee Stadium, Bronx, N.Y., Oct. 16
LAA   0 0 0   1 0 0   0 0 0   - 1 4 3
NYY   2 0 0   0 1 1   0 0 x   - 4 10 0
W – Sabathia   L – Lackey   S – Rivera   A – 48,688

GAME 2 at Yankee Stadium, Bronx, N.Y., Oct. 17
LAA   0 0 0   0 2 0   0 0 0   0 1 0   0 - 3   8 2
NYY   0 1 1   0 0 0   0 0 0   0 1 0   1 - 4 13 3
W – Robertson   L – Santana   S – (none)   A – 49,922

GAME 3 at Angel Stadium, Anaheim, Oct. 19
NYY   1 0 0   1 1 0   0 1 0   0 0 - 4   8 0
LAA   0 0 0   0 1 2   1 0 0   0 1 - 5 13 0
W – Santana   L – Aceves   S – (none)   A – 44,911

GAME 4 at Angel Stadium, Anaheim, Oct. 20
NYY   0 0 0   3 2 0   0 2 3   - 10 13 0
LAA   0 0 0   0 1 0   0 0 0   - 1   5 1
W – Sabathia   L – Kazmir   S – (none)   A – 45,160

GAME 5 at Angel Stadium, Anaheim, Oct. 22
NYY   0 0 0   0 0 0   6 0 0   - 6   9 0
LAA   4 0 0   0 0 0   3 0 x   - 7 12 0
W – Jepsen   L – Hughes   S – Fuentes   A – 45,113

GAME 6 at Yankee Stadium, Bronx, N.Y., Oct. 25
LAA   0 0 1   0 0 0   0 1 0   - 2   9 2
NYY   0 0 0   3 0 0   0 2 x   - 5   9 0
W – Pettitte   L – Saunders   S – Rivera   A – 50,173

2009 WORLD SERIES

The Yankees won their 27th World Championship and first since 2000...Hideki Matsui (.615 avg., 3HR, 8RBI) was the unanimous World Series MVP, marking the first time a Japanese player earned the honor...had 6RBI (single, double, HR) in the Game 6 clincher, tying Bobby Richardson's single-game World Series record (1960 Game 3)...Andy Pettitte became the third-oldest pitcher to win a World Series clinching game (behind Burleigh Grimes-1931 and Eddie Plank-1913) and the first pitcher in baseball history to start and win all three clinching games of a single postseason (DS, CS, WS).

Philadelphia Phillies (NL) 2
New York Yankees (AL)   4

GAME 1 at Yankee Stadium, Bronx, N.Y., Oct. 28
PHI   0 0 1   0 0 1   0 2 2   - 6   9 1
NYY   0 0 0   0 0 0   0 0 1   - 1   6 0
W – Lee   L – Sabathia   S – (none)   A – 50,207

GAME 2 at Yankee Stadium, Bronx, N.Y., Oct. 29
PHI   0 1 0   0 0 0   0 0 0   - 1   6 0
NYY   0 0 0   1 0 1   1 0 x   - 3   8 0
W – Burnett   L – Martinez   S – Rivera   A – 50,181

GAME 3 at Citizens Bank Park, Philadelphia, Oct. 31
NYY   0 0 0   2 3 1   1 1 0   - 8   8 1
PHI   0 3 0   0 0 1   0 0 1   - 5   6 0
W – Pettitte   L – Hamels   S – (none)   A – 46,061

GAME 4 at Citizens Bank Park, Philadelphia, Nov. 1
NYY   2 0 0   0 2 0   0 0 3   - 7   9 1
PHI   1 0 0   1 0 0   1 0 0   - 4   8 1
W – Chamberlain   L – Lidge   S – Rivera   A – 46,145

GAME 5 at Citizens Bank Park, Philadelphia, Nov. 2
NYY   1 0 0   0 1 0   0 3 1   - 6 10 0
PHI   3 0 3   0 0 0   2 0 x   - 8   9 0
W – Lee   L – Burnett   S – Madson   A – 46,178

GAME 6 at Yankee Stadium, Bronx, N.Y., Nov. 4
PHI   0 0 1   0 0 2   0 0 0   - 3   6 0
NYY   0 2 2   0 3 0   0 0 x   - 7   8 0
W – Pettitte   L – Martinez   S – (none)   A – 50,315

Yankees Postseason Award Winners

ALCS MVP

YEAR	PLAYER	AGE	POS	G	AB	R	H	2B	3B	HR	RBI	AVG
1981	Graig Nettles	37	3B	3	12	2	6	2	0	1	9	.500
1996	Bernie Williams	28	CF	5	19	6	9	3	0	2	6	.474
2000	David Justice	34	LF	6	26	4	6	2	0	2	8	.231

YEAR	PITCHER	AGE	POS	G	GS	IP	W	L	SV	H	R	ER	SO	BB	ERA
1998	David Wells	35	LHP	2	2	15.2	2	0	0	12	5	5	18	2	2.87
1999	Orlando Hernandez	30	RHP	2	2	15.0	1	0	0	12	4	3	13	6	1.80
2001	Andy Pettitte	29	LHP	2	2	14.1	2	0	0	11	4	4	8	2	2.51
2003	Mariano Rivera	33	RHP	4	0	8.0	1	0	2	5	1	1	6	0	1.13
2009	CC Sabathia	29	LHP	2	2	16.0	2	0	0	9	2	2	12	3	1.13

World Series MVP

YEAR	PLAYER	AGE	POS	G	AB	R	H	2B	3B	HR	RBI	AVG
1960	Bobby Richardson	25	2B	7	30	8	11	2	2	1	12	.367
1977	Reggie Jackson	31	RF	6	20	10	9	1	0	5	8	.450
1978	Bucky Dent	26	SS	6	24	3	10	1	0	0	7	.417
1998	Scott Brosius	32	3B	4	17	3	8	0	0	2	6	.471
2000	Derek Jeter	26	SS	5	22	6	9	2	1	2	2	.409
2009	Hideki Matsui	35	DH	6	13	3	8	1	0	3	8	.615

YEAR	PITCHER	AGE	POS	G	GS	IP	W	L	SV	H	R	ER	SO	BB	ERA
1956	Don Larsen	27	RHP	2	2	10.2	1	0	0	1	4	0	7	4	0.00
1958	Bob Turley	28	RHP	4	2	16.1	2	1	1	10	5	5	13	7	2.76
1961	Whitey Ford	32	LHP	2	2	14.0	2	0	0	6	0	0	7	1	0.00
1962	Ralph Terry	26	RHP	3	3	25.0	2	1	0	17	5	5	16	2	1.80
1996	John Wetteland	30	RHP	5	0	4.1	0	0	4	1	1	1	6	1	2.08
1999	Mariano Rivera	29	RHP	3	0	4.2	1	0	2	3	0	0	3	1	0.00

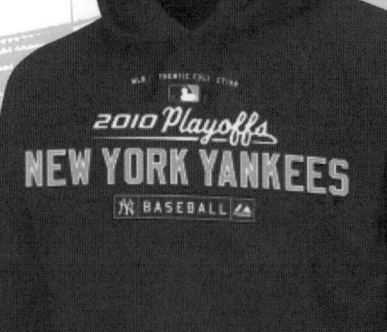